ISO 9000
Quality Systems
Handbook

ONE WEEK LOAN

ISO 9000
Quality Systems
Handbook

Fourth Edition

Completely revised in response to ISO 9000:2000

David Hoyle

BUTTERWORTH
HEINEMANN

OXFORD AUCKLAND BOSTON JOHANNESBURG MELBOURNE NEW DELHI

Butterworth-Heinemann
Linacre House, Jordan Hill, Oxford OX2 8DP
225 Wildwood Avenue, Woburn, MA 01801-2041
A division of Reed Educational and Professional Publishing Ltd

A member of the Reed Elsevier plc group

First published 1994
Second edition 1994
Third edition 1998
Reprinted 1999
Fourth edition 2001
Reprinted 2002

British Library Cataloguing in Publication Data
A catalogue record for this book is available from the British Library

Library of Congress Cataloguing in Publication Data
A catalogue record for this book is available from the Library of Congress

ISBN 0 7506 4451 6

For more information on all Butterworth-Heinemann
publications please visit our website at www.bh.com

Composition by Genesis Typesetting, Laser Quay, Rochester, Kent
Printed and bound in Great Britain by Biddles Ltd, *www.biddles.co.uk*

FOR EVERY TITLE THAT WE PUBLISH, BUTTERWORTH-HEINEMANN
WILL PAY FOR BTCV TO PLANT AND CARE FOR A TREE.

Contents

Preface and acknowledgements

Since the third edition of this handbook was published in 1998 there has been a radical change to the ISO 9000 family of standards. The standards have changed in structure from 20 elements to 8 sections; they have changed in intent from quality assurance to customer satisfaction; the terminology has changed so as to suit all types of organizations and there has been a change in direction from a focus on planning, inspection and test and the removal of nonconformity to a focus on objectives, processes, measurement, analysis and improvement.

This meant that the handbook that had evolved over the previous eight years required a complete rewrite. However, I have maintained the basic purpose of the handbook – that of providing the reader with an understanding of each requirement of ISO 9001 through explanation, examples, lists, tables and diagrams. As there were over 300 requirements in the 1994 version of ISO 9001, this led to a book of considerable size – it was not intended as a quick read! It was and remains a source of reference and although I was tempted to restructure the book as an A-Z of ISO 9000 to reduce duplication, I have adhered to following the structure of the standard, adding clause numbers to the headings to make it user-friendly. The handbook is therefore laid out so as to follow the section numbers of ISO 9001.

Most of the requirements of the 1994 version are included in the 2000 version of ISO 9001, but few remain exactly the same. Many have been reworded or condensed to remove over-prescriptive requirements and focus on general concepts. The differences between the 1994 and 2000 versions are shown in text boxes by the side of the new requirement. In revising this handbook a lot of detail had to be omitted primarily as it was focused on manufacturing examples or detail requirements that are no longer included in the standard. Previous versions of this handbook therefore remain relevant and a useful source of information for those interested in seeking such detail.

In the previous editions the approach taken was to identify a requirement and then explain its meaning followed by some examples to illustrate how it could be implemented. In this new edition I have followed a more structured approach and for each requirement answered three basic questions: *What does it mean? Why is it important? How is it implemented?* This is so that the requirements may be perceived as reflecting concepts valid outside the context of ISO 9000.

At the end of each chapter there is a Questionnaire built from the requirements of the standard. It is not intended that these questions be used by auditors but by users of the standard in order to test the completeness of the system they have formalized. In place of the lists of do's and don'ts and the task list of previous editions, I have included a section on *Food for Thought*. This is intended to cause the reader to reflect on the previous chapter, perhaps even change perceptions but mostly confirm understanding. The do's and don'ts and task lists are within the text and will be consolidated in a new edition of the ISO 9000 Pocket Guide.

Throughout the book a common approach has been taken to the require-ments of ISO 9000. This approach is a development of that what was used in the previous editions. The standard has become more generic, it now presents the requirements in a more user-friendly format and has adopted the process approach to management. While the requirements of ISO 9001 are expressed in a way that takes the reader through a cycle starting with the quality policy, leading onto quality objectives and ending with performance being reviewed against objectives, there remain many inconsistencies that could lead to confusion. Many of the linkages between policy, objectives, processes and results are inferred – they are not expressed unambiguously. It is only by studying ISO 9000, ISO 9001 and ISO 9004 and searching for understanding that a clear logic emerges. The use of the word *quality* creates an anomaly and tends to represent the standard as simply a tool to meet customer quality requirements and no others. This is not to say that the standard is flawed. It is only saying that the concepts could be presented more clearly. Consequently I have taken an approach that requires the principles and requirements contained in the ISO 9000 family to be perceived as general business concepts and not simply limited to the achievement of *quality* in its narrowest sense. While the arguments for taking this approach are addressed in the book, the theme of the book is reflected in the following principles.

The *quality policy* exists to shape behaviour and establish the core values in an organization and therefore equates with the corporate policy – no benefits are gained from specifically expressing a quality policy and ignoring other policies because all policies influence the behaviours that are key to satisfying the needs of interested parties.

Quality is a strategic objective that is established to fulfil the needs and expectations of all interested parties and therefore equates with the corporate objectives – no benefits are gained from ranking quality equally with other objectives.

The *quality management system* is *the* management system that enables the organization to fulfil its purpose and mission. Consequently in this handbook the term *management system* is used throughout (except when referring to the requirements of the standard) rather than terms *quality system, quality management system* or simply *QMS*. Organizations have only one system – no benefits are gained from formalizing part of a system that focuses on quality. By dropping the word quality from this term, it is hoped that the reader will begin to perceive a system that is significantly more beneficial than the quality system addressed by ISO 9000:1994.

The *adequacy, suitability and effectiveness* of the management system is judged by how well the system enables the organization to achieve its objectives, operate efficiently and fulfil its purpose and mission – no benefits are gained from simply focusing on one aspect of performance when it is a combination of factors that deliver organizational performance.

If you read the handbook from cover to cover you will discover that these principles are repeated regularly throughout in one form or another Hopefully this is not too irritating but the handbook is intended as a reference book and I felt that the alternative of frequent cross references would be just as irritating. However, we rarely learn by a chance observation and it often requires frequent exposure to ideas presented in different forms and context before our beliefs or perceptions are changed.

The first three chapters provide background information with the subsequent five chapters dealing with the sections of ISO 9001 that contain the requirements. In this way the chapter numbers of the book mirror the section headings of the ISO 9001.

Chapter 1 addresses the issues that have arisen in the use of ISO 9000, the various perceptions surrounding the standard and the associated infrastructure as well as some of the negative influences and misconceptions. This sets the scene for the approach taken in the remainder of the book.

Chapter 2 is a revised and much enhanced chapter on basic concepts. The opportunity has been taken to place the more general concepts and principles in this chapter and provide greater alignment with the topics covered by the standard. Following the style of the first edition, I have included management theory drawn from authors in the field of both general management and quality management.

Chapter 3 addresses the role of the family of standards and answers frequently asked questions about its purpose, uses, application and origin.

Having discovered the misconceptions surrounding the use of the standard I was prompted to explore a little more of the history, not of the standard itself but of the concepts that are expressed in the standard and applied to its use. Many criticize the standard for the burden of bureaucracy that has arisen since its introduction but what I have found is that ISO 9000 is not a cause but a symptom of an age in which prescription and regulation has dominated business relationships for centuries.

Chapters 4 – 8 address the requirements of ISO 9001. As the 1987 and 1994 versions of ISO 9001 were structured around twenty elements, the chapters were not exceedingly long. As there are now only five sections of requirements in ISO 9001 covering some 250 requirements with most of the original 20 elements being crammed into Section 7 on *Product Realization*, Chapter 7 of the handbook is unfortunately very long. However, the clause numbers added to the headings together with a comprehensive index should make finding topics relatively easy.

Finally an appendix contains a glossary of terms used in ISO 9000 and in this handbook. Definitions contained in ISO 9000 have not been repeated except for the purpose of comparison.

Other than for comparisons between the 1994 and the 2000 version of the standard, all references to ISO 9000, ISO 9001 and ISO 9004 refer to the 2000 versions. In view of the differing perceptions, when the term ISO 9000 is used in this book it means the standard and not its attendant infrastructure. Comment on any aspect of the infrastructure will be referred to it by its usual name – auditing, consulting, certification, training or accreditation.

I have retained the direct style of writing referring to the reader as 'you'. You may be a manager, an auditor, a consultant, an instructor, a member of staff, a student or simply an interested reader. You may not have the power to do what is recommended in this book but may know of someone who does whom you can influence.

The interpretations are those of the author and should not be deemed to be those of the International Organization for Standardization, any National Standards Body or any Certification Body.

As a result of the radical changes reflected in ISO 9000:2000 many thousands of organizations that committed to ISO 9000 certification now face a dilemma. In order to keep their certificates they may have to make some significant changes to the way their organization is managed and will therefore need to decide whether to maintain certification or to abandon it. ISO 9000 merely brings together concepts that have been applied in organizations for many years – not some unique concepts of management that only exist to put a 'badge on the wall'. By all means reconsider the value of ISO 9000 certification but it would be foolish to abandon concepts that have been proven to sustain and improve an organization's performance in the belief that they are inextricably linked with certification. The fact that some ISO 9000 certified organizations perform worse than non-certified organizations is no more reason to denounce the concepts embodied in ISO 9000 than to denounce Newtonian Physics formulated in the 17th century because several road and rail bridges collapsed in the 20th century. This book is written for those who want to improve the performance of their organization and whether or not certification is a goal, I hope the book will continue to provide a source of inspiration in the years ahead.

I am grateful to my associate John Thompson whose ideas and insight provided the clarity needed to explain the requirements of ISO 9000 in the wider context of business management and for his teachings on process management, to my wife Angela for her constructive comment and editing of the manuscript and to Claire Harvey of Butterworth-Heinemann for her continual encouragement and patience as one deadline after another passed by. I am indebted to the many clients and associates I have talked with particularly in the months upto and shortly after the publication of ISO 900:2000. The teachings of P. F. Drucker have been a constant inspiration particularly in clarifying issues on strategic management. The teachings of W. E. Deming have been particularly useful for this fourth edition in clarifying the theory of variation and confirming my ideas on systems theory. The teachings of J. M. Juran have also been a constant inspiration particularly concerning break-through and control principles and quality planning. The treatment of *competence* in Chapter 6 would not have been possible without the teachings of Shirley Fletcher and contributions from John Thompson.

David Hoyle
Monmouth
E-mail:hoyle@transition-support.com
April 2001

Chapter 1
Introduction

By three methods we may learn wisdom:
First, by reflection, which is noblest;
Second, by imitation, which is easiest; and
third by experience, which is the bitterest.

Confucius

Perceptions

Since the publication of the ISO 9000 family of standards in 1987 a new industry has grown in its shadow. The industry is characterized by Standards Bodies, Accreditation Bodies, Certification Bodies, Consulting Practices, Training Providers, Software Providers and a whole raft of publications, magazines, web sites and schemes – all in the name of quality! But has ISO 9000 fulfilled its promise? There are those with vested interests that would argue that it has improved the efficiency and effectiveness of organizations. Equally others would argue that it has done tremendous damage to industry. One of the problems in assessing the validity of the pros and cons of the debate is the very term ISO 9000 because it means different things to different people.

Perceptions that have been confirmed time and again by consultants, other organizations and frequent audits from the certification bodies over the last 20 years makes these perceptions extremely difficult to change. If ISO 9000 is perceived rightly or wrongly, as a badge on the wall or a set of documents, then that is what it is. If this was not the intent of ISO 9000 then clearly we have to do something about it. But why should these perceptions be changed? After all, can 340,000 organizations have got it wrong? Some organizations in fact did use ISO 9000 wisely but they are likely to be in the minority. Many organizations also chose not to pursue ISO 9000 certification and focused on

TQM but that too led to dissatisfaction with the results. As an introduction to this handbook on ISO 9000:2000 it may be useful to take a look at these perceptions – look at how we have come to think about ISO 9000, quality, quality systems, certification and inspection. A realization of these perceptions will hopefully enable us to approach the new standard with a different perspective or at least provide food for thought.

How we think about ISO 9000

To the advocate, ISO 9000 is a standard and all the negative comments have nothing to do with the standard but the way it has been interpreted by organizations, consultants and auditors. To the critics, ISO 9000 is what it is perceived to be and this tends to be the standard and its support infrastructure. This makes any discussion on the subject difficult and inevitably leads to disagreement.

Some people often think about ISO 9000 as a system. As a group of documents, ISO 9000 is a set of interrelated ideas, principles and rules and could therefore be considered a system in the same way that we refer to the metric system or the imperial system of measurement. ISO 9000 is both an international standard and until December 2000, was a family of some 20 international standards. As a standard, ISO 9000 was divided into 4 parts with part 1 providing guidelines on the selection and use of the other standards in the family. The family of standards included requirements for quality assurance and guidelines on quality management. Some might argue that none of these are in fact standards in the sense of being quantifiable. The critics argue that the standards are too open to interpretation to be standards – anything that produces such a wide variation is surely an incapable process with one of its primary causes being a series of objectives that are not measurable. However, if we take a broader view of standards, any set of rules, rituals, requirements, quantities, targets or behaviours that have been agreed by a group of people could be deemed to be a standard. Therefore by this definition, ISO 9000 is a standard.

←ISO 9000 is also perceived as a label given to the family of standards and the associated certification scheme. However, certification was never a requirement of any of the standards in the ISO 9000 family – this came from customers. Such notions as 'We are going for ISO 9000' imply ISO 9000 is a goal like a university degree and like a university degree there are those who pass who are educated and those who merely pass the exam. You can purchase degrees from unaccredited universities just as you can purchase ISO 9000 certificates from unaccredited certification bodies. The acceptance criteria is the same, it is the means of measurement and therefore the legitimacy of the certificates that differ.

As many organizations did not perceive they had a quality management system before they embarked on the quest for ISO 9000 certification, the programme, the system and the people were labelled 'ISO 9000' as a kind of shorthand. Before long, these labels became firmly attached and difficult to shed and consequently why people refer to ISO 9000 as a 'system'.

How we think about quality management systems

All organizations have a way of doing things. For some it rests in the mind of the leaders, for others it is translated onto paper and for most it is a mixture of the two. Before ISO 9000 came along, organizations had found ways of doing things that worked for them. We seem to forget that before ISO 9000, we had built the pyramids, created the mass production of consumer goods, broken the sound barrier, put a man on the moon and brought him safely back to earth. It was organizational systems that made these achievements possible. Systems, with all their inadequacies and inefficiencies, enabled mankind to achieve objectives that until 1987 had completely revolutionized society. The next logical step was to improve these systems and make them more predictable, more efficient and more effective – optimizing performance across the whole organization – not focusing on particular parts at the expense of the others. What ISO 9000 did was to encourage the formalization of those parts of the system that served the achievement of product quality – often diverting resources away from other parts of the system.

⟶ ⌊ISO 9000 did require organizations to establish a quality system as a means of ensuring product met specified requirements. What many organizations failed to appreciate was that they all have a management system – a way of doing things and because the language used in ISO 9000 was not consistent with the language of their business, many people did not see the connection between what they did already and what the standard required. People may think of the organization as a system, but what they don't do is manage the organization as a system. They fail to make linkages between actions and effects and will change one function without considering the effects on another.⌋

New activities were therefore bolted onto the organization such as management review, internal audit, document control, records control, corrective and preventive action without putting in place the necessary linkages to maintain system integrity. What emerged was an organization with warts as illustrated in Figure 1.1. This was typical of those organizations that merely pursued the 'badge on the wall'. Such was the hype, the pressure and the razzmatazz, that the part that was formalized using ISO 9000 became labelled as the ISO 9000 quality system. It isolated parts of the organization and made them less efficient. Other organizations recognized that quality was an

Figure 1.1 Bolt-on systems

important issue and formalized part of their informal management system. When ISO 14001 came along this resulted in the formalization of another part of their management system to create an Environmental Management System (EMS). In the UK at least, with the advent of BS 8800 on Occupational Health and Safety Management Systems, a third part of the organization's management system was formalized. The effect of this piecemeal formalization is illustrated in Figure 1.2. This perception of ISO 9000, ISO 14000 and any other management system standard is also flawed – but it is understandable.

The 1994 edition of the ISO 9000 family of standards was characterized by its focus on procedures. In almost every element of ISO 9001 there was a requirement for the supplier to establish and maintain documented procedures to control some aspect of an organization's operations. So much did this requirement pervade the standard that it generated the belief that ISO 9000 was simply a matter of documenting what you do and doing what you document. This led to the perception that ISO 9000 built a bureaucracy of procedures, records and forms with very little effect on quality.

The 1994 version also created a perception that quality systems only exist to assure customers that product meets requirements. ISO 9001 was often referred

Figure 1.2 Separate systems

to as a Quality Assurance standard because customers used it for obtaining an assurance of the quality of products being supplied. This perception is illustrated in Figure 1.3, in which the organization is represented as a circle containing islands that serve the assurance of quality and with the remainder of the organization running the business.

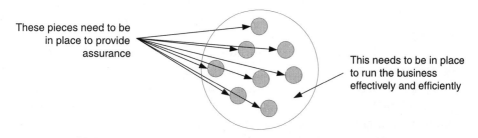

These pieces need to be in place to provide assurance

This needs to be in place to run the business effectively and efficiently

Figure 1.3   Separating assurance activities from management activities

Assurance equates with provision of objective evidence and this equates with the generation and maintenance of documentation i.e. procedures and records. With the pressure from auditors to show evidence, organizations were persuaded to believe that if it wasn't documented it didn't exist and this ultimately led to the belief that quality systems were a set of documents. These systems tended to be sets of documents that were structured around the elements of a standard. None of the standards required this but this is how it was implemented by those who lacked understanding. However, ISO 9001 clause 4. 2. 1 required suppliers to establish a quality system to <u>ensure</u> (not assure) that product met specified requirements. In other words, it required the system to cause conformity with requirements. A set of documents alone cannot cause product to conform to requirements. When people change the system they invariably mean that they update or revise the system documentation. When the system is audited invariably it is the documentation that is checked and compliance with documentation verified. There is often little consideration given to processes, resources, behaviours or results. As few people seem to have read ISO 8402, it is not surprising that the documents are perceived as a system. (NB In talking with over 600 representatives of UK companies in 1999 and 2000 the author discovered that less than 10% had read ISO 8402) But ISO 8402 defined a system rather differently. A quality system was defined as *the organization structure, procedures, processes and resources needed to implement quality management* – clearly not a set of documents. The 1994 version required a system to be established and documented. If the system was a set of documents, why then require it to be established as well as documented?

The persistence of the auditors to require documentation led to situations where documentation only existed in case something went wrong – in case someone was knocked down by a bus. While the unexpected can result in disaster for an organization it needs to be based on a risk assessment. There was often no assessment of the risks or the consequences. This could have been avoided simply by asking the question 'So what?' So there are no written instructions for someone to take over the job but even if there were, would it guarantee there were no hiccups? Would it *ensure* product quality? Often the new person sees improvements that the previous person missed or deliberately chose not to make – often the written instructions are no use without training.

There has also been a perception in the service industries that ISO 9000 quality systems only deal with the procedural aspects of a service and not the professional aspects. For instance in a medical practice, the ISO 9000 quality system is often used only for processing patients and not for the medical treatment. In legal practices, the quality system again has been focused only on the administrative aspects and not the legal issues. The argument for this is that there are professional bodies that deal with the professional side of the business. In other words, the quality system only addresses the non-technical issues, leaving the profession to address the technical issues. This is not *quality management*. The quality of the service depends upon both the technical and non-technical aspects of the service. Patients who are given the wrong advice would remain dissatisfied even if their papers were in order or even if they were given courteous attention and advised promptly. To achieve quality one has to consider both the product and the service. A faulty product delivered on time, within budget and with a smile remains a faulty product!

How we think about certification

When an organization chooses not to pursue ISO 9000 certification or not to retain the ISO 9000 certificate, it should make no difference to the way the organization is managed. It's similar to the man who chooses not to take the course examination. He still has the knowledge he has acquired whether or not he takes the exam and gets a certificate. What he cannot do is demonstrate to others that he has reached a certain level of education without having to prove it every time. People who know him don't care that he didn't take the exam. It is only those who don't know him that he will have difficulty convincing.

Many organizations were driven to seek ISO 9000 certification by pressure from customers rather than as an incentive to improve business performance and therefore sought the quickest route to certification. The critics called this coercion and like most command and control strategies, believed it resulted in managers cheating just to get the badge. What was out of character was that suppliers that were well known to customers were made to jump through this hoop in order to get a tick in a box in a list of approved suppliers. It became a 'necessary evil' to do business. Certainly when perceived as a means to get a badge, the standard was no more than a marketing tool. It could have been used as a framework for improvement but the way it was imposed on organizations generated fear brought about by ignorant customers who mistakenly believed that imposing ISO 9000 would improve quality. To achieve anything in our society we inevitably have to impose rules and regulations – what the critics regard as *command and control* – but unfortunately, any progress we make masks the disadvantages of this strategy and because we only do what we are required to do, few people learn. When people make errors more rules are imposed until we are put in a straightjacket and productivity plummets. There is a need for regulations to keep sharks out of the bathing area, but if the regulations prevent bathing we defeat the objective, as did many of the customers that imposed ISO 9000.

Certification is not a requirement of ISO 9000, nor is it encouraged by the standard. It is however encouraged by governments and this is where the misunderstanding arises. Governments encouraged organizations to use ISO 9000 alongside product standards in their purchasing strategy so as to raise the standard of quality in national and international trade (Department of Trade and Industry, 1982)[1]. Certification became a requirement of customers – they mandated it through contracts. ISO 9000 was a convenient standard to use in order for customers to gain an assurance of quality. ISO 9000 was launched at a time when customers in the western world took an adversarial approach to their suppliers. It came out of the defence industry where there was a long tradition of command and control. As a consequence, ISO 9000 followed the same pattern of imposing requirements to prevent failures that experience had shown led to poor product quality. ISO 9000 did not require purchasers to impose ISO 9000 on their suppliers. What it *did* require was for purchasers to determine the controls necessary to ensure purchased product met their requirements. But the easy way of meeting this requirement was to impose ISO 9000. It saved the purchaser from having to assess for themselves the capability of suppliers. Unfortunately the assessment process was ineffective because it led to suppliers getting the badge that were not capable of meeting their customer's requirements. ISO 9001 required suppliers to establish a quality system to ensure that product met specified requirements but it allowed organizations to specify their *own requirements* – provided they did what they said they did, they could receive the certificate. As there were no specific requirements in the standard that caused the auditors to verify that these requirements were those needed to meet the needs and expectations of customers, organizations could produce rubbish and still receive the badge. Consistency was being checked – not quality.

Before ISO 9000, organizations were faced with meeting all manner of rules and regulations. Government inspectors and financial auditors frequently examined the books and practices for evidence of wrong-doing but none of this resulted in organizations creating something that was not integrated within the routines they applied to manage the business. When ISO 9000 came along, many organizations embarked upon a course of action that was perceived to have no value except to keep the badge – the ISO 9000 certificate. Activities were only documented and performed because the standard required it. Take away the certification and there was no longer a business need for many of these procedures and activities.

ISO 9000–1 in fact suggested that there were two approaches to using ISO 9000: 'management-motivated' and 'stakeholder-motivated'. It suggested that the supplier should consult ISO 9000–1 to understand the basic concepts but few organizations did this. It suggested that with the management-motivated approach organizations should firstly design their systems to ISO 9004–1 and then choose an appropriate assessment standard. It also suggested that with the stakeholder-motivated approach an organization should initially implement a quality system in response to the demands of customers and then select ISO 9001, ISO 9002 or ISO 9003 as appropriate for assessment. It suggested that having found significant improvements in product quality, costs and internal operating results from this approach, the organization would initiate a management-motivated approach based on ISO 9004. Those suppliers that actually obtained such benefits no doubt did initiate a management-motivated approach but many only focused on getting a certificate and therefore did not gain any benefits apart from the marketing advantage that ISO 9000 certification brought.

Believing that ISO 9000 was only about 'documenting what you do', organizations set to work on responding to the requirements of the standard as a list of activities to be carried out. Again, this belief became so widespread that ISO co-ordinators or ISO 9000 project managers were appointed to establish and maintain the quality system. In some organizations, managers were assigned responsibility for meeting the requirements of a particular element of the standard even though there was not only no requirement to do so, but also no business benefit from doing so. Consultants were engaged to write the documents and apart from some new procedures governing internal audits, management review and document control, very little changed. There was a lot of money thrown at these projects in the quest to gain certification, However, none of the surveys conducted since 1987 have shown any significant improvement in an organization's overall performance – quite simply because nothing changed, not the processes, not the people nor the culture. The 'system' existed just to keep the badge on the wall. The ninth ISO survey (International Organization of Standardization, 2000)[2] indicated that 9862 certificates had been withdrawn at the end of 1999 and of these 473 were for reasons of either insufficient return on investment or no business advantage. However some 7186 organizations discontinued certification for reasons unknown, indicating that certification was probably perceived as not adding value.

To make matters worse, the certification scheme established to assess the capability of organizations perpetuated this belief. These third party auditors would reinforce the message by commencing their interviews with the question 'Have you got a procedure for . . . ?' Audits would focus on seeking evidence that the organization was implementing its procedures. Desperate to put the 'badge on the wall' organizations responded to the auditor's expectations and produced quality manuals that mirrored the structure of the standard – manuals containing nothing more than the requirements of section 4 of ISO 9001 or ISO 9002, reworded as policy statements. The auditor would therefore establish an organization's readiness for the audit by the closeness with which the quality manual addressed the requirements of the standard rather than by examining performance. A more sensible approach might have been to ask for the last three months data for the key processes to establish if the processes were stable.

Instead of using the whole family of standards as a framework, the standards became a stick with which to beat people. Managers would ask, where does it say that in the standard and if the auditor or consultant could not show them, the manager did nothing. The astute manager would ask, why would I want to do that and if the auditor or consultant could not give a sound business case for doing it, the manager did nothing.

Customers of auditor training courses behaved as though all they wanted was a training certificate. This led to lower standards. The auditors were poorly trained and the trainers became a victim of the system. Rules forced training bodies to cover certain topics in a certain time. Commercial pressure resulted in training bodies cutting costs to keep the courses running. Customers would not pay for more than they thought they needed but they did not know what they needed. Tell them what is required to convert a novice into a competent auditor and they wince! When there are providers only too willing to relieve them of their cash, customers opt for the cheaper solution. The training auditors received focused on auditing for conformity and led to auditors learning to catch people out. It did not lead to imparting the skills necessary for them to conduct audits that added value for organizations.

Certification bodies were also in competition and this led to auditors spending less time conducting the audit that was *really* needed. They focused on the easy things to spot – not on whether the system was effective. Had the provision of certification services not been commercialized, there would not have been pressure to compromise quality. Organizations stayed with their certification body because they gave them an easy ride. What certification body would deliberately do things to lose customers? They will do everything they can to keep customers – even if it means turning a blind eye. Certification bodies were also barred from making suggestions on improvement because it was considered to be consulting. They therefore stuck to familiar ground. The accreditation bodies were supposed to be supervising the certification bodies but they also needed revenue to be able to deploy assessors in sufficient numbers to maintain the integrity of the certification scheme. It had to be commercially viable at the outset otherwise the whole certification scheme would not have got off the ground because governments would not have been prepared to sponsor it. It is interesting that in the UK, there has been considerable protest against privatising the National Air Traffic Service for fear that profits will compromise air space safety. There was no outcry against commercially operated quality system certification but equally unsafe products could emerge out of an ineffective quality system and enter the market.

The certification scheme also added another dimension – that of scope. The scope of certification was determined by the organization so that only those parts of the quality system that were in the scope of certification were assessed. The quality system may have extended beyond the scope of certification and the scope of the standard but been far less than the scope of the business. This is illustrated in Figure 1.4.

Quality managers scurried around before and after the assessor and in doing so led everyone else to believe that all that was important to the assessor was documentation. This led others in the organization to focus on the things the auditor looked for not on the things that mattered – they became so focused on satisfying the auditor they lost sight of their objectives. They focused on surviving the audit and not on improving performance. It has the same effect as the student who crams for an examination. The certificate may be won but an education is lost. What would the organization rather have – a certificate or an effective management system? (Organizations had it in their power to terminate the contract with their Certification Body if they did not like the way they handled the assessment. They had it in their power to complain to the

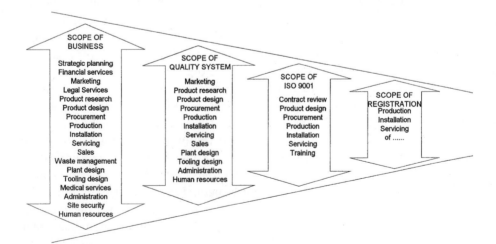

Figure 1.4 The scoping effect

Accreditation Body if they were not satisfied with the Certification Body but on both counts they failed to take any action. Certification Bodies are suppliers – not regulators. What went wrong with ISO 9000 assessments is that the auditors lost sight of the objective to improve the quality of products and services. They failed to ask themselves whether the discrepancies they found had any bearing on the quality of the product. Many of the nonconformities were only classified as such

> Is our goal to survive the audit or to improve our performance?

because the organization had chosen to document what it did regardless of its impact on quality. Auditors often held the view that if an organization took the trouble to document *it, it* must be essential to product quality and therefore by not doing *it*, product quality must be affected!

How ISO 9000 made us think about quality

ISO 9000 was conceived to bring about an improvement in product quality. It was believed that if organizations were able to demonstrate they were operating a quality system that met international standards, customers would gain greater confidence in the quality of products they purchased. It was also believed that by operating in accordance with documented procedures, errors would be reduced and consistency of output ensured. If you find the best way of achieving a result, put in place measures to prevent variation, document it and train others to apply it, it follows that the results produced should be consistently good.

The requirements of the standard were perceived to be a list of things to do to achieve quality. The ISO co-ordinator would often draw up a plan based on the following logic:

- We have to identify resource requirements so I will write a procedure on identifying resource requirements
- We have to produce quality plans so I will write a procedure on producing quality plans
- We have to record contract review so I will write a procedure on recording contract reviews
- We have to identify design changes so I will write a procedure on identifying design changes

The requirements in the standard were often not expressed as results to be achieved. Requirements for a documented procedure to be established resulted in just that. Invariably the objectives of the procedure were to *define something* rather than to *achieve something*. This led to documentation without any clear purpose that related to the achievement of quality. Those producing the documentation were focusing on meeting the standard not on achieving quality. Those producing the product were focusing on meeting the customer requirement but the two were often out of sync. As quality assurance became synonymous with procedures, so people perceived that they could achieve quality by following procedures. The dominance of procedures to the exclusion of performance is a misunderstanding of the implementers. The standard required a documented system *that ensured product met specified requirements* – a clear purpose. Once again the implementers lost sight of the objective. Or was it that they knew the objective but in order to meet it, the culture would have to change and if they could get the badge without doing so, why should they?

Issuing a procedure was considered to equate to task completed. Unfortunately, for those on the receiving end, the procedures were filed and forgotten. When the auditor came around, the individual was found to be totally unaware of the 'procedure' and consequently found noncompliant with it. However, the auditor would discover that the individual was doing the right things so the corrective action was inevitably to change the procedure. The process of issuing procedures was not questioned, the individual concerned was blamed for not knowing the procedure and the whole episode failed to make any positive contribution to the achievement of quality. But it left the impression on the individual that quality was all about following procedures. It also left the impression that quality was about consistency and providing you did what you said you would do regardless of it being in the interests of satisfying customers, it was OK. One is left wondering whether anyone consulted the dictionary in which quality is defined as *a degree of excellence*?

Another problem was that those who were to implement requirements were often excluded from the process. Instead of enquiring as to the best way of meeting a requirement, those in charge of ISO 9000 implementation assumed that issuing procedures would in fact cause compliance with requirements. It requires a study of the way work gets done to appreciate how best to meet a requirement. Procedures were required to be documented and the range and detail was intended to be appropriate to the complexity of the work, the methods used and the skills and training needed. The standard also only required work instructions where their absence would adversely affect quality. It is as though the people concerned did not read the requirement properly or had no curiosity to find out for themselves what ISO had to say about procedures – they were all too ready to be told what to do without questioning why they should be doing it.

More often than not, the topics covered by the standard were only a sample of all the things that need to be done to achieve the organization's objectives. The way the standard classified the topics was also often not appropriate to the way work was performed. As a consequence, procedures failed to be implemented because they mirrored the standard and not the work. ISO 9000 may have required documented procedures but it did not insist that they be produced in separate documents, with titles or an identification convention that was traceable to the requirements.

Critics argue (Seddon, John, 2000)[3] that ISO 9000 did not enable organizations to reduce variation as a result of following the procedures. It is true that ISO 9000 did not explain the theory of variation – it could have done, but perhaps it was felt that this was better handled by the wealth of literature available at the time. However, ISO 9000 did require organizations to identify where the use of statistical techniques was necessary for establishing, controlling and verifying process capability but this was often misunderstood. Clause 4.14 of ISO 9001 required corrective action procedures – procedures to identify variation and eliminate the cause so this should have resulted in a reduction in variation. The procedures did not always focus on results – they tended to focus on transactions – sending information or product from A to B. The concept of corrective action was often misunderstood. It was believed to be about fixing the problem and preventive action was believed to be about preventing recurrence. Had users read ISO 8402 they should have been enlightened. Had they read Deming they would have been enlightened but in many cases the language of ISO 9000 was a deterrent to learning. Had the auditors understood variation, they too could have assisted in clarifying these issues but they too seemed ignorant – willing to regard clause 4.20 as not applicable in many cases.

Clause 4.6 of the undervalued and forgotten standard ISO 9000–1 starts with 'The International Standards in the ISO 9000 family are founded upon the understanding that all work is accomplished by a process.' In clause 4.7 it starts with 'Every organization exists to accomplish value-adding work. The work is accomplished through a network of processes' In clause 4.8 it starts with 'It is conventional to speak of quality systems as consisting of a number of elements. The quality system is carried out by means of processes which exist both within and across functions' Alas, few people read ISO 9000–1 and as a result the baggage that had amassed was difficult to shed especially because there were few if any certification bodies suggesting that the guidance contained in ISO 9000–1 should be applied. Unfortunately, this message from ISO 9000–1 was not conveyed through the requirements of ISO 9001. ISO 9001 was not intended as a design tool. It was produced for contractual and assessment purposes but was used as a design tool instead of ISO 9000–1 and ISO 9004–1.

How we think about reviews, inspections and audits

Audits of the quality system were supposed to determine its effectiveness but effectiveness seemed to be judged by the extent to which procedures were being followed. ISO 9001 clause 4.1.3 did state that *the system should be reviewed for its continuing suitability and effectiveness in satisfying the requirements of the standard and the supplier's quality policy and objectives.* The words underlined were added in the 1994 revision. Clause 4.17 did require internal audits to *verify whether quality activities and related results comply with planned arrangements and to determine the effectiveness of the quality system.* Again the words underlined were added in the 1994 revision. But the original and modified wording seemed to have had no effect. Quality systems continued to be judged on product nonconformities, audit findings and customer complaints.

The management review was supposed to question the validity of these procedures, the validity of the standards and the performance of the system. It was supposed to determine whether the system was effective – i.e. whether the system enabled people to do the right things right. But effectiveness was not interpreted as doing the right things; it was interpreted as conforming to the standard. It led to quality being thought of as conformity with procedures. The reviews and audits therefore focused on deficiencies against the requirements of the standard and deviations from procedure rather than the results the system was achieving. But as the system was not considered to be the way the organization achieved its results, it was not surprising that these totally inadequate management reviews continued in the name of keeping the badge on the wall. Audits did not establish that people were doing the right things – had they done so the system would have been changed to one that caused people to do the right things right without having to be told.

It was often thought that the standard required review, approval, inspection and audit activities to be performed by personnel independent of the work. Critics argue that as a consequence both worker and inspector assumed the other would find the errors. ISO 9000 does not require independent inspection. There is no requirement that prohibits a worker from inspecting his or her own work or approving his or her own documents. It is the management that chooses a policy of not delegating authority for accepting results to those who produce them. There will be circumstances when independent inspection is necessary either as a blind check or when safety, cost, reputation or national security could be compromised by errors. What organizations could have done, and this would have met ISO 9000 requirements, is to let the worker decide on the need for independent inspection except in special cases. However, inspection is no substitute for getting it right first time and it is well known that you cannot inspect quality into an output if it was not there to start with.

Is ISO 9000:2000 any different?

There are those who want to believe that the standard has not changed very much (if at all) and do not believe it has changed in its intent and as a consequence do not have to change their approach The sad thing is that if the standard is perceived as not having significantly changed, it will continue to wreak havoc by being interpreted and used in the same inappropriate way that it has been for the last 14 years. But there is another way. By looking at ISO 9000 as a framework upon which can be built a successful organization (rather than as a narrow set of minimum requirements) significant benefits can be gained. There are real benefits from managing organizations as a set of interconnected processes focused on achieving objectives that have been derived from an understanding of the needs of customers and other interested parties.

In the next chapter you will get re-acquainted with the concepts – so important if you are to avoid repeating the mistakes of the past, but first let us summarize the key messages from Chapter 1.

Summary

In this chapter we have examined the various perceptions about ISO 9000 and its infrastructure. These have arisen from personal observation, discussion with clients and colleagues and studying John Seddon's contribution in – *The case against ISO 9000*.

Where appropriate the perceptions are challenged from a basis of what the standard actually requires. This is no excuse for the resultant confusion. The standard could have been better written but it is unfair to put all the blame on the standard. The standards bodies, certification bodies, accreditation bodies, training providers, consultants, software providers and many others have contributed to this confusion. Commercial interests have as usual compromised quality. We have followed like sheep, pursued goals without challenging whether they were the right goals but most of all we have forgotten why we were doing this. It was to improve quality, but clearly it has not.

ISO 9000 merely brings together concepts that have been applied in organizations for many years – not some unique concepts of management that only exist to put a 'badge on the wall', but it appears that the use of international standards to consolidate and communicate these concepts has not been as effective as we believed it would be. The BNFL problems with fake quality control records, the Firestone problem with unqualified materials, the SA 80 rifle that jams in cold weather, laser guided bombs that miss the target and the recent spate of problems with the railways in the UK all send the signal that we have not solved the problem of effectively managing quality. This is despite ISO 9000 and the teachings of Juran, Deming, Feigenbaum, Ishikawa, Crosby and many others. ISO 9000:2000 is unlikely to change this situation because all these problems are caused by people who for one reason or another chose not to do the right things. All we can hope for is that ISO 9000:2000 will raise the bar enough to enable more organizations to satisfy more customers and do less harm to society.

Introduction – Food for thought

- Does ISO 9000 mean different things to different people?
- If ISO 9000 is perceived rightly or wrongly, as a badge on the wall, a system, a label, a goal or a set of documents, is that what it is?
- If any set of rules, rituals, requirements, quantities, targets or behaviours that have been agreed by a group of people could be deemed to be a standard – is ISO 9000 a standard?
- Do managers think of the organization as a system – if so how come they don't manage the organization as a system?
- Was ISO 9000:1994 simply a matter of documenting what you do and doing what you document?
- Do quality systems only exist to assure customers that product meets requirements?
- Do you believe that if it's not documented it doesn't exist and that's why your quality system is a set of documents?
- Do you believe that you can write instructions that don't rely on the user being trained?
- Can a faulty product delivered on time, within budget and with a smile be anything other than a faulty product?
- If your organization chooses not to pursue ISO 9000 certification or not to retain the certificate, will it make any difference to the way the organization is managed?
- Did *you* cheat to get the ISO 9000 certificate?
- Did your application of ISO 9000 prevent you from producing non-conforming product or did it simply prevent you from producing product?
- Is your organization one of those that coerced its suppliers into seeking ISO 9000 certification because it was believed that the standard required it?
- Did you establish a quality system to ensure that product met your customer's requirements or did you simply use it to ensure you met your own requirements?
- If you were to take away the ISO 9000 certification would there be a business need for all the procedures?
- Did your third party auditor establish your organization's readiness for the audit by the closeness with which the quality manual addressed the requirements of the standard?
- Did you focus on the things the auditor looked for – not on the things that mattered?
- Were your management more interested in surviving the audit than improving performance?
- Were those producing the documentation focusing on meeting the standard or achieving quality?

- Did your management believe the system was effective if it conformed to the standard?
- Do you believe there are real benefits from managing organizations as a set of interconnected processes focused on achieving objectives that have been derived from an understanding of the needs of customers and other interested parties?

If so read on!

Bibliography

1. Department of Trade and Industry, (1982). *White Paper on Quality, standards and competitiveness*, HMSO.
2. International Organization of Standardization, (2000). *The ISO Survey of ISO 9000 and ISO 14000 Certificates Ninth cycle 1999*, ISO.
3. Seddon, John, (2000). *The case against ISO 9000*, Oak Tree Press.

Chapter 2
Basic concepts

Don't throw away the old bucket until you know
whether the new one holds water.

Swedish Proverb

Principles or prescription

One of the great problems in our age is to impart understanding in the minds of those who have the ability and opportunity to make decisions that affect our lives. There is no shortage of information – in fact there is too much now we can search a world of information from the comfort of our armchair. We are bombarded with information but it is not knowledge – it does not necessarily lead to understanding. With so many conflicting messages from so many people, it is difficult to determine the right thing to do. There are those whose only need is a set of principles from which they are able to determine the right things to do. There are countless others who need a set of rules derived from principles that they can apply to what they do and indeed others who need a detailed prescription derived from the rules for a particular task. In the translation from principles to prescription, inconsistencies arise. Those translating the principles into rules or requirements are often not the same as those translating the rules into a detailed prescription. The principles in the field of quality management have not arisen out of academia but from life in the work place. Observations from the work place have been taken into academia, analysed, synthesized and refined to emerge as universal principles. These principles have been expressed in many ways and in their constant refreshment the language is modernized and simplified, but the essence hardly changed.

Without a set of principles, achieving a common understanding in the field of quality management would be impossible. Since Juran, Deming and Feigenbaum wrote about quality management in the 1950s there has been considerable energy put into codifying the field of quality management and a set of principles from which we can derive useful rules, regulations and requirements has emerged. This chapter addresses these principles in a way that is intended to impart understanding not only in the minds of those who prefer principles to prescription, but also in the minds of those who prefer prescriptions. There is nothing intrinsically wrong with wanting a prescription. It saves time, it's repeatable, it's economic and it's the fastest way to get things done but it has to be right. The receivers of prescriptions need enough understanding to know whether what they are being asked to do is appropriate to the circumstances they are facing.

The concepts expressed in this chapter embody universal principles and have been selected and structured in a manner that is considered suitable for users of the ISO 9000 family of standards. It is not intended as a comprehensive guide to quality management – some further reading is given in the Bibliography. ISO 9000:2000 also contains concepts some of which are questionable but these will be dealt with as they arise. The aim is to give the reader a balanced view and present a logical argument that is hoped will lead to greater understanding. As ISO 9000 is supposed to be about the achievement of quality, there is no better place to start than with an explanation of the word *quality*.

Quality

We all have needs, wants, requirements and expectations. Needs are essential for life, to maintain certain standards, or essential for products and services, to fulfil the purpose for which they have been acquired. According to Maslow (Maslow, Abraham H., 1954)[1], man is a wanting being; there is always some need he wants to satisfy. Once this is accomplished, that particular need no longer motivates him and he turns to another, again seeking satisfaction. Everyone has basic physiological needs that are necessary to sustain life. (Food, water, clothing, shelter). Maslow's research showed that once the physiological needs are fulfilled, the need for safety emerges. After safety come social needs followed by the need for esteem and finally the need for self-actualization or the need to realize ones full potential. Satisfaction of physiological needs is usually associated with money – not money itself but what it can buy. The hierarchy of needs is shown in Figure 2.1.

These needs are fulfilled by the individual purchasing, renting or leasing products or services. Corporate needs are not too dissimilar. The physiological needs of organizations are those necessary to sustain survival. Often profit

Figure 2.1 Hierarchy of needs

comes first because no organization can sustain a loss for too long but functionality is paramount – the product or service must do the job for which it is intended regardless of it being obtained cheaply. Corporate safety comes next in terms of the safety of employees and the safety and security of assets followed by social needs in the form of a concern for the environment and the community as well as forming links with other organizations and developing contacts. Esteem is represented in the corporate context by organizations purchasing luxury cars, winning awards, badges such as ISO 9000, superior offices and infrastructures and possessing those things that give it power in the market place and government. Self-actualization is represented by an organization's preoccupation with growth, becoming bigger rather than better, seeking challenges and taking risks. However, it is not the specific product or service that is needed but the benefits that possession brings that is important. This concept of benefits is most important and key to the achievement of quality.

Requirements are what we request of others and may encompass our needs but often we don't fully realize what we need until after we have made our request. For example, now that we own a mobile phone we discover we really need hands-free operation when using the phone while driving a vehicle. Our requirements at the moment of sale may or may not therefore express all our needs. By focusing on benefits resulting from products and services, needs can be converted into wants such that a need for food may be converted into a want for a particular brand of chocolate. Sometimes the *want* is not essential but the higher up the hierarchy of needs we go, the more a *want* becomes essential to maintain our social standing, esteem or to realize our personal goals. Our requirements may therefore include such wants – what we would like to have but are not essential for survival.

Expectations are *implied needs* or *requirements*. They have not been requested because we take them for granted – we regard them to be understood within our particular society as the accepted norm. They may be things to which we are accustomed, based on fashion, style, trends or previous experience. One therefore expects sales staff to be polite and courteous, electronic products to be safe and reliable, policemen to be honest, coffee to be hot etc. One would like politicians to be honest but in some countries we have come to expect them to be corrupt, dishonest or at least, economical with the truth!

In supplying products or services there are three fundamental parameters that determine their saleability. They are price, quality and delivery. Customers require products and services of a given quality to be delivered by or be available by a given time and to be of a price that reflects value for money. These are the requirements of customers. An organization will survive only if it creates and retains satisfied customers and this will only be achieved if it offers for sale products or services that respond to customer needs and expectations as well as requirements. While price is a function of cost, profit margin and market forces, and delivery is a function of the organization's efficiency and effectiveness, quality is determined by the extent to which a product or service successfully serves the purposes of the user during usage (not just at the point of sale). Price and delivery are both transient features, whereas the impact of quality is sustained long after the attraction or the pain of price and delivery has subsided.

> **Quality**
> The degree to which a set of inherent characteristics fulfils a need or expectation that is stated, general implied or obligatory.

The word *quality* has many meanings:

- A degree of excellence
- Conformance with requirements
- The totality of characteristics of an entity that bear on its ability to satisfy stated or implied needs
- Fitness for use
- Fitness for purpose
- Freedom from defects imperfections or contamination
- Delighting customers

These are just a few meanings; however, the meaning used in the context of ISO 9000 was concerned with the totality of characteristics that satisfy needs but in the 2000 version this has changed. Quality in ISO 9000:2000 is defined as the degree to which a set of inherent characteristics fulfils requirements. The former definition focused on an entity that was described as a product or service but with this new definition, the implication is that quality is relative to what something should be and what it is. The something maybe a product, service, decision, document, piece of information or any output from a process. In describing an output, we express it in terms of its characteristics. To comment on the quality of anything we need a measure of its characteristics and a basis for comparison. By combining the definition of the terms *quality* and *requirement* in ISO 9000:2000, quality can be expressed as *the degree to which a set of inherent characteristics fulfils a need or expectation that is stated, generally implied or obligatory.*

Having made the comparison we can still assess whether the output is 'fitness for use'. In this sense the output may be of poor quality but remain fit for use. The specification is often an imperfect definition of what a customer needs; because some needs can be difficult to express clearly and it doesn't mean that by not conforming, the product or service is unfit for use. It is also possible that a product that conforms to requirements may be totally useless. It all depends on whose requirements are being met. For example, if a company sets its own standards and these do not meet customer needs, its claim to producing quality products is bogus. On the other hand, if the standards are well in excess of what the customer requires, the price tag may well be too high for what customers are prepared to pay – there probably isn't a market for a gold-plated mousetrap, for instance, except as an ornament perhaps!

The interested parties

Organizations exist because of their ability to satisfy their customers and other interested parties. There are parties other than the customer that have an interest in the organization and what it does but may not receive a product. The term quality is not defined relative to customers but to requirements and the interested parties do have requirements. ISO 9000:2000 defines an interested party as *a person or group having an interest in the performance or success of an organization*. However, the organization may not have an interest in all of them! Such parties are customers, owners, employees, contractors, suppliers, investors, unions, partners or society. When you produce products you are producing them within the intent that all these parties benefit but particularly for the benefit of customers. The other parties are not particularly interested in the products and services themselves but may be interested in their effects on their investment, their well-being and the environment.

> **Interested party**
>
> Person or group having an interest in the performance or success of an organization – includes:
>
> Customers, owners, employees, contractors, suppliers, investors, unions, partners or society

The customer

A product that possesses features that satisfy customer needs is a quality product. Likewise, one that possesses features that dissatisfy customers is not a quality product. So the final arbiter on quality is the customer. The customer is the only one who can decide whether the quality of the products and services you supply is satisfactory and you will be conscious of this either by direct feedback or by loss of sales, reduction in market share and, ultimately, loss of business. This brings us back to benefits. The customer acquires a product for the benefits that possession will bring. Therefore if the product fails to deliver the expected benefits it will be considered by the customer to be of poor quality. So when making judgements about quality, the requirement should be expressed in terms of benefits not a set of derived characteristics. In the foregoing it was convenient to use the term customer but the definition of *quality* does not only relate to customers.

> **Customer**
>
> Organization that receives a product or service – includes:
>
> Purchaser, consumer, client, end user, retailer or beneficiary

The internal customer

We tend to think of products and services being supplied to customers and in the wake of TQM, we also think of internal and external customers but in reality there is no such thing as an internal customer. A customer is a stakeholder; they have entered into a commitment in return for some benefits that possession of a product or experience of a service may bring. The internal receivers of products are not stakeholders therefore they are not customers. ISO 9000:2000 defines the customer as an organization or person that receives a product. It is implied that the organization and person referred to is external to the organization supplying the product because to interpret the term customer as either internal or external would make nonsense of requirements in ISO 90001 where the term customer is used.

> **Stakeholder**
>
> A person or organization that has freedom to provide something to or withdraw something from an enterprise.

The supply chain

The transaction between the customer and the supplier is often a complex one. There may be a supply chain from original producer through to the end user. At each transaction within this supply chain, the receiving party needs to be satisfied. It is not sufficient to simply satisfy the first receiver of the product or service. All parties in the supply chain need to be satisfied before you can claim to have supplied a quality product. Admittedly, once the product leaves your premises you may lose control and therefore cannot be held accountable for any damage that may become the product, but the inherent characteristics are your responsibility.

Society

Society is a stakeholder because it can withdraw its support for an organization. It can protest or invoke legal action. Society is represented by the regulators and regardless of whether or not a customer specifies applicable regulations *you* are under an obligation to comply with those that apply. The regulator is not interested in whether you satisfy your customers, your employees or your investors – the regulator couldn't care less if you went bankrupt! Its primary concern is the protection of society. The regulators takes their authority from the law that should have been designed to protect the innocent. Regulators are certainly stakeholders because they can withdraw their approval.

> **Regulator**
> A legal body authorized to enforce compliance with the laws and statutes of a national government.

Employees

Employees may not be interested in the products and services, but are interested in the conditions in which they are required to work. Employees are stakeholders because they can withdraw their labour.

Suppliers

Suppliers are interested in the success of the organization because it may in turn lead to their success. However, suppliers are also stakeholders because they can withdraw their patronage. They can choose their customers. If you treat your suppliers badly such as delaying payment of invoices for trivial mistakes, you may find they terminate the supply at the first opportunity putting your organization into a difficult position relative to its customer commitments.

Investors

Often the most common type of stakeholder, owners, investors including banks and shareholders are interested in protecting their stake in the business. They will withdraw their stake if the organization fails to perform. Poorly conceived products and poorly managed processes and resources will not yield the expected return and the action of investors can directly affect the supply chain – although they are not customers, they are feeding the supply chain with much needed resources. In the event that this supply of resource is terminated, the organization ceases to have the capability to serve its customers.

The success of any organization therefore depends upon understanding the needs and expectations of all the interested parties, not just its customers and

Table 2.1 Criteria used by interested parties to judge organization effectiveness

Interested party	Effectiveness criteria
Owner	Financial return
Employees	Job satisfaction, pay and conditions and quality of leadership
Customers	Quality of products and services
Community	Contribution to the community – jobs, support for other traders in the community – care for the local environment
Suppliers	Satisfactory mutual trading
Investors	Value of shares
Government	Compliance with legislation

upon managing the organization in a manner that leads to the continued satisfaction of all parties. Table 2.1 (Rollinson, D., Broadfield, A. and Edwards, D. J., 1998)[2] shows the criteria used by different interested parties. It tends to suggest that for an organization to be successful it needs to balance (not trade-off) the needs of the interested parties such that all are satisfied. There are those who believe that a focus on customers alone will result in the other parties being satisfied. There are those who believe that a focus on shareholder value will result in all other parties being satisfied. The problem is that the interested party is motivated by self interest and may not be willing to compromise.

The characteristics of quality

Classification of products and services

If we group products and services (entities) by type, category, class and grade we can use the subdivision to make comparisons on an equitable basis. But when we compare entities we must be careful not to claim one is of better quality than the other unless they are of the same grade. Entities of the same type have at least one attribute in common. Entities of the same grade have been designed for the same functional use and therefore comparisons are valid. Comparisons on quality between entities of different grades, classes, categories or types are invalid because they have been designed for a different use or purpose.

Let us look at some examples to illustrate the point. Food is a type of entity. Transport is another entity. Putting aside the fact that in the food industry the terms *class* and *grade* are used to denote the condition of post-production product, comparisons between *types* is like comparing fruit and trucks – there are no common attributes. Comparisons between *categories* are like comparing fruit and vegetables. Comparisons between *classes* are like comparing apples and oranges. Comparisons between *grades* is like comparing eating apples and cooking apples.

Now let us take another example. Transport is a type of entity. There are different categories of transport such as airliners, ships, automobiles and trains; they are all modes of transport but each has many different attributes. Differences between categories of transport are therefore differences in *modes* of transport. Within each category there are differences in class. For manufactured products, differences between classes imply differences in *purpose*. Luxury cars, large family cars, small family cars, vans, trucks, four-wheel drive vehicles etc. fall within the same category of transport but each was designed for a different purpose. Family cars are in a different class to luxury cars; they were not designed for the same purpose. It is therefore inappropriate to compare a Cadillac with a Chevrolet or a Rolls Royce Silver Shadow with a Ford Mondeo. Entities designed for the same purpose but having different specifications are of different grades. A Ford Mondeo GTX is a different grade to a Mondeo LX. They were both designed for the same purpose but differ in their performance and features.

Now let us take an example from the service industry: accommodation. There are various categories, such as rented, leased and purchased. In the rented category there are hotels, inns, guesthouses, apartments etc. It would be inappropriate to compare hotels with guesthouses or apartments with inns. They are each in a different class. Hotels are a class of accommodation within which are grades such as 5 star, 4 star, 3 star etc., indicating the facilities offered.

You can legitimately compare the quality of entities if comparing entities of the same grade. If a low-grade service meets the needs for which it was designed, it is of the requisite quality. If a high-grade product or service fails to meet the requirements for which it was designed, it is of poor quality, regardless of it still meeting the requirements for the lower grade. There is a market for such differences in products and services but should customer expectations change then what was once acceptable for a particular grade may no longer be acceptable and regrading may have to occur.

Where manufacturing processes are prone to uncontrollable variation it is not uncommon to grade products as a method of selection. The product that is free of imperfections would be the highest grade and would therefore command the highest price. Any product with imperfections would be downgraded and sold at a correspondingly lower price. Examples of such practice arise in the fruit and vegetables trade and the ceramics, glass and textile industries. In the electronic component industry, grading is a common practice to select devices that operate between certain temperature ranges. In ideal conditions all devices would meet the higher specification but due to manufacturing variation only a few may actually reach full performance. The remainder of the devices has a degraded performance but still offer all the functions of the top-grade component at lower temperatures. To say that these differences are not differences in *quality* would be misleading, because the products were all designed to fulfil the higher specification. As there is a market for such products it is expedient to exploit it. There is a range over which product quality can vary and still create satisfied customers. Outside the lower end of this range the product is considered to be of poor quality.

Quality and price

Most of us are attracted to certain products and services by their price. If the price is outside our reach we don't even consider the product or service, whatever its quality, except perhaps to form an opinion about it. We also rely on price as a comparison, hoping that we can obtain the same characteristics at a lower price. In the luxury goods market, a high price is often a mark of quality but occasionally it is a confidence trick aimed at making more profit for the supplier. When certain products and services are rare, the price tends to be high and when plentiful the price is low, regardless of their quality. One can purchase the same item in different stores at different prices, some as much as 50% less, many at 10% less than the highest price. You can also receive a discount for buying in bulk, buying on customer credit card and being a trade customer rather than a retail customer. Travellers know that goods are more expensive at the airport than from the country craft shop. However, in the country craft shop, defective goods or 'seconds' may well be on sale, whereas at the airport the supplier will as a rule, want to display only the best examples. Often an increase in the price of a product may indicate a better after-sales service, such as free on-site maintenance, free delivery, free telephone support line. The discount shops may not offer such benefits.

The price label on any product or service should be for a product or service free of defects. If there are defects the label should say as much, otherwise the supplier may well be in breach of national laws and statutes. Price is therefore not an inherent feature or characteristic of the product. It is not permanent and as shown above varies without any change to the inherent characteristics of the product. Price is a feature of the service associated with the sale of the product. Price is negotiable for the same quality of product. Some may argue that quality is expensive but in reality, the saving you make on buying low-priced goods could well be eroded by inferior service or differences in the cost of ownership.

Quality and cost

Philip Crosby published his book *Quality Is Free* in 1979 and caused a lot of raised eyebrows among executives because they always believed the removal of defects was an in-built cost in running any business. To get quality you had to pay for inspectors to detect the errors! What Crosby told us was that if we could eliminate all the errors and reach zero defects, we would not only reduce our costs but also increase the level of customer satisfaction by several orders of magnitude. In fact there is the cost of doing the right things right first time and the cost of *not* doing the right things right first time. The latter are often referred to as *quality costs* or the cost incurred because failure is possible. Using this definition, if failure of a product, a process or a service is not possible, there would be no *quality costs*. It is rather misleading to refer to the cost incurred because failure is possible as *quality costs* because we could classify the costs as avoidable costs and unavoidable costs. We have to pay for labour, materials, facilities, machines, transport etc. These costs are unavoidable but we are also paying in addition some cost to cover the prevention, detection and removal of errors. Should customers have to pay for the errors made by others? There is a basic cost if failure is not possible and an additional cost in preventing and detecting failures and correcting errors because our prevention and detection programmes are ineffective. However, there is variation in all processes but it is only the variation that exceeds the tolerable limits that incurs a penalty. If you reduce complexity and install failure-prevention measures you will be spending less on failure detection and correction. There is an initial investment to be paid, but in the long term you can meet your customer requirements at a cost far less than you were spending previously. Some customers are now forcing their suppliers to reduce internal costs so that they can offer the same products at lower prices. This has the negative effect of forcing suppliers out of business. While the motive is laudable the method is damaging to industry. There are inefficiencies in industry that need to be reduced but imposing requirements will not solve the problem. Co-operation between customer and supplier would be a better solution and when neither party can identify any further savings the target has been reached. Customers do not benefit by forcing suppliers out of business.

High quality and low quality; poor quality and good quality

When a product or service satisfies our needs we are likely to say it is of good quality and likewise when we are dissatisfied we say the product or service is of poor quality. When the product or service exceeds our needs we will probably say it is of high quality and likewise if it falls well below our expectations we say it is of low quality.

These measures of quality are all subjective. What is good to one may be poor to another. In the under-developed countries, any product, no matter what the quality, is welcomed. When you have nothing, even the poorest of goods is better than none. A product may not need to possess defects for it to be regarded as poor quality – it may not possess the features that we would expect, such as access for maintenance. These are design features that give a product its saleability. Products and services that conform to customer requirements are considered to be products of acceptable quality. However, we need to express our relative satisfaction with products and services and as a consequence use subjective terms such as high, low, good or poor quality. If a product that meets customer requirements is of acceptable quality, what do we call one that does not quite meet the requirements, or perhaps exceeds the requirements? An otherwise acceptable product has a blemish – is it now unacceptable? Perhaps not because it may still be far superior to other competing products in its acceptable features and characteristics.

While not measurable, these subjective terms enable customers to rate products and services according to the extent to which they satisfy their requirements. However, to the company supplying products and services, a more precise means of measuring quality is needed. To the supplier, a quality product is one that meets in full the perceived customer requirements.

Quality characteristics

Any feature or characteristic of a product or service that is needed to satisfy customer needs or achieve fitness for use is a *quality characteristic*. When dealing with products the characteristics are almost always technical character-istics, whereas service quality characteristics have a human dimension. Some typical quality characteristics are given below.

Product characteristics

Accessibility	Functionality	Size
Availability	Interchangeability	Susceptibility
Appearance	Maintainability	Storability
Adaptability	Odour	Strength
Cleanliness	Operability	Taste
Consumption	Portability	Testability
Durability	Producibility	Traceability
Disposability	Reliability	Toxicity
Emittance	Reparability	Transportability
Flammability	Safety	Vulnerability
Flexibility	Security	Weight

Service quality characteristics

Accessibility	Credibility	Honesty
Accuracy	Dependability	Promptness
Courtesy	Efficiency	Responsiveness
Comfort	Effectiveness	Reliability
Competence	Flexibility	Security

These are the characteristics that need to be specified and their achievement controlled, assured, improved, managed and demonstrated. These are the characteristics that form the subject matter of the product requirements referred to in ISO 9000. When the value of these characteristics is quantified or qualified they are termed *product requirements*. We used to use the term *quality requirements* but this caused a division in thinking that resulted in people regarding quality requirements as the domain of the quality personnel and technical requirements being the domain of the technical personnel. All requirements are *quality* requirements – they express needs or expectations that are intended to be fulfilled by a process output that possesses inherent characteristics. We can therefore drop the word *quality*. If a modifying word is needed in front of the word requirements it should be a word that signifies the subject of the requirements. Transportation system requirements would be requirements for a transportation system, Audio speaker design requirements would be requirements for the design of an audio speaker, component test requirements would be requirements for testing components, and management training requirements would be requirements for training managers. ISO 9000 requirements are often referred to as *quality requirements* as distinct from other types of requirements but this is misleading. ISO 9000 is no more a quality requirement than is ISO 1000 on SI units, ISO 2365 for Ammonium nitrate or ISO 246 for Rolling Bearings. The requirements of ISO 9000 are quality management system requirements – requirements for a quality management system.

Quality, reliability and safety

There is a school of thought that distinguishes between quality and reliability and quality and safety. Quality is thought to be a non-time-dependent characteristic and reliability a time-dependent characteristic. Quality is thought of as conformance to specification regardless of whether the specification actually meets the needs of the customer or society. If a product or service is unreliable, it is clearly unfit for use and therefore of poor quality. If a product is reliable but emits toxic fumes, is too heavy or not transportable when

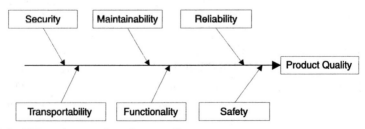

Figure 2.2 Determinants of product quality

required to be, it is of poor quality. Similarly, if a product is unsafe it is of poor quality even though it may meet its specification in other ways. In such a case the specification is not a true reflection of customer needs. A nuclear plant may meet all the specified safety requirements but if society demands greater safety standards, the plant is not meeting the requirements of society, even though it meets the immediate customer requirements. You therefore need to identify the interested parties in order to determine the characteristics that need to be satisfied. The needs of all these parties have to be satisfied in order for *quality* to be achieved. Figure 2.2 shows some of the characteristics of product quality – others have been identified previously.

Quality parameters

Differences in design can be denoted by grade or class but can also be the result of poor attention to customer needs. It is not enough to produce products that conform to the specifications or supply services that meet management's requirements. Quality is a composite of three *parameters*: quality of design, quality of conformance and quality of use:

- *Quality of design* is the extent to which the design reflects a product or service that satisfies customer needs and expectations. All the necessary characteristics should be designed into the product or service at the outset.
- *Quality of conformance* is the extent to which the product or service conforms to the design standard. The design has to be faithfully reproduced in the product or service.
- *Quality of use* is the extent by which the user is able to secure continuity of use from the product or service. Products need to have a low cost of ownership, be safe and reliable, maintainable in use and easy to use.

Products or services that do not possess the right features and characteristics either by design or by construction are products of poor quality. Those that fail to give customer satisfaction by being uneconomic to use are also products of poor quality, regardless of their conformance to specifications. Often people might claim that a product is of good quality but of poor design, or that a product is of good quality but it has a high maintenance cost. These notions result from a misunderstanding because product quality is always a composite of the quality of design, conformance and use.

Dimensions of quality

In addition to quality parameters there are three *dimensions of quality* which extend the perception beyond the concepts outlined previously:

- *The business quality dimension.* This is the extent to which the business serves the needs of all interested parties and is the outward facing view of the organization. The interested parties are not only interested in the quality of particular products and services but judge organizations by their potential to create wealth, the continuity of operations, the sustainability of supply, care of the environment, and adherence to health, safety and legal regulations.
- *The product quality dimension.* This is the extent to which the products and services provided meet the needs of specific customers.
- *The organization quality dimension.* This is the extent to which the organization maximizes its efficiency and effectiveness and is the inward facing view of the organization. Efficiency is linked with productivity which itself is linked with the motivation of personnel and the capability and utilization of resources. Effectiveness is linked with the utilization of knowledge focusing on the right things to do. This directly affects all aspects of quality.

Many organizations only concentrate on the product quality dimension, but the three are interrelated and interdependent. Deterioration in one leads to a deterioration in the others, perhaps not immediately but eventually.

As mentioned previously, it is quite possible for an organization to satisfy the customers for its products and services and fail to satisfy the other interested parties. Some may argue that the producers of pornographic literature, nuclear power, non-essential drugs, weapons etc. harm society and so regardless of these products and services being of acceptable quality to their customers, they are not regarded by society as benefiting the quality of life. Within an organization, the working environment may be oppressive – there may be political infighting – the source of revenue may be so secure that no effort is made to reduce waste. In such situations organizations may produce products and services that satisfy their customers. We must separate the three concepts above to avoid confusion. When addressing quality, it is necessary to be specific about the object of our discussion. Is it the quality of products or services, or the quality of organization in which we work, or the business as a whole, about which we are talking? If we only intend that our remarks apply to the quality of products, we should say so.

Achieving sustaining and improving quality

Several methods have evolved to *achieve, sustain and improve quality*; they are quality control, quality improvement and quality assurance, which collectively are known as *quality management*. Techniques such as quality planning, quality costs, 'Just-in-time' and statistical process control are all elements of these three methods.

Quality management

There are two schools of thought on quality management. One views quality management as the management of success and the other the elimination of failure. They are both valid. Each approaches the subject from a different angle.

The 'success' school is characterized by five questions (Hoyle, David and Thompson, John, 2001)[3]:

1 What are you trying to do?
2 How do you make it happen?
3 How do you know it's right?
4 How do you know it's the best way of doing it?
5 How do you know it's the right thing to do?

The 'failure elimination' school is characterized by five different questions

1 How do you know what is needed?
2 What could affect your ability to do it right?
3 What checks are made to verify achievement?
4 How do you ensure the integrity of these checks?
5 What action is taken to prevent a recurrence of failure?

In an ideal world, if we could design products, services and processes that could not fail we would have achieved the ultimate goal. Success means not only that products, services and processes fulfil their function but also that the function is what customers' desire. Failure means not only that products, services and processes would fail to fulfil their function but also that their function was not what customers desired. A gold-plated mousetrap that does not fail is not a success if no one needs a gold-plated mousetrap!

The introductory clause of ISO 9001:1994 contained a statement that the aim of the requirements is to achieve customer satisfaction by prevention of nonconformities. (This was indicative of the failure school of thought.) The introductory clause of ISO 9001:2000 contains a statement that the aim is to enhance customer satisfaction through the effective application of the quality management system and the assurance of conformity to customer and applicable regulatory requirements. (This is indicative of the success school of thought.)

In reality you cannot be successful unless you know of the risks you are taking and plan to eliminate, reduce or control them. A unification of these approaches is what is therefore needed for organizations to achieve, sustain and improve quality. You therefore need to approach the achievement of quality from two different angles and answer two questions. What do we need to do to succeed and what do we need to do to prevent failure?

Quality does not appear by chance, or if it does it may not be repeated. One has to design quality into the products and services. It has often been said that one cannot inspect quality into a product. A product remains the same after inspection as it did before, so no amount of inspection will change the quality of the product. However, what inspection does is measure quality in a way that allows us to make decisions on whether or not to release a piece of work. Work that passes inspection should be quality work but inspection unfortunately is not 100% reliable. Most inspection relies on human judgement and this can be affected by many factors, some of which are outside our control (such as the private life, health or mood of the inspector). We may also fail to predict the effect that our decisions have on others. Sometimes we go to great lengths in preparing organization changes and find to our surprise that we neglected something or underestimated the effect of something. We therefore need other means to deliver quality products – we have to adopt practices that enable us to achieve our objectives while preventing failures from occurring.

Quality management principles

As explained at the beginning of this chapter, we need principles to help us determine the right things to do and understand why we do what we do. The more prescription we have the more we get immersed in the detail and lose sight of our objectives – our purpose – our reason for doing what we do. Once we have lost sight of our purpose, our actions and decisions follow the mood of the moment. They are swayed by the political climate or fear of reprisals. We can so easily forget our purpose when in heated discussion, when it's not who you are but what you say and to whom you say it that is deemed important. Those people who live by a set of principles often find themselves cast out of the club for saying what they believe. However, with presence of mind and recollection of the reasons why the principles are important for survival, they could just redeem themselves and be regarded as an important contributor.

> **Did you know?**
> Neither the definition of a quality management principle nor the eight principles themselves contain the word **QUALITY**

A quality management principle is defined by ISO/TC 176 as *a comprehensive and fundamental rule or belief, for leading and operating an organization, aimed at continually improving performance over the long term by focusing on customers while addressing the needs of all other interested parties.* Eight principles (see Figure 2.3) have emerged as fundamental to the management of quality.

All the requirements of ISO 9001:2000 are related to one or more of these principles. These principles provide the reasons for the requirements and are thus very important. Each of these is addressed below. Further guidance on the application of these principles is provided in (Hoyle, David and Thompson, John, 2000)[4].

Figure 2.3   The eight quality management principles

Customer focus

This principle is expressed as follows:

> Organizations depend on their customers and therefore should understand current and future customer needs, meet customer requirements and strive to exceed customer expectations.

Customers are the lifeblood of every organization. All organizations provide something to others – they do not exist in isolation. We should remember that customers are not simply purchasers but any person or organization that receives a product or service. Not-for-profit organizations therefore have customers. Customer focus means putting your energy into satisfying customers and understanding that profitability or avoidance of loss comes from satisfying customers. Profit is not the reason for an organization's existence. Profit is needed in order to grow the organization so that it may satisfy more customers. A profit focus is an inward seeking focus, a customer focus is an outward seeking focus. Customer focus means organizing work as a process that converts customers needs into satisfied customers. It means that all processes possess a customer focus.

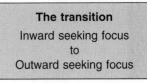

> **The transition**
> Inward seeking focus
> to
> Outward seeking focus

The principle means that everyone in the organization needs to be customer-focused – not simply the top management or the sales personnel. If people were to ask themselves before making a decision, what does the customer need? – the organization would begin to move its focus firmly in the direction of its customers. Customer focus is also about satisfying needs rather than wants. A customer may want ISO 9000 certification but in reality, it is business improvement that may be needed. While an ISO 9000 certificate may appear to give satisfaction initially, this may be short lived as the customer slowly realizes that possession of the ISO 9000 certificate did not result in the growth of business that was expected.

The customer focus principle is reflected in ISO 9001 through the requirements addressing:

- Communication with the customer
- Care for customer property
- The determination of customer needs and expectations
- Appointment of a management representative
- Management commitment

Leadership

This principle is expressed as follows:

> Leaders establish unity of purpose and direction for the organization. They should create and maintain the internal environment in which people can become fully involved in achieving the organization's objectives.

Leaders exist at all levels in an organization – they are not simply the ones at the top. Within every team there needs to be a leader – one who provides a role-model consistent with the values of the organization. It is the behaviour of leaders (our role models) that influence our lives – not just in the business world but also in our family and leisure activities. People naturally concentrate on what they are measured. It is therefore vital that leaders measure the right things. Without a good leader an organization will go where the tide takes it, and as is so predictable with tides, they will be cast upon the shoreline like the flotsam and jetsam of our society. Strong leadership will drive an organization in its chosen direction – away from disasters towards success. But leadership alone will not bring the right success. It needs to be in combination with all the other principles. Leadership without customer-focus will drive organizations towards profit for its own sake. Leadership without involving people will leave behind those who do not share the same vision – hence the second part of the principle. *Leaders are responsible for the internal environment*. If the workforce is unhappy, de-motivated, dissatisfied, it is the fault of the leaders. The culture, vision, values, beliefs and motivation in an organization arise from leadership. Good leadership strives to bring about a set of shared values – a shared vision so that everyone knows what the organization is trying to do and where it is going. A lack of vision and a

> **The transition**
>
> Aggravation
> to
> Motivation

disparate mix of values create conflict. A happy ship comes about by having good leadership. Regardless of Captain Blyth's orders, the crew's mutiny on the Bounty in 1789 was down to a failure in leadership – a failure to create the conditions that motivated people to meet the organization's objectives.

The leadership principle is reflected in ISO 9001 through the requirements addressing:

- The setting of objectives and policies
- Planning
- Internal communication
- Creating an effective work environment

Involvement of people

This principle is expressed as follows:

> People at all levels are the essence of an organization and their full involvement enables their abilities to be used for the organization's benefit.

It is not uncommon for those affected by decisions to be absent from the discussions with decision makers. Decisions that stand the test of time are more likely to be made when those affected by them have been involved. Employees cannot employ a part of a person – they take the whole person or none at all. Every person has knowledge and experience beyond the job he or she has been assigned to perform. Some are leaders in the community, some architects of

The transition
Operate
to
Cooperate

social events, building projects and expeditions. No one is limited in knowledge and experience to the current job they do. This principle means that management should tap this source of knowledge, encourage personnel to make a contribution and utilize their personal experience. It also means that management should be open – not hide its discussions unless national or business security could be threatened. Closed-door management leads to distrust among the workforce. Managers should be seen to operate with integrity and this means involving the people.

The involvement of people principle is reflected in ISO 9001 through the requirements addressing:

- Participation in design reviews
- Defining objectives, responsibilities and authority
- Creating an environment in which people are motivated
- Internal communication
- Identifying competence needs

Process approach

This principle is expressed as follows:

> A desired result is achieved more efficiently when related resources and activities are managed as a process.

All work is a process because it takes inputs and converts these into outputs. In the organizational sense, such processes add value to the input. Processes are therefore dynamic – they cause things to happen. An effective process would be one where the results were those that were required to fulfil the purpose of the organization. Every job involves people or machines equipped with resources performing a series of tasks to produce an output. No matter how simple the task, there is always an objective or a reason for doing it, the consumption of resources and expenditure of energy, a sequence of actions, decisions concerning their correctness, a judgement of completeness and an output which should be that which was expected. The organization exists to create and satisfy customers and other interested parties therefore the organization's processes must serve the needs of these interested parties. (See also *Process Management* later in this chapter.)

> **The transition**
>
> Procedure approach
> to
> Process approach

A process is as capable of producing rubbish as a procedure is capable of wasting resources – therefore processes need to be managed effectively for the required results to be produced. The process approach to management is therefore not simply converting inputs into outputs that meet requirements but about managing processes:

- that have a clearly defined purpose and objective that is based on the needs of the interested parties
- that are designed to achieve these objectives through tasks that use capable human, physical and financial resources and information
- that produce outputs that satisfy the interested parties
- that measure, review and continually improve process efficiency and effectiveness

The process approach principle is reflected in ISO 9001 through the requirements addressing:

- The identity of processes
- Defining process inputs and outputs
- Providing the infrastructure, information and resources for processes to function

System approach to management

This principle is expressed as follows:

> Identifying, understanding and managing interrelated processes as a system contributes to the organization's effectiveness and efficiency in achieving its objectives.

A system is an ordered set of ideas, principles and theories or a chain of operations that produce specific results. To be a chain of operations, the operations need to work together in a regular relationship. Taking a systems approach to management means managing the organization as a system of processes so that all the processes fit together, the inputs and outputs are connected, resources feed the processes, performance is monitored and sensors transmit information which cause changes in performance and all parts work together to achieve the organization's objectives.

This view of a system clearly implies a system is dynamic and not static. The system is not a random collection of elements, procedures and tasks but a set of interconnected processes. The systems approach recognizes that the behaviour of any part of a system has some effect on the behaviour of the system as a whole. Even if the individual processes are performing well, the system as a whole is not necessarily performing equally well. For example, assembling the best electronic components regardless of specification may not result in a world-class computer or even one that will run, because the components may not fit together. It is the interaction between parts and in the case of a management system, between processes, and not the actions of any single part or process that determines how well a system performs. Systems developed to meet the 1994 version of the standard were often based on a functional approach to management i.e. the systems were collection of functions or departments – not processes.

The system approach principle is reflected in ISO 9001 through the requirements addressing:

● Establishing, implementing and maintaining the management system
● Interconnection, interrelation and sequence of processes
● The links between processes
● Establishing measurement processes

Continual improvement

This principle is expressed as follows:

> Continual improvement of the organization's overall performance should be a permanent objective of the organization.

This means that everyone in the organization should be continually questioning its performance and seeking ways to reduce variation, continually questioning their methods and seeking better ways of doing things, continually questioning their targets and seeking new targets that enhance the organization's capability. Performance – methods – targets; three key areas where improvement is necessary for organizations to achieve and sustain success.

> **The transition**
>
> Error correction
> to
> Course correction

ISO 9000:2000 defines continual improvement as a recurring activity to increase the ability to fulfil requirements. Improvement is therefore relative to a timescale. If the improvement recurs once a week, once a month, once a year or once every five years, it can be considered as 'recurring'. The scale of the improvement is also relative. Improvement can be targeted at specific characteristics, specific activities, specific products, specific processes or specific organizations. When targeted at a specific characteristic it may involve reducing variation in the measured characteristic. When targeted at specific products it may involve major modification – product upgrade. When targeted at the organization it may involve major re-organization or reengineering of processes. To appreciate the scope of meaning you need to perceive requirements as a hierarchy of needs. At the lowest level are the needs of the task, passing through to the needs of the process, the needs of the system and ultimately the needs of the organization. At each level continual improvement is about improving efficiency and improving effectiveness.

It has become fashionable in certain sectors to use the term 'Continuous Improvement' rather than 'Continual Improvement'. Continuous means without breaks or interruption such as continuous stationery. 'Continual' means repeated regularly and frequently – a term that fits the concept of improvement rather better and is used in ISO 9000:2000.

The continual improvement principle is reflected in ISO 9001 through the requirements addressing:

- Improvement processes
- Identifying improvements
- Reviewing documents and processes for opportunities for improvement

Factual approach to decision making

This principle is expressed as follows:

> Effective decisions are based on the analysis of data and information.

Facts are obtained from observations performed by qualified personnel using devices, the integrity of which is known. The factual approach to decision-making leads us to take certain actions. To make decisions on the basis of facts we need reliable mechanisms for collecting facts such as measurement systems. We need valid methods for interpreting the facts and producing information in a form that enables sound decisions to be made. The factual approach leads us to control activities based on fact rather than opinion or emotion. It means using statistical techniques to reveal information about a process, rather than

The transition
Subjective
to
Objective

reacting to variation that is an inherent characteristic of the system. However, used in isolation this principle can be dangerous.

An obsession with numbers tends to drive managers into setting targets for things that the individual is powerless to control. A manager may count the number of designs that an engineer completes over a period. The number is a fact, but to make a decision about that person's performance on the basis of this fact is foolish – the engineer has no control over the number of designs completed and even if she did, what does it tell us about the quality of the designs? Nothing! Each design is different so the time to complete each one varies. Each customer is different so the time taken to establish customer needs varies. Setting a target for the number of designs to be completed over a period might lead to the engineer rushing them, injecting errors in order to fulfil a meaningless target. It is therefore necessary to approach the decision in a different way. Firstly decide what decision you want to make and then determine what facts you need in order to make the decision. When you know what facts you need, determine how such facts will be obtained and what methods need to be used to obtain them. Assess the risks of the information being bogus or invalid and put in place measures to ensure its integrity. Work backwards from the decision you need to make to the information you require, not forward from the information to a decision you might make with it. This gives data collection a purpose, for without purpose, data collection is a waste of resources. Don't collect data for the sake of it, just because you can on the pretext that it might come in useful.

The factual approach principle is reflected in ISO 9001 through the requirements addressing:

- Reviews, measurements and monitoring to obtain facts
- Control of measuring devices
- Analysis to obtain facts from information
- Records for documenting the facts
- Approvals based on facts

Mutually beneficial supplier relationships

This principle is expressed as follows:

> An organization and its suppliers are interdependent and a mutually beneficial relationship enhances the ability of both to create value.

The customer-focus principle drew our attention to the fact that organizations depend on their customers. It is also valid to state that organizations depend on

> **The transition**
>
> Adversarial approach
> to
> Alliance approach

their suppliers. Suppliers provide the materials, resources and often many services that were once provided by internal functions. The organizations of the 21st century are more dependent upon their suppliers than ever before. The quest for lower and lower costs with higher and higher performance has caused many organizations to consider the economics of continuing to operate their own support services. There has been a recognition that organizations were trying to be good at everything rather than being good at their core business. This has led to single-function organizations serving many customers where there is entirely mutual dependency. However, there is another reason that has led to stronger supplier relationships.

Over the last 100 years the market for goods and services has changed dramatically. Prior to the 1920s most firms focused on production in the belief that a quality product will sell itself. From the 1920s to the 1950s, many firms focused on selling what they could make regardless of whether the customer actually needed it. From the 1950s to the 1990s the market turned around from a seller's market to a buyers market as customers became more discerning and firms began to focus on identifying customer needs and producing products and services that satisfied these needs. During the last 10 years, customer orientation has been taken one step further by focusing on establishing and maintaining relationships with both customers and suppliers (Boone, Louise, E. and Kurtz, David, L., 2001)[17]. From a simple exchange between buyer and seller, there evolved strategic alliances and partnerships that cut inventory, packaging and most importantly cut the costs of acquiring new customers and suppliers. There is a net benefit to both parties. For the customer, the supplier is more inclined to keep its promises because the relationship secures future orders. There is more empathy – the customer sees the supplier's point of view and vice versa. There is more give and take that binds the two organizations closer together and ultimately there is trust that holds the partnership together. Absent will be adversarial relationships and one-off transactions when either party can walk away from the deal. The partnerships will also encourage better after sales care and more customer focus throughout the organization (everyone knows their customers because there are fewer of them).

The mutually beneficial supplier relationships principle is reflected in ISO 9001 through the requirements addressing:

- Control of suppliers
- Evaluation of suppliers
- Analysis and review of supplier data

Using the principles

The principles can be used in validating the design of processes, in validating decisions, in auditing system and processes. You look at a process and ask:

- Where is the customer focus in this process?
- Where in this process is there leadership, guiding policies, measurable objectives and the environment that motivates the workforce to achieve these objectives?
- Where in this process is the involvement of people in the design of the process, the making of decisions, the monitoring and measurement of performance and the improvement of performance?
- Where is the process approach to the accomplishment of these objectives?
- Where is the systems approach to the management of these processes, the optimization of performance, the elimination of bottlenecks?
- Where in the process are the facts collected and transmitted to the decision makers?
- Where is there continual improvement in performance, efficiency and effectiveness of this process?
- Where is there a mutually beneficial relationship with suppliers in this process?

Alignment of principles with the Business Excellence Model

There is a very close match between the eight quality management principles and the Business Excellence Model used by British Quality Foundation and the EFQM. The Excellence Model consists of nine criteria that are used to assess the overall strengths of an organization and measure its progress towards 'best in class'. The model is based on the premise that *Customer Satisfaction, People* (employee) *Satisfaction* and *Impact on Society* are achieved through *Leadership* driving *Policy and Strategy, People Management, Partnerships & Resources* and *Processes* leading ultimately to excellence in *Business Results*. These are the nine criteria and supporting these are eight fundamental concepts that have some similarity with the eight quality management principles as shown in Table 2.2.

The differences between the business excellence model and ISO 9000:2000 are small enough to be neglected if you take a pragmatic approach. If you take a pedantic approach you can find many gaps but there are more benefits to be gained by looking for synergy rather than for conflict.

Quality control (QC)

The ISO definition states that *quality control* is part of quality management focused on fulfilling requirements. What the definition fails to tell us is that

Table 2.2   Comparison between ISO 9000 and Business Excellence Principles

Business Excellence Concepts	*ISO 9000 principles*
Customer Focus The customer is the final arbiter of product and service quality and customer loyalty, retention and market share gain are best optimized through a clear focus on the needs of current and potential customers.	**Customer Focus** Organizations depend on their customers and therefore should understand current and future customer needs, meet customer requirements and strive to exceed customer expectations.
Leadership and Constancy of Purpose The behaviour of an organization's leaders creates a clarity and unity of purpose within the organization and an environment in which the organization and its people can excel.	**Leadership** Leaders establish unity of purpose and direction for the organization. They should create and maintain the internal environment in which people can become fully involved in achieving the organization's objectives.
People development and Involvement The full potential of an organization's people is best released through shared values and a culture of trust and empowerment, which encourages the involvement of everyone.	**Involvement of people** People at all levels are the essence of an organization and their full involvement enables their abilities to be used for the organization's benefit.
Management by processes and Facts Organizations perform more effectively when all interrelated activities are understood and systematically managed and decisions concerning current operations and planned improvements are made using reliable information that includes stakeholder perceptions	**Process approach** A desired result is achieved more efficiently when related resources and activities are managed as a process. **Factual approach to decision making** Effective decisions are based on the analysis of data and information. **Systems approach** Identifying, understanding and managing interrelated processes as a system contributes to the organization's effectiveness and efficiency in achieving its objectives.
Continuous learning, innovation and improvement Organizational performance is maximized when it is based on the management and sharing of knowledge within a culture of continuous learning, innovation and improvement	**Continual improvement** Continual improvement of the organization's overall performance should be a permanent objective of the organization.

Table 2.2 Continued

Business Excellence Concepts	*ISO 9000 principles*
Partnership development An organization works more effectively when it has mutually beneficial relationships, built on trust, sharing of knowledge and integration with its partners.	**Mutually beneficial supplier relationships** An organization and its suppliers are interdependent and a mutually beneficial relationship enhances the ability of both to create value.
Public responsibility The long-term interest of the organization and its people are best served by adopting an ethical approach and exceeding the expectations and regulations of the community at large.	There is no equivalent principle in ISO 9000 however, ISO 9004 clause 5.2.2 stresses that the success of the organization depends on understanding and considering current and future needs and expectations of the interested parties.
Results orientation Excellence is dependent upon balancing and satisfying the needs of all relevant stakeholders.	There is no equivalent principle in ISO 9000 however, ISO 9004 clause 5.2.2 does recommend that the organization should identify its interested parties and maintain a balanced response to their needs and expectations.

controls regulate performance. Control is sometimes perceived as undesirable as it removes freedom, but if everyone were free to do just as they liked there would be chaos. Controls prevent change and when applied to quality they regulate quality performance and prevent undesirable changes being present in the quality of the product or service being supplied. When operations are under control they are predictable and predictability is a factor that is vital for any organization to be successful. If you cannot predict what might happen when a process is initiated, you are relying on chance. The quality of products and services cannot be left to chance.

The simplest form of quality control is illustrated in Figure 2.4. Quality control can be applied to particular products, to processes that produce the products or to the output of the whole organization by measuring the overall quality performance of the organization.

Quality control is often regarded as a post-event activity: i.e. a means of detecting whether quality has been achieved and taking action to correct any deficiencies. However, one can control results by installing sensors before, during or after the results are created. It all depends on where you install the sensor, what you measure and the consequences of failure.

Figure 2.4 Generic control model

The progressive development of controls from having no control of quality to installing controls at all key stages from the beginning to the end of the product cycle is illustrated in Figure 2.5. As can be seen, if you have no controls, quality products are produced by chance and not design. The more controls you install the more certain you are of producing products of consistent quality but more control does not mean more inspection.

Figure 2.5 Development of controls

Control before the event

Some failures cannot be allowed to occur and so must be prevented from happening through rigorous planning and design. One example is the use of reliability prediction performed before the design is complete to predict whether product reliability will meet the specification. Another is the use of competence-based assessment techniques where personnel are under close supervision until they demonstrate competences following which supervisory controls are removed. This allows you to remove output checks because you know that if you were to inspect the work you would find it to be correct. Instead of checking every product produced, you check competency periodically and assign responsibility to personnel for checking their own work.

Control during the event

Some failures must be corrected immediately using automatic controls or mistake proofing. By continuous monitoring of parameters in a processing plant the temperature, pressure, quantities etc, are adjusted to maintain output within specified limits. Electronic components are designed so that they can only be inserted in the correct orientation. Computer programs are designed so that routines will not run unless the correct type of data is entered in every field.

Control after the event

Where the consequences of failure are less severe or where other types of sensors are not practical or possible, output verification can be used as a means of detecting failure. Product inspection and test is *control after the event* because it occurs after the product is produced. Where failure cannot be measured without observing trends over longer periods, you can use information controls. They do not stop immediate operations but may well be used to stop further operations when limits are exceeded.

It is often deemed that quality assurance serves prevention and quality control detection, but a control installed to detect failure before it occurs serves prevention, such as reducing the tolerance band to well within the specification limits. So quality control can prevent failure. Assurance is the result of an examination whereas control produces the result. *Quality assurance* does not change the product, *quality control* does.

Quality control as a label

'Quality control' is also the term used as the name of a department. In most cases Quality Control Departments perform inspection and test activities and the name derives from the authority that such departments have been given. They sort good products from bad products and authorize the release of the good products. It is also common to find that Quality Control Departments perform supplier control activities, which are called Supplier Quality Assurance or Vendor Control. In this respect they are authorized to release products from suppliers into the organization either from the supplier's premises or on receipt in the organization.

To control anything requires the ability to effect change, therefore the title Quality Control Department is a misuse of the term, because such departments do not in fact change the quality of the product they inspect. They do act as a regulator if given the authority to stop release of product, but this is control of supply and not of control of quality. Authority to change product usually remains in the hands of the producing departments. It is interesting to note that similar activities within a Design Department are not called 'quality control' but 'design assurance' or some similar term. 'Quality control' has for decades been a term applied primarily in the manufacturing areas of an organization and it is therefore difficult to change people's perceptions after so many years of the term's incorrect use.

In manufacturing, inspection and test activities have been transferred into the production departments of organizations, sometimes retaining the labels and sometimes reverting to the inspection and test labels. However, the term quality control is used less frequently in the west probably because of the decline of manufacturing. It has not been widely used in the service sector. A reason for this could be that it is considered more of a concept than a function.

Universal sequence of steps

The following steps can accomplish control of quality, or anything else for that matter:

1 Determine what parameter is to be controlled.
2 Establish its criticality and whether you need to control before, during or after results are produced.
3 Establish a specification for the parameter to be controlled which provides limits of acceptability and units of measure.
4 Produce plans for controls that specify the means by which the characteristics will be achieved and variation detected and removed.
5 Organize resources to implement the plans for quality control.
6 Install a sensor at an appropriate point in the process to sense variance from specification.
7 Collect and transmit data to a place for analysis.
8 Verify the results and establish whether the variance is within the range expected for a stable process (the status quo).
9 Diagnose the cause of any variance beyond the expected range.
10 Propose remedies and decide on the action needed to restore the status quo.
11 Take the agreed action and check that process stability has been restored.

Variation

Variation is present in all systems. Nothing is absolutely stable. If you monitor the difference between the measured value and the required value of a characteristic and plot it on a horizontal timescale in the order the products were produced, you would notice that there is variation over time. There does not have to be a required value to spot variation. If you monitor any parameter over time (duration, resource consumption, strength, weight etc) you will see a pattern of variation that with an appropriate scale will show up significant deviations from the average. If you plot the values as a histogram you will observe that there is a distribution of results around the average. As you repeat the plot for a new set of measurements of the same characteristic, you will notice that there is variation between this second set and the first. In studying the results you will observe:

- Variation in the location of the average for each plot
- Variation in the spread of the values
- Variation in the shape of the distribution

The factors causing these variations are referred to as 'assignable' or 'special causes'.

Special cause

The cause of variations in the location, spread and shape of a distribution are considered special or assignable because the cause can be assigned to a specific or special condition that does not apply to other events. They are causes that are not always present. Wrong material, inaccurate measuring device, worn out tool, sick employee, weather conditions, accident, stage omitted – all one-off events that cannot be predicted. When they occur they make the shape, spread or location of the average change. The process is not predictable while special cause variation is present. Eliminating the special causes is part of quality control – steps 9–11 above.

Once all the special causes of variation have been eliminated the shape and spread of the distribution and the location of the average become stable, the process is under control – the results are predictable. However, it may not be producing conforming product. You may be able to predict that the process could produce one defective product in every 10 produced. There still may be considerable variation but it is random. A stable process is one with no indication of a special cause of variation and can be said to be in *statistical control*. Special cause variation is not random – it is unpredictable. It occurs because something has happened that should not have happened so you should search for the cause immediately and eliminate it. The person running the process should be responsible for removing special causes unless these causes originate in another area when the source should be isolated and eliminated.

Common cause

Once the special cause of variation has been removed, the variation present is left to chance, it is random or what is referred to as common causes. This does not mean that no action should be taken but to treat each deviation from the average as a special cause will only lead to more problems. The random variation is caused by factors that are inherent in the system. The operator has done all she can to remove the special causes, the rest are down to management. This variation could be caused by poor design, working environment, equipment maintenance or inadequacy of information. Some of these events may be common to all processes, all machines, all materials of a particular type, all work performed in a particular location or environment or all work performed using a particular method. This chain of events is illustrated in Figure 2.6.

Figure 2.6   Stabilizing processes

This shows that by removing special causes, the process settles down and although nonconformities remain, performance becomes more predictable. Further improvement will not happen until the common causes are reduced and this requires action by management. However, the action management takes should not be to look for a scapegoat – the person whom they believe caused the error, but to look for the root cause – the inherent weakness in the system that causes this variation.

Common cause variation is random and therefore adjusting a process on detection of a common cause will destabilize the process. The cause has to be removed, not the process adjusted. When dealing with either common cause or special cause problems the search for the root cause will indicate whether the cause is random and likely to occur again or a one-off event. If it is random, only action on the system will eliminate it. If it is a one-off event, no action on the system will prevent its recurrence – it just has to be fixed. Imposing rules will not prevent a nonconformity caused by a worn out tool that someone forgot to replace. A good treatment of common cause and special cause variation is given in (Deming, W. Edwards, 1982)[5].

With a stable process the spread of common cause variation will be within certain limits. These limits are not the specification limits but are limits of natural variability of the process. These limits can be calculated and are referred to as the Upper and Lower Control Limits (UCL & LCL). The control limits may be outside the upper and lower specification limits to start with but as common causes are eliminated, they close in and eventually the spread of variation is all within the specification limits. Any variation outside the control limits will be rare and will signal the need for corrective action. This is illustrated in Figure 2.7.

Figure 2.7 Control limits and specification limits

Keeping the process under control is process control. Keeping the process within the limits of the customer specification is quality control. The action needed to make the transition from process control to quality control is an improvement action and this is dealt with next.

Quality improvement (QI)

Firstly we need to put *quality improvement* in context because it is minefield of terms and concepts that overlap one another. There are three things that are certain in this life, death, taxes and change! We cannot improve anything unless we know its present condition and this requires measurement and analysis to tell us whether improvement is both desirable and feasible. Improvement is always relative. Change is improvement if it is beneficial and a retrograde step if it is undesirable but there is a middle ground where change is neither desirable nor undesirable – it is inevitable and there is nothing we could or should do about it. Change is a constant. It exists in everything and is caused by physical, social or economic forces. Its effects can be desirable, tolerable or undesirable. Desirable change is change that brings positive benefits to the organization. Tolerable change is change that is inevitable and yields no benefit or may have undesirable effects when improperly controlled. The challenge is to cause desirable change and to eliminate, reduce or control undesirable change so that it becomes tolerable change. Juran writes on improvement thus 'Putting out fires is not improvement of the process – Neither is discovery and removal of a special cause detected by a point out of control. This only puts the process back to where it should have been in the first place (Deming, W. Edwards, 1982)[6].' This we call *restoring the status quo*. If eliminating special causes is not improvement but maintaining the status quo, that leaves two areas where improvement is desirable – the reduction of common cause variation and the raising of standards.

Figure 2.8 illustrates the continuing cycle of events between periods of maintaining performance and periods of change. The transition from one target to another may be gradual on one scale but considered a breakthrough on another scale. The variation around the target value is due to common causes that are inherent in the system. This represents the expected performance of the process. The spike outside the average variation is due to a special cause – a one-off event that can be eliminated. These can be regarded as fires and is commonly called *fire fighting*. Once removed the process continues with the average variation due to common causes.

When considering improvement by raising standards, there are two types of standards – one for results achieved and another for the manner in which the results are achieved. We could improve on the standards we aim for, the level of performance, the target or the goal but use the same methods. There may come a point when the existing methods won't allow us to achieve the

Figure 2.8 Continual improvement

standard, when we need to devise a new method, a more efficient or effective method or due to the constraints upon us, we may choose to improve our methods simply to meet existing standards.

This leads us to ask four key questions:

1 Are we doing it right?
2 Can we keep on doing it right?
3 Are we doing it in the best way?
4 Is it the right thing to do?

The ISO definition of *quality improvement* states that it is that part of quality management focused on increasing the ability to fulfil quality requirements. If we want to reduce the common cause variation we have to act upon the system. If we want to improve efficiency and effectiveness we also have to act upon the system and both are not concerned with correcting errors but concerned with doing things better and doing different things.

There is a second dimension to improvement – it is the rate of change. We could improve 'gradually' or by a 'step change'. Gradual change is also referred to as incremental improvement, continual improvement or *kaizen.'* Step change' is also referred to as 'breakthrough' or a 'quantum leap'. Gradual change arises out of refining the existing methods, modifying processes to yield more and more by consuming less and less. Breakthroughs often require innovation, new methods, techniques, technologies and new processes.

Are we doing it right?

Would the answer be this?   No we are not because every time we do it we get it wrong and have to do it again.

Or would it be this?   Yes we are because every time we do it we get it right – we never have to do it over again.

Quality improvement in this context is for better control and is about improving the rate at which an agreed standard is achieved. It is therefore a process for reducing the spread of common cause variation so that all products meet agreed standards. This is illustrated in Figure 2.9. It is not about removing special cause variation – this requires the corrective action process.

This type of improvement is only about reducing variation about a mean value or closing the gap between actual performance and the target. This is improvement by better control. The target remains static and the organization gets better and better until all output meets the target or falls between the acceptance limits.

When a process is stable the variation present is only due to random causes. There may still be unpredictable excursions beyond the target due to a change

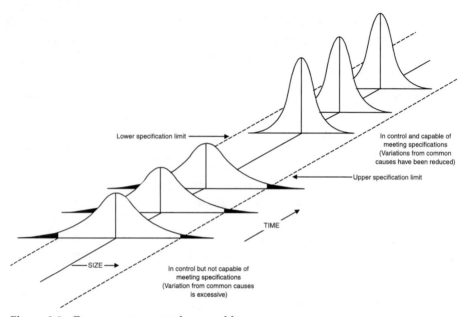

Figure 2.9   From process control to capable process

in the process but this is special cause variation. Investigating the symptoms of failure, determining the root cause and taking action to prevent recurrence can eliminate the special cause and reduce random causes. A typical quality improvement of this type might be to reduce the spread of variation in a parameter so that the average value coincides with the nominal value. Another example might be to reduce the defect rate from three sigma to six sigma. The changes that might be needed to meet this objective can be simple changes in working practices or complex changes that demand a redesign of the process or a change in working conditions. These might be achieved using existing methods or technology but it may require innovation in management or technology to accomplish.

Six sigma

In a perfect world, we would like the range of variation to be well within the upper and lower specification limits for the characteristics being measured but invariably we produce defectives. If there were an 80% yield from each stage in a 10-stage process, the resultant output would be less than 11% and as indicated in Table 2.3. we would obtain only 4 good products from an initial batch of 1 million.

Even if the process stage yield was 99% we would still only obtain half of the products we started with. It is therefore essential that multiple stage processes

Table 2.3 10 Step process yield

Stage	Yield/stage	Total % yield	Initial population 1 million
1	0.80	80	800000.00
2	0.80	64	512000.00
3	0.80	51.2	262144.00
4	0.80	41	107374.18
5	0.80	32.8	35184.37
6	0.80	26.2	9223.37
7	0.80	21	1934.28
8	0.80	16.8	324.52
9	0.80	13.4	43.56
10	0.80	10.7	4.68

have a process stage yield well in excess of 99% and it is from this perspective that the concept of six sigma emerges.

The Greek letter σ called sigma is the symbol used to represent standard deviation – a measure of the spread of frequency distributions. It is the root-mean-square deviation of the readings in a series from their average value. Table 2.4 shows the number of products meeting requirements and the equivalent defects/million products for a range of standard deviations.

Assuming a normal distribution of results at the six sigma level you would expect 0.002 parts per million or ppm but when expressing performance in ppm, it is common practice to assume that the process mean can drift 1.5 sigma in either direction. The area of a normal distribution beyond 4.5 sigma from the mean is 3.4 ppm. As control charts will detect any process shift of this magnitude in a single sample, the 3.4 ppm represents a very conservative upper boundary on the non-conformance rate (Pyzdek, Thomas, 2001)[7].

Table 2.4 Process yield at various sigma values

Sigma	% of product meeting requirements	Number of nonconformities per million products	ppm assuming 1.5 sigma drift
1	68.26	317,400	697672.15
2	95.45	45,500	308770.21
3	99.73	2,700	66810.63
4	99.9937	63	6209.70
5	99.999943	0.57	232.67
6	99.9999998	0.002	3.4

Although the concept of six sigma can be applied to non manufacturing processes you cannot assume as was done in Table 2.3 that the nonconformities in a stage output are rejected as unusable by the following stages. A person may pass through 10 stages in a hospital but you cannot aggregate the errors to produce a process yield based on stage errors. Patients don't drop out of the process simply because they were kept waiting longer than the specified maximum. You have to take the whole process and count the number of serious errors per 1 million patients.

Can we keep on doing it right?

Would the answer be this?   No we can't because the supply of resource is unpredictable, the equipment is wearing out and we can't afford to replace it.

Or would it be this?   Yes we can because we have secured a continual supply of resources and have in place measures that will provide early warning of impending changes.

This question is about continuity or sustainability. It is not enough to do it right first time once – you have to keep on doing it right and this is where a further question helps to clarify the issue.

What affects our ability to maintain this performance?

It could be resources as in the example, but to maintain the status quo might mean innovative marketing in order to keep the flow of customer orders of the type that the process can handle. Regulations change, staff leave, emergencies do happen – can you keep on doing it right under these conditions?

Are we doing it in the best way?

Would the answer be this?   We have always done it this way and if it isn't broke why fix it?

Or would it be this?   Yes we think so because we have compared our performance with the best in class and we are as good as they are.

One might argue that any target can be met providing we remove the constraints and throw lots of money at it. Although the targets may be achieved, the achievement may consume too much resource; time and materials may be wasted – there may be a better way of doing it. By finding a better way you release resources to be used more productively. Over 14 years since the introduction of ISO 9000, it is strange that more organizations did not question if there was a better way than writing all those procedures, filling in all those forms, insisting on all those signatures. ISO 9000 did not however, require these things – there was more than one way of interpreting the requirement.

The search for a better way is often more effective when in the hands of those doing the job and you must therefore embrace the 'leadership' and 'involvement of people' principles in conjunction with continual improvement.

Is it the right thing to do?

Would the answer be this?   I don't know – we always measure customer satisfaction by the number of complaints

Or would it be this?   Yes I believe it is because these targets relate very well to the organizations objectives.

Quality improvement in this context is accomplished by raising standards and is about setting a new level of performance, a new target that brings additional benefits for the interested parties. These targets are performance targets for products, processes and the system. They are not targets established for the level of errors such as nonconformities, scrap, and customer complaints.

One needs to question whether the targets are still valid. These new targets have to be planned targets as exceeding targets sporadically is a symptom of out of control situations. Targets need to be derived from the organization's goals but as these change the targets may become disconnected. Targets that were once suitable are now obsolete – they are not the right things to do any longer. Functions are often measured by their performance against budget. We need to ask whether this is the right thing to do – does it lead to optimizing organizational performance? You may have been desensitized to the level of nonconformities or customer complaints – they have become the norm – is this the right level of performance to maintain or should there be an improvement programme to reach such a lower level of rejects.

New standards are created through a process that starts at a feasibility stage and progresses through research and development to result in a new standard, proven for repeatable applications. Such standards result from innovations in technology, marketing and management. A typical quality improvement of this type might be to redesign a range of products to increase the achieved reliability from 1 failure every 5,000 hours to 1 failure every 100,000 hours. Another example might be to improve the efficiency of the service organization so as to reduce the guaranteed call-out time from the specified 36 hours to 12 hours or improve the throughput of a process from 1,000 components/week to 10,000 components/week. Once again, the changes needed may be simple or complex and might be achieved using existing technology but it may require innovation in technology to accomplish.

The transition between where quality improvement stops and quality control begins is where the level has been set and the mechanisms are in place to keep quality on or above the set level. In simple terms, if quality improvement reduces quality costs from 25% of turnover to 10% of turnover, the objective of quality control is to prevent the quality costs rising above 10% of turnover. This is illustrated in Figure 2.10.

Figure 2.10 Breakthrough and control

Improving quality by better control or raising standards can be accomplished by the following steps.

1 Determine the objective to be achieved, e.g. new markets, products or technologies, or new levels of organizational efficiency or managerial effectiveness, new national standards or government legislation. These provide the reasons for needing change.
2 Determine the policies needed for improvement, i.e. the broad guidelines to enable management to cause or stimulate the improvement.
3 Conduct a feasibility study. This should discover whether accomplishment of the objective is feasible and propose several strategies or conceptual solutions for consideration. If feasible, approval to proceed should be secured.
4 Produce plans for the improvement that specifies the means by which the objective will be achieved.

5 Organize the resources to implement the plan.
6 Carry out research, analysis and design to define a possible solution and credible alternatives.
7 Model and develop the best solution and carry out tests to prove it fulfils the objective.
8 Identify and overcome any resistance to the change in standards.
9 Implement the change, i.e. put new products into production and new services into operation.
10 Put in place the controls to hold the new level of performance.

This improvement process will require controls to keep improvement projects on course towards their objectives. The controls applied should be designed in the manner described previously.

Quality assurance (QA)

The ISO definition states that *quality assurance* is part of quality management focused on providing confidence that quality requirements will be fulfilled. Both customers and managers have a need for quality assurance because they are not in a position to oversee operations for themselves. They need to place trust in the producing operations, thus avoiding constant intervention.

Customers and managers need:

1 Knowledge of what is to be supplied. (This may be gained from the sales literature, contract or agreement.)
2 Knowledge of how the product or service is intended to be supplied (This may be gained from the supplier's proposal or offer.)
3 Knowledge that the declared intentions will satisfy customer requirements if met. (This may be gained from personal assessment or reliance on independent certifications.)
4 Knowledge that the declared intentions are actually being followed. (This may be gained by personal assessment or reliance on independent audits.)
5 Knowledge that the products and services meet the specified requirements. (This may be gained by personal assessment or reliance on independent audits.)

You can gain an assurance of quality by testing the product/service against prescribed standards to establish its capability to meet them. However, this only gives confidence in the specific product or service purchased and not in its continuity or consistency during subsequent supply. Another way is to assess the organization that supplies the products/services against prescribed standards to establish its capability to produce products of a certain standard. This approach may provide assurance of continuity and consistency of supply.

Quality assurance activities do not control quality, they establish the extent to which quality will be, is being or has been controlled. All quality assurance activities are post-event activities and off-line and serve to build confidence in results, in claims, in predictions, etc. If a person tells you they will do a certain job for a certain price in a certain time, can you trust them or will they be late, overspent and under spec? The only way to find out is to gain confidence in their operations and that is what quality assurance activities are designed to do. Quite often, the means to provide the assurance need to be built into the process, such as creating records, documenting plans, documenting specifications, reporting reviews etc. Such documents and activities also serve to control quality as well as assure it. ISO 9001 provides a basis for obtaining an assurance of quality, if you are the customer, and a basis for controlling quality, if you are the supplier.

Quality assurance is often perceived as the means to prevent problems but this is not consistent with the definition in ISO 9000. In one case the misconception arises due to people limiting their perception of quality control to control after the event; not appreciating that you can control an outcome before the event by installing mechanisms to prevent failure, such as automation, mistake-proofing and failure prediction.

In another case, the misconception arises due to the label attached to the ISO 9000 series of standards. They are sometimes known as the quality assurance standards when in fact, as a family of standards, they are quality management system standards. The requirements within the standards do aim to prevent problems, and consequently the standard is associated with the term *quality assurance*. ISO 9001 is designed for use in assuring customers that suppliers have the capability of meeting their requirements. It is true that by installing a quality management system, you will gain an assurance of quality, but assurance comes about through knowledge of what will be, is being or has been done, rather than by doing something. Assurance is not an action but a result. It results from obtaining reliable information that testifies to the accuracy or validity of some event or product.

Labelling the prevention activities as quality assurance activities may have a negative effect, particularly if you have a Quality Assurance Department. It could send out signals that the aim of the Quality Assurance Department is to prevent things from happening! Such a label could unintentionally give the department a law enforcement role.

Quality Assurance Departments are often formed to provide both customer and management with confidence that quality will be, is being and has been achieved. However, another way of looking upon Quality Assurance Departments is as Corporate Quality Control. Instead of measuring the quality of products, they are measuring the quality of the business and by doing so are able to assure management and customers of the quality of products and services. The following steps can obtain an assurance of quality:

1 Acquire the documents that declare the organization's plans for achieving quality.
2 Produce a plan that defines how an assurance of quality will be obtained, i.e. a quality assurance plan.
3 Organize the resources to implement the plans for quality assurance.
4 Establish whether the organization's proposed product or service possesses characteristics that will satisfy customer needs.
5 Assess operations, products and services of the organization and determine where and what the quality risks are.
6 Establish whether the organization's plans make adequate provision for the control, elimination or reduction of the identified risks.
7 Determine the extent to which the organization's plans are being implemented and risks contained.
8 Establish whether the product or service being supplied has the prescribed characteristics.

In judging the adequacy of provisions you will need to apply the relevant standards, legislation, codes of practice and other agreed measures for the type of operation, application and business. These activities are quality assurance activities and may be subdivided into design assurance, procurement assurance, manufacturing assurance etc. Auditing, planning, analysis, inspection and test are some of the techniques that may be used.

Level of attention to quality

Whilst the decision to make the *management of quality* a strategic issue will be an executive decision, the attention it is given at each level in the organization will have a bearing on the degree of success attained. There are three primary organization levels: the *enterprise level, the business level* and the *operations level*(Watson, Gregory H., 1994)[8]. Between each level there are barriers.

At the enterprise level, the executive management responds to the 'voice' of ownership and is primarily concerned with profit, return on capital employed, market share etc. At the business level, the managers are concerned with products and services and so respond to the 'voice' of the customer. At the operational level, the middle managers, supervisors, operators etc. focus on processes that produce products and services and so respond to the 'voice' of the processes carried out within their own function.

In reality, these levels overlap, particularly in small organizations. The CEO of a small company will be involved at all three levels whereas in the large multinational, the CEO spends all of the time at the enterprise level, barely touching the business level, except when major deals with potential customers

Table 2.5 Attention levels

Organizational level	Principle Process Focus	Basic Team Structure	Performance Issue Focus	Typical Quality System Focus	Ideal Quality System Focus
Enterprise Business Operations	Strategic Business Work	Cross-Business Cross-Functional Departmental	Ownership Customer Process	Market Administrative Task Process	Strategic Business Process Work Process

are being negotiated. Once the contract is won, the CEO of the multinational may confine his or her involvement to monitoring performance through metrics and goals.

Quality should be a strategic issue that involves the owners because it delivers fiscal performance. Low quality will cause fiscal performance ultimately to decline.

The typical focus for a quality management system is at the operations level. ISO 9000 is seen as an initiative for work process improvement. The documentation is often developed at the work process level and focused on functions. Much of the effort is focused on the processes within the functions rather than across the functions and only involves the business level at the customer interface, as illustrated in Table 2.5. For the application of ISO 9000 to be successful quality has to be a strategic issue with every function of the organization embraced by the management system that is focused on satisfying the needs of all interested parties.

Quality management systems

Philosophy

A system is an ordered set of ideas, principles and theories or a chain of operations that produce specific results and to be a chain of operations, the operations need to work together in a regular relationship. Shannon defined a system as a group or set of objects united by some form or regular interaction or interdependence to perform a specified function (Shannon, R. E., 1975)[9]. Deming defines a system as a series of functions or activities within an organization that work together for the aim of the organization. These three definitions appear to be consistent although worded differently.

A quality management system is not a random collection of procedures, tasks or documents (which many quality systems are). Quality management systems are like air conditioning systems – they need to be designed. All the components need to fit together, the inputs and outputs need to be connected, sensors need to feed information to processes which cause changes in performance and all parts need to work together to achieve a common purpose.

ISO 9000 defines a quality management as a set of interrelated or interacting processes that achieve the quality policy and quality objective. But the word quality gets in the way of our thinking. It makes us think that quality management systems operate alongside environmental management systems, safety management systems, and financial management systems. In clause 3.11 of ISO 9000 it is stated that the quality management system is 'that part of the organization's management system that focuses on the achievement of outputs in relation to the quality objectives', therefore the quality management system must exist to achieve the organization's quality objectives. This concept was unclear in the 1994 version with the result that many quality systems were focused on procedures for their own sake rather than on serving objectives. It would appear therefore that other parts of the management system are intended to serve the achievement of specific objectives. For example we could establish:

- Safety systems to serve safety objectives
- Environmental systems to serve environmental objectives
- Security systems to serve security objectives
- Human resource systems to serve human resource objectives
- Marketing systems to serve marketing objectives
- Innovation systems to serve innovation objectives
- Financial systems to serve financial objectives

However, several questions arise; Are quality objectives, objectives of the same kind as the other objectives or are these other objectives a subset of quality objectives?' and 'Is the quality management system just one of a series of systems or is it the parent system of which the others are a part?'

To find the answer it is necessary to go back a step. Which comes first an objective or a need? We don't set financial objectives because we think its a good idea, there is a need that has its origins in the organization's mission statement. The mission statement tells us what our goal is – where are we going. Without customers there is no business therefore the basic purpose of a business is to satisfy a particular want in society and so create a customer. Its mission is related to these wants and is expressed in specific terms. To be effective, a mission statement should always look outside the business not inside (Seddon, John, 2000)[10]. For example a mission that is focused on increasing market share is an inwardly seeking mission whereas a mission that is focused on bringing cheap digital communication to the people is an outwardly seeking mission statement. From the mission statement we can ask, 'What affects our ability to accomplish our goal?' The answers we get become our critical success factors and it is these factors that shape our objectives.

The QMS is not part of the management system – IT IS the management system

- If our success depends upon the safety of our products then we need safety objectives.
- If our success depends upon securing the integrity of information entrusted to us by our customers, then we need security objectives.
- If our success depends upon the impact our operations have on the environment, we need environmental objectives.
- If our success depends upon capital investment in modern plant and machinery, we need financial objectives.

This list is incomplete, but if we were to continue, would we find a reason for having quality objectives? Business will only create customers if they satisfy their needs therefore success in all businesses depends upon fulfilling customer needs and expectations. Quality is defined in ISO 9000 as the degree to which a set of inherent characteristics fulfils requirements. Note that the definition is not limited to customer requirements and that the inherent characteristics are limited to products. It could apply

Outputs and Outcomes
Outputs tend to imply products and services whereas outcomes include impacts of the business on its surroundings, its employees etc.

to any set of requirements – internal or external, technical or non-technical including health, safety and environmental requirements. It could also apply to any process outcome – products, services, decisions, information, impacts etc. It extends to all those with an interest in the business. Quality is therefore a term that describes the condition of business outcomes. Everything a business does must directly or indirectly affect the condition of its outcomes and therefore all business objectives are quality objectives. Therefore we do not need quality objectives in addition to all the other objectives because all objectives are quality objectives and the quality management system is not part of the management system – it *is* the management system. We can therefore describe the relationship between the management system and the organization diagrammatically as shown in Figure 2.11.

The management system is the way the organization operates, the way it carries out its business, the way thing are. Its purpose is to enable the organization to accomplish its mission, it purpose, its goals and its objectives. All organizations possess a management system. Some are formal – some are informal. Even in a one-person business, that person will have a way of working – a way of achieving his or her objectives. That way is the system and comprises the behaviours, processes and resources employed to achieve those objectives. The system comprises everything that affects the results. It only has

Figure 2.11   The business management cycle

to be formalized when the relationships grow too large for one person to manage by relying on memory.

It is unlikely that you will be able to produce and sustain the required quality unless you organize yourselves to do so. Quality does not happen by chance – it has to be managed. No human endeavour has ever been successful without having been planned, organized and controlled in some way.

Scope of the system

As the quality management system is the means by which the organization achieves its objectives, it follows that the scope of the system (what it covers) is every function and activity of the organization that contributes to these objectives. This should leave no function or activity outside the system. The system must also include suppliers because the organization depends upon its suppliers to achieve its objectives. The chain of processes from the customer interface and back again includes the suppliers.

Including every function and activity within the system should not be interpreted as compelling every function and activity to certification to ISO 9001 – far from it. The scope of the system does not need to be the same as the scope of certification as was explained in Chapter 1 and addressed further in Chapter 3.

Design of the system

Imagine you are designing an air-conditioning system. You would commence by establishing the system requirements, then designing a system that meets the requirements, documenting the design and building a prototype. You would then test it and when satisfied it functions under the anticipated operating conditions, launch into production. If problems are detected during production, solutions would be developed and the design documentation changed before recommencing production. If problems were experienced during maintenance, the design documentation would be consulted to aid in the search for the fault. If improvements are to be made, once again the design documentation would be consulted and design changes made and the documentation revised before implementation in production. This traditional cycle for products therefore has some redeeming features:

- Design does not commence without a specification of requirements – if it does, the wrong product is likely to be designed.
- Designs are documented before product is manufactured – if they are not documented, it is likely that the product cannot be manufactured or will not fit together or function as intended.
- Designs are proven before launching into production – if production commences before design proving, the product will probably fail on test or in service.
- Design documentation is changed before changes are implemented in production – if documentation is not changed before implementation, the product will be different each time it is made; solved problems will recur and no two installations will be alike.

If we apply the same logic to the design and implementation of a management system, we would

- Define the requirements before commencing management system design i.e. we would establish the objectives the system is required to achieve.
- Document the management system design before implementation.
- Verify that the management system meets the requirements before commitment to full operation.
- Document changes to the management system before implementation in practice.

But what often happens is:

- Management system development commences without a specification of requirements or a clear idea of the objectives that need to be achieved.
- The management system is documented before it has been designed.
- The management system is made fully operational before being verified it meets the requirements.
- Changes are made to practices before they are documented.
- Improvements are made to the management system without consulting the documentation because it is often out of date.

As the management system is the means by which the organization achieves its objectives, the management system delivers the organization's products. (This includes hardware, software, services and processed material including information products.)

If we analyse the factors upon which the quality of these products depend we would deduce they include:

- The style of management – autocratic, democratic, participative, directive etc;
- The attitude and behaviour of the people – positive, negative etc.;
- The capability of the available resources – capacity, responsiveness, technology;
- The quantity and quality of the available resources – materials, equipment, finance, people;
- The condition and capability of the facilities, plant and machinery;
- The physical environment in which people work – heat, noise, cleanliness etc.;
- The human environment in which people work – freedom, empowerment, health and safety.

It follows therefore that a management system consists of the processes required to deliver the organization's products and services as well as the resources, behaviours and environment upon which they depend. It is therefore not advisable to even contemplate a management system simply as a set of documents or if we do go someway towards ISO 9000:2000, a set of processes that simply converts inputs into outputs. Three out of the seven factors above relate to the human element – we therefore cannot afford to ignore it.

Process management

The 1994 version of ISO 9000 created a notion that quality management was about following procedures. This is regrettable because quality management has always focused on the result – the outputs of the organization and on whether they meet customer requirements. The endeavours of those involved in quality management have been focused on the engine that produces these results – trying to make it deliver results that met customer needs and expectations. This focus has become somewhat blurred by all the campaigns, initiative and slogans that have handicapped the field. They have caused us to take our eye off the ball. Often good intentioned initiatives, they have only focused on one aspect of quality management. Many have only focused on the production operations and those that focused on management have not been associated with quality management. But that is changing – quality is now a strategic issue. We just have to change the way we perceive various aspects of quality management if these various tools, techniques and ideas are to be successful.

As indicated previously, the management system consists of a series of processes interconnected in a manner that enables the organization to achieve its objectives.

Until the spread of ISO 9000, organizations focused on fixing processes and problems with the output not on refining procedures. However, in view of the confusion that has arisen between processes and procedures a short diversion to explain the differences is appropriate. This is illustrated in Table 2.6.

A view that is emerging in the literature supporting ISO 9000:2000 is that the procedural approach is about how you do things and processes are about what you do. This is misleading as it places the person outside the process when in fact the person is part of the process. It also sends out a signal that processes are just a set of instructions rather than a dynamic mechanism for achieving results. This message could jeopardise the benefits that could be gained from using the process approach.

Table 2.6 Contrasting procedures with processes (Hoyle, David and Thompson, John, 2000)[16]

Procedures	*Processes*
Procedures are driven by completion of the task	Processes are driven by achievement of a desired result
Procedures are implemented	Processes are operated
Procedure steps are completed by different people in different departments with different objectives	Process stages are completed by different people with the same objectives – departments do not matter
Procedures are discontinuous	Processes flow to conclusion
Procedures focus on satisfying the rules	Processes focus on satisfying the interested parties
Procedures define the sequence of steps to execute a task	Processes transform inputs into outputs through use of resources
Procedures may be used to process information	Information is processed by use of a procedure
Procedures exist – they are static	Processes behave – they are dynamic
Procedures cause people to take actions and decisions	Processes cause things to happen

Finding a definition

There are different schools of thought on what constitutes a process.

A process is defined in ISO 9000 as *a set of interrelated or interacting activities which transforms inputs into outputs* and goes on to state *that processes in an organization are generally planned and carried out under controlled conditions to add value.* The inclusion of the word *generally* tends to suggest that organizations may have processes that are not planned, not carried our under controlled conditions and do not add value and indeed they do!

Juran defines a process (Juran, J. M., 1992)[11] as a systematic series of actions directed to the achievement of a goal. In Juran's model the inputs are the goals and product features and the outputs are product features required to meet customer needs. The ISO 9000 definition does not refer to goals or objectives.

Hammer defines a process (Hammer, Michael and Champy, James, 1993)[12] as a collection of activities that takes one or more kinds of inputs and creates an output that is of value to the customer. Hammer places customer value as a criterion for a process unlike the ISO 9000 definition.

Davenport defines a 'process (Davenport, T. H., 1993)[13] as a structured measured set of activities designed to produce a specified output for a particular customer or market.

> **Procedures versus Processes**
>
> *The procedural approach* is about doing a task, conforming to the rules, doing what we are told to do.
>
> *The process approach* is about, understanding needs, doing whatever it takes to make it happen, finding the best way of fulfilling these needs even if it means changing the way we do our job.

The concept of adding value and the party receiving the added value is seen as important in these definitions. This distinguishes processes from procedures (see below).

It is easy to see how these definitions can be misinterpreted and result in people simply drawing flowcharts and calling them processes. They may describe the process flow but they are not in themselves processes because they simply define transactions. A series of transactions can represent a chain from input to output but it does not cause things to happen. Add the resources, the behaviours, the constraints and make the necessary connections and you might have a process that will cause things to happen.

Business process reengineering

Most organizations are structured into functions that are collections of specialists performing tasks. The functions are like silos into which work is passed and executed under the directive of a function manager before being passed into another silo where it waits its turn because the people in that silo have different priorities and were not lucky enough to receive the resources they requested. Each function competes for scarce resources and completes a part of what is needed to deliver product to customers. This approach to work came out of the industrial revolution influenced firstly by Adam Smith and later by Frederick Taylor, Henry Fayol and others. When Smith and Taylor made their observations and formulated their theories, workers were not as educated as they are today. Technology was not as available and machines not as portable as they are today. Transportation of goods and information in the 18th and 19th centuries was totally different from today. As a means to transform a domestic economy to an industrial economy the theory was right for the time. Mass production would not have been possible under the domestic systems used at that time.

Reengineering is the fundamental rethinking and radical redesign of business processes to achieve dramatic improvements in critical contemporary measures of performance such as costs, quality, service and speed (Hammer, Michael and Champy, James, 1993)[14]. Business process reengineering is about turning the organization on its head. Abandoning the old traditional way of organizing work as a set of tasks to organizing it as a process. Reengineering means scrapping the organization charts and starting again.

ISO 9001 is not requiring reengineering. It is requiring that work be managed as a process so that its performance is evaluated on resultant customer value. In identifying the business processes, the sub-processes, the tasks and the functions through which work passes opportunities for improvement may be detected. These can be prioritized for action as part of a continual improvement programme.

Process characteristics

We can conceive of three different types of processes:

- Processes that convert inputs into outputs without adding value (i.e. a process without a specified purpose, a procedure the purpose of which is to define a series of activities, the middleman in a supply chain who simply bills a handling charge but adds no value)
- Processes that convert inputs into outputs with perceived added value for the internal customer but no added value for external parties (i.e. the manager who sets up processes to produce reports that protect the manager from blame but do not add value for customers)
- Processes that convert inputs into outputs of added value for the external interested party (i.e. a process that creates products or services possessing benefits that add value for customers, a process that provides employees with greater skills and adds value for employees, a process that reduces airborne emissions from the facility and adds value for the community)

Process purpose

From the definitions of a process it is clear that every process needs a purpose for it to add value. The purpose provides a reason for its existence. The purpose statement should be expressed in terms of what the process does and in doing so identify what is to be converted. The purpose of a sales process may be to convert prospects into orders for the organizations products. Instead of calling the process a sales process you could call it the *prospect to order process*. Similarly the purpose of a design process may be to convert customer needs into product features that satisfy these needs.

Process objectives

Process objectives provide a means to measure the effectiveness with which the process fulfils its purpose. The objectives of the sales process might be to maintain the rate at which prospects are converted into orders at or above 45%. Another objective might be to induce 50% of the market segment to be aware of organization's products and services. A human resource process objective might be to ensure 80% of staff receives the training that has been identified within the budget period. A technique often used to test the soundness of objectives is SMART (Specific, Measurable, Achievable, Realistic and Timely). Further details of SMART are provided in Chapter 5 under *Setting objectives*.

Process inputs

The inputs of a process are considered to be those things that are transformed by the process into outputs. Under these conditions, the input has to change in some way. This implies that instructions, requirements, objectives or any documents are not *inputs* because they are not transformed. They are the same at the end of the process as they were when they entered it. It is not the requirement that is changed but a product generated from the requirement. However, if you enquire of a person as to what the process inputs are, they will no doubt tell you of all the things that are needed for the process to commence. Within the items mentioned would be the information that triggers the work – the instruction, the order, the phone call etc. In reality, therefore, anything received by a process is an input whether or not it is transformed.

Process outputs

The outputs of a process are considered to be the tangible or intangible results such as a product or advice. However, in addition to outputs, processes have outcomes. There is an effect that the process has on its surroundings. An outcome of a process may be a detrimental affect on the environment. Satisfaction of either customers or employees is an outcome not an output.

Process resources

The resources in a process are the supplies that can be drawn upon when needed by the process. Resources are classified into human, physical and financial resources. The physical resources include materials, equipment, plans, machinery but also include time. Human resources include managers and staff including employees, contractors, volunteers and partners. The financial resources include money, credit and sponsorship. Resources are used or consumed by the process. There is a view that resources to a process are used (not consumed) and are those things that don't change during the process. People and machinery are resources that are used (not consumed) because they are the same at the start of the process as they are at the end, i.e. they don't lose anything to the process. Whereas materials, components and money are either lost to the process, converted or transformed and are therefore process inputs. People would be inputs not resources if the process transforms them.

Process constraints

The constraints on a process are the things that limit its freedom. Actions should be performed within the boundaries of the law, regulations impose conditions on hygiene, emissions and the internal and external environment. They may constrain resources (including time), effects, methods, decisions and many other factors depending on the type of process, the risks and its significance with respect to the business and society. Some people call these things **controls** rather than constraints but include among them, the customer requirements that trigger the process and these could just as well be inputs.

Views differ and whilst a purist might argue that requirements are controls not inputs, and materials are inputs not resources, it matters not in the

Figure 2.12 Conceptual process

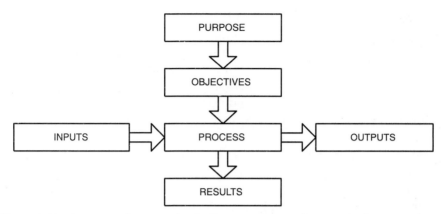

Figure 2.13 A managed process (excluding resources and constraints)

management of quality. All it might affect is the manner in which the process is described diagrammatically. The requirements would enter the process from above and not from the side if you drew the chart as a horizontal flow. The symbolic view of a process given in Figure 2.12 is only one view of a process. The danger in drawing the process as a flow from input to output is that you might omit the provisions that need to be in place to manage the process. This is illustrated in Figure 2.13. The resources and constraints are not shown for clarity.

Process results

The outputs are things, they do result from a process – of that there is no doubt – but the measurable results of the process are the outcomes:

- Is the process delivering outputs that meet the input requirements?
- Is the process operating efficiently?
- Is the process effective?

These questions are not answered by a single process output but by monitoring and measurement taken of the outcomes – not the output.

Process classes

There are two classes of organizational processes – macro-processes and micro-processes. Macro-processes are multi-functional in nature consisting of numerous micro-processes. Macro-processes deliver business outputs and have been referred to as *Business Processes* for nearly a decade or more. For processes to be classed as business processes they need to be in a chain of processes having the same stakeholder at each end of the chain. The input is an input to the business and the output is an output from the business. This is so that the outputs can be measured in terms of the inputs. If the outputs were a translation of the inputs they could not be measured against the inputs.

There is a view that design is not a business process because the stakeholders are different at each end. On the input end could be marketing and the output end could be production. Under this logic, production would not be a business process because on the input could be sales and the output could be the customer. Therefore the business process flow is: customer – sales – production – distribution – finance – customer.

The sales process takes the order from the customer and routes it to the production process. The production process supplies product to the distribution process and the distribution process delivers product to the customer, collects the cheque and routes it to the finance process where it is put into the bank and turned into cash. The business process is therefore 'order to cash' or order fulfilment. With this convention, there would be only four business processes in most organizations. These are displayed diagrammatically in Figure 2.14 with Table 2.7 showing the stakeholders.

Micro-processes deliver departmental outputs and are task oriented. In this book these are referred to as *Work Processes*. A management system is not just a collection of work processes, but also the interconnection of business processes. The relationship between these two types of processes is addressed in Table 2.8 (Juran, J. M., 1992)[15].

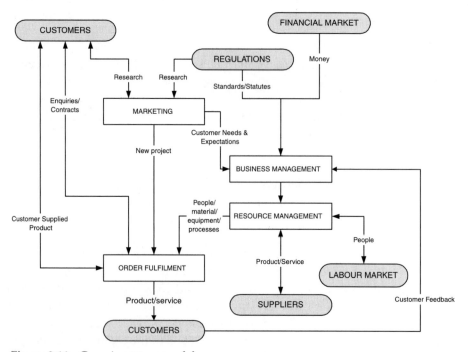

Figure 2.14 Generic system model

Table 2.7 Business process stakeholders

Business process	Input stakeholder	Output stakeholder
Business management	Shareholders, Owners	Shareholders, Owners
Marketing	MD	MD
Order fulfilment	Customer	Customer
Resource management	Resource user	Resource user

Table 2.8 Relationship of business process to work processes

Scope	Business process	Work process
Relationship to organization hierarchy	Unrelated	Closely related
Ownership of process	No natural owner	Departmental head or supervisor
Level of attention	Executive level	Supervisory or operator level
Relationship to business goals	Directly related	Indirectly related and sometimes (incorrectly) unrelated
Responsibility	Multifunctional	Single function
Customers	Generally external or other business processes	Other departments or personnel in same department
Suppliers	Generally external or other business processes	Other departments or personnel in same department
Measures	Quality, cost delivery	Errors, quantities, response time
Units of measure	Customer satisfaction, shareholder value, cycle time	% Defective, % Sales cancelled, % Throughput

Making the connections

It is important to visualize the complete picture when setting out to define and manage your processes. Processes exist in a context to deliver against an objective that also serves to deliver a strategic objective. As illustrated in Figure 2.11, there is a continuum from interested parties to mission through the system to results and back to the mission. The arrows form connections so that there is a clear line of sight from the results to the mission and this will only be accomplished if those carrying out strategic planning realize that processes cause results. Processes will not cause the right results unless the process objectives have been derived from the mission. The measures employed to indicate work process performance need to relate to the measures employed in the related business process so that when all the measures indicate that the system is performing as it should, the strategic objectives are being achieved.

Process effectiveness

A process should be effective but what determines its effectiveness? How would you know whether a process is effective? Effectiveness is about doing the right things – so what should a process do? Firstly and most obviously the process should deliver the required output – a decision, a document, a product or a service. But there is much more. It is not sufficient merely to deliver output. Output that is of poor quality is undesirable as is output that is late. But even when the output is of good quality and on time there are other factors to be considered. If in producing the output the laws of the land are breached, the process is clearly not effective. If in producing the output, the producers are exploited, are forced to work under appalling conditions or become de-motivated and only deliver the goods when stimulated by fear, the process is again not effective. So we could fix all these factors and deliver the required output on time and have satisfied employees.

Employees are but one of the stakeholders – customers are the most important and although an output may be of good quality to its producers, it may not be a product that satisfies customers. The costs of operating the process may not yield a profit for the organization and its shareholders, and even if in compliance with current environmental laws, it may waste natural resources, dissatisfy the community and place unreasonable constraints upon suppliers such that they decline to supply the process's material inputs. There is therefore only one measure of process effectiveness – that the process outcomes satisfy all interested parties.

Summary

In this chapter we have examined the basic concepts that underpin the body of knowledge of quality management relative to ISO 9000. We have discovered that knowledge of ISO 9000 alone is insufficient to be able to apply the concepts and principles of quality management that are expressed in ISO 9000. We demonstrated that the terms used in ISO 9000 are much more than words but labels for universal principles that help us discover the right things to do. With a clear understanding of these principles we should not only be able to determine the rationale for the ISO 9000 requirements but determine the actions needed where the requirements are less detailed and in so doing use ISO 9000 in a manner that will bring lasting benefits to the organization.

Basic concepts – Food for thought

1 Without a set of principles, achieving a common understanding in the field of quality management would be impossible.
2 In supplying products or services there are three fundamental parameters that determine their saleability – price, quality and delivery.
3 Organizations exist because of their ability to satisfy their customers and other interested parties.
4 It is quite possible for an organization to satisfy its customers and fail to satisfy the needs of the other interested parties.
5 The needs of all parties have to be satisfied in order for *quality* to be achieved.
6 Products or services that do not possess the right features and characteristics either by design or by construction are products of poor quality.
7 A gold-plated mousetrap that does not fail is not a success if no one needs a gold-plated mousetrap!
8 The more prescription we have the more we get immersed in the detail and lose sight of our objectives.
9 Customer focus means putting your energy into satisfying customers and understanding that profitability or avoidance of loss comes from satisfying customers.
10 People naturally concentrate on what is measured – it is therefore vital that leaders measure the right things.
11 Processes are dynamic – they cause things to happen.
12 The behaviour of any part of a system has some effect on the behaviour of the system as a whole.
13 Everyone in the organization should be continually questioning its performance and seeking ways to reduce variation, improve their methods and seeking better ways of doing things.
14 The factual approach leads us to control activities based on fact rather than opinion or emotion.
15 Organizations depend on their suppliers as much they depend on their customers.

16 Control is sometimes perceived as undesirable as it removes freedom, but if everyone were free to do just as they liked there would be chaos.

17 Keeping the process under control is process control. Keeping the process within the limits of the customer specification is quality control.

18 Putting out fires is not improvement of the process; it only puts the process back to where it should have been in the first place.

19 Quality assurance activities do not control quality, they establish the extent to which quality will be, is being or has been controlled.

20 Quality should be a strategic issue that involves the owners because it delivers fiscal performance.

21 We do not need quality objectives in addition to all the other objectives because all objectives are quality objectives.

22 All organizations possess a management system. Some are formal – some are informal.

23 The quality management system is the means by which the organization achieves its objectives and therefore no function or activity should be exist outside the system.

24 A series of transactions can represent a chain from input to output but it does not cause things to happen.

25 Only when you add the necessary resources, behaviours and constraints and make the necessary connections will you have a process that will cause things to happen.

26 There is only one measure of process effectiveness – that the process outcomes satisfy all interested parties.

Bibliography

1. Maslow, Abraham, H., (1954). *Motivation and Personality*, New York Harper & Row.
2. Rollinson, D., Broadfield, A. and Edwards, D. J., (1998). *Organizational behaviour and analysis*, Addison Wesley Longmans.
3. Hoyle, David and Thompson, John, (2001). *ISO 9000:2000 Auditor Questions*, Transition Support.
4. Hoyle, David and Thompson, John, (2000). *ISO 9000:2000 Quality Management Principles ~ A Self Assessment Guide*, Transition Support.
5. Deming, W. Edwards, (1982). *Out of the crisis*, MITC.
6. Deming, W. Edwards, (1982). *Out of the crisis*, MITC. Juran as observed by Edwards Deming
7. Pyzdek, Thomas, (2001). *The Complete Guide to Six Sigma*, McGraw-Hill.
8. Watson, Gregory, H. (1994). *Business Systems Engineering*, Wiley.
9. Shannon, R. E., (1975). *Systems Simulation*, Prentice-Hall.
10. Seddon, John, (2000). *The case against ISO 9000*, Oak Tree Press.
11. Juran, J. M., (1992). *Juran on Quality by design*, The Free Press.
12. Hammer, Michael and Champy, James, (1993). *Reengineering the corporation*, Harper Business.

13. Davenport, T. H., (1993). *Process Innovation: Reengineering work through Information Technology*, Harvard Business School Press.
14. Hammer, Michael and Champy, James, (1993). *Reengineering the corporation*, Harper Business.
15. Juran, J. M., (1992). *Juran on Quality by design*, The Free Press.
16. Hoyle, David and Thompson, John, (2000). *Converting a Quality Management System using the Process Approach*, Transition Support.
17. Boone, Louise, E. and Kurtz, David, L., (2001). *Contemporary Marketing 10th Edition*, Hartcourt College Publishers, pp. 11–13.

Chapter 3
Role, origins and application of ISO 9000

The past has only got us to where we are today;
it may not necessarily get us to where we want to be

John Thompson

The role of ISO 9000

What is ISO 9000?

ISO 9000:2000 is a series of three International Standards for Quality Management Systems. They specify requirements and recommendations for the design and assessment of management systems. ISO 9000 is not a product standard. None of the standards in the family contain requirements with which a product or service can comply. There are no product acceptance criteria in ISO 9000 so you can't inspect a product against the standard.

What is the purpose of ISO 9000?

The purpose of these standards is to assist organizations of all types to implement and operate effective quality management systems. These standards provide a vehicle for consolidating and communicating concepts in the field of quality management that have been approved by an international committee of representatives from national standards bodies. It is not their purpose to fuel the certification, consulting, training and publishing industries. The primary users of the standards are intended to be organizations acting as either customers or suppliers.

What is the ISO 9000 family of standards?

The three standards in the family are

ISO 9000 Quality management systems – Fundamentals and vocabulary
ISO 9001 Quality management systems – Requirements
ISO 9004 Quality management systems – Guidelines for performance
improvements

What is the purpose of these standards?

Each standard fulfils a different purpose.

The purpose of ISO 9000 is to provide an appreciation of the fundamental principles of quality management systems and an explanation of the terminology used in the family of standards.

The purpose of ISO 9001 is to provide requirements which if met will enable organizations to demonstrate they have the capability to consistently provide product that meets customer and applicable regulatory requirements. ISO 9001 states that *the standard can be used to assess the organization's ability to meet customer, regulatory and the organization's own requirements.*

The purpose of ISO 9004 is to provide guidance for improving the efficiency, effectiveness and overall performance of an organization.

ISO 9001 and ISO 9004 have been developed as a consistent pair of standards that complement each other. They have a common structure but can be used independently. ISO 9004 is not intended as a guide to ISO 9001. Although ISO 9004 includes the requirements of ISO 9001 it does not contain an explanation of these requirements or guidance in meeting them.

Why would we need to use these standards?

It is imperative that all three standards are studied for the following reasons:

ISO 9000 contains the definitions of terms used in the family of standards. Without an understanding of the terms, the standards are prone to mis-interpretation. ISO 9000 also contains the general concepts and principles that apply to quality management and quality management systems in particular. Although they are not requirements, the context and interpretation of the requirements will not be understood without an appreciation of the concepts that underpin the requirements.

ISO 9001 contains requirements for a quality management system. This standard should be used in contractual situations where the customer requires its suppliers to demonstrate they have the capability to consistently produce product that meets customer requirements. The theory is that if suppliers can show they do all the things in ISO 9001, only conforming product would be shipped to customers. This would (in theory) reduce the need for customers to verify product on receipt. Third parties can also use the standard to assess the capability of organizations to provide product that meets customer and regulatory requirements. Organizations can use ISO 9001 as a model in designing their management systems providing they also use ISO 9000 and ISO 9004. On its own ISO 9001 does not define everything an organization needs to do to satisfy its customers.

ISO 9004 contains guidance on developing and improving a quality management system. This standard should be used as guidance in designing, operating and improving a management system. It is not intended for contractual or assessment purposes but when used internally there may be benefits in using the standard as a basis for assessing current capability. There is no doubt that if an organization were to follow the guidance given in ISO 9004, it would have no problem in demonstrating it had an effective management system.

Why was ISO 9000 created?

The standards were created to facilitate mutual understanding of quality management system requirements in national and international trade. The associated certification schemes that are not a requirement of any of the standards in the ISO 9000 family were launched to reduce costs of customer-sponsored audits performed to verify the capability of their suppliers. The schemes were born out of a reticence of customers to trade with organizations that had no credentials in the market place.

The standard was primarily intended for situations where customers and suppliers were in a contractual relationship. It was not intended for use where there was no contractual relationship. However, the 1994 version has been applied in non-contractual situations with the result that organizations created over complicated systems with far more documentation than they needed. In non-contractual situations there is usually no need to demonstrate potential capability. Customers normally purchase on the basis of recommendation or prior knowledge. Even in contractual situations, demonstration of capability is often only necessary when the customer cannot verify the quality of the products or services after delivery. The customer may not have any way of knowing that the product or service meets the agreed requirements until it is put into service by which time it is costly in time, resource and reputation to make corrections. In cases where the customer has the capability to verify conformity, the time and effort required is an added burden and its elimination helps reduce costs to the end user.

It is clear that customers need confidence in the quality of products supplied and would require some evidence that addressed this need. ISO 9000 was a neat solution to this problem as it embodied most of the requirements customers needed to obtain an assurance of quality. Any additional requirements could be put into the contract. Standardization in this case improved efficiency in getting orders out. However, in the mad rush to use ISO 9000, the buyers in the purchasing departments overlooked a vital step. Having determined the product or service to be procured and the specification of its characteristics, they should have asked themselves a key question:

> Are the consequences of failure such that we need the supplier to demonstrate it has the capability to meet our requirements or do we have sufficient confidence that we are willing to compensate for any problems that might arise?

In many cases, using ISO 9000 as a contractual requirement was like using a sledgehammer to crack a nut – it was totally unnecessary and much simpler models should have been used.

What does ISO 9000 apply to?

The ISO 9000 family of standards can be applied to all organizations regardless of type, size and product provided. The 1994 versions were particularly focused on the manufacturing sector, but this has largely been remedied in the 2000 version.

They are standards that apply to the management of an organization and only the management can and should decide how it will respond to these standards and recommendations.

Origin of ISO 9000

The story of ISO 9000 is a story of standards, methods and regulation. The brief history that follows is in no way comprehensive but is intended to illustrate four things:

- that standards are an ancient concept that survived several millennia;
- that a means of verifying compliance often follows the setting of standards;
- that the formalizing of working practices is centuries old and seen as a means to consistently meet standards;
- that market regulation (relative to the standard of goods and services) has been around for centuries for the protection of both craftsmen and traders.

ISO 9000 is a symptom of practices that were around centuries before anyone coined the term quality management. It is in some respects a natural progression that will continue to evolve. The story is told from a British viewpoint.

3000 BC

One cannot be certain when the concepts that underpin ISO 9000 were first derived. The principles of inspection against standards have been around since the Egyptians built the Pyramids. Imhotep is believed to have set standards for stones to ensure they were uniform and used wooden gauges for measurement. The practices used in organizations have been documented in one form or another since the Sumerians developed written language around 3100 BC and much of what was written at that time was almost exclusively for business and administrative purposes.

Third century AD

There is some evidence to suggest that associations of traders and craftsmen called *collegia* existed in ancient Rome as a means of monopolizing trade and establishing trading practices. They were sanctioned by the central government and were subject to the authority of the magistrates. With the fall of the western Roman Empire, guilds disappeared from European society for more than six centuries (Guilds, © 1994–1999)[1].

Tenth century AD

The *collegia* did survive in the Byzantine Empire and particularly in what is now Istanbul. The *Book of the Prefect*, a manual of government probably drawn up around the year 900, describes an elaborate guild organization whose primary function was the imposition of rigid controls, especially for financial and tax-raising purposes on every craft and trade in the city (Guilds, © 1994–1999)[2].

Eleventh century AD

As communities grew in size and formed towns, craftsmen or merchants formed guilds for mutual aid and protection and for the furtherance of their professional interests. By the 11th century in Europe, guilds performed a variety of important functions in the local economy among which were their monopoly of trade, the setting of standards for the quality of goods and the integrity of trading practices. Guilds came to control the distribution and sale of food, cloth, and other goods and compelled foreign merchants to pay a fee if they wanted to participate in local trade. Some outside merchants were prohibited altogether from participating in that trade – not too dissimilar from the use to which ISO 9000 has been put in the 20th century. Because medieval craftsmen employed simple hand tools, the skill of the workman rather than his equipment determined the quantity and quality of his output. There was therefore a long period of learning for the apprentice and journeyman. Boys were taken into the guild, served a 5–9 year apprenticeship and became a journeyman (a paid craftsman who worked for a master). A journeyman who provided proof of technical competence might become a master and establish his own workshop and hire and train apprentices. The guild system was not limited to Europe and could be found in India, China, Japan, and the Islamic world well into the 20th century.

Thirteenth century AD

In 1300, Edward I, King of England brought in a statute that no gold or silver be sold until tested by the 'Gardiens of the Craft' and struck with the leopard's head first known as the king's mark (Hallmark, © 1994–1999)[3].

Sixteenth century AD

By the 16th century the guild system was in decline with the emergence of regulated companies and other associations of wealthy merchant-capitalists.

Eighteenth century AD

In 1776 Adam Smith, a Scottish social philosopher wrote *Inquiry into the nature and causes of the Wealth of Nations* which changed the way work was organized for the next 200 years. Smith observed that a number of specialist workers each performing a single step in the manufacture of a pin could make far more pins in a day than the same number of generalists each engaged in making whole pins. Under the influence of Adam Smith the age of the specialist was born. Work was broken down into its simplest tasks and each task assigned to a specialist. No single worker ever completes a whole job – they pass their output to others to perform further tasks until the whole job is complete. In the economics and education of the day, this principle of the division of labour was the perfect solution to mass production. During the industrial revolution in Europe rigid systems of inspection were established particularly in the textile industry where it was realized that a reputation for supplying fault-free goods encouraged repeat orders. No doubt the inspectors were appointed on the basis of Smith's division of labour principle. We can trace the origin of the quality specialist to this period and from the same principles the armies of inspectors deployed by the military in the 19th and 20th centuries.

Nineteenth century

Frederick Winslow Taylor conducted studies at Bethlehem Steel in North America with the aim of increasing output. Taylor formulated the task concept where the work of every worker is fully planned in advance and each man receives in most cases written work instructions describing in detail the task which he is to accomplish as well as the means to be used in doing the work. However, with Taylor's task concept it was intended that work was planned not by the management alone but often by the joint effort of the worker and management. The instructions specified not only what was to be done but also how it was to be done and the exact time allowed for doing it. It should be appreciated that at the turn of the 20th century, the average workers were not well educated and lacked the knowledge to perform administrative tasks.

1900–20

In 1911, Taylor developed his principles of scientific management that are often condemned today as the cause of industrial strife and inefficiency but there are a number of principles that still hold true today and have found their way into ISO 9000. Taylor's principles (Hodgetts, Richard M., 1979)[4] were as follows:

1 'Develop a science for each element of a man's work, which replaces the old rule of thumb method'. Nothing intrinsically wrong with this and clearly in line with the principles of ISO 9000 – understanding the nature of the task and planning for a successful outcome rather than relying on chance.
2 'Scientifically select and then train, teach and develop the workman, whereas in the past he chose his own work and trained himself as best he could'. Again in general this principle remains valid today and is embodied in the Excellence Model and ISO 9000. The only difference is that employees have more opportunities now to train themselves and there is more of a partnership between employee and manager.
3 'Heartily cooperate with the men so as to ensure all of the work is being done in accordance with the principles of the science that have been developed'. This is about doing the right things right and again embodied within ISO 9000 and the Excellence Models. Many managers probably did not fully apply this principle as there was not always cooperation between workers and managers. Also this principle does not preclude workers controlling their own output.
4 'There is an almost equal division of the work and the responsibility between the management and the workers. The management takes over all of the work for which it is better fitted than the worker, while in the past almost all of the work and the greater part of the responsibility were thrown upon the men'. At the time this was a practical division of labour. Where it went

wrong was that when workers became more educated and thus had the ability to take on the management jobs, they were denied the opportunity – but apparently this was not what Taylor had intended.

Taylor also advocated a piecework system whereby workers received a certain price for each piece produced based on a standard devised from a time-and-motion study. Taylor believed that the worker could indeed benefit from this scheme in an environment in which management took a systematic approach to conducting its business. However, the followers of the piecework system chose not to honour their side of the deal and devoted their attention to the payment plan with its system of penalties for poor output. Taylor clearly recognized that in an industrial age, work needed to be managed as a system and that management and workers are partners within it and not adversaries. His second principle clearly shows how important he felt training to be but those that followed his teachings chose to ignore those principles that would commit them to spending money. This remains true in the 21st century although many organizations do see the benefits of investing in staff development and for incentive schemes that do not penalize the worker for management failures.

With the outbreak of the First World War in 1914, the British government established a Ministry of Munitions to co-ordinate the production of armaments because difficulties arose as a result of variation in the methods of inspection. This led to a growing force of ministry inspectors. It may not have been the right solution to the problem but in time of war it was perceived as the only solution.

It was Henri Fayol's contribution to management theory around 1916 that separated work into functions. Fayol recognized the need to separate technical activities from administrative activities in industry on the basis that a worker's chief characteristic is technical ability and the administrator's ability is planning, organizing, command, coordination and control. Fayol believed that separating the planning, organizing and controlling of work from performing work, increases in efficiency could be achieved (Hodgetts, Richard M., 1979)[5]. As a result, the control of work was separated from performing work because it left workers to concentrate their abilities on production. This separation of work by ability rather than process has continued to be the basis of organization structures upto the present day. Most organizations are structured by function where the functions comprise staff assigned tasks that have a common purpose.

1950s

Formal quality systems did not appear until the early 1950s. Quality Control, as an element of quality management emerged as a function in industry after

WWII and the principles were codified by J M Juran in his Quality Control Handbook of 1951, now in its fourth edition and still the most notable book on the subject today. In 1959 the first national standard, Mil Std 9858 on quality program requirements was issued by the American Department of Defense. This standard formed the foundation of all quality system standards that followed. The requirements for corrective and preventive action, data analysis, improvement, removal of special cause variation, contract review, work instructions, records, document control and many more were all in this standard of the 1950s.

1960s

Mil-Q-9858 was followed by a number of military standards relating to the management of product quality. Procurement in the UK defence industry was governed by contracts that invoked general inspection requirements (Form 649). This required a 'firm' to appoint a Chief Inspector and operate an inspection system that applied to purchasing and production. The UK Government posted Inspectors on defence contractor's premises and operated a final inspection policy. Product design was also subject to regulation through technical standards and codes of practice but administered by a different branch to the Inspectorate. Firms had to have Design Approval and Inspection Approval to trade with the government. With the growth of the arms race in the 1960s, the US Military flooded industry with standards and in 1968 Mil-Q-9858 was used as a basis for the NATO Allied Quality Assurance Publications (AQAP) for application to all member countries engaged in joint defence programmes.

1970s

Shortly after the publication of NATO Quality Assurance Standards, the UK Ministry of Defence brought out Def Stan 05–08 in 1970 which was a UK version of AQAP-1 and in 1972 the British Standards Institution (BSI) brought out BS 4891, 'A guide to Quality Assurance'. Def Stan 05–08 was revised in 1973 and several standards were issued to match the AQAP standards; these were Def Stan 05–21, 05–24 and 05–29 with corresponding guides. BSI then issued BS 5179 in 1974 to complement the UK MoD standards. This was heavily based on the Defence Standards but was aimed at the non-military market, although it was only a guide. During the 1970s, the US Military continued to publish standards governing elements of a quality system such as Drawing Systems, Systems Engineering, Configuration Management, Corrective Action, Supplier QA, Software QA and Calibration.

Contracting in the defence industry used quality assurance models to rate the capability of suppliers and made it a condition that those not registered to the appropriate defence standards would not be invited to tender for work. In an industry where national security was at stake, it paid not to take risks. The lessons of two world wars from ammunition and equipment that failed in service led to a series of solutions embodied within defence standards that experience had shown would prevent failure. Failure prevention was the driving force but cost was also an issue. In the commercial sector, contracts were often awarded on lowest price. When you are about to jump out of an aircraft into the jungle to suppress the enemy, it is comforting to know that the parachute and ammunition contracts were awarded on the basis of assured quality – not lowest price! In the commercial sector at the time, the profit motive was very strong. Quality would be compromised for profits and this was definitely not what the military wanted. As a result equipment was over-engineered and overpriced but in general the equipment did the job for which it was designed.

In 1975, Canada was the first nation to develop and publish quality system standards for commercial (non-military) use. This took the form of the Canadian Standards Association's Z299 Series. In 1979, BSI published BS 5750 in three parts for contractual purposes matching the three UK Defence Standards and the three AQAP Standards. Meanwhile contemporary standards were published in other countries covering the same scope and by 1983 many more countries had joined the procession but there were slight differences between them.

1980s

In 1982 the UK Government's white paper on Standards, Quality and International Competitiveness encouraged British Industry to pursue Certification to quality standards. In those days, quality assurance systems were seen as a means to achieve product standards that were perceived as central to international competitiveness. The White Paper triggered the birth of the Quality System Certification infrastructure and with it the drive for BS 5750 certification. Believing that BS 5750 would relieve them of supplier assessment, purchasers began to require their suppliers to register to BS 5750 some putting pressure to achieve certification by a certain date or they would be removed from the list of approved suppliers – echoes of the Guilds in the 11th century and of the military programmes of the 1960s. In order to bump start this drive for competitiveness, the UK's Department of Trade and Industry launched a scheme that offered grants to offset the costs of using consultants to help them achieve BS 5750 registration. This scheme gained momentum on release of ISO 9000 in 1987 and lasted well into the 1990s but on being terminated, the demand for ISO 9000 certification in the UK levelled off.

By 1984 BSI had drafted a revision to BS 5750 1979 and in view of the international interest in the subject encouraged the International Organization of Standardization (ISO) to embark on an International Standard for Quality Systems. Over 26 countries were involved in its development and whilst the standard still bears evidence of its military pedigree, it did break the mould and set a new world standard for quality management. ISO 9000 was published in 1987 as a set of six standards. ISO 8402, ISO 900–1, ISO 9001, ISO 9002, ISO 9003 and ISO 9004–1 all bearing a strong resemblance to the BS 5750 family of standards. Each country connected with its development then brought out a national equivalent. As would be expected from a standard that met with the agreement of 26 countries, one does not achieve a standard that is the state of the art. There had to be compromises and the result is the minimum standard acceptable to the majority. There followed additional standards and guides in the ISO 9000 series as it seemed appropriate at the time to attempt to codify the body of knowledge on quality management through international standards.

1990s

Throughout the 1990s, the popularity of ISO 9000 grew. Initially it was used entirely within the manufacturing sector. Having a military pedigree it was still intended only for contractual situations but the badge that came with certification and the drive by governments brought about a shift from manufacturing to the service sector. Initially being used in product-related services it soon took off among the professions, schools, health care, transport, agriculture etc. Although there are many disadvantages, there is however one tremendous advantage that should not be overlooked. By 1993 the number of certifications has risen to 27,000 and by 1999 the number was 274,040 worldwide. This was some achievement because over a period of 40 years, the teachings of Juran and Deming had apparently not reached as many organizations – if they had, there would have been less of a demand for ISO 9000 certification.

By 1995 the US Military had cancelled hundreds of Military Standards among them Mil-Q-9858 from which ISO 9000 was first developed. The UK MoD published Def Stan 05–91, 05–92 and 05–93 as their equivalents to ISO 9000, however, they only replace the material omitted when AQAP-1 was converted to ISO 9001. They added nothing new and regrettably the standards perpetuate their manufacturing bias.

The Technical Committee of ISO responsible for the ISO 9000 family of standards (TC/176) had a vision of what they desired the standards to become and published this as Vision 2000. Being international standards, the ISO 9000 family would be subject to review every five years and so as part of the plan the first review in 1992 was fairly superficial – a few changes in detail but no change in concept. The second edition was published in 1994 and since then a further 200,000 organizations gained certification. It is a pity TC 176 could not have made the major change when the use of the standard was relatively low. To wait until a quarter of a million organizations have based their quality management systems on a standard and then change it does seem irresponsible especially as the concepts upon which the revision was based were known and in use by 1990. TQM had been around for 10 years. Juran wrote about the universal principles of Breakthrough and Control in 1966 and Deming wrote *Out of the crisis* in 1982 addressing the key principles that should be used in organizations to turn around the flagging economy. Both of these eminent people had helped Japan turn around its production systems in the 1950s. But TC/176 needed much longer to realize their vision! The vision is illustrated in Figure 3.1 as a transition from little q to Big Q.

Figure 3.1   Big Q to little q

Changes to ISO 9000
Changes in titles

The titles have changed – moving away from models to requirements and guidance.

Changes in scope

The scope of the standard has changed from those activities that impact the product to embrace all activities in an organization that serve the satisfaction of customers. This leaves little if any activity of an organization that would be outside the scope of the quality management system.

Changes in structure

By far the most significant change is the change in structure – away from 20 elements to a model based on five elements. The ISO 9000:2000 family of standard is based on a process model – a model that is intended to represent

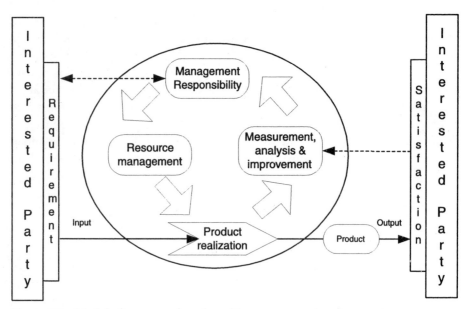

Figure 3.2   Model of a process based quality management system

a process-based quality management system. A version of this is illustrated in Figure 3.2.

This diagram is different to that in the standard for one simple reason. In the standard it shows continual improvement shooting out of the cycle and implying that it is somehow separate. It could be merely pointing out that within the cycle is continual improvement but it is confusing. Figure 3.2 also takes the model from ISO 9004 not ISO 9001. The figure title in both ISO 9001 and ISO 9004 is identical and the only difference is that customers are shown in the outside boxes in ISO 9001 and Interested Parties in ISO 9004. This clearly indicates that ISO 9001 remains focused on customers and supply of product to meet customer requirements. It conflicts with the text of the standard because regulations and the working environment are addressed which must include interested parties. However, the model is a symbolic representation of the standard rather than a management system because it bears only a vague relationship with how organizations operate. There are however, two significant advantages of this model.

There are no processes or systems between the needs of interested parties and satisfying them other than are shown within the ellipse i.e. the management system. There are no other systems shown on the model – no environmental management system, no financial management system, and no health and safety management system – in fact only one system. However, to confuse matters it refers to this system as a quality management system rather than the management system.

Figure 3.3   End-to-end processes

There are stakeholders at either end of the processes. Another way of drawing this part of the model is shown in Figure 3.3.

Changes in content

The content has changed from 20 elements organized on the basis of what could go wrong to four groups of requirements that focus on elements of process management. It is however, not the fact that the original elements have been placed onto a new structure, but that the principles upon which the standard has been based have changed.

Changes in intent

The intent of ISO 9001 has changed from a model for quality assurance to a set of requirements for an effective quality management. The standard is now based on eight management principles not on what requirements were necessary to prevent failures that experience had shown led to poor product quality. The forgotten standard ISO 8402 is brought into the family of ISO 9000 thus making it more likely that people will use it. However, in the author's opinion, all three standards should have been merged into one standard thus ensuring that everyone who possessed the requirements also possessed the concepts, terminology and guidelines to refer to as necessary.

Much damage can be done when the requirements of ISO 9000 are taken out of context, taken in isolation and taken literally. ISO 9000 is not a product standard therefore it is subject to interpretation as appropriate to the conditions in which it is being used. Whatever the initial understanding of a requirement of ISO 9001 might be, the intent is that:

- organizations design and manage their processes effectively to achieve corporate objectives, not that they create functional silos that compete for resources.
- organizations choose the right things to do based on an objective analysis of the environment in which they operate, not slavishly follow procedures that serve no practical purpose.
- management create an environment in which people will be motivated, not create bureaucratic systems of documentation that stifle initiative and creativity.

It is not the intent of the standard to imply uniformity in the structure of quality management systems or uniformity of documentation. Although this principle has not changed it is worth emphasizing that by moving away from 20 elements and focusing on processes, the model sends out a much stronger signal that the management system should be built around the organization not the standard.

Changes in language

The language in ISO 9000 has changed to reflect pressure from the user community for a user-friendlier standard. In some cases the changes are insignificant but in others the changes have a wider impact as indicated below:

Subcontractor has changed to supplier and supplier changed to organization so that there is now a supply chain represented by customer – organization – supplier.

In ISO 9001 the term **customer** is used but in ISO 9004 the term, *interested party* is used in order to embrace customers, employees, investors and other parties.

Executive management has been changed to Top Management indicating that when the standard uses the term management responsibility it is the people who *direct* the organization that should address these requirements.

Specified requirements have changed to customer and regulatory requirements or product requirements depending on the context.

Procedures have not exactly been changed to processes but presented in a different way that makes procedures only one element of managing an effective process. Procedures have lost their dominance in the standard to be replaced by the concept of managed processes.

Changes in requirement

ISO 9001 still contains 136 'shall' statements, 2 less than the 1994 version so in some respects it is no different. There were roughly 323 requirements in ISO 9001:1994 (Hoyle, David, 1996)[6]. In ISO 9001:2000 there are roughly 250 requirements. This is still too many especially if we are trying to get across the fundamental requirements of the standard. The following summarizes the requirement of ISO 9001 at two levels: firstly as a single requirement, secondly as a series of generic requirements.

The basic requirement

If ISO 9001 were to be resolved into a single requirement it would be phrased along the following lines:

> The organization shall determine what it needs to do to satisfy its customers, establish a system to accomplish its objectives and measure, review and continually improve its performance.

Generic requirements

If the 250 or so requirements of ISO 9001 and the intentions of ISO 9004 were to be condensed into just five simple requirements they might read as follows:

> The organization shall:
>
> - Determine the needs and expectations of customers and other interested parties;
> - Establish policies, objectives and a work environment necessary to motivate the organization to satisfy these needs;
> - Design, resource and manage a system of interconnected processes necessary to implement the policy and attain the objectives;
> - Measure and analyse the adequacy, efficiency and effectiveness of each process in fulfilling its purpose and objectives and;
> - Pursue the continual improvement of the system from an objective evaluation of its performance.

Key changes

There are many changes in ISO 9001. Some phrases from the 1994 version have been retained although only 17 instances could be found. In a great many cases, the wording has changed but not the intent. In the majority of cases, the wording represents a new requirement often as a new topic not only addressed in the 1994 version but also as a modification of the previous requirement extending its scope or application. Of the new requirements the following list presents those that are considered key to understanding the differences.

Audits   Audits of management system design, processes and conformity with ISO 9001 – no longer limited to procedure audits

Communication   Processes for internal communication rather than systems of documentation

Continual improvement   The effectiveness of the management system to be continually improved – not merely reviewed

Contract Review   Replaced by a wide-ranging review of all product requirements including customer, organizational and regulatory requirements – no longer limited to contracts and tenders. The standard has moved away from the original intention of it being used in a contractual situation to one in which there might be no contract until after a product or service has been developed.

Customer satisfaction   Customer perceptions of the organization's performance to be monitored as one of the measures of management system performance

Design   If the organization designs its own products and services, design and development processes must be included in the management system (see *Exclusions* below)

Documentation   Determined by the organization as necessary for effective operation of its processes – not simply as required by the standard

Linkages   Organization purpose, policy, objectives, processes and results to be linked to demonstrate effective process management

Management review   Top management to review the system for its effectiveness in enabling the organization to meet requirements of customers and other interested parties – no longer limited to a review of audit results and customer complaints

Marketing   The processes employed to determine customer needs and expectations must form part of the management system – no longer limited to contract review activities

Measurement   Required for all processes not only production, servicing and installation processes

Procedures   Only six procedures specified as requirements, others as needed for effective operation and control of the processes

Processes   All processes that serve the achievement of the organization's objectives to comprise the management system – no longer limited to production, installation and servicing

QMS   To be designed around the organization's processes not the elements and clauses of the standard

Quality Manual   Needs to describe the interaction between processes – is not to be a response to each clause of the standard

Quality objectives   Separate from the policy but consistent with it and established at relevant levels and functions – the driver of continual improvement in performance

Quality policy   To be appropriate to the purpose of the organization and provides a framework for quality objectives – not a motherhood statement

Records   As needed to provide evidence of effective operation – all types of records not simply those referred to as quality records

Requirements   Commitment to meeting requirements of customer and other interested parties – no longer limited to the organization's own requirements

System effectiveness   To be measured, analysed and continually improved and judged by the degree to which customers are satisfied – not judged on conformity with standard

Top management   Must be involved in establishing, developing, reviewing and improving the management system

The 1994 version was primarily aimed at quality assurance. The 2000 version is aimed at customer satisfaction. System effectiveness is therefore not measured on whether conformity with requirement could be demonstrated but on whether customers are satisfied with the product.

The 1994 version required procedures to be established, documented and maintained. The 2000 version requires processes to achieve defined objectives. Conformity is therefore not measured on the basis of following procedures but on whether defined objectives are achieved and whether these objectives serve the needs of customers and other interested parties.

The 1994 version focused on correcting errors. The 2000 version focuses on continual improvement not only by better control but also by finding better ways of doing things (improving effectiveness).

The 1994 version required management with executive responsibility to define its commitment to quality. The 2000 version requires top management to demonstrate its commitment to developing, implementing and improving a system of interrelated processes that will enable the organization to achieve its objectives.

There is a tremendous impact from these few differences alone. Picking out the new clauses will illustrate this even further.

4.1   General requirement on process management
5.2   Customer focus
5.4.1   Quality objectives
5.4.2   Quality management system planning
5.5.3   Internal communication
6.3   Infrastructure
6.4   Work environment
7.2.1   Determination of requirement relating to product
7.2.3   Customer communication
8.2.1   Customer satisfaction
8.2.3   Monitoring and measurement of processes
8.4   Analysis of data
8.5.1   Continual improvement

The detail of each of these clauses is covered in chapters 4 to 8, but the important message is that ISO 9001:2000 is not more of the same. It is a completely different standard – so much so that it is questionable whether it should have retained the same number. The scope and title have both changed and according to the ISO rules, if this happens a new standard should be developed. ISO 9000 was born out of the need for customers to have a common standard to control their suppliers and to reduce multiple assessment. What is emerging now is a standard to improve competitiveness. A standard that goes beyond assuring quality to assuring best practice – a prescription for achieving business excellence is therefore a new standard and not a revision. (In the author's opinion, the standard is so different that it should have been given a new number. By retaining the number ISO 9000, it carries with it the baggage collected by the previous versions, when it should be trying to create a new direction. The number ISO 9000 will retard progress and it will be interesting to observe the outcome).

Impact

These requirements will have considerable impact on organizations that only saw ISO 9000 as a 'badge on the wall', a means of getting recognition for what they were doing without changing anything.
    It means that:

● If organizations wish to obtain or retain certification, they will need to look outwards towards their customers. It will not be permissible to simply meet the organization's specified requirements.

- The system can no longer be a bolt-on system; in existence only to serve the certification body and only to get the badge. The system has to cause results and for this to happen the system and the organization are synonymous.
- Organizations can no longer choose the parts of the structure or select functions or operations that will be subject to ISO 9000 certification. All parts, functions, operations and activities that serve the achievement of the organization's objectives must be included.
- The performance of the organization relative to customer satisfaction will be monitored as a measure of the effectiveness of the system.
- Audits will need to focus on processes not procedures and will need to monitor performance against objectives.
- Management can no longer delegate out of sight to another person. They have only one system; the QMS is this system. They created the system so they must resource it, ensure it fulfils its purpose and strive for its continual improvement.

What's happened to the 20 elements?

When the 1994 version is compared with the 2000 version of ISO 9001, it is easy to see why many readers would reach the conclusion that little has changed. All the elements can be located in the new structure – albeit in a reduced form.

4.1 Management responsibility

This element remains but has been renumbered and clause 4.1.2.2 on resources has been expanded into a new section on resource management.

4.2 Quality system

This element has been divided up into 4 separate clauses, 3 of which are placed in section 4 under *Quality management system* and the fourth in clause 7.1 under *Planning of product realization*.

4.3 Contract review

This element has been placed in clause 7.2 under *Customer related processes* and remains virtually unchanged.

4.4 Design control

This element remains and has been placed in section 7 under *Product realization* with little change.

4.5 Document and data control

This element has been placed in section 4 under *Quality management system* and substantially reduced but retaining the original intent.

4.6 Purchasing

This element has been placed in clause 7.5 under *Product realization* retaining the original intent and absorbing receiving inspection.

4.7 Customer supplied product

This element has been placed in clause 7.5 under *Production and service provision* retaining the original intent. Had the architects recognized that customer supplied property is as much a design issue as it is a production issue, they might have raised its level in section 7.

4.8 Product identification and traceability

This element has been placed in clause 7.5 under *Production and service provision* retaining the original intent. Had the architects recognized that product identification is as much a design and purchasing issue as it is a production issue, they might have raised its level in section 7.

4.9 Process control

This element has been placed in section 7 under *Production and service provision* and substantially reduced but retains the same intent as in the original version.

4.10 Inspection and testing

This element has been placed in section 8 under *Monitoring and measurement*. The seven clauses have been reduced to three short paragraphs that retain the same intent as in the original version.

4.11 Inspection, measuring and test equipment

This element has been placed in section 7 under *Product realization* so that it could be included in the clause where exclusions were permitted. It should have been placed in section 8 along with measurement, analysis and improvement. This is because the principles involved are not really about controlling measuring devices but about maintaining the integrity of measurements. Had the architects recognized that measurement integrity applies to all measurement – not only physical measurements – they may have rewritten the clause and not made it optional.

4.12 Inspection and test status

This element has been reduced to one line and placed in clause 7.5.3 on *Identification and traceability.*

4.13 Control of nonconforming product

This element remains but is now placed under *Measurement, analysis and improvement* in clause 8.3. This is not in fact the correct location for this requirement as it is more to do with product realization than measurement. Its new position is as a result of section 7 being designated as the only section where exclusions may be permitted. Clearly control of nonconforming product could not be excluded so the architects relocated the requirement to section 8.

4.14 Corrective and preventive action

This element has been split into two and placed in section 8 under *Improvement.* The wording remains very similar and does not change the meaning of these two confusing concepts. Corrective action remains an action to prevent recurrence of nonconformity and preventive action remains and action to prevent the occurrence of nonconformity.

4.15 Handling storage, packaging, preservation and delivery

This element has been placed in section 7 under *Product realization.* It has been reduced to two requirements of less than three lines primarily because all six clauses addressed the same principle of controlling conforming product and preventing deterioration.

4.16 Quality records

This element has been placed in section 4 under *General quality* management system *requirements* and reduced to a few lines.

4.17 Internal quality audits

This element has been moved under *Monitoring and measurement* and largely retains the original wording.

4.18 Training

This element has been placed under section 6 on *Resource management* and enhanced to cover competency and awareness.

4.19 Servicing

This element has been eliminated.

4.20 Statistical techniques

This element has been reduced to one line and placed in clause 8.1 under *Measurement, analysis and improvement*.

Exclusions

Clause 1.2 of ISO 9001 states that where any requirement cannot be applied due to the nature of an organization and its product, this can be considered for exclusion. In the past organizations were able to register parts of their system or parts of their organization and product ranges. Certification applied to some product lines but not others. This is no longer applicable. However, *exclusion* is a certification issue – not an issue with using ISO 9001 as a basis for designing a management system.

Exclusions are limited to requirements within clause 7 meaning that you cannot exclude requirements contained in clauses 4, 5 and 8. If you want certification against ISO 9001, clauses 4, 5 and 8 are mandatory and any exclusion in clause 7 are only acceptable if they do not affect the organization's ability or responsibility to provide product that meets customer and applicable regulatory requirements. You cannot exclude requirements of clause 7 simply because you do not want to meet them.

IQNet provides some useful advice for auditors for interpreting the applicability of the requirements in clause 7.

● What is the idea or principle behind this requirement?
● What kind of problem could be prevented from meeting this requirement?
● Why would meeting the requirements provide confidence to customers?

The International Accreditation Forum has issued guidelines on the application of ISO 9001:2000 which addresses the issue of exclusions (International Accreditation Forum, 2001)[7].

Examining of each sub-clause in clause 7 may serve to explain the impact of this requirement.

7.1 Planning of product realization

Every organization provides outputs of one kind or another and therefore needs processes to deliver these outputs that obviously need to be planned. It is therefore inconceivable that this clause could be excluded.

7.2 Customer related processes

Every organization has customers, people or organizations they serve with their outputs. Organizations do not have to be profit-making to have customers because the term customer is not used in ISO 9000 to imply only those that make purchases. It is therefore inconceivable that this clause could be excluded.

7.3 Design and development

Every organization provides outputs that can be in the form of tangible or intangible products (computers, materials, software or advice), services that may process product supplied from elsewhere or services that develop, distribute, evaluate or manipulate information such as in finance, education or government.

With every product there is a service. If the product is provided from elsewhere, a service still needs to be designed to process it. While not every organization may provide a tangible product, every organization does provide a service. Some organizations manufacture products designed by their customers and therefore product design could be excluded. However, they still provide a service possibly consisting of sales, production and distribution and so these processes need to be designed. In franchised operations, the service is designed at corporate headquarters and deployed to the outlets but it is not common for an outlet alone to seek ISO 9000 certification – it would be more common for ISO 9000 certification to be a corporate policy and therefore the scope of certification would include service design. The IAF guidance (IQNet, 2001)[8] is that if you are not provided with the product/service characteristics necessary to plan product/service realization and have to define those characteristics; this is product design and development.

It is therefore inconceivable that this clause could be excluded for anything other than for product design meaning that it must be included for service design.

7.4 Purchasing

Every organization purchases products and services because no organization is totally self-sufficient except perhaps a monastery and it is doubtful that ISO 9000 would even enter the thoughts of a monk! Some purchases may be incorporated into products supplied to customers or simply passed onto customers without any further processing. Other purchases may contribute to the processes that supply product or deliver services to customers and there are perhaps some purchases that have little or no effect on the product or service supplied to customers but they may affect other interested parties. It is therefore inconceivable that this clause could be excluded in an organization that was considering certification to ISO 9001.

7.5 Production and service provision

Every organization provides outputs and these outputs need to be either produced or distributed. If the organization only designs products, it provides a design service and therefore this clause would apply. If the organization only moves product, it provides a distribution/shipment/transportation service and therefore this clause would apply. If the organization provides a service that some other organization designed, this clause *would* apply. There are however sub clauses within this clause that could be excluded.

7.5.2 Validation of processes

This clause applies to processes where the resulting output cannot be verified by subsequent monitoring or measurement. Firstly if we apply the provisions of clause 7.3 to all processes, this clause is redundant. Secondly, there is nothing within these requirements that should not apply to all processes.

(a) Defined criteria for review and approval of processes is addressed by clause 4.1c for all processes where it requires criteria and methods needed to ensure operation and control of processes

(b) Approval of equipment is addressed by clause 4.1d for all processes where it requires resources necessary to support the operation and monitoring of processes to be available. The qualification of personnel is addressed by clause 6.2.1 for all processes where it requires personnel to be competent on the basis of appropriate education, training, skills and experience

(c) Use of specific methods and procedures is addressed by clause 4.1d for all processes where it requires information necessary to support the operation and monitoring of processes to be available

(d) Requirements for records is addressed by clause 4.2.4 for all processes where it requires records to be established and maintained to provide evidence of conformity to requirements

(e) Revalidation is addressed by clause 8.2.3 for all processes where it requires methods to demonstrate the ability of processes to achieve planned results

It is therefore inconceivable that this clause could be excluded.

7.5.3 Identification and traceability

This clause only applies where product identification is appropriate and where traceability is a requirement – there is therefore no need to exclude it.

7.5.4 Customer property

Not every organization receives customer property but such property does take a variety of forms. It is not only product supplied for use in a job or for incorporation into supplies, but can be intellectual property, personal data or effects. Even in a retail outlet where the customer purchases goods, customer property is handed over in the sales transaction perhaps in the form of a credit card where obviously there is a need to treat the card with care and in confidence. In other situations the customer supplies information in the form of requirements and receives a product or a service without other property belonging to the customer being supplied. Information about the customer obtainable from public sources is not customer property neither is information given freely but there may be constraints on its use.

It is therefore conceivable that this clause could be excluded.

7.5.5 Preservation of product

This clause applies to organizations handling tangible product and would include documentation shipped to customers. It applies in service organizations that handle product, serve food and transport product or people. It does not apply to organizations that deal in intangible product such as advisers although if the advice is documented and the documents are transmitted by post or electronic means, preservation requirements would apply.

Although in theory it is conceivable that this clause could be excluded, in practice it is unlikely.

7.6 Control of monitoring and measuring devices

Every organization measures the performance of its products, services and processes. It uses devices for such measurement. They may be physical, financial or human and while calibration may not be appropriate, validation certainly is. Whatever the method of measurement, it is important that the integrity of measurement is sound. It is therefore inconceivable that this clause could be excluded. If however, we take individual requirements within this clause, the specific requirements for calibration could be excluded if no physical measuring devices are employed.

It is inconceivable therefore that this clause could be excluded but conceivable that certain requirements within it could be excluded.

Summary

This analysis has shown that in only one instance could a clause in section 7 of ISO 9001 be excluded (Customer property) and in only two other instances could requirements within a clause be excluded. It is therefore not the big loophole that it may have appeared to be at first glance.

An alternative structure

While ISO 9000:2000 is a step forward there are several weaknesses with the model illustrated in Figure 3.2 and the resultant structure of the standard.

- Management responsibility is not a process but a commitment.
- Resource Management is a series of processes
- Measurement, Analysis and Improvement is not a process but a series of sub-processes within every process.
- Product Realization is a series of processes that have interfaces with resource management processes and which embody measurement, analysis and improvement processes.
- Purchasing is a process that could fit as comfortably under resource management as product realization because it is not limited to the acquisition of components. It is a process that is used outside product realization as well as inside it.
- Control of measuring devices is more related to measurement processes than realization processes and should thus be in section 8.
- Control of nonconforming product is more to do with handling product than measurement so should be in section 7.

Including a provision for exclusions and a desire to make this as simple as possible brought about some of the anomalies. A quest for simplicity can unfortunately result in destroying logic, order and meaning. The structure of the standard also contains a lot of duplication that those using it as a prescription may struggle in discovering the differences in wording. Within chapters 4 to 8 of this book is guidance on the linkages and differences to facilitate understanding.

As the process model has its limitations an alternative model is shown in Figure 3.4 that is oriented around the elements of a process and not the standard.

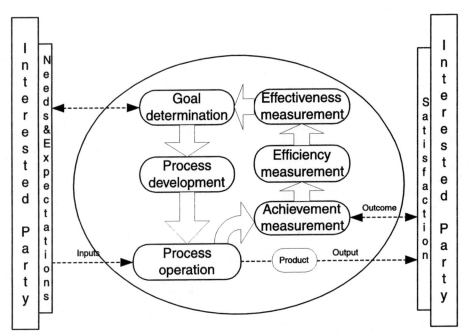

Figure 3.4 Alternative model of a process based management system

This shows the six stages of process management linked between the needs and expectations of interested parties and their satisfaction. It is clear in this model that process management is not simply about converting inputs into outputs. Effective management results from:

- setting goals that serve the interested parties;
- developing processes to achieve these goals;
- operating and maintaining the processes as designed;
- measuring achievement of the process goals;
- improving efficiency by finding better ways of doing things and;
- improving effectiveness by validating the goals and changing them if they are no longer relevant to the needs and expectations of the interested parties.

Management responsibility is not represented in the model because everything in the model is the responsibility of management.

Resource management is not represented in the model because processes cannot operate without resources and are therefore an integral characteristic of every process.

The linkage between these six stages and the clauses of ISO 9001 is shown in Table 3.1.

Table 3.1 Linkage between process stages and clauses

PROCESS STAGE	BASE CLAUSE		RELATED CLAUSES	
Determine the goal	5.3	Establish organization's purpose	5.1	Management responsibility
	5.1	Establish Quality policy	5.3	Quality policy
	5.4.1	Establish Quality objectives	5.1	Management responsibility
			5.2	Customer focus
			7.1	Planning of product realization
			7.2.1	Determination of requirement related to the product
			7.3.2	Design and development inputs
Develop processes to achieve the goal	4.1a	Identify processes	5.4.2	QMS planning
			7.1	Planning of product realization
			7.3.1	Design and development planning
	4.1b	Determine sequence and interaction of processes	7.1	Planning of product realization
			7.3.1	Design and development planning
			7.4.1	Purchasing process
			7.5.1	Control of production and service provision
			8.1	General
	4.1c	Develop criteria and methods	5.5.1	Responsibility and authority
			5.5.2	Management representative
			7.1	Planning of product realization
			7.4.1	Purchasing process
			7.5.1	Control of production and service provision
			7.5.3	Identification and traceability
			7.5.4	Customer property
			7.5.5	Preservation of product
			8.1	General
			8.3	Control of nonconforming product

	4.1d	Provide information	4.2.1 General documentation requirements
			4.2.2 Quality manual
			4.2.3 Control of documents
			4.2.4 Control of records
			5.1 Management commitment
			5.5.3 Internal communication
			7.1 Planning of product realization
			7.2.3 Customer communication
			7.3.3 Design and development outputs
			7.4.2 Purchasing information
	4.1d	Provide resources	6.1 Provision of resources
			6.2 Human resources
			6.3 Infrastructure
			6.4 Work environment
			7.1 Planning of product realization
Operate and maintain processes	4.1	Implement and maintain QMS	4.2.2 Quality manual
			4.2.3 Control of documents
			5.1 Management commitment
			5.4.2 Quality management system planning
			5.5.2 Management representative
			6.3 Infrastructure
			7.2.3 Customer communication
			7.5.1 Control of product and service provision
Establish that goal is being achieved	8.2.4	Monitor and measure product	7.2.2 Review of requirements related to the product
			7.3.4 Design and development review
			7.3.5 Design and development verification
			7.3.6 Design and development validation
			7.4.3 Verification of purchased product
			7.5.1 Control of production and service provision
			7.6 Control of monitoring and measuring devices
			8.1 General
			8.2.1 Customer satisfaction
			8.2.2 Internal audit

Table 3.1 Continued

PROCESS STAGE	BASE CLAUSE		RELATED CLAUSES	
Establish that goal is being achieved (continued)	8.4	Analyse product	8.1	General
			8.5.2	Corrective action
			8.5.3	Preventive action
			8.3	Control of nonconforming product
	4.1f	Implement actions to achieve planned results	5.6	Management review
			7.3.7	Control of design and development changes
			8.1	General
			8.2.3	Monitoring and measurement of processes
			8.5.1	Continual improvement
			8.5.2	Corrective action
			8.5.3	Preventive action
Establish goal is achieved in the best way	4.1e	Monitor and measure processes	5.6	Management review
			7.5.2	Validation of processes for production and service provision
			7.6	Control of monitoring and measuring devices
			8.1	General
			8.2.2	Internal audit
			8.2.3	Monitoring and measurement of processes
	4.1e	Analyse processes	8.1	General
			8.4	Analysis of data
	4.1f	Continually improve processes	8.1	General
			8.5.1	Continual improvement
Establish if it's the right goal	8.4	Analyse suitability, adequacy and effectiveness	5.6.2	Review input
			7.6	Control of monitoring and measuring devices
	5.6.1	Review system effectiveness	5.6	Management review
	4.1f	Continually improve processes	8.5.1	Continual improvement

Certification to ISO 9001:2000

A number of documents are available from ISO, IAF, IQNet and BSI web sites covering issues related to certification to ISO 9001:2000 (See Appendix B).

- ISO (International Organization of Standardization) is the body issuing the standard. They do not perform audits or accredit certification bodies
- IAF (International Accreditation Forum) is an association of national accreditation bodies and sets policies for mutual recognition of certificates by member bodies. If your certification body is accredited by a member of IAF, the CBs certificates will be recognized everywhere else in the world
- IQNet is an association of Certification Bodies but does not include all CBs

Organizations have until 15 December 2003 to upgrade their certificate to ISO 9001:2000. Certificates to ISO 9001:1994, ISO 9002:1994 and ISO 9003:1994 may be issued upto the cut-off date of 14 December 2003.

It is recommended by IQNet that auditors should perform audits using the process approach and that the audit reports should address the ability of the processes to meet customer requirements and the effectiveness in achieving customer satisfaction. This is far different from the conformity approach taken with the 1994 version of ISO 9000.

An issue of concern to organizations choosing certification to ISO 9001:2000 is the variability of the certification process and the validity of the resultant certificate. There are certification bodies that are not accredited by a recognized accreditation body. In principle this should make a difference because the accredited certification body has proven that it is competent to assess certain types of organizations to ISO 9001:2000. However, the process itself is not capable. There is a wide variation in the competence of certification body auditors meaning that there is no guarantee that an auditor from an accredited certification body will be any better than one from an unaccredited certification body. The only difference is that one can show evidence of nationally recognized independent review and the other can't.

From the IQNet position paper (IQNet, 2001)[9] and response from UK certification bodies(LRQA, NQA, BSI, DNV, BM TRADA, 2001)[10] it appears that there will also be wide variation in the scope of certification that is not made evident through the certificate. Apart from the permissible exclusions that will be stated on the certificate, it appears that some certification bodies will audit the management system in its entirety if requested and others will only audit those processes having a direct impact on product meeting customer requirements. This implies that those organizations that choose to use the management system as a means to enable the organization meet all its objectives and thus include finance, marketing, administration etc will receive the same certificate as those organizations that chose to limit their management system to processes that directly affect the product.

The three pillars of ISO 9000

ISO 9000 Certification is only of any value in markets where it provides the confidence needed for free trade. ISO 9000 as a symbol has become synonymous with certification, quality management systems, documentation and internal audits to such an extent that if one were to dispense with ISO 9000 certification, one also ceases to maintain a quality management system, ceases to conduct audits and ceases to use documentation. We have to divorce certification from systems and systems from standards and correct a few misconceptions.

ISO 9000 Certification is optional and whether or not your organization is ISO 9000 certificated, it does not by itself affect the performance of an organization. It is a flag of confidence that is visible to others with whom you trade. Certification is inextricably linked to the standard.

ISO 9000 is a series of standards and their use is optional. They do not affect the performance of an organization although their use can assist organizations improve performance. The standards can be used without being linked with certification.

All organizations have a quality management system but its formalization is optional. The system enables the organization to achieve its objectives and therefore exists independently of whether or not ISO 9000 is used and whether or not ISO 9000 Certification is obtained.

These three pillars are illustrated in Figure 3.5 showing that an organization can sustain and improve its performance without using ISO 9000 as a standard and without using ISO 9000 Certification. Remove the two outer pillars and the

Figure 3.5   The three pillars of ISO 9000

organization remains stable! The foundation upon which the three pillars stand is the body of knowledge that represents the field of quality management. Most of this knowledge is channelled through the management system, somewhat less is channelled through the standard (ISO 9000) and a particular branch of the body of knowledge is channelled through certification. An organization could absorb and apply all relevant knowledge and therefore obtain no additional support from ISO 9000 standards or ISO 9000 certification. Another organization may absorb and apply some knowledge directly from the foundation but require the support of the ISO 9000 standards to help understanding and application. A third organization may absorb and apply little knowledge directly from the foundation and require both the support of the ISO 9000 standards and ISO 9000 certification to maintain a stable and robust management system.

Summary

In this chapter we have explored the role of the standard and its origins and discovered that it continues a long tradition of setting standards, verifying compliance and the formalized working practices as a means of meeting customer expectations. Although a concept of the late 20th century, system certification also follows a long tradition of voluntary regulation of trade within market sectors. However, ISO 9000 is among the first of a group of standards to attempt standardization of management systems on an international scale. We have examined the changes that have been made to the ISO 9000 family of standards and discovered that they are substantially different. The standard now reflects a set of concepts and principles that moves away from procedures and conformity audits as a means of assuring customers of quality. ISO 9000 now requires organizations to identify customer needs and expectations, manage a series of interconnected processes to achieve these requirements and to measure, analyse and continually improve performance. For many organizations this will require significant change not only in the system documentation but also in the way the organization is managed.

Many of the terms used in ISO 9000:2000 may appear the same as those in the 1994 version. If you want to see the same requirements you will see them – but a word of warning: make no assumption about the terminology! Recognition of the terms is no guarantee that 'we already do that'!

Consult ISO 9000:2000

Do not assume that ISO 9000 will cause improvement in business performance. ISO 9000 is a standard but standards cannot cause people to do the right things right first time. People produce the products and services supplied by organizations and standards merely serve to guide these people in choosing the right things to do. It is the quality of leadership in an organization that creates an environment in which people will do the right things right without having to be told.

> *Customer focused leadership*
> *produces satisfied customers*
> *not standards*

Role, origins and application – Food for thought

1 Don't simply go for the badge on the wall
2 If you are going to use ISO 9000, use it as an aid not a slave
3 Go for certification only if it is essential for you to win business
4 Don't label things or positions within your organization with ISO 9000 – it gives the impression that they exist only to serve the standard
5 Do read and use all three standards in the ISO 9000 family
6 Don't get hung up on the words – seek the purpose of the requirement that transcends the words
7 Don't assume the terms are used in the same way as you use them – apply the terms as they are defined in ISO 9000
8 Don't impose ISO 9001 on your suppliers unless you cannot verify the quality of the goods yourself
9 Don't coerce your suppliers into seeking ISO 9001 certification when you already have confidence in the quality of their supplies
10 Don't rely on ISO 9001 certificates to give you an assurance of quality – check them out
11 Don't assume that a non-accredited certification body is any worse than an accredited one – check them out
12 Don't create separate systems – there is only one
13 Don't assume that because a clause is in section 7 you can exclude it – would it impact the organization if you did not do this?
14 Don't forget that contract review has gone – it is now product review and not dependent on you having a contract
15 Do use the process approach to develop and audit your system
16 Don't ask what benefit do we get from implementing ISO 9000 – ask what benefit do we get from managing our processes effectively
17 If you choose to withdraw from ISO 9000 certification don't forget that you still need to manage your processes effectively

Bibliography

1. Subject – Guilds, (© 1994–1999). *Britannica® CD 99 Multimedia Edition,* Encylopædia Britannica, Inc.
2. Subject – Guilds, (© 1994–1999). *Britannica® CD 99 Multimedia Edition,* Encylopædia Britannica, Inc.
3. Subject – Hallmark, (© 1994–1999). *Britannica® CD 99 Multimedia Edition,* Encylopædia Britannica, Inc.
4. Hodgetts, Richard M., (1979). *Management; Theory, process and practice,* W B Saunders Company.
5. Hodgetts, Richard M., (1979). *Management; Theory, process and practice,* W B Saunders Company.
6. Hoyle, David, (1996). *ISO 9000 Quality System Assessment Handbook,* Butterworth Heinemann.
7. International Accreditation Forum, (2001). www.iaf.nu.
8. IQNet, (2001). www.iqnet-certification.com.
9. IQNet, (2001). www.iqnet-certification.com.
10. LRQA, NQA, BSI, DNV, BM TRADA, (2001). Question time, *Quality World,* **27**, (3), pp. 38–39.

Chapter 4
Quality management system

A system must have an aim. A system must create
something of value, in other words results.
Management of the system requires knowledge of
the interrelationships between all the components
within the systems and of the people that work in it

W. Edwards Deming

Summary of requirements

Section 4 of ISO 9001 contains the basic requirements for establishing a management system rather than any particular component of the system. In some respects they are duplicated in other clauses of the standard but this is no bad thing because it emphasizes the principal actions necessary to develop, implement, maintain and improve such a system. Unlike the 1994 version, the focus has moved away from documentation towards processes and therefore these general requirements capture some of the key activities that are required to develop an effective system.

Although the clauses in section 4 are not intended as a sequence there is a relationship that can be represented as a cycle, but first we have to lift some clauses from section 5 to commence the cycle. The words in bold indicate the topics covered by the clauses within sections 4 of the standard. The cycle commences with the Organization's purpose from which are developed objectives. In planning to meet these objectives the *processes are identified* and their *sequence and interaction* determined. Once the relationship between processes is known, the *criteria and methods* for effective operation and control can be developed and *documented*. The processes are described in terms that enable their effective communication and a suitable way of doing this would be compile the process descriptions into a *quality manual* that not only references the associated *procedures* and *records* but also shows how the processes interact. Before implementation the processes need to be *resourced* and the *information* necessary to operate and control them deployed and brought under *document control*. Once operational the processes need to be *monitored* to ensure they are functioning as planned. *Measurements* taken to verify that the processes are delivering the required output and actions taken to *achieve the planned results*. The data obtained from monitoring and measurement that is captured on *controlled records* needs to be *analysed* and opportunities for *continual improvement* identified and the agreed actions *implemented*.

Establishing a quality management system (4.1)

The standard requires the organization *to establish a quality management system in accordance with the requirements of ISO 9001.*

What does this mean?

To *establish* means to set up on a permanent basis, install, or create and therefore in establishing a management system, it has to be designed, constructed, resourced, installed and integrated into the organization signifying that a management system on paper is not a management system.

Establishing a system in accordance with the requirements of ISO 9001 means that the characteristics of the system have to meet the requirements of ISO 9001. However, the requirements of ISO 9001 are not expressed as system requirements of the form 'The system shall . . .' but are expressed as organization requirements of the form 'The organization shall . . .' It would appear, therefore, that the system has to cause the organization to comply with the requirements and this will only happen if the system has been integrated into the way the organization does things. Some organizations regard the management system as the way they do things but merely documenting what you do does not equate with establishing a system for the reasons given in Chapter 2 under *Quality management systems*.

> **1994–2000 Differences**
> Previously the standard required the supplier to establish a quality system as a means of ensuring that product conforms to specified requirements. There is no difference in intent but the new wording (in accordance with) implies that the standard defines how the management system should be established but it loses the reasons for doing it.

Why is this necessary?

This requirement responds to the System Approach Principle.

ISO 9001 contains a series of requirements which if met will provide the management system with the capability of supplying products and services that satisfy the organization's customers. All organizations have a management system – a way of working, but in some it is not formalized – in others it is partially formalized but not effective and in a few organizations the management system really enables its objectives to be achieved year after year. In such organizations, a management system has been established rather than evolved and if an organization desires year after year success, it needs a formal mechanism to accomplish this – it won't happen by chance or even by the brute force and determination of one man or woman – it requires an effective management system. This requires management to think of a system as a set of interconnected processes that include tasks, resources and behaviours as explained in Chapter 2.

How is this implemented?

The terms 'establish', 'document', 'implement', 'maintain' and 'improve' are used in the standard as though this is a sequence of activities when in reality, in order to establish a system it has to be put in place and putting a system in place requires two separate actions:

- Design the system using a process that transforms the system requirements into specific characteristics that results in a clear definition of all the processes that meet the system requirements.
- Construct the system using a process that documents, installs, commissions and integrates the processes to deliver the required business outputs.

The way in which these phases of quality system development are related is illustrated in the management system process model shown in Figure 4.1. This diagram has some important features. Note that the design input to the system comprises internal and external requirements. On the right side there are four improvement routes:

- Improvements in conformity during operation of the system arise through enforcing policy and practices – doing what you say you do
- Improvements in conformity during system construction arise through enforcing policy and design rules on the system – reworking the system to comply with the established policies and objectives
- Improvements in efficiency during system construction arise through finding better ways of implementing the system design – shorter, less wasteful routines, less complexity, lower skill levels, fewer resources
- Improvements in effectiveness arise as a result of identifying different policies and objectives – higher targets, new objectives, new requirements, regulations, and new technologies

As indicated above, establishing a system means designing and constructing it, which can be referred to as *system development*. System design is dealt with under *Identifying processes*. Constructing the system covers documentation, resourcing, installation, commissioning, qualification and integration. Documentation is dealt with under *Documenting a quality management system*, resourcing is dealt with in Chapter 6 and the other actions are addressed below.

Process installation

Process installation is concerned with bringing information, human resources and physical resources together in the right relationship so that all the components are put in place in readiness to commence operation. In many cases the process will be installed already because it existed before formalization. In some cases process installation will require a cultural change. There is little point in introducing change to people who are not prepared for it. Installing a dynamic process-based system into an environment in which people still believe in an element-based system or in which management still think in terms of functions, is doomed to fail. Therefore a precursor to *process installation* is the preparation of sound foundations. Everyone concerned needs to understand the purpose and objectives of what is about to happen – they all need to perceive the benefits and be committed to change and understand the concepts and principles involved.

Installation is not a term that is often used with respect to a management system. One generally refers to management system *implementation*, but this implies that the management system is a set of rules, not a dynamic system. (You do not implement a product – you implement product design). As stated previously, in order to establish a management system one needs to design, resource and install it, therefore installation is concerned with implementing the design.

A common failing with the implementation of documented practices is that they are not sold to the workforce before they become mandatory. Also, after spending much effort in their development, documented practices are often issued without any thought given to training or to verifying that practices have in fact been changed. As a result, development is often discontinued after document release. It then comes as a shock to managers to find that all their hard work has been wasted. An effectively managed programme of introducing new or revised practices is a way of overcoming these shortfalls.

The process of installing a new process or one that requires a change in practice is one that is concerned with the management of change. It has to be planned and resourced and account taken of attitudes, culture, barriers and any other resistance there may be (Juran, J. M., 1995)[1]. You must remember that not all those who are to use the process may have participated in its development and may therefore be reluctant to change their practices.

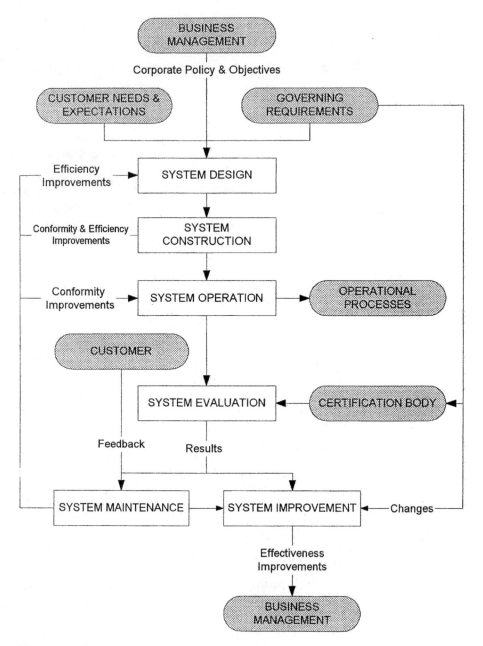

Figure 4.1 System management process model

Process commissioning

Process commissioning is concerned with getting all the new processes working following installation. The people will have been through reorientation and will have received all the necessary process information. Any new resources will have been acquired and deployed and the old processes decommissioned. Installation and commissioning of new processes take place sequentially usually without a break so that current operations are not adversely affected.

Process integration

Process integration is concerned with changing behaviour so that people do the right things right without having to be told. The steps within a process become routine, habits are formed and beliefs strengthened. The way people act and react to certain stimuli becomes predictable and produces results that are required. Improvement does not come about by implementing requirements – it comes about by integrating principles into our behaviour.

System integration

System integration is concerned with making the interconnections between the processes, ensuring that all the linkages are in place and that the outputs from a process feed the interfacing processes at the right time in the right quality. The system will not be effective if the process linkages do not function properly.

Identifying processes (4.1a)

1994–2000 Differences

Previously the standard required the supplier to identify the production, installation and servicing processes which directly affect quality. The difference is a widening of the requirement to all processes needed for the management of quality and therefore removing its limitation to product realization processes.

The standard requires the organization *to identify the processes needed for the quality management system and their application throughout the organization.*

What does this mean?

Processes produce results of added value. Processes are not procedures (see Chapter 2 on Basic Concepts). The results needed are those that serve the organization's objectives. Processes needed for the management system might be all the processes needed to achieve the organization's objectives and will therefore form a chain of processes from corporate goals to their accomplishment. However, as we discovered in Chapter 2, the business processes need to add value for the interested parties. The chain of processes

Figure 4.2   End-to-end processes

is a *value chain* and therefore should extend from the needs of the interested parties to the satisfaction of these needs. This is illustrated by the process model of Figure 3.4.

Traditionally work has been organized into functions of specialists, each performing tasks that serve functional objectives. This has the effect of suboptimization – pursuit of local goals at the expense of organizational goals. By thinking of a system as a collection of interconnected processes rather than a series of interconnected functions, each focused on the needs of interested parties, the chain of processes cuts across the functions. The processes needed for the management system are those processes with a purpose that is aligned to the organization's objectives. (See Figure 4.2.)

Why is this necessary?

This requirement responds to the Process Approach Principle.

The management system consists of a series of interconnected processes and therefore these processes need to be identified.

How is this implemented?

As the standard is not specific as to the types of processes, we must assume it is all processes and this would therefore include both business processes and work processes. This distinction is important for a full appreciation of this requirement. The relationship between these two types of processes is addressed further in Chapter 2.

In many cases, organizations have focused on improving the work processes believing that as a result there would be an improvement in business outputs but often such efforts barely have any effect. It is not until you stand back that the system comes into view. A focus on work processes and not business processes is the primary reason why ISO 9000, TQM and other quality initiatives fail. They resulted in sub-optimization – not optimization of the organizational performance. If the business objectives are functionally ori-ented, they tend to drive a function-oriented organization rather than a process-oriented organization. Establish process-oriented objectives, measures and targets, focused on the needs and expectations of external stakeholders, the functions will come into line and you will be able to optimize organizational performance. When Texas Instruments reengineered its processes in 1992, their process map showed only six processes(Hammer, Michael and Champy, James 1993)[2]. Hammer remarks that hardly any company contains more then ten or so principal processes.

There are several ways of identifying processes but the two that we will discuss here are the top down approach and the bottom up approach.

Top down approach

From the organization's mission statement determine the factors upon which accomplishment of the mission depend – these are the critical success factors (CSF). The CSFs indicate the capabilities needed and consequently identify the processes required to delivery these capabilities. In order to fulfil the mission, an organization might need a design capability, a production capability and a distribution capability. This results in a need for a design process, a production process and a distribution process. These processes depend upon an available supply of capital, competent staff, equipment and materials and well-equipped facilities. Delivery of this capability requires a capable resource management process that manages human, physical and financial resources. Another CSF would be the ability of the organization to identify customer needs and expectations in its chosen markets and consequently a need for an effective marketing process is identified. A further CSF would be the rate at which customer enquiries were converted into sales and consequently a need for an effective sales process is identified. By identifying CSFs and the associated processes a list of core processes will emerge. However, these processes do not operate in isolation. They need to be linked and this is where the context diagram is useful (see Figure 4.4). From a context diagram of the organization that indicates the external inputs, outputs, constraints and resources, you could take each interface and position the identified processes in a relationship that represents a value chain from inputs to outputs. The result will be a system model similar to that illustrated in Figure 2.14. Now, analyse each core process and identify the key stages from input to output in order to identify the key sub-processes. Decomposing the layers further, by analysing each sub-process will identify the work processes and eventually the tasks performed by specific individuals. This is as deep in the hierarchy that you should need to go.

Bottom up approach

Take any group of tasks within a function and establish the processes to which they contribute, keeping the focus on the external party. Bring in other groups when it is realized that there is a gap in the chain. Extend the chain until you reach the tasks that interface with the external party. This approach can commence at the functional level and grow outwards until all groups are represented in the chain. In taking this approach you may well find some tasks do not link with any other tasks or an external party and should be marked for action because clearly they appear to add no value. However, a task may not add value to one external party but may add value to another. If you focus only on customers, you will find a number of tasks that do not contribute to the achievement of customer needs but do contribute to satisfying the needs of other interested parties.

The processes you identify may not be like those of any other organization – they don't have to be, as every organization is different – even those that appear to be in the same business.

The processes you identify might include:

- Marketing process that converts customer needs into an interest in the organization's products and services. This process might also be known as *Understanding customer needs.*
- Business management process that converts the needs of the interested parties into policies and objectives for their fulfilment, provides the system for meeting them and ensures continued satisfaction of all interested parties. This process might also be known as *Mission management.*
- Resource management process that converts organization's objectives into a facility that is fully equipped with the human, physical and financial resources needed to achieve the objectives. This process might also be known as *Asset management.*
- Order fulfilment process that converts sales prospects into satisfied customers. This process might also be known as *Order to cash.*

Order fulfilment is obviously a major process in any organization because it creates wealth. It may include the sub-processes of sales, design, production and distribution.

'Identifying processes' means more than just naming them. A name is a label that triggers perceptions, some of which may differ from what we intended. It is therefore necessary to define the processes in terms that will form clear understanding of the boundaries, purpose and outputs of each process. The above list identifies groups of processes and there may therefore be several processes that deliver marketing objectives, resource objectives and other objectives.

However, naming is important in order to avoid confusion between processes and functions. There are two conventions used for naming processes one is verb focused and the other is noun focused. The verb-focused construction of a process name commences with a verb such as produce, define, acquire. The noun-focused construction may simply be one word such as marketing, design, production. This distinction is illustrated in Figure 4.3. The noun focused convention can give the impression that the chain of processes is a chain of functions having these titles, when in reality several

Figure 4.3 Distinction between process naming conventions

functions will contribute to each process. In order to avoid the confusion, it may be more appropriate to use the verb-focused convention. In Figure 4.3 both product and service are treated differently because in practice the chain of end-to-end processes is different.

In every organization there are sets of activities but each set or sequence is not necessarily *a process*. If the result of a sequence of activities adds no value, continue the sequence until value is added for the benefit of customers – then you have defined a *business* or *work process*.

A technique frequently used to design management systems is process mapping or flow-charting which is outlined below. (Hoyle, David and Thompson, John, 2000)[3]

A process chart is a diagrammatic representation of the sequence and interaction of the tasks and activities required to convert process inputs into the desired outputs. Charting commences with a context diagram that puts the organization in context with its surroundings and identifies the various business inputs and outputs (see Figure 4.4).

By expanding the interfaces on the context diagram, the primary processes that convert these business inputs into the required business outputs are identified and displayed in a System Model (Figure 2.14). Taking each Business Process sequentially, the sub-processes required to convert process inputs into the required process outputs are displayed in a Business Process Model. If necessary, each sub-process can be analysed to define the tasks required to convert the process inputs into process outputs and displayed in a Work Process Model (Hoyle, David and Thompson, John, 2000)[4].

Another technique is IDEF (Integrated Definition) developed by the US Air Force (US Department of Defense, 2001)[5]. The objective of the model is to provide a means for completely and consistently modelling the functions (activities, actions, processes, operations) required by a system or enterprise,

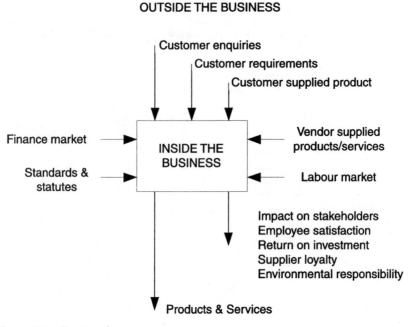

OUTSIDE THE BUSINESS

Customer enquiries

Customer requirements

Customer supplied product

Finance market → INSIDE THE BUSINESS ← Vendor supplied products/services

Standards & statutes → ← Labour market

Impact on stakeholders
Employee satisfaction
Return on investment
Supplier loyalty
Environmental responsibility

Products & Services

Figure 4.4   Context diagram

and the functional relationships and data (information or objects) that support the integration of those functions. Four models were developed:

IDEF0, used to produce a 'function model'. A function model is a structured representation of the functions, activities or processes within the modelled system or subject area.

IDEF1, used to produce an 'information model'. An information model represents the structure and semantics of information within the modelled system or subject area.

IDEF2, used to produce a 'dynamics model'. A dynamics model represents the time-varying behavioural characteristics of the modelled system or subject area.

IDEF3 used to produce a 'process model'. A process model represents the structured method by which a domain expert can express knowledge about the operation of a particular system or organization.

IDEF is a systematic method of modelling that can reveal all there is to know about a function, activity, process or system. Considering its pedigree it is more suited to very complex systems but can result in *paralysis from too much analysis!* Many management systems do not require such rigorous techniques. There can be a tendency to drill down through too many layers such that at the lowest level you are charting movements of a person performing an activity or identifying pens and pencils in a list of required resources. For describing the management system processes it is rarely necessary to go beyond an activity performed by a single individual. As a rough guide you can cease the decomposition when the charts stop being multifunctional.

Sequence and interaction of processes (4.1b)

The standard requires the organization *to determine the sequence and interaction of the identified processes.*

What does this mean?

Sequence refers to the order in which the processes are connected to achieve a given output. Interaction

1994–2000 Differences

This is a new requirement that has no equivalent in the 1994 version.

refers to the relationship between the processes and their dependencies, the source of inputs and destination of the outputs. The system model shown in Figure 2.14 illustrates the sequence and interaction of the business processes.

Why is this necessary?

This requirement responds to the System Approach Principle.

Objectives are achieved through processes, each delivering an output that serves as an input to other processes along a chain that ultimately results in the objective being achieved. It is therefore necessary to determine the sequence of processes. Some will work in parallel; others in a direct line but all feeding results that are needed to accomplish the objective. There will therefore be interactions between processes that need to be determined.

How is this implemented?

A practical way to show the sequence of processes is to produce a series of flow charts. However, charting every activity can make the charts appear very complex but by layering the charts in a hierarchy, the complexity is reduced into more digestible proportions.

Many processes will not only require inputs from other processes to start, but will require other inputs or conditions for tasks to be executed. For example, a verification process requires trained people, calibrated equipment and perhaps certain environmental conditions and therefore relies upon the

Resource Management process to deliver trained people, calibrated equipment and facilities in which the environment is maintained. The interface between the verification process and resource management process creates an inter-action when the processes are active. The reliance upon resource management to provide inputs creates a dependency. A verification process will also require documentation and therefore relies upon the document control process feeding only up to date documents. The verification process has outputs and therefore relies upon material handling processes and data storage processes to take away the outputs. Some of the interactions occur on demand and are therefore dynamic, others are passive and are often taken for granted but without which the process cannot deliver its required output. To test whether you have identified all the interactions, just ask yourself what would happen if a particular condition were not available – would the process still be able to deliver the required outputs?

Criteria and methods for effective operation and control (4.1c)

1994–2000 Differences
This is a new requirement that has no equivalent in the 1994 version.

The standard requires the organization *to determine criteria and methods required to ensure the effective operation and control of the identified processes.*

What does this mean?

The criteria that ensure effective operation are the standard operating conditions, the requirements or success criteria that need to be met for the process to fulfil its objectives.

The methods that ensure effective operation are those regular and systematic actions that deliver the required results. In some cases the results are dependent upon the method used and in other cases, any method might achieve the desired results. Use of the word 'method' in this context is interesting. It implies something different than had the standard simply used the word 'procedure'. Procedures may cover both criteria and methods but have often been limited to a description of methods. Methods are also ways of accomplishing a task that are not procedural. For example, information may be conveyed to staff in many ways – one such method might be an electronic display that indicates information on calls waiting, calls completed and call response time. The method of display is not a procedure although there may be an automated procedure for collecting and processing the data.

Why is this necessary?

This requirement responds to the Process Approach Principle.

A process that is operating effectively delivers the required outputs of the required quality, on time and economically, while meeting the policies and regulations that apply to the process. A process that delivers the required quantity of outputs that do not possess the required characteristics, are delivered late, waste resources and breach policy and safety, environmental or other regulations is not effective. It is therefore necessary to determine the criteria for the acceptability of the process inputs and process outputs and the criteria for acceptable operating conditions. Thus it is necessary to ascertain the characteristics and conditions that have to exist for the inputs, operations and outputs to be acceptable.

How is this implemented?

In order to determining the criteria for effective operation and control you need to identify the factors that affect success. Just ask yourself the question: What are the factors that affect our ability to achieve the required objectives? In a metal machining process, material type and condition, skill, depth of cut, feed and speed affect success. In a design process input requirement adequacy, designer competency, resource availability and data access affect success. In an auditing process, objectives, method, timing, auditor competency, site access, data access and staff availability affect success. In a computer activated printing process, the critical factor may be the compatibility of the input data with the printer software, the format of the floppy disk and the resolution of the image. There are starting conditions, running conditions and shutdown conditions for each process that need to be specified. Get any one of these wrong, and whatever the sequence of activities, the desired result will not be achieved.

Determining the methods can mean determining the series of actions to deliver the results or simply identifying a means to do something. For example there are various methods of control:

- Supervisors control the performance of their work groups by being on the firing line to correct errors.
- Automatic machines control their output by in-built regulation.
- Manual machines control their output by people sensing performance and taking action on the spot to regulate performance.
- Managers control their performance by using information.

The method is described by the words following the word 'by' as in the above list. A method of preventing failure is by performing a Failure Mode and

Effects Analysis (FMEA). You don't have to detail how such an analysis is performed to have determined a method. However, in order to apply the method effectively, a procedure may well be needed. The method is therefore the way the process is carried out which together with the criteria contributes to the description of the process.

Documenting a quality management system (4.1, 4.2.1)

1994–2000 Differences

Previously the standard required the supplier to document a quality system as a means of ensuring product conforms to specified requirements.

There is no difference in intent but the new wording 'in accordance with' implies that the standard defines how the management system should be documented but it loses the reasons for doing it.

The standard requires the organization to *document a quality management system in accordance with the requirements of ISO 9001*.

What does this mean?

A document (according to ISO 9000 clause 2.7.1) is *information and its supporting medium*. A page of printed information, a CD ROM or a computer file is a document, implying that recorded information is a document and verbal information is not a document. Clause 4.2 requires the management system documentation to include certain types of documents and therefore does not limit the management system documentation to the types of documents listed.

As a management system is the means to achieve the organization's objectives, and a system is a set of interrelated processes, it follows that what has to be documented are all the processes that constitute the system.

While there is a reduction in emphasis on documentation in ISO 9001:2000 compared with the 1994 version, it does not imply that organizations will need less documentation to define their management system. What it does mean is that the organization is left to decide the documentation necessary for effective operation and control of its processes. If the absence of specific documentation does not adversely affect operation and control of processes, such documentation is unnecessary.

Why is this necessary?

This requirement responds to the System Approach Principle.

Before ISO 9000 came along, organizations prospered without masses of documentation and many still do. Those that have chosen not to pursue the ISO 9000 path often only generate and maintain documents that have a useful purpose and will not produce documents just for auditors unless there is a legal requirement. Most of the documentation that is required in ISO 9000 came about from hindsight – the traditional unscientific way organizations learn and how management systems evolve.

ISO 9000 contains a list of valid reasons for why documents are necessary and here is a list used in previous editions of this handbook.

- To communicate requirements, intentions, instructions, methods and results effectively
- To convert solved problems into recorded knowledge so as to avoid having to solve them repeatedly
- To provide freedom for management and staff to maximize their contribution to the business
- To free the business from reliance on particular individuals for its effectiveness
- To provide legitimacy and authority for the actions and decisions needed
- To make responsibility clear and to create the conditions for self-control
- To provide co-ordination for inter-departmental action
- To provide consistency and predictability in carrying out repetitive tasks
- To provide training and reference material for new and existing staff
- To provide evidence to those concerned of your intentions and your actions
- To provide a basis for studying existing work practices and identifying opportunities for improvement
- To demonstrate after an incident the precautions which were taken or which should have been taken to prevent it or minimize its occurrence

If only one of these reasons make sense in a particular situation, the information should be documented. In some organizations, they take the view that it is important to nurture freedom, creativity and initiative and therefore feel that documenting procedures is counterproductive. Their view is that documented procedures hold back improvement, forcing staff to follow routines without thinking and prevent innovation. While it is true that blindly enforcing procedures that reflect out-of-date practices coupled with bureaucratic change mechanisms is counter productive, it is equally short-sighted to ignore past experience, ignore decisions based on valid evidence and encourage staff to reinvent what were perfectly acceptable methods. Question by all means, encourage staff to challenge decisions of the past, but encourage them to put forward a case for change. That way it will cause them to study the old methods, select the good bits and modify the parts that are no longer appropriate. It is often said that there is nothing new under the sun – just new ways of packaging the same message. The *six sigma* initiative is a case in point (see Chapter 1). It is no different to the quality improvement programmes of the 1980s or in fact the teachings of Shewart of the 1930s and Juran and Deming of the 1950s – it is just a different way of packaging the message.

How is this implemented?

Before deciding to document anything, there is something more important to consider. Documents, as stated previously are *information and its support medium*. The important matter is the transmission of information rather than its documentation and therefore you need firstly to decide the best method of transmitting the information. There are several choices:

- Convey it through documents – suitable for information that needs to be referred to when performing a task
- Convey it verbally – suitable for instructions intended for immediate action
- Convey it so that it is observed visually – suitable for warnings
- Convey it through education – suitable for values, beliefs and principles
- Convey it through training – suitable for methods and routines
- Convey it through example – suitable for values, beliefs, methods

There is no right or wrong answer; it depends on the simplicity or complexity of the information being transmitted and the degree of spontaneity required by the user. Written instructions on how to fire a gun are of no use in battle – you have to be trained. Values such as honesty, integrity have to be internalized as a set of morals – no procedure would cause you to behave differently.

Clause 4.2.1 requires management system documentation to include 5 types of document:

(a) Quality policy and objectives
(b) Quality manual
(c) Documented procedures
(d) Documents needed to ensure the effective planning, operation and control of processes
(e) Records

Other than the requirements in clause 4 for documentation, there are 14 other references requiring documentation. These are as follows:

(a) The output of the planning
(b) The quality manual
(c) A documented procedure for document control
(d) A documented procedure for the identification, storage, retrieval, protection, retention time and disposition of records

(e) Planning of the realization processes
(f) Inputs relating to product requirements
(g) The outputs of the design and development process
(h) Design and development changes
(i) The results of the review of changes and subsequent follow up actions
(j) A documented procedure for conducting audits that includes the responsibilities and requirements
(k) Evidence of conformity with the acceptance criteria characteristics of the product
(l) A documented procedure for nonconformity control activities
(m) A documented procedure for corrective action
(n) A documented procedure for preventive action

This list is somewhat inadequate for our purposes because it does not tell us what types of things we should document or provide criteria to enable us to decide what we need to document. ISO 9000 clause 2.7.2 includes a more useful list of document types that are classified as follows:

(a) Quality manuals
(b) Quality plans
(c) Specifications
(d) Guidelines
(e) Procedures, work instructions and drawings
(f) Records

This list is similar to that in clause 4.2.1 with some notable differences. The policy and objective could form part of the quality manual and the quality plans, work instructions, guidelines, drawings and specifications could be the documents needed to ensure the effective planning, operation and control of processes.

Obviously the size, type and complexity of the organization and the competency of personnel will have an effect on the depth and breadth of the documentation but the subject matter other than that which is product, process or customer specific is not dependent on size, type and complexity of the organization etc. There is no single method that will reveal all the things that should be documented but there are several approaches that can be used to reveal the documentation necessary.

(a) Documentation analysis
(b) Applying the control model
(c) Applying Kipling's Law
(d) Applying the process approach

Documentation analysis

There are three approaches you can take to identify the documentation required(Hoyle, David, 1996)[15]:

- Conduct a search of the relevant standards for references to documentation
- Respond to the requirements of the standard with operational policies then identify where documents would be needed to implement these policies
- Chart the processes and identify where documents are needed to convey inputs and outputs, record actions and results and carryout the tasks and activities identified.

Of these the most effective approach is to adopt the third option and then apply the other two options to identify any documents that have been omitted. Having identified a missing document, assess whether the process would be improved by its inclusion and what new tasks or activities would need to be inserted into the process to integrate the activities into the system.

Applying the control model

Control of anything follows a universal sequence of tasks illustrated by the generic control model in Figure 4.5.

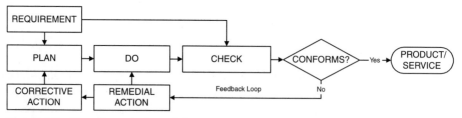

Figure 4.5 Generic control model

By asking some key questions derived from the model we can reveal the essential documents:

- What do we have to do? . . . A statement of requirements, objectives, success criteria
- How will we make it happen? . . . A plan of action or work to be undertaken and preparation to be made
- What did we do? . . . A record of the work carried out
- How will we know it's right? . . . A definition of the measurements that are to be performed
- How can we prove its right? . . . A record of the results of measurement

- What did we decide to do with the rejects? . . . A plan of the remedial action to be taken
- How do we know the reject was fixed? . . . A record of the remedial action taken
- How will we stop it happening again? . . . A plan of the corrective action to be taken
- How do we know it won't happen again? . . . A record testifying to the effectiveness of the corrective action taken.

The generic control model could be applied at four levels:

- At the system level – so as to reveal the system requirements, system measurements and system changes and thus identify business requirements, business plans, business performance reviews and changes in the business strategy and structure. The system level is at the level of the whole organization.
- At the business process level – so as to reveal the process requirements, process measurements and process changes and thus identify customer requirements, quality plans, compliance checks, and customer feedback. The process level is at the level of the functions that make up the business that may be discharged through one or more departments.
- At the task level – so as to reveal the task requirements, task measurements and task changes thus identify the product requirements, product plans, inspections, test, reviews and modification actions. The task level is at the level of a group or department that may assign people to perform the various activities that make up the task.
- At the activity level – so as to reveal the activity requirements, activity measurements and activity changes and thus identify work instructions, work plans, checks and rework actions. The activity level is at the level of the individual.

Applying Kipling's law

In the poem The Elephant Child, the English writer Rudyard Kipling wrote 'I had six honest serving friends, they taught me all I knew, they are what, where, why, when, how and who.' This I have called Kipling's Law because it is not just the words but also what can be obtained by using them. E.g. auditors use these words to discover information that will enable them to establish compliance with requirements. It follows therefore that system developers should use the same words to identify the types of information that users of the management system documentation will need to know to perform their jobs as effectively as possible. However, the 6 friends also need a trigger in order to focus on an object and this is where the process model in Figure 2.12 is useful.

For each entry and exit apply Kipling's Law and establish Who does What, When, Where, Why and How such that you answer the questions in Table 4.1.

Table 4.1 Applying Kipling's law

Inputs	Resources	Process	Constraints	Outputs
What are the inputs?	What resources are required?	What tasks are performed?	What are the constraints?	What are the outputs?
Where do they come from?	Where do they come from?	Where are they performed?	Where in this process are they applied?	Where do they go?
Who supplies them?	Who supplies them?	Who performs the tasks?	Who imposes the constraints?	Who receives them?
How are they supplied?	How are they supplied?	How are the tasks performed?	How are they addressed?	How are they supplied?
When are they supplied?	When are they supplied?	When are the tasks performed?	When do they apply?	When are they supplied?
Why are they needed?	Why are they needed?	Why are the tasks performed?	Why are the constraints necessary?	Why are they needed?

The process approach method (Hoyle, David and Thompson, John, 2001)[6]

The fourth method is to use five key questions that establish whether a process is being managed effectively.

(a) What are you trying to do?
(b) How do you make it happen?
(c) How do you know it's right?
(d) How to you know it's the best way to do it?
(e) How do you know it's the right thing to do?

There are many subsidiary questions each exploring the process in more detail. The questions can be asked of top management at the enterprise level, of functional management at the managerial level and of professionals, administrators and technicians at the operations level.

Documented procedures (4.2.1c)

The standard requires the management system documentation *to include documented procedures required by ISO 9001.*

> **1994–2000 Differences**
> Previously the standard required the supplier to prepare procedures consistent with the requirements of the standard and the supplier's stated quality policy. This was a much more general requirement than its replacement.

What does this mean?

ISO 9000 defines a procedure as *a specified way to carry out an activity or a process.* This definition is ambiguous because an activity is on a different scale than a process. Process outputs are dependent upon many factors of which activities are but one. An activity is the smallest unit of work. Several activities accomplish a task and several tasks reflect the stages in a process but there is more to a process than a series of tasks as addressed in Chapter 2. This definition also results in a belief that procedures are documented processes but this too is inaccurate. Procedures tell us how to proceed – they are a sequence of steps to execute a routine activity and result in an activity or a task being performed regardless of the result.

There are very few procedures actually required by the standard but this does not imply you don't need to produce any others. The specific procedures required are:

(a) A documented procedure for document control
(b) A documented procedure for the control of records

(c) A documented procedure for conducting audits

(d) A documented procedure for nonconformity control

(e) A documented procedure for corrective action

(f) A documented procedure for preventive action

These areas all have something in common. They are what the authors of the early drafts of ISO 9000:2000 referred to as system procedures – they apply to the whole system and are not product, process or customer specific although it is not uncommon for customers to specify requirements that would impact these areas. Why procedures for these aspects are required and not for other aspects of the management system is unclear but it seems that the authors of ISO 9000 felt these were not processes – a conclusion I find difficult to justify. They are certainly not business processes but could be work processes. However, there is another message that this requirement conveys. It is that procedures are not required for each clause of the standard. Previously, countless organizations produced a manual of 20 procedures to match the 20 elements of ISO 9001. Some limited their procedures to the 26 procedures cited by the standard and others produced as many as were necessary to respond to the requirements.

Why is this necessary?

This requirement responds to the Process Approach Principle.

It is uncertain why the authors of ISO 9001:2000 deemed it necessary to require any specific procedures when there is a general requirement for the system to be documented. This should have been sufficient. Clearly procedures are required so that people can execute tasks with consistency, economy, repeatability and uniformity but there is no logical reason why procedures are required for only the above six subjects. One possible reason is that none of the six subjects are addressed in clause 7, which is the only clause where exclusions may be permitted.

How is this implemented?

One solution is to produce the six procedures as required. In fact many ISO 9000:1994-based systems are likely to include such procedures so there is nothing new here. The question is, why would you want to do this when in all other aspects, you may have documented your processes?

Document control is a work process or a number of work processes because the inputs pass through a number of stages each adding value to result in the achievement of defined objectives. These are the acquisition, approval, publication, distribution, storage, maintenance, improvement, and disposal stages. These are not tasks but processes that achieve defined objectives and involve both physical, financial and human resources. Within these processes are tasks, each of which may require documented procedures as they are initiated.

Control of records is also a work process similar to document control. There are the preparation, storage, access, maintenance and disposal stages. This is not one uninterrupted flow but a life cycle. There is not one task but several performed at different times for different reasons.

Auditing is certainly a process with a defined objective. Without the provision of competent personnel and a suitable environment, audits will not achieve their objectives no matter how many times the procedure is implemented.

Nonconformity control like *records control* is a work process for the same reasons. The sequence of tasks is not in the form of an uninterrupted sequence. The sequence of stages may be identification, documentation, segregation, review, remedial action and disposal but this is not a continuous sequence. There are breaks and different procedures may apply at each stage depending on what it is that is nonconforming.

There is little merit in having one corrective action procedure when the source of problems that require corrective action is so varied. One Corrective Action Form might be appropriate but its application will be so varied that it is questionable whether one size fits all. Presenting top management with a nonconformity report because it has been detected that the organization charts are not promptly updated following a change, will not motivate them into action. Corrective action forms part of every process rather than being a separate process. It is unreasonable to force all actions aimed at preventing the recurrence of problems through one process. Many problems are prevented from recurring not by following a procedure, but by the designer, the producer, supplier, manager remembering they had a problem last time and doing it differently the next – i.e. they learn from their mistakes. No forms filled in, no procedures followed – just people using their initiative – this is why corrective action is part of every process operation.

Preventive action remains one of the most misunderstood requirements of ISO 9001 because it is mistaken for corrective action but more on this in Chapter 8. There is even less justification for one preventive action procedure because the source of potential problems is so varied. Preventive actions are taken in design, in planning, in training and in maintenance under the name of FMEA, Reliability Prediction, Quality Planning, Production Planning, Logistic Planning, Staff Development, Equipment Maintenance – preventive actions are built into these processes and similar to corrective action are part of every process design.

Documents that ensure effective planning, operation and control of processes (4.2.1d)

The standard requires management system documentation *to include documents required by the organization to ensure the effective planning, operation and control of its processes.*

What does this mean?

The documents required for effective planning, operation and control of the processes would include several different types of documents. Some will be product and process specific and others will be common to all processes. Rather than stipulate the documents that are needed, ISO 9001 now provides for the organization to decide what it needs for *the effective operation and control of its processes.* This phrase is the key to determining the documents that are needed.

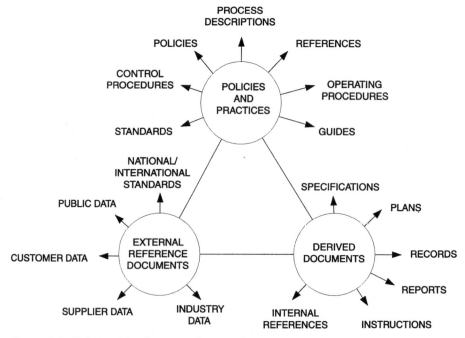

Figure 4.6 Relationships between documents

There are three types of controlled documents, as illustrated in Figure 4.6:

- Policies and practices (these include process descriptions, control procedures, guides, operating procedures and internal standards)
- Documents derived from these policies and practices, such as drawings, specifications, plans, work instructions, technical procedures and reports
- External documents referenced in either of the above

There will always be exceptions to this model but in general the majority of documents used in a management system can be classified in this way.

Figure 4.7 Classification of documents

Derived documents are those that are derived by executing processes; for example, audit reports result from using the audit process, drawings result from using the design process, procurement specifications result from using the procurement process. There are, however, two types of derived document: prescriptive and descriptive documents. *Prescriptive documents* are those that prescribe requirements, instructions, guidance etc. and may be subject to change. They have issue status and approval status, and are implemented in doing work. *Descriptive documents* result from doing work and are not implemented. They may have issue and approval status. Specifications, plans, purchase orders, drawings are all prescriptive whereas audit reports, test reports, inspection records are all descriptive. This distinction is only necessary because the controls required will be different for each class of documents.

Figure 4.7 shows some examples of the different classes of documents and their relationship.

Why is this necessary?

This requirement responds to the Process Approach Principle.

The degree of documentation varies from a simple statement of fact to details of how a specific activity is to be carried out. To document *everything* you do would be impractical and of little value. Several good reasons for documenting information are listed under – *What should be documented*.

How is this implemented?

The identification of documentation needs was addressed under – *Documenting a quality management system*. In this section, the specific types of documents are described in more detail.

Policies and practices

The relationship between these various types of policies and practices is illustrated in Figure 4.8.

Policies

Policies are essential in ensuring the effective planning of processes because they lay down the rules to be followed to ensure that actions and decisions taken in the design and operation of processes serve the business objectives.

Any statement made by management at any level that is designed to constrain the actions and decisions of those it affects is a *policy*. There does not have to be a separate document containing policies. The policies can be integrated within any of the documents.

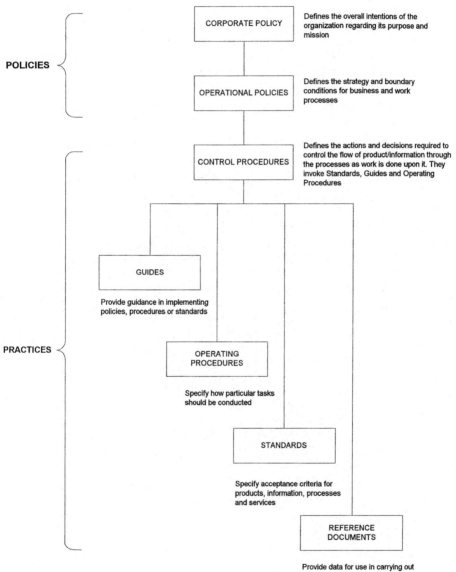

POLICIES

CORPORATE POLICY — Defines the overall intentions of the organization regarding its purpose and mission

OPERATIONAL POLICIES — Defines the strategy and boundary conditions for business and work processes

CONTROL PROCEDURES — Defines the actions and decisions required to control the flow of product/information through the processes as work is done upon it. They invoke Standards, Guides and Operating Procedures

PRACTICES

GUIDES — Provide guidance in implementing policies, procedures or standards

OPERATING PROCEDURES — Specify how particular tasks should be conducted

STANDARDS — Specify acceptance criteria for products, information, processes and services

REFERENCE DOCUMENTS — Provide data for use in carrying out actions and making decisions

Figure 4.8   Relationship between policies and practices

There are different types of policy that may impact the business processes:

- Government policy, which when translated into statutes applies to any commercial enterprise
- Corporate policy, which applies to the business as a whole and may cover, for example:
    - Environmental policy – our intentions with respect to the conservation of the natural environment
    - Financial policy – how the business is to be financed
    - Marketing policy – to what markets the business is to supply its products
    - Investment policy – how the organization will secure the future
    - Expansion policy – the way in which the organization will grow, both nationally and internationally
    - Personnel policy – how the organization will treat its employees and the labour unions
    - Safety policy – the organization's intentions with respect to hazards in the work place and to users of its products or services
    - Social policy – how the organization will interface with society
- Operational policy, which applies to the operations of the business, such as design, procurement, manufacture, servicing and quality assurance. This may cover, for example:
    - Pricing policy – how the pricing of products is to be determined
    - Procurement policy – how the organization will obtain the components and services needed
    - Product policy – what range of products the business is to produce
    - Inventory policy – how the organization will maintain economic order quantities to meet its production schedules
    - Production policy – how the organization will determine what it makes or buys and how the production resources are to be organized
    - Servicing policy – how the organization will service the products its customers have purchased
- Department policy, which applies solely to one department, such as the particular rules a department manager may impose to allocate work, review output, monitor progress etc.
- Industry policy, which applies to a particular industry, such as the codes of practice set by trade associations for a certain trade

All policies set boundary conditions so that actions and decisions are channelled along a particular path to fulfil a purpose or achieve an objective. Many see policies as requirements to be met – they are requirements but only in so far as an enabling mechanism. Policies serve to guide the actions and decisions required to achieve objectives and are not therefore objectives in themselves. Policies enable management to operate without constant intervention and once established enable others to work within a framework without seeking decisions or guidance from above. The larger and more complex an organization the more policies it may have. Small lean organizations will have few documented policies because guidance can be given verbally.

Staff do not work to policies but in fact work in accordance with procedures which themselves direct actions and decisions within the framework of the stated policies. In order to make the decisions required in the procedures, staff will often need to know the company policy on a particular subject, such as procurement, recruitment, release of product, licensing agreements, agreeing design changes etc. Can they or can they not do something and if so what criteria should they satisfy?

When one deviates from procedure one may not in fact be violating a policy because the procedure may describe one of several ways of doing something. Where top management dictates that all work be conducted in accordance with certain procedures, it puts itself in a position of having to authorize deviations when the procedures cannot be followed. It is therefore more effective if top management prescribes the policies to be met by its direct subordinates rather than by all levels, and leaves the procedures to be decided by those responsible for achieving objectives.

There are many sound reasons for documenting your operational policies:

- Corporate policy needs to be translated into practical terms that can be implemented through procedures.
- Every job has constraints surrounding it – without written policies people would be left to discover them by trial and error, the organization would become a disorganized mess, its managers lacking any means to direct and harmonize their staff's activities.
- Policies enable managers and their workforce to be left in no doubt about what they are actually responsible for, the boundaries within which they need to work and the demands upon them to which they will be expected to respond.
- Policies set clear boundaries for people's jobs so that everyone knows in advance what response they are to expect from others when making decisions.
- Policies create a baseline to which subsequent change can be referred and enable changes in the way things are done to be clearly defined.
- Policies enable managers to determine whether a subordinate's action or decision was justified or simply poor judgement or an infringement of the rules. If no rule exists, subordinates cannot be criticized for using their judgement, however well or poorly it is used. If a rule exists, one has to establish whether it was accidentally or deliberately broken, for the latter is a disciplinary offence. Without written policy no one knows where he or she stand and any decision may create an unwanted precedent.

- Policies provide freedom to individuals in the execution of their duties to make decisions within defined boundaries and avoid over-control by managers. If people are uncertain about where the limits of their job lie they cannot feel free to act. Without a clearly defined area of freedom there is no real freedom at all.
- Policies enable managers to exercise control by exceptions rather than over every action and decision of their subordinates and therefore enable self-control by subordinates.
- Policies enable managers to control events in advance. Before the action begins, people know the rules and so are more likely to produce the right results first time. Without policies, one is forced to control events in arrears, after something has happened to cause dissatisfaction. Alternatively, one has to be on the scene of the event to respond as soon as the situation approaches the limits. This is a costly use of managers' time.

The reasons above may not be appropriate in organizations that have a strong value-based culture. Rules are appropriate to a command and control culture. Therefore, these principles need to be applied with care. In all cases you need to ask; what would be the effect on our performance as an organization if this were not documented? If the answer is nothing or a response such as – well somebody might do xyz – forget it! But is it likely? If you cannot predict with certainty that something will happen that should be prevented, leave people free to choose their own path.

However, even in a command and control culture one does not need to write *everything* down, as policies are needed only for important matters where the question of right or wrong does not depend upon circumstances at the time, or when the relevance of circumstances only rarely come into the picture.

A common practice is to paraphrase the requirements of ISO 9001 as operational policy statements. Whilst this approach does provide direct correlation with ISO 9001 it renders the exercise futile because users can read the same things by referring to ISO 9001. Operational policies should respond to the needs of the organization, not paraphrase the standard.

Process descriptions

Process descriptions are necessary in ensuring effective operation and control of processes because they contain or reference everything that needs to be known about a process.

Process descriptions may be maintained as discrete documents or combined into a manual. Process descriptions would include:

- Process objectives
- Process owner
- Process inputs in terms of the materials and information to be processed

- Process outputs in terms of the products, services and information delivered
- Set-up and shut down conditions
- Process flow charts indicating the sequence of actions and decisions identifying those responsible and the interacting processes, actions and references to supporting documentation
- Resources – physical and human resources required to deliver process outputs
- Dependencies – the known factors upon which the quality of the process output depends (skills, competencies, behaviours, capabilities)
- Key performance indicators – the indicators by which the achievement of the process objectives will be measured
- Performance measurement methods – measures to detect variation in product and process performance
- Preventive measures – measures in place to prevent process and product error or failure

Clearly this description goes well beyond the content of a procedure. It also goes well beyond flow charts. Flow charts depict the steps in a process but do not fully describe a process. We could have two processes each with the same sequence of steps and therefore the same flow chart. Process A performs well while Process B constantly under performs, reject rates are high, morale is low etc. The procedures, equipment and controls are identical. What causes such a difference in performance? In Process B the people have not been trained, the supervisors are in conflict and rule by fear and there is high absenteeism. There is poor leadership and because of the time spent on correcting mistakes, there is no time for maintaining equipment, cleanliness and documentation. In process A, the supervisors spend time building relationships before launching the process. They plan ahead and train their staff. They are constantly looking for opportunities for improvement and because the process runs smoothly, they have time for maintaining equipment, documentation and cleanliness – morale is high so there is no absenteeism. Therefore to describe a process in a way that will show how the process objectives are achieved, it is necessary to describe the features and characteristics of the process that cause success and this warrants more than can be depicted on a flow chart. It is not intended that behaviours should be documented but the activities that reflect appropriate behaviours such as planning, preparing, checking, communicating, advising can be reflected in the process description.

The difference between a rule-based culture and a values-based culture provides another example of why flow charts alone do not describe processes. In a rule based culture (or command and control culture) people will follow the rules or procedures regardless of the consequences. Conformity is paramount and produces consistency but not necessarily customer satisfaction. For example – a hotel has a procedure for maintaining the facilities and this requires annual maintenance of the air conditioning system. Maintenance staff perform exactly as required by the procedure but take no account of the effect of their actions on customers using the conference facilities. The conference department performs exactly in accordance with the conference management procedure but takes no account of facility maintenance. The result is that a conference is held in the summer while the air-conditioning is out of action due to maintenance. This causes dissatisfaction to customers. Other examples result in the classic retort from service providers 'It's more than my job's worth to . . .' The staff only focus on doing what they are told and following the procedure. Their training concentrates on equipping them with the skills to perform the task. Initiative is not a requirement and can result in a reprimand from management when staff deviate from the rules. Staff are trained to perform the task and not trained to achieve objectives – otherwise they would weigh up the circumstances and apply their common sense.

Previously, procedures were established to meet a specific requirement defined by the standard e.g. contract review. However contract review is a task that is part of the sales process the objectives of which are different. The objective of contract review is to prevent the organization entering into a commitment with its customers that it is incapable of fulfilling, whereas the objective of the sales process is to secure business for the organization that meets the business objectives. Previously the success indicators for many parts of the management system were based on whether the task had been carried out, not whether the objective of the task had been accomplished. Therefore a success indicator for contract review was a tick in a box when it should have been the number of orders accepted that fully met customer expectations.

Procedures

Procedures are necessary in ensuring the effective operation and control of processes because they layout the steps to be taken in setting up, operating and shutting down the process.

A procedure is a sequence of steps to execute a routine task. It prescribes how one should proceed in certain circumstances in order to produce a desired output. Sometimes the word can imply formality and a document of several pages but this is not necessarily so. A procedure can be five lines, where each line represents a step in the execution of a task. (See also *Plans* below.)

Procedures can only work, however, where judgment is no longer required or necessary. Once you need to make a judgement, you cannot prescribe what you might or might not do with the information in front of you. A form of judgement-based procedure is a decision tree that flows down a chain of questions to which either a yes or a no will route you down a different branch. The chart does not answer your questions but is a guide to decision-making.

There are various types of documented practices:

- Divisional procedures apply to more than one division of a company and regulate common activities.
- Control procedures control work on product as it passes between departments or processes. These should contain the forms that convey information from department to department and reference the operating procedures that apply to each task.
- Operating procedures prescribe how specific tasks are to be performed. Subcategories of these procedures may include test procedures, inspection procedures, installation procedures etc. These should reference the standards and guides (see below) which are needed to carry out the task, document the results and contain the forms to be used on which information is to be recorded.

Standards

Standards are essential in ensuring the effective operation and control of processes because they define the criteria required to judge the acceptability of the process capability and product quality.

Standards define the acceptance criteria for judging the quality of an activity, a document, a product or a service. There are national standards, international standards, standards for a particular industry and company standards. Standards may be in diagrammatic form or narrative form or a mixture of the two. Standards need to be referenced in control procedures or operating procedures. These standards are in fact *your* quality standards. They describe features and characteristics that *your* products and services must possess. Some may be type-specific, others may apply to a range of products or types of products and some may apply to all products whatever their type. These standards are not the drawings and specifications that describe a particular product but are the standards that are invoked in such drawings and specifications and are selected when designing the product.

In the process context, standards are essential for defining the acceptance criteria for a capable process.

Guides

Guides are necessary in ensuring the effective operation and control of processes because they provide information of use during preparation, operation, shut down and troubleshooting.

Guides are aids to decision-making and to the conduct of activities. They are useful as a means of documenting your experience and should contain examples, illustrations, hints and tips to help staff perform their work as well as possible.

Derived documents

Specifications

Specifications are crucial in ensuring the effective planning and control of processes because they govern the characteristics of the inputs and outputs and are thus used in process and product design and measurement.

Specifications according to ISO 9000 are *documents stating requirements* and may be in the form of:

- Performance specifications ~ defining the performance requirements for a product, process or service without limiting the solution or the technology or prescribing particular characteristics – the basic goal
- Design specifications ~ a more definitive version of a performance specification which defines the criteria to be satisfied in designing a particular product, service or process. (Typical criteria for a product include performance requirements under specified environments, interface requirements, size, weight, ruggedness, safety margins, derating factors and apportioned reliability goal.)
- Test specifications ~ stating requirements for verifying by test certain prescribed characteristic of an item under simulated operational conditions to verify the item meets the design specification
- Procurement specifications ~ defines for a specific item of supply the requirements for performance, design, construction and packaging of the item and the requirements for verifying that the requirements have been achieved

Plans

Plans are crucial in ensuring the effective operation and control of processes because they lay out the work that is to be carried out to meet the specification.

A plan is a statement of the provisions that have been made to achieve a certain objective. It describes the work to be done and the means by which the work will be done. Plans are often produced for specific one-off events not routine events – they require imagination and original thought to produce. When work becomes routine, the provisions will have been made, staff trained etc and so work can be executed using procedures – these don't generally require original thought or imagination. If, however you have not done something before, you cannot write a procedure – a plan is needed first of all to set-up the conditions that will subsequently become routine.

The process of producing a plan is a process of decision-making and once produced its provisions can be put to work to yield the desired result. A good plan possesses unity, continuity, flexibility and precision.

The producer of the plan gains an in depth knowledge of the work to be done. The plan provides to others a statement that will enable them to predict whether the provisions will, if implemented yield the desired result and so provides a measure of confidence in the success of the provisions.

Reports

Reports are useful in ensuring the effective operation and control of processes because they contain information about the process or the product being processed. They may be used to guide decision-making both in the design and operation of processes and in product-realization.

Reports are the result of some activity and differ from records in that reports will contain background data, conclusions and recommendations from a study of certain conditions, situations or records. Examples of topics for which reports will be produced are:

- Market research
- Competition analysis
- Benchmarking study
- Reliability prediction
- Process capability
- Warranty returns
- Productivity analysis
- Environmental effects analysis
- Failure mode effects analysis

Records

Records are essential in ensuring the effective operation and control of processes because they capture factual performance from which decisions on process performance can be made.

Records are defined in ISO 9000 as *documents stating the results achieved or providing evidence of activities performed.* Records are therefore produced during an event or immediately afterwards. Records do not arise from contemplation. They contain facts, the raw data as obtained from observation or measurement and produced manually or automatically. The information may have been received verbally, visually or as a printout from a machine. There could be notes taken during an interview, or results recorded from observing a test. Records are not reports in that there is no interpretation, comment or opinion expressed by the recorder. There are many types of records that may be generated by a process, some of which are identified in ISO 9001 and are addressed under the section on the *Control of records.*

Instructions

Instructions are crucial in ensuring the effective operation and control of processes because they cause processes to be initiated and define variables that are specific to the date and time, location, product or customer concerned.

Work instructions define the work required in terms of who is to perform it, when it is to commence and when it is to be completed. They also include what standard the work has to meet and any other instructions that constrain the quality, quantity, delivery and cost of the work required. Work instructions are the product of implementing a control procedure, an operating procedure or a document standard (see further explanation below).

Instructions and work instructions are not defined in ISO 9000 and only mentioned once in ISO 9001 (clause 7.5.1) and twice in ISO 9004 (Clauses 5.5.5 and 7.5.1) and in both cases the term procedure could just as well have been used.

In simple terms, *instructions* command work to be done, *procedures* define the sequence of steps to execute the work to be done. Instructions may or may not refer to procedures that *define how an activity is performed*. In some cases an instruction might be a single command such as 'Pack the goods'. Procedures, on the other hand, define how one should proceed to execute a task. Procedures are documented when the activities that need to be performed are likely to be performed regularly or routinely.

For example, you may issue an instruction for certain goods to be packed in a particular way on a specified date and the package to be marked with the contents and the address to which it is to be delivered. So that the task is carried out properly you may also specify the methods of packing in a *procedure*. The procedure would not contain specific details of a particular package – this is the purpose of the instruction. The procedure is dormant until the instruction to use it is initiated or until personnel are motivated to refer to it.

Not all instructions need to be documented – it depends upon the nature of the message being conveyed. Many types of forms have been conceived to convey instructions. Purchase Orders, Change Requests, Amendment Instructions, Engineering Orders and Print Requisitions are all instructions that cause people to do work and are work instructions rather than procedures.

It follows therefore that the idea of calling documents *procedures* when they only apply to interdepartmental activities and calling documents *work instructions* when they only apply to departmental activities is ill conceived. Both types of documents are in fact *procedures*. In both cases work instructions may be needed to initiate work and procedures may be needed to define the sequence in which the work is to be executed, where the instructions alone are insufficient.

Internal references

Internal reference documents are useful in ensuring the effective operation and control of processes because they will contain data relevant to the equipment, people, facilities or other factors upon which set-up or operation of the process depends.

Reference documents differ from other types of documents in that they should be neither prescriptive nor instructional. They should not be descriptive like reports, proposals or records but should contain data that is useful in carrying out a task.

Examples of internal reference documents are:

- Organization charts
- Telephone directories
- Shift roster
- Equipment lists
- Staff lists

External reference documents

External reference documents are those not produced by the organization but used by the organization as a source of information, consequently the categories of external reference documents are identified by their source.

National and international standards

National and international standards are essential in ensuring the effective planning, operation and control of processes because they contain the agreed conditions, requirements, parameters etc that govern various aspects of a process or the resultant product. Such standards are also essential in reducing variation and choice and thus ensuring safety, interchangeability and compatibility between components.

However, useful as national and international standards are, they have several limitations. They are rarely read in detail, often just quoted in a specification and both customers and users assume the organization is capable of meeting them. One cannot negotiate an external standard because it cannot be changed, only supplemented, or replaced. They force people to require only work that meets the standard and reject work that does not even if such work would be otherwise acceptable. They therefore reduce flexibility. The wide circulation of standards makes their change lengthy and costly both to the standard producers and their users and therefore standards cannot be made to react quickly enough to meet customer needs. For example it has taken 14 years to revise the ISO 9000 family of standards and during this time the knowledge that was being standardized has changed enormously.

The only standards that work effectively are those subject to continual surveillance such as product standards where tests are routinely performed to verify that process outputs meet national or international standards.

Public data

Public data is useful in ensuring the effective planning, operation and control of processes because it is a source of data useful in marketing, business planning, product design, human resource management etc.

Public data is that which is publicly available in the form of books and reports. It could come from public libraries, newspapers, the Internet, government departments and bureaux. Such data may include demographic data, scientific data, financial data, reports from studies into working conditions, environmental pollution, management style etc.

Customer data

Customer data is useful in ensuring the effective planning, operation and control of processes because it is a source of customer needs, expectations and requirements. Without customer data, the organization cannot plan to satisfy its customers.

Customer data may include:

● Contracts and orders specifying the product or service to be supplied and the conditions under which it has been agreed to supply them
● Customer specifications and drawings detailing the product or service characteristics that are to be satisfied
● Customer plans describing the programme of work (of which the contracted items form a part), required delivery milestones etc.

Supplier data

Supplier data is useful in ensuring the effective operation and control of processes because it is a source of information necessary to make purchasing decisions, maintain purchased equipment and components, verify compliance with requirements and monitor supplier performance.

Supplier data may include:

● Proposals for the supply of products and services
● Data sheets describing the supplier's products and services
● Reports of supplier activities in response to contract requirements
● Instructions and manuals on the installation, handling, maintenance and disposal of the equipment or components supplied

Industry data

Industry data is useful in ensuring the effective planning, operation and control of processes because it is a source of guidance and best practice. The data is generally only available to those organizations that subscribe to particular trade associations.

Industry data may include:

● Brochures, guides and leaflets on sector specific tools, techniques and practices
● Reports on the industry sector, its growth, decline, opportunities, etc.

- Benchmarking data
- Catalogues and directories of organizations, products and services

What should be documented? (4.2)

The standard requires *the extent of quality management system documentation to be dependent on the size and type of organization, complexity of the processes, and the competency of personnel.*

Clause 4.9 of ISO 9001:1994 required procedures only where the absence of such procedures would adversely affect quality. This phrase, now omitted from the 2000 version, used to be taken out of context and used as a valid reason for not documenting aspects of the management system. The requirement only applied to procedures but could just as easily have applied to other types of documentation. The factors mentioned in the standard apply equally to documentation generated by a process and documentation supporting the process. For example, a person may need documented policies and practices to execute the processes reliably and also may produce documents that are required inputs for other processes. In both cases the factors of size, complexity etc., apply to the extent of the supporting documentation as well as to the extent of the output documentation – therefore documentation producers need to be aware of the documentation needs of the interconnecting processes.

> **1994–2000 Differences**
>
> Previously the range and detail of the procedures that form part of the quality system was required to be dependent upon the complexity of the work, the methods used and the skills and training needed by personnel involved in carrying out the activity. The intent of the requirement is the same but it introduces organization size and competency of personnel as determining factors.

Size of organization

If we think about it, what has size of the organization got to do with the amount of information you document? A large organization could be large because of the quantity of assets – 2000 offices with 2 people in each. Or it could be large because it employs 6,000 people, 5,500 of whom do the same job. Or we could find that of the 6,000, there are 200 departments, each providing a different contribution and each staffed with people of different disciplines. Therefore size in itself is not a factor and size without some units of measure is meaningless.

Type of organization

The type of organization will affect what you document and what documents you use but again not the amount of information you document. An organization that deals primarily with people may have little documentation. One that moves product may also have little documentation but one that processes information may have lots of documentation. A software house is different from a gas installation service, a bank is different from a textile manufacturer and therefore the content of the documentation will differ but they may use the same types of documents.

Complexity of processes

Complexity is a function of the number of processes and their interconnections in an organization. The more processes, the greater the number of documents. The more interconnections the greater the detail within documents. Complexity is also a function of the relationships. The more relationships there are, the greater the complexity and channels of communication. Reducing the number of relationships can reduce complexity. Assigning work to fewer people reduces the number of transactions. Many documents exist simply to communicate information reliably and act as a point of reference should our memory fail us, which introduces another factor – that of the man's limited ability to handle unaided large amounts of data.

In the simplest of processes, all the influencing facts can be remembered accurately. As complexity increases, it becomes more difficult to remember all the facts and recall them accurately. A few extraordinary people have brilliant memories, some have learnt memory skills but the person of average ability cannot always remember a person's name or telephone number. It would therefore be unreasonable to expect people to perform their work without the use of recorded information of some kind. What you should record and what you remember is often a matter of personal choice but in some cases you cannot rely on people remembering facts by chance. You therefore need to identify the dependencies in each process and perform a risk assessment to establish what must be documented.

Competence

Competence is the ability to demonstrate the skills, behaviours, attributes and qualifications to the level required for the job. Competency may depend upon the availability of documentation. For example a lawyer will refer to documented case law to assist in preparing a case for defence or prosecution not because of a lack of competency but because of man's limited memory and a desire for accuracy. The lawyer can remember where to look for the relevant case law, but not the details. If the document containing the relevant case law cannot be found, the lawyer is unable to do the job and therefore cannot demonstrate competence.

When personnel are new to a job, they need education and training. Documentation is needed to assist in this process for two reasons. Firstly to make the process repeatable and predictable and secondly to provide a memory bank that is more reliable than the human memory. As people learn the job they begin to rely less and less on documentation to the extent that in some cases, no supporting documentation may be used at all to produce the required output. This does not mean that once the people are competent you can throw away your documentation. It may not be used on a daily basis, but you will inevitably have new staff to train and improvements to make to your existing processes. You will then need the documentation as a source of information to do both.

Factors affecting the amount of information you document

There has to be a limit on what you document. At school we are taught reading, writing and arithmetic so documents should not attempt to define these activities. The documents in regular use need only detail what would not be covered by education and training. A balance should be attained between training and procedures. If you rely on training rather than employing documented procedures, you will need to show that you have control over the quality of training to a level that will ensure its effectiveness. We expect staff to know how to do the various tasks that comprise their trade or profession, how to write, how to design, how to type, answer the telephone, how to paint, lay bricks etc. etc. You may feel it necessary to provide handbooks with useful tips on how to do these tasks more economically and effectively and you may also use such books to bridge gaps in education and training but these are not your procedures.

ISO 9001:1994 required the quality manual to cover the requirements of the standard but this requirement has been removed. There is therefore no requirement to respond to the requirements of the standard in the order in which they are stated either in a quality manual or in documented procedures.

You can combine several procedures in one document, the size of which depends on the complexity of your business. The more complex the business the greater is the number of documents. The more variations in the ways that work is executed, the larger the description of management system will need to be. If you have a small business and only one way of carrying out work, your system description will tend to be small. Your management system may be described in one document of no more than 30 pages. On the other hand a larger business may require several volumes and dozens of documents of over 10 pages each to adequately describe the system.

Control procedures need to be user-friendly and so should be limited in size. Remember you can use other documents such as guides, standards, and operating procedures to extend what you have written in the control procedures. The procedures should not, however, be so short as to be worthless as a means of controlling activities. They need to provide an adequate degree of direction so that the results of using them are predictable. If you neglect to adequately define what needs to be done and how to do it, don't be surprised that staff don't know what to do or constantly make mistakes. It is also important to resist the desire to produce manuals that are impressive rather than practical. Printing the documents on expensive paper with coloured logo does not improve their effectiveness and if they are not written simply and understood by a person of average intelligence, they will not be used.

Reasons for not documenting information

There are also several reasons for not documenting information.

- If the course of action or sequence of steps cannot be predicted a procedure or plan cannot be written for unforeseen events.
- If there is no effect on performance by allowing freedom of action or decision, there is no mandate to prescribe the methods to be employed.
- If it cannot be foreseen that any person might need to take action or make a decision using information from a process, there is no mandate to require the results to be recorded. (However you need to look beyond your own organization for such reasons if demonstrating due diligence in a product liability suit requires access to evidence.)
- If the action or decision is intuitive or spontaneous, no manner of documentation will ensure a better performance.
- If the action or decision needs to be habitual, documentation will be beneficial only in enabling the individual reach a level of competence.

Implementing a quality management system (4.1)

1994–2000 Differences

Previously the standard required the supplier to effectively implement the quality system and its documented procedures. There is no difference in intent but the new wording implies that the standard defines how the management system should be implemented but it loses the reasons for doing so. However, internal audits (clause 8.2.2) now have to verify that the system has been effectively implemented, therefore the intent of the previous wording is retained.

The standard requires the organization *to implement a quality management system in accordance with the requirements of ISO 9001*.

What does this mean?

The notion of implementing a management system seems to imply that the management system is a set of rules, a procedure or a plan. One implements procedure but the management system is far more than a collection of procedures. Also the standard requires a management system to be established and as stated previously, to establish a management system you need to design and construct it and integrate it into the organization. Implementation therefore applies to the use and operation of the management system following its construction and integration and is therefore concerned with the routine operation of an already established, documented and resourced system. Effective implementation means adhering to the policies and practices, following what is stated, not changing your procedures after changing your practice.

Why is this necessary?

This requirement responds to the Leadership principle.

It goes without saying that it is necessary to implement the management system that has been established because the benefits will only arise from using the system.

How is this implemented?

There is no magic in meeting this requirement. You simply need to do what you said you would do, you have to keep your promises, honour your commitments, adhere to the policies, meet the objectives, follow the procedures – in other words manage your processes effectively.

Managing processes (4.1)

The standard requires the organization *to manage the identified processes in accordance with the requirements of ISO 9001.*

What does this mean?

The first stage in managing a process is to establish what it is you are trying to achieve, what requirements you need to satisfy, what goals you are aiming at; then establish how you will measure your achievements. The next stage is to define the process you will employ to deliver the results. Managing the process then involves managing all the inherent characteristics of the process in such a manner that the requirements of customers and interested parties are fulfilled by the process outcomes. This means:

1994–2000 Differences
Previously the standard required the supplier to plan the production, installation and servicing processes that directly affect quality and ensure that these processes are carried out under controlled conditions. The difference is a widening of the requirement to all processes and extension of scope beyond mere planning to include organizing and controlling all processes.

- Managing the process inputs
- Managing the work
- Managing the physical resources
- Managing the financial resources
- Managing the human resources
- Managing the constraints
- Managing the outputs

Process management is therefore much more than managing activities and therefore when describing processes, one needs more than a flow chart of activities. The chart is a diagrammatical representation of a process but only one aspect. One can also add numerical data to the charts to indicate resources, cycle times, delays, costs etc. but the intangible factors of the human environment cannot be reduced to numerical data to add to the charts.

The notes to clause 4.1 of ISO 9001 need some explanation. It is stated that the processes needed for the management system include *management activities, provision of resources, product realization and measurement.* This note could cause confusion because it suggests that these are the processes that are needed for the management system. It would be unwise to use this as the model and far better to identify the processes from observing how the business operates. The term *provision of resources* should be *Resource Management,* which is the collection of processes covering financial, human and physical resources. *Product realization* is also a collection of processes such as design, production, service delivery, etc. *Measurement* is not a single process but a sub-process within each process. Grouping all the measurement processes together serves no useful purpose except it matches the standard – a purpose of little value in managing the organization.

The second note refers to *outsourcing processes* although it is difficult to imagine that management activities, product realization or measurement would be outsourced in its entirety. It is likely that market research; design, product verification, equipment calibration and other specialized services may be outsourced. While outsourcing comes under purchasing, it is correct to point out that the organization should control *any* outsourced processes. The supplier of the process is usually referred to as a subcontractor because they provide services to the organization's requirements not their own. Control of subcontractors is covered by clause 7.4 but in meeting clause 7.4.3, you need to treat suppliers and subcontractors differently (see chapter 7).

Why is this necessary?

This requirement responds to the Process Approach Principle.

Desired results will not be achieved by chance – their achievement needs to be managed and as the processes are the means by which the results are achieved, this means managing the processes.

How is this implemented?
Managing the inputs

This means making sure that:

- the process is capable of producing the required outputs of the required quality, on time, with the human physical and financial resources available

- the processes providing the required inputs are capable of supplying them on time, in the right quantity and quality and if not, adjusting the process to accommodate known variations.

Managing the work

This means that the activities have to be planned, organized and controlled in a way that will deliver the desired outputs. To do this one has to:

- Determine the process objectives and establish performance measures of success
- Determine the activities required to achieve the objectives and design the process so that the sequence and interaction of the activities and use of resources will achieve the process objectives
- Determine the stages in the process where checks need to be made to verify work and detect variance
- Organize the assignment of responsibility and delegation of authority for the actions and decisions required
- Install communication mechanisms for feeding the process with changes in the inputs and for obtaining information on the behaviour of the process
- Install sensors to detect variance in process capability
- Monitor and measure process performance against process objectives, taking account of measurement capability
- Take action to improve the efficiency and effectiveness with which the process produces results

Managing the physical resources

This means that the physical resources needed by the process are planned, organized and controlled in a way that enables the process to deliver the desired results. To do this one has to:

- Determine the physical resources required and establish objectives for their acquisition, utilization and productivity;
- Establish performance measures for physical resource acquisition, utilization and productivity;
- Develop or acquire physical resources of the right type, quantity and quality at the right time;
- Deploy these resources to the stage in the process where they are required, when they are required;
- Maintain the physical resources necessary for efficient and effective performance;
- Install sensors for measuring physical resource acquisition, utilization and productivity;
- Monitor and measure the acquisition, utilization and productivity of physical resources against the established objectives;

- Dispose of those assets that are no longer required that are diverting resources away from productive operations;
- Take action to improve the acquisition, utilization and productivity of physical resources.

Managing the financial resources

This means that the financial resources needed by the processes are planned, organized and controlled in a way that the other resources are acquired on time, of the right quality and in the right quantity to feed the process with the means to deliver the desired performance. Starve the process of financial resources and the process will cease to produce the desired results. Financial control processes have in general not formed part of the documented management system, but clearly one cannot manage processes without control of the finances. The success of any enterprise depends on their being sufficient capital and cost control.

To manage the financial resources one has to:

- Develop a financial budget for setting up the process as designed. This may require investment capital the source of which needs to be secured;
- Develop a financial budget for operating and maintaining the process that projects spend over time. The cost of raw materials, consumables and labour, of out-sourced services such as laboratories, cleaning, maintenance etc.;
- Set up cost control mechanisms that regulate expenditure on capital, materials, labour and expenses that are commensurate with process objectives;
- Set up revenue collection mechanisms including sales invoicing, receipts and debt collection;
- Set up cost accounting mechanisms that identify all elements of expenditure including capital costs, running costs, maintenance costs and quality costs (costs of prevention, detection, correction and failure);
- Monitor and measure the acquisition and utilization of financial resources against the budgets;
- Recover the cost of surplus or waste physical resources as is practical;
- Divert surplus resources for investment so as to feed the demand for capital;
- Take action to improve the acquisition and utilization of financial resources.

Managing the human resources

This means that the human resources needed by the process are planned, organized and controlled in a way that enables the process to deliver the desired results:

- Determine the human resources required and establish objectives for their acquisition, utilization, capability, competency and productivity;
- Establish performance measures for human resource acquisition, utilization, capability and productivity;
- Develop or acquire human resources of the right competency so as to be available at the right time;
- Assign responsibilities and delegate authority to the human resources commensurate with their abilities;
- Create conditions in which the human resources will be motivated to deliver the desired performance;
- Deploy these human resources to the stage in the process where they are required, when they are required and in the required number;
- Develop the capability of human resources necessary for efficient and effective performance;
- Install sensors for measuring human resource acquisition, utilization, capability, competency and productivity;
- Monitor and measure the acquisition, utilization and productivity of human resources against the established objectives;
- Retire or retrain those human resources that are no longer required for current process operations;
- Take action to improve the acquisition, utilization, capability, competency and productivity of human resources.

Managing the constraints

Process constraints are forces that prevent, restrict, limit or regulate a process. There are two types of constraints on a process; one is controllable and the other isn't because of a legal requirement or corporate policy you cannot change. Each constraint has to be managed differently. The legal and policy constraints have to be satisfied otherwise the process will be in breach of the law or policy and will be shut down unless compliance is restored. The controllable constraint is an inherent characteristic of the process that can be changed provided that the effects can be measured. The force constraining the process can be identified and either removed, reduced or controlled. These forces may be of a technical, political, physical or behavioural nature and therefore the measures taken will differ in each case. In order to manage the controllable constraints one has to:

- Verify that the performance measures provide meaningful data upon which to judge process performance;
- Determine the inherent characteristics upon which the performance measures depend (e.g. throughput may be limited by capacity or by approval stages);

- Identify the forces that prevent, restrict limit or regulate some aspect of process performance (e.g. what is constraining capacity or delaying approval);
- Determine the stage in the process where the constraint impacts performance (e.g. the binding machine in a printing process or the plant manager's approval of a purchase order);
- Establish the root cause of the technical, political, physical or behavioural constraint (e.g. glue temperature control or plant manager's distrust of subordinates);
- Take action to remove the constraint (e.g. fit new thermostat to glue reservoir or counsel the manager or the subordinates);
- Act upon the next force that constrains process performance and so on until process capability is assured.

Managing the outputs

The most common form of management is output management. Financial management is often output management – all the focus is on the bottom line without regard to the processes that deliver it. All the kicking, whipping and instruction does little to improve the output because the focus is in the wrong place. People complain they cannot deliver more because of a lack of capable resources, problems with the inputs or the constraints imposed by management. If the inputs, activities, resources and constraints have been managed effectively, the outputs should be predictable and should satisfy customers and therefore the outputs are being managed indirectly. However, you can still manage the outputs directly. To do this you should:

- Define the output required in terms of quantity, quality and timeliness – often the customer specification
- Translate the requirements into characteristics of the output that are measurable and determine the units of measure and the standard values
- Install sensors in the process to measure these characteristics and detect variance
- Install communication mechanisms to feedback information on the output to the stage in the process where correction can be effected
- Monitor and measure the outputs to verify conformity and feedback information to those responsible for remedial action
- Take action to correct outputs that are nonconforming
- Determine the causes of variation and take corrective action to prevent recurrence of unacceptable variation

Ensuring information availability (4.1d)

The standard requires the organization *to ensure the availability of information necessary to support the operation and monitoring of the identified processes.*

What does this mean?

Information to support the operation of processes would include that related to:

- Process inputs
- Planning activities
- Preparatory activities
- Result-producing activities
- Routing activities
- Process outputs

> **1994–2000 Differences**
> Previously the standard required the supplier to plan the production, installation and servicing processes which directly affect quality. The difference here is to remove the limitation on process control by the widening of the requirement to all processes.

Information to support the monitoring of processes would include that related to:

- Past and current performance, throughput, response time, downtime etc
- Operating conditions
- Verification activities
- Diagnostic activities

Such information would include plans, specifications, standards, records and any other information required to be used in operating and monitoring the process.

Why is this necessary?

This requirement responds to the Leadership principle.

All processes require information whether they are automated or manually operated.

How is this implemented?

Ensuring the availability of information is part of process management and was also addressed above. One would expect personnel to have information available in order to plan their work, prepare facilities, or set up equipment, to perform operations, measure results, make decisions on the results, resolve problems, prepare the output for delivery and to route the output to its intended destination.

To ensure availability of information you need to provide access at point of use and this is addressed under *Control of documents*.

Ensuring the availability of resources (4.1d)

1994–2000 Differences
Previously the standard required the supplier to identify resource requirements and provide adequate resources for management, performance of work and verification activities.

The standard requires the organization *to ensure the availability of resources necessary to support the operation and monitoring of the identified processes.*

What does this mean?

The resources necessary to support the operation of processes would include:

- Raw materials and consumables
- Personnel
- Utilities such as heat, light, power, water
- Time
- Equipment, plant machinery, facilities, work space
- Money to fund the needs of the process

The resources necessary to support the monitoring of processes would include:

- Instrumentation, equipment
- Verification and certification services to ensure measurement integrity
- Personnel to perform monitoring
- Computers and other tools to analyse results
- Utilities to energize the monitoring facilities
- Money to fund the needs of monitoring

Why is this necessary?

This requirement responds to the Leadership principle.

Without the necessary resources processes cannot function as intended. All processes consume resources. If there are insufficient resources to monitor processes, it is hardly worthwhile operating them because you will not know how they are performing.

How is this implemented?

The process owner or manager is responsible for ensuring the availability of resources. This commences with identifying resource needs, securing an available and qualified supply, providing for their deployment into the process when required and monitoring their utilization. Further guidance is given in Chapter 6.

Measuring, monitoring and analysing processes (4.1e)

The standard requires the organization *to measure, monitor and analyse the identified processes.*

What does this mean?

Measuring processes is rather different to measuring the output of processes – this is commonly referred to as inspection or product verification. Figure 4.9 illustrates this difference.

Measuring is concerned with determination of the quantities of an entity such as time, speed, and capability indices whereas monitoring is concerned with continual observation aside from periodic measurement.

1994–2000 Differences
Previously the standard required controlled conditions to include the monitoring and control of suitable process parameters and product characteristics and limited application to production, installation and servicing processes. There is no change in intent but a significant change in applicability.

Analysing processes is concerned with under-standing the nature and behaviour of processes for the purpose of their design, development and improvement. Measuring and monitoring take place following installation of the process whereas process analysis can be used as a design tool (Hoyle, David and Thompson, John, 2000)[7].

Why is this necessary?

This requirement responds to the Factual Approach Principle.

You can't manage a process unless equipped with the facts about its performance. Observations from monitoring provide this useful information.

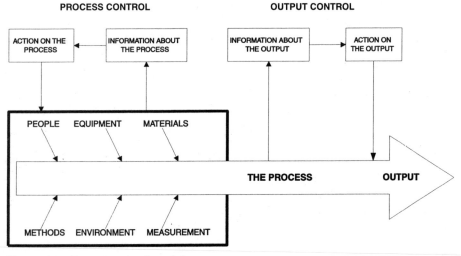

Figure 4.9 Process control model

You cannot claim success, failure or make improvements unless you know the current performance of your processes. It is therefore necessary to install sensors to gather this data. The facts may tell you where you are, but further analysis is needed to establish whether it is an isolated occurrence, an upward or a downward trend and whether improvement is feasible. Process analysis is performed to enable the decision makers to make decisions based on fact.

How is this implemented?

Process measurement

In order to measure the process you need (Juran, J. M., 1995) [8]:

1 Process objectives (what the process is designed to achieve) e.g. a sales process may be designed to convert customer enquiries into sales orders and accurately convey customer requirements into the product/service generation process
2 Indicators of performance (the units of measure) e.g. for a sales process measures may be:
   • The ratio of confirmed orders to enquiries
   • The ratio of customer complaints relative or order accuracy to total orders completed
   • The ratio of orders lost due to price relative to total order won. Similar indicators could be applied for quality and delivery
   There may be other indicators related to the behaviour of sales staff in dealing with customers and internal functions such as whether the sales promise matched the true capability of the organization etc.
3 Defined performance standard (the level above or below which performance is deemed to be sub standard or inferior)
4 Sensors to detect variance before, during or after operations. There may be human or physical sensors each of which has an element of measurement uncertainty
5 Calibrated sensors so that you can be assured the results are accurate and precise. There are two types of measurements to be made:
   • Measurements that tell us whether the process is operating as intended
   • Measurements that tell us whether the process is effective

The former measurements are taken using the process indicators and the later measurements are taken using process analysis.

Process monitoring

For process monitoring to be effective, the staff involved need to understand the process objectives and how they are measured. They need to be vigilant to potential and actual variations from the norm. A typical type of process monitoring takes place in a ship's engine room where there are lots of dials, gauges and data logging on a continuous basis. The watch engineers scan the log at the start of the watch for unusual occurrences that might account for variation in engine temperature. In monitoring a staff deployment process it may be noticed that staff are trained but there follows prolonged periods before the new skills are deployed. In the invoicing process it may be observed that a number of invoices go missing and have to be resent thus delaying receipt of revenue. In observing the design change process, it may be noticed that there is a burst in activity immediately prior to a holiday period without any additional resources being provided. Monitoring is looking for unusual occurrences or indicators of a potential change in performance.

Process analysis

Process analysis can be used to implement clauses 4.1a, 4.1b and 4.1c of ISO 9001 as well as clause 4.1e and 4.1f.

Analysis in process design

Process analysis is performed to design a process and understand the behaviour of a process (Hoyle, David and Thompson, John, 2000)[9]. In this regard there are a number of activities that may be undertaken and there follows a sequence in which they could be implemented:

- Define the key performance indicators
- Define the method of measurement
- Establish current performance against the indicators
- Produce a process flow chart
- Perform a task analysis to determine who does what, when, where, how and why
- Identify constraints on the process and test their validity
- Perform a control analysis to determine/verify the controls to be/being applied
- Deploy the system requirements (ISO 9001 + any relevant regulations, statutes) to identify any gaps
- Deploy known customer requirements (e.g. using QFD) to establish that the process will deliver the right output
- Identify failure modes and effects to establish the issues that could jeopardize success
- Install failure prevention features to reduce, contain or eliminate potential failure modes
- Conduct relationship analysis to establish conflicts of responsibility and authority and thus potential constraints

- Perform productivity assessment to identify the number of transactions and their validity
- Identify resources required to establish any deficiencies
- Perform information needs analysis to identify/validate all the documentation needed
- Perform a cultural analysis to establish the behavioural factors that will/are causing success or failure

This analysis enables decisions to be made on the design or modification of processes and the conditions for their successful operation.

Analysis in process operation

In constructing the process, the identified measuring and monitoring stations should be installed. Process analysis is performed on the data generated by these sensors and includes several activities as follows, (Juran, J. M., 1995)[10]:

- Collect the data from monitoring activities
- Sort, classify, summarize, calculate, correlate, present, chart and otherwise simplify the original data
- Transmit the assimilated data to the decision makers
- Verify the validity of the variation
- Evaluate the economical and statistical significance of the variation
- Discover the root cause of the variation
- Evaluate the alternative solutions that will restore the status quo

This analysis enables decisions to be made on the continued operation of the processes and whether to modify the conditions under which they operate. (See also *Variation* in Chapter 2.)

1994–2000 Differences

Previously the standard required the supplier to maintain a quality system as a means of ensuring that product conforms to specified requirements. There is no difference in intent but the new wording implies that the standard defines how the management system should be maintained but it loses the reasons for doing it.

Maintaining a quality management system (4.1)

The standard requires the organization *to maintain a quality management system in accordance with the requirements of ISO 9001.*

What does this mean?

For many working to the 1994 version of ISO 9000, this was interpreted as maintaining documents, but as the management system is the means by which the organization's objectives are achieved, it clearly

means much more than this. Maintenance is concerned with both retaining something in and restoring something to a state in which it can perform its required function. In the context of a management system this entails maintaining processes and their capability.

Why is this necessary?

This requirement responds to the Process Approach Principle.

Without maintenance any system will deteriorate and management systems are no exception. A lack of attention to each of the factors mentioned above will certainly result in a loss of capability and therefore poor quality performance, financial performance and lost customers. Even to maintain performance a certain degree of improvement is necessary – in fact even raising standards can be perceived as a means of maintaining performance in a dynamic environment in which you adapt or die.

How is this implemented?

In maintaining processes you need to keep:

- reducing variation
- physical resources operational
- human resources competent
- financial resources available for replenishment of consumables, replace worn out or obsolete equipment
- the process documentation up-to-date as changes in the organization, technology, resources occur
- space available to accommodate input and output
- buildings, land and office areas clean and tidy – remove the waste
- benchmarking processes against best in the field

In maintaining capability you need to keep:

- replenishing human resources as staff retire, leave the business or are promoted
- renewing technologies to retain market position and performance
- surplus resources available for unforeseen circumstances
- upto date with the latest industry practices
- refreshing awareness of the vision, values and mission

Another set of actions that can be used is the Japanese 5-S technique (Imai, Masaaki, 1986)[11].

1 Seiri (straighten up)
2 Seiton (put things in order)
3 Seido (clean up)
4 Seiketsu (personal cleanliness)
5 Shitsuke (discipline)

Continual improvement in the quality management system and its processes (4.1 and 4.1f)

1994–2000 Differences
This is a new requirement that has no equivalent in the 1994 version.

The standard requires the organization *to continually improve the effectiveness of the quality management system in accordance with the requirements of ISO 9001 and to implement action necessary to achieve planned results and continual improvement of the identified processes.*

What does this mean?

ISO 9000 defines continual improvement as a recurring activity to increase the ability to fulfil requirements. As the organization's objectives are its requirements, continually improving the effectiveness of the management system means continually increasing the ability of the organization to fulfil its objectives.

Why is this necessary?

This requirement responds to the Continual Improvement principle.

If the management system is enabling the organization to accomplish its objectives when that is its purpose, why improve? The need for improvement arises out of a need to become more effective at what you do, more efficient in the utilization of resources so that the organization becomes best in its class. The purpose of measuring process performance is to establish whether or not the objectives are being achieved and if not to take action on the difference. If the performance targets are being achieved, opportunities may well exist to raise standards and increase efficiency and effectiveness.

How is this implemented?

Action necessary to achieve planned results is addressed under correction action in Chapter 8.

If the performance of a process parameter is currently meeting the standard that has been established, there are several improvement actions you can take:

- Raise the standard e.g. if the norm for the sales ratio of orders won to all orders bid is 60%, an improvement programme could be developed for raising the standard to 75% or higher
- Increase efficiency e.g. if the time to process an order is within limits, identify and eliminate wasted resources
- Increase effectiveness e.g. if you bid against all customer requests, by only bidding for those you know you can win you improve your hit rate

You can call all these actions improvement actions because they clearly improve performance. However, we need to distinguish between being better at what we do now and doing new things. Some may argue that improving efficiency is being better at what we do now, and so it is – but if in order to improve efficiency we have to be innovative we are truly reaching new standards. Forty years ago, supervisors in industry would cut an eraser in half in the name of efficiency rather than hand out two erasers. Clearly this was a lack of trust disguised as efficiency improvement and it had quite the opposite effect. In fact they were not only increasing waste but also creating a hostile environment.

Each of the improvement actions is dealt with later in the book and the subject of continual improvement addressed again under *Quality planning in Chapter 5*.

There are several steps to undertaking continual improvement (Juran, J. M., 1995)[12].

1 Determine current performance
2 Establish the need for change
3 Obtain commitment and define the improvement objectives
4 Organize diagnostic resources
5 Carry out research and analysis to discover the cause of current performance
6 Define and test solutions that will accomplish the improvement objectives
7 Product improvement plans which specify how and by whom the changes will be implemented
8 Identify and overcome any resistance to change
9 Implement the change
10 Put in place controls to hold new levels of performance and repeat step one

Preparing the quality manual (4.2.2)

The standard requires *a quality manual to be established and maintained that includes the scope of the quality management system, the documented procedures or reference to them and a description of the sequence and interaction of processes included in the quality management system.*

What does this mean?

ISO 9000 defines a quality manual as *a document specifying the quality management system of an organization.* It is therefore not intended that the manual be a response to the requirements of ISO 9001. As the top-level document describing the management system it is a system description describing how the organization is managed.

Countless quality manuals produced to satisfy ISO 9000:1994, were no more than 20 sections that paraphrased the requirements of the standard. Such documentation adds no value. They are of no use to managers, staff or auditors. Often thought to be useful to customers, organizations would gain no more confidence from customers than would be obtained from their registration certificate.

Why is this necessary?

This requirement responds to the System Approach Principle.

A description of the management system is necessary as a means of showing how all the processes are interconnected and how they collectively deliver the business outputs. It has several uses as :

- a means to communicate the vision, values, mission, policies and objectives of the organization
- a means of showing how the system has been designed
- a means of showing linkages between processes
- a means of showing who does what
- an aid to training new people
- a tool in the analysis of potential improvements
- a means of demonstrating compliance with external standards and regulations

How is this implemented?

When formulating the policies, objectives and identifying the processes to achieve them, the manual provides a convenient vehicle for containing such information. If left as separate pieces of information, it may be more difficult to see the linkages.

The requirement provides the framework for the manual. Its content may therefore include the following:

1 Introduction
   (a) Purpose (of the manual)
   (b) Scope (of the manual)
   (c) Applicability (of the manual)
   (d) Definitions (of terms used in the manual)

2 Business overview
   (a) Nature of the business/organization – its scope of activity, its products and services
   (b) The organization's interested parties (customers, employees, regulators, shareholders, suppliers, owners etc.)
   (c) The context diagram showing the organization relative to its external environment
   (d) Vision, values
   (e) Mission

3 Organization
   (a) Function descriptions
   (b) Organization chart
   (c) Locations with scope of activity

4 Business processes
   (a) The system model showing the key business processes and how they are interconnected
   (b) System performance indicators and method of measurement
   (c) Business planning process description
   (d) Resource management process description
   (e) Marketing process description
   (f) Product/service generation processes description
   (g) Sales process description
   (h) Order fulfilment process description

5 Function matrix (Relationship of functions to processes)

6 Location matrix (Relationship of locations to processes)

7 Requirement deployment matrices
   (a) ISO 9001 compliance matrix
   (b) ISO 14001 compliance matrix
   (c) Regulation compliance matrices (FDA, Environment, Health, Safety, CAA etc.)

8 Approvals (List of current product, process and system approvals)

The process descriptions can be contained in separate documents and should cover the topics identified previously (see *Documents that ensure effective planning, operation and control of processes*).

As the manual contains a description of the management system a more apt title would be a Management System Manual (MSM) or maybe a title reflecting its purpose might be Management System Description (MSD).

In addition a much smaller document could be produced that does respond to the requirements of ISO 9001, ISO 14001, and the regulations of regulatory authorities. Each document would be an exposition produced purely to map your management system onto these external requirements to demonstrate how your system meets these requirements. When a new requirement comes along, you can produce a new exposition rather than attempt to change your system to suit all parties. A model of such relationships is illustrated in Figure 4.10. The process descriptions that emerge from the Management System Manual describe the core business processes and are addressed in Chapter 4 under the heading of *Documents that ensure effective operation and control of processes*.

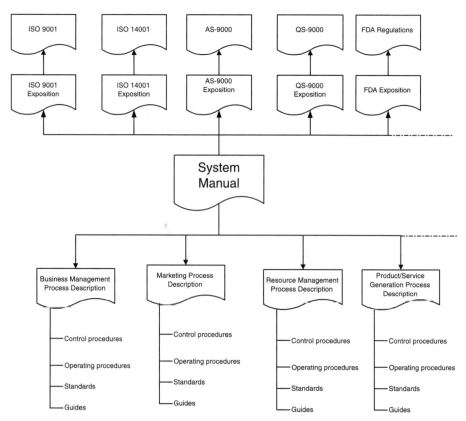

Figure 4.10 Relationship of external standards to the management system

Scope of the quality management system (4.2.2)

The standard requires the quality manual *to include the scope of the quality management system including details of justification for any exclusion.*

1994–2000 Differences

Previously the standard required the quality manual to cover the requirements of the standard. The difference is that by virtue of the nature of its business, the manual does not need to address requirements that do not apply to the organization.

What does this mean?

The standard addresses activities that may not be relevant or applicable to an organization. The permissible exclusions are explained in section 1.2 of ISO 9001. Here it states that the organization may only exclude requirements that *neither affect the organization's ability, nor its responsibility to provide product that meets customer and applicable regulatory requirements.* The requirements for which exclusion is permitted are limited to those in section 7 of the standard. Exclusions are addressed in Chapter 3.

Under ISO 9000:1994, it was possible for organizations to exclude functions and processes of their organization that may have been difficult to control or were not part of the order fulfilment cycle. Organizations that designed their own products but not for specific customers could escape bringing these operations into the management system. Marketing was omitted because it operated before placement of order. Accounting, Administration, Maintenance, Publicity, Public Relations and After Sales Support functions were often omitted because there were no requirements in the standard that specifically dealt with such activities. As there is no function in an organization that does not directly or indirectly serve the satisfaction of interested parties, it is unlikely that any function or process will now be excluded from the management system.

Why is this necessary?

This requirement responds to the System Approach Principle.

It is sensible to describe the scope of the management system so as to ensure effective communication. The scope of the management system is one area that generates a lot of misunderstanding particularly when dealing with auditors, consultants and customers. When you claim you have a management system that meets ISO 9001 it could imply that you design, develop, install and service the products you supply, when in fact you may only be a distributor. Why you need to justify specific exclusions is uncertain because it is more practical to justify inclusions.

How is this implemented?

The scope of the management system is the scope of the organization. There is no longer any reason to exclude locations, activities, functions or processes for which there is no requirement in the standard. The reason is because the ISO 9000 family now serves customer satisfaction and is not limited to quality assurance as were the 1994 versions of ISO 9001, ISO 9002 and ISO 9003.

It is not appropriate to address exclusions by inserting pages in the manual corresponding to the sections of the standard and adding justification if not within the scope of the management system – such as 'We don't do this!'. It is much more appropriate to use an appendix as indicated previously in the manual contents list. By describing the nature of the business, you are establishing boundary conditions. If in doing so you do not mention that you design products, it will be interpreted that design is not applicable. For exclusions relative to detail requirements, the Compliance Matrix may suffice but for an unambiguous solution, it is preferable to produce an exposition that addresses each requirement of the standard as illustrated in Figure 4.10.

Referencing procedures in the quality manual (4.2.2)

> **1994–2000 Differences**
>
> Previously the standard required the quality manual to include or make reference to the quality system procedures. There is no difference in requirement.

The standard requires the quality manual *to include the documented procedures established for the quality management system or reference to them.*

What does this mean?

As the standard now only requires six documented procedures it is unclear whether it is these procedures that should be included or referenced or all procedures. A practical interpretation is to include or reference the Process Descriptions which themselves reference all the other documents used to manage processes.

Why is this necessary?

This requirement responds to the Process Approach Principle.

By including or referencing the documentation that describes the management system, you are providing a road map that will help people navigate through the system. Take the road map away and people won't know which documents to use. All documentation in the management system should be related and serve a defined purpose. By expressing the documentation in a hierarchy you provide a baseline and thus a means of configuration control. This will prevent new documents being created or existing documents withdrawn without reference to the baseline.

How is this implemented?

The retention of a requirement for the manual to include or refer to documented procedures indicates that management system documentation is still perceived by the standard makers as primarily comprising procedures. It is as though every requirement constitutes an activity that requires a documented procedure rather than a process. However, the requirement for the interaction of processes to be described in the manual provides a means for correcting this inconsistency. If the manual is structured as suggested previously, each business process will be described and in doing so the relevant procedures for performing tasks within the process can be listed or included. One way is to refer to procedures when detailing some aspect of a process. Another way is to list the procedures in an annex to each process description. A third way is to include an appendix in the manual that lists all the procedures. Alternatively a reference can be made to a database or number of databases that contain the procedures. With electronic documentation it is often not practical to duplicate lists of documents that would appear in a directory of a computer. Duplication creates a need for the synchronization of two or more lists to be maintained – thus causing additional effort and the possibility of error. Adding a new document to a file structure on a computer is the same as adding a new document to a list. A problem with file structures is that the configuration is changed when a document is added or deleted and therefore the status at any time in the past cannot be established unless a record is kept. Auditors and investigators certainly need to be able to establish the status of the system documentation at intervals so that they can determine the documentation that was current when a particular event took place. Ideally, the database containing the documents needs the capability to reconstruct the file structure that existed at a particular date in the past.

Describing the processes and their interaction (4.2.2)

The standard requires the quality manual *to include a description of the interaction between the processes of the quality management system.*

What does this mean?

Each of these processes within the management system interacts with the others to produce the required outputs. A description of this interaction means that the linkages between processes, the source and destination of these linkages and what passes along these channels should be described. In

> **1994–2000 Differences**
>
> Previously the standard required the quality manual to outline the structure of the documentation used in the quality system. This new requirement implies a change from the typical documentation pyramid to process descriptions.

describing an air conditioning system, for example, the system drawing would show all the components and how they linked together to form the system. Any component not linked into the system would have no function in the system and therefore would not be essential to its performance. Similarly with a management system, any process not connected to the system cannot perform a useful purpose within the system and can therefore be ignored.

Why is this necessary?

This requirement responds to the System Approach Principle.

The management system comprises the processes required to achieve the organization's objectives and therefore they are linked together. It is necessary to describe these linkages so that it can be demonstrated that a coherent system exists and how it operates.

How is this implemented?

The sequence and interaction of processes was addressed previously. In this case the interaction is required to be described and one way of doing this is through process flow charts arranged in a hierarchy. You could include all the process descriptions in the manual or merely include the business process flow charts and reference the process descriptions. The advantage of including all the process descriptions is that the manual becomes much more of a useful document and avoids duplicating information already contained in the process descriptions.

Control of documents (4.2.3)

Documents required for the management system (4.2.3)

1994–2000 Differences

Previously the standard required the supplier to control all documents and data that relate to the requirements of ISO 9001 including, to the extent applicable, documents of external origin such as standards and customer drawings.

The intent of the new requirement remains the same.

The standard requires *documents required by the quality management system to be controlled.*

What does this mean?

Documents required by the management system are those documents used by or generated by a process that forms part of the management system. The documentation used by a process could include policy documents, process descriptions, procedures, work instructions, contractual documents and standards. Those generated by a process could include product specifications, subcontracts, plans, orders, instructions, reports, and records. However records are subject to different controls from the other types of documents because they are time-related and once produced they must not be changed unless they contain errors (see under *Control of records*).

The term document should be taken to include data or any information that is recorded and stored either on paper or magnetic media in a database or on disk. It may be both an audio and visual record although the controls that will be applied will vary depending on the media. The requirement is not limited to documented procedures. These are only one type of document that needs to be controlled. There is often confusion between quality system documents and quality documents and also between technical documents and quality documents. Such fine distinctions are unnecessary. Whether the document has the word *quality* in its title is irrelevant. The only question of interest is 'Is the document used or generated by this process?' If the answer is 'yes' the document should be controlled. Notes that you make when performing a task and then discard are not documents generated by a process – they are merely an aide-memoire. Someone else may not make any notes at all or make different notes.

Controlling documents means regulating the development, approval, issue, change, distribution, maintenance, use, storage, security, obsolescence or disposal of documents.

Why is this necessary?

This requirement responds to the Process Approach Principle.

It is necessary to regulate the documentation to ensure that:

- documents fulfil a useful purpose in the organization;
- resources are not wasted in the distribution of non-essential information ;
- only valid information is used in the organization's processes;
- people have access to appropriate information for them to perform their work;
- information is kept up-to-date;
- information is in a form that can be used by all relevant people;
- classified information is restricted to only those with a need to know;
- information important to the investigation of problems, improvement opportunities or potential litigation is retained.

How is this implemented?

For those using document control software with the documents located on a secure server, many of the recommendations in this part of the book may seem unnecessary. However, even proprietary software claiming to meet the requirements of ISO 9000 for document control may not contain all the features you need. There are also many organizations that still use paper for good reasons. Paper does not crash without warning. Paper can be read more easily at a meeting or on a train. Comments can be added more easily to paper.

In the world of documents there are two categories: those that are controlled and those that are not controlled. A controlled document is one where requirements have been specified for its development, approval, issue, change, distribution, maintenance, use, storage, security, obsolescence or disposal. You do not need to exercise control over each of these elements for a document to be designated as a controlled document. Controlling documents may be limited to controlling their revision. On the other hand, you cannot control the revision of national standards but you can control their use, their storage, their obsolescence etc. Even memoranda can become *controlled documents* if you impose a security classification upon them.

The standard acknowledges that records are indeed documents but require different controls to those that apply to other documents.

In order to control documents a document control process needs to be established that provides an adequate degree of control over all types of documents generated and used in the management system.

The process stages are common to all documents but the mechanisms for controlling different types of documents may differ. There are many software packages available that can be used to develop documents and control their issue, access, storage, maintenance and disposal. Unfortunately few can handle all types. You may not wish to trust all your documentation to one package. The software has automated many of the procedural issues such that it is no longer the Achilles heel of a management system.

Document control procedures (4.2.3)

The standard requires that *a documented procedure be established to define the controls needed.*

1994–2000 Differences

Previously the standard required the supplier to establish and maintain documented procedures to control all documents and data.

The difference is the removal of 'data' and making the term procedures singular. The intent however remains the same.

What does this mean?

This requirement means that the methods for performing the various activities required to control different types of documents should be defined and documented.

Although the standard implies that a single procedure is required, should you choose to produce several different procedures for handling the different types of documents it is doubtful that any auditor would deem this noncompliant. Where this might be questionable is in cases where there is no logical reason for such differences and where merging the procedures and settling on a best practice would improve efficiency and effectiveness.

Why is this necessary?

This requirement responds to the Process Approach Principle.

Documents are recorded information and the purpose of the document control process is to firstly ensure the appropriate information is available where needed and secondly to prevent the inadvertent use of invalid information. At each stage of the process are activities to be performed that may require documented procedures in order to ensure consistency and predictability. Procedures may not be necessary for each stage in the process.

How is this implemented?

Every process is likely to require the use of documents or generate documents and it is in the process descriptions that you define the documents that need to be controlled. Any document not referred to in your process descriptions is therefore, by definition, not essential to the achievement of quality and not required to be under control. It is not necessary to identify uncontrolled documents in such cases. If you had no way of tracing documents to a governing process, a means of separating controlled from uncontrolled may well be necessary.

The procedures that require the use or preparation of documents should also specify or invoke the procedures for their control. If the controls are unique to the document, they should be specified in the procedure that requires the document. You can produce one or more common procedures that deal with the controls that apply to all documents. The stages in the process may differ depending on the type of document and organizations involved in its preparation, approval, publication and use. One procedure may cater for all the processes but several may be needed.

The aspects you should cover in your document control procedures, (some of which are addressed further in this chapter) are as follows

- Planning new documents, funding, prior authorization, establishing need etc.
- Preparation of documents, who prepares them, how they are drafted, conventions for text, diagrams, forms etc.
- Standards for the format and content of documents, forms and diagrams.
- Document identification conventions.
- Issue notation, draft issues, post approval issues.
- Dating conventions, date of issue, date of approval or date of distribution.

- Document review, who reviews them and what evidence is retained.
- Document approval, who approves them and how approval is denoted.
- Document proving prior to use.
- Printing and publication, who does it and who checks it.
- Distribution of documents, who decides, who does it, who checks it.
- Use of documents, limitations, unauthorized copying and marking.
- Revision of issued documents, requests for revision, who approves the request, who implements the change.
- Denoting changes, revision marks, reissues, sidelining, underlining.
- Amending copies of issued documents, amendment instructions, and amendment status.
- Indexing documents, listing documents by issue status.
- Document maintenance, keeping them current, periodic review.
- Document accessibility inside and outside normal working hours.
- Document security, unauthorized changes, copying, disposal, computer viruses, fire and theft.
- Document filing, masters, copies, drafts, and custom binders.
- Document storage, libraries and archive, who controls location, loan arrangements.
- Document retention and obsolescence.

With electronically stored documentation, the document database may provide many of the above features and may not need to be separately prescribed in your procedures. Only the tasks carried out by personnel need to be defined in your procedures. A help file associated with a document database is as much a documented procedure as a conventional paper based procedure.

Document approval (4.2.3a)

The standard requires that *documents be approved for adequacy prior to issue.*

What does this mean?

Approval prior to issue means that designated authorities have agreed the document before being made available for use. Whilst the term *adequacy* is a little vague it should be taken as meaning that the document is judged as fit for the intended purpose. In a paper based system, this means approval before the document is distributed. With an electronic system, it means that the

1994–2000 Differences

Previously the standard required that documents and data be approved for adequacy by authorized personnel prior to issue.

Although this requirement no longer requires approval by authorized personnel there is no difference in the intent because authority of functions is required to be defined by 5.5.2.

documents should be approved before they are published or made available to the user community.

Why is this necessary?

This requirement responds to the Factual Approach Principle.

By subjecting documentation to an approval process prior to its use you can ensure that the documents in use have been judged by authorized personnel and found fit for purpose. Such a practice will also ensure that no unapproved documents are in circulation, thereby preventing errors from the use of invalid documents.

How is this implemented?

Adequacy of documents

The document control process needs to define the process by which documents are approved. In some cases it may not be necessary for anyone other than the approval authority to examine the documents. In others it may be necessary to set up a panel of reviewers to solicit their comments before approval is given. It all depends on whether the approval authority has all the information needed to make the decision and is therefore 'competent'. One might think that the CEO could approve any document in the organization but just because a person is the most senior executive does not mean he or she is competent to perform any role in the organization.

Users should be the prime participants in the approval process so that the resultant documents reflect their needs and are fit for the intended purpose. If the objective is stated in the document, does it fulfil that objective? If it is stated that the document applies to certain equipment, area or activity, does it cover that equipment, area or activity to the depth expected of such a document? One of the difficulties in soliciting comments to documents is that you will gather comment on what you have written but not on what you have omitted. A useful method is to ensure that the procedures requiring the document specify the acceptance criteria so that the reviewers and approvers can check the document against an agreed standard.

To demonstrate documents have been deemed as adequate prior to issue, you will need to show that the document has been processed through the prescribed document approval process. Where there is a review panel, a simple method is to employ a standard comment sheet on which reviewers can indicate their comments or signify that they have no comment. During the drafting process you may undertake several revisions. You may feel it necessary to retain these in case of dispute later, but you are not required to do so. You also need to show that the current issue has been reviewed so your comment sheets need to indicate document issue status.

Approval authorities

The standard no longer contains a specific requirement for documents to be approved by authorized personnel. The person approving a document derives his or her authority from the process. The process descriptions or procedures should identify who the approval authorities are by their role or function, preferably not their job title and certainly not their name because both can change. The procedure need only state that the document be approved, for example by the Chief Designer prior to issue. Another method is to assign each document to an owner. The owner is a person who takes responsibility for its contents and to whom all change requests need to be submitted. A separate list of document owners can be maintained and the procedure need only state that the Owner approves the document. It is not necessary for all approval authorities to be different from the author. You only need separate approval authorities where there is added value by having an extra pair of eyes. Admiral Rickover US Navy formulated some 'Basic rules for doing your job' in 1948 in which he wrote: 'An essential element of carrying out my work is the need to have it checked by an independent source. Even the most dedicated individual makes mistakes.'

Denoting approval

The standard doesn't require that documents visibly display approval but it is necessary to be able to show that the designated authorities have in fact approved documents in use. Electronic systems of control differ significantly in this area. With paper-based systems, approval can be denoted directly on the document, on a change or issue record, in a register or on a separate approval record. The presence of a coloured header or the stamp of the issuing authority can substitute for actual signatures on documents. Providing signatures and front sheets often adds an extra sheet but no added value. The objective is to employ a reliable means of indicating to users that the document is approved. Some organizations maintain a list of authorized signatories where there are large numbers of people whose signatures and names are unknown to users. If you are dealing with a small group of people who are accessible and whose signatures are known, a list of authorized signatures is probably unnecessary. All you need is a means of checking that the person who signed the document was authorized to do so. If below the signature you indicate the position of the person and require his or her name to be printed alongside his or her signature, you have exercised due diligence.

With electronic systems, indication of approval is accomplished by electronic signature captured by the software as a function of the security provisions. These can be set up to permit only certain personnel to enter data in the approval field of the document. The software is often not as flexible as paper-based systems and therefore provisions need to be made for dealing with situations where the designated approval authority is unavailable. If you let competency determine authority rather than position, other personnel will be able to approve documents because their electronic signature will provide traceability.

Issuing documents

The term *issue* in the context of documents means that copies of the document are distributed. You will of course wish to *issue* draft documents for comment but obviously they cannot be reviewed and approved beforehand. The sole purpose of issuing draft documents is to solicit comments. The ISO 9001 requirement should have been that the documents are reviewed and approved prior to *use*. Some organizations insist that even drafts are approved for issue. Others go further and insist that copies cannot be taken from unapproved documents. This is nonsense and not what is intended by the standard. Your draft documents need to look different from the approved versions either by using letter issue notation (a common convention) or by printing the final versions on coloured or watermark paper. If the approved document would carry signatures, the absence of any signature indicates that the document is not approved. With electronic systems, the draft documents should be held on a different server or in a different directory and provisions made to prohibit draft documents being published into the user domain.

Approving external documents

The requirements for document approval do not distinguish between internal and external documents. However, there is clearly a need to review and approve external documents prior to their internal release in order to establish their impact on the organization, the product, the process or the management system. The external document control procedure should make provision for new documents and amendments to such documents to be reviewed and approved for use prior to their issue into the organization.

Approving data

ISO 9000 defines a document *as information and its support medium*. This means that databases containing contacts, problems, sales, complaints, inventory etc., are documents and yet we don't call them 'document bases'; we prefer the term database. The term data is not defined in ISO 9000 but is commonly understood to be information organized in a form suitable for manual or computer analysis. When data is recorded it becomes information and should therefore be controlled. All data should be examined before use otherwise you may inadvertently introduce errors into your work. The standard does not require common controls for all information so you are at liberty to pitch the degree of control appropriate to the consequences of failure.

Regarding approval of data, you will need to define which data needs approval before issue as some data may well be used as an input to a document which itself is subject to approval. It all depends on how we interpret 'approved prior to issue'. This should be taken to mean 'issue to someone else'. Therefore if you use data that you have generated yourself it does not need approval prior to use. If you issue data to someone else, it should be approved before distributing in a network database. If your job is to run a computer program in order to test a product, you might use the data resulting from the test run to adjust the computer or the program. You should be authorized to conduct the test, your approval of the data is not required because the data has not in fact been issued to anyone else. The danger hiding in this requirement is that an eagle-eyed auditor may spot data being used without any evidence that it has been approved. As a precaution, ensure you have identified in your procedures those type of data that require formal control and that you know the origin of the data you are using.

Document review (4.2.3b)

1994–2000 Differences

Previously the standard required documents to be reviewed for adequacy by authorized personnel prior to issue.

The intent of the new requirement for document review is to establish whether the document remains suitable for its intended purpose following a period of use. The previous requirement did not prohibit documents remaining in use after they have become inadequate through neglect.

The standard requires that *documents be reviewed.*

What does this mean?

Previously the implication was that the review was a check by potential users that the document was fit for purpose before it was offered for approval. It could be construed that for a document to receive approval it must be checked and therefore 'review and approval' in this context are one and the same and the requirement is in this instance enhanced rather than relaxed.

A review is another look at something. Therefore document review is a task that is carried out at any time following the issue of a document.

Why is this necessary?

This requirement responds to the Continual Improvement principle.

Reviews may be necessary when:

- Taking remedial action (i.e. Correcting an error)
- Taking corrective action (i.e. Preventing an error recurring)
- Taking preventive action (i.e. Preventing the occurrence of an error)

- Taking maintenance action (i.e. Keeping information current)
- Validating a document for use (i.e. When selecting documents for use in connection with a project, product, contract or other application)
- Taking improvement action (i.e. Making beneficial change to the information)

How is this implemented?

Reviews may be random or periodic. Random reviews are reactive and arise from an error or a change that is either planned or unplanned. Periodic reviews are proactive and could be scheduled once each year to review the policies, processes, products, procedures, specification etc. for continued suitability. In this way obsolete documents are culled from the system. However, if the system is being properly maintained there should be no outdated information available in the user domain. Whenever a new process or a modified process in installed the redundant elements including documentation and equipment should be disposed of.

Revision of documents (4.2.3b)

The standard requires that *documents be updated as necessary and re-approved following their review.*

> **1994–2000 Differences**
> This is a new requirement that has no equivalent in the 1994 version.

What does this mean?

Following a document review, action may or may not be necessary. If the document is found satisfactory, it will remain in use until the next review. If the document is found unsatisfactory there are two outcomes.

- The document is no longer necessary and should be withdrawn from use – this is addressed by the requirement dealing with obsolescence.
- The document is necessary but requires a change – this is addressed by this requirement.

The standard implies that updating should follow a review. The term *update* also implies that documents are reviewed only to establish whether they are current when in fact document reviews may be performed for many different reasons. A more appropriate term to *update* would be *revise*. Previously the standard addressed only the review and approval of changes and did not explicitly require a revision process. However, a revision process is executed before a document is subject to re-approval.

Why is this necessary?

This requirement responds to the Continual Improvement principle.

It is inevitable that during use a need will arise for changing documents and therefore provision needs to be made to control not only the original generation of documents but also their revisions.

How is this implemented?

The change process

The document change process consists of a number of key stages some of which are not addressed in ISO 9001.

- Identification of need (addressed by document review)
- Request for change (not addressed in the standard)
- Permission to change (not addressed in the standard)
- Revision of document (addressed by document updates)
- Recording the change (addressed by identifying the change)
- Review of the change (addressed under quality planning)
- Approval of the change (addressed by document re-approval)
- Issue of change instructions (not addressed in the standard)
- Issue of revised document (addressed by document availability)

As stated previously, to control documents it is necessary to control their development, approval, issue, change, distribution, maintenance, use, storage, security, obsolescence or disposal and we will now address those aspects not specifically covered by the standard.

What is a change?

In controlling changes it is necessary to define what constitutes a change to a document. Should you allow any markings on documents, you should specify those that have to be supported by change notes and those that do not. Markings that add comment or correct typographical errors are not changes but annotations. Alterations that modify instructions are changes and need prior approval. The approval may be in the form of a change note that details changes that have been approved.

Request for change

Anyone can review a document but approved documents should only be changed/revised/amended under controlled conditions. The document review will conclude that either a change is necessary or unnecessary. If a change is necessary, a request for change should be made to the issuing authorities. Even when the person proposing the change is the same as would approve the change, other parties may be affected and should therefore be permitted to comment. The most common method is to employ Document Change Requests. By using a formal change request it allows anyone to request a change to the appropriate authorities.

Change requests need to specify:

- The document title, issue and date
- The originator of the change request (who is proposing the change, his or her location or department)
- The reason for change (why the change is necessary)
- What needs to be changed (which paragraph, section, etc. is affected and what text should be deleted)
- The changes in text required where known (the text which is to be inserted or deleted)

By maintaining a register of such requests you can keep track of who has proposed what, when and what progress is being made on its approval. You may of course use a memo or phone call to request a change but this form of request becomes more difficult to track and prove you have control. You will need to inform staff where to send their requests.

Permission to change

On receipt of the request you need to provide for its review by the change authority. The change request may be explicit in what should be changed or simply report a problem that a change to the document would resolve. Someone needs to be nominated to draft the new material and present it for review but before that, the approval authorities need to determine whether they wish the document to be changed at all. There is merit in reviewing requests for change before processing in order to avoid abortive effort. You may also receive several requests for change that conflict and before processing you will need to decide which change should proceed. While a proposed change may be valid, the effort involved may warrant postponement of the change until several proposals have been received – it rather depends on the urgency (see below).

As with the review and approval of data you need to be careful how you control changes to data. Data that have not been issued to anyone does not require approval if changed. Only the data that have been issued to someone other than its producer need be brought under change control. If you are using data provided by someone else, in principle you can't change it without that person's permission. However, there will be many circumstances where formal change control of data is unnecessary and many where it is vital as with scientific experiments, research, product testing etc. One way of avoiding seeking approval to change data is to give the changed data a new identity thereby creating new data from old data. It is perfectly legitimate for internal data (but not copyrighted data) because you have not changed the original data provided that others can still access it. If you use a common database for any activities you will need to control changes to the input data.

Making the change

The technology available for producing and controlling documents has changed dramatically over the last 50 years. There are three levels of technology in use.

- Documents produced, stored and distributed manually (Handwritten or typed on paper)
- Documents produced and stored electronically but distributed manually (Printed on paper)
- Documents produced, stored, distributed locally and controlled electronically (Intranet)
- Documents produced, stored, distributed worldwide and controlled electronically (Internet)

Each technology requires its own controls such that the controls applied to one type of technology would be totally inappropriate for another technology. Although we live in an age of Information Technology, all four types operate concurrently. The pen and paper are not obsolete and have their place alongside more sophisticated technologies. Maintenance personnel require documentation that may only be available in paper form although many might be equipped with laptop computers with a radio link to a central database. Document controls therefore need to be appropriate to the technology used to produce, store, distribute and control the documents.

The 1987 version of the ISO 9001 required that *documents be re-issued after a practical number, of changes have been made* but this provision was removed in the 1994 version. The requirement stems from the days before word-processing when changes were promulgated by amendment leaflet or change notes and one had to stick additional paragraphs over ones which were crossed out. In such circumstances there were only so many changes of this nature that you could make before the document became unusable and consequently a potential source of error. If you still operate in this fashion, the number of changes may well be a limiting factor but if you use word processors, other factors ought to be taken into account. However, there are practical reasons with documents distributed in paper medium (whether or not they are electronically produced documents) why it may not be prudent to reissue a document after each change. There are several types of changes you may need to consider.

- Changes affecting a whole range of documents
- Changes affecting many pages of a single document
- Changes affecting a few pages of a single document

For the change that affects a whole range of documents you will either need to reissue the complete set of documents or employ a Global Change Notice. When the cost and time required to process a change that affects many documents is prohibitive, something like a Global Change Notice (GCN) is a useful tool to have in your management system. With a GCN you can instruct document holders to make changes to certain documents in their possession without having to identify every document. For example, if a component specification changes, a GCN can authorize the new information to be added to any documents that specify that particular component without having to process hundreds of documents. When the document is subsequently revised for other reasons, the GCN can be embodied so that over a period of time all documents will eventually be brought up-to-date. You will need a means of alerting staff to the issue of a GCN but if you control your distribution lists this should not present a problem. With electronic systems, a macro can be run on the database to update all references to a particular aspect thus updating automatically all affected documents. Where this mechanism gets complicated is in cases where there are different forms of data capture and storage. E.g the CAD data will probably not be generated using the same software tools as the management procedures. Advertising literature may be generated using drawing packages or DTP software not word processing software. Flow charts may not be generated using word processing software. The technology is not yet available to search and replace information held in different forms on multiple platforms.

Where a change affects many pages, the document should be reissued. Even if the substantive change is minor, the knock-on effect in double-sided documents with diagrams etc. can be to change every page. With modern word processing techniques, even adding a full stop can throw out several pages.

Where a change affects only a few pages, you can issue the changed pages with an amendment instruction informing the recipient which pages to change. Alternatively you can use the Document Change Notice (DCN) to add new pages and amend text at the same time.

If only a few words or figures are affected, the DCN is by far the least expensive and the quickest method.

As an alternative to actually issuing changes, you may wish to process the change requests to the master and hold reissue of the document until a suitable number of changes, or a significant proportion of the document has been changed. It is not the number of changes that is significant because a single change could have far greater effect than 20 minor changes. With small documents, say 3–6 pages, it is often easier to reissue the whole document for each change.

Identifying the change (4.2.3c)

<table>
<tr>
<td>

1994–2000 Differences

Previously, the standard required the nature of change to be identified in the document or the appropriate attachment.

The intent of the requirement remains unchanged.

</td>
<td>

The standard requires that *changes to documents be identified.*

What does this mean?

The requirement means that it should be possible to establish what has been changed in a document following its revision.

</td>
</tr>
</table>

Why is this necessary?

This requirement responds to the Factual Approach Principle.

There are several benefits in identifying changes:

- Approval authorities are able to identify what has changed and so speed up the approval process
- Users are able to identify what has changed and so speed up the implementation process
- Auditors are able to identify what has changed and so focus on the new provisions more easily
- Change initiators are able to identify what has changed and so verify whether their proposed changes were implemented as intended

How is this implemented?

There are several ways in which you can identify changes to documents:

- By sidelining, underlining, emboldening or similar technique
- By a change record within the document (front or back) denoting the nature of change
- By a separate change note that details what has changed and why
- By appending the change details to the initiating change request

If you operate a computerized documentation system, your problems can be eased by the versatility of the computer. Using a database you can provide users with all kinds of information regarding the nature of the change, but be careful. The more you provide the greater the chance of error and the harder and more costly it is to maintain. Staff should be told the reason for change and you should employ some means of ensuring that where changes to documents require a change in practice, adequate instruction is provided. A system that promulgates change without concern for the consequences is out of control. The changes are not complete until everyone whose work is affected by them both understands them and are equipped to implement them when necessary. Although not addressed under document control, the requirement for the integrity of the management system to be maintained during change in clause 5.4.2 implies that changes to documents should be reviewed before approval to ensure compatibility between documents is maintained. When evaluating the change you should assess the impact of the requested change on other areas and initiate the corresponding changes in the other documents.

Identifying the current revision of documents (4.2.3c)

The standard requires the *current revision status of documents to be identified*.

What does this mean?

When a document is revised its status changes to signify that it is no longer identical to the original version. This status may be indicated by date, by letter or by number or may be a combination of issue and revision. Every change to a document should revise the revision index. Issue 1 may denote the original version. Upon changing the document an incremental change to the revision index is made so that the new version is now Issue 2 or issue 1.1 depending on the convention adopted.

> **1994–2000 Differences**
>
> Previously, the standard required that a master list or equivalent document control procedure identifying the current revision status of documents be established and be readily available to preclude the use of invalid and/or obsolete documents.
>
> Although less prescriptive the requirement meets the same intent.

Why is this necessary?

This requirement responds to the Factual Approach Principle.

It is necessary to denote the revision status of documents so that firstly planners can indicate the version that is to be used and secondly, that users are able to clearly establish which version they are using or which version they require so as to avoid inadvertent use of incorrect versions.

How is this implemented?

There are two aspects to this requirement. One is the identity denoted on the document itself and the other is the identity of documents referred to in other documents.

Revision conventions

Changes may be *major* causing the document to be reissued or re-released, or they may be *minor* causing only the affected pages to be revised. You will need to decide on the revision conventions to use. Software documents often use a different convention to other documents such as release 1.1, or version 2.3. Non-software documents use conventions such as Issue 1, Issue 2 Revision 3, and Issue 4 Amendment 2. A convention often used with draft documents is the letter revision status whereby the first draft is Draft A, second draft is Draft B and so on. When the document is approved, the status changes to Issue 1. During revision of an approved document, drafts may be denoted as Issue 1A, 1B etc and when approved the status changes to Issue 2. Whatever the convention adopted, it is safer to be consistent so as to prevent mistakes and ambiguities.

Revision letters or numbers indicate maturity but not age. Dates can also be used as an indication of revision status but dates do not indicate whether the document is new or old and how many changes there have been. In some cases this is not important, but in others there are advantages in providing both date and revision status therefore denoting date and revision status is often the simplest solution.

Document referencing

Staff should have a means of being able to determine the correct revision status of documents they should use. You can do this through the work instructions, specification or planning documents, or by controlling the distribution, if the practice is to work to the latest issue. However, both these means have weaknesses. Documents can get lost, errors can creep into specifications and the cost of changing documents sometimes prohibits keeping them up to date. The issuing authority for each range of documents should maintain a register of documents showing the progression of changes that have been made since the initial issue. With configuration documents (documents which prescribe the features and characteristics of products and services) the relationship between documents of various issue states may be important. For example a Design Specification at issue 4 may equate with a Test Specification at issue 3 but not with the Test Specification at issue 2. This record is sometimes referred to as a Master Record Index or MRI but there is a distinct difference between a list of documents denoting issue state and a list of documents denoting issue compatibility state. The former is a Document Record Index and the later a Configuration Record Index. If there is no relationship between the document issues care should be taken not to imply a relationship by the title of the index.

The index may be issued to designated personnel or so as to preclude use of obsolete indices, it may be prudent not to keep hard copies. With organizations that operate on several sites using common documentation it may well be sensible to issue the index so that users have a means of determining the current version of documents.

It is not necessary to maintain one index. You can have as many as you like. In fact if you have several ranges of documents it may be prudent to create and index for each range.

Regarding electronically controlled documents, arranging them so that only the current versions are accessible is one solution. In such cases and for certain type of documents, document numbers, issues and dates may be of no concern to the user. If you have configured the security provisions so that only current documents can be accessed, providing issue status, approval status, dates etc adds no value for the user, but is necessary for those maintaining the database. It may be necessary to provide access to previous versions of documents. Personnel in a product-support function may need to use documentation for various models of a product as they devise repair schemes and perform maintenance. Often documentation for products no longer in production carries a different identity but common components may still be utilized in current models.

Re-approving documents after change (4.2.3b)

The standard requires that documents *be re-approved after revision*.

What does this mean?

Following a change the revised document needs to be subject to approval as verification of its fitness for purpose.

Why is this necessary?

This requirement responds to the Factual Approach Principle.

As the original document was subject to approval prior to issue it follows that any changes should also be subject to approval prior to issue of the revised version. The approval does not have to be by the same people or functions that approved the original although this may be the case in many situations. The criteria are not whether the people or functions are the same, but whether the approvers are authorized. Organizations change and therefore people and functions may take on different responsibilities.

> **1994–2000 Differences**
> Previously the standard required changes to documents and data be reviewed and approved by the same functions/ organizations that performed the original review and approval unless specifically designated otherwise. Although the requirement is less prescriptive it meets the same intent simply because the authority of functions is required to be defined by 5.5.2.

How is this implemented?

Depending on the nature of the change, it may be necessary to provide the approval authorities with factual information upon which a decision can be made. The change request and the change record should provide this information. The change request provides the reason for change and the change note provides details of what has changed.

The change should be processed in the same way as the original document and submitted to the appropriate authorities for approval. If approval is denoted on the front sheet of your documents, you will need to reissue the front sheet with every change. This is another good reason to use separate approval sheets. They save time and paper. With electronically controlled documents, archived versions provide a record of approvals providing they are protected from revision.

Ensuring the availability of controlled documents (4.2.3d)

1994–2000 Differences
Previously the standard required the supplier to ensure that the pertinent issues of appropriate documents are available at all locations where operations essential to the effective functioning of the quality system are performed.

There is no difference in the intent of the previous requirement.

The standard requires that *relevant versions of applicable documents are available at points of use.*

What does this mean?

The relevant version of a document is the version that should be used for a task. It may not be the latest version because you may have reason to use a different version of a document such as when building or repairing different versions of the same product. Applicable documents are those that are needed to carry out work. *Availability at points of use* means the users have access to the documents they need at the location where the work is to be performed. It does not mean that users should possess copies of the documents they need, in fact this is undesirable because the copies may become outdated and not withdrawn from use.

Why is this necessary?

This requirement responds to the Process Approach Principle.

This requirement exists to ensure that access to documents is afforded when required. Information essential for the performance of work needs to be accessible to those performing it otherwise they may resort to other means of obtaining what they need that may result in errors, inefficiencies and hazards.

How is this implemented?

Availability

In order to make sure that documents are available you should not keep them under lock and key (or password protected) except for those where restricted access is necessary for security purposes. You need to establish who wants which documents and when they need them. The work instructions should specify the documents that *are* required for the task so that those documents not specified are not essential. It should not be left to the individual to determine which documents are essential and which are not. If there is a need for access out of normal working hours, access has to be provided. The more copies there are the greater the chance of documents not being maintained so minimize the number of copies. A common practice is to issue documents to managers only and not the users. This is particularly true of management system documents. One finds that only the managers hold copies of the Quality Manual. In some firms all the managers reside in the same building, even along the same corridor and it is in such circumstances that one invariably finds that these copies have not been maintained. It is therefore impractical to have all the copies of the Quality Manual in one place. Distribute the documents by location, not by named individuals. Distribute to libraries, or document control centres so that access is provided to everyone and so that someone has responsibility for keeping them up to date. If using an *intranet*, the problems of distribution are less difficult but there will always be some groups of people who need access to hard copy (Hoyle, David, 1996)[13].

The document availability requirement applies to both internal and external documents alike. Customer documents such as contracts, drawings, specifications and standards need to be available to those who need them to execute their responsibilities. Often these documents are only held in paper form and therefore distribution lists will be needed to control their location. If documents in the public domain are required, they only need be available when required for use and need not be available from the moment they are specified in a specification or procedure. You should only have to produce such documents when they are needed for the work being undertaken at the time of the audit. However, you would need to demonstrate that you could obtain timely access when needed. If you provide a lending service to users of copyrighted documents, you would need a register indicating to whom they were loaned so that you can retrieve them when needed by others.

A document that is not ready for use or is not used often may be archived. But it needs to be accessible otherwise when it is called for it won't be there. It is therefore necessary to ensure that storage areas, or storage mediums provide secure storage from which documents can be retrieved when needed. Storing documents off-site under the management of another organization may give rise to problems if they cannot be contacted when you need the documents.

Archiving documents on magnetic tape can also present problems when the tape cannot be found or read by the new technology that has been installed! Electronic storage presents very different problems to conventional storage and gives rise to the retention of 'insurance copies' in paper should the retrieval mechanism fail.

Relevant versions of internal documents

A question often asked by Assessors is 'How do you know you have the correct issue of that document?' The question should not arise with an electronically controlled documentation system that prohibits access to archived versions. If your system is not that sophisticated, one way of ensuring the latest issue is to control the distribution of documents so that each time a document changes, the amendments are issued to the same staff who received the original versions. If you identify authentic copies issued by the issuing authority in some way, by coloured header, red stamp or other means, it will be immediately apparent which copies are authentic and under control and which are uncontrolled. Another way is to stamp uncontrolled documents with an 'Uncontrolled Document' stamp. All paper documents should carry some identification as to the issuing authority so that you can check the current issue if you are in doubt. The onus should always rest with the user. It is his or her responsibility to check that he or she has the correct issue of a document before work commences. One way of signifying authenticity is to give documents copy numbers in red ink as a practical way of retaining control over their distribution. If documents are filed in binders by part or volume, the binder can be given a copy number, but you will need a cross-reference list of who holds which copy.

Where different versions of the same document are needed, you will need a means of indicating which issue of which document is to be used. One method is to specify the pertinent issues of documents in the specifications, drawings, work instructions or planning documents. This should be avoided if at all possible because it can cause maintenance problems when documents change. It is sometimes better to declare that staff should use the latest version unless otherwise stated and provide staff with a means of determining what the latest version is.

Relevant versions of external documents

In some cases the issues of public and customer specific documents are stated in the contract and therefore it is important to ensure that you possess the correct version before you commence work. Where the customer specifies the issue status of public domain documents that apply you need a means of preventing their withdrawal from use in the event that they are revised during the term of the contract.

Where the issue status of public domain documents is not specified in a contract you may either have a free choice as to the issue you use or, as more likely, you may need to use the latest issue in force. Where this is the case you will need a means of being informed when such documents are revised to ensure you can obtain the latest version. The ISO 9000 series for instance is reviewed every 5 years so could well be revised at 5-year intervals. With national and international legislation the situation is rather different because this can change at *any* time. You need some means of alerting yourself to changes that affect you and there are several methods from which to choose:

- Subscribing to the issuing agency of a standards updating service;
- Subscribing to a general publication which provides news of changes in standards and legislation;
- Subscribing to a trade association which provides bulletins to its members on changes in the law and relevant standards;
- Subscribing to the publications of the appropriate standards body or agency;
- Subscribing to a society or professional institution that updates its members with news of changes in laws and standards;
- Joining a business club which keeps its members informed of such matters;
- As a registered company you will receive all kinds of complementary information from government agencies advising you of changes in legislation.

As an ISO 9000 registered company you will receive bulletins from your certification body on matters affecting registration and you can subscribe to ISO 9000 News (International Organization of Standardization, 2001)[17] to obtain worldwide news of events and changes in the ISO 9000 arena.

The method you choose will depend on the number and diversity of external documents you need to maintain and the frequency of usage.

Issuing change instructions

If you require an urgent change to a document, a legitimate means of issuing change instructions is to generate a Document Change Note. The Change Note should detail the changes to be made and be authorized by the appropriate authorities. On receipt of the Change Note the recipients make the changes in manuscript or by page replacement, and annotate the changes with the serial number of the Change Note. This practice primarily applies to paper systems but with electronically controlled documents, changes can be made to documents in a database without any one knowing and therefore it is necessary to provide an alert so that users are informed when a change has been made that may affect them. If the information is of a type that users invariably access rather than rely on memory, change instructions may be unnecessary.

Ensuring documents are legible and identifiable (4.2.3e)

1994–2000 Differences

Previously requirements for legibility, identification and access applied only to quality records.

The impact of these changes should be negligible.

The standard requires documents *to remain legible and readily identifiable.*

What does this mean?

Legibility refers to the ease with which the information in a document can be read or viewed. A document is readily identifiable if it carries some indication that will quickly distinguish it from similar documents. Any document that requires a reader to browse through it looking for clues is clearly not readily identifiable.

Why is this necessary?

This requirement responds to the Process Approach Principle.

The means of transmission and use of documents may cause degradation such that they fail to convey the information originally intended. Confusion with document identity could result in a document being misplaced, destroyed or otherwise being unobtainable. It can also result in incorrect documents being located and used.

How is this implemented?

Legibility

This requirement is so obvious it hardly needs to be specified. As a general rule, any document that is printed or photocopied should be checked for legibility before distribution. Legibility is not often a problem with electronically controlled documents. However, there are cases where diagrams cannot be magnified on screen so it would be prudent to verify the capability of the technology before releasing documents. Not every user will have perfect eyesight! Documents transmitted by fax present legibility problems due to the quality of transmission and the medium on which the information is printed. Heat sensitive paper is being replaced with plain paper but many organizations still use the old technology. You simply have to decide your approach. For any communication required for reference, it would be prudent to use photocopy or scan the fax electronically and dispose of the original.

Documents used in a workshop environment may require protection from oil and grease. Signatures are not always legible so it is prudent to have a policy of printing the name under the signature. Documents subject to frequent photocopying can degrade and result in illegible areas.

Identification

Although a new requirement, it is unusual to find documents in use that carry no identification at all. Three primary means are used for document identification – classification, titles and identification numbers. Classification divides documents into groups based on their purpose – policies, procedures, records, plans, etc are classes of documents. Titles are acceptable providing there are no two documents with the same title in the same class. If you have hundreds of documents it may prove difficult to sustain uniqueness. Identification can be made unique in one organization but outside it may not be unique. However, the title as well as the number is usually sufficient. Electronically controlled documents do not require a visible identity other than the title in its classification. Classifying documents with codes enables their sorting by class (Hoyle, David, 1996)[16].

Control of external documents (4.2.3f)

The standard requires *documents of external origin to be identified and their distribution controlled*.

What does this mean?

An external document is one produced externally to the organization's management system. There are two types of external documents, those in the public domain and those produced by specific customers and/or suppliers. Controlling distribution means designating those who need external documents and ensuring that any change of ownership is known about and approved.

1994–2000 Differences

Previously the standard required the supplier to establish and maintain documented procedures to control documents of external origin such as standards and customer drawings.

Although an additional requirement for distribution to be controlled has been inserted, the intent remains unchanged as control of documents should include control of their distribution.

Why is this necessary?

External documents are as much part of the management system as any other document and hence require control although the control that can be exercised over external documents is somewhat limited. You cannot for instance control the revision, approval or identification of external documents therefore all the requirements concerning document changes will not apply. You can, however, control the use and amendment of external documents by specifying which versions of external documents are to be used and you can remove invalid or obsolete external documents from use or identify them in a way that users recognize as invalid or obsolete. You can control the amendment of external documents by controlled distribution of amendment instructions sent to you by the issuing agency.

How is this implemented?

External documents are likely to carry their own identification that is unique to the issuing authority. If they do not carry reference number, the issuing authority is normally indicated which serves to distinguish them from internal documents. Where no identification is present other than a title, the document may be invalid. This sometimes happens with external data and forms. If the source cannot be confirmed and the information is essential, it would be sensible to incorporate the information into an appropriate internal document.

In order to control the distribution of external documents you need to designate the custodian in the appropriate process descriptions or procedures and introduce a mechanism for being notified of any change in ownership. If the external documents are classified, prior approval should be granted before ownership changes. This is particularly important with military contracts because all such documents have to be accounted for. Unlike the internal documents, many external documents may only be available in paper form so that registers will be needed to keep track of them. If electronic versions are provided, you will need to make them 'read only' and put in place safeguards against inadvertent deletion from the server.

Preventing unintended use of obsolete documents (4.2.3g)

The standard requires *the unintended use of obsolete documents to be prevented and a suitable identification to be applied to obsolete documents retained for any purpose.*

What does this mean?

In simple terms an obsolete document is one that is no longer required for operational purposes. If an obsolete document has not been removed from the workplace there remains a possibility that it could be used. A suitable identification is one that readily distinguishes a current version of a document from an obsolete version.

Regrettably the standard no longer refers to invalid documents as well as obsolete documents. Invalid documents may not be obsolete and may take several forms. They may be:

- Documents of the wrong issue status for a particular task
- Draft documents which have not been destroyed
- Documents which have not been maintained up to date with amendments
- Documents which have been altered or changed without authorization
- Copies of documents which have not been authenticated
- Unauthorized documents or documents not traceable through the management system
- Illegal documents

> **1994–2000 Differences**
>
> Previously the standard required
>
> (a) the supplier to ensure that invalid and/or obsolete documents are promptly removed from all points of issue or use, or otherwise assured against unintended use.
>
> (b) any obsolete document retained for legal and/or knowledge preservation purposes be suitably identified.
>
> There is no difference in the intent of this new requirement – it is less verbose.

Why is this necessary?

This requirement responds to the Process Approach Principle.

A means of distinguishing current documents from obsolete documents is needed to prevent their unintended use. Use of obsolete information may lead to errors, failures and hazards.

There are several reasons why you may wish to retain documents that are replaced by later versions:

- As a record of events (what did we do last time?)
- For verifying that the correct changes were made (what did it say in the last version or the first version?)
- For justifying rejection of a discarded solution (we've had this one before – what did we decide on that occasion?)
- For investigating problems that did not occur previously (what was it that we did differently?)
- For preparing a defence in a product liability case (what controls were in place when we made this product?)
- For learning from previous designs (how did we solve that problem?)
- For restoring/refurbishing a product (they don't make them like they used to – do they?)
- For reference to explanations, descriptions, translations etc in order to preserve consistency in subsequent revisions or new documents (what wording did we use last time we encountered this topic or term?)

How is this implemented?

With an electronic documentation system, access to obsolete documents can be barred to all except the chosen few. All it needs is for operational versions to be held in an operational directory and archived versions to be transferred into an archive directory automatically when a new version is released. On being transferred the revision status should be changed automatically to 'obsolete' indicating that later versions have been released.

With paper documents, it is more difficult. There are two options. You either remove the obsolete documents or mark them in some way that they are readily recognizable as obsolete.

It is unnecessary to remove invalid or obsolete documents if you provide staff with the means of determining the pertinent issues of documents to use. There are often valid reasons for retaining obsolete documents. One may need to remove copies of previous versions of a document but retain the master for reference purposes. You cannot demonstrate to an assessor that you corrected a deficiency if you don't retain the version that contained the deficiency as well as the subsequent version. If you do not have a means of readily distinguishing the correct version of a document, amendment instructions should require that the version being replaced is destroyed or returned to the document controller. If you allow uncontrolled copies to be taken, you will need to provide a means of distinguishing controlled and uncontrolled documents.

One way of identifying obsolete documents is to write SUPERSEDED or OBSOLETE on the front cover, but doing this requires that the custodian is informed. When a version of a document is replaced with a new version, the withdrawal of the obsolete version can be accomplished in the amendment instructions that accompany the revision. When documents become obsolete by total replacement, their withdrawal can also be accomplished with the amendment instruction. However where a document becomes obsolete and is not replaced there needs to be a Document Withdrawal Notice which informs the custodian of the action to be taken and the reason for withdrawal.

There is no simple way of identifying invalid documents because the reasons that they are invalid will vary. By printing authentic documents on coloured paper or providing paper with a special header one can inject a degree of control. Placing the approval signatures on the front sheet will immediately identify an unapproved document. However, the onus must rest with the user who if properly trained and motivated will instinctively refrain from using invalid documents.

With electronically controlled documents the invalid documents can be held in a database with access limited to those managing the documents. In such cases, an approved document becomes invalid when its status is denoted as draft or withdrawn.

Control of records (4.2.1e and 4.2.4)

Establishing and maintaining records (4.2.4)

The standard requires records *to be established and maintained to provide evidence of conformity to requirements and the effective operation of the quality management system.*

What does this mean?

A record is defined in ISO 9000 as *a document stating results achieved or providing evidence of activities performed.*

Although a record is a document, the document control requirement of clause 4.2.3 do not apply to *records* primarily because records are not issued, neither do they exhibit revision status simply because they are results that are factual when recorded. If the facts change, a new record is usually created rather than the previous record revised. Even where a record is revised and new facts added, the old facts remain identified as to their date. The only reason for revising facts contained in a record without changing the identity of the record or the date when they were collected is where the facts were incorrectly recorded. This subtle difference demands different treatment for documents that are classed as records to those that are classed as informative. As with other types of documents, records result from processes and may be used as inputs to other processes.

Records required by the management system means records used or generated by the management system. There is therefore no requirement to produce records solely to satisfy an auditor. The records required are those for the effective operation of the organization's processes (see clause 4.1d of ISO 9001). If a record has no useful purpose within the management system there is no requirement that it be established or maintained.

This does not mean that a record is required to prove conformity with every single requirement for every product and service. There are those records required by the standard (see below) that are required for every product and service where applicable and in all other cases, audit records showing compliance on a sample of operations would be sufficient.

Compliance with many requirements can be demonstrated by observation, analysis, interview or examination of documentation. If a result or an activity is not required to be recorded in order to manage the organization effectively and satisfy the interested parties, it is not necessary to maintain records of it.

Why is this necessary?

This requirement responds to the Factual Approach Principle.

The reason for establishing records is to provide information necessary for managing processes, meeting objectives and demonstrating compliance with requirements – both customer requirements and legal requirements.

The reason for maintaining records is to secure their access, integrity, durability and disposal. If information of this nature cannot be located, or is illegible, or its integrity is suspect, or is obsolete, the decisions that require this information cannot be made on the basis of fact and will therefore be unsound or not as robust as intended. Lost, altered or illegible records can result in an inability to prove or disprove liability.

How is this implemented?

Establishing records

Records that are governed by the requirements of clause 4.2.4 should be classified as *controlled records* so as to distinguish them from other records. If information needs to be recorded in order to manage the organization effectively, these records should be identified in the governing procedures as being required. This will then avoid arguments on what is or is not a controlled record, because once you have chosen to identify a record as a controlled record you have invoked all the requirements that are addressed in clause 4.2.4. The references to clause 4.2.4 give some guidance to the types of records required but should not be interpreted as definitive. In the 1994 version of ISO 9001 there were 20 references to records. In ISO 9001:2000 although now reduced to 19 they are not 19 of the original 20 as there are 5 new ones. The numbers don't compute because there were 3 types of records required for special process whereas only a general requirement is now stated. These are identified as follows:

1 Management review records (Clause 5.6.3)
2 Records of education, experience, training and qualifications (Clause 6.2.2)
3 Records needed to provide evidence that realization processes and resultant product meet requirement (Clause 7.1) – This is new
4 Customer requirement review records (Clause 7.2.2)
5 Design and development inputs (clause 7.3.2) – This is new and does not fit the criteria for a record (see Chapter 7)
6 Design and development review records (Clause 7.3.4)
7 Design verification records (Clause 7.3.5)
8 Design validation records (Clause 7.3.6) – This is new

9 Design and development change review records (Clause 7.3.7) – This is new
10 Supplier evaluation records (Clause 7.4.1)
11 Validation arrangements for processes to include requirements for records (Clause 7.5.2)
12 Product identification records (Clause 7.5.3)
13 Records of unsuitable customer property (Clause 7.5.4)
14 Calibration records (Clause 7.6)
15 Internal audit results are to be recorded (Clause 8.2.2)
16 Product verification records (Clause 8.2.4)
17 Nonconformity records (Clause 8.3)
18 Results of corrective actions taken are to be recorded (Clause 8.5.2) – This is new
19 Results of preventive actions taken are to be recorded (Clause 8.5.3) – This is new

There are 4 instances where records required by ISO 9001:1994 are not addressed directly by ISO 9001:2000:

1 Positive recall records (These are now addressed by product identification records in Clause 7.5.3)
2 Verification records for test hardware and test software (These are now addressed by validation of processes in Clause 7.5.2)
3 Nonconformity investigation records (These are not records of Type A or B)
4 Subcontract records (These are addressed by Clause 7.5.3)

Such an analysis is only useful to illustrate that not all records required for effective quality management are identified in ISO 9001. It is unnecessary to produce a record testifying that each requirement of ISO 9001 has been met. For example there is no obvious benefit from *maintaining* records that a document is legible (clause 5.5.6e), that a customer enquired about some information that was later provided (clause 7.2.3) or that a particular filing system was improved (clause 8.1). At the time, the facts may be recorded temporarily but disposed of as the event passes into history. Such information may not be needed for future use. However, there are obvious benefits from requiring records to be established for:

- Customer complaints
- Warranty claims
- Failure analysis reports
- Process capability studies
- Service reports
- Concessions

- Change requests
- Subcontractor assessments
- Performance analysis
- Deviations and waivers
- Contract change records
- Quality cost data
- External quality audit records

Regarding the effectiveness of the management system, the very existence of a document is not evidence of effectiveness but it could be regarded as a record. To be a *record*, the document would need to contain results of an examination into the effectiveness of the system.

One can demonstrate the effective operation of the management system in several ways:

- By examination of customer feedback
- By examination of system, process and product audit results
- By examination of the management review records
- By examination of quality cost data
- By examination of results against the organization's objectives

Showing records that every requirement of the standard has been met will not however, demonstrate that the system is effective. You may have met the requirement but not carried out the right tasks or made the right decisions. The effectiveness of the management system should be judged by how well it fulfils its purpose. Although there is no specific requirement for you to do this, you can deduce this meaning from the requirement in clause 5.6.1 for the system to be reviewed for its continuing suitability. Some Assessors may quote this requirement when finding that you have not recorded a particular activity that is addressed in the standard. They are not only mistaken but also attempting to impose an unnecessary burden on companies that will be perceived as bureaucratic nonsense. One can demonstrate the effectiveness of the system simply by producing and examining one or more of the above records.

The subcontractor records that are delivered to you should form part of your records. However, the controls you can exercise over your subcontractor's records are somewhat limited. You have a right to the records you have paid for but no more unless you invoke the requirements of this clause of the standard in your subcontract. Your rights will probably only extend to your subcontractor's records being made available for your inspection on their premises therefore you will not be able to take away copies. It is also likely that any subcontractor records you do receive are *copies* and not originals. Before placing the contract you will need to assess what records you will require to be delivered and what records the contractor should produce and retain.

Maintaining records

The standard requires records to be maintained.

There are three types of maintenance regarding records.

- Keeping records up to date
- Keeping the information in the records upto date
- Keeping the records in good condition (see under *protection and storage*)

Some records are designed to collect data because they pass through the process and need to be promptly updated with current information. Remember:

The filing provisions should enable your records to be readily retrievable, however, you need to maintain your files if the stored information is to be of any use. In practice, records will collect at the place they are created and unless promptly removed to secure files may be mislaid, lost or inadvertently destroyed. Once complete, records should not be changed. If they are subsequently found to be inaccurate, new records should be created. Alterations to records should be prohibited because they bring into doubt the validity of any certification or authentication because no one will know whether the alteration was made before or after the records were authenticated. In the event that alterations are unavoidable due to time or economic reasons, errors should be struck through in order that the original wording can still be read, and the new data added and endorsed by the certifying authority.

Records held electronically present a different problem and why a new requirement for the protection of records is introduced (see later).

Establishing a records procedure (4.2.4)

The standard requires records *to remain legible, readily identifiable and retrievable* and that *a procedure defines the controls needed for the identification, storage, protection, retrieval, retention time and disposition of records.*

What does this mean?

Records have a life cycle. They are generated during which time they acquire an identity and are then assigned for storage for a prescribed period. During use and storage they need to be protected from inadvertent or malicious destruction and as they may be required to support current activities or investigations, they need to be brought out of storage

1994–2000 Differences

Previously the standard required the supplier to establish and maintain documented procedures for identification, collection, indexing, access, filing, storage, maintenance and disposition of quality records.

Requirements for record collection, indexing, access and filing have been dropped.

quickly. When their usefulness has lapsed, a decision is made as to whether to retain them further or to destroy them.

Readily retrievable means that records can be obtained on demand within a reasonable period (hours not days or weeks) Readily identifiable means that the identity can be discerned at a glance.

Although the requirement implies a single procedure, several may be necessary because there are several unconnected tasks to perform. A procedure cannot in fact ensure a result. It may prescribe a course of action which if followed may lead to the correct result, but it is the process that ensures the result not the procedure.

Why is this necessary?

This requirement responds to the Process Approach Principle.

The requirement for a procedure is not as important as the topics the procedure is required to address. Records are important in the management of processes and building customer confidence, therefore it is important that they be maintained, retained and accessible.

How is this implemented?

Records procedures

The revised requirement omits several aspects covered in clause 4.16 of the 1994 version.

- Collection of records is now addressed by Analysis of data (clause 8.4)
- Indexing of records is a specific form of identification and is therefore already addressed
- Access is now addressed by the requirement for record retrieval
- Filing is a specific form of storage and is therefore already addressed

You may only need one procedure which covers all the requirements but this is not always practical. The provisions you make for specific records should be included in the documentation for controlling the activity being recorded. For example, provisions for inspection records should be included in the inspection procedures; provisions for design review records should be included in the design review procedure. Within such procedures you should provide the forms (or content requirement for the records), the identification, collection/ submission provisions, the indexing and filing provisions. It may be more practical to cover the storage, disposal and retention provisions in separate procedures because they may not be type-dependent. Where each department retains their own records, these provisions may vary and therefore warrant separate procedures.

Legibility of records

Unlike prescriptive documents, records may contain handwritten elements and therefore it is important that the handwriting is legible. If this becomes a problem, you either improve discipline or consider electronic data capture. Records also become soiled in a workshop environment so may need to be protected to remain legible. With electronically captured data, legibility is often not a problem. However, photographs and other scanned images may not transfer as well as the original and lose detail so care has to be taken in selecting appropriate equipment for this task.

Identification of records

Whatever the records, they should carry some identification in order that you can determine what they are, what kind of information they record and what they relate to. A simple way of doing this is to give each record a reference number and a name or title in a prominent location on the record.

Records can take various forms – reports containing narrative, computer data, and forms containing data in boxes, graphs, tables, lists and many others. Where forms are used to collect data, they should carry a form number and name as their identification. When completed they should carry a serial number to give each a separate identity. Records should also be traceable to the product or service they represent and this can be achieved either within the reference number or separately, provided that the chance of mistaken identity is eliminated. The standard does not require records to be identifiable to the product involved but unless you do make such provision you will not be able to access the pertinent records or demonstrate conformance to specified requirements.

> **1994–2000 Differences**
>
> Previously the standard covered retrieval in four ways. It required:
>
> (a) that quality records be made available for evaluation by the customer or his representative for an agreed period, where agreed contractually
> (b) procedures for the filing of quality records
> (c) procedures for the access of quality records
> (d) procedures for the indexing of quality records.
>
> The intent of the requirements has not changed.

Retrieving records

You need to ensure that the records are accessible to those who will need to use them. This applies not only to current records but also to those in the archive and any 'insurance copies' you may have stored away. A balance has to be attained between security of the records and their accessibility. You may need to consider those who work outside normal working hours and those rare occasions when the troubleshooters are working late, perhaps away from base with their only contact via a computer link. In providing for record retrieval you need to consider two aspects. You need to enable authorized retrieval of records and prohibit unauthorized retrieval. If records are held in a locked room or filing cabinet, you need to nominate certain persons as key holders and ensure that these people can be contacted in an emergency. Your procedures should define how you provide and prohibit access to the records. With electronically held records, password protection will accomplish this objective provided that you control the enabling and disabling of passwords in the records database. For this reason it is advisable to install a personnel termination/movement process that ensures passwords are disabled or keys returned on departure of staff from their current post.

Remember these records are not personal property or the property of a particular department. They belong to the organization and are a record of the organization's performance. Such records should not be stored in personal files. The filing system you create should therefore be integrated with the organization's main filing system and the file location should either be specified in the procedure that defines the record or in a general filing procedure.

If you operate a computerized record system, filing will be somewhat different although the principles are the same as for paper records. Computerized records need to be located in named directories for ease of retrieval and the locations identified in the procedures.

Storage of records

Records soon grow into a mass of paper and occupy valuable floor space. To overcome this problem you may choose to microfilm the records but keep them in the same location or archive them in some remote location. In both cases you need to control the process and the conditions of storage. With paper archives you will need to maintain records of what is where and if the archive is under the control of another group inside or outside the organization, you will need adequate controls to prevent loss of identity and inadvertent destruction.

A booking in/out system should be used for completed records when they are in storage in order to prevent unauthorized removal.

You will need a means of ensuring that you have all the records that have been produced and that none are missing or if they are, you know the reason. One solution is to index records and create and maintain registers listing the records in numerical order as reference or serial numbers are allocated. The records could be filed in sequence so that you can easily detect if any are missing, or you can file

---

1994–2000 Differences

Previously the standard required the supplier to establish and maintain documented procedures for maintenance of quality records and for records to be stored in facilities that provide a suitable environment to prevent damage or deterioration and to prevent loss.

The intent of the requirements has not changed and is less verbose.

the records elsewhere providing your registers or your procedures identify the location.

Records should also be stored in a logical order (filed numerically or by date) to aid retrieval. With electronically held records their storage should be secure from inadvertent deletion. If archived on CD ROM, floppy disk or tape, protection methods should be employed (see below).

Protection of records

The protection of records applies when records are in use and in storage and covers such conditions as destruction, deletion, corruption, change, loss and deterioration arising from wilful or inadvertent action.

On the subject of loss, you will need to consider loss by fire, theft, and unauthorized removal. If using computers you will also need to consider loss through computer viruses and unauthorized access, deletion or the corruption of files.

It is always risky to keep only one copy of a document. If computer-generated, you can easily take another copy provided you always save it, but if manually generated, its loss can be very costly. It is therefore prudent to produce additional copies of critical records as an insurance against inadvertent loss. These 'insurance copies' should be stored in a remote location under the control of the same authority that controls the original records. Insurance copies of computer disks should also be kept in case of problems with the hard disk or file server. Data back-up at defined periods should be conducted and the backed-up data stored securely at a different location than the original data.

Records, especially those used in workshop environments can become soiled and therefore provisions should be made to protect them against attack by lubricants, dust, oil and other materials which may render them unusable. Plastic wallets can provide adequate protection whilst records remain in use.

Retention of records

It is important that records are not destroyed before their useful life is over. There are several factors to consider when determining the retention time for records.

- *The duration of the contract* – some records are only of value whilst the contract is in force.
- *The life of the product* – access to the records will probably not be needed for some considerable time, possibly long after the contract has closed. On defence contracts the contractor has to keep records for up to 20 years and for product liability purposes, in the worst-case situation (taking account of appeals) you could be asked to produce records up to 17 years after you made the product.

● *The period between management system assessments* – assessors may wish to see evidence that corrective actions from the last assessment were taken. If the period of assessment is three years and you dispose of the evidence after 2 years, you will have some difficulty in convincing the assessor that you corrected the deficiency.

You will also need to take account of the subcontractor records and ensure adequate retention times are invoked in the contract.

Where the retention time is actually specified can present a problem. If you specify it in a general procedure you are likely to want to prescribe a single figure, say 5 years for all records. However, this may cause storage problems – it may be more appropriate therefore to specify the retention times in the procedures that describe the records. In this way you can be selective.

You will also need a means of determining when the retention time has expired so that if necessary you can dispose of the records. The retention time doesn't mean that you must dispose of them when the time expires – only that you must retain the records for at least that stated period. Not only will the records need to be dated but the files that contain the records need to be dated and if stored in an archive, the shelves or drawers also dated. It is for this reason that all documents should carry a date of origin and this requirement needs to be specified in the procedures that describe the records. If you can rely on the selection process a simple method is to store the records in bins or computer disks that carry the date of disposal.

While the ISO 9001 requirement applies only to records, you may also need to retain tools, jigs, fixtures, test software – in fact anything that is needed to repair or reproduce equipment in order to honour your long-term commitments.

Should the customer specify a retention period greater than what you prescribe in your procedures, special provisions will need to be made and this is a potential area of risk. Customers may choose not to specify a particular time and require you to seek approval before destruction. Any contract that requires you to do something different creates a problem in conveying the requirements to those who are to implement them. The simple solution is to persuade your customer to accept your policy. You may not want to change your procedures for one contract. If you can't change the contract, the only alternative is to issue special instructions. You may be better off storing the records in a special contract store away from the normal store or alternatively attach special labels to the files to alert the people looking after the archives.

Disposition of records

Disposition in this context means the disposal of records once their useful life has ended. The requirement should not be confused with that on the retention of records. Retention times are one thing and disposal procedures quite another.

As stated previously, records are the property of the organization and not personal property so their destruction should be controlled. Controls should ensure that records are not destroyed without prior authorization and, depending on the medium on which data are recorded and the security classification of the data, you may also need to specify the method of disposal. The management would not be pleased to read details in the national press of the organization's performance, collected from a waste disposal site by a zealous newspaper reporter – a problem often reported as encountered by government departments!

Validation of records

The standard does not specifically require records to be authenticated, certified or validated other than product verification records in clause 8.2.4. A set of results without being endorsed with the signature of the person who captured them or other authentication lacks credibility. Facts that have been obtained by whatever means should be certified for three reasons:

- They provide a means of tracing the result to the originator in the event of problems.
- They indicate that the provider believes them to be correct.
- They enable you to verify whether the originator was appropriately qualified.
- They give the results credibility.

If the records are generated by computer and retained in computerized form, a means needs to be provided for the results to be authenticated. This can be accomplished through appropriate process controls by installing provisions for automated data recording or preventing unauthorized access.

Summary

In this chapter we have examined the requirements contained in section 4 of ISO 9001. Although clause 4.1 is quite short, the six requirements addressing processes encapsulate the essence of the standard. We have explored the ways in which a management system may be defined and documented and discovered a range of methods that can be used. Perhaps one of the most significant differences between the 1994 and 2000 versions of ISO 9001 is that organizations are now free to choose the documents they need to manage the business. This simple change should signal an end to mountains of paperwork created simply to satisfy auditors. It should result in a change in perception. The system should no longer be perceived as a set of documents but as a means to achieve the organization's objectives. Effort should be seen to be directed towards improving performance rather than towards improving documents.

Quality Management System Questionnaire

General requirements

1 What process did you employ to establish the management system?
2 How did you identify the processes needed for the management system?
3 How did you determine the sequence and interaction of the identified processes?
4 How did you determine criteria and methods required to ensure the effective operation and control of the identified processes?
5 How do you ensure the management system is implemented in accordance with the organization's policies?
6 How do you manage the identified processes so they deliver outcomes that satisfy the interested parties?
7 How do you ensure the availability of information necessary to support the operation and monitoring of the identified processes?
8 How do you ensure the availability of resources necessary to support the operation and monitoring of the identified processes?
9 How do you measure, monitor and analyse the identified processes?
10 How do you maintain a management system so that it continually fulfils the purpose for which it was established?
11 How do you ensure the effectiveness of the management system is continually improved?
12 How do you ensure that the actions necessary to achieve planned results and the continual improvement of the identified processes are implemented?

Documentation requirements

13 What documents describe the management system?
14 How do you ensure that management system documentation includes documents required by the organization to ensure the effective planning, operation and control of its processes?
15 What criteria have been used to determine the extent of management system documentation required?
16 In what document is the scope of the management system described?
17 In what document is the sequence and interaction of organization's processes defined?
18 In what document is justification given for any exclusion to the requirements of ISO 9001?
19 In what document are the documented procedures established for the management system identified?
20 How do you ensure that documents required by the management system are controlled?

21 In what document are the provisions needed to control the organization's documents defined?

22 How do you ensure that documents are approved for adequacy prior to issue?

23 How do you ensure that documents are periodically reviewed for adequacy?

24 How do you ensure that documents are updated as necessary and re-approved following their review?

25 How do you ensure that changes to documents are identified?

26 How do you ensure that the current revision status of documents is identified?

27 How do you ensure that documents are re-approved after their revision?

28 How do you ensure that relevant versions of applicable documents are available at points of use?

29 How do you ensure documents remain legible and readily identifiable?

30 How do you ensure that documents of external origin are identified?

31 How do you control distribution of documents of external origin?

32 How do you prevent the unintended use of obsolete documents?

33 How do you identify obsolete documents retained for any purpose?

34 What records have been established to provide evidence of conformity to requirements?

35 What records have been established to provide evidence of the effective operation of the management system?

36 How do you ensure records remain legible, readily identifiable and retrievable?

37 In what document are the controls needed for the identification, storage, protection, retrieval, retention and disposition of records defined?

Quality Management System – Food for Thought

1 Is your system thought of as a set of documents or a set of interconnected processes that deliver the organizations objectives?

2 Is your system integrated into the environment so that people do the right things right without having to be told?

3 Is your system a collection of interconnected processes rather than a series of interconnected functions?

4 Does every process in the chain of processes from requirements to their satisfaction add value?

5 Are your business objectives functionally oriented driving a functional oriented organization or are they process oriented?

6 If you have simply changed the names of your procedures to reflect processes, where have you defined the process objectives, the resources and the

behaviours required to cause these objectives to be achieved and the measures required to determine process adequacy, efficiency and effectiveness?

7 Are your processes described simply as a series of transactions or are there provisions in the process to manage its performance?

8 Do the outputs from one process connect with other processes?

9 Do all the inputs to a process have their origin in other processes or external organizations?

10 Do you have measures that enable you to determine how well each process is performing and are these known to those controlling the process?

11 Is there any activity, task or processes that exists only to meet the requirements of ISO 9001?

12 Are you sure that all the documentation in place is needed for the effective operation and control of your processes?

13 There are six ways of conveying information. Before you document, have you eliminated the other five ways as being unsuitable for the particular situation?

14 If a person moves onto another job, how much of what is removed from the process is essential for the process to maintain its capability?

15 How much of what affects your ability to achieve results is dependent upon staff following documented procedures?

16 How much of what affects your ability to achieve results is dependent upon the physical and human environment in which your staff work?

17 How much of what affects your ability to achieve results is dependent upon your staff's ability to do the right things right?

18 How much of what affects your ability to achieve results is dependent upon your staff's motivation to do the right things right?

19 Do you question the effectiveness of established policies and procedures first when the customer complains or do you look for someone to blame?

20 What causes the actions and decisions for which there are no documented policies or procedures?

21 Are you managing a set of functions or a series of processes and do you know the difference?

22 Do you know what each process aims to achieve?

23 Do you know how each process causes the observed results?

24 Do you know whether the process is producing outcomes that satisfy the process objectives?

25 Do you know how to change process performance to bring it into line with the objectives?

Bibliography

1. Juran, J. M., (1995). *Managerial Breakthrough Second Edition*, McGraw-Hill.
2. Hammer, Michael and Champy, James (1993). *Reengineering the corporation*, Harper Business.

3. Hoyle, David and Thompson, John (2000). *Converting a Quality Management System using the Process Approach*, Transition Support.
4. Hoyle, David and Thompson, John (2000). *Converting a Quality Management System using the Process Approach*, Transition Support.
5. US Department of Defense, (2001). www.idef.com.
   All IDEF models can be downloaded from this web site
6. Hoyle, David and Thompson, John (2001). *ISO 9000:2000 Auditor Questions*, Transition Support.
7. Hoyle, David and Thompson, John (2000). *Converting a Quality Management System using the Process Approach*, Transition Support.
8. Juran, J. M., (1995). *Managerial Breakthrough Second Edition*, McGraw-Hill.
9. Hoyle, David and Thompson, John (2000). *Converting a Quality Management System using the Process Approach*, Transition Support.
10. Juran, J. M., (1995). *Managerial Breakthrough Second Edition*, McGraw-Hill.
11. Imai, Masaaki (1986). *KAIZEN, The key to Japanese Competitive Success*, McGraw-Hill.
12. Juran, J. M., (1995). *Managerial Breakthrough Second Edition*, McGraw-Hill.
13. Hoyle, David (1996). *ISO 9000 Quality System Development Handbook*, Butterworth Heinemann.
14. Hoyle, David (1996). *ISO 9000 Quality System Development Handbook*, Butterworth Heinemann.
15. Hoyle, David (1996). *ISO 9000 Quality System Development Handbook*, Butterworth Heinemann.
16. Hoyle, David (1996). *ISO 9000 Quality System Development Handbook*, Butterworth Heinemann.
17. International Organization of Standardization, (2001). www.iso.ch.

Chapter 5
Management responsibility

***

Attention to quality can become the
organization's mind-set only if all of its
managers – indeed all of its people – live it

Tom Peters

Summary of requirements

While the implementation of *all* requirements in ISO 9001 are strictly management's responsibility, those in section 5 of the standard are indeed the responsibility of top management. All clauses in this section commence with the phrase "Top management shall . . ." The first four clauses clearly apply to the strategic planning processes of the organization rather than to specific products. However, it is the Board of Directors that should take note of these requirements when establishing their vision, values, mission and objectives. These requirements are amongst the most important in the standard. There is a clear linkage between customer's needs, policy, objectives and processes. One leads to the other in a continuous cycle as addressed previously in Chapter 2. Although the clauses in section 5 are not intended as a sequence, each represents a part of a process that establishes direction and keeps the organization on course. The cycle commences with a *Vision* – a statement of what we want to be or do, and then a *Focus on customers* for it is the customer that will decide whether or not the organization survives. It is only when you know what your market is, who your customers will be and where they will be that you can define the *Purpose* or *Mission* of the organization. From the purpose or mission you can devise a *Vision* (where you want to get to – what you want to become) and from the mission come the *Policies or Values* that will guide you on your journey. These policies help frame the *Objectives,* the milestones en route towards your destination. The policies won't work unless there is *Commitment* so that everyone pulls in the same direction. *Plans* have to be made to achieve the objectives and these plans need to identify and lay out the *Processes* that will be employed to deliver the results – for all work is a process and without work nothing will be achieved. The plans also need to identify the *Responsibilities and Authority* of those who will be engaged in the endeavour. As a consequence it is essential that effective channels of *Internal Communication* be established to ensure that everyone understands what they are required to achieve and how they are performing. No journey should be undertaken without a means of knowing where you are, how far you have to go, what obstacles are likely to lie in the path ahead or what forces will influence your success. It is therefore necessary to collate the facts on current performance and predictions of what lies ahead so that a *Management Review* can take place to determine what action is required to keep the organization on course or whether any changes are necessary to the course or the capability of the organization in order to fulfil its purpose and mission.

Management commitment (5.1)

Commitment to the QMS (5.1)

The standard requires that top management *provide evidence of its commitment to the development and implementation of the quality management system and continually improving its effectiveness.*

> **1994–2000 Differences**
> Previously the standard required the supplier's management with executive responsibility to define and document its commitment to quality. This change places the emphasis on providing evidence of commitment that is more to do with top management's actions and decisions than with documentation.

What does this mean?

Top management

Throughout this section of the standard the term *Top management* is used. Previously ISO 9001:1994 used the term Management with executive responsibility. Although it is customary to only grant executive responsibility to department level managers and above, the requirement did not compel the top managers and directors to take any of the actions implied by the standard because executive responsibility could in fact be held by personnel at any level in an organization's hierarchy. This change is therefore significant because it does bring the actions and decisions of top management into the quality management system and makes them full partners in the development, operation and improvement of the system. Top management is defined in ISO 9000 as *the person or group of people who direct and control an organization* and therefore sit at the top of the tree.

Commitment

A commitment is an obligation that a person (or a company) takes on in order to do something. It is very easily tested by examination of the results. It is also easy for you to make promises to resolve immediate problems hoping that the problem may go away in due course. This is dishonest and although you may mean well, the problem will return to haunt you if you can't deliver on your promise.

A commitment exists if a person agrees to do something and informs others of their intentions. A commitment that is not communicated is merely a personal commitment with no obligation except to one's own conscience.

Commitment therefore means:

- Doing what you need to do to meet the organization's objectives
- Doing what you say you will do
- Not accepting work below standard
- Not shipping product below standard
- Not walking by problems, not overlooking mistakes
- Improving processes
- Honouring plans, procedures, policies, promises
- Listening to the workforce
- Listening to the interested parties

Commitment to a management system

Although the standard does indicate how commitment to a management system should be demonstrated it presupposes that top management understands what it is committing itself to. There is a presumption in that a management that is committed to the development, implementation and continual improvement of a management system will be committed to quality because it believes that the management system is the means by which quality will be achieved. This is by no means obvious because it depends upon top management's perception of the management system. To some the management system may be a set of documents, instructions for performing administrative tasks, a collection of procedures etc. Many managers have given a commitment to quality without knowing what impact it would have on their business. Many have given a commitment without being aware that their own behaviour may need to change let alone the behaviour of their managers and staff. The phrase "continually improving its effectiveness" clearly implies that top management has to ensure the management system continually fulfils its purpose and hence need to understand what its purpose is. A study of clauses 4.1 and 5.1 together with the definitions in ISO 9000 should leave one in no doubt that the purpose of the management system is to enable the organization to satisfy its customers. Expressing a commitment to the development and improvement of the management system means a belief that the management system is the means by which quality is achieved and that resources will be provided for its development, implementation, maintenance and improvement.

As the revised requirement now moves the focus from quality to the means for its achievement it has the tendency for creating even greater mis-understanding than previously. The perceptions of quality may well be customer focused but the managers may perceive the management system as only applying to the quality department and consequently may believe that a commitment to the development of a management system implies that they have to commit to maintaining a quality department. This is not what is intended. A quality department is the result of structuring a particular organization to meet its business objectives. There are several other solutions that would not result in the formation of a department dedicated to quality. There is certainly no requirement in ISO 9000 for a department that is dedicated to quality.

Why is this necessary?

This requirement responds to the Leadership Principle.

Management must be seen to do what it says it will do so as to demonstrate its understanding. There is no doubt that actions speak louder than words for it is only when the words are tested that it is revealed whether the writers are serious. It is not about whether management can be trusted but whether they understand the implications of what they have committed themselves to. The wording of this requirement is no accident. The requirements of the 1994 version were clearly not interpreted as intended and it has therefore been necessary to strengthen the message that the management system is supposed to make the right things happen and not simply be regarded as a set of procedures.

How is this implemented?

Defining top management

In order to clarify who in the organization is a member of top management it will be advantageous to specify this in the Quality Manual. It is then necessary to ensure that the positions of the personnel performing the specified actions are from top management.

A search of section 5 of the standard will reveal that Top management are required to:

● Provide evidence of commitment to the development and improvement of the management system

- Communicate the importance of meeting customer requirements
- Establish the quality policy and ensure it meets prescribed criteria
- Ensure that customer needs and expectations are determined, converted into requirements and fulfilled to achieve customer satisfaction
- Establish quality objectives and ensure they are established at each relevant function and level
- Ensure that resources needed to achieve the objectives are identified, planned and are available
- Appoint members of management who shall have responsibility for ensuring the management system is established etc
- Review the management system to ensure its continuing suitability and effectiveness

Merging requirements in sections 5.1 to 5.5 of the standard produced this list. It is interesting that in some of the above references top management is required to *ensure* something rather than *do* something. To ensure means to make certain and top management can't make certain that something will happen unless it is in control. However, it does mean that it can delegate to others the writing of the policy, the objectives and provision of resources.

In some organizations, there are two roles, one of Management Representative and another of Quality Manager with the former only being in top management. It is clear that in such cases, the Quality Manager should not be the person carrying out these actions but the person who is a member of top management.

Commitment

Once communicated, a commitment can be tested by:

- Establishing if resources have been budgeted for discharging the commitment.
- Establishing that resources are allocated when needed.
- Establishing that performance of the tasks to which the person has given his or her commitment are progressed, monitored and controlled.
- Establishing that deviations from commitment are not easily granted.

In managing a management system, such tests will need to be periodically carried out even though it will be tedious to both the person doing the test and the person being subjected to it. It is less tedious if such tests are a feature of the programme that the management has agreed to, thereby making it impersonal and by mutual consent.

The management has to be committed to quality, in other words it must not knowingly ship defective product, give inferior service or in any other way dissatisfy its stakeholders. It must do what it says it will do and what it says it will do must meet the needs and expectations of the stakeholders. A manager who signs off waivers without customer agreement is not committed to quality whatever the reasons. It is not always easy, however, for managers to honour all their commitments when the customer is screaming down the phone for supplies that have been ordered or employees are calling for promised pay rises. Unlike the 1994 version, the standard now requires proof that managers are committed to quality through their actions and decisions. When they start spending time and money on quality, diverting people to resolve problems, motivating their staff to achieve performance standards, listening to their staff and to customers, there is *commitment*. It will also be evident from customer feedback, internal and external audits and sustained business growth. Increased profits do not necessarily show that the company is committed to quality. Profits can rise for many reasons not necessarily because of an improvement in quality. Managers should not just look at profit results to measure the success of the improvement programme. Profits may go down initially as investment is made in management system development. If managers abandon the programme because of short-term results, it shows not only a lack of commitment but a lack of understanding. Every parent knows that a child's education does not bear fruit until he or she is an adult. It is therefore much better to tailor the programme to available resources than abandon it completely.

Commitment to a management system

Although the standard defines how top management should demonstrate its commitment there are some obvious omissions. Commitment to the development and improvement of a management system could be demonstrated by evidence that top management:

- understands the role of the management system in relation to achieving business objectives and customer satisfaction
- is steering management system development and improvement effort and monitoring its performance
- is promoting core values, adherence to policy, best practice and continual improvement
- undertakes the top management actions in a timely manner
- does not defer decisions that are impeding progress in management system development and improvement
- is implementing the processes that have been developed to achieve business objectives
- is actively stimulating system improvements

Communicating the importance of requirements (5.1a)

1994–2000 Differences
This is a new requirement that has no equivalent in the 1994 version.

The standard requires that top management *communicate to the organization the importance of meeting customer as well as statutory and regulatory requirements.*

What does this mean?

Communication

This is a new requirement and is the primary application of the *customer focus principle.* Effective communication consists of four steps; attention, understanding, acceptance and action. It is not just the sending of messages from one source to another. It is therefore not enough for top management to publish a quality policy that declares the importance of meeting customer, regulatory and legal requirements – this is only the first step and depending on how this is done it may not even accomplish the first step.

Statutory and regulatory requirements

Although the ISO 9000 family addresses all interested parties, ISO 9001 focuses on customers and therefore the statutory and regulatory requirements referred to in this requirement are those pertaining directly or indirectly to the product or service supplied. However, there are few regulations that in some way would not impact the customer if not complied with. Customers not only purchase products and services but also often desire a sustaining relationship so that they can rely on consistent quality, delivery and cost. If the operations are suspended through non-compliance with environmental, health and safety legislation, existing customers will be affected and potential customers lost. The absence of key personnel due to occupational health reasons may well impact deliveries and relationships. Some customers require their suppliers to operate ethically and conserve the environment. If the financial laws are breached causing the organization to cut costs to pay the fines, credit worthiness may also be affected. Such breaches also distract management from focusing on customers; therefore it is not only the product related regulations that can affect customer satisfaction.

There is also a secondary meaning. Some customers may require the organization to provide products and services that do not comply with statutory and regulatory requirements.

Why is this necessary?

This requirement responds to the Customer Focus Principle.

Top management need to attract the attention of the workforce and this requires much more then pinning-up framed quality policy statements all over the place. In organizations in which the producers are remote from the customer, it is necessary to convey customer expectations down the line so that decisions are made primarily on the basis of satisfying these expectations and not on the secondary internal requirements. It is also necessary for management to signal its intentions with respect to customer requirements so that personnel know of the factors affecting the work priorities.

How is this implemented?

Before embarking on a communication programme top management should examine its culture relative to profit. If asked why the organization exists, many would say it is to make a profit – clearly indicating they are a profit-focused organization – not a customer-focused organization. Profits are important but are the *result* of what we do – not the *reason* for doing it. Profits are needed to pay off loans, for investment in new technology, new plant, and new skills and to award higher salaries but they come from satisfying customers and operating efficiently and effectively. Focusing on profit creates a situation where people constantly observe the bottom line rather than the means to achieve it so that most decisions are based on cost rather than quality. Managers in such organizations rule by fear and treat a lack of capability as an excuse rather than a valid reason why targets are not met. It is right to question the value of any activity but with the focus on customer satisfaction not profit. It is vital therefore that top management consider the culture they have created before communicating the importance of customer requirements. Where profit is the first priority, stressing the importance of customer requirements will create a conflicting message. Management needs to make employees understand that the priorities have changed so that the aim is to satisfy customers profitably. If the customer's requirements cannot be satisfied profitably, business should not be transacted unless there are opportunities for recovering the loss in another transaction. It is also important that before accepting a commitment to supply, a clear understanding of customer needs and expectations as well as regulatory and legal requirements is established – hence sales personnel need to understand that they should not make promises the organization cannot honour.

Meeting this requirement may therefore require a realignment of priorities and careful consideration as to the way management will attract the attention, understanding, acceptance and correct action of the workforce.

Establishing quality policy (5.1b)

The standard requires that top management *establish the quality policy.*

What does this mean?

ISO 9000 defines a quality policy as the overall intentions and direction of an organization related to quality as formally expressed by top management. It also suggests that the policy be consistent with the overall policy of the organization and provide a framework for setting quality objectives. Furthermore ISO 9000 advises that the eight quality management principles be used as a basis for forming the quality policy. The quality policy can therefore be considered as the values, beliefs and rules that guide actions, decisions and behaviours. A value may be 'integrity' and expressed as: *We will be open and honest in our dealings with those inside and outside the organization.* A rule may be 'confidentiality' and expressed as *Company*

Corporate terminology

There are so many similar terms that are used by upper management that it is not surprising that their use is inconsistent. We use the term *goal* when we mean purpose or perhaps we really did mean goal or should we use the term *mission* or *objective*, or perhaps a better term would be *target* . . . and so on. The problem is that we often don't know the intention of the user. Did he or she carefully select the term to impart a specific meaning or would the alternatives have been equally appropriate?

Purpose	Why we exist, why we do what we do
Mission	Where we are going – the journey
Goals	Our intended destination
Vision	What we want to become
Values	What beliefs will guide our behaviour
Strategy	How we are going to get there
Policy	Rules that guide our actions and decisions – the signposts en route
Principles	Fundamental truth
Objectives	What we want to achieve – the results
Targets	What we aim at to achieve objectives

information shall not be shared with those outside the organization. Both these are also beliefs because it might be believed that deceiving people only leads to failure in the long run. It might also be believed that disclosing confidential information fuels the competition and will drive the organization out of business. Both values guide actions, decisions and behaviours and hence may be termed *policies.* They are not objectives because they are not achieved – they are demonstrated by the manner in which actions and decisions are taken and the way your organization behaves towards others.

The detail of quality policy will be addressed later. What is important in this requirement is an understanding of why a quality policy is needed, what is required to *establish* a quality policy and where it fits in relation to other policies.

Why is this necessary?

This requirement responds to the Leadership Principle.

Defining the purpose or mission of the business is one thing but without some guiding policies, the fulfilment of this mission may not happen unless effort is guided in a common direction. If every manager chooses his or her direction, and policies, the full potential of the organization would not be realized. A shared vision is required that incorporates shared values and shared policies.

The purpose of corporate policies is to influence the short and long-term actions and decisions and to influence the direction in which the mission will be fulfilled. If there were policies related to the organization's customers, they could be fulfilled at the expense of employees, shareholders and society. If there were policies related to profit, without other policies being defined, profit is positioned as a boundary condition to all actions and decisions. Clearly this may not direct the organization towards its mission.

How is this implemented?

To establish means to put in place permanently. A quality policy that is posted in the entrance hall – published yes, but not established. For a policy to become established, it has to reflect the vision of the organization and underpin every conscious thought and action. This will only arise if everyone believes in the policy. For this to happen, managers need to become the role model so that by their actions and decisions they exemplify the policy. Belief in the policy is unlikely if the quality policy is merely perceived as something written only to satisfy ISO 9000.

With the 1994 version of ISO 9000, the focus was on product quality and consequently quality was associated with order-driven processes that delivered goods to customer requirements. The new definition of quality in

ISO 9000 clearly goes beyond relations with the purchaser and embraces all interested parties. The eight quality management principles also go far beyond the mechanical processes for achieving product quality and embrace the softer factors that influence the behaviour of people in an organization. Clearly, a quality policy that addresses all these issues comes close to reflecting all the policies of the organization and hence can be termed the corporate policy. While organizations may have a safety policy, an environmental policy, a personnel policy, a servicing policy etc, these are really topics within the corporate policy. Quality is not just another topic but a term that embraces all the topics. It is hard to think of any policy that could not be classed as a quality policy when quality is defined as *the degree to which a set of inherent characteristics fulfils requirements*. This definition does not limit *quality* to the fulfilment of customer requirements, but extends it to the fulfilment of any requirements including employees, suppliers, in fact any interested party. Safety policies are quality policies because they respond to employees and customers as interested parties. Environmental policies are quality policies because they respond to society as an interested party. There is therefore no advantage in issuing a separate quality policy – it is more effective if the organization formulates its corporate policies and within them addresses the topics covered by the eight quality management principles.

Establishing quality objectives (5.1c)

1994–2000 Differences
Previously the standard required the supplier's management with executive responsibility to define and document its policy for quality including objectives for quality. The new wording clarifies the original intent that quality objectives are separate from and not the same as quality policy.

The standard requires that top management *ensure that quality objectives are established*.

What does this mean?

ISO 9000 defines quality objectives as *results sought or aimed for related to quality*. It also suggests that these objectives be based on the quality policy and be specified at different levels in the organization, being quantified at the operational level. As with quality policy the details will be addressed later and here we will focus on what it means to establish quality objectives and how they relate to other objectives.

As the quality policy equates to the corporate policy, it follows that quality objectives equate to corporate objectives. All of the organization's objectives should in some way serve to fulfil requirements of customers and other interested parties. It is also interesting to note that in ISO 9000, the term *requirement* is defined as *a need or expectation that is stated, customarily implied or obligatory*. While an investor may not specify a requirement for growth in share value, it would certainly be an expectation. While an employee does not express requirements for salary increases when profits rise, it would certainly be an expectation and while society has no way other than to protest or invoke the law to impose its desires upon an organization, it certainly has the power to make organization's comply and even change the law in extreme cases. So quality objectives *do* equate to corporate objectives.

Why is this necessary?

This requirement responds to the Leadership Principle.

Management needs to ensure that the objectives are established as a basis for action. All work serves an objective and it is the objective that stimulates action. The reason for top management setting the objectives is to ensure that everyone channels their energies in a positive direction that serves the organizations purpose and mission.

How is this implemented?

For an objective to be established it has to be communicated, translated into action and become the focus of all achievement. Objectives are not wish lists. The starting point is the purpose and mission statement and the factors identified as affecting the ability of the organization to accomplish its mission. It is in these areas the organization needs to excel and therefore they become the focus for action and consequently the setting of objectives. Although ISO 9000 suggests that the quality objectives should be based on the quality policy, it is more likely to be current performance, competition and opportunities arising from new technology that drive the objectives. The setting of objectives is addressed further under *Quality objectives* (5.4.1).

Conducting management reviews (5.1d)

The standard requires that top management *conduct management reviews.*

What does this mean?

The term *review* is defined in ISO 9000 as *an activity undertaken to ensure the suitability, adequacy, effectiveness and efficiency of the subject matter to achieve established objectives.* The addition of the term *management* means that the management review can be perceived as a review *of* management rather than a

> **1994–2000 Differences**
> Previously the standard required the supplier's management with executive responsibility to review the quality system with the implication that it could be delegated. This new requirement means that top management must conduct the reviews and not delegate them.

review *by* management, although both meanings are conveyed in the standard. The rationale for this is that the examples given in ISO 9000 such as design review and nonconformity review clearly indicate it is design and non-conformity that is being reviewed. If the system was to be reviewed then the action should be called a *system review*. It is no doubt unintentional in the standard but, if the management system is perceived as the way in which the organization's objectives are achieved, a review of management is in fact a review of the way achievement of objectives is being managed because the organization exists to achieve objectives and so both meanings are correct.

Why is this necessary?

This requirement responds to the Factual Approach Principle.

Top management has set the policies and agreed the objectives and means for their achievement i.e. the management system. It follows therefore that periodic checks are needed to establish that the management system continues to fulfil its purpose. Failure to do so will inevitably result in deterioration of standards and performance as inherent weaknesses in the system build up to eventually cause catastrophic failure i.e. customer satisfaction will decline and orders, markets and business will be lost. It may be argued that this won't happen because people won't let it happen – they will take action. If these conditions persist, what will emerge is not a managed system but an unmanaged system that is unpredictable, unreliable with erratic performance. A return to the days before the management system (as defined in this book) was established.

How is this implemented?

Top management will not regard the management review as important unless they believe it is essential to running the business. The way to do this is to treat it as a business performance review. This is simpler than it may appear. If the quality policy is now accepted as corporate policy and the quality objectives are accepted as corporate objectives, any review of the management system becomes a performance review and no different to any other executive meeting. The problem with the former management reviews was that they allowed discussion on the means for achieving objectives to take place in other management meetings leaving the management review to a review of errors, mistakes and documentation that no one was interested in anyway. The management system *is* the means for achieving objectives therefore it makes sense to review the *means* when reviewing the *ends* so that actions are linked to results and commitment secured for all related changes in one transaction.

The requirement emphasizes that top management conduct the review – not the quality manager, not the operational manager – but *top management* – those who direct and control the organization at the highest level. In many ISO 9000 registered organizations, the management review is a chore, an event held once each year, on a Friday afternoon before a national holiday – perhaps a cynical view but nonetheless often true. The reason the event has such a low priority is that management have not understood what the review is all about. Tell them it's about reviewing nonconformities, customer complaints and internal audit records and you will be lucky if anyone turns up. The quality manager produces all the statistics so the others managers are free of any burden. By careful tactics, these managers may come away with no actions, having delegated any in their quarter to the quality manager.

In order to provide evidence of its commitment to conducting management reviews, management would need to demonstrate that it planned for the reviews, prepared input material in the form of performance results, metrics and explanations, decided what to do about the results and accepted action to bring about improvement.

Ensuring availability of resources (5.1e)

The standard requires that top management *ensure the availability of necessary resources.*

What does this mean?

A resource is something that can be called upon when needed and therefore includes time, personnel, skill, machines, materials, money, plant, facilities, space, information, knowledge etc. *To ensure* means to make certain. For top management *to ensure the availability of necessary resources*, it has to:

1994–2000 Differences
Previously the standard required the supplier to provide adequate resources. The change in emphasis to ensure necessary resources changes the intent. Resource adequacy was concerned with maintaining the status quo – necessary resources implies those needed to meet organizational goals including continuous improvement.

- know what objectives it is committed to achieve
- know what resources are required to achieve these objectives
- know when the resources will be needed
- know of the availability of such resources
- know the cost of acquiring these resources
- know that all of the above is feasible

Why is this necessary?

This requirement responds to the Leadership Principle.

No plans will be achieved unless the resources to make them happen are provided. It is therefore incumbent upon top management to not only require a management system to be developed, implemented and maintained but provide the means by which this is accomplished. In many organizations, the quest for ISO 9000 certification has resulted in an existing manager being assigned additional responsibilities for establishing the management system without being provided with additional resources. Even if this person did have surplus time available, it is not a job for one person. Every manager should be involved and they too need additional resources. In the long term, the total resources required to maintain the organization will be less with an effective management system than without but to start with, additional time and skills are required and need to be made available.

How is this implemented?

One of the problems with implementing the 1994 requirements was that it did not require management to link resource provision with objectives. It is not uncommon for management to budget for certain resources and when the time comes to acquire them, the priorities have changed and the ambitious plans are abandoned. Top management will need to be more careful when agreeing to objectives and plans for their accomplishment. It will need to have confidence that, excluding events beyond its control, funds will be available to acquire the resources committed in the improvement plans. This does not mean that management will be forced to fund plans when it clearly has no funding available but such circumstances need to be monitored. Any lack of funding should be reviewed to establish whether it was poor estimating, forces outside the organization's control or a genuine lack of commitment. Opportunities often change and it would be foolish to miss a profitable business opportunity while pursuing an improvement programme that could be rescheduled. The risks need to be assessed and the objectives adjusted. It could also be that such business opportunities remove the need for the improvement programme because it removes the process or product line that is in need of improvement. However, managers at all levels need to be careful about approving plans which are over ambitious, impractical or not feasible with the anticipated resources that will be available.

Customer focus (5.2)

Determining customer requirements (5.2)

The standard requires top management *to ensure that customer requirements are determined.*

What does this mean?

A customer is defined in ISO 9000 as an organization or person that receives a product. This could be a consumer, client, end-user, retailer, beneficiary or purchaser. The meaning has therefore changed considerably from the 1987 version of ISO 9000 that was primarily focused on purchasers.

In the Committee Drafts of ISO 9001, this requirement was expressed differently. It required that customer needs and expectation be determined – which to many is very different from determining customer requirements. The former implies that the organization should be pro-active and seek to establish customer needs and expectations before commencing the design of products and services and offering them for sale. The latter implies that the organization should react to the receipt of an order

> **1994–2000 Differences**
>
> Previously the standard required the tender, contract or order to be reviewed to ensure that the requirements are adequately defined and documented. The implication of the new requirement is a change from an order driven management system to a market driven system.

by determining what the customer wants. However, the original meaning has not been lost because ISO 9000 defines a requirement as *a need or expectation that is stated, customarily implied or obligatory*. We can therefore use the term *requirement* or the terms *needs, expectations and obligations* as synonymous. As there is no indication in the statement that such requirements are limited to those in an order or contract, it can be interpreted as requiring both proactive and reactive action.

The requirement is specific in that it requires top management *to ensure* customer requirements are determined – meaning that it has to ensure an effective process is in place for determining customer requirements.

Why is this necessary?

This requirement responds to the Customer Focus Principle.

All organizations have customers. Organizations exist to create and retain satisfied customers – those that do not do so, fail to survive. Not-for-profit organizations have customers even though they may not purchase anything, they give and they take and if the organization fails to fulfil their needs, it ceases to exist. Governments are a prime example. If they fail to satisfy the voters they fail to be re-elected. It is therefore essential for the survival of an organization that it determines customer requirements.

How is this implemented?

The requirement is implemented through two processes – the marketing process and the sales process. This requirement extends the management system beyond the processes required to satisfy current customers and clearly brings the marketing process as well as the sales process into the management system.

The marketing process is primarily concerned with finding out what customers want and attracting them to the organization so that these wants are satisfied. In this process it is important to keep the organization's purpose and mission in focus because all too easily, the organization may become entangled in pursuing opportunities that others may be far better equipped to satisfy – 'stick to the knitting' as Tom Peters would say (Peters, Tom and Waterman, Robert, 1995)[1]. There are millions of opportunities out there. The key is to discover those that your organization can exploit better than any other and generate a profit by doing so.

The sales process is primarily concerned with making contact with customers for existing products and services and converting enquiries into firm orders. In this process, it is important that the customer requirements are determined so as to match the benefits of existing products and service with the needs and expectations of customers. The tender/contract review process is therefore important in ensuring needs are understood before a commitment to supply is accepted.

Understanding customer needs

In order to determine customer needs and expectations you need to answer some important questions.

- What is our business?
- What will our business be?
- What should our business be?

Answers to questions above are obtained by answering the following questions:

- Who are our customers?
- Where are our customers?
- What do customers buy?
- What is value to the customer?
- Which of the customer's wants are not adequately satisfied?

The change in direction of the American people that quickly came about with the mass production of the automobile made Amtrak think long and hard about what business they were in. If they stayed in the railroad business for much longer they would cease to exist. They therefore came to the conclusion that they were not in the railroad business but in the transportation business and as a result they adapted and prospered.

The answers to the above questions will enable marketing objectives to be established for:

- existing products and services in present markets
- abandonment of obsolete products, services and markets
- new products and services for existing markets

- new markets
- service standards and service performance
- product standards and product performance

The results of market research will be a mix of things. It will identify:

- new potential customers for existing products and services
- new potential markets
- opportunities for which no technology exists
- opportunities for which no product or service solution exists
- enhancements to existing products and services

The organization needs to decide which of these to pursue and this requires a marketing process that involves all the interested parties. Marketing processes that only involve the marketers will not exploit the organization's full potential. The contributions from design, production, service delivery, legal and regulation experts are vital to formulating a robust set of customer requirements from which to develop new markets, new products and new services. The research may identify a need for improvement in specific products or a range of products, but the breakthroughs will come from studying customer behaviour. For example, research into telecommunications brought about the mobile phone and technology has reduced it in size and weight so that the phone now fits into a shirt pocket. Further research on mobile phones has identified enhancements such as access to e-mail and the Internet through the mobile phone but whether these are essential improvements is debatable. The fear of radiation and driving laws means that a breakthrough will arise by eliminating manual interaction so that the communicator is worn like a hat, glove or a pair of spectacles, being voice activated and providing total hands free operation.

Determining customer needs and expectations should not be limited to your present customer-base. Customers may want your products but may be unable to obtain them. If your products and services are limited to the home market either due to import regulations or distribution policies you could satisfy a new sector of the market with your existing products and extend their life. Austin Morris did this in the 1960s with their Morris Cowley and Oxford by exporting the technology to India.

From analysing the results of the research a design brief or requirement can be developed that translates customer needs and expectations into performance, physical and functional characteristics for a product or service. This forms the basis of the input into the product and service design processes. Often this requirement is no more than a couple of lines on a memorandum. In the 1970s, the MD of Ferranti Computer Systems issued an instruction to the design staff that a 16 bit digital computer was required. No more information was provided but in subsequent discussions the target customers (Royal Navy) and functional purpose (Command and Control Systems) were established and by further research the detail performance, physical and functional characteristics and regulatory standards were identified. The process of converting needs into requirements can therefore be quite protracted and iterative. With military projects, establishing requirements is a distinct phase that is put out for tender and where the winner may not necessarily win a subsequent contract to develop the product.

If you misunderstand customer needs and expectations you will produce an inadequate set of requirements, often not knowing they are inadequate until you launch the product into the market. It is therefore the most important stage in the product realization process where ideas and beliefs are tested and retested to ensure they really do reflect customer needs and expectations.

Gathering the data

Decisions affecting the future direction of the organization and its products and services are made from information gleaned through market research. Should this information be grossly inaccurate, over optimistic or pessimistic the result may well be the loss of many customers to the competition. It is therefore vital that objective data is used to make these decisions. The data can be primary data (data collected for the first time during a market research study) or secondary data (previously collected data). However, you need to be cautious with secondary data because it could be obsolete or have been collected on a different basis than needed for the present study.

The marketing information primarily identifies either *problems* or *opportunities*. *Problems* will relate to your existing products and services and should indicate why there has been a decline in sales or an increase in returns. In order to solve these problems a search for possible causes should be conducted and one valid method for doing this is to use the Fishbone Diagram or Cause and Effect Diagram. *Opportunities* will relate to future products and services and should indicate unsatisfied wants. There are three ways of collecting such data; by observation, survey and experiment.

Observation studies are conducted by actually viewing the overt actions of the respondent. In the automotive industry this can either be carried out in the field or in the factories where subcontractors can observe their customer using their materials or components.

Using surveys is the most widely used method for obtaining primary data. Asking questions that reveal their priorities, their preferences, their desires, their unsatisfied wants etc., will provide the necessary information. Information on the profile of the ultimate customers with respect to location, occupation, life style, spending power, leisure pursuits etc. will enable the size of market to be established. Asking questions about their supplier preferences and establishing what these suppliers provide that you don't provide is also necessary. Knowing what the customer will pay more for is also necessary, because many may expect features that were once options, to be provided as standard.

A method used to test the potential of new products is the *controlled experiment*. – using prototypes, alpha models etc, distributed to a sample of known users. Over a limited period these users try out the product and compile a report that is returned to the company for analysis.

A source of secondary data can be trade press reports and independent reviews. Reading the comments about other products can give you some insight into the needs and expectations of potential customers.

Meeting requirements (5.2)

The standard requires *customer requirements to be met with the aim of enhancing customer satisfaction.*

What does this mean?

For many, ISO 9000 has been perceived as a standard that allows organizations to consistently supply rubbish. After all, the auditors merely establish that you do what you say you do. If your products are not intended to be good quality, having a system that meets the requirements of ISO 9000 could be perceived as allowing you to produce substandard goods under an ISO 9000 certified management system! This argument succeeds if the term "specific requirements" in ISO 9000 is limited to the organization's requirements. If the term *specified requirements* had been interpreted as indicated in ISO 8402, it would be clear that such requirements are those of the market or of specific customers not the organization's internal requirements. This requirement changes the focus from *doing what you say you do* to *doing what you need to do to satisfy your customers*. It also means that if your interpretation of customer requirements is incorrect in some way, you have an obligation to go beyond the requirements and aim for customer satisfaction. It does not mean however, that you must satisfy customers regardless of their demands. Some customers are unreasonable and expect something for nothing so it is your choice not to supply them if that is the case.

> **1994–2000 Differences**
> The previous version required the supplier to meet specified requirements. The implication is that the supplier can no longer specify its own requirements where such requirements could neglect to take into account the needs and expectations of customers.

Why is this important?

This requirement responds to the Customer Focus Principle.

Organizations only stay in business by satisfying their customers. Even the Inland Revenue has customers and, in the UK at least, it has a customer charter that commits it to providing services to agreed standards. ISO 9001 focuses on customers but organizations can fail to survive if they do not also satisfy other interested parties such as their employees, regulators and society. People will only continue to work for organizations that treat them fairly. Regulators can close down businesses if they breach the rules and if all else fails, society can influence government and so change the law to stop organizations behaving in a way that harms the population not only of the host country but even the earth itself.

How is this implemented?

The whole standard addresses the elements of a management system that aims to achieve customer satisfaction and therefore by constructing and operating a system that meets the intent of ISO 9000, this goal will be achieved.

Quality Policy (5.3)

Ensuring policy is appropriate (5.3a)

1994–2000 Differences
Previously the standard required the quality policy to be relevant to the supplier's organizational goals. There has been a change in emphasis from *goals* to *purpose* requiring there to be a clear linkage between the achievement of the quality policy and the organization's purpose.

The standard requires the quality policy *to be appropriate to the purpose of the organization.*

What does this mean?

The purpose of an organization is quite simply the reason for its existence and as Peter Drucker so eloquently put it – "there is only one valid definition of business purpose: to create a customer"(Drucker, Peter F., 1977)[2]. In ensuring that the quality policy is appropriate to the purpose of the organization, it must be appropriate to the customers the organization desires to create. It is therefore necessary to establish who the customers are, where the customers are, what they buy or wish to receive and what these customers regard as value.

Why is this necessary?

This requirement responds to the Leadership Principle.

As stated above, the quality policy is the corporate policy and such policies exist to channel actions and decisions along a path that will fulfil the organization's purpose and mission. A goal of the organization may be the attainment of ISO 9000 certification and thus a quality policy of meeting the requirements of ISO 9000 would be consistent with such a goal, but goals are not

---

Examples of corporate policies

On customers
We will listen to our customers, understand and balance their needs and expectations with those of our suppliers, employees, investors and society and endeavour to give full satisfaction to all parties.

On leadership
We will establish and communicate our vision for the organization and through our leadership exemplify core values to guide the behaviour of all to achieve our vision.

On people
We will involve our people in the organization's development, utilize their knowledge and experience, recognize their contribution and provide an environment in which they are motivated to realize their full potential.

On processes and systems
We will take a process approach towards the management of work and manage our processes as a single system of interconnected processes that delivers all the organization's objectives.

On continual improvement
We will provide an environment in which every person is motivated to continually improve the efficiency and effectiveness of our products, processes and our management system.

On decisions
We will base our decisions on the logical and intuitive analysis of data collected where possible from accurate measurements of product, process and system characteristics.

On supplier relationships
We will develop alliances with our suppliers and work with them to jointly improve performance.

---

the same as purpose as indicated in the box to the right. Clearly no organization would have ISO 9000 certification as its purpose because certification is not a reason for existence – an objective maybe but not a purpose.

Policies expressed as short catchy phrases such as "to be the best" really do not channel actions and decisions. They become the focus of ridicule when the organization's fortunes change. There has to be a clear link from mission to policy.

How is this implemented?

Policies are not expressed as vague statements or emphatic statements using the words *may, should* or *shall*, but clear intentions by use of the words *'we will'* – thus expressing a commitment or by the words *'we are, we do, we don't, we have'* expressing shared beliefs. Very short statements tend to become slogans which people chant but rarely understand the impact on what they do. Their virtue is that they rarely become outdated. Long statements confuse people because they contain too much for them to remember. Their virtue is that they not only define what the company stands for but how it will keep its promises.

In the ISO 9000 definition of quality policy it is suggested that the eight quality management principles be used as a basis for establishing the policy. One of these principles is the *Customer Focus principle*. By including in the quality policy the intention to identify and satisfy the needs and expectations of customers and other interested parties and the associated strategy by which this will be achieved, this requirement would be fulfilled. The inclusion of the strategy is important because the policy should guide action and decision. Omitting the strategy may not ensure uniformity of approach and direction.

Expressing a commitment (5.3b)

1994–2000 Differences

Previously the standard stipulated that the quality policy should include a commitment to quality. The new wording implies that a commitment to quality means a commitment to meeting requirements and to continual improvement.

The standard requires that the quality policy *include a commitment to comply with requirements and continually improve the effectiveness of the quality management system.*

What does this mean?

A commitment to comply with requirements means that the organization should undertake to meet the requirements of all interested parties. This means meeting the requirements of customer, suppliers, employees, investors, owners and society. Customer requirements are those either specified or implied by customers or determined by the organization and these are dealt with in more detail under clauses 5.2 and 7.2.1. The requirements of employees are those covered by legislation such as access, space, environmental conditions, equal opportunities and maternity leave but also the legislation appropriate to minority groups such as the disabled and any agreements made with unions or other representative bodies. Investors have rights also and these will be addressed in the investment agreements. The requirements of society are those obligations resulting from laws, statutes, regulations etc.

An organization accepts such obligations when it is incorporated as a legal entity, when it accepts orders from customers, when it recruits employees, when it chooses to trade in regulated markets and when it chooses to use or process materials that impact the environment.

The effectiveness of the management system is judged by the extent to which it fulfils its purpose. Therefore improving effectiveness means improving the capability of the management system. Changes to the management system that improve its capability i.e its ability to deliver outputs that satisfy all the interested parties, are a certain types of change and not all management system changes will accomplish this. This requirement therefore requires top management to pursue changes that bring about an improvement in performance.

Why is this necessary?

This requirement responds to the Leadership Principle.

Policies guide action and decision. It is therefore necessary for top management to impress upon their workforce that they have entered into certain obligations that commit everyone in the enterprise. Such commitments need to be communicated through policy statements in order to ensure that when taking actions and making decisions, staff give top priority to meeting the requirements of the interested parties. This is not easy. There will be many difficult decisions where the short term interests of the organization may need to be subordinated to the needs of customers. Internal pressures may tempt people to cut corners, break the rules and protect their own interests. Committing the organization to meet requirements may be an easy decision to take – but difficult to honour.

Some 300,000 organizations worldwide have obtained ISO 9000 certification but many (perhaps the majority) have not improved their performance as a result. They remain mediocre and not top performers primarily because the management system is not effective. If it were effective the organization would meet its objectives year on year and grow the number of satisfied customers. Resources, technology, market conditions, economical conditions and customer needs and expectations continually change, thus impacting the organization's capability. The effectiveness of the management system in meeting this challenge therefore needs to be continually improved.

How is this implemented?

A policy containing a commitment to meeting the needs and expectations of all interested parties would meet the first part of this requirement. In making a commitment to meet all these requirements the organization is placed under an obligation to

- identify the relevant requirements
- design and install processes that will ensure the requirements are met
- verify compliance with the identified requirements
- demonstrate to relevant authorities that the requirements have been met

The second part can be dealt with by including a policy that commits the organization to improve the effectiveness of the system by which the organization's objectives are achieved. Policies are more easily understood when expressed in terms that are understood by the employees. Some organizations use the terms *internal* and *external* customers but even this can be ambiguous because not everyone will think of themselves as internal customers. The term *interested parties* is "ISO speak" and may not be readily understood. Spell it out if necessary – in fact it is highly desirable where relevant to state exactly what you mean rather than use the specific words from the standard.

Providing a framework for quality objectives (5.3c)

1994–2000 Differences

Previously the standard required the policy for quality to include objectives for quality. The implication of the change is that the quality objectives should not form part of the quality policy but that the policy be used as a basis for establishing quality objectives.

The standard requires the quality policy *to provide a framework for establishing and reviewing quality objectives.*

What does this mean?

The quality policy represents a set of guiding principles and therefore when setting as well as reviewing quality objectives, these principles should be employed to ensure the objectives are appropriate to the purpose of the organization.

Why is this necessary?

This requirement responds to the Leadership Principle.

The quality policy statements arising from ISO 9001:1994 were often stand-alone statements with little or no relationship to the operations of the business. The following are some typical quality policy statements:

- *We will perform exactly like the requirements or cause the requirements to be officially changed.*
- *We will satisfy our customer's requirements on time, every time and within budget.*
- *Our aim is to give customer satisfaction in everything we do.*
- *We shall not knowingly ship defective product.*

If we take just one of the above policy statements *"Our aim is to give customer satisfaction in everything we do"* on its own it is a motherhood statement. Nice, looks good in the lobby – visitors are impressed but the bottom line is that actual performance does not meet the expectations set. The reason is that no one thought out the process for accomplishing this – the links between the policy, the objectives and the processes for realizing it were not put in place.

Without being linked to the business processes, these policies remain dreams. There has to be a means to make these policies a reality and it is by setting objectives that are derived from the policy that this is accomplished. For the first time in these standards, a link has been made between policy and objectives so that policies are not merely motherhood statements but intentions for action. By deriving objectives from the policy you initiate a process for bringing about compliance with policy.

How is this implemented?

ISO 9000 recommends that the eight principles of quality management are used as the basis for establishing the quality policy and therefore these can provide the basis for setting objectives. However, it is not common practice for top management to derive its objectives from policies. Objectives are normally derived from needs, not guiding principles. The relationship between objectives and the management system was explained in chapter 4 and here it was shown that objectives are derived from the mission statement resulting in objectives for marketing, innovation, productivity, human organization, financial resources, social responsibility and profit. If the objectives are based on the policy and the policy is based on the eight quality management principles, there is a mismatch because there are no principles covering profit. (See also *Expressing objectives*.)

Ensuring policy is communicated and understood (5.3d)

The standard requires that the quality policy *is communicated and understood within the organization*.

What does this mean?

For a policy to be communicated it has to be brought to the attention of personnel. Personnel have to be made aware of how the policy relates to what they do so that they understand what it means before action is taken. Without action there is no demonstration that communication has been effective. If you

> **1994–2000 Differences**
>
> Previously the standard required that the supplier ensured that its quality policy is understood at all levels of the organization. The change from *all* levels to *appropriate* levels acknowledges that there will be some levels in the organization where understanding of the quality policy is not vital to what they do.

are already doing it, publishing the policy merely confirms that this is your policy. If the organization does not exhibit the right characteristics, there will need to be a change in culture to make the policy a reality.

Why is this necessary?

This requirement responds to the Leadership Principle.

As has been stated previously, a policy in a nice frame positioned in the lobby of an organization may impress the visitors but unless it is understood and adhered to, it will have no effect on the performance of the organization.

How is this implemented?

It is difficult to imagine how a policy could be understood if it wasn't communicated but the change in requirement signifies that the understanding has to come about by top management communicating the policy rather than the policy being deployed via the grape vine.

Whilst it is important that management shows commitment towards quality, policy statements can be one of two things – *worthless* or *obvious*. They are worthless if they do not reflect what the organization already believes and is currently implementing. They are obvious if they do reflect the current beliefs and practices of the organization. It is therefore foolish to declare in your policy what you would like the organization to become.

This is perhaps the most difficult requirement to achieve. Any amount of documentation, presentations by management, and staff briefings will not necessarily ensure that the policy is understood. Communication of policy is about gaining understanding but you should not be fooled into believing that messages delivered by management are effective communication. Effective communication consists of four steps; attention, understanding, acceptance and action. It is not just the sending of messages from one source to another. So how do you *ensure* that the policy is understood?

Within your management system you should prescribe the method you will employ to ensure that all the policies are understood at all appropriate levels in the organization. There will be levels in the organization where a clear understanding of the corporate policy is necessary for the making of sound decisions. At other levels, staff may work to instructions, having little discretion in what they can and cannot do. At these levels relevant aspects of the policy may be translated by the local manager into words that the staff understand. These can be conveyed through local procedures or notices.

One method to ensure understanding is for top management to do the following:

- Debate the policy together and thrash out all the issues. Don't announce anything until there is a uniform understanding among the members of the management team. Get the managers to face the question, "Do we intend to adhere to this policy?" and remove any doubt before going ahead.
- Ensure the policy is presented in a user-friendly way.
- Announce to the workforce that you now have a policy that affects everyone from the top down.
- Publish the policy to the employees (including other managers).
- Display the policy in key places to attract peoples' attention.
- Arrange and implement training/instruction for those affected.
- Test understanding at every opportunity e.g. at meetings, when issuing instructions/procedures, when delays occur, when failures arise, when costs escalate.
- Audit the decisions taken that affect quality and go back to those who made them if they do not comply with the stated policy.
- Take action every time there is misunderstanding. Don't let it go unattended and don't admonish those who may have misunderstood the policy. It may not be their fault!
- Every time there is a change in policy, go through the same process. Never announce a change and walk away from it. The change may never be implemented!
- Give time for the understanding to be absorbed. Use case studies and current problems to get the message across.

The audit programme is another method of testing understanding and is a way of verifying whether the chosen method of ensuring understanding is being effective.

In determining whether the policy is understood, auditors should not simply ask "What is the quality policy?" All this will prove is whether the auditee remembers it! The standard does not require that everyone knows the policy, only that it be communicated and understood. To test understanding therefore, you need to ask, for example:

- How does the quality policy affect what you do?
- What happens if you can't accomplish all the tasks in the allotted time?
- What would you do if you discovered a nonconformity immediately prior to delivery?
- How would you treat a customer who continually complains about your products and services?
- What action would you take if someone asked you to undertake a task for which you were not trained?
- What are your objectives and how do they relate to the quality policy?

- What action would you take if you noticed that someone was consuming food and drink in a prohibited area?
- What action would you take if you noticed that a product for which you were not responsible was in danger of being damaged?

Ensuring that the policy is reviewed (5.3e)

1994–2000 Differences

Previously the standard did not require the policy to be reviewed. This change will impact those organizations that simply created a policy addressing an organizational goal of compliance with ISO 9000 rather than with achieving customer satisfaction. The policy will need to be reviewed for its suitability to deliver the organization's purpose.

The standard requires the quality policy *to be reviewed for continuing suitability.*

What does this mean?

This requirement means that the policy should be examined in light of planned changes in the organization to establish whether it will remain suitable for guiding the organization towards its mission i.e. will this policy guide us to where we now want to go?

Why is this necessary?

This requirement responds to the Leadership Principle.

Nothing remains static for very long. As the organization grows and seeks new opportunities, its size and characteristics will need to change as it responds to the markets and economic climate in which it currently operates. A policy established under different circumstances may therefore not be appropriate for what the organization needs to become to meet these challenges – it may not be suitable for guiding the future organization towards its mission. The policy is required to be appropriate to the organization's purpose and while the purpose may not change, the environment in which the organization operates does change. These changes will impact the corporate policy. The policy will need to be reviewed in light of changes in the economic, social and technological environment for its suitability to enable the organization to fulfil its purpose.

How is this implemented?

The quality policy should be reviewed whenever a change in the market, the economic climate, statutory and legal requirements, technology or a major change in the organizational structure is contemplated. This review may be conducted at the *management review* but it rather depends upon the type of review that is conducted (see under Management review). Changes in policy have wide impact and therefore should not be taken lightly. They should be reviewed by top management with the full participation of the management team and therefore should be debated at the Corporate Planning Review or Business Review meeting. We are not talking about tinkering with the wording but a real change in direction. Changes in technology might mean that the workforce ceases to be predominantly on site as it becomes more effective to promote home or remote working. This change will impact the policy regarding leadership and people. Changes in the economic climate might mean that the workforce ceases to consist primarily of employees as it becomes more effective to outsource work to subcontractors and consultants. This change will impact the policy regarding leadership, suppliers and people.

Once the decision is made to change the policy it has to be communicated and the process for educating the workforce initiated.

Quality objectives (5.4.1)

Establishing objectives (5.4.1)

The standard requires that top management *ensure that quality objectives, including those needed to meet requirements for product, are established at relevant functions and levels within the organization.*

What does this mean?

An objective is a result that is aimed for and is expressed as a result that is to be achieved. Objectives are therefore not policies. The requirement should also not be interpreted as applicable only to organizational functions and levels. Objectives are required at levels within the organization not levels within the organization *structure*. This is clarified by the requirement for objectives to include those needed to meet requirements for product. There are therefore five levels at which control and improvement objectives need to be established:

> **1994–2000 Differences**
>
> Previously the standard required the policy for quality to include objectives for quality – the levels or functions at which objectives be established were not stipulated. The difference is that previously one statement of quality objectives would have been compliant whereas the new version implies that quality objectives should be set at corporate, divisional, departmental levels and perhaps for each function, process, product and individual when relevant.

- Corporate level where the objectives are for the whole enterprise to enable it to fulfil its vision
- Process level where the objectives are for specific processes to enable them to fulfil corporate goals
- Product or service level where the objectives are for specific products/ services or ranges of products/services to enable them to fulfil *or create* customer needs and expectations

- Departmental or function level where the objectives are for an organizational component to enable it to fulfil corporate goals
- Personal level where the objectives are for the development of individual competency

Why is this necessary?

This requirement responds to the Leadership Principle.

The requirement for defining objectives is one of the most important requirements. Without quality objectives there can be no improvement and no means of measuring how well you are doing. Without objectives any level of performance will do. If you don't know where you are going, any destination will do! Objectives are therefore necessary as a basis for measuring performance, to give people something to aim for, to maintain the status quo in order to prevent decline and to advance beyond the status quo for the enterprise to grow.

How is this implemented?

Objectives for control and improvement

A management system is not a static system but a dynamic one and if properly designed and implemented can drive the organization forward towards world-class quality. All managerial activity is concerned either with maintaining performance or with making change. Change can retard or advance performance. That which advances performance is beneficial. In this regard, there are two classes of quality objectives, those serving the control of quality (maintaining performance) and those serving the improvement of quality (making beneficial change).

The objectives for quality control should relate to the standards you wish to maintain or to prevent from deteriorating. To maintain your performance and your position in the market you will have to continually seek improvement. Remaining static at whatever level is not an option if your organization is to survive. Although you will be striving for improvement it is important to avoid slipping backwards with every step forwards. The effort needed to prevent regression may indeed require innovative solutions. While to the people working on such problems, it may appear that the purpose is to change the status quo, the result of their effort will be to maintain their present position not raise it to higher levels of performance. Control and improvement can therefore be perceived as one and the same thing depending on the standards being aimed for and the difficulties in meeting them.

The statements of objectives may be embodied within business plans, product development plans, improvement plans, process descriptions and even procedures.

Process for establishing objectives

Achievable objectives do not necessarily arise from a single thought even when the policies provide a framework. There is a process for establishing objectives. At the strategic level, the subjects that are the focus for setting objectives are the factors that affect the organization's ability to accomplish its mission – the critical success factors such as marketing, innovation, human resources, physical and financial resources, productivity and profit. There may be other factors such as the support of the community, of unions, of the media as certain businesses depend on continued support from society (see Table 5.1). Customer needs, regulations, competition and other external influences shape these objectives and cause them to change frequently. The measures arise from an analysis of current performance, the competition and there will emerge the need for either improvement or control. The steps in the objective setting process are as follows (Juran, J. M., (1995). *Managerial Breakthrough*, Second Edition. McGraw-Hill)[3]:

- Identifying the need
- Drafting preliminary objectives
- Proving the need to the appropriate level of management in terms of:
  - whether the climate for change is favourable
  - the urgency of the improvement or controls
  - the size of the losses or potential losses
  - the priorities
- Identifying or setting up the forum where the question of change or control is discussed
- Conducting a feasibility study to establish whether the objective can be achieved with the resources that can be applied
- Defining achievable objectives for control and improvement
- Communicating the objectives

The standard does not require that objectives be achieved but it does require that their achievement be planned and resourced. It is therefore prudent to avoid publishing objectives for meeting an unproven need and which has not been rigorously reviewed and assessed for their feasibility. It is wasteful to plan for meeting objectives that are unachievable and it diverts resources away from more legitimate uses.

Objectives are not established until they are understood and therefore communication of objectives must be part of this process. Communication is incomplete unless the receiver understands the message but a simple yes or no is not an adequate means of measuring understanding. Measuring employee understanding of appropriate quality objectives is a subjective process. Through the data analysis carried out to meet the requirements of clause 8.4 you will have produced metrics that indicate whether your quality objectives are being achieved. If they are being achieved you could either assume your employees understand the quality objectives or you could conclude that it doesn't matter. Results alone are insufficient evidence. The results may have been achieved by pure chance and in six months time your performance may have declined significantly. The only way to test understanding is to check the decisions people make. This can be done with a questionnaire but is more effective if one checks decisions made in the work place. Is their judgement in line with your objectives or do you have to repeatedly adjust their behaviour?

For each objective you should have a plan that defines the processes involved in its achievement. Assess these processes and determine where critical decisions are made and who is assigned to make them. Audit the decisions and ascertain whether they were contrary to the objectives. A simple example is where you have an objective of decreasing dependence upon inspection. By examining corrective actions taken to prevent recurrence of nonconformities you can detect whether a person decided to increase the level of inspection in order to catch the nonconformities or considered alternatives. Any person found increasing the amount of inspection has clearly not understood the objective.

Corporate Goals

At the corporate level the objectives are concerned with business performance and will often be expressed as business goals or a mission statement addressing markets, the environment and society.

Goals reflect the intended destination of the organization. They could be such destinations as:

- To be a world class airline
- To capture 50% of the market in high temperature lubricants
- To be first to market with innovative solutions in automobile safety
- To be an organization that people like doing business with

These destinations capture the imagination but without planning they are mere pipe dreams. You need ask: "How will we know when we have got there?" If you can't define what success looks like, you have the wrong objectives.

These are objectives for improvement – for changing the status quo. They also focus on intentions that are optional. For instance, meeting customer needs and expectations is not an option and therefore not a goal. If you make it a goal you would send out the wrong signal. It gives the impression that you do not currently intend to meet customer needs and expectations but intend to do so at some point in the future. This is an intention, not a destination and therefore a policy.

In order to establish your corporate goals you need to:

- analyse competitor products where available
- benchmark inside and outside the industry

There are many books (Codling, Sylvia., 1998)[4] and organizations you can turn to for advice on benchmarking. With benchmarking you analyse your current position, find an organization that is performing measurably better and learn from them what they are doing that gives them the competitive edge. You then change your processes as a result of what you learn and then implement the changes.

Corporate objectives for control might include those for maintaining the market share, maintaining market penetration, maintaining the values system, maintaining supplier relationships, maintaining ISO 9000 registration.

Process objectives

There are two types of processes, business processes and work processes. Business processes deliver business outputs and work processes deliver product or information required by business processes. At the process level the objectives are concerned with process performance – addressing process capability, efficiency and effectiveness, use of resources, and controllability. As a result objectives for control may focus on reducing errors and reducing waste, increasing controllability but may require innovative solution to achieve such objectives. Objectives for improvement might include increasing throughout, turnaround times, response times, resource utilization, environmental impact, process capability and use of new technologies, etc.

Product objectives

At the product level, objectives are concerned with product or service performance addressing customer needs and competition. Again these can be objectives for control or improvement. Objectives for control might include removing nonconformities in existing products (improving control) whereas objectives for improvement might include the development of new products with features that more effectively satisfy customer needs (improving performance), use of new technologies, and innovations. A product or service that meets its specification is only of good quality if it satisfies customer needs and requirements. Eliminating all errors is not enough to survive – you need the right products and services to put on the market. With the 1994 version of ISO 9000 quality management was perceived as applying after the organization had decided where it is going, what customers needed and what products and services will be supplied. However with ISO 9000:2000 this perception needs to change because the purpose of the family of standards is to enable organizations to satisfy their customers not just at the point of sale but in the product and service features they offer. This means finding out what customers want, what they need and what benefits they expect to gain from owning the organization's products or using their services. Objectives for satisfying the identified needs and expectations of customers with new product features and new service features are thus quality objectives.

Departmental objectives

At the departmental level objectives are concerned with organizational performance – addressing the capability, efficiency and effectiveness of the organization, its responsiveness to change, the environment in which people work etc. Control objectives might be to maintain expenditure within the budget, to keep staff levels below a certain level, to maintain moral, motivation or simply to maintain control of the department's operations. Objectives for improvement might be to improve efficiency by doing more with less resources, improving internal communication, interdepartmental relationships, information systems etc.

Personal objectives

At the personal level objectives will be concerned with worker performance addressing the skills, knowledge, ability, competency, motivation and development of people. Objectives for control might include maintaining time-keeping, work output and objectivity. Objectives for improvement might include improvement in work quality, housekeeping, interpersonal relationships, decision-making, computer skills etc.

Expressing quality objectives (5.4.1)

1994–2000 Differences
This is a new requirement that has no equivalent in the 1994 version.

The standard requires quality objectives *to be measurable and consistent with the quality policy.*

What does this mean?

There should be a tangible result from meeting an objective and a defined time period should be specified. The objective should therefore be expressed in the form – *what is to be achieved and by when*. It is measurable if it can be determined when the objective has or has not been achieved – the passing of a date, a level of performance, or the absence of a problem, a condition, a situation.

Each statement within the quality policy should also have an associated quality objective and each quality objective should be traceable to higher-level quality objectives that have a clear relationship with a statement within the quality policy.

Why is this necessary?

This requirement responds to the Leadership Principle.

Where objectives are not measurable there is often some difficulty in establishing whether they have been achieved. Achievement becomes a matter of opinion and therefore variable. Measures provide consistency and predictability and produce facts upon which decisions can be made.

Objectives need to be consistent with the quality policy so that there is no conflict. For example if the policy is "We will listen to our customers, understand and balance their needs and expectations with those of our suppliers, employees, investors and society and endeavour to give full satisfaction to all parties" an objective which penalizes suppliers for poor performance would be inconsistent with the policy.

How is this implemented?

Setting Objectives

A technique has evolved to test the robustness of objectives and is identified by the letters SMART meaning that objectives should be Specific, Measurable, Achievable, Realistic and Timely.

S	Specific	Objectives should be *specific* actions completed in executing a strategy. They should be derived from the mission and relevant to the process or task to which they are being applied. They should be specified to a level of detail that those involved in their implementation fully understand what is required for their completion – not vague or ambiguous and defining precisely what is required.
M	Measurable	Objectives should be *measurable* actions that have a specific end condition. Objectives should be expressed in terms that can be measured using available technology. When setting objectives you need know how achievement will be indicated, the conditions or performance levels that will indicate success.
A	Achievable	Objectives should be *achievable* with resources that can be made available – they should be achievable by average people applying average effort.
R	Realistic	Objectives should be *realistic* in the context of the current climate and the current and projected workload. Account needs to be taken of the demands from elsewhere that could jeopardize achievement of the objective.
T	Timely	Objectives should be *time-phased* actions that have a specific start and completion date. Time-phased objectives facilitate periodic review of progress and tracking of revisions.

Table 5.1 Matching objectives with the quality management principles

Objective Category	Subject	Quality Management Principles							
		Customer Focus	Leadership	Involvement of People	Process Approach	Systems Approach	Continual Improvement	Factual Approach	Supplier Relationships
Marketing	Existing products in current markets	●							
	Abandoning products	●							
	New products in current markets	●							
	New markets	●							
	New products in new markets	●							
	Standards and performance	●					●		
Innovation	Reaching market goals in near future						●		
	Taking advantage of technological advances in the distant future						●		
Human resources	Supply of managers and their development		●						
	Supply of staff and their development		●						
	Relationships with representative bodies		●						
	Relationship with suppliers								●
	Employee attitudes and competencies			●					

Category		
Physical resources	Supply of raw materials and components	●
	Supply of capital equipment	●
	Supply of buildings and facilities	●
Financial resources	Investment and attracting capital	●
	Obtaining financial resources	●
Productivity	Utilization of knowledge	●
	Utilization of physical resources	●
	Utilization of time	●
	Utilization of financial resources	●
	Making workers productive	●
	Utilizing experience and ability	●
	Utilizing reputation	●
Social responsibility	Disadvantaged people	●
	Protection of the environment	●
	Education of potential employees	●
	Contribution to professions	●
	Health and safety of employees at work	●
	Minimizing impact on society, economy, community and individual	●
Profit requirement	Producing the minimum profit needed to accomplish the other objectives	●

Although the SMART technique for objective setting is used widely, there is some variance in the words used. If you search the Internet on the key words "SMART Objectives" you will discover several variations on this theme. The S of SMART has been used to denote Small meaning not too big to be unachievable – one small step at a time. The A of SMART has been used to denote Attainable, Accountable and Action oriented and the R of SMART has been used to denote Resource – consuming action and Relevant. These differences could arise out of different uses of the technique.

Consistency with policy

The subject matter of quality objectives arises from an analysis of the factors that affect the organization's ability to accomplish its mission as stated previously. The quality policy may influence the wording of these objectives to some extent but it is doubtful that you would want to derive specific objectives from the policy itself. Let us say you have a policy that addresses customer focus. Your objectives would include marketing objectives that were customer focused thereby linking the policy with the objectives. You may have a human resource objective for improving employee motivation. However, in this instance the process designed to achieve this objective would need to demonstrate adherence to a policy for the involvement of people. Here the process and not the objective links with the policy.

Policies condition behaviour so that objectives are achieved so they may each cover different topics. Drucker identified eight categories of corporate objectives (Drucker, Peter F., 1977)[5] and these have been matched with the eight quality management principles in Table 5.1. The match is not perfect because there is no match for profit requirement, however if you were to establish your objectives based upon Drucker's categories, you would be able to show that your objectives were consistent with a quality policy that was based on the eight quality management principles.

Measures

It is important to determine the measures that will be used to verify achievement of the objectives. If you have an objective for being World Class, what measures will you use that indicate when you are World Class? You may have an objective for improved delivery performance. What measures will you use that indicates delivery performance has improved? You may choose to use % delivered on time. You will also need to set a target relative to current performance. Let us say that currently you achieve 74% on-time delivery so you propose a target of 85%. However, targets are not simply figures better than you currently achieve. The target has to be feasible and therefore it is necessary to take the steps in the process described previously for setting objectives.

In the last 30 years or so there has emerged an approach to management that focuses on objectives. Management by objectives (MBO) or management by results (MBR) has dominated boardrooms and management reports. In theory management by objectives or results is a sensible way to manage an organization but in practice this has led to internal competition, sub-optimization and punitive measures being exacted on staff that fail to perform. Deming's 14 points (Deming, W. Edwards, 1982)[6] included the elimination of management by objectives for the simple reason that management derives the goals from invalid data. They observe that a goal was achieved once and therefore assume it can be achieved every time. If they understood the process they would realize that the highs and lows are a characteristic of natural variation. They observe what the competition achieves and raise the target for the organization without any analysis of capability or any plan for its achievement. Management sets goals and targets for results that are beyond the capability of staff to control. Targets for the number of invoices processed, the number of orders won, the hours taken to fix a problem. Such targets not only ignore the natural variation in the system but also are set without any knowledge about the processes that deliver the results. If a process is unstable, no amount of goal-setting will change its performance. If you have a stable process, there is no point in setting a goal beyond the capability of the process – you will get what the process delivers.

Quality management system planning (5.4.2)

Planning to meet quality objectives (5.4.2a)

The standard requires top management *to ensure that the planning of the quality management system is performed to meet the quality objectives and the requirement in clause 4.1.*

What does this mean?

Planning is performed to achieve objectives and for no other purpose and therefore the requirement clearly indicates that the purpose of the management system is to enable the organization to meet its quality objectives. This is reinforced by the definition of quality planning in ISO 9000 which states that *it is part of quality management focused on setting objectives and specifying necessary operational processes and related resources to fulfil the quality objectives.*

The additional requirement for management system planning to meet the requirements of clause 4.1

> **1994–2000 Differences**
>
> Previously, the standard required the supplier to identify resource requirements both in general and relative to meeting the specified requirements for products, projects or contracts.
>
> When taken in conjunction with the requirement for establishing quality objectives, the new requirement implies that there has to be a clear linkage between objectives and resources to achieve them.

means that in planning the processes of the management system, you need to put in place provisions to measure, monitor and analyse processes, determine their sequence and interaction and determine criteria and methods to ensure effective operation and control. In addition you will need to provide resources and information necessary to support the operation and monitoring of these processes. The focus has clearly moved away from procedures as a means to establish a management system.

Why is this necessary?

This requirement responds to the Process Approach Principle.

The link between planning of the management system and quality objectives was not clearly expressed in the ISO 9001:1994 and consequently there was often a disconnect between the management system and quality objectives and the quality policy. This resulted in systems of documentation that served no useful purpose apart from appeasing the auditors. Now there is a clear linkage from policy to objectives and from objectives to processes that are established to meet such objectives. This means that the management system should now be more results-oriented with the objectives employed as measures of performance.

How is this implemented?

The process of defining objectives was outlined above indicating that planning proceeds only after the feasibility of achieving an objective has been established. One plans only to achieve an objective and remembering that planning consumes resources, an effective management system would need to ensure that dreams, wish lists and ambitions do not become the subject of any formal planning.

As objectives are required to be defined at relevant functions and levels, it follows that planning is also required at relevant functions and levels thereby requiring planning at corporate, divisional and department levels, product, process and system level.

The planning referred to in this clause is focused on that needed to meet the organization's objectives and not on that needed to meet specific contracts or orders or for specific products and services. This type of planning is addressed under product realization. The organizational and resource planning needed for developing a new range of products or services would be considered to be part of corporate planning.

Objectives are achieved through processes and therefore in planning to meet an objective, the planner should identify the process or processes involved. At a high level this may be no more than an outline strategy for achieving the objectives, minimizing risks and measuring success. Responsibilities may identify no more than a function or department although in some organizations ownership is deemed paramount and individual managers are named. At the lower level, the plan may extend to detail activities with a bar chart showing timescales and responsibilities.

Processes for planning

In Taylor's Scientific Management, there was a planning function that did all the planning. In the complex organizations created since Taylor's time, it has become too unwieldy for one function to do all the planning. Planning has been deployed to the function that will achieve the objective. At the corporate level there will be a corporate planning process that runs on a cycle of one, three and five years. Every function will be involved in providing their inputs. As each cycle ends a new one begins. The planning process includes the objective setting process and it is quite common for the ideas to come from below, float to the top where selections are made and passed down again for feasibility studies which go to the Board for approval and return to the source for detailed budgets and justification. Depending on the resources involved and the urgency the process may take months or even years to gain approval for the plans. The sanction to spend is often based on approval levels requiring budgets and detail plans before approval can be given. Even after such a lengthy process, there is likely to be another process for acquiring the resources that also requires approval, indicating that approved plans do not necessarily signify that permission to spend has been granted. This is often because of timing. When the time comes to acquire the resources, the priorities may have changed and plans once approved may be put on ice. It is interesting that ISO 9001 does not require plans to be implemented – it requires the *system* to be implemented and within this system may be provisions to abort plans when circumstances dictate that necessity for the survival of the organization.

It is therefore necessary to define the planning processes so that there is a clear linkage between objectives and plans to meet them.

Corporate planning

Corporate Plans should contain provisions made to accomplish corporate objectives. It is quite common to produce separate business plans of the following types:

- Annual Business Plan
- Three year Business Plan
- Five year plus Business Plan

Such plans may exist for each profit centre and consolidate the plans of all functions within that profit centre. These plans typically contain the budgets and other provisions such as head count and inventory required meeting the declared objectives. Corporate planning is not usually referred to as corporate quality planning, although in the larger enterprises, corporate quality planning may be one part of the corporate plan. In such cases, the corporate quality plan may address objectives related to improvement by better control leaving the objectives related to improvement by innovation to be defined in product development or process development plans. The labels are not important. The scope of the set of plans should address all the defined objectives regardless of what they are called.

Department planning

Corporate objectives need to be deployed to each relevant department. Some objectives may be achieved wholly within the confines of one department whereas other objectives may have one department as the primary responsibility with other departments providing a contribution. In some cases, objectives will cascade to all departments and subdivisions within each department. Departmental budgets form part of this planning and contribute to corporate planning. Departmental plans should define the provisions made for achieving departmental objectives and this may typically include the acquisition and development of physical and human resources, re-organization of staff, development of new practices, application of new technologies.

Product and process development planning

Although each department will include in its budgets provisions associated with product and process development, for large developments it is often necessary to coordinate these budgets on a corporate level to ensure nothing is overlooked. Such developments apply to innovations targeted at improving the organization's capability and not those arising from specific contracts. Product development plans will typically define provisions for research, design, development, production and launch of new products and services. At the corporate level these plans will be of a strategic nature with resources budgets, risk analysis, assumptions, dependencies, major work packages and timescales. Process development plans will typically define provisions for research, design, development, acquisition, installation and commissioning of new processes. At the corporate level these plans will again be of a strategic nature with resources budgets, risk analysis, assumptions, dependencies, major work packages and timescales. Detail plans should be created from these corporate plans to address the operational aspects from research through to in-service. These plans are addressed under product realization in Chapter 7.

Product and service objectives will clearly involve the design, development, production/delivery processes but other objectives may require re-organization, new facilities, new technology etc. The processes for achieving such objectives should form part of the management system even though there may be no clauses in ISO 9001 that directly refer to such processes.

Personal planning

The organization's objectives should be deployed down to individuals where relevant and translated into the knowledge, skills and competencies required. This often takes place during annual appraisals but it is important that the timing of such appraisals matches the corporate planning cycle so that any personnel development serves the corporate objectives. Personnel planning may be carried out at corporate, departmental and individual level. The organization may have a need for improving its capability in a new area and may therefore require all its people trained in particular subjects and skills. The quest for ISO 9000 certification may well create such a demand. Equally at departmental level, new technology may be planned for installation and all staff will require instruction and training. Both these types of change may occur outside the staff appraisal cycle and require additional personnel development planning.

Planning for change (5.4.2b)

The standard requires the integrity of the quality management system *to be maintained when changes to the quality management system are planned and implemented.*

1994–2000 Differences
This is a new requirement that has no equivalent in the 1994 version.

What does this mean?

This requirement refers to *change* in general not simply changes to the management system documentation. As the management system is the means by which the organization's objectives are achieved (not just a set of documents), it follows that that any change in the enabling mechanism should be planned and performed without adversely affecting its capability. Changes needed to accomplish these objectives should be managed and the processes required to execute the changes should be part of the management system.

It means that the linkages and the compatibility between interfaces should be maintained during a change. By being placed under *planning*, there is recognition that the plans made to meet the defined objectives may well involve changing the organization, the technology, the plant, machinery, the processes, the competency levels of staff and perhaps the culture.

Why is this necessary?

This requirement responds to the Process Approach Principle.

If changes in the management system are permitted to take place without consideration of their impact on other elements of the management system, there is likely to be a deterioration in performance. In the past it may have been common for changes to be made and some months later the organization charts and procedures to be updated indicating that these documents are perceived as historical records – certainly not documents used in executing the change. The updating activities were often a response to the results of the change process creating in people's minds that it was a housekeeping or administrative chore. To meet this new requirement, change management processes need to be designed and put in place. The integrity of the management system will be maintained only if these processes are made part of the management system so that in planning the changes, due consideration is given to the impact of the change on the organization, resources, processes and products and any resulting or associated documentation.

How is this implemented?

To control any change there are some basic steps to follow and these are outlined in Chapter 2 under quality improvement. To maintain the integrity of the management system you need to do several things:

- Use the change processes defined in the management system documentation to plan and execute the change. If they don't exist, the management system does not reflect how the organization operates. These processes should be part of the business management subsystem.
- Determine the impact of the change on the existing system and identify what else need to change to maintain system effectiveness.
- Plan and execute the change concurrently with associated changes to documentation.
- Don't remove the old processes until the new processes have been proven effective.
- Measure performance before, during and after the change.
- Don't revert to routine management until the changes have been integrated into the culture – i.e. People perform the new tasks without having to be told.

The management system should not be perceived as a set of discrete processes – all should be connected, therefore change one process and there is likely to be an effect on others. For example, if new technology is to be introduced, it may not only affect the process in which it is to be used but also the staff development process, the equipment maintenance process and the design process. It will also affect the marketing process because the new technology will improve the organization's capability and thus enabling it to create new markets, attract different customers etc. On a more mundane level, if a new form is introduced, it is not only the process in which the form is used that may be affected but also the interfacing processes that receive the form when complete. It is the information management processes that make the form available and secure its contents.

Responsibility and authority (5.5.1)

Defining responsibilities and authority (5.5.1)

The standard requires that *the responsibilities and authority be defined*.

What does this mean?

The term responsibility is commonly used informally to imply an obligation a person has to others. However, the term authority has increasingly become associated with power and public bodies but in principle one cannot have responsibility without authority and vice versa. Problems arise when these two are not matched, where one is greater or less than the other.

Responsibility is in simple terms an area in which one is entitled to act on one's own accord. It is the obligation of staff to their managers for performing the duties of their jobs. It is thus the obligation of a person to achieve the desired conditions for which they are accountable to their managers. If you cause something to happen, you must be responsible for the result just as you would if you cause an accident – so to determine a person's responsibility ask, "What can you cause to happen?"

> **1994–2000 Differences**
> Previously the standard required the responsibility and authority and interrelationship of personnel who manage, perform and verify work affecting quality to be defined and documented.
>
> The effect of the change is a move away from job descriptions to function descriptions thereby allowing more flexibility and bringing in all personnel not just those whose work affects "quality".
>
> The omission of 'interrelationships' moves away from organization charts having any role in the management of processes.

Authority is, in simple terms, the right to take actions and make decisions. In the management context it constitutes a form of influence and a right to take action, to direct and co-ordinate the actions of others and to use discretion in the position occupied by an individual, rather than in the individuals themselves. The *delegation of authority* permits decisions to be made more rapidly by those who are in more direct contact with the problem.

Why is this necessary?

This requirement responds to the Leadership Principle.

It is necessary for management to define who should do what in order that the designated work is assigned to specific individuals for it to be carried out.

In the absence of the delegation of authority and assignment of responsibilities, individuals assume duties that may duplicate those duties assumed by others. Thus jobs that are necessary but unattractive will be left undone. It also encourages decisions to be made only by top management which can result in an increased management workload but also engender a feeling of mistrust by the workforce.

How is this implemented?

An organization may respond to these requirements in several ways. The standard no longer requires responsibility and authority to be documented – instead it needs to be communicated and this may be through documentation or verbally. For anything other than a minor temporary assignment of short duration the responsibilities and authority should be documented so as to effect reliable communication. The rationale for documentation is no different than in other cases (see Chapter 4 – *What should be documented (4.2)*).

A person's job can be divided into two components: actions and decisions. Responsibilities and authority should therefore be described in terms of the actions assigned to an individual to perform and discretion delegated to an individual i.e. the decisions they are permitted to take together with the freedom they are permitted to exercise. Each job should therefore have core responsibilities that provide a degree of predictability and innovative responsibilities that in turn provide the individual with scope for development.

In defining responsibilities and authority there are some simple rules that you should follow:

- Through the process of delegation, authority is passed downward within the organization and divided among subordinate personnel whereas responsibility passes upwards.
- A manager may assign responsibilities to a subordinate and delegate authority, however he or she remain responsible for the subordinates use of that authority.
- When managers delegate responsibility for something, they remain responsible for it. When managers delegate authority they lose the right to make the decisions they have delegated but remain responsible and accountable for the way such authority is used. Accountability is one's control over the authority one has delegated to one's staff.
- It is also considered unreasonable to hold a person responsible for events caused by factors that they are powerless to control.
- Before a person can be in a state of control they must be provided with three things:
  - Knowledge of what they are supposed to do i.e. the requirements of the job, the objectives they are required to achieve

- Knowledge of what they are doing, provided either from their own senses or from an instrument or another person authorized to provide such data
- Means of regulating what they are doing in the event of failing to meet the prescribed objectives. These means must always include the authority to regulate and the ability to regulate both by varying the person's own conduct and varying the process under the persons authority. It is in this area that freedom of action and decision should be provided
- The person given responsibility for achieving certain results must have the right (i.e. the authority) to decide how those results will be achieved, otherwise, the responsibility for the results rests with those who stipulate the course of action.
- Individuals can rightfully exercise only that authority which is delegated to them and that authority should be equal to that persons' responsibility (not more or less than it). If people have authority for action without responsibility, it enables them to walk by problems without doing anything about them. Authority is not power itself. It is quite possible to have one without the other! A person can exert influence without the right to exert it.

Communicating responsibilities and authority (5.5.1)

The standard requires that the responsibilities and authority *be communicated within the organization.*

What does this mean?

Communication of responsibility and authority means that those concerned need to be informed and to understand their obligations so that there is no doubt about what they will be held accountable for.

Why is this necessary?

This requirement responds to the Leadership Principle.

There are also several reasons why it is necessary to communicate this information:

> **1994–2000 Differences**
>
> Previously the standard required the responsibility and authority of personnel who manage, perform and verify work affecting quality to be defined and documented.
>
> The effect of the change is a move away from job descriptions to function descriptions thereby allowing more flexibility and bringing in all personnel not just those whose work affects "quality".

- to convey consistency and avoid conflict
- to show which functions make which contributions and thus serve to motivate staff
- to establish channels of communication so that work proceeds smoothly without unplanned interruption

- to indicate from whom staff will receive their instructions, to whom they are accountable and to whom they should go to seek information to resolve difficulties

How is this implemented?

There are four principal ways in which responsibilities and authority can be communicated:

- In an organization structure diagram or *organigram*
- In function descriptions
- In job descriptions
- In terms of reference
- In procedures

The standard does not stipulate which method should be used. In very small companies a lack of such documents defining responsibility and authority may not prove detrimental to quality provided people are made aware of their responsibilities and adequately trained. However, if you are going to rely on training, then there has to be some written material that is used so that training is carried out in a consistent manner.

Organigrams are a useful way of showing interrelationships but imprecise as a means of defining responsibility and authority. They do illustrate the lines of authority and accountability but only in the chain of command. Although it can define the area in which one has authority to act, it does not preclude others having responsibilities within the same area e.g. the title Design Manager-Computer Products, implies the person could be responsible for all aspects of computer product design when in fact they may not have any software, mechanical engineering or reliability engineering responsibilities. Titles have to be kept brief because they are labels for communication purposes and are not usually intended for precision on the subject of responsibilities and authority. One disadvantage of organigrams is that they do not necessarily show the true relationships between people within the company. Horizontal relationships can be difficult to depict with clarity in a diagram. They should therefore not be used as a substitute for policy.

Function descriptions are useful in describing the role and purpose of a function, its objective and its primary responsibilities and authority. Function in this context refers to business functions rather than product functions and is a collection of activities that make a common and unique contribution to the purpose and mission of a business. Function is determined by the contribution made rather than the skill that the contributors possess. The marketing function in a business generates revenue and the people contributing to marketing may possess many different skills e.g. planning, organizing, selling, negotiating, data analysis etc. It is quite common to group work by its contribution to the business and to refer to these groupings as functions so that there is a marketing function, a design function a production function etc. However, it should not be assumed that all those who contribute to a function reside in one department. The marketing department may contain many staff with many skills, but often the design staff contributes to marketing. Likewise, the design function may have the major contribution from the design department but may also have contributors from research, test laboratory, trials and customer support. Therefore the organization chart may in fact not define functions at all but a collection of departments that provide a mixture of contributions. In a simple structure the functions will be clear but in a complex organization, there could be many departments concerned with the marketing function, the design function, the production function etc. For example the Reliability Engineering Department may be located in the Quality Department for reasons of independence but contributes to the design function. A Function/Department/Group description is needed to define the role the function executes in each process to which it contributes. These become useful in staff induction as a means of making new staff aware of who is who and who does what without getting into too much detail. They are also useful to analysts and auditors because they enable a picture of who does what to be quickly assimilated.

Job descriptions or job profiles are useful in describing what a person is responsible for, however it rather depends upon the reason for having them as to whether they will be of any use in managing quality. Those produced for job evaluation, recruitment, salary grading, etc. may be of use in the management system if they specify the objectives people are responsible for achieving and the decisions they are authorized to take.

Terms of reference are not job descriptions but descriptions of the boundary conditions. They act as statements that can be referred to in deciding the direction in which one should be going and the constraints on how to get there. They are more like rules than a job description and more suited to a committee than an individual. They rarely cover responsibilities and authority except by default.

Procedures are probably the most effective way of defining peoples' responsibilities and authority because it is at the level of procedures that one can be specific as to what someone is required to do and what results they are responsible for. Procedures specify individual actions and decisions. By assigning actions or decisions to a particular person or role a person carries out you have assigned to them a responsibility or given them certain authority. They do present problems however. It may be difficult for a person to see clearly what his or her job is by scanning the various procedures because procedures often describe tasks rather than objectives. When writing procedures never use names of individuals because they will inevitably change. The solution is to use position or role titles and have a description for a particular position or role that covers all the responsibilities assigned through the procedures. Individuals only need to know what positions they occupy or roles they perform. Their responsibilities and authority are clarified by the procedures and the position or role descriptions (Hoyle, David, 1996)[7].

In organizations that undertake projects rather than operate continuous processes or production lines, there is a need to define and document project related responsibilities and authority. These appointments are often temporary, being only for the duration of the project. Staff are assigned from the line departments to fulfil a role for a limited period. To meet the requirement for defined responsibility, authority and interrelationships for project organizations you will need Project Organization Charts and Project Job Descriptions for each role, such as Project Manager, Project Design Engineer, Project Systems Engineer, Project Quality Engineer etc.

As project structures are temporary, there need to be systems in place that control the interfaces between the line functions and project team. Such a system would include:

- Policies that govern the allocation of work to the divisions
- Policies that govern the allocation of work to staff in these divisions
- Job descriptions for each role stating responsibilities, authority and accountability
- Procedures that identified the roles responsible for each task and for ensuring that information is conveyed to and from these staff at the appropriate time
- Procedures that consolidate information from several disciplines for transmission to the customer when required
- Monitoring procedures to track progress and performance
- Procedures that ensure the participation of all parties in decisions affecting the product, its development and production
- Procedures for setting priorities and securing commitment
- Procedures that include the management of subcontractor programmes during development and deal with the transmission of information to and from the subcontractors, what is to be transmitted, by whom, in what form and with whose approval

Some organizations have assigned responsibility for each element of the standard to a person, but such managers are not thinking clearly. Now the elements have been reduced from 20 to 5 with ISO 9000:2000, such allocations will need to be reviewed. There are 51 clauses and many are interrelated. Few can be taken in isolation therefore such a practice is questionable. When auditors ask 'Who is responsible for purchasing?' ask them to specify the particular activity they are interested in. Remember you have a system which delegates authority to those qualified to do the job.

Management Representative (5.5.2)

Appointing management representatives (5.5.2)

The standard requires the top management *to appoint a member of management who has certain defined responsibility and authority for ensuring the quality management system is established, implemented and maintained.*

What does this mean?

This means that one manager in particular is delegated the authority and responsibility to plan, organize and control the management system. Clearly this is not a one-man job and cannot be performed in isolation because the management system comprises all the processes required to create and retain satisfied customers. It does not mean that this manager must also manage each of the processes but should act as a coordinator, a facilitator, a change agent and induce change through others who in all probability are responsible to other managers.

> **1994–2000 Differences**
>
> Previously the standard required the supplier's management with executive responsibility to appoint a member of the supplier's own management with certain defined authority. The difference is the recognition that this appointment need not be to a single individual as all members of management should bear responsibility for the QMS.

There is a note in clause 5.5.3 of ISO 9001, which states: *The responsibility of a management representative may also include liaison with external parties on matters relating to the supplier's quality management system.*

Logically a representative carries the wishes of the people they represent to a place where decisions are taken that affect them – Members of Parliament, Union Representatives, Committee Members etc. The 'note' would appear to address the need for representation outside the business. Inside the business, the person represents management to the workforce but not in the same sense. The person carries the wishes of management (i.e. the policies) to the workforce so that the workforce makes decisions that take into account the wishes of management. However, the requirement matches more closely the role of a director rather than an external representative because this person is not only representing management but also directing resources in a way that will enable the company to achieve its objectives. What the organization needs is not so much a representative but a director who can represent management when necessary and influence other managers to implement and maintain the system. Such a person is unlikely to be under the direct authority of anyone other than the CEO.

In the standard the term 'management representative' appears only in the title of the requirement. The emphasis has been put on management appointing a member of its own management, indicating that the person should have a managerial appointment in the organization. This implies that a contractor or external consultant cannot fill the role. It also implies that the person should already hold a managerial position and be on the pay roll. However, it is doubtful that the intention is to exclude a person from being promoted into a managerial position as a result of a person being available for the appointment or in fact preclude the authority of the management representative being delegated to a contractor, provided that responsibility for the tasks is retained within the company.

Why is this necessary?

This requirement responds to the Systems Approach Principle.

As everyone in some way contributes to the quality of the products and services provided, everyone shares the responsibility for the quality of these products and services. The achievement of quality, however, is everyone's job but only in so far as each person is responsible for the quality of what they do. You cannot hold each person accountable for matters over which they have no control. It is a trait of human nature that there has to be a leader for an organization to meet an objective. It does not do it by itself or by collective responsibility – someone has to lead.

In principle the Management Representative or Quality Director role is similar to the roles of the Financial Director, Security Director, Safety Director etc. It is a role that exists to set standards and monitor performance thus giving an assurance to management, customers and regulators that specified objectives are being achieved. The role takes the title from the subject that is vital to the survival of the company. If security is vital, then a director is given the task of establishing security policy and putting in a system that will ensure security is not compromised. The security staff do not implement the system – that is the duty of all other managers. The same is true for finance, personnel, quality and any other critical success factor. If quality is vital to survival then it makes sense to appoint someone to direct the programme that will ensure quality is not compromised. As with finance, security and personnel these directors do not implement the policies, they regulate compliance. The other functional managers are appointed to deal with other factors critical to the company's survival and each is bound by the others' policies. This way of delegating authority works because it establishes a champion for each key factor who can devote resources to achieving specified objectives. Each manager is responsible for some aspect of security, finance, quality, personnel etc. Their responsibilities extend to implementing policy and achieving objectives. This means that the Production Director for example, is responsible for implementing the quality policy and achieving quality objectives within a system that is under the control of the Quality Director. Likewise the Production Director is responsible for implementing the design solution that is under the control of the Design Director.

If you were to make every manager responsible for setting policy, setting up systems and ensuring compliance then you would have as many management systems as there were managers This is not an effective way to run a business. In such a structure, you would not have one company but as many companies as there were managers. If each manager is to serve common objectives, then we have to divide the objectives between them and permit one manager to impose requirements on other managers. This is what is known as functional authority.

How is this implemented?

There are two schools of thought: One is that the management representative is a figurehead rather than a practitioner and has a role established solely to meet ISO 9000. It is doubtful that any organizations not registered to ISO 9000 will have made such an appointment. Those organizations not registered would not perceive there was a system to be managed. The CEO would either take on the role or would appoint one of the executive directors as the management representative in addition to his or her regular job – the role being to ascertain that a quality management system is being established, implemented and maintained. Such a person may not necessarily employ the resources to do this. These resources would be dispersed throughout the organization. While the system is being developed, a project manager is assigned to coordinate resources and direct the project towards its completion. After the system is fully operational, a management system manager takes over to maintain and improve the system who, with a small staff, manages the audit and improvement programmes.

The other school of thought views the management representative as a practitioner and not a figurehead. Here you would appoint a senior manager as a quality director and assign him/her the role of management representative. This director takes on the role of project manager during the development phase, management system manager during the maintenance and improvement phase. He/she acts as the management representative with the customer and registrar and in effect is the eyes of the customer inside the organization. Depending on the size and complexity of the organization, there may be one person doing all of these jobs. In some cases a fairly large team of engineers, auditors, analysts, statisticians etc. may be appropriate. Before ISO 9000, organizations appointed quality managers not management representatives. The difference is that being a quality manager is a job whereas being a management representative is a role.

To give this appointment due recognition, an appointment at executive level would be appropriate. The title chosen should reflect the position and as stated previously need not be a full time job. Often companies appoint a member of the executive to take on the role in addition to other responsibilities. It could be the Marketing, Sales, Engineering, Production or any other position. The notion that there has to be independence is one that is now dated and a reflection of an age when delivery was more important than quality. A person with responsibility for delivery of product or service also carries a responsibility for the quality of his or her actions and decisions. A person who therefore subordinates quality to delivery is unfit to hold the position and should be enlightened or replaced.

If you have one management system, the role of management representative and job of quality director become difficult to separate and can cause a conflict of interest unless the management representative is the CEO. In large organizations with multiple sites, each with separate ISO 9000 registrations, a more appropriate solution is to have a management representative for each site and one quality director for the whole organization.

As with all assignments of responsibility one has to:

- define the actions and decisions for which the person is to be responsible ensuring no conflict with others
- define the competency needed
- select a person with the necessary abilities
- ensure that you give the person the necessary authority to control the results for which they are responsible
- provide and environment in which the person is motivated to achieve the results for which he/she is responsible
- evaluate and develop his or her competency to perform the role effectively

Responsibility for establishing and maintaining processes (5.5.2)

The standard requires the management representative *to ensure that processes needed for the quality management system are established, implemented and maintained.*

What does this mean?

The management system consists of interconnected processes each of which needs to be established, implemented and maintained. This requirement means that top management being responsible for the system, delegates authority to one manager (the Quality Director/Manager/Management Representative) to orchestrate the design, development, construction, maintenance and improvement of these processes.

Why is this necessary?

This requirement responds to the Leadership Principle.

If the CEO assigned responsibility for this task to each functional manager, it is likely that a fragmented system would emerge rather than a coherent one. Someone has to lead the effort required, to direct resources and priorities and judge the resultant effectiveness.

> **1994–2000 Differences**
>
> Previously the standard required the management representatives to ensure that a quality system is established, implemented and maintained and to report on the performance of the quality system to the supplier's management.
>
> Key differences are that the MR no longer is responsible for implementing the system (presumably because that is line management responsibility) and has a new responsibility for promoting awareness of customer requirements.

How is this implemented?

Primarily, the designated person is the system designer for the management system appointed by top management. This person may not design all the processes and produce the documentation but may operate as a system designer. He/she lays down the requirements needed to implement the corporate quality policy and verifies that they are being achieved. As system designer, the person would also define the requirements for processes so as to ensure consistency and lead a team of process owners who develop, implement and validate business processes. Previously the emphasis was on the management representative establishing the system that had the implication that the task was concerned with documenting procedures. This new requirement clearly changes the focus to establishing processes and with it brings in a responsibility for process management. In this regard the person needs the authority to:

- Manage the design, development, construction and evaluation of the processes of the management system including the necessary resources;
- Determine whether the processes meet the requirements of the standard, are suitable for meeting the business needs, are being properly implemented and cause non-compliances to be corrected;
- Manage the change processes for dealing with changes to the processes of the system.

Responsibility for reporting on QMS performance (5.5.2)

<table>
<tr><td>

1994–2000 Differences

Previously the standard required the management representative to report on the performance of the quality system to the supplier's management for review and as a basis for improvement of the quality system.

The requirement is more succinct without any change in intent.

</td><td>

The standard requires the management representative *to report to top management on the performance of the quality management system and the need for improvement.*

What does this mean?

This requirement means that the Quality Director collects and analyses factual data across all the organization's operations to determine whether the quality objectives are being achieved and if not, to identify opportunities for improvement.

</td></tr>
</table>

Why is this necessary?

This requirement responds to the Factual Approach Principle.

Each manager cannot measure the performance of the company relative to quality although individually they carry responsibility for the utilization of resources within their own area. The performance of the company can only be measured by someone who has the ability and authority to collect and analyse the data across all company operations. All managers may contribute data, but this needs to be consolidated in order to assess performance against corporate objectives just as a Finance Director consolidates financial data.

How is this implemented?

To report on management system performance and identify opportunities for improvement in the management system the Quality Director needs the right to:

- Determine the effectiveness of the management system;
- Report on the quality performance of the organization;
- Identify opportunities for improvement in the management system;
- Cause beneficial changes in quality performance.

By installing data collection and transmission nodes in each process, relevant data can be routed to the Quality Director for analysis, interpretation, synthesis and assessment. It can then be transformed into a language suitable for management action and presented at the management review. However, this requirement imposes no reporting time period, therefore performance should also be reported when considered necessary or on request of top management.

Responsibility for promoting awareness of customer requirements (5.5.2)

The standard requires the management representative *to ensure the awareness of customer requirements throughout the organization.*

1994–2000 Differences
This is a new requirement that has no equivalent in the 1994 version.

What does this mean?

This means that the management representative encourages and supports initiatives by others to make staff at all levels aware of customer requirements. This is not necessarily the detail requirements as would be contained in specifications, but their general needs and expectations, what is important to them, what the product being supplied will be used for and how important the customer is to sustaining the business.

Why is this necessary?

This requirement responds to the Customer Focus Principle.

Unless staff are aware of customer requirements it is unlikely they will be achieved. Customer satisfaction is the aim of the management system and hence it is important that all staff at all levels do not lose sight of this. Clearly all managers are responsible for promoting awareness of customer requirements but this does not mean it will happen as internal pressures can cause distractions. Constant reminders are necessary when making decisions in which customer satisfaction may be directly or indirectly affected. Often staff at the coalface are remote from the end user and unaware of the function or role of their output relative to the final product or service. Heightened awareness of customer requirements and the role they play in achieving them can inject a sense of pride in what they do and lead to better performance.

How is this implemented?

There are general awareness measures that can be taken and awareness for specific customers. General awareness can be accomplished through:

- the quality policy and objectives
- induction and training sessions

- instructions conveyed with product and process documentation
- bulletins, notice boards and staff briefings
- brochures of the end product in which the organization's product features
- videos of customer products and services featuring the organization's products

It is also a responsibility of designers to convey (through the product specifications) critical features and special customer characteristics. Also production planners or service delivery planners should denote special requirements in planning documents so that staff are alerted to requirements that are critical to customers (see also Chapter 6 under *Training awareness and competency*).

Responsibility for external liaison

Although a note in clause 5.5.3 of the standard, it is necessary to have someone who can liase with customers on quality issues, who can co-ordinate the assessment and subsequent surveillance visits, who can keep abreast of the state of the art in quality management through conferences, publications and exhibitions.

Internal communication (5.5.3)

Establishing communication processes (5.5.3)

1994–2000 Differences
This is a new requirement that has no equivalent in the 1994 version.

The standard requires *appropriate communication processes to be established within the organization*.

What does this mean?

Communication processes are those processes that convey information and impart understanding upwards, downwards and laterally within the organization. They include the people transmitting information, the information itself, the receivers of the information and the environment in which it is received. They also include all auditory and visual communication, the media that convey the information and the infrastructure for enabling the communication to take place. The medium of communication such as telephone, e-mail and video is the means of conveying information and forms part of the process of communication. Examples of such processes are briefings, announcements, meetings, conferences, presentations, internal publishing and distribution process (paper and intranet), internal mailing process, (paper and electronic) and display boards.

Why is this necessary?

This requirement responds to the Leadership Principle.

The operation of a management system is dependent upon effective transmission and reception of information and it is the communication processes that are the enablers. Information needs to be communicated to people for them to perform their role as well as possible. These processes need to be effective otherwise:

- the wrong information will be transmitted
- the right information will fail to be transmitted
- the right information will go to the wrong people
- the right information will reach the right people before they have been prepared for it
- the right information will reach the right people too late to be effective
- the communication will not be understood
- the communication will cause an undesirable result

How is this implemented?

As the requirement focuses on processes rather than the subject of communication it follows that whatever the information that needs to be communicated, the communicator needs to select an appropriate communication process. There needs therefore to be some standard processes in place that can be used for communicating the majority of information. There needs to be a communication policy that facilitates downwards communication and encourages upwards and lateral communication.

A simple solution would be to identify the various types of information that need to be conveyed and the appropriate process to be used. In devising such a list you need to consider the audience and their location along with the urgency, sensitivity, impact and permanency of the message.

- Audience influences the language, style and approach to be used (who are they?)
- Location influences the method (where are they?)
- Urgency influences the method and timing when the information should be transmitted (when is it needed?)
- Sensitivity influences the distribution of the information (who needs to know?)
- Impact influences the method of transmission and the competency of the sender (how should they be told and who should tell them?)
- Permanency influences the medium used (is it for the moment or the long-term?)

Communication processes should be established for communicating:

- **The vision, mission and values of the organization** – while displaying this information acts as a reminder, this does not communicate. You need to establish a process for gaining understanding, getting commitment and forming the culture.
- **Operating policies**. These are often conveyed through manuals and procedures but a communication process is needed to ensure they are understood at all levels.
- **The corporate objectives**. A process is needed for conveying these down the levels in the hierarchy with translation possibly at each level as they are divided into departmental, group, section and personal objectives.
- **Plans for entering new markets, for new products and processes and for improvement.** A process is needed for communicating plans following their approval so that all engaged in the project have a clear understanding of the strategy to be adopted.
- **Customer requirements, regulations and statutory requirements**. A process is needed for ensuring that these requirements reach the point at which they are implemented and are understood by those who will implement them.
- **Product and process objectives**. These are often conveyed through plans but a communication process is needed to ensure they are understood by those who are to use them or come into contact with them.
- **Product and process information**. A process is needed to ensure that all product and process information gets to those who need it, when they need it and in a form that they can understand.
- **Problems**. A process is needed for communicating problems from their source of detection to those who are authorized to take action.
- **Progress**. Managers need to know how far we are progressing through the plan and therefore a communication process is needed to ensure the relevant managers receive the appropriate information.
- **Change**. All change processes should incorporate communication processes in order to gain commitment to the change.
- **Results and measurements**. A process is needed for communicating financial results, quality and delivery performance, accomplishments, good news, bad news and customer feedback.

Clearly not everything can be communicated to all levels because some information will be sensitive, confidential or simply not relevant to everyone. Managers therefore need to exercise a 'need to know' policy that provides information necessary for people to do their job as well as creating an environment in which people are motivated. Other than national and commercial security, too much secrecy is often counterproductive and creates an atmosphere of distrust and suspicion that affects worker performance.

In communication processes there needs to be a feedback loop to provide a means for conveying questions and queries as well as acceptance. These feedback loops should be short – to the next level only. An Executive who demands to be kept informed of progress will soon stop reading the reports and if the process continues without change, the reports will just pile up in his or her office (Juran, J. M., 1995)[8]. This is not an uncommon phenomenon. A manager may demand reports following a crisis but fail to halt further submissions when the problem has been resolved. The opposite is also not uncommon where a local problem is not communicated outside the area and action subsequently taken which adversely affects the integrity of the management system.

Communicating the effectiveness of the QMS (5.5.3)

The standard requires communication *to take place regarding the effectiveness of the quality management system.*

> **1994–2000 Differences**
> This is a new requirement that has no equivalent in the 1994 version.

What does this mean?

This means that there should be communication from top management and from those on the scene of action (two way communication) as to whether the management system is enabling achievement of the organization's objectives. Information from above should initiate improvement action. Information from below should prompt investigation and analysis in order to identify improvement actions.

Why is this necessary?

This requirement responds to the Leadership Principle.

It is important that staff are kept informed of how effective the management system is to encourage continuation of the status quo or to encourage change. Also staff should be encouraged to report system effectiveness or ineffectiveness whenever it is encountered.

How is this implemented?

After each management review, the results can be communicated to staff but care should be taken with the format of the message. Charts against each major objective showing how performance has changed are the most effective. New improvement initiatives should also be communicated indicating the project name, the project leader or champion, the project objectives and timescales. However, the application of this requirement should not be restricted to annual communication briefings. Update the charts monthly and display on notice boards or on the intranet. Provide means for staff to alert management of ineffectiveness in the management system by opening channels through to the Quality Director. It is not uncommon for a particular practice to be changed locally or ignored altogether and subsequently discovered on periodic audit. There should be free communication so no one takes such action without consultation and agreement.

Management Review (5.6)

Purpose of review (5.6)

<table>
<tr><td>

1994–2000 Differences
Previously the standard required that the quality system be reviewed to ensure its continuing suitability and effectiveness in satisfying the requirements of ISO 9001 and the supplier's stated quality policy and objectives.

There is no difference in the intent of this requirement however, the effectiveness of the system was previously determined by the extent by which it satisfied the requirements of the standard and the quality policy – now the focus is on the QMS achieving the organization's objectives.

</td><td>

The standard requires top management *to review the quality management system to ensure its continuing suitability, adequacy and effectiveness.*

What does this mean?

A review is another view of something. Although termed a management review the requirement is strictly referring to a review of the management system (see also under *Management commitment*).

The three terms; adequacy, suitability and effectiveness are not included as three alternatives but as three different concepts. However their meanings vary as illustrated in Table 5.2.

The adequacy of the management system is judged by its ability to deliver product or service that satisfies requirements, standards and regulations. It does what it was designed to do. In some cases this condition is referred to as effectiveness.

The suitability of the management system is judged by its ability to enable the organization to

</td></tr>
</table>

sustain current performance. If the management system is inefficient, the organization may no be able to continue to feed a resource hungry system. In such cases we would be justified in claiming that the management system is not suitable for its purpose even though customers may be satisfied by the outputs, other interested parties will soon express dissatisfaction. A better term would be efficiency.

The effectiveness of the management system is judged by how well it enables the organization to fulfil the needs of society. The system may deliver satisfied customers and minimize use of resources but if it is not responding to the changing needs of society, of customers, of regulators and of other

Table 5.2 Elements of management system performance

Concept	ISO term	Other terms
Output meets requirements	Adequacy	Effectiveness
Results achieved in best way	Suitability	Efficiency
System fulfils needs	Effectiveness	Adaptability

interested parties, it is not an effective system. In some cases this concept is referred to as adaptability. However, effectiveness is about doing the right things, not doing things right. Doing things right is about satisfying the customer. Doing the right things is choosing the right objectives. If the corporate objectives change or the environment in which the organization operates changes, will the system enable the organization to achieve these new objectives or operate successfully in the new environment? If the purpose of the system is merely to ensure customers are supplied with products and services which meet their requirements, then its effectiveness is judged by how well it does this and not how much it costs to do it. If the purpose of the management system is to enable the organization to fulfil its purpose, its effectiveness is judged by how well it does this. The measures of effectiveness are therefore different.

Why is this necessary?

This requirement responds to the Systems Approach Principle.

There is a need for top management, as the sponsors of the system, to look again at the data the system generates and determine whether the system they installed is actually doing the job they wanted it to do. It is necessary that top management rather than the management representative review the system because the system serves the organization's objectives not just those of the management representative. Financial performance is reviewed regularly and a statement of accounts produced every year. There are significant benefits to be gained if quality performance is treated in the same way because it is quality performance that actually causes the financial performance. Under-performance in any area will be reflected in the financial results.

Treating the review as a chore, something that we do because we want to keep our ISO 9000 certificate, will send out the wrong signals. It will indicate that members of top management are not serious about quality or about the system they commissioned to achieve it – it will also indicate they don't understand and if they don't understand they clearly cannot be committed.

How is this implemented?

In any organization, management will conduct reviews of performance so as to establish how well the organization is doing in meeting the defined objectives. As the objectives vary it is often more practical to plan reviews relative to the performance characteristic being measured. As a result, organizations may convene strategic reviews, divisional reviews, departmental reviews, product reviews, process reviews, project reviews etc. They all serve the same purpose, that of establishing whether performance is in line with objectives. Such reviews should be part of the management system and will to some extent examine the capability of the system to deliver against objectives. The management review referred to in ISO 9001 is a review of the complete management system by top management and in a hierarchy of reviews is the top level review which should capture the results of all the lower level reviews. The standard does not require only one review. In some organizations, it would not be practical to cover the complete system in one review. It is often necessary to consolidate results from lower levels and feed into intermediate reviews so that departmental reviews feed results into divisional reviews that feed results into corporate reviews. The fact that the lower level reviews are not performed by top management is immaterial providing the results of these reviews are submitted to top management as part of the system review. It is also not necessary to separate reviews on the basis of ends and means. A review of financial performance is often separated from technical performance and both of these separate from management system reviews. This situation arises in cases where the management system is perceived as procedures and practices. The management system is the means the organization employs to achieve the ends. A review of results without review of the capability to achieve them (the means) would therefore be ineffective. For these reasons the management review as referred to in ISO 9001 could well be the Strategic Review or Business Performance Review with separate committees or focus groups targeting specific aspects. In organizations that separate their performance reviews from their management system reviews, one has to question whether they are gaining any business benefit or in fact whether they have really understood the purpose of the management system.

In determining the effectiveness of the management system you should continually ask:

- Does the system fulfil its purpose?
- To what extent are our customers satisfied with our products and services?
- Are the corporate objectives being achieved as intended?
- Do measurements of process performance indicate the processes are effective?

- Do the results of the audits indicate that the system is effective?
- Are procedures being used properly?
- Are policies being adhered to?

If the answer is 'Yes' your system is operating effectively. If your answer is 'No' to any of these questions, your management system has not been effectively designed or is not being effectively implemented.

The management review is not a meeting. Management review is an activity aimed at assessing information on the performance of the management system. When you have a real understanding of the intentions of the review you will realize that its objectives cannot be accomplished entirely by a meeting. The review should be in three stages. Stage one is collecting and analysing the data, stage two is reviewing the data and stage three is a meeting to discuss the results and decide on a course of action. One of the reasons that the management review may not work is when it is considered something separate to management's job, separate to running the business, a chore to be carried out just to satisfy the standard. This is partially due to perceptions about quality. If managers perceive quality to be about the big issues like new product or service development, major investment programmes for improving plant, for installing computerization etc., then the management review will take on a new meaning. If on the other hand it looks only at audit results it will not attract a great deal of attention unless of course the audits also include the big issues.

Planning the review (5.6.1)

The standard requires *management reviews at planned intervals*.

What does this mean?

Planned intervals means that the time between the management reviews should be determined in advance e.g. annual, quarterly or monthly reviews. The plan can be changed to reflect circumstances but should always be looking forward.

> **1994–2000 Differences**
>
> Previously the standard required management review at defined intervals. Implies that the intervals should be defined with foresight and not some arbitrary period.

Why is this necessary?

Previously the standard required reviews at defined intervals that allowed for reviews to be scheduled after each review on an ad hoc basis. The change indicates that more forethought is needed so that performance is measured on a regular basis thus enabling comparisons to be made.

How is this implemented?

This requirement responds to the Process Approach Principle.

A simple bar chart or table indicating the timing of management reviews over a given period will meet this requirement. The frequency of management reviews should be matched to the evidence that demonstrates the effectiveness of the system. Initially the reviews should be frequent say monthly, until it is established that the system is effective. Thereafter the frequency of reviews can be modified. If performance has already reached a satisfactory level and no deterioration appears within the next three months, extend the period between reviews to six months. If no deterioration appears in six months extend the period to twelve months. It is unwise to go beyond twelve months without a review because something is bound to change that will affect the system. Shortly after reorganization, (the launch of a new product/service, breaking into a new market, securing new customers etc.) a review should be held to establish if performance has changed. After new technology is planned, a review should be held before and afterwards to measure the effects of the change.

Scope of review (5.6.1)

1994–2000 Differences This is a new requirement that has no equivalent in the 1994 version.

The standard requires the review *to include assessing opportunities for improvement and the need for changes to the quality management system including quality policy and quality objectives.*

What does this mean?

The review is of current performance and hence there will be some parameters where objectives or targets have not been accomplished thus providing opportunities for improvement and some areas where the status quo is not good enough to grow the organization or meet new challenges.

Why is this necessary?

This requirement responds to the Continuous Improvement Principle.

Top management should never be complacent about the organization's performance. Even maintaining the status quo requires improvement, just to maintain market position, keep customers, retain capability. If the management review restricts its agenda to examining audit results, customer complaints and nonconformities month after month without a commitment to improvement, the results will not get any better – they will more than likely get worse.

There will be reports about new marketing opportunities, reports about new legislation, new standards, the competition and benchmarking studies. All these may provide opportunities for improvement. In this context improvement means improvement by better control (doing this better) as well as improvement by innovation (doing new things). These changes may affect the quality policy (see also under *Ensuring the policy is reviewed*) and will certainly affect the objectives. Objectives may need to change if they prove to be too ambitious or not far reaching enough to beat the competition.

How is this implemented?

The implication of this new requirement is that performance data on the implementation of quality policy and the achievement of quality objectives should be collected and reviewed in order to identify the need to change the system, the quality policy and quality objectives.

As the management system is the means by which the organization achieves its objectives, it follows that the management review should evaluate the need for changes in the objectives and the processes designed to achieve them. It is therefore insufficient to limit the review to documentation as was often the case when implementing ISO 9000:1994. In fact as no function, process or resource in the organization would exist outside the management system, the scope of the review is only limited by the boundary of the organization and the market and environment in which it operates.

The approach you take should be described in your quality manual – but take care! What you should describe is the process by which you determine the suitability, adequacy and effectiveness of the management system and in doing so describe all the performance reviews conducted by management and show how they serve this objective. Describing a single management review without reference to all the other ways in which performance is reviewed sends out the signal that there isn't an effective process in place.

Records of management reviews (5.6.1)

The standard requires the results of management reviews *to be maintained*.

What does this mean?

A record of the results of the review means the outcome of the review but the outcome won't be understood unless it is placed in the right context. The records therefore also need to include the criteria for the review and who made what decisions.

1994–2000 Differences

Previously the standard required records of management review to be maintained. The new requirement for records of the results of reviews rather than records of reviews does have implications. A record of a review could be the minutes of a meeting whereas a record of the results of the review is much more and could include the input data, analysis, conclusions, recommendations and decisions in addition to minutes of any meetings that took place.

Why is this necessary?

This requirement responds to the Factual Approach Principle.

Recorded results of management reviews are necessary for several reasons:

- to convey the actions from the review to those who are to take them
- to convey the decisions and conclusions as a means of employee motivation
- to enable comparisons to be made at later reviews when determining progress
- to define the basis upon which the decisions have been made
- to demonstrate system performance to interested parties

How is this implemented?

Although the intent of the requirement may appear unchanged, the new requirement for records of the results of reviews rather than records of reviews does have some implications. Using an analogy, test records would not only indicate a pass or fail but would indicate the acceptance criteria, the actions taken on the failures, the identity of those performing the tests, the location of the test etc. Therefore the records of management reviews need to contain:

- Date and location review
- Contributors to the review (The process owners, functional managers, management representative, auditors etc.)
- Criteria against which the management system is being judged for effectiveness (The organization's objectives)
- Criteria against which the management system is to be judged for continued suitability (Future changes in the organization, legislation, standards, customer requirements, markets)
- The evidence submitted, testifying the current performance of the management system (Charts, tables and other data against objectives)
- Identification of strengths, weaknesses, opportunities and threats (SWOT – the analysis of: What are we good at? What we are not good at? What can we change? What can't we change? What must we change?)
- Conclusions (Is the management system effective or not and if not in what way?)

- Actions and decisions (What will stay the same and what will change?)
- Responsibilities and timescales for the actions (Who will do it and by when will it be completed?)

Review inputs (5.6.2)

The standard requires inputs to management review *to include information about various aspects of the system.*

1994–2000 Differences

This is a new requirement that has no equivalent in the 1994 version.

What does this mean?

This means that data from audits, product measurements, process measurements, customers, suppliers, regulators, etc has to be analysed relative to defined objectives to establish current performance (How are we doing?) and identify improvement opportunities (Can we do better?). Data on planned changes in the organization, resources, the infrastructure, legislation and standards have to be examined for their impact.

Why is this necessary?

This requirement responds to the Factual Approach Principle.

It is necessary to gather sufficient data relative to the objectives being measured to provide a sound basis for the review. Any review of the management system needs to be based on fact. The factors identified in this clause cover most of the parameters influencing the effectiveness of the management system.

How is this implemented?

The key questions to be answered are; 'Is the system effective?' and 'Is it suitable for continued operations without change?' At every meeting of the review team these questions should be answered and the response recorded. In order to answer these questions certain inputs are required. The standard identifies several inputs to the review, which are addressed below, but these should not be seen as limiting. The input data should be that which is needed to make a decision on the effectiveness of the system. Rather than use a generic list as is presented in the standard, a list tailored to business needs should be developed and continually reviewed and revised as necessary.

System performance

The most important factor has been omitted from the list of inputs in clause 5.6.2 of ISO 9001. System performance data should be used to establish whether the defined quality objectives are being met. It may also be used to establish whether there is conflict between the stated quality policy, the quality objectives and the organizational purpose and the expectations and needs of the interested parties. There may be a small number of factors upon which the performance of the organization depends and these above all others should be monitored. For example in a telephone datacentre, processing thousands of transactions each day, system availability is paramount. In a fire department or an ambulance service, response time is paramount. In an air traffic control centre the number of near misses is paramount because the centre exists to maintain aircraft separation in the air. Analysis of the data that the system generates should reveal whether the targets are being achieved. It is also important to establish whether the system provides useful data with which to manage the business. This can be done by providing evidence showing how business decisions have been made. Those made without using available data from the management system show either that poor data is being produced or management is unaware of its value. One of eight quality management principles is the *factual approach to decision making* and therefore implies decisions should be made using data generated from the management system.

Improvement opportunities may cover:

- the identification of major projects to improve overall performance
- the setting of new objectives and targets
- the revision of the quality policy
- the adequacy of the linkages between processes

Audit results

Audit results should be used to establish whether the system is being used properly and whether the commitments declared in the quality policy are being honoured. You can determine this by providing the results of all quality audits of the system, of processes and of products. An analysis of managerial decisions should reveal whether there is constancy of purpose or lip service being given to the policy. Audit results should also be used to establish whether the audit programme is being effective and you can determine this by providing the evidence of previous audit results and problems reported by other means. Current performance from audit results should compare the results with the quality objectives you have defined for the system as a whole and for the audit programme in particular.

Improvement opportunities relative to audit results may cover:

- the scope and depth of the audit programme
- the suitability of the audit approach to detecting problems worthy of management attention

- the competency of the auditors to add value and discover opportunities that enhance the organization's capability
- the relevance of audit results to the organization's objectives

Customer feedback

Customer feedback should be used to establish whether customer needs are being satisfied. You can determine this by providing the evidence of customer complaints, market share statistics, competitor statistics, warranty claims, customer satisfaction surveys etc. Current performance from customer feedback should compare the results with the quality objectives you have set for customer needs and expectations.

Improvement opportunities relative to customer feedback may cover:

- the extent to which products and services satisfy customer needs and expectations
- the adequacy of the means used to assess customer satisfaction and collect data
- the need to develop new or enhanced products or services
- the need to explore new markets or obtain more accurate data of current markets

Process performance

Process performance data should be used to establish whether process objectives are being achieved. Current performance of processes should compare process data with the quality objectives you have set for the processes. Improvement opportunities relative to process performance may cover:

- the efficiency of processes relative to the utilization of resources (physical, financial and human resources and the manner in which they are structured)
- the effectiveness of processes relative to the utilization of knowledge, experience in achieving process objectives
- the need to change process design, methods and techniques including process measurement
- the need to reduce variation
- the need to meet or exceed new legal and regulatory requirements that apply to the process

Product performance

Product performance data should be used to establish whether products fulfil their intended purpose in both design and build quality. Current performance of products should compare product data with product specifications and product specifications with design intent (what the product was intended to accomplish). Improvement opportunities relative to product performance may cover:

- the need to change product design, technology and materials
- the need to change product literature to match actual performance (reset expectations)
- the adequacy of the means used to measure product performance and collect data
- the conditions of use and application

Corrective actions

Corrective action data should be used to establish whether the recurrence of problems is being prevented. Current performance on the status of corrective actions should compare the results with the quality objectives you have set for dealing with corrective actions such as closure time and degree of recurrence. Improvement opportunities relative to corrective actions may cover:

- the adequacy of problem analysis and resolution techniques
- the need for new training programmes
- the capability of the system to maintain performance in line with objectives (its sensitivity to change)

Preventive actions

Current performance on the status of preventive actions should compare the results with the quality objectives you have set for dealing with preventive actions such as closure time and degree of occurrence. Remember that preventive actions are supposed to prevent the occurrence of problems therefore a measure of status is the extent to which problems occur. However, this is an area that often causes confusion. Preventive action is often not an action identified as preventive but an action identified under guise of planning, training, research and analysis. Why else would you plan but to achieve objectives and hence to prevent failure? Why else do you perform an FMEA, but to prevent failure? Therefore don't just look for actions with the label *preventive*.

Improvement opportunities relative to preventive actions may cover:

- the adequacy of techniques to identify potential problems
- the need for new tools and techniques, training programmes etc.
- the re-organization of departments, resources etc

Actions from management reviews

Current performance on follow-up actions from earlier management reviews should address not only whether they are open or closed but how effective they have been and how long they remain outstanding as a measure of planning effectiveness.

Improvement opportunities relative to actions from management reviews may cover:

- the prioritization of actions
- the reclassification of problems relative to current business needs
- the need to re-design the management review process

Changes affecting the management system

It is difficult to foresee any change inside the organization that would not affect the management system in some way or other. However, the management system should be designed to cope with a degree of change without top management intervention. The change in management processes to bring in new products, new processes, new people, new resources and new organization structures should be part of the management system. The system should be designed to handle such changes as a routine. If the management system is perceived as a set of documents, there are many changes that might not affect the management system but as stated previously, the management system is much more than this. Also changes in products, processes, organization structures etc. will all affect the management system documentation but there should be processes in place to manage these changes under controlled conditions. In an environment in which perceptions of the management system have not been harmonized, it is likely that some change mechanisms will be outside the documented management system and in such circumstances, these changes need to be brought to the management review.

Review outputs (5.6.3)

The standard requires the outputs from the management review *to include decisions and actions related to the improvement of the effectiveness of the quality management system and its processes, improvement of product and actions related to resource needs.*

> **1994–2000 Differences**
> This is a new requirement that has no equivalent in the 1994 version.

What does this mean?

Improving the effectiveness of the management system is not about tinkering with documentation but enhancing the capability of the system so that it enables the organization to fulfil its objectives more effectively. The management system comprises processes therefore the effectiveness of these too must be improved. Improvement of product related to customer requirements means not only improving the degree of conformity of existing product but enhancing product features so that they meet changing customer needs and expectations.

Why is this necessary?

This requirement responds to the Continual Improvement Principle.

The outcomes of the management review should cause beneficial change in performance. The performance of products is directly related to the effectiveness of the process that produces them. The performance of these processes is directly related to the effectiveness of the system that connects them. Without resources no improvement would be possible.

How is this implemented?

The implication of this requirement is that the review should result in decisions being made to improve products, processes and the system in terms of the actions required.

Actions related to improvement of the system and its processes should improve the capability of the system to achieve the organization's objectives. Such actions should therefore focus on making beneficial changes in methods, techniques, relationships, measurements, behaviours, capacity, competency etc. A quick fix to overcome a problem is neither a system change nor a system improvement because it only acts upon a particular problem. If the fix not only acts upon the present problem but also will prevent its recurrence, it can be claimed to be a system improvement. This may result in changes to documentation but this should not be the sole purpose behind the change – it is performance that should be improved.

Actions related to improvement of products should improve:

- the quality of design i.e. the extent to which the design reflects a product that satisfies customer needs
- the quality of conformity i.e. the extent to which the product conforms to the design
- the quality of use i.e. the extent to which the user is able to secure continuity of use and low cost of ownership from the product

Such actions may result in providing different product features or better-designed product features as well as improved reliability, maintainability, durability and performance. Product improvements may also arise from better packaging, better user instructions, clearer labelling, warning notices, handling provisions etc.

Actions related to resource needs are associated with the resource planning process that should be part of the management system. If this process were operating effectively, no work would commence without adequate resources being available. If the resources cannot be provided, the work should not proceed. It is always a balance between time, effort and materials. If the effort cannot be provided the time has to expand accordingly.

Summary

In this chapter we have examined the requirements contained in section 5 of ISO 9001. All these requirements apply to top management and their implementation reflects the leadership style of the organization. We have shown that an understanding of customer needs and expectations is vital for organizations to prosper and essential for developing an effective management system. We have also discovered that success is not simply about getting results. The manner in which these results are obtained is important if we are to satisfy all interested parties. We have learnt that this is where policies are needed to guide our actions and decisions and our behaviour in accomplishing the purpose and mission of the organization. We have seen that objectives are important in focusing the efforts of people so that they all pull in the same direction. But we have also seen that setting objectives and targets without a plan for meeting them is futile just as setting an objective or a target beyond the capability of the system will create frustration and low moral. Lastly we have realized the importance of evaluating system effectiveness and recognized that we must change the approach taken towards management review. We now know there is only one system and therefore our management review is a review of the way we manage the organization.

Management Responsibility Questionnaire

Management commitment

1 What evidence can top management provide of its commitment to the development and implementation of the quality management system?
2 What evidence can top management provide of its commitment to continually improve the effectiveness of the quality management system?
3 How has top management communicated to the organization the importance of meeting customer requirements?
4 How has top management communicated to the organization the importance of meeting statutory and regulatory requirements?

5 What evidence can top management provide that it has established a quality policy?

6 How does top management ensure that quality objectives are established?

7 What evidence can top management provide that it has conducted management reviews?

8 What evidence can top management provide that the necessary resources have been available to implement the quality policy and achieve the quality objectives?

Customer focus

9 How does top management ensure that customer requirements are determined?

10 How does top management ensure that customer requirements are met with the aim of enhancing customer satisfaction?

Quality policy

11 How do you ensure that the quality policy is appropriate to the purpose of the organization?

12 How does the quality policy cause a commitment to comply with requirements?

13 How does the quality policy cause continual improvement in the effectiveness of the management system?

14 In what way does the quality policy provide a framework for establishing and reviewing quality objectives?

15 How do you ensure that the quality policy is communicated and understood within the organization?

16 How often is the quality policy reviewed for continuing suitability?

Planning

17 How does top management ensure that quality objectives are established at relevant functions and levels within the organization?

18 How do you ensure quality objectives are measurable and consistent with the quality policy?

19 How does top management ensure that the planning of the management system is performed to meet the quality objectives and the requirement in clause 4.1?

20 How do you ensure that the integrity of the management system is maintained when changes to the management system are planned and implemented?

Responsibility, authority and communication

21 In what documents have the responsibilities and authority been defined?

22 How do you communicate responsibilities and authority within the organization?

23 Whom has top management appointed as the member of management with defined responsibility and authority for ensuring the management system is established, implemented and maintained?

24 How does the management representative ensure that processes needed for the management system are established, implemented and maintained?

25 What information does the management representative report to top management concerning the performance of the management system?

26 What information does the management representative report to top management on the need for improvement?

27 How does the management representative ensure the awareness of customer requirements throughout the organization?

28 What communication processes have been established within the organization?

29 How do you communicate the effectiveness of the management system?

Management review

30 How does top management ensure the quality management system is suitable, adequate and effective?

31 What intervals have been planned for conducting management reviews of the quality management system?

32 What opportunities for improvement and changes to the management system have been identified as a result of management reviews?

33 What changes to the quality policy and quality objectives have been made as a result of management reviews?

34 What records are maintained of management reviews?

35 What information is used as inputs to management review?

36 What are the outputs from the management review?

Management Responsibility – Food for Thought

1 Does your quality management system make the right things happen or is it just a set of procedures?

2 Does your management perceive the quality management system as the means by which the organization's objective are achieved?

3 Does your organization exist to make profit or to create and retain satisfied customers?

4 Does your quality policy affect how people behave in your organization or is it simply a slogan?

5 Do all your quality objectives relate to the organization's purpose and mission or are they focused only on what the quality department will achieve?

6 Does your management review examine the way the organization is managed or does it simply focus on conformity issues?

7 Do you struggle to obtain the necessary resources to do your job, or have you designed your job so that you get all the resources necessary for you to achieve your objectives?

8 Do you wait to receive a customer enquiry before identifying customer needs and expectations or have you researched the market in which you operate so that your offerings respond to customer needs?

9 What made you think that by simply publishing your quality policy, anything would change?

10 If you didn't know your current performance, how did you manage to set meaningful objectives?

11 When you set your objectives, was there any discussion on how they might be achieved and did it result in changing the way you do things?

12 If you don't think you need to change, how come you didn't meet these objectives last year?

13 How will you know when you have achieved your objectives?

14 Are you sure that none of the managers' objectives relate to extracting more performance from unstable processes?

15 Are you sure that none of the managers are tasked with meeting objectives for which no plans have been agreed for their achievement?

16 How many plans are the managers working on that have an objective that is not derived from the business plan?

17 Are you sure that managers are not pursing objectives that will cause conflict with those of others managers?

18 Are you sure you have not imposed a target on a member of staff for performance improvement when it is the system that requires improvement?

19 Do you always consider the impact of change on other processes before you proceed?

20 Does your staff know of the results for which they are accountable and are their job descriptions limited to such responsibilities?

21 If your management representative is unable to influence the other managers to implement, maintain and improve the management system, are you sure you have appointed the right person?

22 How often do you check that messages conveyed from management are actually understood by those they are intended to affect?

23 How often do you check that messages conveyed by workers are actually given due consideration by management and interpreted as the consequence of their own actions and decisions?

24 If the person with the most interest in the effectiveness of the management system is not your CEO, is there not something wrong with the way the management system is perceived in the organization?

Bibliography

1. Peters, Tom and Waterman, Robert, (1995). *In Search of Excellence,* Harper Collins.
2. Drucker, Peter F., (1977). *Management,* Harper's College Press.
3. Juran, J. M., (1995). *Managerial Breakthrough Second Edition.* McGraw-Hill. (1995).
4. Codling, Sylvia, (1998). *Benchmarking,* Gower.
5. Drucker, Peter F., (1977). *Management,* Harper's College Press.
6. Deming, W. Edwards, (1982). *Out of the crisis,* MITC.
7. Hoyle, David, (1996). *ISO 9000 Quality System Development Handbook,* Butterworth Heinemann.
8. Juran, J. M., (1995). *Managerial Breakthrough Second Edition,* McGraw-Hill.

Chapter 6
Resource management

Only the orchestra playing a joint score makes music

Peter F. Drucker

Summary of requirements

Section 6 of ISO 9001 draws together all the resources-related requirements that were somewhat scattered in the 1994 version. Resource management is a key business process in all organizations. In practice, resource management is a collection of related processes that are often departmentally oriented.

- Financial resources are controlled by the Finance Department.
- Purchased materials, equipment and supplies are controlled by the Purchasing Department.
- Measuring equipment maintenance is controlled by the Calibration Department.
- Plant maintenance is controlled by the Maintenance Department.
- Staff development is controlled by the Human Resources or Personnel Department.
- Building maintenance is controlled by the Facilities Management Department.

These departments control the resources but do not manage them. They therefore only perform a few of the tasks necessary to manage resources. Collectively they control the human, physical and financial resources of the organization.

The resource management process has a number of distinct stages as shown in Figure 6.1.

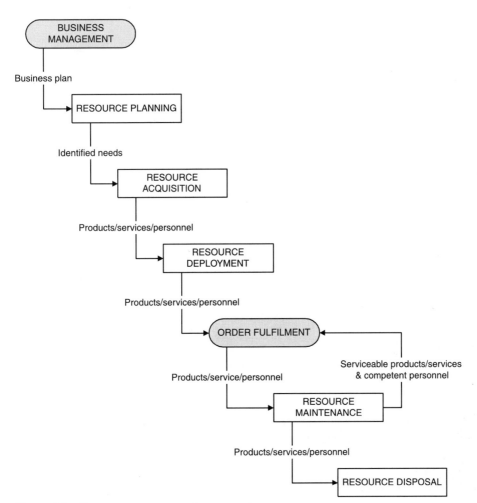

Figure 6.1   Resource management process stages

Whatever the resource, it firstly has to be planned, then acquired, deployed, maintained and eventually disposed of. The detail of each process will differ depending on the type of resource being managed. Human resources are not 'disposed off' but their employment or contract terminated although the standard does not address disposal of any resources. Resource disposal impacts the environment and other interested parties. Only measuring devices need calibration but other devices need verification. The standard does not address financial resources specifically but clearly they are required to implement and maintain the management system. Purchasing is not addressed under resource management but under product realization. However, the location of clauses should not be a barrier to the imagination because their location is not governed by the process approach but by user expectations. The clauses of ISO 9001 are related to these processes as indicated in Table 6.1.

Table 6.1   Clause alignment with process model

Resource management processes	Human	Physical				Finance
	Personnel	Plant, equipment & materials	Buildings	Utilities and Support Services	Measuring devices	Finance
Resource Planning	6.1 6.2.2a 7.1	6.1 6.3 7.1	6.1 6.3 7.1	6.1 6.3 7.1	7.1 7.6	6.1 7.1
Resource Acquisition	6.1 7.4	6.1 6.3 7.4	6.1 6.3	6.1 6.3 7.4	7.4	6.1
Resource Deployment	4.1d 6.1 6.2.1	4.1d 6.1 6.3	4.1d 6.1 6.3	4.1d 6.1 6.3	4.1d 7.5.1	4.1d 6.1
Resource Maintenance	6.2.2b	6.3	6.3	6.3	7.6	NA
Resource Disposal	NA	NA	NA	NA	NA	NA

Note that there are no clauses that address resource disposal. This is probably because the standard only focuses on intended product, whereas ISO 14001 would address resource disposal and unintended product.

Determining resources (6.2.1)

The standard requires the organization *to determine the resources needed to implement and maintain the quality management system, continually improve its effectiveness and enhance customer satisfaction by meeting customer requirements.*

What does this mean?

Determination of resources means identifying resource needs. The resources needed to implement the management system include all human, physical and financial resources needed by the organization for it to function. The resources needed to maintain the management system are those needed to maintain a level of performance. The resources needed to continually improve the effectiveness of the management system are those needed to implement change in the organization's processes. Those resources needed to enhance customer satisfaction are no more than those needed to achieve the organization's objectives because of the linkage between customer requirements, policy, objectives and processes. What is missing is the determination of resources to establish the management system that includes the human, physical and financial resources to design and construct the processes needed to enable the organization to achieve its objectives. As clause 4.1 requires the organization to establish, implement, maintain and continually improve the management system this could be more of an oversight than intentional.

If you put a boundary around the management system and perceive it only as a part of the overall management system, there will be those resources which serve the management system and those which serve other purposes, but such boundaries are not useful because they divert attention from the basic goal of satisfying the interested parties. If you are faced with making a decision as to what to include and exclude, the question you need to answer is 'Why would we want to exclude a particular resource from the management system? What business benefit is derived from doing so? Hopefully, you will conclude there are no benefits from their exclusion and many benefits from their inclusion.

Why is this necessary?

This requirement responds to the Process Approach Principle.

Without adequate resources, the management system will not function. As addressed previously, the management system is more than a set of documents. It is a dynamic system and requires human, physical and financial resources for it to deliver the required results. Starve it of resources and the planned results will not be achieved.

How is this implemented?

Resource management is a common feature of all organizations and whilst it may be known by different titles, the determination and control of the resources to meet customer needs is a fundamental requirement and fundamental to the achievement of all other requirements.

There are two types of resource requirements: those needed to set up and develop the organization and those needed to execute particular contracts or sales. The former is addressed in clause 6.1 and the latter in clause 7.1.

The way many companies identify resource requirements is to solicit resource budgets from each department covering a 1 to 5 year period.

However, before the managers can prepare budgets they need to know what requirements they will have to meet. They will need access to the corporate plans, sales forecasts, new regulations and statutes, new product development plans, marketing plans, production plans etc. as well as the quality policies, objectives, process descriptions and procedures.

In specifying resource needs for meeting product requirements there are three factors that need to be defined – the quantity, delivery and quality expressed by questions such as: How many do you want? When do you want them? To what specification/standard do they need to be? These factors will affect cost directly and if not determined when establishing the budgets, you could have difficulty later when seeking approval to purchase. In specifying resource needs for meeting organizational requirements there are three factors that need to be defined. These are the objectives for maintaining the status quo, objectives for improving efficiency and objectives for improving effectiveness.

Although resources are normally configured around the organization's departments not its processes, departmental resource budgets can divert attention away from process objectives. A more effective way to determine resources is by process and not by department. In this way the resources become focused on process objectives and overcome conflicts that can arise due to internal politics and the power structure. It then becomes less of a problem convincing top management of the need when it can be clearly demonstrated that the requested resource serves the organization's objectives.

A practical way of ensuring that you have adequate resources is to assign cost codes to each category of work and divide them into two categories: *maintenance* and *improvement*. Include all costs associated with maintaining the status quo under maintenance and all costs associated with change under improvement. You can then focus on reducing maintenance costs for the same level of sales without jeopardizing improvement. It is often difficult to obtain additional resources after the budget has been approved but provided they can be justified against the organization's objectives, it should not be a problem.

There are four types of change that affect resources.

- The unplanned loss of capability (staff leave or die, equipment/software obsolescence, major breakdown, fuel shortage, man-made or natural disaster)
- An increase or reduction in turnover (doing more/less of what we do already)
- A change in the organization's objectives (aiming at new targets, new products, new processes)
- A change in the external standards, regulations, statutes, markets, customer expectations (we have to do this to survive)

Providing resources (6.2.1)

The standard requires the organization *to provide the resources needed to implement and maintain the quality management system, and continually improve its effectiveness and enhance customer satisfaction by meeting requirements.*

> **1994–2000 Differences**
>
> Previously the standard required that the supplier:
>
> (a) provide adequate resources, including the assignment of trained personnel;
>
> (a) acquire any resources that may be needed to achieve the required quality.
>
> There is now clarification of the intent.

What does this mean?

Providing resources means acquiring and deploying the resources that have been identified as being needed. The acquisition process, should deliver the resource in the right quantity and quality when they are needed. The deployment process should transport and prepare the resource for use. Therefore, if there is an identified need for human resources, they have been provided only when they are in position ready to assume their duties i.e. deemed competent or ready to take up a position under supervision. Likewise with equipment, it has been provided only when it is installed, commissioned and ready for use. The maintenance process should maintain stock levels, equipment, people, facilities etc. so that there is no shortage of supply of capable and suitable physical and human resources.

Why is this necessary?

This requirement responds to the Process Approach Principle.

For plans to be implemented resources have to be provided but the process of identifying resources can be relatively non-committal. It establishes a need, whereas the provision of resources requires action on their acquisition which depending on prevailing circumstances may not lead to all needs being provided for when originally required.

How is this implemented?

As indicated above, providing resources requires the implementation of the acquisition processes. The physical resources will be initiated through the purchasing process; the human resources through the recruitment process and the financial resources through the funding process. The purchasing process is dealt with further under Purchasing in Chapter 7. An example of a recruitment process is illustrated in Figure 6.2. The acquisition of financial resources is beyond the scope of this book because such methods are so varied and

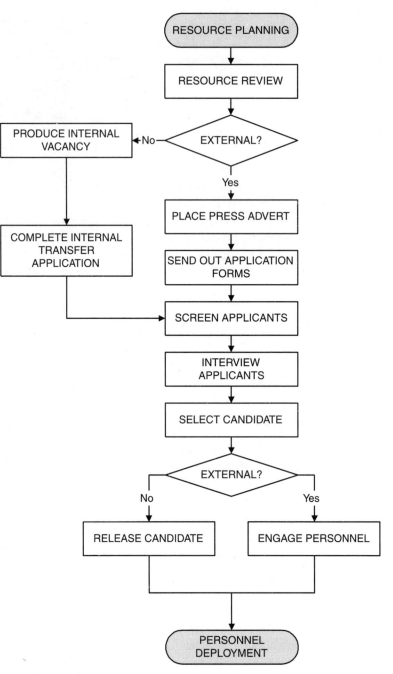

Figure 6.2   Personnel acquisition process flow

specialized. For example funds can be acquired by cutting costs, eliminating waste, downsizing, selling surplus equipment, stocks and shares or seeking a bank loan.

Inventory

Inventory is not addressed in ISO 9001 but clearly an adequate supply of materials and components is necessary for the organization to produce the required products and deliver the required services.

To enable you to achieve delivery requirements you may need adequate stocks of parts and materials to make the ordered products in the quantities required. In typical commercial situations, predicting the demand for your products is not easy – organizations tend to carry more inventory than needed to cope with unexpected demand. The possibility of an unexpected increase in demand leads to larger inventories as an out-of-stock situation may result in lost customer orders. Most companies have to rely on forecasts and estimates. Some customers may protect you to some extent from fluctuations in demand by giving you advanced notification of their production and service require-ments in order that your production schedule can be 'order driven'. In the event that an increase in demand is necessary you should be given adequate warning in order that you can increase your inventory in advance of the need. If adequate warning cannot be given, you need suitable clauses in your contract to protect you against any unexpected fluctuations in demand that may cause you to fail to meet the delivery requirement.

Inventory management is concerned with maintaining economic order quantities in order that you order neither too much stock nor too little to meet your commitments. The stock level is dependent upon what it costs both in capital and in space needed to maintain such levels. Even if you employ a 'ship-to-line' principle, you still need to determine the economic order quantities. Some items have a higher value than others thereby requiring a higher degree of control. Use of the Pareto principle will probably reveal that 20% of inventory requires a higher degree of control to enable you to control 80% of the inventory costs.

Whether or not 100% on-time delivery is a requirement of your customers, you won't retain customers for long if you continually fail to meet their delivery requirements regardless of the quality of the products you supply. It is only in a niche market that you can retain customers with a long waiting list for your products. In competitive markets you need to exceed delivery expectations as well as product quality expectations to retain your market position.

In addition to establishing an inventory management system, you should optimize turnover time – meaning that the time an item goes through the system from receipt to use should be an optimum. To achieve optimum turnover you will need metrics for receiving and storage times. You should also assure stock rotation, meaning that parts and materials are used on a first-in-first-out (FIFO) basis. The picking system will need to be date sensitive to operate FIFO.

Competence of personnel (6.2.1)

1994–2000 Differences

Previously the standard required:

(a) that trained personnel be assigned for management, performance of work and verification activities including internal quality audits;

(b) personnel performing specific assigned tasks to be qualified on the basis of appropriate education, training and/or experience, as required;

(c) design and development activities to be assigned to qualified personnel equipped with adequate resources.

There is change from trained personnel to competent personnel and a narrowing of applicability to those affecting product quality.

The standard requires *personnel performing work affecting product quality to be competent on the basis of appropriate education, training, skills and experience.*

What does this mean?

If a person has the appropriate education, training and skills to perform a job the person can be considered qualified. If a person demonstrates the ability to achieve the desired results the person can be considered competent. Qualified and competent are therefore not the same. Qualified personnel may not be able to deliver the desired results. While they may have the knowledge and skill, they may exhibit inappropriate behaviours (The expert who knows everything but whose interpersonal skills cause friction with staff!).

A competent person may not be appropriately educated, trained or possess what are perceived to be the required skills (The pragmatist who gets the job done but can't explain how he does it). This requirement therefore presents a dichotomy because you can't be competent on the basis of appropriate education, training and skills unless you can also demonstrate you can achieve the required results. The standard fails to specify whether competence in this context is about what individuals *know* or what individuals *can do*. Taking a pragmatic approach, it would not serve the intent of the standard to simply focus on what people know therefore competence in the context of ISO 9000 must be about what people *can do*.

Competence is the ability to demonstrate *use* of knowledge, skills and behaviours to achieve the results required for the job. It is the ability to perform the whole work role not just specific tasks, the ability to meet standards that apply in the particular job not in a classroom or examination and the ability to perform in real working environments with all the associated variations, pressures, relationships and conflicts. Competence is not a probability of success in the execution of one's job; it is a real and demonstrated capability. ISO 9000 defines competence as the demonstrated ability to apply knowledge and skills. The subtle difference in this definition is that the frame of reference is not present by there being no reference to the results required for the job and behaviours have been omitted but we must assume this is an oversight and not intentional.

Competence is concerned with outcomes rather than attributed abilities. Competence is more than a list of attributes. A person may claim to have certain ability but proof of competence is only demonstrated if the desired outcomes are achieved. While the opposite of competence is incompetence we tend to use the phrase 'not yet competent' to describe those who have not reached the required standard of competence. Competence does not mean excellence. Competence is meeting the established performance or behavioural standards. Excellence is exceeding the established standards. Competence is a quality of individuals, groups and organizations. Corporate competence empowers an organization to build a competitive advantage and is the result of having capable processes that deliver corporate goals. Core competences are the things the organization is good at and these are dependent upon employing competent human resources.

The requirement makes a distinction between those personnel whose work affects product quality and those personnel whose work does not affect product quality. Why would you not want all your personnel to be competent? It makes no sense! In principle, everyone's work affects the quality of the products and services supplied by the organization, some directly, others indirectly.

Why is this necessary?

This requirement responds to the Leadership and Involvement of People Principles.

Traditionally personnel have been selected on the basis of certificated evidence of qualifications, training and experience rather than achievement of results. Here are some examples showing the inadequacy of this method:

- A person may have received training but not have had the opportunity to apply the knowledge and skills required by the job.
- A person may have practiced the acquired skills but not reached a level of proficiency to work unsupervised.
- A person may possess the knowledge and skills required for a job but may be temporarily or permanently incapacitated (A professional footballer with a broken leg is not competent to play the game until his leg has healed and he is back on top form).

- A person may have qualified as a chemist 30 years ago but not applied the knowledge since.
- Airline pilots who spend years flying one type of aircraft will require some period in the flight simulator before flying another type because they are not deemed competent until they have demonstrated competency.
- A person may have been competent in maintaining particular air traffic control equipment but has not had occasion to apply the skills in the last 12 months – in this industry the engineers need to demonstrate competence before being assigned to maintain a particular piece of equipment because flight safety is at risk.

The above examples illustrate why the possession of qualifications, training certificates and years of experience are not necessarily adequate proof of competence. With the 1994 version of ISO 9001, all that was needed was to demonstrate that personnel had the qualifications, training and experience required for the work – not that they were competent to perform it although in may cases, the staff appraisal system was offered as proof that staff were suitable for the job. However, staff appraisal systems are notoriously inadequate because the standards are not measurable and performance is based on the subjective and sometimes biased judgement of the managers and not the measured performance and behaviours of their staff.

How is this implemented?

In any organization there are positions that people occupy, jobs they carry out and roles they perform in these positions. For each of these certain outcomes are required from the occupants. The starting point is therefore to define the outcomes required from a job and then define what makes those performing it successful and agree these with the role/job holder. However, having set these standards, they become the basis for competence assessment and competence development. The education and training provided should be consistent with enabling the individual concerned to achieve the agreed standards.

The outcomes required of a role or job has two dimensions. There are the hard results such as products and decisions and the soft results such as behaviours, influence and stamina. The outcomes are also dependent upon the conditions or context in which the role/job is performed. For instance manager of a large enterprise may produce the same outcomes as the manager of a small enterprise but under entirely different conditions. It follows therefore that a competent manager in one context may not be competent in another.

For instance, a person who occupies the position of production manager in a glass factory performs the role of a manager and therefore needs to be competent in achieving the required results through use of appropriate physical and human resources. This person also performs several different jobs concerned with the production of glass and therefore may need to be competent to negotiate with suppliers, use computers, produce process specifications, blow glass, drive trucks, test chemicals, administer first aid etc. depending on the scale of the operations being managed. Each job comprises a number of tasks that are required to deliver a particular result. Having a fork lift truck driving certificate is not a measure of competence. All this does is prove that the person can drive a forklift truck. What the organization may need is someone who can move 4 tons of glass from point A to point B safely in 5 minutes using a fork lift truck. The management role may occupy some people 100% of the time and therefore the number of competencies needed is less than those who perform many different types of jobs in addition to management. For this reason there is no standard set of competencies for any particular position because each will vary but there are national schemes for assessing competence relative to specific occupations. In the UK the National Vocational Qualification (NVQ) scheme has been operating since 1986. The central feature of NVQs is the National Occupational Standards (NOS) on which they are based. NOS are statements of performance standards that describe what competent people in a particular occupation are expected to be able to do. They cover all the main aspects of an occupation, including current best practice, the ability to adapt to future requirements and the knowledge and understanding that underpin competent performance. NVQs are work-related, competence-based qualifications. They reflect the skills and knowledge needed to do a job effectively and represent national standards recognized by employers throughout the country. Five levels of competence are defined covering knowledge, complexity, responsibility, autonomy and relationships.

While ISO 9001 does not require vocational qualifications such as the UK NVQ scheme, the implication of this requirement for competence is that managers will need to select personnel on the basis of their ability to deliver the outcomes required. Selecting a person simply because they are related to the boss would not be appropriate unless of course they could also deliver the required outcomes!

The standard requires:

- personnel to be competent
- the necessary competence to be determined
- actions to be taken to satisfy these needs
- the evaluation of the effectiveness of actions taken

The standard is therefore implying that organizations should employ competence-based assessment techniques but as indicated previously, it is not explicit nor is it clarified in ISO 9004 whether competence in this context is based on what people know or what they can do. The current method of selection may be on the basis of past performance but without performance standards in place and a sound basis for measurement, this method is not capable of delivering competent people to the workplace.

You will need to maintain documentary evidence that personnel are competent to perform the jobs assigned to them and to do this you need to identify the competence needed and demonstrate that a competence assessment process is employed to validate competence. This is addressed in the next section. Fletcher (Fletcher, Shirley, 2000)[1] provides useful guidance on designing competence-based assessment programmes. Competence-based assessment has a number of uses:

- Assessment for certification (not required for ISO 9001 but regulations or customers may require this. Airline pilots, welders, gas fitters are some examples)
- Performance appraisal (indirectly required by ISO 9001 from the requirement for an evaluation of actions take to satisfy needed competence)
- Identification of training needs (required by ISO 9001)
- Skills audit (indirectly required by ISO 9001 from the requirement to ensure the organization has the ability to meet product requirements and from the requirement for selecting competent personnel)
- Accreditation of prior learning (not required by ISO 9001)
- Selection and recruitment (required by ISO 9001)
- Evaluating training (required by ISO 9001)

There is also considerable information on competence from the International Labour Organization (ILO)(International Labour Organization, 2001)[3] founded in 1919 and an agency of the United Nations.

Training, awareness and competence (6.2.2)

Determining competence necessary (6.2.2a)

The standard requires the organization *to determine the necessary competence for personnel performing work affecting product quality.*

1994–2000 Differences

Previously the standard required the supplier to establish and maintain documented procedures for identifying training needs.

The new requirement has a wider implication than its predecessor.

What does this mean?

Individual competence is concerned with the ability of a person to achieve a result whereas training is concerned with the acquisition of skills to perform a task and education is concerned with the acquisition of knowledge. It is therefore not a question of whether a person has the skills and knowledge to do a job but on whether a person is able to achieve the desired outcome. This is known as the competence-based approach. Academic qualifications tend to focus on theory or application of theory to work situations. In contrast, the competence-based approach focuses on the results the individuals are achieving. People are either competent or not yet competent. There are no grades, percentages or ratings. People are deemed competent when they have demonstrated performance that meets all the requirements standards. A person who is appropriately educated, trained and experienced is competent only if they have the ability to produce the desired results when required. If for some reason a competent person became incapacitated they would no longer be deemed competent to perform the job they were performing prior to the incapacity.

Why is this necessary?

This requirement responds to the Leadership and Involvement of People principles.

When assigning responsibility to people we often expect that they will determine what is needed to produce a good result and perform the job right first time. We are often disappointed. Sometimes it is our fault because we did not adequately explain what we wanted or more likely, we failed to select a person that was competent to do the job. We naturally assumed that because the person had a college degree, had been trained in the job and had spent the last two years in the post, that they would be competent. But we would be wrong, primarily because we had not determined the necessary competence for the job and assessed whether the person had reached the standard of competence we had defined as necessary. In theory we should select only personnel who are competent to do a job but in practice we select the personnel we have available and compensate for their weaknesses either by close supervision or by providing the means to detect and correct their failures.

The competence-based movement developed in the 1960s out of a demand from businesses for greater accountability and more effective means of measuring and managing performance. This led to research into what makes people effective and what constitutes a competent worker. Two distinct competence-based systems have emerged. The British model focuses on standards of occupational performance and the American model focuses on competency development. In the UK the standards reflect the outcomes of workplace performance. In the USA, the standards reflect the personal attributes of individuals who have been recognized as excellent performers (Fletcher, Shirley, 2000)[4] but what individuals achieved in the past is not necessarily an indication of what they achieve in the future; they age, they forget and they may not be as agile both physically and mentally as they once were.

Competence is particularly important in the professions because the outputs result from an intellectual process rather than an industrial process. We put our trust in professionals and expect them to be competent but methods of setting standards of competence and their evaluation have only been developed over the last 10 years. It was believed that education, training and experience were enough, but the recent cases of malpractice particularly in the medical profession have caused the various health authorities to look again at clinical competence.

How is this implemented?

Determining the competence necessary for performing a job is a matter of determining the outcomes required of a job, the performance criteria or standards to be achieved, the evidence required and the method of obtaining it. It is important that the individuals whose performance is to be assessed are involved in the setting of these standards.

The jobs that people perform must be related to the organization's objectives and as these objectives are achieved through processes, these jobs must contribute to achievement of the process objectives. In the decomposition from the system level where the business processes are identified through to work processes and sub-processes you will arrive at a level where the results are produced by a single person. The objectives for these processes or sub-processes describe outcomes 'What must be achieved? If you then ask, 'What must be done for this to be achieved?' These are termed *units of competence*. Several units of competence will be necessary to achieve a given outcome. For example a front line operator's primary output is conforming product. The operator needs to possess several competences for conforming product to be produced consistently.

For example an operator might need the ability to:

- Understand and interpret technical specifications
- Set up equipment
- Operate the equipment so as to produce the required output
- Undertake accurate measurements
- Apply variation theory to the identification of problems
- Apply problem-solving methods to maintain control of the process

Simply possessing the ability to operate a machine is not a mark of competence.

Table 6.2 shows the key questions to be asked, the terms used and one example. It should be noted that there may be several performance criteria and a range of methods used to collect the evidence. It should also be noted that the evidence should be against the unit of competence not against each performance criteria because it is competence to deliver the specified outcome that is required not an ability to produce discrete items of evidence (Fletcher,

Table 6.2 Competence-based assessment

Key Question	What this is called	Example
What must be achieved?	Outcome	Conforming product
What must be done for this to be achieved?	Unit of Competence	The ability to apply variation theory to the identification of problems (this is one of several)
How well must this be achieved?	Performance criteria	Distinguishes special cause problems from common cause problems (this is one of several)
How should assessment be conducted?	Assessment method	Observation of performance
What evidence should be collected?	Evidence requirement	Run charts indicating upper and lower control limits with action taken only on special causes (this is one of several)

Shirley, 2000)[5]. Terminology in this area is not yet standardized and therefore there are some differences in the terms between the British and American competence-based systems. For instance, performance criteria seem to be clustered into Elements of Competence in the British system.

When considering the introduction of a competence-based assessment system Fletcher provides a useful check list (Fletcher, Shirley, 2000)[6].

Is the proposed system:

- based on the use of explicit statements of performance?
- focused on the assessment of outputs or outcomes of performance?
- independent of any specified learning programme?
- based on a requirement in which evidence of performance is collected from observation and questioning of actual performance as the main assessment method?
- one which provides individualized assessment?
- one which contains clear guidance to assessors regarding the quality of evidence to be collected
- one which contains clear guidelines and procedures for quality assurance?

The determination of competence requires that we have defined a standard for competence, measured performance and acquired evidence of attainment.

We therefore need to ask:

- What are the key results or outcomes for which the person is responsible? (The units of competence)
- What are the principal tasks the individual is expected to perform and the expected behaviours the individual is required to exhibit to achieve these outcomes? (The elements of competence)
- What evidence is required to demonstrate competence?
- What method of measurement will be used to obtain the evidence?

The methods for setting competence standards are quite complex therefore the reader should consult the various references in Appendix B.

The purpose in determining competence is to identify the requirements for the job. Requirements for new competencies arise in several ways as a result of:

- job specifications
- process specifications, maintenance specifications, operating instructions etc.
- development plans for introducing new technologies
- project plans for introducing new equipment, services, operations etc.
- marketing plans for launching into new markets, new countries, new products and services
- contracts where the customer will only permit trained personnel to operate customer owned equipment
- corporate plans covering new legislation, sales, marketing, quality management etc.
- an analysis of nonconformities, customer complaints and other problems
- developing design skills, problem-solving skills or statistical skills
- introducing a quality system thus requiring awareness of the topics covered by ISO 9000, the quality policies and objectives and training in the implementation of quality system procedures, standards, guides etc.

Once the competency requirements have been specified, managers should plan the development needed for their staff.

Providing for training (6.2.2b)

The standard requires the organization *to provide training or take other actions to satisfy these needs.*

What does this mean?

Having identified the competence needs, this requirement addresses the competence gap but this gap is only established after assessing competence.

Therefore there are two types of action needed to satisfy these needs – competence assessment and competence development.

Why is this necessary?

This requirement responds to the Leadership and Involvement of people principles.

Having identified the competence needed to achieve defined outcomes, it is necessary to determine the current level of competence and provide the means to develop the competence of personnel where it is found that staff are not yet competent in some areas of their job.

> **1994–2000 Differences**
>
> Previously the standard required the supplier to:
>
> (a) provide for the training of all personnel performing activities affecting quality;
>
> (b) acquire any skills that may be needed to achieve the required quality.
>
> The requirement removes the limitation of training as a means to provide competence.

How is this implemented?

To operate a competence-based approach to staff selection, development and assessment it is necessary to:

- Set criteria for the required performance
- Collect evidence of competence
- Match evidence to standards
- Plan development for areas in which a 'not yet competent' decision has been made

A number of questions arise when considering the collection and assessment of evidence.

- What do we want to assess?
- Why do we want to assess it?
- Who will perform the assessment?
- How will we ensure the integrity of the assessment?
- What evidence should be collected?
- Where will the evidence come from?
- How much evidence will be needed?
- When should the assessment commence?
- Where should the assessment take place?
- How will we conduct the assessment?
- How will we record and report the findings?

Answers to these questions can be found in Fletcher's book on Competence-based assessment techniques and also on the ILO web site.

Once the results of the competence assessment are known, the gap may be bridged by a number of related experiences:

- Training courses where an individual undertakes an internal or external course
- Mentoring where a more senior person acts as a point of contact to give guidance and support
- Coaching where a more experienced person transfers knowledge and skill
- Job rotation where a person is temporarily moved into a complementary job to gain experience or relieve boredom
- Special assignments where a person is given a project that provides new experiences
- Action learning where a group of individuals work on their own but share advice with others and assist in solving each other's problems
- On the job learning where the individual explores new theories and matches these with organizational experience

Beware of training courses that are no more than talk and chalk sessions where the tutor lectures the students, runs through hundreds of slides and asks a few questions! There is little practical gain from these kinds of courses. A course that enables the participants to learn by doing, to learn by self-discovery and insight is a *training* course. The participants come away having had an experience. Just look back on your life, and count the lessons you have learnt by listening and watching and compare that number with those you have learnt by doing. The latter will undoubtedly outnumber the former.

Encourage your staff to make their mistakes in the classroom not on the job or if this is not practical, provide close supervision on the job. Don't reprimand staff under training – anyone can make mistakes. An environment in which staff are free to learn is far better than one in which they are frightened of doing something wrong.

If training is necessary to improve skills involving the operation or maintenance of tools or equipment, you need to ensure that any practical aids used during training:

- represent the equipment that is in operational service;
- adequately simulate the range of operations of the service equipment;
- are designated as training equipment and only used for that purpose;
- are recorded and maintained indicating their serviceability and their design standards including records of repairs and modifications.

Students undertaking training may inadvertently damage equipment. It may also be necessary to simulate or inject fault conditions so as to teach diagnostic skills. Training activities may degrade the performance, reliability and safety of training equipment and so it should be subject to inspection before and after training exercises. The degree of inspection required would depend on whether the equipment has been designated for use only as training equipment or whether it will be used either as test equipment or to provide operational spares. If it is to be used as test or operational equipment, it will need to be re-certified after each training session. During the training sessions, records will need to be maintained of any fault conditions injected, parts removed and any other act which may invalidate the verification status of the equipment. In some cases it may be necessary to refurbish the equipment and subject it to the full range of acceptance tests and inspections before its serviceability can be assured. Certification can only be maintained while the equipment remains under controlled conditions. As soon as it passes into a state where uncontrolled activities are being carried out, its certification is immediately invalidated. It is for such reasons that it is often more economical to allocate equipment solely for training purposes.

Evaluating the effectiveness of personnel development activities (6.2.2c)

The standard requires *the organization to evaluate the effectiveness of the actions taken.*

> **1994–2000 Differences**
> This is a new requirement – it has no equivalent in the 1994 version. The implication is that whatever the means used to develop competency, the results need to be evaluated and action taken should the person remain incompetent.

What does this mean?

All education, training, experience or behavioural development should be carried out to achieve a certain objective. The effectiveness of the means employed to improve competence is determined by the results achieved by the individual doing the job. Regardless of how well the education, training or behavioural development has been designed; the result is wholly dependent on the intellectual and physical capability of the individual. Some people learn quickly others learn slowly and therefore personnel development is incomplete until the person has acquired the appropriate competence i.e. is delivering the desired outcomes.

Why is this necessary?

This requirement responds to the Factual Approach and Involvement of people principles.

The mere delivery of education or training is not proof that it has been effective. Many people attend school only to leave without actually gaining an education. They may pass the examinations but are not educated because they are often unable to apply their knowledge in a practical way except to prescribed examples. The same applies with training. A person may attend a training course and pass the course exam but may not have acquired the necessary proficiency – hence the necessity to evaluate the effectiveness of the actions taken.

How is this implemented?

Competence is assessed from observed performance and behaviours in the workplace not from an examination of education and training programmes far removed from the workplace.

Having established and agreed standards of competence for each role and job in the organization, those who can demonstrate attainment of these standards are competent. Thus competent personnel have the opportunity to prove their competence.

Fletcher (Fletcher, Shirley, 2000)[7] identifies the following key features of a competence-based assessing system:

- Focus on outcomes
- Individualized assessment
- No percentage rating
- No comparison with other individual's results
- All standards must be met
- Ongoing process
- Only 'competent' or 'not yet competent' judgements made

There are three parts to the evaluation:

- An evaluation of the personnel performance activity before development
- An evaluation of the personnel performance immediately on completion of development activity
- An evaluation of the personnel development activity within weeks of its completion

Deming illustrates this as a run chart (Deming, W. Edwards, 1982)[8] an example of which is shown in Figure 6.3.

Development activity evaluation (the initial stage)

Activity evaluation by the students themselves can only indicate how much they felt motivated by the event. It is not effective in evaluating what has been learnt. This is more likely to be revealed by examination at the end of the event or periodically throughout the development period. However, the type of examination is important in measuring the effectiveness of the personnel

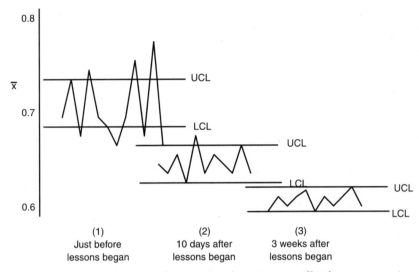

Figure 6.3 Average daily scores for a patient learning to walk after an operation

development e.g. a written examination for a practical course may test the theories behind the skills but not the practical mastery of the skills themselves. A person may fail an exam by not having read the question correctly, so examination by itself cannot be a valid measure of training effectiveness. You need to examine the course yourself before sending your staff on it. If you want information to be conveyed to your staff, a lecture with accompanying slide show may suffice. Slide shows are good for creating awareness but not for skill training. Skills cannot be acquired by any other means than by doing.

Development activity effectiveness short term (the intermediate stage)

We often think of training as a course away from work. We go on training courses. But the most effective training is performed on the job. Training should be primarily about learning new skills not acquiring knowledge – that is education. On returning to work or normal duties after a course it is important that the skills and knowledge learnt are put to good effect as soon as possible. A lapse of weeks or months before the skills are used will certainly reduce the effectiveness. Little or no knowledge or skill may have been retained. Training is not about doing something once and once only. It is about doing something several times at frequent intervals. One never forgets how to ride a bicycle or drive a car regardless of the time-lapse between each attempt, because the skill was embedded by frequency of opportunities to put the skill into practice in the early stages. Therefore to ensure effectiveness of training you ideally need to provide opportunities to put into practice the newly acquired skills as soon as possible. The person's supervisor should then examine the students' perform-ance through sampling work pieces, reading documents he or she produces and observing the person doing the job. If you have experts in the particular skills then in addition to appraisals by the supervisor, the expert should also be involved in appraising the person's performance. Pay particular attention to the person's understanding of customer requirements. Get this wrong and you could end up in trouble with your customer!

Development activity effectiveness long term (the final stage)

After several months of doing a job and applying the new skills, a person will acquire techniques and habits. The techniques shown may not only demonstrate the skills learnt but also those being developed through self-training. The habits may indicate that some essential aspects of the training have not been understood and that some reorientation is necessary. It is also likely that the person may have regressed to the old way of doing things and this may be due to matters outside his or her control. The environment in which people work and the attitudes of the people they work with can have both a motivating and de-motivating effect on an individual. Again the supervisor should observe the person's performance and engage the expert to calibrate his or her judgement. Pay particular attention to customer requirements and whether the trainee really understands them. If there are significant signs of regression you will need to examine the cause and take corrective action.

Increasing sensitivity to the impact of activities (6.2.2d)

1994–2000 Differences

Previously this topic was limited to requiring the supplier to ensure that the quality policy is understood at all levels in the organization.

The implication is that managers have to take responsibility for their staff perceptions – if staff perceive their work to be unimportant or an action to have no effect when the opposite is true then managers have failed to educate their staff.

The standard requires the organization *to ensure that its personnel are aware of the relevance and importance of their activities and how they contribute to the achievement of the quality objectives.*

What does this mean?

Every activity an individual is required to perform should serve the organization's objectives either directly or indirectly. All activities impact the organization in some way and the quality of results depends on how they are perceived by the person performing them. In the absence of clear direction, personnel use intuition, instinct, knowledge and experience to select the activities they perform and how they should behave. Awareness of the relevance of an activity means that individuals are more able to select the right activities to perform in a given context. Awareness of the importance of an activity means that individuals are able to approach the activity with the appropriate behaviour. Some activities make a significant contribution to the achievement of objectives and others make less of a contribution but all make a contribution. Awareness of this contribution means that individuals are able to apportion their effort accordingly.

Why is this necessary?

This requirement responds to the Customer Focus and Involvement of People principles.

Other than those at the front end of the business, personnel often don't know why they do things, why they don't do other things, why they should behave in a certain way and why they should or should not put a lot of effort into a task. Some people may work very hard but on activities that are not important, not relevant or not valued by the organization. Working smart is much better and is more highly valued and why awareness of the relevance and importance of activities and their contribution to the organization's objectives is essential for enabling an organization to function effectively.

Awareness of contribution also puts a value on the activity to the organization and therefore awareness of the contribution that other people make puts a job in perspective, overcomes grievances and discontent. Personnel can sometimes get carried away with their sense of self-importance that may be based upon a false premise. When managers make their personnel aware of the context in which activities should be performed, it helps redress the balance and explain why some jobs are paid more than others, or more highly valued than others.

There are perhaps thousands of activities that contribute to the development and supply of products and services some of which create features that are visible to the customer or are perceived by the customer as important. They may be associated with the appearance, odour, sound, taste, function or feel of a product where the activity that creates such features is focused on a small component within the product the customer purchases. They may also be associated with the actions, appearance or behaviour of service delivery personnel where the impact is immediate because the personnel come face to face with the customer. However close to or remote from the customer and seemingly insignificant, the result of an activity will impact customer satisfaction. Explaining the relationship between what people do and its effect on customers can have a remarkable impact on how personnel approach the work they perform. Awareness creates pride, a correct sense of importance and serves to focus everyone on the organization's objectives.

How is this implemented?

An obvious way of implementing this requirement is for managers to advise staff before an event of the type of actions and behaviours that are considered appropriate. Also managers should advise staff during or immediately after an event that their action or behaviour is inappropriate and explain the reasons for this. If done in a sympathetic and sensitive manner the effect can be productive and people will learn. If done insensitively, abruptly and in a condescending manner, the effect can be counterproductive and people will not learn. However, the success of this method depends upon managers being on the scene of action to observe intended or actual behaviour.

There are other ways of building awareness.

- Induction to a new job
- Training for a new or changed job
- Product briefings
- Chart displays and warning notices
- Performance results briefings
- Videos showing activities in context, where components are used, safety incidents etc.
- Coaching of personnel by demonstrating appropriate behaviour that they may follow

A source of information is the Failure Modes and Effects Analysis carried out on the product and process as a means of identifying preventive action. In this analysis the possible modes of failure are anticipated and measures taken to eliminate, reduce or control the effect. Such measures may include staff training and awareness as to the consequence of failure or nonconformity. However, it is sometimes not enough to explain the consequences of failure, you may need to enable them to see for themselves the effect using simulations, prototypes or case studies. Staff may have no idea of the function that the part they are producing performs, where it fits, how important it is. This education is vital to increasing sensitivity. In many organizations this sensitivity is low. The manager's task is to heighten sensitivity so that everyone is in no doubt what effect nonconformity has on the customer.

You can take a horse to water but you can't make it drink so the saying goes! It is the same with people! Making personnel aware of the quality issues and how important they are to the business and to themselves and the customer may not motivate certain individuals. The intention should be to build an understanding of the collective advantages of adopting a certain style of behaviour. It is therefore more important to modify behaviour than promote awareness. A good example is to look at what has happened with smoking in the USA. Once an expected behaviour in all but places of worship, it has now been driven out of most public places by pressure from society. It has become, certainly in some states, unacceptable behaviour of the worst kind. However smokers have been *aware* of the dangers and unsociable effects for years but have not been motivated to change their behaviour. Those that changed did so either because they were ostracized by their friends or acknowledged that they were damaging their health or they had no option because they realized their life was in immediate danger unless they stopped. Therefore awareness is only one step to take – it is by no means the only step to changing behaviour.

Maintaining training records (6.2.2e)

The standard requires the organization *to maintain records of education, training, skills and experience.*

What does this mean?

As the requirement references clause 4.2.4, the records referred to are records that provide:

- evidence of the extent to which a person's abilities fulfil certain competence requirements
- evidence of activities performed to specify, develop or verify the abilities of a person who is intended to fulfil certain competence requirements

> **1994–2000 Differences**
> Previously the standard required the supplier to maintain appropriate records of training.
> The difference here is that records of training alone are insufficient and that any actions taken to improve competency should be recorded.

Such records will include a personal development plan indicating the actions to be taken by the organization and the individual in meeting competence requirements as well as the records of the actions taken and records of any measurement and verification of competence. Therefore the records required need to extend beyond lists of training courses, academic qualifications and periods of experience because these only record actions taken and not whether they were planned or whether they achieved the desired result.

Calling these records training records becomes misleading because they will contain evidence of other activities as well as training. They are part of the personnel records but do not constitute all the personnel records because these will undoubtedly include confidential information such as promotions, grading, disciplinary records etc. A more suitable label for the records that contain the results of competence assessment would be Personnel Competence Records.

Why is this necessary?

This requirement responds to the Factual Approach Principle.

The justification for records is provided in Chapter 4.

How is this implemented?

The standard is somewhat inconsistent in this requirement. Previously it required personnel to be competent, next it required the necessary competence to be determined but instead of requiring records of competence it reverts back to requiring only records of education, skills, training and experience. It would be more useful to generate records of the competence assessments.

Comparing product records with personnel records can be a useful way to determine the information required in competence records.

The Job Specification identifies the competence needed and the Personnel Development Plan identifies the education, training and behavioural development required to bridge the gap in terms of courses of study, training and development together with dates. Re-verification therefore provides evidence of education, training and behavioural development undertaken together with dates completed. The Certification of Competence provides evidence that the actions were effective. However, certification of competence is not required unless it is necessary for regulatory purposes. With this method you will also need to maintain separately in the personnel records, historical records of education, training and experience to provide a database of capability that can be tapped when searching for potential candidates for new positions.

Whenever any personnel development is carried out you should record on the individual's personal file, details of the course taken, the dates, duration and exam results (if one was taken). Copies of the certificate should be retained on file as evidence of training but these are not necessarily evidence of competence. You may find it useful to issue each individual with a PDP that includes personal development log, but do not rely on this being maintained or retained by the person in question. Often personnel development records are

Table 6.3 Contrasting product records and personnel records

Product record	*Personnel record*
Identity of product	Identity of person
Product specification reference	Job specification reference
Required characteristics	Required competences
Product verification stages	Competence assessment stages
Product verification method	Competence assessment method
Inspector or tester	Competence assessor
Product verification results	Assessment results
Nonconformity Reports	Opportunities for Improvement
Remedial action plan	Personal development plan
Re-verification results	Re-assessment results
Certification of conformity	Certification of competence
Certifying authority	Certifying authority

held at some distance away from an individual's place of work and in certain cases, especially for certificated personnel performing special processes, individuals should carry some identification of their proficiency so as to avoid conflict if challenged.

The records should indicate whether the prescribed level of competence has been attained. In order to record competence, formal training needs to be followed by on-the-job assessment. The records should also indicate who has conducted the education, training or behavioural development and there should be evidence that this person or organization has been assessed as competent to deliver and evaluate such activities.

Competence records should contain evidence that the effectiveness of action taken has been evaluated and this may be accomplished by a signature and date from the assessor against the stages of evaluation.

Periodic reviews of Competence records should be undertaken to clearly identify personnel development needs.

You will need two types of competence records – those records relating to a particular individual and those relating to particular activities. The former is used to identify an individual's competence and the latter to select competent people for specific assignments.

Infrastructure (6.3)

The standard requires the organization *to determine, provide and maintain the infrastructure needed to achieve conformity to product requirements.*

What does this mean?

ISO 9000 defines infrastructure as the system of permanent facilities and equipment of an organization. Infrastructure also includes basic facilities, equipment, services and installations needed for growth and functioning of the organization. Such basics would include the buildings and utilities such as electricity, gas, water and telecommunications. Within the buildings it would include the office accommodation, furniture, fixtures and fittings, computers, networks, dining areas, medical facilities, laboratories, plant, machinery and on the site it would include the access roads and transport. In fact everything an organization needs to operate other than the financial, human and consumable resources. In many organizations infrastructure is classified

1994–2000 Differences

Previously the standard required:

(a) the identification and acquisition of any equipment (including inspection and test equipment), fixtures and resources that may be needed to achieve the required quality;

(b) the identification of any measuring requirements that exceeds the known state of the art in sufficient time for the needed capability to be developed;

(c) suitable maintenance of equipment to ensure continuing process capability.

under the heading of *capital expenditure* because it is not order-driven i.e. it does not change on receipt of an order.

The identification and provision of the infrastructure needs no explanation but in maintaining the infrastructure the implications go beyond the maintenance of what exists. Maintenance is more to do with maintaining the capability the infrastructure provides. Plant and facilities can be relatively easily maintained, but maintaining their capability means continually providing a capability even when the existing plant and facilities are no longer serviceable. Such situations can arise due to man-made and natural disasters. Maintaining the infrastructure means maintaining output when there is a power cut, a fire, a computer virus, a flood, a gas explosion or when an aircraft crashes onto the facility. Maintaining the infrastructure therefore means making provision for disaster recovery and therefore maintaining business continuity.

The emphasis in this requirement is on infrastructure needed to achieve conformity to product requirements. As the conforming product is the organization's output, it follows that most of the infrastructure exists for this purpose. However, there will be areas, buildings, facilities etc. that may not be dedicated to this purpose but to meeting requirements of interested parties other that the customer of the organization's products. The requirement is not implying that these other facilities do not need to be identified, provided and maintained, but that such provision is not essential to meet ISO 9001. As with determining resources previously ask; 'Why would we want to exclude a particular resource from the management system? What business benefit is derived from doing so?

Why is this necessary?

This requirement responds to the Process Approach Principle.

The design, development and supply of products and services do not exist in a vacuum. There is always an infrastructure within which these processes are carried out and upon which these processes depend for their results. Without an appropriate infrastructure and appropriate maintenance of that infrastructure the desired results will not be achieved. A malfunction in the infrastructure can directly affect results.

How is this implemented?

Identifying infrastructure

In identifying the resources needed to implement the quality system, some are product, project, contract, order specific, others are needed for maintenance and growth of the organization. These are likely to be classified as capital assets. The management of the infrastructure is a combination of asset management (knowing what assets you have, where they are, how they are depreciating and what value they could realize) and of facilities management (identifying, acquiring, installing and maintaining the facilities).

As the infrastructure is a critical factor in the organization's capability to meet customer requirements, and ability to continually meet customer requirements, its management is vital to the organization's success. Within the resource management process there are therefore several sub-processes related to the management of the infrastructure. It would be impractical to put in place one process because the processes will differ depending upon the services required. Based on the generic model for resource management (see Figure 6.1) several planning processes will be needed for identifying and planning the acquisition, deployment, maintenance and disposal of the various assets. In describing these processes, you need to cover the aspects addressed in Chapter 4 under Process Descriptions and in doing so, identify the impact of failure upon the organization's ability to achieve conforming product.

Providing infrastructure

Providing the infrastructure is associated with the acquisition and deployment of resources and therefore processes addressing the acquisition and deployment of buildings, utilities, computers, plant, transport etc. need to be put in place. Many will use the purchasing process but some require special versions of this process because provision will include installation and commissioning and all the attendant architectural and civil engineering services. Where the new facility is required to provide additional capability so that new processes or products can be developed, the time to market becomes dependent upon the infrastructure being in place for production to commence. Careful planning is often required because orders for new products may well be taken on the basis of projected completion dates and any delays can adversely affect achievement of these goals and result in dissatisfied customers. Customers may have bought tickets for a flight to a new destination, a rail journey through a new tunnel, a football match at a new stadium relying on the airport, the tunnel or the stadium being open for business on time. A new microprocessor, television, automobile may be dependent on a new production plant and orders may be taken on the basis of projected completion dates. With major capital works, plans are made years in advance with predictions of completion dates based on current knowledge. A new Air Traffic Control Centre at Swanwick in the UK was planned to replace West Drayton ATC outside London because when the plans were made in the late 1980s it was predicted that capacity would be exceeded by the mid 1990s. By the summer of 2000 it is still not operational and therefore the problem that it was designed to solve remains and air traffic congestion continues to delay flights and dissatisfy customers. These examples as do others illustrate the importance of infrastructure on performance and the link with customer satisfaction. A model facility maintenance process flow is illustrated in Figure 6.4

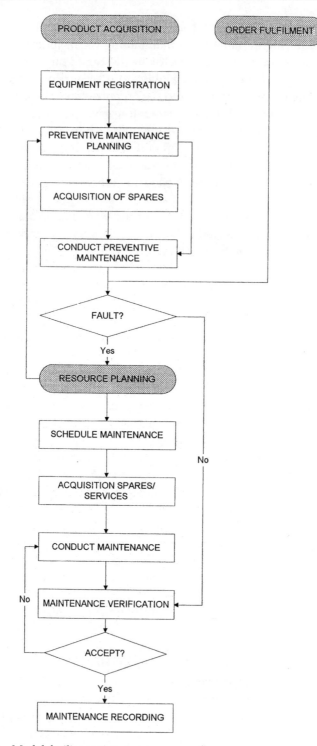

Figure 6.4 Model facility maintenance process flow

Maintaining infrastructure

There are two aspects to maintenance as addressed previously. Maintaining the buildings, utilities and facilities in operational condition is the domain of planned preventive and corrective maintenance. Maintaining the capability is the domain of contingency plans, disaster recovery plans and business continuity provisions. In some industries there is no obligation to continue operations as a result of *force majeure* i.e. an event, circumstance or effect that cannot be reasonably anticipated or controlled including natural disasters caused by weather and land movement, war, riots, air crash, labour stoppage, illness, disruption in utility supply by service providers etc. However, in other industries, provisions have to be made to continue operations albeit at a lower level of performance in spite of force majeure.

Although such events cannot be prevented, their effects can be reduced and in some cases eliminated. Contingency plans should therefore cover those events that can be anticipated where the means to minimize the effects are within your control. What may be a force majeure situation for your suppliers does not need to be the same for you.

Start by doing a risk assessment and identify those things on which continuity of business depends – power, water, labour, materials, components, services etc. Determine what could cause a termination of supply and estimate the probability of occurrence. For those with a relatively high probability (1 in 100) find ways to reduce the probability. For those with lower probability (1 in 10,000 chance) determine the action needed to minimize the effect. The FMEA technique works for this as well as for products and processes.

If you are located near an airport and a Boeing 747 descends upon your factory, can you claim it to be an event outside your control when you chose to site your plant so close to the airport? You may have chosen to outsource manufacture to a supplier in a poorer country and now depend on them for your supplies. They may ship the product but because it is seized by pirates it doesn't reach its destination – you may therefore need an alternative source of supply!

Maintenance of equipment

In a manufacturing environment the process plant, machinery and any other equipment upon which process capability depends need to be maintained and for this you will need:

- A list of the equipment upon which process capability depends
- Defined maintenance requirements specifying maintenance tasks and their frequency
- A maintenance programme which schedules each of the maintenance tasks on a calendar

- Procedures defining how specific maintenance tasks are to be conducted
- Procedures governing the decommissioning of plant prior to planned maintenance
- Procedures governing the commissioning of plant following planned maintenance
- Procedures dealing with the actions required in the event of equipment malfunction
- Maintenance logs that record both the preventive and corrective maintenance work carried out

In a service environment if there is any equipment upon which the capability of your service depends, this equipment should be maintained. Maintenance may often be subcontracted to specialists but nevertheless needs to be under your control. If you are able to maintain process capability by bringing in spare equipment or using other available equipment, your maintenance procedures can be simple. You merely need to ensure you have an operational spare at all times. Where this is not possible you can still rely on the Call-out Service if you can be assured that the anticipated down time will not reduce your capability below that which you have been contracted to maintain.

The requirement does not mean that you need to validate all your word-processing software or any other special aids you use. Maintenance means retaining in an operational condition and you can do this by following some simple rules.

There are several type of maintenance:

Planned maintenance is maintenance carried out with forethought as to what is to be checked, adjusted, replaced etc.

Preventive maintenance is maintenance carried out at predetermined intervals to reduce the probability of failure or performance degradation. An effective maintenance system should be one that achieves its objectives in minimizing down time i.e. the period of time in which the equipment is not in a condition to perform its function.

Corrective maintenance is maintenance carried out after a failure has occurred and is intended to restore an item to a state in which it can perform its required function.

Predictive maintenance is part of planned preventive maintenance. In order to determine the frequency of checks you need to predict when failure may occur. Will failure occur at some future time, after a certain number of operating hours, when being operated under certain conditions or some other time. An example of predictive maintenance is vibration analysis. Sensors can be installed to monitor vibration and thus give a signal when normal vibration levels have been exceeded. This can signal tool wear and wear in other parts of the machine in advance of the stage where nonconforming product will be generated.

The manuals provided by the equipment manufacturer's should indicate the recommended preventive maintenance tasks and the frequency they should be performed covering such aspects as cleaning, adjustments, lubrication, replacement of filters and seals, inspections for wear, corrosion, leakage, damage etc.

Another source of data is from your own operations. Monitoring tool wear, corrective maintenance, analysing cutting fluids and incident reports from operators you can obtain a better picture of a machines performance and predict more accurately the frequency of checks, adjustments and replacements. For this to be effective you need a reporting mechanism that causes operators to alert maintenance staff to situations where suspect malfunctions is observed. In performing such monitoring you cannot wait until the end of the production run to verify whether the tools are still producing conforming product. If you do you will have no data to show when the tool started producing nonconforming product and will need to inspect the whole batch.

An effective maintenance system depends upon it being adequately resourced. Maintenance resources include people with appropriate skills, replacement parts and materials with the funds to purchase these material and access to support from OEMs when needed. If the OEM no longer supports the equipment, you may need to cannibalize old machines or manufacture the parts yourself. This can be a problem because you may not have a new part from which to take measurements. At some point you need to decide whether it is more economical to maintain the old equipment than to buy new. Your inventory control system needs to account for equipment spares and to adjust spares holding based on usage.

For the system to be effective there also has to be control of documentation, maintenance operations, equipment and spare parts. Manuals for the equipment should be brought under document control. Tools and equipment used to maintain the operational equipment should be brought under calibration and verification control. Spare parts should be brought under identity control and the locations for the items brought under storage control. The maintenance operations should be controlled to the extent that maintenance staff should know what to do, know what they are doing and be able to change their performance should the objectives and requirements not be met. Whilst the focus should be on preventive maintenance, one must not forget corrective maintenance. The maintenance crew should be able to respond to equipment failures promptly and restore equipment to full operational condition in minimum time. The function needs resourcing to meet both preventive and corrective demands because, it is down time that will have most impact on production schedules.

The exact nature of the controls should be appropriate to the item concerned, the emphasis being placed upon that which is necessary to minimize operational equipment down time. It would be far better to produce separate procedures for these tasks rather than force fit the operational procedures to maintenance applications.

Jigs, tools and fixtures

Drawings should be provided for jigs, fixtures, templates and other hardware devices and they should be verified as conforming with these drawings prior to use. They should also be proven to control the dimensions required by checking the first-off to be produced from such devices. Once these devices have been proven they need checking periodically to detect signs of wear or deterioration. The frequency of such checks should be dependent on usage and the environment in which they are used. Tools which form characteristics such as crimping tools, punches, press tools etc. should be checked prior to first use to confirm they produce the correct characteristics and then periodically to detect wear and deterioration. Tools that need to maintain certain temperatures, pressures, loads etc. in order to produce the correct characteristics in materials should be checked to verify that they will operate within the required limits.

Steel rules, tapes and other indicators of length should be checked periodically for wear and damage and although accuracy of greater than 1mm is not normally expected, the loss of material from the end of a rule may result in inaccuracies that affect product quality.

While you may not rely entirely on these tools to accept product, the periodic calibration or verification of these tools may help prevent unnecessary costs and production delays. While usage and environment may assist in determining the frequency of verification hardware checks, these factors do not affect software. Any bugs in software have always been there or were introduced when it was last modified. Software therefore needs to be checked prior to use and after any modifications have been carried out, so you cannot predetermine the interval of such checks.

Work environment (6.4)

The standard requires the organization *to identify and manage the work environment needed to achieve conformity of product.*

What does this mean?

The word environment is very topical at the dawn of the 21st century. The protests in the 1980s and 1990s made us all more aware of the damage being done to the natural environment by human activity. The boom and bust years from the 1970s onwards made us aware of the fragile nature of the business environment and the decline of lifetime employment so prevalent in the first half of the 20th century. However, trade union protests in the 1970s and 1980s also made us aware of the environment in which people work and the breakdown in relations between management and workers. With the 1990s came the growth in violence in the home, a sharp rise in single parent families, homelessness and issues within the home environment that spilled over into classrooms and urban areas. These four types of environment are important and although only work environment is addressed directly in ISO 9001, they are all inter-related. They all involve people and it's the same people that populate the work environment.

> **1994–2000 Differences**
>
> Previously the standard required:
>
> (a) controlled conditions for production, installation and servicing processes which directly affect quality to include the use of a suitable working environment;
>
> (b) the supplier to ensure that the environmental conditions are suitable for the calibration, inspections, measurements and tests being carried out.

The natural environment describes the physical conditions that affect the development of the living organisms on the planet. In the context of environmental management systems, it is the natural environment that is being managed. The natural environment is addressed through legislation and therefore covered by clause 5.1 of ISO 9001.

The home environment is the physical, human and economic conditions that affect the development of the family unit. It is in the home environment where family values are developed, the code of ethics, the difference between right and wrong and the religious and racial beliefs that the individual takes into the work place. The home is also an environment where abuse, violence, poverty can exist that affect an individual's attitude towards and treatment of others. Although outside the scope of ISO 9000, we cannot ignore the home environment when dealing with interpersonal relationships because it is often a source of problems that an individual brings into the workplace and affects his or her performance.

The business environment is the economic, political and market conditions under which an organization operates. Unlike the natural and the home environment, there is little that organizations can do to change the economic, political and market factors. Even protests, pickets and lobbying members of parliament have little immediate effect – certainly not sufficient to prevent economic failure of an organization. Organizations have to learn to predict these conditions, turn them into a force for good, manoeuvre the organization around them or adapt. The business environment needs to be taken into account when formulating the quality policy and the quality objectives in clauses 5.3 and 5.4 of ISO 9001 so that the organization adapts to the environment in which it operates. In essence here we are concerned about the environmental impact on the organization. Although these factors are outside the organization's control, smart tactics can minimize their impact.

The work environment is a set of conditions under which people operate and include physical, social and psychological environmental factors (ISO 9000). The social and psychological factors can be considered to be human factors as both are related to human behaviour. There are two dimensions to the work environment however. Organizational design and job design. A job exists within an organization and there are factors that arise from performing the job such as physical movement, the man–machine interface, the physical environment and the psychological factors of the job. These form the basis of ergonomics (see BS 3138:1979). Even when the ergonomics of the job have been optimized, performance can still be adversely affected by wider influence of factors inherent in the organization caused by the way it functions or the way things get done – its culture and climate (see below).

In essence, the organization impacts the natural environment and the work environment and both the business environment and the home environment impact the organization.

Physical factors of the work environment include space, temperature, noise, light, humidity, hazards, cleanliness, vibration, pollution, accessibility, physical stress and airflow. In addition to visible light, other types of radiation across the whole spectrum impact the physical environment.

Social factors of the work environment are those that arise from interactions between people and include the impact of an individual's family, education, religion and peer pressure as well as the impact of the organization's ethics, culture and climate.

Psychological factors of the work environment are those that arise from an individuals inner needs and external influences and include recognition, responsibility, achievement, advancement, reward, job security, interpersonal relations, leadership, affiliation, self esteem, and occupational stress. They tend to affect or shape the emotions, feelings, personality, loyalty and attitudes of people and therefore the motivation of people towards the job to which they have been assigned.

While this grouping serves to identify related factors, it is by no means comprehensive or exclusive. Each has an influence on the other to some extent. Relating the identification of such factors to the achievement of conformity of product tends to imply that there are factors of the work environment that do not affect conformity of product. Whether people produce products directly or indirectly, their behaviour affects their actions and decisions and consequently the results of what they do. It is therefore difficult to exclude any factor on the basis that it is not needed to achieve conformity of product in some way or other.

Managing such factors means creating, monitoring and adjusting conditions in which the physical and human factors of the work environment act positively towards achievement of the planned results.

Why is this necessary?

This requirement responds to the Leadership and Involvement of People principles.

The work environment is critical to worker performance and extends beyond the visible and audible factors commonly observed in a place of work. All the above factors influence individual behaviour and individual behaviour has a direct impact on organizational performance and consequently product quality. It is the duty of management to control the physical factors firstly within the levels required by law and as necessary for people to perform their jobs as efficiently and effectively as possible. It is also the task of management to create conditions in which personnel are motivated to achieve the results for which they are responsible and therefore remove or contain any de-motivating elements such as friction and conflict in the workplace.

The physical factors of the work environment influence individual behaviour by causing fatigue, distraction, accidents and a series of health problems. There are laws governing many of the physical factors such as noise, air pollution, space and safety. There are also laws related to the employment of disabled people that impact the physical environment in terms of access and ergonomics. The social interactions in the work place influence interpersonal relationships. The worker – boss, worker – subordinate, worker – colleague, worker – peer relationship. The social factors if disregarded cause unpredictable effects and some of these are the subject of legislation such as discrimination on the basis of religion, gender, race and disability. The issue is not whether product will be affected directly, but whether performance will be affected. It requires no more than common sense (rather than scientific evidence) to deduce that intimidation, sexual harassment, invasion of privacy and similarly unfair treatment by employees and employers, will adversely affect the performance of people and consequently the quality of their output. Social factors can have a psychological effect on employees causing de-motivation and mental stress. This is not to say that employees have to be mollycoddled, but it is necessary to remove the negative forces in the work environment if productivity is to be maximized and business continuity maintained.

The information produced to support ISO 9000 from the standards and certification bodies seems to restrict the work environment to those aspects that directly affect the product such as cleanliness, temperature and regulations relating to the product. This narrow view overlooks the principal factors that affect product quality – that of human behaviour and adds little to the movement to enhance customer satisfaction. A more progressive organization would realize that the influence of the physical factors of the environment is small in comparison with the human factors and place their improvement effort on this.

How is this implemented?

Previously the work environment was limited to its effect on the product and although not explicit in ISO 9001, it is clear from ISO 9004–1 that this was the intent. The implication here is that personnel safety, job security, recognition, relationships, responsibility etc. influence the performance of people in an organization and that managers have to manage these factors to provide an environment in which personnel will be motivated. This is a wide subject and beyond the scope of this book but it is important that the reader appreciates the breadth and scope of the factors that influence the working environment in preparing for further study.

For a solution we can use a similar approach to that taken towards the natural environment. Environmental management is the control over activities, products and processes that cause or could cause environmental impacts. The approach taken is based on the management of cause and effect where the activities, products and processes are the causes or 'aspects', and the resulting effects or potential effects on the environment are the impacts. All effort is focused on minimizing or eliminating the impacts. In the context of the work environment, the causes or aspects would be the physical and human factors and the impacts would be the changes in working conditions. However, unlike management of the natural environment, the effort would not all be focused on reducing or eliminating impacts where a state of zero impact is ideal. In the working environment, the effort should be focused on eliminating negative impact and creating positive or beneficial impacts that also lead to an improvement in performance.

Dealing with the physical factors

The physical factors are more easily dealt with than the human factors primarily because they are more tangible, measurable and controllable. To manage the physical factors they firstly need to be identified and this requires a study of the work environment to be made relative to its influence on the worker. We are not necessarily dealing only with safety issues although these are very important. The noise levels do not need to cause harm for them to be a factor that adversely affects worker performance. Libraries are places of silence simply to provide the best environment in which people can concentrate on reading. No harm arises if the silence is broken!

In dealing with physical factors there is a series of steps you can take to identify and manage these factors.

- Use an intuitive method such as brainstorming to discover the safety related and non safety related factors of the environment such as noise, pollution, humidity, temperature, light, space, accessibility etc.
- Research legislation and associated guidance literature to identify those factors that could exist in the work environment due to the operation of certain processes, use of certain products or equipment. We do X, therefore, from historical and scientific evidence there will be Y impact. (VDUs, RSI, airborne particles, machinery etc.)
- Determine the standard for each factor that needs to be maintained to provide the appropriate environment.
- Establish whether the standard can be achieved by work space design, by worker control or by management control or whether protection from the environmental impact is needed (protection of ears, eyes, lungs, limbs, torso or skin).
- Establish what could fail that would breach the agreed standard using FMEA or Hazards analysis, identify the cause and the effect on worker performance.
- Determine the provisions necessary to eliminate, reduce or control the impact.
- Put in place the measures that have been determined.
- Measure and monitor the working environment for compliance with the standards and implementation of the provisions defined.
- Periodically repeat the previous steps to identify any changes that would affect the standards or the provisions currently in place. Ask – Is the standard still relevant? Are there better methods now available for dealing with this environmental impact?

Dealing with the human factors

Managers are often accused of ignoring the human factors but such factors are not easily identified or managed. With physical factors you can measure the light level and adjust it if it's too bright or too dim. You can't measure ethics, culture, climate, occupational stress – all you see are its effects and the primary effect is employee motivation.

Managers need to understand and analyse human behaviour and provide conditions in which employees are motivated to achieve the organization's objectives.

Ethics

Ethics concern a person's behaviour towards others and therefore within a particular work environment there will be some accepted norms of right and wrong. These values or standards vary from group to group and culture to culture. For example bribery it is an accepted norm in some countries but in others it is illegal. When the work environment includes employees of different races and religions, conflict can arise simply due to an individual behaving in a way that to them is normal but to another in the group is unethical.

Ethical standards therefore vary and change with time. Family, religion, and education will influence an individual's code of ethics and this may conflict with that of the work environment that the person joins. Unfortunately it is often not until a situation arises that challenges the ethical standards of the individual or the group that the conflict becomes apparent. People may be content to abide by the unwritten code of ethics under normal conditions but when an important prize is within reach, the temptation to put the principles to one side is too great and some will succumb to the pressure and put self interest or profits first causing harm to other interested parties. Employees may be easily led by other less ethical employees in a desire to follow the pack and those that do challenge their peers and their managers get accused of 'rocking the boat' and being 'troublemakers'. Management may turn a blind eye to unethical practices if in doing so they deliver the goods and no one appears to be harmed thus strengthening the beliefs of the instigator of such practices. Sometimes managers are simply unaware of the impact of their decisions. A one-off instruction to let a slightly defective product be despatched because it was needed urgently, gets interpreted by the employees as permission to deviate from requirements. A one-off instruction to take the previous test results as evidence of conformity instead of waiting until the test equipment has been repaired, gets interpreted as permission to do this every time. Employees naturally take the lead from the leader and can easily misread the signals. They can also be led by a manager who does not share the same ethical values and under threat of dismissal; an otherwise law-abiding citizen can be forced into falsifying evidence.

Questions of right and wrong in the work environment can arise between two individuals or between an individual and the group or the top management. There is also the wider perspective of the relationship between the organization and society. Social responsibility is becoming more dominant in the boardroom because investors look for 'green' companies and those that do not support apartheid or purchase from producers that use child labour. While the organization's behaviour with respect to its interested parties is outside the work environment the internal and external relationships cannot be isolated. The behaviour of the organization externally will undoubtedly influence internal behaviour.

The moral maze created by attempting to satisfy all interested parties within an environment in which there are so many variables calls for a code of ethics. Some companies have ethical policies that are intended to guide employees in dealing with a wide range of issues and assist managers to manage the work environment. However, writing down the code of ethics is fraught with problems.

- They have to be followed in all circumstances – there are no exceptions.
- If an employee 'blows the whistle' on the company for unethical behaviour, it must not reprimand that individual but accept the situation as a consequence of its unethical behaviour.
- It cannot put 'gagging' conditions in contracts of employment because this itself would be indicative of unethical behaviour.

Motivation

Everything achieved in or by an organization ultimately depends upon the activities of its workforce. It is therefore imperative that the organization is staffed by people who are motivated to achieve its goals. Everyone is motivated but not all are motivated to achieve their organization's goals. Many may be more interested in achieving their personal goals. Motivation is key to performance. The performance of a task is almost always a function of three factors. Environment, Ability and Motivation. To maximize performance of a task, personnel have not only to possess the necessary ability or competence to perform it but also need to be in the right surroundings and have the motivation to perform it. (Vroom, V.H., 1964)[9] Motivation comes from within. A manager cannot alter employees at will despite what they may believe is possible.

So what is motivation? It has been defined as an inner mental state that prompts a direction, intensity and persistence in behaviour (Rollinson, Broadfield and Edwards, 1998)[10]. It is therefore a driving force within an

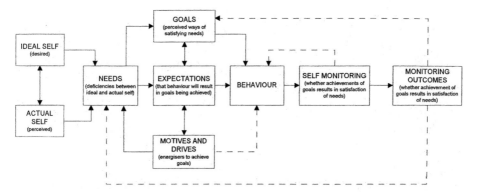

Figure 6.5 Motivation process

individual that prompts him or her to achieve some goal. There is a motivation process – not an organizational process but a process operating inside to the individual. This process is illustrated in Figure 6.5.

From this diagram it will be observed that motivation comes from satisfying personal needs and expectations of work, therefore the motivation to achieve quality objectives must be triggered by the expectation that achievement of objectives will lead to a reward that satisfies a need of some sort. This does not mean that you can motivate personnel solely by extrinsic rewards such as financial incentives. It requires a good understanding of an individual's pattern of needs. People desire psychological rewards from the work experience or like to feel a part of an organization or team. People can be motivated by having their efforts recognized and appreciated or included in discussions. However, this will only occur if the conditions they experience allow them to feel this way.

Culture

If we ask people to describe what it is like to work for a particular organization, they often reply in terms of their feelings and emotions that are their perceptions of the essential atmosphere in the organization. This atmosphere is encompassed by two concepts – culture and climate (Rollinson, Broadfield and Edwards, 1998)[11]. Rollinson, Broadfield and Edwards observe that Schein conceptualizes culture as a layered phenomenon that has three interrelated levels of meaning. The observations of Schein, Peters, Waterman and Ouchi have been integrated to illustrate a more diverse range of cultural characteristics.

1 **Artefacts and creations**
   (a) Rites and ceremonies e.g. morning exercises, celebrations of success
   (b) Symbols e.g. status symbols
   (c) Taboos e.g. addressing the boss by his or her first name, parking in the manager's parking space
   (d) Myths and stories – e.g. how the founder grew the company
   (e) Language e.g. how managers address subordinates and vice versa, jargon and verbal signals
   (f) Norms e.g. behaviour that is accepted as being normal for various levels
2 **Values and beliefs**
   (a) Honesty
   (b) Basis of reward and punishment
   (c) Effort
   (d) Trust
   (e) Commitment to employees
   (f) Evaluation of employees e.g. evaluation on quantitative or qualitative criteria

    (g) Career paths

    (h) Employee control e.g. rules, procedures or mentoring and coaching

    (i) Decision making e.g. decisions by individuals or by groups, based on fact or intuition, consensus or dictate

    (j) Concern for people

    (k) Management contact e.g. managers work behind closed doors or walk about and make contact

    (l) Autonomy e.g. small autonomous units rather than large bureaucracy

    (m) Customer focus not self interest

3 **Basic assumptions**

    (a) Respect for the individual

    (b) Responsibility for actions and decisions

    (c) Internal cooperation

    (d) Freedom

Culture evolves and can usually be traced back to the organization's founder. The founder gathers around people of like mind and values and these become the role models for new entrants. Culture has a strong influence on people's behaviour but is not easily changed. It is an invisible force that consists of deeply held beliefs, values and assumptions that are so ingrained in the fabric of the organization that many people might not be conscious that they hold them. Unless the recruitment process recognizes the importance of matching people with the culture, mavericks may well enter the organization and either cause havoc in the work environment or be totally ineffective due to a lack of cultural awareness. People who are oblivious to the rites, symbols, customs, norms, language etc., may not advance and will become demotivated. There is however, no evidence to suggest a right or wrong culture. What is important is that the culture actually helps an organization to achieve its goals – that it is pervasive and a positive force for good.

    The role of management relative to culture is to set a good example and ensure that personnel are likely to fit in with the existing culture before being offered employment. It is also important for management not to reprimand staff for failing to observe the protocols when they may not understand them and to take time to induct new staff in a way that reduces any anxieties associated with the new job. New entrants often don't know what to ask. It doesn't occur to them to ask about the culture, what the rites and customs are and in effect discover information that will be vital to their performance. They are often more concerned about the who, what where when and how of the job. Even if it is explained on induction, it will not become significant to the individual until something happens that reinforces the culture. For many people, the culture in an organization has to be discovered – it is not something that is necessarily articulated by the managers. Statements of the vision and values help but the rites, symbols and taboos are all learnt mainly by observation.

Climate

Climate is allied to culture and although people experience both, climate tends to be something of which there is more awareness. Culture provides a code of conduct that defines acceptable behaviour whereas climate tends to result in a set of conditions to which people react. Culture is more permanent whereas climate is temporary and is thought of as a phase the organization passes through. In this context therefore, the work environment will be affected by a change in the organizational climate. Several external forces cause changes in the climate such as economic factors, political factors and market factors. These can result in feelings of optimism or pessimism, security or insecurity, complacency or anxiety. There are also several internal characteristics of the organization that impact the climate.

- Job design – do these limit freedom, stifle initiative and innovation?
- Technology – high manual input and personal control or extensive automation and little personal involvement
- Management philosophies – the roles and functions of subordinates, employee performance measurement
- Authority – autocratic, democratic, strong delegation or little delegation, multiple approvals
- Local practices – supervision manipulates policies to serve their own purpose, varying rules to exert power
- Accessibility – supervision being accessible or inaccessible for support, help, discussion
- Fear – workers frightened of reporting problems, stopping the process, owning up to mistakes

These and probably many more climatic factors influence the behaviour of people in the work environment and therefore it is important to avoid those factors that lead to poor performance and employee dissatisfaction.

Ergonomics

An employee's body movement in performing a job has important implications on the work environment.

The study of the relationship between a person and his or her job is referred as Ergonomics (see BS 3138) and it deals principally with the relationship between a person and his or her job, equipment and environment and particularly the anatomical, physiological and psychological aspects arising thereon. The layout of the work place, the distances involved the areas of reach, seating, frequency and type of movement all impact the performance of the worker. These factors require study to establish the optimum conditions that minimize fatigue, meet the safety standards while increasing productivity.

Where people are an integral part of a mechanized process the man–machine interface is of vital importance and has to be carefully considered in process design. The information on display panels should be clear and relevant to the task. The positioning of instruments, input, output devices and monitoring devices should allow the operator to easily access information without abnormal movement. The emergency controls should be within easy reach and the operating instructions accessible at the workstation. Legislation and national standards cover many of these aspects.

Managing the human factors

Identifying the barriers

The role of the manager in enabling a person to be motivated is that of removing barriers to work motivation. There are two types of barriers that cause the motivation process to break down. The first barrier is job-related i.e. there is something about the job itself that prevents the person performing it from being motivated – e.g. boring and monotonous work in mass production assembly lines. The second barrier is goal-related i.e. attainment of the goals is thwarted in some way – e.g. unrealistic goals, insufficient resources and insufficient time for preparation. When targets are set without any regard for the capability of processes this often results in frustration and a decline in motivation. (See also Chapter 5 under *Expressing quality objectives*.)

Common barriers are:

- Fear of failure, of reprisals, of rejection, of losing, of conflict, of humiliation, of exploitation
- Distrust of management, favouritism, discrimination
- Work is not challenging or interesting
- Little recognition, respect, reward for a job well done
- No authority and responsibility

Empowerment

Empowerment is said to motivate employees because it offers a way of obtaining higher level of performance without the use of strict supervision. However, it is more theory and rhetoric than a reality. To *empower* employees, managers not only have to delegate authority but to release resources for employees to use as they see fit and to trust their employees to use the resources wisely. If you are going to empower your employees, remember that you must be willing to cede some of your authority but also as you remain responsible for their performance, you must ensure your employees are able to handle their new authority. Employees have to be trained not only to perform tasks but also need a certain degree of experience in order to make the right judgements and therefore need to be competent. Some employees may acknowledge that they are willing to accept responsibility for certain decisions but beware, they may not be ready to be held accountable for the results when they go sour. It is also important that any changes arising from the empowering of employees to improve the process, be undertaken under controlled conditions. However, empowerment does not mean that you should give these individuals the right to change policies or practices that affect others without due process.

Measuring employee satisfaction

Within the work environment the bottom line is whether the objectives are being achieved and the employees satisfied. It is not enough just to achieve objectives. The first 200 years of the industrial revolution did that but in response to worker exploitation the labour unions were born and thus commenced 100 years of strife. The very idea that employees should be satisfied at work is a comparatively recent notion but clearly employee dissatisfaction leads to lower productivity. The measurement of employee satisfaction together with the achievement of the organization's objectives would therefore provide an indication of the quality of the work environment i.e. whether the environment fulfils its purpose.

Many companies carry out employee surveys in an attempt to establish their needs and expectations and whether they are being satisfied. It is a fact that unsatisfied employees may not perform at the optimum level and consequently product quality may deteriorate. As with customer satisfaction surveys, employee satisfaction surveys are prone to bias. If the survey hits the employee's desk following a reprimand from a manager, the result is likely to be negatively biased. The results of employee satisfaction surveys are also often disbelieved by management. Management believe their decisions are always in their employees best interests whereas the employees may not believe if management says its track record has not been all that great. Employee satisfaction has less to do with product quality and more to do with relationships. However employee relationships can begin to adversely affect product quality if no action is taken.

You will need a process for measuring employee satisfaction but design the survey with great care and treat the results with an open mind because they cannot be calibrated. A common method for measuring satisfaction is to ask questions that require respondents to check the appropriate box on a scale from 'strongly agree' to 'strongly disagree'. An alternative is for an outsider appointed by management to conduct a series of interviews. In this way you will obtain a more candid impression of employee satisfaction. The interviewer needs some knowledge of the management style, the efforts management has actually made to motivate their workforce – not the rhetoric they have displayed through newsletters, briefings etc. On hearing what management has actually done, the employees may react differently. They also have short memories and are often reacting to immediate circumstances forgetting the changes that were made some time ago. The interviewer is also able to discover whether the employee has done anything about the feelings of dissatisfaction. It could be that a supervisor or middle manager is blocking communication. Whatever the method, management needs unbiased information of the level of employee satisfaction to do the job.

The forgoing treatment of the work environment may appear at odds with the current interpretation of the requirement in ISO 9001. But to claim that the human factors of the work environment have nothing to do with quality would be a spurious argument. Most of Deming's 14 points focus on the human factors, the constancy of purpose, leadership, driving out fear, removing barriers etc. If you are serious about quality, you cannot ignore the human factors – they are key to your success. If you want to adopt the minimalist approach and do only what lies in the words of the standard, you will miss the point completely. You will not succeed as an organization and be constantly trying to reduce variation as though each deviation from the norm has a unique cause. When you have eliminated the impossible, whatever remains, however improbable, must be the truth (Arthur Conan Doyle). The improbable is the human factor.

Summary

In this chapter we have examined the requirements contained in section 6 of ISO 9001. Although still a relatively short set of requirement in ISO 9001, they are among the most important, for without adequate resources no organization will fulfil its purpose and mission. We have discovered that we cannot exclude any of the organization's resources as all either directly or indirectly affect our ability to satisfy the needs and expectations of the interested parties. We have learnt that there is a significant difference between qualified personnel and competent personnel. We now know we need people who can deliver results not people who can provide evidence of certain academic qualifications, training and experience. Recognizing that we need to take a new approach to the selection and development of our human resources, we have examined some proven methods used to identify competence needs and assess competence. We have learnt that the infra- structure is important in sustaining the organization's capability and that customer satisfaction depends on maintaining continuity of supply when disaster strikes. Lastly we have looked deeply into the work environment and discovered that this is not simply a question of managing physical conditions of the work place but of managing the culture and climate within the organization. We have shown that product quality depends upon maintaining a motivated workforce and that motivation is affected by both human and physical factors that can be identified and managed. Effective management of human resources therefore arises from deploying competent personnel into a work environment in which they are motivated to achieve the organization's goals.

Resource Management Questionnaire

Provision of resources

1 How do you determine the resources needed to implement and maintain the management system?
2 How do you determine the resources needed to continually improve the effectiveness of the management system and enhance customer satisfaction?
3 How do you ensure that resources needed to implement and maintain the management system, and continually improve its effectiveness and enhance customer satisfaction are provided?

Human resources

4 How do you ensure that personnel performing work affecting product quality are competent on the basis of appropriate education, training, skills and experience?
5 How do you determine the necessary competence of personnel performing work affecting product quality?
6 How do you ensure that training or other actions are taken to close the identified gap in personnel competence?
7 How do you evaluate the effectiveness of the actions taken to develop personnel competence?
8 How do you ensure that your personnel are aware of the relevance and importance of their activities and how they contribute to the achievement of the quality objectives?
9 What records are maintained of personnel education, training, skills, experience and competence?

Infrastructure

10 What elements of the infrastructure have been identified as needed to achieve conformity to product requirements?
11 How do you ensure that the infrastructure needed to achieve conformity to product requirements is provided and maintained?

Work environment

12 What physical and human factors of the work environment have been identified as being needed to achieve conformity of product?
13 How do you manage the physical and human factors of the work environment needed to achieve conformity of product?

Resource Management – Food for thought

1 Are there any activities in an organization that require no human or financial resources?
2 What business benefit is derived from excluding particular resources from the management system?
3 Why are the costs of maintaining the management system different from those of maintaining the organization?
4 Are functional budgets justified when in reality the organization's objectives are achieved through a series of interconnected processes?
5 If your staff are your most important asset, why are staff development programmes a prime target for cost reduction?
6 Do you select people on what they demonstrate they know or what they demonstrate they can do?
7 How do you know that your staff are competent to achieve the objectives you have agreed with them?
8 From where does the evidence come from to assess staff competence?
9 There are seven ways of developing staff. Before you send them on a training course have you eliminated the other six ways as being unsuitable for the particular situation?
10 What action was taken the last time your staff returned from an external training course that resulted in an improvement in their performance?
11 How do you ensure that staff work on those things that add value to the organization?
12 What's the second thing you do on receipt of a customer complaint?
13 How much information is contained in your personnel training records to help you make decisions on staff development needs?
14 Do you know of all the ways in which an infrastructure failure might impact customer satisfaction?
15 How much of what affects individual performance depends on the relationship between management and staff?
16 In describing what it is like to work in your organization, would you identify any factors that were detrimental to overall performance?
17 Would anyone in your organization take an action or make a decision that might be considered unethical in your society?

18 What actions do managers take to create conditions in which their staff are motivated to achieve their objectives?

19 When did you last examine the organization's culture for its relevance to the current conditions in which the organization operates?

20 When did you last recognize or appreciate the efforts of your staff in contributing towards improved performance?

21 When did you last reprimand a member of staff for something that was symptomatic of the natural variation inherent in the process?

22 If every employee were to follow the examples set by the management, in what way would the organization's performance change?

23 Do you wait until you have no option but to take drastic action to restore financial stability or do you involve your workforce in seeking ways in which to lessen the impact?

24 When did you last calculate the time lost by the inappropriate location of tools, information, equipment and facilities?

25 If an employee was dissatisfied with the working environment, could you be sure that he or she would approach the manager with confidence that the matter would be dealt with objectively and sympathetically?

Bibliography

1. Fletcher, Shirley, (2000). *Competence-based assessment techniques,* Kogan Page.
2. Fletcher, Shirley, (2000). *Competence-based assessment techniques,* Kogan Page.
3. International Labour Organization, (2001). http://www.ilo.orgpublic/spanish/region/ampro/cinterfor/temas/complab/xxxx/ing/index.htm#a.
4. Fletcher, Shirley, (2000). *Competence-based assessment techniques,* Kogan Page.
5. Fletcher, Shirley, (2000). *Competence-based assessment techniques,* Kogan Page.
6. Fletcher, Shirley, (2000). *Competence-based assessment techniques,* Kogan Page.
7. Fletcher, Shirley, (2000). *Competence-based assessment techniques,* Kogan Page.
8. Deming, W. Edwards, (1982). *Out of the crisis,* MITC.
   Chapter 8 page 253
9. Vroom, V. H., (1964). *Work and Motivation,* John Wiley.
10 Rollinson, Broadfield and Edwards, (1998). *Organizational behaviour and analysis,* Addison Wesley Longmans.
11 Rollinson, Broadfield and Edwards, (1998). *Organizational behaviour and analysis,* Addison Wesley Longmans.

Chapter 7
Product realization

> Quality must be built into each design and each process.
> It cannot be created through inspection.
>
> *Kaoru Ishikawa*

Summary of requirements

ISO 9001:2000 is stated as being structured around a revised process model but the language is misleading. Management responsibility is not a process but a commitment. However, the requirements address aspects such as policy, objectives and planning for which processes will be required. Resource Management is a series of processes and Measurement, Analysis and Improvement is not a process but a series of sub-processes within every process. Product Realization is also a series of processes that have interfaces with resource management processes and which embody measurement, analysis and improvement processes. Product realization requirements include requirements for purchasing, a process that could fit as comfortably under resource management because it is not limited to the acquisition of components but is a process that is used for acquiring all physical resources including services. Section 7 also includes requirements for control of measuring devices which would fit more comfortably into section 8 but it omits the control of nonconforming product which is more to do with handling product than measurement.

If we link the requirements together in a cycle (indicating the headings in bold type) as we did with Management Responsibility, the cycle commences by scanning the environment to gain an understanding of customer needs and expectations. In doing so we need to *communicate with customers* and *determine the requirements* of customers, of regulators and of the organization relative to the product or service to be supplied. This will undoubtedly involve more *customer communication* and once requirements have been determined we need to *review the requirements* to ensure they are understood and confirm we have the capability to achieve them. If we have identified a need for new products and services, we would then need to *plan product realization* and in doing so use *preventive action* methods to ensure the success of the project and take care of any *customer property* on loan to us. We would undertake product *design and development* and in doing so we would probably need to *identify product, purchase* materials, components and services, build prototypes using the process of *production provision* and *validate* new *processes.* After *design validation* we would release product information into the market to attract customers and undertake more *customer-communication.* As customers enquire about our offerings we would once more *determine the requirements* in order to match customer needs with product offerings and our ability to supply.

Now faced with real customers demanding our products, we would *review the requirements* and confirm we had the capability to supply a product that matched their needs before entering into a commitment to supply. We would then proceed to *plan product realization* once again and undertake *production or service provision.* During production or service delivery we would maintain *traceability* of the product if applicable, perform *measurement and monitoring* and *control the measuring and monitoring devices.* We would *monitor and measure processes* and *monitor and measure products* at each stage of the process. If we found variations we would undertake the *control of non-conforming product* and *analyse data* to facilitate *corrective action.* Through-out production or service delivery we would seek the *preservation of product* and take care of *customer property.* Once we had undertaken all the *product verification* and *preserved* the product for delivery, we would ship the product to the customer or complete the service transaction. To complete the cycle *customer communication* would be initiated once more to obtain feedback on our performance.

Here we have linked together all the clauses in section 7 and many in section 8 of the standard because the two cannot be separated. The relationship between the primary product realization processes is illustrated in Figure 7.1

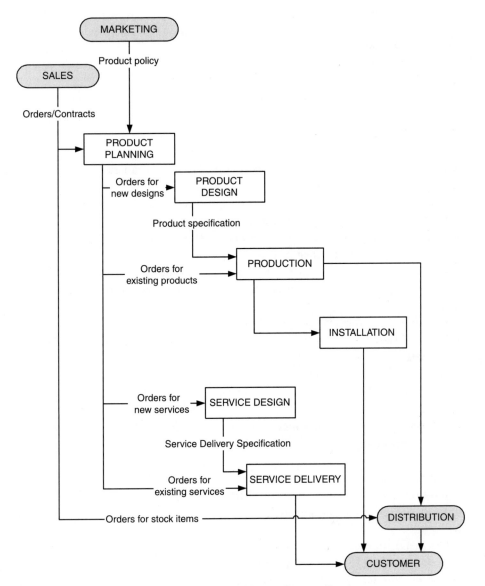

Figure 7.1   Relationship between processes in product realization

Planning product realization processes (7.1)

Planning and developing product realization processes (7.1)

<table>
<tr><td>

1994–2000 Differences

This is a new requirement that has no equivalent in the 1994 version.
</td><td>

The standard requires the organization to *plan and develop the processes required for product realization.*

What does this mean?
</td></tr>
</table>

The product realization processes are the processes needed to identify, create and supply the product or service and would include those needed to:

- Identify the products and services required by the organization's customers (the sales process).
- Plan the provision of the identified products and services (the project, contract or order planning process).
- Design the identified products and services so as to meet customer needs and expectations (the design process).
- Procure the materials, components, services needed to accomplish the design and/or generate or deliver the product or service (the procurement process).
- Generate the product (the production process).
- Supply the product or service (the distribution or service delivery processes).
- Install the product on customer premises (the installation process).
- Maintain and support the product in service (the product and service support process).
- Provide support to customers (the after sales, technical support or customer support process).

These processes are all product or service specific and take the input from the marketing process, where new products and services have been identified, through the chain of related processes that deliver such products or services to customers.

Product design may not have formed part of the organization's management system under ISO 9001:1994 if the products were not designed for specific customers but were proprietary designs (to the organization's own specifications). However, ISO 9001:2000 removes this constraint and requires the processes to realize the product to be included in the management system whether or not the products are provided to the organization's specification or to a specification defined by a customer.

Planning these processes means identifying the processes required for a specific project, contract or order and determining their sequence and interrelation. In many cases the processes will have been designed and will form part of the management system. However, the nature and complexity of specific projects, contracts or orders may require these processes to be developed i.e. tailored or enhanced to suit particular needs. As the nature of planning will vary significantly from organization to organization, the generic term for this type of planning is *product realization planning* thus distinguishing it from specific planning activities such as design planning, production planning, installation planning etc. Product realization planning is therefore the overall planning activities needed to meet all requirements for a project, product, contact or order.

Why is this necessary?

This requirement responds to the Process Approach Principle.

In designing the management system the core processes needed to produce the organization's products and services should have been developed so that planning to meet specific orders does not commence with a blank sheet of paper. These core processes provide a framework that aids the planners in deciding upon the specific processes, actions and resources required for specific projects, contracts or orders. The process descriptions may not contain details of specific products, dates, equipment, personnel or product characteristics. These may need to be determined individually for each product – hence the need to plan and develop processes for product realization.

How is this implemented?

Planning product realization processes

There are too many variations in the product realization process to provide much more than an overview.

Product planning is driven by two processes – the sales process and the marketing process. The sales process promotes the organization's existing products and service and attracts enquiries, thus creating a need for an enquiry conversion process to convert customer enquiries into orders or contracts. This may require a project planning process in order to provide the customer with a viable proposal. On receipt of a contract or order an order processing process is then needed to confirm and agree customer requirements and the terms and conditions for the supply of product or service. Once the contract or order has been agreed, a project or order planning process is needed to establish the provisions needed to meet the contract/order requirements.

The marketing process searches for new opportunities that will result in the development of new products and service and thus its output will lead into project planning which subsequently supplies the sales process with proven products and service to sell.

Product planning can therefore be driven by customer specific requirements as well as requirements determined by the organization that will reflect or create customer needs and expectations. The product realization planning process therefore includes the sales process and the product planning process. The sales process may not require tailoring for specific enquiries but with major projects for the large procurement agencies, this process often varies depending on the nature of the project and may require careful planning for the organization to be successful. The product planning process will often require tailoring for specific projects or contracts as the nature of the work involved will vary. Where the organization takes orders for existing products or services which the customer selects from a catalogue, no special planning may be needed other than the creation of work orders.

In planning product realization, there are several factors involved – task, timing, responsibility, resources, constraints, dependencies and sequence. The flowcharts for each process that were developed in establishing the management system identify the tasks. The planners job is to establish whether these tasks, their sequence and the process characteristics in terms of throughput, resources, capacity and capability require any modification to meet the requirements of a particular project, contract or order. A typical product planning process is illustrated in Figure 7.2.

Tools often used in product realization planning are Gannt Charts and PERT Charts. The Gannt chart depicts the tasks and responsibilities on a timescale showing when the tasks are to commence and when they are to be complete. PERT charts display the same information but show the relationship between the tasks. These tools are useful in analysing a programme of work, determining resources and determining whether the work can be completed by the required end date using the allocated resources. It is not the purpose here to elaborate on project planning techniques but merely to indicate the scope of the requirement and what is needed to implement it.

A common method of planning projects is to prepare a Project Plan that includes the following:

1 Project objectives
2 System requirements
3 Project strategy
4 Critical success factors and success criteria
5 Project milestones
6 Project timeline
7 Project organization (chart and team responsibilities and authority)
8 Work breakdown structure (Major tasks, work packages, deliverables)
9 Resource provision in terms of space, development tools, equipment
10 Supplier control plan
11 Information system (Strategy, tools and their development)

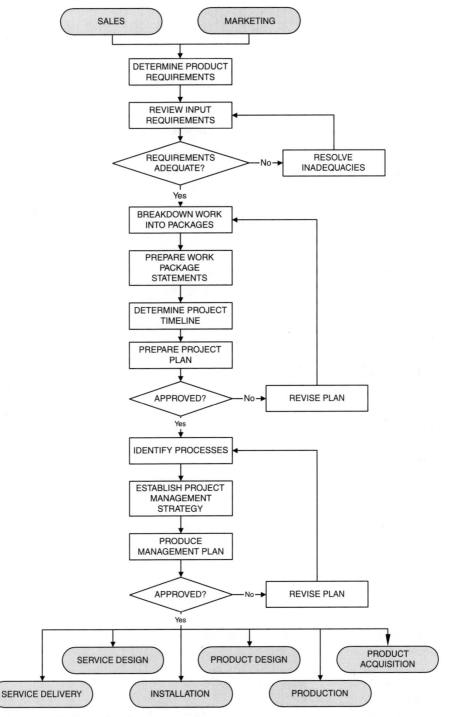

Figure 7.2 Product planning process flow

12 Communication plan (Strategy, methods and tasks)

13 Personnel development plan (Strategy, education and training for those engaged on the project)

14 Evaluation plan (Audits, design reviews and assessments)

15 Project reviews (Strategy, project reviews and team reviews)

16 Contract management

Developing product realization processes

There is a note that suggests that the design and development requirements may be applied to the development of product realization processes. This note means that these processes may be developed in the same way as products. There is no logical reason why the requirements of section 7.3 should not be applied to all processes; in fact other references imply this. The standard does require the operation and control of *processes* to be effective (clause 4.1c) and that *processes* are measured and monitored (clause 4.1e) and that their ability to achieve planned results is demonstrated (clause 8.2.3). Therefore process inputs and outputs need to be defined, process design reviews need to be performed, process verification and validation needs to be carried out and process changes need to be controlled – otherwise it is unlikely that the process will be effective. So how would you go about this?

Process development planning

This would involve identifying:

- the process objectives
- the process specification (parameters, targets and success criteria)
- the process development stages
- the responsibilities for the actions and decisions in developing the process
- the procedures, instructions needed to execute the process development tasks
- the stages where verification and validation of process and product take place, the acceptance criteria and methods of measurement
- the conditions that have to be satisfied for the process to be deemed operational (who make the decision and on what basis)
- the timescales required for each task in each stage

The processes referred to are not only the making and moving processes. New processes may be needed for:

- Communicating with overseas customers
- Processing military orders
- Managing a multinational project
- Configuration management

- Managing a centralized procurement programme
- System design involving new technologies
- Installing a new IT system
- Managing major subcontractors
- Setting-up a remote servicing unit.

A process development team should be established to manage the development of any new processes. If several new processes are to be developed, several teams will be needed. By building a team for each process you will focus the efforts of staff more clearly than loading several new jobs onto the same individuals, but if you lack resources you may have no option.

Process development inputs

This would consist of the input data required to design the process and the actions taken to verify and validate these inputs (whether the right inputs had been received and were correct).

Process development

Curiously the standard does not address the activity of design itself, only the boundary activities of input and output but in the middle, the process has to be designed and this requires several important steps.

It would involve determining:

- the process stages, their sequence and interrelation, the inputs and outputs and their destination
- the procurement and/or construction activities (make or buy)
- the methods for performing the tasks in the process
- the means of conveying product and information through the process
- the means of storing product or data awaiting processing
- the means of disposing of process waste
- the potential failure modes and eliminating, reducing or controlling the effects including mistake-proofing measures
- the resources required (equipment, tooling, facilities, personnel competency, finance, physical and human environment)
- the measures necessary to maintain the equipment, facilities and environment
- the installation and commissioning activities including layout and access

Process development outputs

This would consist of the process development deliverables (the specifications, floor plans, layouts, procedures, set-up and operating instructions, forms, notices, guides, standards, certificates, competency requirements, handling requirements, samples needed to operate and maintain the process).

Process development reviews

This would be the review stages where process development is assessed i.e. planning, construction, verification and validation in terms of risks, costs, utilization, lead-times, critical paths etc.

Process verification

This would be the action needed to verify that the process is being fed with the correct inputs and resources and that it is producing the required results at each stage. Verification is also a period when parameters are optimized and special cause variation is removed. This would also involve the monitoring of resource consumption in terms of time, materials and labour, verification of mistake-proofing provisions, measurement system capability, packaging, health, safety and environmental requirements and other regulations that apply to the process.

Process validation

This would be the action needed to determine the capability of the process to produce consistent output that meets the requirements in terms of quality, cost and delivery. In some cases this may require product approval by the customer or the designer.

Process change control

This would be the action needed to propose, review, evaluate, approve and implement changes in the process design.

Creating consistency in process planning (7.1)

> **1994–2000 Differences**
>
> Previously the standard required that quality planning be consistent with all other requirements of the quality system. There is no change in intent.

The standard requires planning of the realization processes to *be consistent with the other requirements of the organization's quality management system.*

What does this mean?

This means that the processes employed for specific products and services should either be those that form part of the management system, are developments of those that form part of the management system or are new processes that fit into the set of management system processes and meet the same organizational objectives.

Why is this necessary?

This requirement responds to the Process Approach Principle.

 The management system developed to meet the requirements of ISO 9001 is likely to be a generic system, not specific to any particular product, project or contract other than the range of products and services which your organization supplies. By implementing the processes of the management system, product, project or contract specific plans, procedures, specification etc. are generated. However specific variants, modifications or even new processes may be required for particular projects, contracts or orders. It is therefore essential that the provisions made for any particular product, service, project or contract do not conflict with the authorized policies and practices so that the integrity of the system is maintained. Also, if staff are familiar with one way of working, by receiving conflicting instructions staff may apply the incorrect policies and practices to the project.

How is this implemented?

There is often a temptation when planning for specific contracts to change the policies and processes where they are inflexible, invent new forms, change responsibilities, by-pass known bottlenecks etc. You need to be careful not to develop a mutant management system for specific contracts. If the changes needed are good for the business as a whole, they should be made using the prescribed management system change procedures.

Quality objectives and requirement for product (7.1a)

The standard requires the organization to *determine the quality objectives and requirements for the product.*

What does this mean?

This means that for every product or service that is to be supplied there has to be a specification of requirements which if met will deliver a product or service that meets customer requirements.

1994–2000 Differences
This is a new requirement that has no equivalent in the 1994 version. Previously it was assumed that the customer supplied the product quality requirements.

The quality objectives for the product are those inherent characteristics of the product or service that aims to satisfy customers. For products these would include objectives for functional performance and physical attributes, reliability, maintainability, durability etc. Those for services would include accessibility, responsiveness, promptness, reliability etc. Quality requirements for the product are the inherent characteristics that are required to be met and may equal the quality objectives, but quality objectives may aim higher than the requirements either in an attempt to delight customers or simply to ensure requirements are met. In some cases, the characteristic may be prone to variation due to factors that are not easily controllable and therefore targets are set higher to be certain of meeting the requirement. In other cases the objective may be stated in subjective or non-specific terms such as high reliability or relevant medical device directives whereas the requirement will be specific and quantifiable such as requiring an MTBF of 100,000 hrs or requiring compliance with EU Directive 90/385/EEC Annex 1. These quality objectives are for specific products whereas the quality objectives referred to in clause 5.4.1 relate to the whole organization.

Why is this necessary?

This requirement responds to the Leadership Principle.

The objective of product realization processes is to deliver product or service that meets requirements. It is therefore necessary to establish exactly what requirements the product must satisfy in order to determine whether the processes to be employed are fit for their purpose i.e. are capable of delivering a product that meets the requirements.

How is this implemented?

A specification should be produced or supplied for each product or service that is designed, produced and delivered. This specification should not only define the characteristics of the product but should define its purpose or function so that a product possessing the stated characteristics can be verified as being fit for its purpose. It is of little use for a product to meet its specification if the specification does not accurately reflect customer needs.

Determining the need for specific processes (7.1b)

1994–2000 Differences

Previously the standard required consideration to be given to the identification and acquisition of any controls and processes that may be needed in meeting the specified requirements for products, projects or contract.

The intent of the requirement remains unchanged.

The standard requires the organization to *determine the need to establish processes specific to the product.*

What does this mean?

There are two classes of processes – those that are product specific and those that are not. The none-product specific processes are generally the management and support processes such as business management and resource management. These are used for all the organization's products and services. Design, production and delivery processes are in general product specific because their characteristics may change depending on the nature of the product or service being produced or supplied. However, there are many design, production and delivery processes that do not require customization to deliver the required outputs other than when initially established. An organization that designs electronic circuits can use the same design process regardless of the specific characteristic of particular products. The same is true with respect to production processes where there are many making and moving processes that do not change with the product. Each of the processes has a performance range within which it can process product, therefore design processes for electronic circuits would probably be inappropriate for designing ships. Fabrication processes for telephones would probably be inappropriate for washing machines etc.

Why is this necessary?

This requirement responds to the Process Approach Principle.

When planning for specific products it is necessary to determine whether the intended product characteristics are within the design limits of the existing processes. If the product is similar to existing products no change to the processes may be needed. If the nature of the product is different or if the performance required is beyond the capability of existing processes, new or modified processes will be required. Many problems arise where managers load product into processes without being aware of the process's limitations. Often because people are so flexible, it is assumed that because they were successful at producing the previous product they will be successful with any other products. It is only when the differences are so great as to be glaringly obvious that they stop and think.

How is this implemented?

In planning for a contract or new product or service, the existing processes need to be reviewed against the customer or market requirements. One can then identify whether the system provides an adequate degree of control. Search for unusual requirements and risks to establish whether any adjustment to processes is necessary. This may require you to introduce new processes, procedures and forms or provide additional verification stages and feedback loops or prepare contingency plans.

When defining your processes you need not only to give them a name but also qualify their capabilities. This should be contained in the Process Description. Another way is to produce a list of existing processes identifying:

- The process by name
- The process specification
- Existing qualification data

For each new or modified product select the product specific processes that will be used and produce a product specific process list adding an additional column for inserting the additional qualification requirements for the intended application.

One technique you can use to identify the new controls is to establish a list of critical items or areas by analysing the design. Such items may include:

- Long lead items, i.e. items that need to be procured well in advance of the main procurement
- Risky suppliers i.e. single source suppliers or suppliers with a poor quality record for which there is no alternative
- High reliability items and single point failure items
- Limited life items, fragile items or hazardous items

For each item you should:

- Provide a description
- State the nature of criticality
- Identify the failure modes and the effects
- Determine the action required to eliminate, reduce or control the criticality

New controls may also be needed if there are unusual contractual relationships such as overseas suppliers, international consortia, in-plant surveillance by the customer etc. There may be language problems, translation work, harmonization of standards and other matters arising from international trade.

Once the criticality has been eliminated or reduced by design, choosing the right quality controls is key to the achievement of quality. You need to:

- Analyse the items or activities to determine the key characteristics the measurement and control of which will ensure quality
- Install provisions that will ensure that these characteristics are achieved
- Define methods for evaluating the selected characteristics
- Establish when to perform the measurements and what to do if they are not achieved

Another method of identifying the controls needed is to describe the result-producing processes in flow diagram format. This will enable you to identify where the verification stages need to be added and the feedback loops inserted(Hoyle, David, 1996)[1].

Determining the need for documentation (7.1b)

The standard requires the organization to *determine the need to establish documents specific to the product.*

What does this mean?

Documentation specific to the product is any documentation that is used or generated by the product realization processes. Such documents include specifications, drawings, plans, standards, datasheets, manuals, handbooks, procedures, instructions, records, reports etc. that refer to the product or some aspect of the product. Determining the need to establish documentation means that in planning product realization you need to determine the information carriers that will feed each of the processes and be generated by each of the processes.

Why is this necessary?

This requirement responds to the Process Approach Principle.

The process descriptions will specify the types of information required to operate the process and required to be generated by the process. However, depending on the nature of the product, contract or project, these may need to be customized for the specific product so that they carry the required information to the points of implementation. Information required for one project may not be required for another project. Product configuration, organization structure and locations may all be different and require specific documents that are not used on other projects.

How is this implemented?

A common method for project work is to establish a Work Breakdown Structure (WBS) that identifies all the major packages of work to be carried out. For each Major Task a Work Statement is produced that defines the inputs, tasks and outputs required. The outputs are described and a series of deliverables. Some of these will be documents, particularly in the design and planning phases. For less complex projects a list of deliverables may be all that is required, identifying the document by name, the author and delivery date.

Determining the need for resources (7.1b)

1994–2000 Differences

Previously the standard required consideration to be given to:

(a) the identification and acquisition of any resources that may be needed to achieve the required quality;

(b) the development of new instrumentation;

(c) the identification of any measuring requirements that exceeds the known state of the art in sufficient time for the needed capability to be developed.

The intent of the requirement remains unchanged.

The standard requires the organization to *provide resources specific to the product*.

What does this mean?

Resources are an available supply of equipment, environment, machines, materials, processes, labour, documentation and utilities such as heat, light, water and power etc. that can be drawn upon when needed. This therefore requires detailed planning and logistics management and may require many lists and sub-plans so that the resources are available when required. Inventory management is an element of such planning.

Why is this necessary?

This requirement responds to the Process Approach Principle.

All businesses are constrained by their resources. No organization has an unlimited capability. It is therefore necessary when planning new or modified products to determine what resources will be required to design, develop, produce and supply the product or service. Even when the requirement is for existing products, the quantity or delivery required might strain existing resources to an extent where failure to deliver becomes inevitable.

How is this implemented?

Successful implementation of this requirement depends on managers having current details of the capability of the process at their disposal. At the higher levels of management, a decision will be made as whether the organization has the inherent capability to meet the specific requirements. At the lower levels, resources planning focuses on the detail, identifying specific equipment, people, materials, capacity and most important, the time required. A common approach is to use a project-planning tool such as Microsoft Project that facilitates the development of Gannt Charts and PERT Charts and the ability to predict resources levels in terms of manpower and programme time. Other planning tools will be needed to predict process throughput and capability. The type of resources to be determined might include any of the following:

- Special equipment tools, test software and test or measuring equipment
- Equipment to capture, record and transmit information internally or between the organization and its customers

- New technologies such as CAD/CAM
- Fixtures, jigs and other tools
- New instrumentation either for monitoring processes or for measuring quality characteristics
- New measurement capabilities
- New skills required to operate the processes, design new equipment, perform new roles
- New research and development facilities
- New handling equipment, plant and facilities

Determining verification, validation and monitoring activities (7.1c)

The standard requires the organization to *determine the required verification, validation, monitoring, inspection and test activities specific to the product.*

What does this mean?

The required verification activities are those activities necessary to establish that a product meets or is meeting the defined and agreed requirements. There are several methods of verification that include inspection, test, monitoring, analysis, simulation, observation or demonstration each serving the same purpose but each being different in the manner in which it is conducted and the conditions under which it is appropriate.

> **1994–2000 Differences**
>
> Previously the standard required consideration to be given to the identification of suitable verification at appropriate stages in the realization of product.
>
> The intent of the requirement remains unchanged.

Why is this necessary?

This requirement responds to the Factual Approach Principle.

Provision should be made in the management system for verification of product at various stages through the realization processes. The stage at which verification needs to be performed and the characteristics to be verified at each stage are dependent on the requirements for the particular product. It is therefore necessary to determine the verification required for each product and process.

How is this implemented?

Product verification

If all the key features and characteristics of your product/service can be verified by a simple examination on final inspection or at the point of delivery, the requirement is easily satisfied. On the other hand if you can't do this, whilst the principle is the same, it becomes more complex.

Generically there are two types of requirements – *Defining requirements* and *Verification requirements*. Defining requirements specify the features and characteristics required of a product, process or service. These may be wholly specified by the customer or by the organization or a mixture of the two. *Verification requirements* specify the requirements for verifying that the defining requirements have been achieved and again may be wholly specified by the customer or by the organization or a mixture of the two. With verification requirements, however, other factors need to be taken into consideration depending on what you are supplying and to whom you are supplying it. In a contractual situation, the customer may specify what he wants to be verified and how he wants it verified. In a non-contractual situation, there may be statutory legal requirements, compliance with which is essential to avoid prosecution. Many of the national and international standards specify the tests that products must pass rather than performance or design requirements, so identifying the verification requirements can be quite a complex issue. It is likely to be a combination of:

● what your customer wants to be verified to meet the need for confidence (the customer may not demand you demonstrate compliance with all customer requirements, only those which are judged critical)
● what you need to verify to demonstrate that you are meeting all your customer's defining requirements (you may have a choice as to how you do this so it is not as onerous as it appears) and
● what you need to verify to demonstrate that you are meeting your own defining requirements (where your customer defines the product/service in performance terms, you will need to define in more detail the features and characteristics that will deliver the specified performance and these will need to be verified) and
● what you need to verify to demonstrate that you are complying with the law (product safety, personnel health and safety, conservation, environmental and other legislation) and
● what you need to verify to obtain confidence that your suppliers are meeting your requirements

Verification requirements are not limited to product/service features and characteristics. One may need to consider who carries out the verification, where and when it is carried out and under what conditions and on what quantity (sample or 100%) and standard of product (prototype or production models).

You may find that the only way you can put your product on the market is by having it tested by an independent test authority. You may need a licence to manufacture it, to supply it to certain countries and this may only be granted after independent certification. Some verification requirements only apply to the type of product/service, others to the process or each batch of product and others to each product or service delivery. Some requirements can only be verified under actual conditions of use. Others can be verified by analysis or similarity with other products that have been thoroughly tested. The range is so widespread it is not possible in this book to explore all examples, but as you can see, this requirement contains a minefield unless you have a simple product or unless the customer has specified everything you need to verify.

There are a number of ways of documenting verification requirements:

- By producing defining specifications which prescribe requirements for products or services and also the means by which these requirements are to be verified in-house in terms of the inspections, tests, analyses, audits, reviews, evaluations and other means of verification
- By producing separate verification specifications which define which features and characteristics of the product or service are to be verified and the means by which such verification is to be carried out
- By producing a quality plan or a verification plan that identifies the verification stages from product conception to delivery and further as appropriate, and refers to other documents that define the specific requirements at each stage
- By route card referencing drawings and specifications
- By inspection and test instructions specific to a production line, product or range of products.

In fact you may need to employ one or more of the above techniques to identify all the verification requirements.

Document verification

It is necessary to verify that all the documentation needed to produce and install the product is compatible; that you haven't a situation where the design documentation requires one thing and the production documents require another or that details in the design specification conflict with the details in the test specification. Incompatibilities can arise in a contract that has been compiled by different groups. For example the contract requires one thing in one clause and the opposite in another. Many of the standards invoked in the contract may not be applicable to the product or service required. Production processes may not be qualified for the material specified in the design – the designer may have specified materials that are unavailable!

In order to ensure compatibility of these procedures, quality-planning reviews need to be planned and performed as the new documentation is produced. Depending on the type of contract, several quality planning reviews may be necessary, each scheduled to occur prior to commencing subsequent stages of development, production, installation or servicing. The quality planning reviews during product development can be held in conjunction with the design stage reviews required in section 7.3.4 of ISO 9001. At these reviews the technical and programme requirements should be examined to determine whether the existing provisions are adequate, compatible and suitable to achieve the requirements and if necessary additional provisions put in place.

Determining the criteria for product acceptance (7.1c)

1994–2000 Differences

Previously the standard required:

(a) consideration to be given to the clarification of standards of acceptability for all features and requirements, including those which contain a subjective element;

(b) criteria for workmanship to be stipulated in the clearest practical manner.

The intent of the requirement remains unchanged.

The standard requires the organization to *determine the criteria for product acceptance.*

What does this mean?

The criteria for product acceptability are those characteristics that the product or service needs to exhibit for it to be deemed acceptable to the customer or the regulator. These are those standards, references, and other means used for judging compliance with defined requirements. In some cases the requirements can be verified directly such as when a measurable dimension is stated. In other cases the measurements to be made have to be derived, such as in the food industry where there is a requirement for food to be safe for human consumption. Standards are established for levels of contamination, microbes etc. which if exceeded are indicative of food is not safe for human consumption. Another example is in traffic management systems where speed limits are imposed for certain roads because they have been proved to represent a safe driving speed under normal conditions. The requirement is for people to drive safely but this is open to too much interpretation consequently measurable standards are imposed for effective communication and to ensure consistency in the application of the law.

Why is this necessary?

This requirement responds to the Factual Approach Principle.

In order to verify that the products or services meet the specified requirements there needs to be unambiguous standards for making acceptance decisions. These standards need to be expressed in terms that are not open to interpretation so that any qualified person using them would reach the same decision when verifying the same characteristics in the same environment using the same equipment. In some cases the requirement is expressed definitively and in other cases subjectively. It is therefore necessary to establish how reliable is 'reliable', how safe is 'safe', how clean is 'clean', how good is 'good quality'. Specifications often contain subjective statements such as good commercial quality, smooth finish etc., and require further clarification in order that an acceptable standard can be attained.

How is this implemented?

A common method of determining acceptance criteria is to analyse each requirement and establish measures that will indicate that the requirement has been achieved. In some cases national or international standards exist for use in demonstrating acceptable performance. The secret is to read the statement then ask yourself, 'Can I verify we have achieved this?' If not, select a standard that is attainable, unambiguous and acceptable to both customer and supplier that if achieved will be deemed as satisfying the intent of the requirement.

The results of some processes cannot be directly measured using gauges, tools, test and measuring equipment and so an alternative means has to be found of determining what is conforming product. The term given to such means is 'Workmanship Criteria', criteria that will enable producers and inspectors to gain a common understanding of what is acceptable and unacceptable. Situations where this may apply in manufacturing are soldering, welding, brazing, riveting, deburring etc. It may also include criteria for finishes, photographs, printing, blemishes and many others. Samples indicating the acceptable range of colour, grain and texture may be needed and if not provided by your customer, those that you provide will need customer approval.

The criteria need to be defined by documented standards or by samples and models that clearly and precisely define the distinguishing features that represent both conforming and nonconforming product. In order to provide adequate understanding it may be necessary to show various examples of workmanship from acceptable to unacceptable so that the producer or inspector doesn't strive for perfection or rework product unnecessarily. These standards like any others need to be controlled. Documented standards should be governed by the document control provisions. Samples and models need to be governed by the provision for controlling measuring devices and be subject to periodic examination to detect deterioration and damage. They should be certified as authentic workmanship samples and measures taken to preserve their integrity. Ideally they should be under the control of the inspection authority or someone other than the person responsible for using them so that there is no opportunity for them to be altered without authorization. The samples represent your company's standards, they do not belong to any individual and if used by more than one person you need to ensure consistent interpretation by training the users.

Determining the need for records (7.1d)

1994–2000 Differences

Previously the standard required:

(a) consideration to be given to the identification and preparation of quality records in meeting the specified requirements for products, projects or contracts;

(b) the inspection and testing records to be established to be detailed in the quality plan or documented procedures.

The intent of the requirement remains unchanged.

The standard requires the organization to *determine the records needed to provide evidence that the realization processes and resulting product meet requirements.*

What does this mean?

Countless verification activities will be carried out at various levels of product and service development, production and delivery. These activities will generate data and this data needs to be collected in a form that can be used to demonstrate that processes and products fulfil requirements. This does not mean that every activity needs to be recorded but the manner in which the data is recorded and when it is to be recorded should be determined as part of the planning activity.

Why is this necessary?

This requirement responds to the Factual Approach Principle.

Without records indicating the results that have been obtained from product and process verification, compliance cannot be demonstrated to those on the scene of the action such as customers, managers and analysts. When investigating failures and plotting performance trends, records are also needed for reference purposes.

While procedures should define the records that are to be produced, these are the records that will be produced if these procedures are used. On particular contracts, only those procedures that are relevant will be applied and therefore the records to be produced will vary from contract to contract. Special conditions in the contract may make it necessary for additional records to be produced.

How is this implemented?

There are two parts to this requirement. One concerning product records and the other concerning process records.

Product records

By assessing the product requirements and identifying the stage in the process where these requirements will be verified, the type of records needed to capture the results should be determined. In some cases common records used for a variety of products may suffice but in others, product specific records may be needed that prescribe the characteristics to be recorded and the corresponding acceptance criteria to be used to indicate pass or fail conditions.

Process records

The records required for demonstrating process performance should be identified during process development (see previously). Continued operation of the process should generate further records that confirm that the process is functioning properly – i.e. meeting the requirements for which it was designed. Periodically, process managers should review their processes and establish that the process continues to function as planned. These reviews should apply to the office processes as well as the shop floor processes so that sales, design and purchasing processes are subject to the same reviews as production, distribution, installation and service delivery.

Process records should indicate the process objectives and exhibit performance data showing the extent to which these objectives are being achieved. These may be in the form of bar charts, graphs, pie charts etc.

Documenting product realization planning (7.1)

The standard requires the product realization planning to *be in a form suitable for the organization's method of operations.*

> **1994–2000 Differences**
>
> Previously the standard required quality planning to be documented in a format to suit the supplier's method of operation.
>
> There is no change in intent.

What does this mean?

The output of planning can be in a variety of forms depending on the nature of the product, project, contract or service and its complexity. For simple products, the planning output may be in tabular form on a single page. For complex products, the planning output may take the form of a project plan and several supplementary plans each being in the form of a manual with several sections. What it is called is immaterial.

Why is this necessary?

This requirement responds to the Process Approach Principle.

The standard does not impose a particular format for the output of the planning activity or insist that such information carriers are given specific labels. Each product is different and therefore the planning outputs need to match the input requirements of the processes they feed.

How is this implemented?

Discrete plans are needed when the work to be carried out requires detailed planning beyond that already planned for by the management system. The system will not specify everything you need to do for every job. It will usually specify only general provisions that apply in the majority of situations. You will need to define the specific processes that will be used, the producing activities to be performed, the documentation to be produced, the verification activities to be performed and resources to be employed. The contract may specify particular standards or requirements that you must meet and these may require additional provisions to those defined in the documented management system.

The planning outputs are dependent upon the work that is required and therefore may include:

- Project plans
- Product development plans
- Production plans
- Procurement plans
- Reliability and maintainability programme plans
- Control plans or verification plans
- Installation plans
- Commissioning plans
- Performance evaluation plans

It is not necessary to produce a separate quality plan if the processes of the management system that are to be utilized are identified in the project plan. Sometimes the project is so complex that separate quality or quality assurance plans may be needed simply to separate the subject matter into digestible chunks. The disadvantage in giving any document a label with the word *quality* in the title is that it can sometimes be thought of as a document that serves only the Quality Department rather than a document that defines the provisions for managing the various processes that will be utilized on the project. A useful rule to adopt is to avoid giving documents a title that reflect the name of a department wherever possible.

Customer-related processes (7.2)

Determination of requirements related to the product (7.2.1)

This heading implies there are other requirements that do not relate to the product that may form part of the customer requirements. However, ISO 9000 defines a product as the result of a process and includes services among these.

It is therefore difficult to imagine any aspect of customer requirements that would not relate to the product or service that is being provided. Requirements related to the product or service could include:

- Characteristics that the product is required to exhibit i.e. the inherent characteristics
- Price and delivery requirements
- Procurement requirements that constrain the source of certain components, materials or the conditions under which personnel may work
- Management requirements related to the manner in which the project will be managed, the product developed, produced and supplied
- Security requirements relating to the protection of information
- Financial arrangements for the deposit of bonds, payment conditions, invoicing etc.
- Commercial requirements such as intellectual property, proprietary rights, labelling, warranty, resale, copyright etc.
- Personnel arrangements such as access to the organization's facilities by customer personnel and vice versa

A process for determining product requirements should be designed so that it takes as its input the identified need for a product and passes this through several stages where requirements from various sources are determined, balanced and confirmed as the definitive requirements that form the basis for product realization. The input can either be a customer specific requirement or the market specification that results from market research (See Chapter 5 under *Customer focus*) or a sales order for an existing product. The output may indeed be presented in several documents – the product requirement specification containing the hardware and software requirements and the service requirement specification containing the service requirements. Alternatively where service is secondary, the requirement may be contained the contract.

Products requirements specified by the customer (7.2.1a)

The standard requires the organization to *determine requirements specified by the customer including requirements for delivery and post delivery activities.*

What does this mean?

ISO 9000 defines the customer as the organization that receives the product, however, this is easily taken out of context by referring to internal and

1994–2000 Differences
Previously the standard required the supplier to ensure that the requirements of the tender, contract or order are adequately defined and documented.
This new requirement is no different in intent to that repeated in clause 7.2.2.

378 ISO 9000 Quality Systems Handbook

external customers. The term customer in ISO 9000 is reserved only for the external customer because the organization that is the subject of the standard is the whole organization not its component parts. Customers are also consumers, clients, end users, retailers, purchasers and beneficiaries, therefore requirements specified by the customer need not be limited to the organization that is purchasing the product or the service. ISO 9000 also defines requirements as needs or expectations that are stated, generally implied or obligatory and therefore any information that is expressed by the customer as a need or expectation, whether in writing or verbally is a requirement. To determine such requirements means that the needs and expectations that are either stated verbally, or in writing, implied or obligatory have to be resolved, pinned-down and defined so that neither party is in any doubt as to what is required. The requirements for delivery mean requirements pertaining to the shipment, transportation, transmission or other means for conveying the product or service to the customer in a specified condition. Similarly with post delivery requirements, these are the requirements pertaining to the support the customer requires from the organization to maintain, service, assist or otherwise retain the product or service in a serviceable state.

Why is this necessary?

This requirement responds to the Customer Focus Principle.

The purpose of the requirements is to ensure that you have established the requirements you are obliged to meet before you commence work. This is one of the most important requirements of the standard. The majority of problems down stream can be traced either to a misunderstanding of customer requirements or insufficient attention being paid to the resources required to meet customer requirements. Get these two things right and you are half way towards satisfying your customer needs and expectations.

How is this implemented?

Customers will convey their requirements in various forms. Many organizations do business through purchase orders or simply order over the telephone or by mail. Some customers prefer written contracts others prefer a handshake or a verbal telephone agreement. However a contract does not need to be written and signed by both parties to be a binding agreement. Any undertaking given by one party to another for the provision of products or services is a contract, whether written or not. The requirement for these requirements to be determined rather than documented, places the onus on the organization to understand customer needs and expectations, not simply react to what the customer has transmitted. It is therefore necessary in all but simple transactions to enter into a dialogue with the customer in order to understand what is required. Through this dialogue, assisted by checklists that cover your product and service offerings, you can tease out of the customer all the requirements that relate to the product. Sometimes the customer wants one of your products or services but in fact needs another but has failed to realize it. Customer's wants are not needs unless the two coincide. It is not until you establish needs that you can be certain that you can satisfy the customer. There may be situations when you won't be able to satisfy customer's needs because the customer simply does not have sufficient funds to pay you for what is necessary!

Many customer requirements will go beyond end product or service requirements. They will address delivery, quantity, warranty, payment and other legal obligations. With every product one provides a service, for instance one may provide delivery to destination, invoices for payment, credit services, enquiry services, warranty services etc. and the principal product may not be the only product either – there may be packaging, brochures, handbooks, specifications etc. With services there may also be products such as brochures, replacement parts and consumables, reports, certificates etc.

In ensuring the contract requirements are adequately defined, you should establish where applicable:

- That there is a clear definition of the purpose of the product or service you are being contracted to supply
- That the conditions of use are clearly specified
- That the requirements are specified in terms of the features and characteristics that will make the product or service fit for its intended purpose
- That the quantity, price and delivery are specified
- That the contractual requirements are specified including: warranty, payment conditions, acceptance conditions, customer supplied material, financial liability, legal matters, penalties, subcontracting, licences and design rights
- That the management requirements are specified such as points of contact, programme plans, work breakdown structure, progress reporting, meetings, reviews, interfaces
- That the quality assurance requirements are specified such as quality system standards, quality plans, reports, customer surveillance and concessions

It is wise to have the requirement documented in case of a dispute later. The document also acts as a reminder as to what was agreed but it is vital when either of the parties that made agreement move on to pastures new, leaving their successors to continue the relationship. This becomes very difficult if the agreements were not recorded particularly if your customer representative moves on before you have submitted your first invoice. The document needs to carry an identity and if subject to change, an issue status. In the simple case this is the serial numbered invoice and in more complicated transactions, it will be a multipage contract with official contract number, date and signatures of both parties.

Product requirements not specified by the customer (7.2.1b)

The standard requires the organization to *determine product requirements not specified by the customer but necessary for known intended use.*

What does this mean?

There are two ways of looking at this requirement.

- From the viewpoint of an identified market need
- From the viewpoint of a specific contract or order

Market need

The process of identifying future customer needs and expectations was addressed under Customer focus in Chapter 5. The output of this process will be in the form of a market research report that contains information from which a new product requirement can be developed.

Specific contract or order

The customer is not likely to be an expert in your field. The customer may not know much about the inner workings of your product and service offerings and may therefore specify the requirements only in performance terms. In such cases, the onus is on the organization to determine the requirements that are necessary for the product or service to fulfil its intended use. For example, if a customer requires an electronic product to operate close to high voltage equipment, the electronics will need to be screened to prevent harmful radiation from affecting its performance. The customer may not know that this is necessary but during your dialogue, you establish the conditions of use and as a result identify several other requirements that need to be met. These are requirements not specified by the customer but necessary for known intended use.

Why is this necessary?

This requirement responds to the Customer Focus Principle.

It is necessary to convert the results of market research into definitive product requirements so as to form a basis for new product development.

In the case of specific orders it is important to identify requirements necessary for intended use. For instance, subsequent to delivery of a product, a customer could inform you that your product does not function properly and you establish that it is being used in an environment that is outside its design specification. You would not have a viable case if the customer had informed you that it was going to be placed near high voltage equipment and you took no action.

How is this implemented?

Careful examination of customer needs and expectations is needed in order to identify all the essential product requirements. A useful approach is to maintain a check list or datasheet of the products and services offered which indicate the key characteristics but also indicate the limitations, what it can't be used for, what your processes are not capable of. Of course such data needs to be kept within reasonable bounds but it is interesting to note that a manufacturer of refrigerators was successfully sued under product liability legislation for not providing a warning notice that the item was not safe for a person to stand on the top surface. It is therefore important to establish what the customer intends to use the product for, where and how they intend to use it and for how long they expect it to remain serviceable. With proprietary products many of these aspects can be clarified in the product literature supplied with the goods or displayed close to the point of service delivery. With custom designed products and services, a dialogue with the customer is vital to understand exactly what the product will be used for through its design life.

Statutory and regulatory requirements (7.2.1c)

The standard requires the organization to *determine statutory and regulatory requirements related to the product*.

What does this mean?

Almost all products are governed by regulations that constrain or prohibit certain inherent characteristics. Many of the regulations apply to human safety but some also apply to equipment safety such as those pertaining to electromagnetic radiation. There are also regulations that apply to the import and export of goods and environmental regulations that apply to pollution. While there may be no pollution from using the product, there may be pollution from making, moving or disposing of the product and therefore, regulations that apply to production processes are indeed product-related.

> **1994–2000 Differences**
>
> Previously this requirement was limited to new design where the standard required design input requirements relating to the product including applicable statutory and regulatory requirements, to be identified.
>
> The new requirement extends the applicability of regulatory and legal requirements to the products supplied whether or not the organization designed them.

Why is this necessary?

This requirement responds to the Customer Focus Principle.

The customer may not be aware of all regulations that apply but will expect the supplier of the products and services required to be fully aware and have complied with all of them without exception. It is necessary to be fully aware of such statutes and regulations for the following reasons:

- A failure to observe government health and safety regulations could close a factory for a period and suspend your ability to supply customers.
- Health and safety hazards could result in injury or illness and place key personnel out of action for a period.
- Environmental claims made by your customers regarding conservation of natural resources, recycling etc. may be compromised if environmental inspections of your organization show a disregard for such regulations.
- The unregulated discharge of waste gases, effluent and solids may result in public concern in the local community and enforce closure of the plant by the authorities.
- A failure to take adequate personnel safety precautions may put product at risk.
- A failure to dispose of hazardous materials safely and observe fire precautions could put plant at risk.
- A failure to provide safe-working conditions for personnel may result in public concern and local and national inquiries that may harm the reputation of the organization.

It is therefore necessary to maintain an awareness of all regulations that apply regardless of the extent to which they may or may not relate to the product.

How is this implemented?

In order to determine the applicable statutes and regulations you will need a process for scanning the environment, identifying those that are relevant and capturing them in your management system. The legislators don't know what is relevant to your organization – only you know that so a dialogue with legal experts may be necessary to identify all those regulations that apply.

There are lots of regulations and no guarantees of finding them all. However, you can now search through libraries on the Internet and consult bureaux, trade associations and government departments to discover those that apply to you. Ignorance of the law they say is no excuse.

The requirement also applies to products you purchase that are resold under the original manufacturer's label or re-badged under your label or incorporated into your product. Regulations that would apply to your products apply to products you have purchased. There may be regulations that only apply to products you have purchased because of their particular form, function or material properties and may not apply to your other products. It pays therefore to be vigilant when releasing purchase orders.

Organization's product requirement (7.2.1d)

The standard requires *any additional requirements determined by the organization for the product to be determined.*

What does this mean?

In addition to the requirements specified by the customer and the regulations that apply, there may be requirements imposed by the organization's policies that impinge upon the particular products or services that are to be supplied. The product policy may impose certain style, appearance, reliability and maintainability requirements or prohibit use of certain technologies or materials. Other requirements may serve to aid production or distribution that are of no consequence to the customer but necessary for the efficient and effective realization and supply of the product.

Why is this necessary?

This requirement responds to the Leadership Principle.

The requirement is necessary in order that relevant organizational policies and objectives are deployed through the product and service offerings. A failure to identify such constraints at the requirement definition stage could lead to abortive design work or if left undetected, the supply of products or services that harm the organization's reputation. Often, an organization is faced with the task of balancing customer needs with those of other interested parties. It may therefore be appropriate in some circumstances for the organization to decline to meet certain customer requirements on the grounds that they conflict with the needs of certain stakeholders.

How is this implemented?

The organization's requirements should be defined in technical manuals that are used by designers, production and distribution staff. These will often apply to all the organization's products and services but will however, need to be reviewed to identify the specific requirements that apply to particular products.

Review of requirements related to the product (7.2.2)

Conducting the review (7.2.2)

The standard requires the organization to *review the requirements related to the product.*

1994–2000 Differences

Previously the standard required the supplier to establish and maintain documented procedures for contract review and for the coordination of these activities.

The requirement for procedures is now limited to one general requirement. Where this new requirement differs is that the review has to embrace all identified requirements not only those stated in the order or contract. This changes the review from a *contract review* to a *requirement review*.

What does this mean?

A review of the requirements related to the product means that all the requirements that have been identified through the requirement determination process should be examined together preferably by someone other that those who gathered the information. The review may be quite independent of any order or contract but may need to be repeated should an order or contract for the product be received.

Why is this necessary?

This requirement responds to the Factual Approach Principle.

The process of determining the requirements that relate to the product consists of several stages culminating in a definitive statement of the product requirements. All processes should contain review stages as a means of establishing that the process output is correct and that the process is effective. The review referred to in this requirement is therefore necessary to establish that the output of the requirement determination process is correct.

How is this implemented?

The information gathered as a result of determining the various product requirements should be consolidated in the form of a specification, contract or order and then subject to review. The personnel who should review these requirements depend upon their complexity and there are three situations that you need to consider.

1 Development of new product to satisfy identified market needs – New product development
2 Sales against the organization's requirements – Proprietary sales
3 Sales against specific customer requirements – Custom sales

New product development

In setting out to develop a new product there may not be any customer orders – the need for the product may have been identified as a result of market research and from the data gathered a definitive product requirement developed. The product requirement review is performed to confirm that the requirements do reflect a product that will satisfy the identified needs and expectations of customers. At the end product level, this review may be the same as the design input review, but there other outputs from market research such as the predicted quantities, the manner of distribution, packaging and promotion considerations. The review should be carried out by those functions representing the customer, design and development, production, service delivery and in service support so that all views are considered.

Proprietary sales

In a proprietary sales situation, you may simply have a catalogue of products and services advertising material and a sales office taking orders over the telephone or over the counter. There are two aspects to the review of requirements. The first is the initial review of the requirements and advertising material before they are made available for potential customer to view and the second is where the sales person reviews the customer's request against the catalogue to determine if the particular product is available and can be supplied in the quantity required. We could call these reviews, Requirement Review and Transaction Review. As a customer may query particular features, access to the full product specification or a technical specialist may be necessary to answer such queries.

Custom sales

In custom sales situation the product or service is being produced or customized for a specific customer and with several departments of the organization having an input to the contract and its acceptability. These activities need co-ordinating so that you ensure all are working with the same set of information. You will need to collect the contributions of those involved and ensure they are properly represented at meetings. Those who negotiate contracts on behalf of the company, carry a great responsibility.

One aspect of a contract often overlooked is shipment of finished goods. You have ascertained the delivery schedule, the place of delivery, but how do you intend to ship it – by road, rail and ship or by air. It makes a lot of difference to the costs. Also delivery dates often mean the date on which the shipment arrives not the date it leaves. You therefore need to build into your schedules an appropriate lead-time for shipping by the means agreed to. If you are late you may need to employ speedier means but that will incur a premium for which you may not be paid. Your financial staff will therefore need to be involved in the requirement review.

Having agreed the requirements, you need to convey them to their point of implementation in sufficient time for resources to be acquired and put to work.

Timing of review (7.2.2)

The standard requires the review to *be conducted prior to the decision or commitment to supply a product to the customer (e.g. submission of a tender, acceptance of a contract or order).*

> **1994–2000 Differences**
>
> Previously the standard required that the tender, contract or order be reviewed before submission or acceptance.
>
> There is no change in requirement.

What does this mean?

A tender is an offer made to a potential customer in response to an invitation. The acceptance of a contract is a binding agreement on both sides to honour commitments. Therefore, the period before the submission of a tender or acceptance of a contract or order is a time when neither side is under any commitment and presents an opportunity to take another look at the requirements before legal commitments are made.

Why is this necessary?

This requirement responds to the Factual Approach Principle.

The purpose of the requirement review is to ensure that the requirements are complete, unambiguous and attainable by the organization. It is therefore necessary to conduct such reviews before a commitment to supply is made so that any errors or omissions can be corrected in time. There may not be opportunities to change the agreement after a contract has been signed without incurring penalties. Customers will not be pleased by organizations that have underestimated the cost, time and work required to meet their requirements and may insist that organizations honour their commitments – after all an agreement is a promise and organizations that break their promises do not survive for long in the market place.

How is this implemented?

The simplest method of implementing this requirement is to make provision in the requirement determination process for a requirement review to take place before tenders are submitted, contracts are signed or orders accepted. In order to ensure this happens staff need to be educated and trained to react in an appropriate manner to situations in which the organization will be committed to subsequently honouring its obligations. At one level this means that staff stop, think and check before accepting an order. At another level, this means that staff seek out someone else to perform the checks so that there is another pair of eyes focused on the requirements. At a high level, this means that a review panel is assembled and the requirements debated and all issues resolved before the authorized signatory signs the contract. One means of helping staff to react in an appropriate manner is to provide forms with provision for a requirement review box that has to be checked or signed and dated before the process may continue. With computer-based systems, provision can also be made to prevent the transaction being completed until the correct data has been entered. This process is needed also for any amendments to the contract or order so that the organization takes the opportunity to review its capability with each change.

Ensuring that product requirements are defined (7.2.2a)

The standard requires that the review of requirements *ensure product requirements are defined.*

What does this mean?

This means that the review should verify that all the
requirements specified by the customer, the regulators and the organization have been defined,
there are no omissions, no errors, no ambiguities, no
misunderstandings.

Why is this necessary?

This requirement responds to the Factual Approach
Principle.

> **1994–2000 Differences**
> Previously the standard
> required the review of the
> tender, contract or order
> ensure the requirements
> are adequately defined
> and documented.
>
> The only difference is the
> omission of the words
> 'adequately' and
> 'documented' which does
> not change the intent of
> the requirement but which
> challenges auditors to be
> innovative.

During the requirement determination process there are many variables. The
time allowed, the competence of the personnel involved, the knowledge of the
customer of what is needed and the accessibility of information. A deficiency
in any one of these can result in the inadequate determination of requirements.
It is therefore necessary to subject these requirements to review to ensure they
are correct before a commitment to supply is made.

How is this implemented?

Some organizations deal with orders that are so predictable that a formal
documented review before acceptance adds no value. But however predictable
the order, it is prudent to establish that it is what you believe it to be before
acceptance. Many have been caught out by the small print in contracts or sales
agreements such as the following wording 'This agreement takes precedence
over any conditions of sale offered by the supplier' or 'Invoices must refer to
the order reference otherwise they will be rejected'.

If the customer is choosing from a catalogue or selecting from a shelf of
products, you need to ensure that the products offered for sale are properly
described. Such descriptions must not be unrepresentative of the product
otherwise you may be in breech of national laws and statutes. In other
situations you need some means of establishing that the customer requirements are adequate.

One means of doing this is to use checklists that prompt the reviewers to
give proper consideration to important aspects before accepting contracts.
Another method is to subject the requirements to an independent review by
experts in their field, thus ensuring a second pair of eyes scans the
requirements for omissions, ambiguities and errors.

Resolving differences (7.2.2b)

The standard requires the review to *ensure that contract or order requirements differing from those previously expressed are resolved.*

What does this mean?

Previously expressed requirements are those that may have been included in an invitation to tender issued by the customer. Whether or not you have submitted a formal tender, any offer you make in response to a requirement is a kind of tender. Where a customer's needs are stated and you offer your product, you are implying that it responds to your customer's stated needs. You need to ensure that your 'tender' is compatible with your customer's needs otherwise the customer may claim you have sold a product that is not 'fit for purpose'.

Why is this necessary?

This requirement responds to the Customer Focus Principle.

In situations where the organization has responded to an invitation to tender for a contract, it is possible that the contract when it arrives may differ from the draft conditions against which the tender was submitted. It is therefore necessary to check whether any changes have been made that will affect the validity of the tender. Customers should indicate the changes that have been made but they often don't – they would if there was a mutually beneficial relationship in place.

How is this implemented?

On receipt of a contract that has been the subject of an invitation to tender, or the subject of an unsolicited offer of product or service, it is prudent to check that what you are now being asked to provide is the same as that which you offered. If the product or service you offer is in any way different than the requirement, you need to point this out to your customer and reach agreement before you accept the order. Try and get the contract changed, but if this is not possible, record the differences in your response to the contract. Don't rely on verbal agreements because they can be conveniently forgotten when it suits one party or the other, or as is more common, the person you conversed with moves on and the new person is unable to act without written agreement – such is the world of contracting!

Ensuring that the organization has the ability to meet defined requirements (7.2.2c)

The standard requires that the review *ensure that the organization has the ability to meet defined requirements.*

> **1994–2000 Differences**
>
> Previously the standard required that the review ensure that the supplier has the capability to meet contract or accepted order requirements.
>
> There is no change in requirement.

What does this mean?

The organization needs to be able to honour its obligations made to its customers. Checks therefore need to be made to ensure that the necessary resources including plant, equipment, facilities, technology, personnel, competency and time are available or will be available to discharge these obligations when required.

Why is this necessary?

This requirement responds to the Leadership Principle.

You must surely determine that you have the necessary capability before accepting the contract as to find out afterwards that you haven't the capability to honour your obligations could land you in deep trouble. There may be penalty clauses in the contract or the nature of the work may be such that the organization's reputation could be irrevocably damaged as a result.

How is this implemented?

It is important that those accepting a contract are in a position to judge whether the organization has the capability of executing it. You have to consider the following:

- Do you have access to the products and services required?
- Do you have a licence to supply the required products and services if appropriate?
- Do you have the technology to design, manufacture or install the product?
- Do you have the equipment to utilize the data in the form that the customer may provide to you?
- Do you have the skills, knowledge and competency to execute the work required in the time required and to the specified standards?
- Is there sufficient time to accomplish the task with the resources you have available?
- Do you have access to appropriate suppliers and suppliers?
- It there is a secure supply of the necessary materials and components?
- Can you meet the terms and conditions imposed by your customer?
- Are you prepared to be held to the penalty clause (if specified)?

If you don't have any of the above, you will need to determine the feasibility of acquiring the relevant licence, the skills, the technology etc. within the timescale. Many organizations do not need staff waiting for the next contract. It is a common practice for companies to bid for work for which they do not have the necessary numbers of staff. However, what they need to ascertain is from where and how quickly they can obtain the appropriate staff. If a contract requires specialist skills or technologies that you don't already possess, it is highly probable that you will not be able to acquire them in the timescale. It is also likely that your customer will want an assurance that you have the necessary skills and technologies before the contract is placed. No organization can expect to hire extraordinary people at short notice, all you can expect to be available are average people and you may well have no choice than to accept less than average people. With good management skills and a good working environment you may be able to get these average people to do extraordinary things but it is not guaranteed!

A sales person who promises a short delivery to win an order invariably places an impossible burden on the company. A company's capability is not increased by accepting contracts beyond its current level of capability. You need to ensure that your sales personnel are provided with reliable data on the capability of the organization, do not exceed their authority and always obtain the agreement of those who will execute the contractual conditions before their acceptance.

In telephone sales transactions or transactions made by sales personnel alone, the sales personnel need to be provided with current details of the products and services available, the delivery times, prices and procedures for varying the conditions.

Maintaining records of product requirement reviews (7.2.2)

The standard requires *the results of the review and actions as a consequence of the review to be recorded (see 4.2.4).*

1994–2000 Differences

Previously the standard required records of contract reviews to be maintained.

The difference is that the records now apply to reviews of product requirement regardless of there being a contract or order and that follow-up actions now need to be recorded.

What does this mean?

A requirement review is an action that generates an outcome and this requirement means that the outcome of the review should be recorded. The outcome may be a decision in which case, a record of the decision is all that is necessary. However, the outcome could be a list of actions to be executed to correct the definition of requirement, or a list of concerns that need to be addressed. If the review is conducted with customer representatives present, records of the review could include modifications, interpretations and correction of errors that may be held back until the first contract amendment. In such cases the review records act as an extension to any contract.

Why is this necessary?

This requirement responds to the Factual Approach Principle.

For both new product development and order processing, records of the review are necessary as a means of recalling accurately what took place or as a means of reference in the event of a dispute or to distribute to those having responsibility for any actions that have been agreed. During the processing of orders and contracts, records of the requirement review indicate the stage in the process that has been reached and are useful if the process is interrupted for any reason.

How is this implemented?

There should be some evidence that a person with the authority to do so has accepted each product requirement, order or contract. This may be by signature or by exchange of letters or e-mails. You should also maintain a register of all contracts or orders and in the register indicate which were accepted and which declined for use when assessing the effectiveness of the sales process. If you prescribe in your contract acquisition procedures the criteria for accepting a contract; the signature of the contract or order together with this register can be adequate evidence of requirement review. If requirement reviews require the participation of several departments in the organization, their comments on the contract, minutes of meetings and any records of contract negotiations with the customer will represent the records of product requirement review. It is important however, to be able to demonstrate that the requirement being executed was reviewed for adequacy, differences in the tender and for supplier capability, before work commenced. The minimum you can have is a signature accepting an assignment to do work or supply goods but you must ensure that those signing the document know what they are signing for. Criteria for accepting orders or contracts can be included in the appropriate procedures. It cannot be stressed too strongly the importance of these actions. Most problems are caused by the poor understanding or poor definition of requirements.

Handling undocumented statements of requirements (7.2.2)

The standard requires *that where the customer provides no documented statement of requirement, the customer requirements are to be confirmed by the organization before acceptance.*

> **1994–2000 Differences**
>
> This is a new requirement that has no equivalent in the 1994 version.
>
> Previously the standard required the supplier to ensure that where no written statement of requirement is available for an order received by verbal means, the order requirements are agreed before their acceptance.
>
> There is no change in requirement.

What does this mean?

Customers often place orders by telephone or in face-to-face transactions where no paperwork passes from the customer to the organization. Confirmation of customer requirements is an expression of the organization's understanding of the obligations it has committed to honour.

Why is this necessary?

This requirement responds to the Customer Focus Principle.

Confirmation is necessary because when two people talk, it is not uncommon to find that although they use the same words, they each interpret the words differently. Confirming an understanding will avoid problems later. Either party to the agreement could move leaving the successors to interpret the agreement in a different way.

How is this implemented?

The only way to implement this requirement is for the organization to send a written acknowledgement to the customer confirming the requirements that form the basis of the agreement. In this way there should be no ambiguity, but if later the customer appears to be requiring something different, you can point to the letter of confirmation. If you normally use e-mail for correspondence, obtain an e-mail receipt that it has been read (not merely *received* as it could be overlooked) otherwise always send confirmation by post as e-mails can easily be inadvertently lost or deleted. Keep a copy of the e-mail and the letter and bring them under records control.

1994–2000 Differences
Previously the standard required suppliers to identify how an amendment to a contract is correctly transferred to the functions concerned. Also the requirements previously only applied to changes of requirements contained in a tender, contract or order. This new requirement embraces requirements defined by the organization and hence if these change, the same controls have to be imposed as if they were requirements specified by customers.

Changes to product requirements (7.2.2)

The standard requires that *where product requirements are changed, the organization ensure that relevant documents are amended and that relevant personnel are made aware of the changed requirements.*

What does this mean?

Products requirements may be changed by the customer, by regulators or by the organization itself and this may be made verbally or by changing the affected product requirement documents. This requirement means that all documents affected by the change are amended and that the changes are transmitted to those who need to know.

Why is this necessary?

This requirement responds to the Factual Approach Principle.

When changes are made to product requirements, the documents defining these requirements need to be changed otherwise those using them will not be aware of the changes. Also, changes to one document may have an impact on other related documents and unless these too are changed, the users will be working with obsolete information. It is therefore necessary to promulgate changes in a way that users are able to achieve the desired results.

How is this implemented?

In some organizations *product requirement change control* is referred to as *configuration management* (Lyon, D.D., 2000)[2]. Once a baseline set of requirements has been agreed, any changes to the baseline need to be controlled such that accepted changes are promptly made, and rejected changes are prevented from being implemented. If there is only one product specification and no related information, configuration management is synonymous with document control (see Chapter 4). When there are many specifications and related information, configuration management introduces a further dimension of having to control the compatibility between all the pieces of information. Document control is concerned with controlling the information carriers, whereas configuration management is concerned with controlling the information itself. If a system parameter changes there may be a knock-on effect through the sub-systems, equipments and components. The task is to identify all the items affected and as each item will have a product specification, this task will result in a list of affected specifications, drawings etc. While the list looks like a list of documents, it is really a list of items that are affected by the change. The requirement of ISO 9001 makes it appear a simple process but before documents are amended, the impact on each item may vary and have to be costed before being implemented. Major redesign may be necessary, tooling, handling equipment, distribution methods etc. may be affected and therefore, the process of not only communicating the change, but communicating the effects and the decisions relating to the change is an essential part of configuration management. It is not so much as who should be informed as what is affected. Identify what is affected and you should be able to identify who should be informed.

Customer communication (7.2.3)

Providing product information (7.2.3a)

The standard requires the organization to *determine and implement effective arrangements for communicating with customers relating to product information.*

> **1994–2000 Differences**
>
> This is a new requirement that has no equivalent in the 1994 version.

What does this mean?

Product information could be in the form of advertising material, catalogues, a web site, specifications or any medium for promoting the organization's products and services. Effective arrangements would be the processes that identified, planned, produced and distributed information that accurately describes the product.

Why is this necessary?

This requirement responds to the Customer Focus Principle.

Customers are only aware of product information that is accessible but whether they receive it or retrieve it, it must accurately represent the products and services offered otherwise it is open to misrepresentation and liable to prosecution in certain countries. It is therefore necessary to employ an effective process for communicating production information.

How is this implemented?

This requirement is concerned with the quality of information available to customers and has two dimensions. There is the misleading of customers into perceiving that a product or service provides benefits that it cannot deliver (accuracy) and there is the relationship between information available to customers and information as would need to be to properly represent the product (compatibility).

Accuracy depends on getting the balance right between imaginative marketing and reality. Organizations naturally desire to present their products and services in the best light – emphasizing the strong points and playing down or omitting the weak points. Providing the omissions are not misleading to the customer this is legitimate. What is needed is a product advertizing process that ensures product information accurately represents the product and does not infringe advertizing regulations and sale of goods laws.

Compatibility depends upon maintaining the product information once it has been released. In publishing for instance, advanced information about a new book is released months before publication, partially in order to obtain orders but also because it takes months to process bibliographic data through the ISBN registration process. If one were to wait until the book was published it would be six months before bookshops would have the details on their computers. Product information takes many forms and keeping all of it compatible is not an easy task. An information control process is therefore needed to ensure information compatibility is maintained when changes are made.

Handling enquiries (7.2.3a)

The standard requires the organization to *determine and implement effective arrangements for communicating with customers relating to enquiries.*

What does this mean?

Customer enquiries are the result of the effectiveness of the marketing process. If this has been successful, customers will be making contact with the organization to seek more information, clarify price, specification or delivery or request tenders, proposals or quotations.

1994–2000 Differences

This is a new requirement that has no equivalent in the 1994 version.

Why is this necessary?

This requirement responds to the Customer Focus Principle.

If the personnel receiving a customer enquiry are uninformed or not yet competent to deal effectively with enquiries, a customer may not receive the treatment intended by the organization and either go elsewhere or be misled. Both situations may result in lost business and dissatisfied customers.

How is this implemented?

An enquiry handling process is needed as part of the sales process that ensures customers are fed correct information and treated in a manner that maximizes the opportunity of a sale. Enquiries should be passed through a process that will convert the enquiry into a sale. As the person dealing with the enquiry could be the first contact the customer has with the organization, it is vital that they are competent to do the job. Frequent training and monitoring is therefore necessary to prevent customer dissatisfaction. This has become more apparent with telephone sales where a recorded message informs the customer that the conversation may be monitored for quality assurance purposes. As with all processes, you need to establish what you are trying to achieve, what affects your ability to get it right and how you will measure your success. The potential for error is great, whether customers are dealing with someone in person or cycling through a menu during a telephone transaction or on the Internet. Both human and electronic enquiry-handling processes need to be validated regularly to ensure their continued effectiveness. A typical enquiry conversion process flow is illustrated in Figure 7.3.

Handling contracts and orders (7.2.3b)

The standard requires the organization to *determine and implement effective arrangements for communicating with customers relating to contracts or order handling.*

What does this mean?

When an order or contract is received, several activities need to be performed in addition to the determination and review of product requirements and in each of these activities, communication with

1994–2000 Differences

This is a new requirement that has no equivalent in the 1994 version.

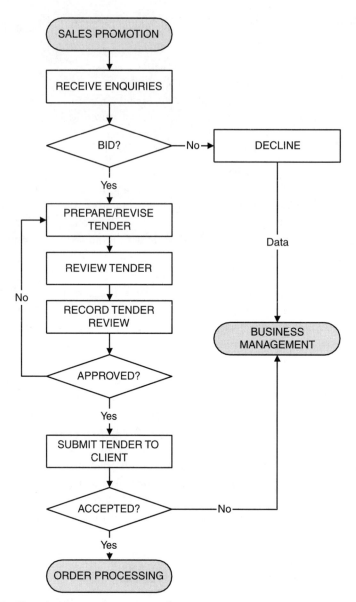

Figure 7.3 Enquiry conversion process flow

the customer may be necessary to develop an understanding that will secure an effective relationship.

Why is this necessary?

This requirement responds to the Customer Focus Principle.

Customer enquiries may or may not result in orders. However, when an order or a contract is received, it is necessary to pass it through an effective process that will ensure both parties are in no doubt as to the expectations under the contract.

How is this implemented?

A process should be established for handling orders and contracts with the objective of ensuring both parties are in no doubt as to the expectations under the contract before work commences. A typical order processing process is illustrated in Figure 7.4.

Apart from the requirement determination and reviews stages, there will be:

● Order/contract registration – recording its receipt

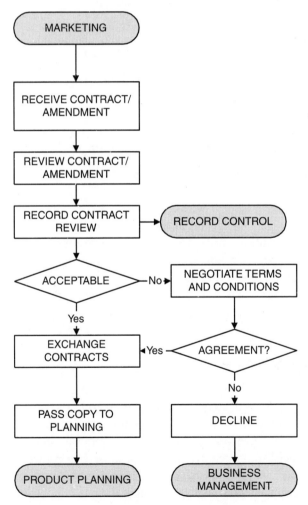

Figure 7.4 Typical order processing process flow

- Order/contract acknowledgement – informing the customer the order has been received and that the organization intends or does not intend to offer a bid or supply a product or service
- Requirement determination (as addressed previously)
- Requirement review (as addressed previously)
- Order/contract negotiation
- Order/contract acceptance
- Order/contract communication

Handling contract amendments (7.2.3b)

1994–2000 Differences

Previously the standard required the supplier to identify how an amendment to a contract is made.

The contract amendment process now needs to go beyond handling amendments received from customers and address the process of generating, issuing, negotiating and agreeing amendments.

The standard requires the organization to *determine and implement effective arrangements for communicating with customers relating to amendments.*

What does this mean?

An order or contract amendment is a change that corrects errors, rectifies ambiguities or otherwise makes improvements.

Why is this necessary?

This requirement responds to the Customer Focus Principle.

The need for an amendment can arise at any time and be initiated by either party to an agreement.

As orders and contracts are primarily a source of reference, it is necessary to ensure that only agreed amendments are made and that any provisional amendments or disagreed amendments are not acted upon or communicated as though they were approved. Otherwise, the basis of the agreement becomes invalid and may result in a dissatisfied customer or an organization that cannot recover its costs.

How is this implemented?

There may be several reasons why a customer needs to amend the original contract – customer needs may change, your customer's customer may change the requirement or details unknown at the time of contract may be brought to light. Whatever the reasons you need to provide a process for amending existing contracts under controlled conditions. On contracts where direct liaison with the customer is permitted between several individuals e.g. a project manager, contract manager, design manager, procurement manager, manufacturing manager, quality assurance manager, it is essential to establish ground rules for amending contracts, otherwise your company may unwittingly be held liable for meeting requirements beyond the funding that was originally predicted. It is often necessary to stipulate that only those changes to contract that are received in writing from the contract authority of either party will be legally binding. Any other changes proposed, suggested or otherwise communicated should be regarded as being invalid. Agreement between members of either project team should be followed by an official communication from the contract authority before binding either side to the agreement.

Having officially made the change to the contract, a means has to be devised to communicate the change to those who will be affected by it. You will need to establish a distribution list for each contract and ensure that any amendments are issued on the same distribution list. The distribution list should be determined by establishing who acts upon information in the contract and may include the managers of the various functions that are involved with meeting the contract/order requirements. Once established the distribution list needs to be under control because the effect of not being informed of a change to contract may well jeopardize delivery of conforming product.

Customer feedback (7.2.3c)

The standard requires the organization to *determine and implement effective arrangements for communicating with customers relating to customer feedback including customer complaints.*

1994–2000 Differences

Previously the standard required the corrective action procedures to include the effective handling of customer complaints.

The customer compliant process needs to be extended to embrace all customer feedback, both positive and negative.

What does this mean?

Customer feedback is any information conveyed by the customer in relation to the quality of the products or services provided. Sometimes this may be positive in the form of compliments, praise, gifts or tips and other times the feedback could be negative in the form of a complaint or an expression of disapproval.

Why is this necessary?

This requirement responds to the Customer Focus Principle.

Without an effective process for capturing customer feedback the organization would be missing opportunities for improving its performance as it is perceived to be by its customers. While not an accurate measure of customer satisfaction, customer feedback provides objective evidence that can be used in such an assessment.

How is this implemented?

You can only handle effectively the customer feedback that you receive and record. Customers may complain about your products and services but not go to the extent of writing a formal complaint. They may also compliment you on your products and services but again not bother to put it in writing. Compliments and complaints may arise in conversation between the customer and your sales and service staff and this is where you need to instill discipline and ensure they are captured. The primary difference between compliments and complaints is that compliments deserve a thank you and complaints deserve action, therefore the processes for dealing with compliments and complaints will differ.

The complaint handling process should cover the following aspects to be effective:

- A definition of when a message from a customer can be classified as a complaint
- The method of capturing the customer complaints from all interface channels with the customer
- The behaviour expected from those on the receiving end of the complaint
- The registration of complaints in order that you can account for them and monitor progress
- A form on which to record details of the complaint, the date, customer name etc.
- A method for acknowledging the complaint in order that the customer knows you care
- A method for investigating the nature and cause of the complaint
- A method for replacing product, repeating the service or for compensating the customer
- A link with other processes to trigger improvements that will prevent a recurrence of the complaint

The compliment handling process should cover the following:

- A definition of when a message from a customer can be classified as a compliment
- The method of capturing the compliments from all interface channels with the customer
- The behaviour expected from those on the receiving end of the compliment
- The registration of compliments in order that you can account for those you can use in your promotional literature
- A method for keeping staff informing of the compliments made by customers
- A method of rewarding staff when compliments result in further business.

Design and development (7.3)

Design and development control (7.3.1)

The standard requires the organization to *control design and development of the product.*

What does this mean?

Design can be as simple as replacing the motor in an existing vehicle with one of a different specification, or as complex as the design of a new automobile or any of its subsystems. Design can be of hardware, software (or a mixture of both) and can be of new services or modified services. Before design commences there is either a requirement or simply an idea. Design is a creative process that creates something tangible out of an idea or a requirement. The controls specified in the standard apply to the design process. There are no requirements that will

> **1994–2000 Differences**
>
> Previously the standard required the supplier to establish and maintain procedures to control the design of the product in order to ensure that the specified requirements are met.
>
> There is no change in this requirement except that the objective of control is now stated elsewhere and the method of control is at the organization's discretion.

inhibit creativity or innovation. In order to succeed, the process of converting an idea into a design that can be put into production or service has to be controlled. Design is often a process which strives to set new levels of performance, new standards or create new wants and as such can be a journey into the unknown. On such a journey we can encounter obstacles we haven't predicted which may cause us to change our course but our objective remains constant. Design control is a method of keeping the design on course towards its objectives and as such will comprise all the factors that may prevent the design from achieving its objectives. It controls the process not the designer, i.e. the inputs, the outputs, the selection of components, standards, materials, processes, techniques and technologies.

To control any design activity there are ten primary steps you need to take in the design process:

- Establish the customer needs.
- Convert the customer needs into a definitive specification of the requirements.
- Plan for meeting the requirements.
- Organize resources and materials for meeting the requirements.
- Conduct a feasibility study to discover whether accomplishment of the requirements is feasible.
- Conduct a project definition study to discover which of the many possible solutions will be the most suitable.
- Develop a specification which details all the features and characteristics of the product or service.

- Produce a prototype or model of the proposed design.
- Conduct extensive trials to discover whether the product or service which has been developed meets the design requirements and customer needs.
- Feed data back into the design and repeat the process until the product or service is proven to be fit for the task.

Control of design and development does not mean controlling the creativity of the designers – it means controlling the process through which new or modified designs are produced so that the resultant design is one that truly reflects customer needs.

Why is this necessary?

This requirement responds to the Process Approach Principle.

Without control over the design and development process several possibilities may occur:

- Design will commence without an agreed requirement.
- Costs will escalate as designers pursue solutions that go beyond what the customer really needs.
- Costs will escalate as suggestions get incorporated into the design without due consideration of the impact on development time and cost.
- Designs will be released without adequate verification and validation.
- Designs will be expressed in terms that cannot be implemented economically in production or use.

The bigger the project, the greater the risk that the design will overrun budget and timescale. Design control aims to keep the design effort on course so that the right design is released on time and within budget.

How is this implemented?

Control of the design and development requires the application of the same principles as any other process. The standard actually identifies the controls that need to be applied to each design but there are other controls that need to be applied to the design process in order to apply the requirements of ISO 9001 clause 4.1. Typical product design and service design process flow charts are illustrated in Figure 7.5 and 7.6 respectively.

The design process is a key process in enabling the organization to achieve its objectives. These objectives should include goals that apply to the design process (see Chapter 5–5.4.1). Consequently there need to be:

- objectives for the design process
- measures for indicating achievement of these objectives
- a defined sequence of sub-processes or tasks that transform the design inputs into design outputs

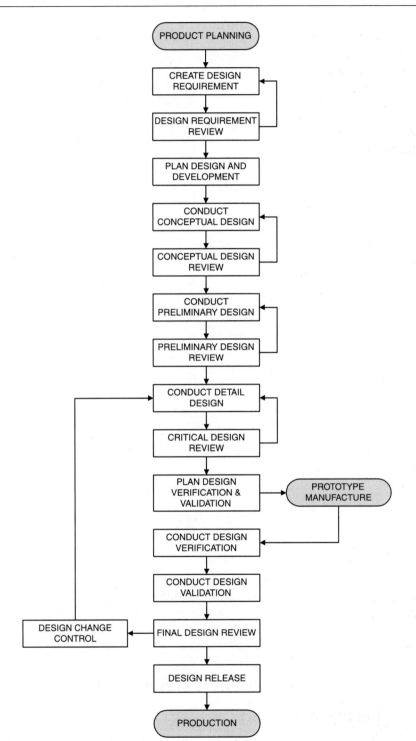

Figure 7.5 Product design process flow

Figure 7.6 Service design process flow

- links with the resource management process so that human and physical resources are made available to the design process when required
- review stages for establishing that the process is achieving its objectives
- processes for improving the effectiveness of the design process

Design and development planning (7.3.1)

Preparing the plans (7.3.1)

The standard requires the organization to *plan design and development of the product*.

What does this mean?

Planning the design and development of a product means determining the design objectives and the design strategy, the design stages, timescales, costs, resources and responsibilities needed to accomplish them. Sometimes the activity of design itself is considered to be a planning activity but what is being planned is not the design but the product.

> **1994–2000 Differences**
>
> Previously the standard required the supplier to prepare plans for each design and development activity.
>
> The requirement is unchanged.

Why is this necessary?

This requirement responds to the Leadership Principle.

The purpose of planning is to determine the provisions needed to achieve an objective. In most cases, these objectives include not only a requirement for a new or modified product but also requirements governing the costs and product introduction timescales (Quality, Cost and Delivery or QCD). Remove these constraints and planning becomes less important but there are few situations when cost and time is not a constraint. It is therefore necessary to work out in advance whether the objective can be achieved within the budget and timescale. One problem with design is that it is often a journey into the unknown and the cost and time it will take cannot always be predicted. It may in fact result in disaster and either a complete reassessment of the design objective or the technology of the design solution. This has been proven time and again with major international projects such as Concorde, the Channel Tunnel and the International Space Station. Without a best guess these projects would not get off (or under!) the ground and so planning is vital firstly to get the funding and secondly to define the known and unknown so that risks can be assessed and quantified.

How is this implemented?

You should prepare a design and development plan for each new design and also for any modification of an existing design that radically changes the performance of the product or service. For modifications that marginally change performance, control of the changes required may be accomplished through the design change process.

Design and development plans need to identify the activities to be performed, by whom they will be perform and when they should commence and be complete. One good technique is to use a network chart (often called a PERT chart), which links all the activities together. Alternatively a bar chart may be adequate. There does need to be some narrative in addition as charts in isolation rarely conveys everything required.

Design and development is not complete until the design has been proven as meeting the design requirements, so in drawing up a design and development plan you will need to cover the planning of design verification and validation activities. The plans should identify as a minimum:

- The design requirements
- The design and development programme showing activities against time
- The work packages and names of those who will execute them (Work packages are the parcels of work that are to be handed out either internally or to suppliers)
- The work breakdown structure showing the relationship between all the parcels of work
- The reviews to be held for authorizing work to proceed from stage to stage
- The resources in terms of finance, manpower and facilities
- The risks to success and the plans to minimize them
- The controls that will be exercised to keep the design on course

Planning for all phases at once can be difficult as information for subsequent phases will not be available until earlier phases have been completed. So, your design and development plans may consist of separate documents, one for each phase and each containing some detail of the plans you have made for subsequent phases.

Your design and development plans may also need to be subdivided into plans for special aspects of the design such as reliability plans, safety plans, electromagnetic compatibility plans, configuration management plans. With simple designs there may be only one person carrying out the design activities. As the design and development plan needs to identify all design and development activities, even in this situation you will need to identify who carries out the design, who will review the design and who will verify the design. The same person may perform both the design and the design verification activities, however, it is good practice to allocate design verification to another person or organization because it will reveal problems overlooked by the designer. On larger design projects you may need to employ staff of various disciplines such as mechanical engineers, electronic engineers, reliability engineers etc. The responsibilities of all these people or groups need to be identified and a useful way of parcelling up the work is to use work packages that list all the activities to be performed by a particular group. If you subcontract any of the design activities, the supplier's plans need to be integrated with your plans and your plan should identify which activities are the supplier's responsibility. While purchasing is dealt with in clause 7.4 of the standard, the requirements also apply to design activities.

Stages of design and development process (7.3.1a)

The standard requires *the stages of design and develop-ment to be determined.*

What does this mean?

A stage in design and development is a point at which the design reaches a phase of maturity. There are several common stages in a design process. The names may vary but the intent remains the same.

> **1994–2000 Differences**
> Previously the standard required the plans to describe or reference each design and development activity. The difference is a recognition that control over design is more easily accomplished by controlling the stages through which the design passes rather than controlling each design activity.

- Feasibility stage – the stage during which studies are made of a proposed objective to determine whether practical solutions can be developed within time and cost constraints. This stage usually terminates with a design brief.
- Conceptual design stage – the stage during which ideas are conceived and theories tested. This stage usually terminates with a preferred solution in the form of a design requirement.
- Design definition stage – the stage during which the architecture or layout takes form and the risks assessed and any uncertainty resolved. This stage usually terminates with definitive design specifications for the components comprising the product, service or process.
- Detail design stage – the stage during which final detail characteristics are determined and method of production/delivery established. This stage usually terminates with a set of specifications for the construction of prototypes.
- Development stage – the stage during which the prototype is proven using models or simulations and refined. This stage usually terminates with a set of approved specifications for the construction, installation and operation of the product, service or process.

Why is this necessary?

This requirement responds to the Process Approach Principle.

Any endeavour is more easily accomplished when undertaken in small stages. By processing a design through several iterative stages, a more robust solution will emerge than if the design is attempted in one cycle.

How is this implemented?

In drawing up your design and development plans you need to identify the principal activities and a good place to start is with the list of ten steps detailed previously of which the last five are explained further above. Any more detail will in all probability be a breakdown of each of these stages initially for the complete design and subsequently for each element of it. If dealing with a system you should break it down into subsystems, and the subsystems into equipments and equipments into assemblies and so on. It is most important that you agree the system hierarchy and associated terminology early on in the development programme otherwise you may well cause both technical and organizational problems at the interfaces.

Planning review, verification and validation activities (7.3.1b)

1994–2000 Differences

Previously the standard required

(a) design verification measures to be recorded.

(b) formal documented reviews of the design results to be planned at appropriate stages of design.

Although the previous requirement was poorly worded, this new requirement has not changed the intent and had merely consolidated three separate requirements.

The standard requires *the review, verification and validation activities appropriate to each design and development stage to be determined.*

What does this mean?

Each design stage is a process that takes inputs from the previous process and delivers outputs to the next stage. Within each process are verification, validation and review points that feedback information into the process to produce a further iteration of the design. At the end of each stage the output needs to be verified, validated and reviewed before being passed on the next stage. The further along the design cycle, the more rigorous and complex the verification, validation and review stages will need to be. The verification stages are those stages where design output of a stage is checked against the design input for that stage to ensure the output is correct. The validation stages occur sequentially or in parallel to confirm that the output is the right output by comparing it with the design brief or requirement. The review stages are points at which the results of verification and validation are reviewed to confirm the design solution, recommend change and authorize or halt further development.

Why is this necessary?

This requirement responds to the Factual Approach Principle.

The checks necessary to select and confirm the design solution need to be built into the design process so that they take place when they will have the most beneficial effect on the design. Waiting until the design is complete before verification, validation or review will in all probability result in extensive rework and abortive effort.

How is this implemented?

The stages of verification, validation and review should be identified in the design and development plan, but at each stage there may need to be supplementary plans to contain more detail of the specific activities to be performed. This may result in a need for a separate design verification plan.

The design verification plan should be constructed so that every design requirement is verified and the simplest way of confirming this is to produce a verification matrix of requirement against verification methods. You need to cover all the requirements, those that can be verified by test, by inspection, by analysis, by simulation or demonstration or simply by validation of product records. For those requirements to be verified by test, a test specification will need to be produced. The test specification should specify which characteristics are to be measured in terms of parameters, limits and the conditions under which they are to be measured.

The verification plan needs to cover some or all of the following details as appropriate:

- A definition of the product design standard that is being verified
- The objectives of the plan (You may need several plans covering different aspects of the requirement.)
- Definition of the specifications and procedures to be employed for determining that each requirement has been achieved
- Definition of the stages in the development phase at which verification can most economically be carried out
- The identity of the various models that will be used to demonstrate achievement of design requirements. (Some models may be simple space models, others laboratory standard or production standard depending on the need.)
- Definition of the verification activities that are to be performed to qualify or validate the design and those which need to be performed on every product in production as a means of ensuring that the qualified design standard has been maintained
- Definition of the test equipment, support equipment and facilities needed to carry out the verification activities
- Definition of the timescales for the verification activities in the sequence in which the activities are to be carried out
- Identification of the venue for the verification activities
- Identification of the organization responsible for conducting each of the verification activities
- Reference to the controls to be exercised over the verification activities in terms of the procedures, specifications and records to be produced, the reviews to be conducted during the programme and the criteria for

commencing, suspending and completing the verification operations. (Provision should also be included for dealing with failures, their remedy, investigation and action on design modifications.)

As part of the verification plan, you should include an activity plan that lists all the planned activities in the sequence they are to be conducted and use this plan to progressively record completion and conformance. The activity plan should make provision for planned and actual dates for each activity and for recording comments such as recovery plans when the program does not proceed exactly as planned. It is also good practice to conduct test reviews before and after each series of tests so that corrective measures can be taken before continuing with abortive tests (see also under design validation).

The designers and those performing the verification activities should approve the verification plan. Following approval the document should be brought under document control. Design verification is often a very costly activity and so any changes in the plan should be examined for their effect on cost and timescale. Changes in the specification can put back the programme by months whilst new facilities are acquired, new jigs, cables, etc. procured. However small your design, the planning of its verification is vital to the future of the product. Lack of attention to detail can rebound months (or even years) later during production.

Determining responsibilities and authority for design and development activities (7.3.1c)

The standard requires *the responsibilities and authorities for design and development activities to be determined.*

1994–2000 Differences

Previously the standard required the design and development plans to define responsibility for the implementation of design and development activities.

The new wording rectifies an inconsistency by adding the word 'authorities' while leaving the intent unchanged.

What does this mean?

To cause the activities in the design and development plan to happen, they have to be assigned to either a person or an organization. Once assigned and agreed by both parties, the assignee becomes responsible for delivering the required result. The authority delegated in each assignment conveys a right to the assignee to make decisions affecting the output. The assignee becomes the design authority for the items designed but this authority does not extend to changing the design requirement – this authority is vested in the organization that delegated or sponsored the design for the item.

Why is this necessary?

This requirement responds to the Leadership Principle.

Responsibility for design activities needs to be defined so that there is no doubt as to who has the right to take which actions and decisions. Authority for design activities needs to be delegated so that those responsible have the right to control their own output. Also the authority responsible for the requirements at each level of the design needs defining so that there is a body to which requests for change can be routed. Without such a hierarchy, there would be anarchy resulting in a design that failed to fulfil its requirements.

How is this implemented?

Within the design and development plan the activities need to be assigned to a person, group or organization equipped with the resources to execute them. Initially the feasibility study may be performed by one person or one group but as the design takes shape, other personnel are required and possibly other external organizations may be required to undertake particular tasks or products.

One way of assigning responsibilities is to use the work package technique. With this approach you can specify not only what is to be done but estimate the required hours, days months or years to do it and then obtain the group's acceptance and consequently commitment to the task.

One of the difficulties with assigning design work is ensuring that those to whom the work is assigned understand the boundary conditions i.e. what is included and what is excluded (see below under *organizational interfaces*).

You also need to be careful that work is not delegated or subcontracted to parties about whom you have little knowledge. In subcontracts, clauses that prohibit subcontracting without your approval need to be inserted, thereby enabling you to retain control.

Managing organizational interfaces (7.3.1)

The standard requires *the interfaces between different groups involved in design and development process to be managed to ensure effective communication and clarity of responsibilities.*

What does this mean?

Where there are many different groups of people working on a design they need to work together to produce an output that meets the overall requirement when all outputs are brought together. To achieve this each party needs to know how the design work has been allocated and to which

> **1994–2000 Differences**
> Previously the standard required that organizational interfaces between different groups which input to the design process be identified and the necessary information documented, transmitted and regularly reviewed.
>
> The intent of the requirement has not changed.

requirements each party is working so that if there are problems, the right people can be brought together.

Why is this necessary?

This requirement responds to the Leadership Principle.

If the interfaces between design groups are not properly managed, there are likely to be technical problems arising from groups changing interface requirement without communicating the changes to those affected, political problems arising from groups assuming the right to do work or make decisions that have been allocated to other groups and cost overruns arising from groups not communicating their difficulties when they are encountered.

How is this implemented?

You should identify where work passes from one organization to another and the means used to convey the requirements such as work instructions, work package descriptions or contracts. Often in design work, the product requirements are analysed to identify further requirements for constituent parts. These may be passed on to other groups as input requirements for them to produce a design solution. In doing so these groups may in fact generate further requirements in the form of development specifications to be passed to other groups and so on. For example, the systems engineer generates the system specification and subsystem specifications and passes the latter to the subsystems engineers. These engineers design the subsystem and generate equipment specifications to pass on to the equipment engineers. To meet the equipment specification new parts may be necessary and so these engineers generate part specifications and pass these to the parts engineers. Some of these transactions may be in-house but some might be subcontracted. Some organizations only possess systems engineering capabilities and subcontract most of the hardware, software or specialist service components to specialists such as the IT architecture and network design. In this way they concentrate on the business they are good at and get the best specialist support through competitive tenders. These situations create organizational interfaces that require effective information control processes.

In managing the organizational interfaces you will need to:

- Define the customer and the supplier in the relationship
- Define the product requirements that the supplier is to meet (the objectives and outputs)
- Define the work that the supplier is to carry out with the budget and time constraints
- Define the responsibility and authority of this work (who does what, who approved what)
- Define the process used for conveying information and receiving feedback

- Define the reporting and review requirements for monitoring the work
- Conduct regular interface review meetings to check progress and resolve concerns
- Periodically review the interface control process for its effectiveness

One mechanism of transmitting technical interface information is to establish and promulgate a set of baseline requirements that are to be used at commencement of design for a particular phase. Any change to these requirements should be processed by a *change control board or* similar body and following approval a change to the baseline is made. This baseline listing becomes a source of reference and if managed properly ensures that no designer is without the current design and interface information.

Interfaces should be reviewed along with other aspects of the design at regular design reviews scheduled prior to the completion of each phase or more often if warranted. Where several large organizations are working together to produce a design, an interface control board or similar body may need to be created to review and approve changes to technical interfaces. Interface control is especially difficult with complex projects. Once underway an organization like a large ship gains momentum and takes some time to stop. The project manager may not know of everything that is happening. Control is largely by information and it can often have a tendency to be historical information by the time it reaches its destination. So it is important to control changes to the interfaces. If one small change goes unreported, it may cause months of delay correcting the error – such as two tracks of a railway or a two ends of a tunnel being misaligned.

Ensuring that plans are updated as the design progresses (7.3.1)

The standard requires planning output to *be updated, as appropriate, as the design and development progresses.*

What does this mean?

Planning commences before work is performed but as work progresses and the unknown becomes the known, its direction may need to change and therefore the plans need to change.

> **1994–2000 Differences**
>
> Previously the standard requires that the design and development plans be updated as the design evolves.
>
> The intent of the requirement is unchanged.

Why is this necessary?

This requirement responds to the Factual Approach Principle.

The design and development plan is a source of reference for those on the project – it communicates the work to be performed, who is to perform it and when. It should form the basis upon which the design and development costs have been estimated and the work is proceeding. Therefore, if the basis for the plan changes, the plan needs to change so that it reflects the design that is being produced and provides legitimacy for the actions and decisions being carried out. If the plan is not updated, those in possession of it may waste valuable effort in performing work that is no longer required or may not be able to provide the resources when needed and therefore additional costs may be incurred.

How is this implemented?

Some design planning needs to be carried out before any design commences, but it is an iterative process and therefore the design plans may be completed progressively as more design detail emerges. It is not unusual for plans to be produced and as design gets underway, problems are encountered which require a change in direction. When this occurs the original plans should be changed. The design and development plan should be placed under control after it has been approved. When a change in the plan is necessary you should use the document change request mechanism to change the design and development plan and not implement the change until the request has been approved. In this way you remain in control.

Design and development input (7.3.2)

Determining and recording design inputs (7.3.2)

1994–2000 Differences
Previously the standard required design input requirements relating to the product to be identified and documented.
There is no change in requirement.

The standard requires inputs relating to product requirements to *be determined and records maintained* (*see 4.2.4*).

What does this mean?

The design inputs are the requirements governing the design of the intended product. They include all the requirements determined from an analysis of customer and regulatory requirements and the organization's requirements. It may appear that this requirement duplicates those addressed in clause 7.2 of the standard, but as the design is decomposed into subsystems, equipments, components, materials and processes, design inputs are the inputs into the design of each of these levels and will therefore become more specific through the hierarchy. The records to be maintained are the resultant specifications that describe these requirements.

Why is this necessary?

This requirement responds to the Factual Approach Principle.

The design input requirements constitute the basis for the design without which there is no criteria to judge the acceptability of the design output.

How is this implemented?

Design inputs should reflect the customer, regulator and organization's needs and be produced or available before any design commences.

To identify design input requirements you need to identify:

- The purpose of the product or service
- The conditions under which it will be used, stored and transported
- The skills and category of those who will use and maintain the product or service
- The countries to which it will be sold and the related regulations governing sale and use of products
- The special features and performance characteristics which the customer requires the product or service to exhibit (including life, reliability, durability and maintainability; see Chapter 2 for list of other typical features and characteristics)
- The constraints in terms of timescale, operating environment, cost, size, weight or other factors
- The standards with which the product or service needs to comply
- The products or service with which it will directly and indirectly interface and their features and characteristics
- The documentation required of the design output necessary to manufacture, procure, inspect, test, install, operate and maintain a product or service.

Organizations have a responsibility to establish their customer requirements and expectations. If you do not determine conditions that may be detrimental to the product and you supply the product as meeting the customer needs and it subsequently fails, the failure is your liability. If the customer did not provide reasonable opportunity for you to establish the requirements, the failure may be the customer's liability. If you think you may need some extra information in order to design a product that meets the customer needs, you must obtain it or declare your assumptions. A nil response is often taken as acceptance in full.

In addition to customer requirements there may be industry practices, national standards, company standards and other sources of input to the design input requirements to be taken into account. You should provide design guides or codes of practice that will assist designers identify the design input requirements that are typical of your business.

The design output has to reflect a product that is producible or a service that is deliverable. The design input requirements may have been specified by the customer and consequently not have taken into account your production capability. The product of the design may therefore need to be producible within your current production capability using your existing technologies, tooling, production processes, material handling equipment etc.

Having identified the design input requirements, you need to document them in a specification that when approved is brought under document control. The requirements should not contain any solutions at this stage so as to provide freedom and flexibility to the designers. If the design is to be subcontracted, it makes for fair competition and removes from you the responsibility for the solution. Where specifications contain solutions, the supplier is being given no choice and if there are delays and problems the supplier may have a legitimate claim against you.

Defining functional and performance requirements (7.3.2a)

The standard requires design inputs to *include functional and performance requirements.*

1994–2000 Differences
Previously functional and performance requirements were implicit in the term 'design input requirements'.
Although not previously specified, such requirements are so fundamental that it is unlikely that it will require any change in the management system.

What does this mean?

Functional requirements are those related to actions that the product is required to perform with or without external stimulus. Performance requirements relate to the results or behaviours required by such actions under stated conditions. Normally a product's characteristics are stated in physical, functional and performance terms rather than functional and performance but no matter, the intent of the requirement is that all characteristics that the product is required to exhibit should be included in the design input requirements and expressed in terms that are measurable.

Why is this necessary?

This requirement responds to the Process Approach Principle.

All the characteristics need to be stated otherwise the resultant design may not reflect a product that fulfils the conditions for intended use. Two products may possess the same physical and functional characteristics but perform differently due to the individual arrangement of their component parts and the materials and processes used in their construction.

How is this implemented?

From the statement of product purpose, the conditions of use and the skills of those who will use it, the most obvious characteristics can be derived and divided into physical, functional and performance requirements. The physical characteristics might include size, mass, appearance, material properties. Functional characteristics might include speed, power, capacity and a wide range of characteristics that give the product distinctive features. Performance characteristics might include reliability, maintainability, durability, flammability, portability, safety etc.

Defining statutory and regulatory requirements (7.3.2b)

The standard requires design inputs to *include applicable statutory and regulatory requirements.*

What does this mean?

At the end product level, the applicable statutory and regulatory requirements are those addressed by clause 7.2.1c. However, as the design unfolds additional statutory and regulatory requirements may become applicable as specific subsystems, equipments, components, materials and processes are identified.

> **1994–2000 Differences**
>
> Previously the standard required design input requirements relating to the product to include applicable statutory and regulatory requirements. The intent of the requirement remains unchanged.

Why is this necessary?

This requirement responds to the Process Approach Principle.

The statutory and regulatory requirements that apply are dependent upon a range of factors that emerge during the design process once it is known what type of device is required. These regulations need to be identified in the design input so that the resultant design is proven to meet them before commitment to production is granted.

How is this implemented?

Statutory and regulatory requirements are those that apply in the country to which the product or service is to be supplied. Whilst some customers have the foresight to specify these, others often don't. Just because such requirements are not specified in the contract doesn't mean you don't need to meet them.

Statutory requirements may apply to the prohibition of items from certain countries, power supply ratings, security provisions, markings and certain notices.

Regulatory requirements may apply to health, safety and environmental emissions, electromagnetic compatibility and these often require accompanying certification of compliance.

If you intend exporting the product or service, it would be prudent to determine the regulations which would apply before you complete the design requirement. Failure to meet some of these requirements can result in no export licence being granted as a minimum and imprisonment in certain cases if found to be subsequently noncompliant.

Defining information from previous designs (7.3.2c)

The standard requires the design inputs to *include applicable information derived from previous similar designs.*

What does this mean?

1994–2000 Differences

This is a new requirement that has no equivalent in the 1994 version.

Most designs are a development of that which was designed previously. It is rare for a design to be completely new. Even if the product concept is new, it may contain design solutions used previously. The history of these previous designs contains a wealth of information that may be applicable to the application that is currently being considered.

Why is this necessary?

This requirement responds to the Continual Improvement Principle.

Using the lessons learnt from previous designs is corrective action – preventing the recurrence of problems that have occurred in the past. If previous design history is not utilized, the problems may recur.

How is this implemented?

In principle the design history of a product should be archived and made available to future designers. Design history can be placed in a database or library that is accessible to future designers. A rather old way of doing this was for companies to create design manuals containing data sheets, fact sheets and general information sheets on design topics – a sort of design guide that captured experience. Companies should still be doing this but many will by now have converted to electronic storage medium with the added advantage of a search engine. Information will also be available from trade associations, libraries and learned societies. Often professional journals, published literature and even newspapers can contain useful information for designers. In your model of the design process you need to install a research process that is initiated prior to commencing design of a system, subsystem, equipment or component. The research process needs to commence with an inquiry such as 'Have we done this or used this before? Has anyone done this or used this before?' The questions should initiate a search for information but to make this structured approach, the database or libraries need to structure the information in a way that it will be used. One advantage of submitting the design to a review by those not involved in the design is that they bring their experience to the review and identify approaches that did not work in the past, or put forward more effective ways of doing such things in the future. A case for keeping the old designers on tap, if not on top!

Within the design input requirements, such information would appear as either as preferred solutions or non-preferred solutions, either directly or by reference to learned papers, standards, guide etc.

Identifying other essential requirements (7.3.2d)

The standard requires design inputs to *include any other requirements essential for design and development*.

What does this mean?

In addition to the requirements identified there may be requirements that are dictated because of the organizational policies, national and international politics as was addressed under clause 7.2.1d.

Why is this necessary?

This requirement responds to the Process Approach Principle.

The organization may wish to maintain a certain profile or reputation through its designs and therefore may impose requirements that may impact the design input requirements.

How is this implemented?

One specific series of requirement that may not emerge from the forgoing are technical interface requirements. Some of these may need to be written around a particular supplier. However, within each

> **1994–2000 Differences**
> Previously the standard required:
> (a) design input requirements relating to the product to be identified and documented;
> (b) technical interfaces between different groups which input into the design process to be identified;
> (c) design input to take into consideration the results of any contract review activities.
>
> The reworded requirement is less prescriptive and does not change the intent of the previous requirements.

development specification the technical interfaces between systems, subsystems, equipments etc. should be specified so that when all these components are integrated they function properly. In some situations it may be necessary to generate separate interface specifications defining requirements that are common to all components of the system. In a large complex design, minor details of a component may be extremely important in the design of another component. Instead of providing designers with specifications of all the components, it may be more economical (as well as more controllable) if the features and characteristics at the interface between components are detailed in separate interface specifications.

Reviewing design input requirements (7.3.2)

The standard requires design inputs to *be reviewed for adequacy* and for the requirements *to be complete, unambiguous and not in conflict with other requirements*.

What does this mean?

Adequacy in this context means that the design input requirements are a true reflection of the customer needs.

Why is this necessary?

1994–2000 Differences

Previously the standard required that:

(a) the selection of design input requirements be reviewed by the supplier for adequacy;

(b) incomplete, ambiguous or conflicting requirements be resolved with those responsible for drawing up these requirements.

The change removes an unnecessary constraint as those who drew up the requirements may in fact be no longer available for discussion.

This requirement responds to the Factual Approach Principle.

The determination of design inputs results in information that needs to be reviewed prior to its release otherwise incorrect information may enter the design process. It is prudent to obtain customer agreement to the design requirements before commencing the design. In this way you will establish whether you have correctly understood and translated customer needs. It is advisable also to hold an internal design review at this stage so that you may benefit from the experience of other staff in the organization.

How is this implemented?

The review of the design input requirements needs to be a systematic review, not a superficial glance. Design work will commence on the basis of what is conveyed in the requirements or the brief, although you should ensure there is a mechanism in place to change the information should it become necessary later. In fact such a mechanism should be agreed at the same time as agreement to the requirement is reached.

In order to detect incomplete requirements you either need experts on tap or check lists to refer to. It is often easy to comment on what has been included but difficult to imagine what has been excluded. It is also important to remove subjective statements.

Ambiguities arise where statements imply one thing but the context implies another. You may also find cross-references to be ambiguous or in conflict. To detect the ambiguities and conflicts you need to read statements and examine diagrams very carefully. Items shown on one diagram may be shown differently in another. There are many other aspects you need to check before being satisfied they are fit for use. Any inconsistencies you find should be conveyed to the appropriate person with a request for action. Any changes to correct the errors should be self-evident so that you do not need to review all the information again.

Design and development output (7.3.3)

Documenting the design and development output (7.3.3)

The standard requires that *the outputs of design and development be provided in a form that enables verification against the design and development inputs.*

What does this mean?

Design output is the product of the design process and will therefore comprise information and/or models and specimens that describe the design in all its detail, the calculations, assumptions and the rationale for the chosen solution. It is not simply the specifications or drawings because should the design need to be changed, the designer may need to revisit the design data to modify parameters and assumptions. By requiring the design output to be in a form that enables verification, the characteristics of the

1994–2000 Differences

Previously the standard required that the design output be documented and expressed in terms that can be verified and validated against design-input requirements.

There is no change in this requirement.

product need to be expressed in measurable terms. One would therefore expect form, fit and function to be specified in units of measure with allowable tolerances or models and specimens to be capable of use as comparative references.

It is interesting to note that the requirement omits validation. This is because design outputs are verified against design inputs whereas, the design is validated against the original product requirement using a product or simulation that accurately reflects the design, thereby by-passing the design input and output as illustrated in Figure 7.7.

Why is this necessary?

This requirement responds to the Process Approach Principle.

Unless the design output is expressed in a form that enables verification, it will not be possible to verify the design with any certainty.

How is this implemented?

The design input requirements should have been expressed in a way that would allow a number of possible solutions. The design output requirements should therefore be expressed as *all* the inherent features and characteristics of the design that reflect a product that will satisfy these requirements. It should therefore fulfil the stated or implied needs, i.e. be fit for purpose.

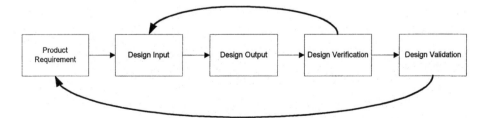

Figure 7.7 Relationship between design output and design validation

Product specifications

Product specifications should specify requirements for the manufacture, assembly and installation of the product in a manner that provides acceptance criteria for inspection and test. They may be written specifications, engineering drawings, diagrams, inspection and test specifications and schematics. With complex products you may need a hierarchy of documents from system drawings showing the system installation to component drawings for piece-part manufacture. Where there are several documents that make up the product specification there should be an overall listing that relates documents to one another.

Service specifications should provide a clear description of the manner in which the service is to be delivered, the criteria for its acceptability, the resources required including the numbers and skills of the personnel required, the numbers and types of facilities and equipment necessary and the interfaces with other services and suppliers.

In addition to the documents that serve product manufacture and installation or service delivery, documents may also be required for maintenance and operation. The product descriptions, handbooks, operating manuals, user guides and other documents which support the product or service in use are as much a part of the design as the other product requirements. Unlike the manufacturing data, the support documents may be published either generally or supplied with the product to the customer. The design of such documentation is critical to the success of the product as poorly constructed handbooks can be detrimental to sales.

The requirements within the product specification need to be expressed in terms that can be verified. You should therefore avoid subjective terms such as 'good quality components', 'high reliability', 'commercial standard parts' etc. as these requirements are not sufficiently definitive to be verified in a consistent manner.

Design calculations

Throughout the design process, calculations will need to be made to size components and determine characteristics and tolerances. These calculations should be recorded and retained together with the other design documentation but may not be issued. In performing design calculations it is important that the status of the design on which the calculations are based is recorded. When there are changes in the design these calculations may need to be repeated. The validity of the calculations should also be examined as part of the design verification activity. One method of recording calculations is in a designer's logbook that may contain all manner of things and so the calculations may not be readily retrievable when needed. Recording the calculations in separate reports or in separate files along with the computer data will improve retrieval.

Design analyses

Analyses are types of calculations but may be in the form of comparative studies, predictions and estimations. Examples are stress analysis, reliability analysis, hazard analysis. Analyses are often performed to detect whether the design has any inherent modes of failure and to predict the probability of occurrence. The analyses assist in design improvement and the prevention of failure, hazard, deterioration and other adverse conditions. Analyses may need to be conducted because the end-use conditions may not be reproducible in the factory. Assumptions may need to be made about the interfaces, the environment, the actions of users etc. and analysis of such conditions assists in determining characteristics as well as verifying the inherent characteristics.

Ensuring that design output meets design input requirements (7.3.3a)

The standard requires that design and development output *meets the design and development input requirements.*

What does this mean?

The characteristics of the resultant design should be directly or indirectly traceable to the design input requirements. In some cases a dimension may be

> **1994–2000 Differences**
>
> Previously the standard required that the design output meet the design input requirements.
>
> There is no change in requirement.

stated in the design input which is easily verified when examining the design specifications, drawings etc. In other cases the input requirement may be stated in performance terms that is translated into a number of functions which when energized provide the required result. In other cases a parameter may be specified above or below the design input requirement so as to allow for production variation.

Why is this necessary?

This requirement responds to the Factual Approach Principle and needs no explanation.

How is this implemented?

The techniques of design verification can be used to verify that the design output meets the design input requirements. However, design verification is often an iterative process. As features are determined, their compliance with the requirements should be checked by calculation, analysis or test on development models. Your development plan should identify the stages at which each requirement will be verified so as to give warning of non-compliance as early as possible.

Providing information for purchasing, production and service provision (7.3.3b)

1994–2000 Differences

This is a new requirement that has no equivalent in the 1994 version.

The standard requires that *design and development output provide appropriate information for purchasing, production and service provision.*

What does this mean?

British Standard BS 7000 defines a design as *a set of instructions (specifications, drawings, schedules etc.) necessary to construct a product.* Therefore the inherent characteristics of the product that facilitates procurement, production and servicing need to be defined. Tooling for production is considered to be part of the production process but information within the design output is needed to enable tooling to be designed.

The instructions needed to produce, inspection, test, install and maintain the product may be produced by the designers but are strictly outputs of the production, installation and servicing processes that are derived from inputs that comprise the design description.

Why is this necessary?

This requirement responds to the Systems Approach Principle.

A design description alone will not result in its realization unless information is provided for procuring the materials and components, preparing the product for production and maintaining the product in service.

How is this implemented?

Products should be designed to facilitate procurement, manufacture, installation and servicing and therefore additional characteristics to those required for end use may be necessary. Examples include, geometric tolerances, specific part numbers, part marking, assembly aids, mistake proofing, lifting points, transportation and storage protection. Techniques used to identify such design provisions are:

- Failure Mode and Effects Analysis (FMEA) (see Chapter 8)
- Producibility Analysis
- Testability Analysis
- Maintainability Analysis

Defining acceptance criteria (7.3.3c)

The standard requires design and development output to *contain or reference product acceptance criteria.*

What does this mean?

Acceptance criteria are the requirements that, if met, will deem the product acceptable. It means that characteristics should be specified in measurable terms with tolerances or limits. These limits should enable all production versions to perform to the product specification, providing such limits are well within the limits to which the design has been tested.

> **1994–2000 Differences**
> The standard required that the design output contains or makes reference to acceptance criteria.
>
> There is no change in requirement.

It means that every requirement should be stated in such a way that it can be verified – that there is no doubt as to what will be acceptable and what will be unacceptable.

Why is this necessary?

This requirement responds to the Factual Approach Principle.

Where product characteristics are specified in terms that are not measurable or are subjective, they lend themselves to misinterpretation and variation such that no two products produced from the design will be the same and will exhibit consistent performance.

How is this implemented?

A common method used to ensure characteristics are stated in terms of acceptance criteria is to define them by reference to product standards. These standards maybe developed by the organization or be of national or international status. Standards are employed to enable interchangeability, repeatability and to reduce variety.

Where there are common standards for certain features, these may be contained in a standards manual. Where this method is used it is still necessary to reference the standards in the particular specifications to ensure that the producers are always given full criteria. Some organizations omit common standards from their specifications. This makes it difficult to specify different standards or to subcontract the manufacture of the product or operation of a service without handing over proprietary information.

Specifying essential characteristic (7.3.3d)

The standard requires design and development output to *define the characteristics of the product that are essential to its safe and proper use.*

> **1994–2000 Differences**
> Previously the standard required that the supplier identify those characteristics of the design that are crucial to the safe and proper functioning of the product.
>
> The intent of the requirement remains unchanged.

What does this mean?

Certain characteristics will be critical to the safe operation of the product. These can be divided into two types. Those characteristics that the product needs to exhibit in order to function correctly and those characteristics that are exhibited when the product is put together, used or maintained incorrectly.

Why is this necessary?

This requirement responds to the Customer Focus Principle.

Alerting assemblers, users and maintainers to safety-critical characteristics increases their sensitivity, provides the awareness to plan preventive measures and thus reduces the probability of an incident or accident.

How is this implemented?

The design output data should identify by use of symbols or codes those characteristics that are safety-critical under normal operating conditions. This will enable the manufacturers to determine the measures needed to ensure no variation from specification when the characteristics are initially produced and ensure no alteration of these characteristics during subsequent processing.

Drawings should indicate the warning notices required, where such notices should be placed and how they should be affixed. Examples that indicate improper function or potential danger are red lines on tachometers to indicate safe limits for engines, audible warnings on computers to indicate an incorrect command or on smoke alarms to indicate the presence of smoke. In some cases it may be necessary to mark dimensions or other characteristics on drawings to indicate that they are critical and employ special procedures for dealing with any variations. In passenger vehicle component design, certain parts are regarded as safety-critical because they carry load or need to behave in a certain manner under stress. Others are not critical because they carry virtually no load so there can be a greater tolerance on deviations from specification.

Failure Modes and Effects Analysis and Hazard Analysis, are techniques that aid the identification of characteristics crucial to the safe and proper functioning of the product.

Approval of design outputs (7.3.3)

> **1994–2000 Differences**
>
> Previously the standard required that the design output documents be reviewed before release.
>
> The new requirement focuses on outputs instead of documents.

The standard requires design and development outputs to be *approved prior to release.*

What does this mean?

Although the requirement for design outputs to be approved prior to release may appear to duplicate the requirement of clause 4.2.3 of the standard on document control, there is a subtle difference. Document approval is not the same as design approval and design release is not the same as document issue. When a design is approved it is the description of that design in whatever form that is approved. Design approval therefore applies to all the documents, models, and specimens etc. that constitute the design description, not as separate entities but as a whole.

Why is this necessary?

This requirement responds to the Factual Approach Principle.

While design documents should pass into the document control process for issue, several iterations may be needed before the design output is complete and ready for release. It is important that these iterations are under control otherwise the full impact of changes in one component may not be reflected in other components. When the design is ready for verification it is released.

How is this implemented?

The requirements in both the 1994 and 2000 versions of ISO 9001 do not recognize that design reviews are not only concerned with reviewing a design but are also concerned with granting design approval. This oversight resulted in design approval being planted under design outputs. Design approval proceeds through three stages:

- Design information should be approved before being presented to a design review – in this way the reviewers only work with information that has been checked and found acceptable.
- Designs should be approved before the design is subject to verification – in this way prototypes are produced, or simulated using a complete set of design information that has been found acceptable.
- Designs should be verified before being subject to validation – in this way trials are only conducted on models representative of those that will enter production.

The design output may consist of many documents each of which fulfils a certain purpose. It is important that these documents are reviewed and verified as being fit for their purpose before release using the documentation controls developed for meeting section 4.5 of ISO 9001. In the software industry, where documentation provides the only way of inspecting the product prior to installation, document inspections called Fagan Inspections, (after Michael Fagan of IBM) are carried out not only to identify the errors, but to collect data on the type of error and the frequency of occurrence. By analysing this data using statistical techniques the results assist in error removal and prevention.

Design documentation reviews can be made effective by providing data requirements for each type of document as part of the design and development planning process. The data requirement can be used both as an input to the design process and as acceptance criteria for the design output documentation review. The data requirements would specify the input documents and the scope, content and format required for the output document. Contracts with procurement agencies often specify deliverable documents and by invoking formal data requirements in the contract, the customer is then assured of the outputs.

As design documents are often produced at various stages in the design process, they should be reviewed against the input requirements to verify that no requirements have been overlooked and that the requirements have been satisfied.

Design reviews (7.3.4)

Planning design reviews (7.3.4)

1994–2000 Differences

Previously the standard required that at appropriate stages of design, formal documented reviews of the design results be conducted.

The reworded requirement focuses on reviews being *systematic* rather than *formal*.

The standard requires that *at suitable stages, systematic reviews of design and development be performed in accordance with planned arrangements.*

What does this mean?

ISO 9000 defines a review as an activity undertaken to determine the suitability, adequacy and effectiveness of the subject matter to achieve established objectives. This is the way the term should be interpreted in the context of ISO 9000. When the term review is used in another context, it simply means to have another look at something. The ISO 9000 definition implies that a design review is an activity undertaken to determine the suitability, adequacy and effectiveness of a design to meet the design requirement. Suitability means 'Has an appropriate design solution been developed?' Adequacy means 'Does the design solution meet all the design requirements?' and effectiveness means 'Have we got the right design objective?' Design reviews are therefore *not* document reviews.

Systematic reviews are those that cover the complete design from the high level down to the smallest component and all the associated requirements in a logical manner. The review has to be stage by stage, methodical with purpose. Systematic reviews probe the design solution and the interfaces between all components for design weaknesses and delves into the detail to explore how requirement are fulfilled.

Suitable stages are at the transition between the various phases of design maturity in the design process. In simple terms designs begin with a conceptual phase, proceed through a definition phase and end with a detail design phase. Development commences with a detail design and proceeds through several iterations involving verification and validation and may continue through several enhancements before the design becomes obsolete and a new design idea is conceived.

The planned arrangements are the stages in the design and development cycle that reviews have been planned and the expected inputs and outputs and the acceptance criteria for proceeding to the next stage.

Why is this necessary?

This requirement responds to the Leadership Principle.

A design represents a considerable investment by the organization. There is therefore a need for a formal mechanism for management and the customer (if the customer is sponsoring the design) to evaluate designs at major milestones. The purpose of the review is to determine whether the proposed design solution is compliant with the design requirement and should continue or should be changed before proceeding to the next phase. It should also determine whether the documentation for the next phase is adequate before further resources are committed. Design review is that part of the design control process which measures design performance, compares it with pre-defined requirements and provides feedback so that deficiencies may be corrected before the design is released to the next phase.

How is this implemented?

Review schedules

A schedule of design reviews should be established for each product/service being developed. In some cases there will need to be only one design review. After completion of all design verification activities but depending on the complexity of the design and the risks, you may need to review the design at some or all of the following intervals:

- Design Requirement Review – to establish that the design requirements can be met and reflect the needs of the customer before commencement of design
- Conceptual Design Review – to establish that the design concept fulfils the requirements before project definition commences
- Preliminary Design Review – to establish that all risks have been resolved and development specifications have been produced for each sub-element of the product/service before detail design commences
- Critical Design Review – to establish that the detail design for each sub-element of the product/service complies with its development specification and that product specifications have been produced before manufacture of the prototypes
- Qualification Readiness Review – to establish the configuration of the baseline design and readiness for qualification before commencement of design proving
- Final Design Review – to establish that the design fulfils the requirements of its development specification before preparation for its production.

Design review input data

The input data for the review should be distributed and examined by the review team well in advance of the time when a decision on the design has to be made. A design review is not a meeting. However, a meeting will often be necessary to reach a conclusion and to answer questions of the participants. Often analysis may need to be performed on the input data by the participants in order for them to determine whether the design solution is the most practical and cost effective way of meeting the requirements.

Conducting design reviews (7.3.4a and b)

1994–2000 Differences

This is a new requirement that has no equivalent in the 1994 version.

The standard requires design reviews to *be conducted to evaluate the ability of the results of the design and development to fulfil requirements, identify problems and propose required actions.*

What does this mean?

Design reviews occur at the end of a design phase when there are results to review. This means that every phase needs an objective, the achievement of which is evaluated at the review. The results of the design may be concepts, models, calculations, drawings, specifications or any output which describes the maturity of the design at a particular stage. During the initial phases, the key performance characteristics will be evaluated and at subsequent design reviews further definition enables the design to be evaluated against more definitive requirements until all requirements are fulfilled. Each review may reveal design weaknesses that need to be resolved before proceeding to the next phase.

Why is this necessary?

This requirement responds to the Factual Approach Principle.

It would be folly to proceed with a design that possesses significant weaknesses and therefore the design review provides an opportunity to identify these weaknesses early on and take action to eliminate them before compounding the errors.

How is this implemented?

Although design documents may have been through a vetting process, the purpose of the design review is not to review documents but to subject the design to an independent board of experts for its judgment as to whether the most satisfactory design solution has been chosen. By using a design review methodology, flaws in the design may be revealed before it becomes too costly to correct them. Design reviews also serve to discipline designers by requiring them to document the design logic and the process by which they reached their conclusions, particularly the options chosen and the reasons for rejecting other options.

The experiences of previous designs provide a wealth of information of use to designers that can alert them to potential problems. In compiling this information designers can feed off the experience of others not only in the same organization but also in different organizations and industries. By using technical data available from professional institutions, associations, research papers etc., checklists can be complied that aid the evaluation of designs.

Participants at design reviews (7.3.4)

The standard requires participants in design reviews to *include representatives of functions concerned with the design and development stage(s) being reviewed.*

> **1994–2000 Differences**
>
> Previously the standard required that participants at each design review include representatives of all functions concerned with the design stage being reviewed as well as other specialist personnel as required.
>
> There is no change to this requirement.

What does this mean?

Representatives of functions concerned with a design include not only the designers but those sponsoring the design such as the customers, marketing personnel or upper management, those that will be responsible for transforming the design into a product or service, those responsible for maintaining the product, using the product or disposing of the product in fact any party that has an interest in the quality of the design solution.

Why is this necessary?

This requirement responds to the Involvement of People Principle.

Design reviews should be performed by management or the sponsor rather than the designers, in order to release a design to the next phase of development. A review is another look at something. The designer has had one look at the design and when satisfied presents the design to an impartial body of experts so as to seek approval and permission to go-ahead with the next phase. Designers are often not the budget holders, or the sponsors. They often work for others. Even in situations where there is no specific customer or sponsor or third party, it is good practice to have someone else look at the design. A designer may become too close to the design to spot errors or omissions and so will be biased towards the standard of his or her own performance. The designer may welcome the opinion of someone else because it may confirm that the right solution has been found or that the requirements can't be achieved with the present state of the art. If a design is inadequate and the inadequacies are not detected before production commences the consequences may well be disastrous. A poor design can lose a customer, a market or even a business so the advice of independent experts should be valued.

How is this implemented?

The review team should have a collective competency greater than that of the designer of the design being reviewed. For a design review to be effective it has to be conducted by someone other than the designer. The requirement for participants to include representatives of all functions concerned with the design stage means those who have an interest in the results.

The review team should comprise as appropriate, representatives of the purchasing, manufacturing, servicing, marketing, inspection, test, reliability, QA authorities etc. as a means of gathering sufficient practical experience to provide advance warning of potential problems with implementing the design. The number of people attending the design review is unimportant and could be as few as the designer and his or her supervisor provided that the supervisor is able to impart sufficient practical experience and there are no other personnel involved at that particular design stage. There is no advantage gained in staff attending design reviews who can add no value in terms of their relevant experience, regardless of what positions they hold in the company. The representation at each review stage may well be different – may be being just the designer and his or her supervisor at the conceptual review and may be representation from manufacturing, servicing etc. at the final review.

The Chairman of the review team should be the authority responsible for placing the development requirement and should make the decision as to whether design should proceed to the next phase based on the evidence substantiated by the review team.

Design review records (7.3.4)

1994–2000 Differences
Previously the standard required records of design reviews to be maintained.
The intent of the requirement remains unchanged.

The standard requires *the results of the reviews and actions arising from the review to be recorded.*

What does this mean?

The results of the design review are not simply minutes of a meeting but all the evidence that has been accumulated in evaluating a particular design, identifying problems and determining actions required to resolve them.

Why is this necessary?

This requirement responds to the Factual Approach Principle.

The results of the design review should be documented in a report rather than minutes of a meeting because they represent objective evidence that may be required later to determine product compliance with requirements, investigate design problems and compare similar designs. Even when no problems are found, the records of the review provide a baseline that can be referred to when making subsequent changes.

How is this implemented?

The report should have the agreement of the full review team and should include:

- The criteria against which the design has been reviewed
- A list of the documentation that describes the design being reviewed and any evidence presented which purports to demonstrate that the design meets the requirements
- The decision on whether the design is to proceed to the next stage
- The basis on which confidence has been placed in the design
- A record of any uncompleted corrective actions from previous reviews
- The recommendations and reasons for corrective action – if any
- The members of the review team and their roles

Design verification (7.3.5)

Performing design verification (7.3.5)

The standard requires design and development verification to *be performed in accordance with planned arrangements to ensure the output meets the design and development inputs.*

What does this mean?

ISO 9000 defines verification as confirmation, through the provision of objective evidence that specified requirements have been fulfilled. There are two types of verification, those verification activities performed during design and on the component parts to verify conformance to specification and

> **1994–2000 Differences**
>
> Previously the standard required that at appropriate stages of design, design verification be performed to ensure that the design stage output meets the design stage input requirements.
> The intent of this requirement remains unchanged.

those verification activities performed on the completed design to verify performance against the design input. When designing a system there should be design requirements for each subsystem, each item of equipment and each unit and so on down to component and raw material level. Each of these design requirements represents acceptance criteria for verifying the design output of each stage. Verification may take the form of a document review, laboratory tests, alternative calculations, similarity analyses or tests and demonstrations on representative samples, prototypes etc. In all these cases the purpose is to prove that the design is right i.e. it meets the requirements. Validation on the other hand serves to confirm that it is the right design i.e. that the requirements were the right requirements for a specific application.

The reference to planned arrangements again means that verification plans should be adhered to.

Why is this necessary?

This requirement responds to the Factual Approach Principle.

Verification is fundamental to any process and unless the design is verified, there will be no assurance that the resultant design meets the requirements.

How is this implemented?

Timing

The standard does not state when design verification is to be performed although verification of the design after launch of product into production would not be appropriate. The stages of verification will therefore mirror the design review schedule but may include additional stages. Design verification needs to be performed when there is a verifiable output.

Verification process

During the design process many assumptions may have been made and will require proving before commitment of resources to the replication of the design. Some of the requirements such as reliability and maintainability will be time-dependent. Others may not be verifiable without stressing the product beyond its design limits. With computer systems, the wide range of possible variables is so great that proving total compliance would take years. It is however necessary to subject a design to a series of tests and examinations in order to verify that all the requirements have been achieved and that features and characteristics will remain stable under actual operating conditions. With some parameters a level of confidence rather than certainty will be acceptable. Such tests are called *qualification tests*. These differ from other tests because they are designed to establish the design margins and prove the capability of the design.

The design verification process should provide for:

- Test specifications to be produced that define the features and characteristics that are to be verified for design qualification and acceptance
- Test plans to be produced that define the sequence of tests, the responsibilities for their conduct, the location of the tests and test procedures to be used
- Test procedures to be produced that describe how the tests specified in the test specification are to be conducted together with the tools and test equipment to be used and the data to be recorded

- All measuring equipment to be within calibration during the tests
- The test sample to have successfully passed all planned in-process and assembly inspections and tests prior to commencing qualification tests
- The configuration of the product in terms of its design standard, deviations, nonconformities and design changes to be recorded prior to and subsequent to the tests
- Test reviews to be held before tests commence to ensure that the product, the facilities, tools, documentation and personnel are in a state of operational readiness for verification
- Test activities to be conducted in accordance with the prescribed specifications, plans and procedures
- The results of all tests and the conditions under which they were obtained to be recorded
- Deviations to be recorded, remedial action taken and the product subject to re-verification prior to continuing with the tests
- Test reviews to be performed following qualification tests to confirm that sufficient objective evidence has been obtained to demonstrate that the product fulfils the requirements of the test specification

Development models

Many different types of models may be needed to aid product development, test theories, experiment with solutions etc. However, when the design is complete, prototype models representative in all their physical and functional characteristics to the production models may need to be produced.

If design is proven on uncontrolled models then it is likely that there will be little traceability to the production models. Production models may therefore contain features and characteristics which have not been proven. The only verification that needs to be performed on production models is for those features and characteristics that are subject to change due to the variability in manufacturing, either of raw materials or of assembly processes.

When building prototypes, the same materials, locations, suppliers, tooling and processes should be used as will be used in actual production so as to minimize the variation.

Development tests will not yield valid results if obtained using uncontrolled measuring equipment, therefore the requirements of clause 7.6 on measuring devices apply to the design process. Design is not complete until the criteria for accepting production versions have been established. Products need to be designed so as to be testable during production using the available production facilities. The proving of production acceptance criteria is therefore very much part of design verification.

Development tests

Where tests are needed to verify conformance with the design specification, development test specifications will be needed to specify the test parameters, limits and operating conditions. For each development test specification there should be a corresponding development test procedure that defines how the parameters will be measured using particular test equipment and taking into account any uncertainty of measurement (see Measurement uncertainty under *Defining measuring processes*). Test specifications should be prepared for each testable item. Whilst it may be possible to test whole units, equipment or subsystems you need to consider the procurement and maintenance strategies for the product when deciding which items should be governed by a test specification. Two principal factors to consider are:

● Testable items sold as spare parts
● Testable items the design and/or manufacture of which are subcontracted.

If you conduct trials on parts and materials to prove reliability or durability, these can be considered to be verification tests. For example, you may conduct tests in the laboratory on metals for corrosion resistance or on hinges for reliability and then conduct validation tests under actual operating conditions when these items are installed in the final product.

Verifying compliance with regulations

Having designed the product to meet the applicable statutes and regulations you need to plan for verifying that they have been met. Verification of compliance can be accomplished through discrete checks combined with other tests, inspections and analyses however, it may be more difficult to demonstrate compliance through the records alone. In some cases tests such as pollution tests, safety tests, proof loading tests, electromagnetic compatibility tests, pressure vessel tests etc., are so significant that separate tests and test specifications are the most effective method of verifying compliance with regulations.

Alternative design calculations

Verification of some characteristics may only be possible by calculation rather than by test, inspection or demonstration. In such cases the design calculations should be checked either by being repeated by someone else or by performing the calculations by an alternative method. When this form of verification is used the margins of error permitted should be specified in the verification plan.

Comparing similar designs

Design verification can be a costly exercise. One way of avoiding unnecessary costs is to compare the design with a similar one that has been proven to meet the same requirements. This approach is often used with designs that use a modular construction. Modules used in previous designs need not be subject to the range of tests and examinations necessary if their performance has been verified either as part of a proven design or has been subject to such in-service use that will demonstrate achievement of the requirements. Care has to be taken when using this verification method that the requirements are the same and that evidence of compliance is available to demonstrate compliance with the requirements. Marginal differences in the environmental conditions and operating loads can cause the design to fail if it was operating at its design limit when used in the previous design.

Recording design verification results (7.3.5)

The standard requires *the results of the verification and any required actions to be recorded.*

What does this mean?

The results of design verification comprise:

- The criteria used to determine acceptability
- Data testifying the standard of the design being subject to verification
- The verification methods
- Data testifying the conditions, facilities and equipment used to conduct the verification
- The measurements
- Analysis of the differences between planned and achieved results
- Actions to be taken on the differences

> **1994–2000 Differences**
>
> Previously the standard required the design verification measures to be recorded.
>
> Although verification measures and verification records are quite different, the intent was that the measures taken to verify the design be recorded and therefore there has been no change in requirement.

Why is this necessary?

This requirement responds to the Factual Approach Principle.

Any decision to proceed either to the next stage of development or into production or operations needs to be based on fact and the records of design verification provide the facts. As the definition of verification explains, it is the provision of objective evidence that requirements have been fulfilled and the records of verification constitute this objective evidence.

How is this implemented?

In planning design verification, consideration needs to be given to the output, its format and content. The basic content is governed by the design specification but the data to be recorded both before, during and after verification need to be prescribed. Some data may be generated electronically and other data may be collected from observation. Often there are lots of different pieces of evidence that need to be collected, collated and assembled into a dossier in a secure format. These factors need to be sorted out before commencing verification so that all the necessary information is gathered at the time. After verification a report of the activities may also be necessary to explain the results, possible causes of any variation and recommendations for action for presentation at a design review.

Design validation (7.3.6)

Performing validation (7.3.6)

<table>
<tr><td>

1994–2000 Differences

Previously the standard required that design validation be performed to ensure that product conforms to defined user needs and/or requirements.

The intent of the requirement remains unchanged.

</td><td>

The standard requires design and development validation to *be performed in accordance with planned arrangements to confirm that resulting product is capable of fulfilling the requirements for the specified application or intended use where known.*

What does this mean?

ISO 9000 defines validation as confirmation through the provision of objective evidence that requirements for a specific intended use or application have been fulfilled. Specified requirements are often an imper-

</td></tr>
</table>

fect definition of needs and expectations and therefore to overcome inadequacies in the manner in which requirements can be specified, the resultant design needs to be validated against intended use or application.

Design validation is a process of evaluating a design to establish that it fulfils the intended use requirements. It goes further than design verification in that validation tests and trials may stress the product of such a design beyond operating conditions in order to establish design margins of safety and performance. Design validation can also be performed on mature designs in order to establish whether they will fulfil different user requirements to the original design input requirements. An example is where software designed for one application can be proven fit for use in a different application or where a component designed for one environment can be shown to possess a capability that would enable it to be used in a different environment. Multiple validations may therefore be performed to qualify a design for different applications.

Why is this necessary?

This requirement responds to the Factual Approach Principle.

Merely requiring that the design output meets the design input would not produce a quality product or service unless the input requirements were a true reflection of the customer needs and this is not always achieved. If the input is inadequate the output will be inadequate: 'garbage-in-garbage-out' to use a common software expression.

How is this implemented?

Design validation may take the form of qualification tests which stress the product upto and beyond design limits – beta tests where products are supplied to several typical users on trial in order to gather operational performance data, performance trials and reliability and maintainability trials where products are put on test for prolonged periods to simulate usage conditions.

In the automobile industry the road trials on test tracks are validation tests as are the customer trials conducted over several weeks or months under actual operating conditions on pre-production models. Sometimes the trials are not successful as was the case of the 'Copper Cooled Engine' in General Motors in the early 1920s. Even though the engine seemed to work in the laboratory, it failed in service. Production was commenced before the design had been validated. The engine had pre-ignition problems and showed a loss of compression and power when hot. As a result many cars with the engine were scrapped. Apart from the technical problems GM experienced with its development, it did prove to be a turning point in GM's development strategy, probably resulting in what is now their approach to product quality planning.

Other examples are beta tests or public testing conducted on software products where tens or hundreds of products are distributed to designated customer sites for trials under actual operating conditions before product launch. Sometimes, commercial pressures force termination of these trials and premature launch of products in order to beat the competition.

As the cost of testing vast quantities of equipment would be too great and take too long, qualification tests particularly on hardware, are usually performed on a small sample. The test levels are varied to take account of design assumptions, variations in production processes and the operating environment.

Products may not be put to their design limits for some time after their launch into service, probably far beyond the warranty period. Customer complaints may appear years after product launch. When investigated this may be traced back to a design fault which was not tested for during the verification programme. Such things as corrosion, insulation, resistance to wear, chemicals, climatic conditions etc. need to be verified as being within the design limits.

Following qualification tests, your customer may require a demonstration of performance in order to accept the design. These tests are called design acceptance tests. They usually consist of a series of functional and environmental tests taken from the qualification test specification supported by the results of the qualification tests. When it has been demonstrated that the design meets all the specified requirements, a Design Certificate can be issued. The design standard that is declared on this certificate is the standard against which all subsequent changes should be controlled and from which production versions should be produced.

Demonstrations

Tests exercise the functional properties of the product. Demonstrations on the other hand, serve to exhibit usage characteristics such as access, maintainability including interchangeability, repairability and serviceability. Demonstrations can be used to prove safety features such as fire escape provisions in aircraft, ships or buildings. However, one of the most important characteristics that need to be demonstrated is producibility. Can you actually make the product economically in the quantities required? Does production yield a profit or do you need to produce 50 to yield 10 good ones? The demonstrations should establish whether the design is robust. Designers may be selecting components at the outer limits of their capability. A worst-case analysis should have been performed to verify that under worst case conditions, i.e. when all the components fitted are at the extreme of their tolerance range, the product will perform to specification. Analysis may be more costly to carry out than a test and by assembling the product with components at their tolerance limits you may be able to demonstrate economically the robustness of the design.

Product approval

A product approval process is often required in large-scale production situations such as the automotive and aerospace sectors. When one considers the potential risk involved in assembling unapproved products into production models, it is hardly surprising that the customers impose such stringent requirements. The process provides assurance that the product meets all design criteria and is capable of production in the qualities required without unacceptable variation. It is intended to validate that products made from production materials, tools and processes meet the customer's engineering requirements and that the production process has the potential to produce product meeting these requirements during an actual production run at the quoted production rate.

The process commences following design and process verification during which a production trial run using production standard tooling, suppliers, materials etc. produces the information needed to make a submission for product approval. Until approval is granted, shipment of production product may not be authorized. If any of the processes change then a new submission is required. Shipment of parts produced to the modified specifications or from modified processes would not be authorized until customer approval is granted.

Timing of validation (7.3.6)

The standard requires validation to *be completed wherever applicable prior to the delivery or implementation of the product.*

1994–2000 Differences
This is a new requirement that has no equivalent in the 1994 version.

What does this mean?

As indicated previously, validation trials may take some considerable time but until confidence in the capability of a design to fulfil intended use requirements is known, any decision to launch into production or into operation involves risk. The requirement however, recognizes that it may not be possible or practical to hold production until all the results of validation have been obtained and assessed.

Why is this necessary?

This requirement responds to the Systems Approach Principle.

There are some characteristics such as safety and reliability that need to be demonstrated before launching into production otherwise unsafe or unreliable products might be put onto the market. One has only to scan the recall programmes accessible on the internet to notice that many products are indeed launched into production with major faults (see Appendix B). Some failures may be due to the quality of conformity but there are also some that are due to design weaknesses that should have been detected in the verification and validation programmes.

It is thought that in the USA alone, there are 30 million product recalls every year. Probably the biggest recall of all time occurred in April 1996 when Ford USA recalled upto 9 million vehicles that may have been equipped with a faulty ignition switch. In July 1999 – General Motors USA recalled 1.1 million vehicles that may have had anti-lock brake problems. Launching into production without sufficient evidence that the decision satisfies all interested parties can therefore be very costly.

How is this implemented?

The simplest approach is to wait until all the evidence from verification and validation trials has been assessed before launching into production or going operational. In practice it depends upon knowing what the risks are and therefore is a balance between risk and the impact any delay in production launch or going operational may have. It would therefore be prudent to conduct a risk assessment in such circumstances. However it should be noted that there is no mean time between failure (MTBF) until you actually have a failure, so you need to keep on testing until you know anything meaningful about the product's reliability.

Recording results. (7.3.6)

The standard requires *the results of the validation and subsequent follow-up actions to be recorded.*

What does this mean?

The results of validation are similar to those required for verification except that duration of testing and trials is important in quantifying the evidence. The results should not only indicate that the product meets intended use requirements but also satisfies market need.

Why is this necessary?

This requirement responds to the Factual Approach Principle.

The reasons for recording validation results are the same as for verification results but the decision based on the results is far more significant. Going into production or going operational with the wrong product will be disastrous. There have been several examples of this over the years. The Ford Edsel was a classic example as was the Sinclair C5 motorized tricycle. There was no market for such a product and sales did not materialize in the quantities anticipated.

How is this implemented?

As with design verification, consideration of the output, its format and content needs to be given early in the design phase so that the correct data is captured during validation trials.

Control of design and development changes (7.3.7)

Identification and recording of design changes (7.3.7)

The standard requires design and development changes to *be identified and records maintained.*

What does this mean?

This clause covers two different requirements involving two quite different control processes. Design changes are simply changes to the design and can occur at any stage in the design process from the stage at which the requirement is agreed to the final certification that the design is proven. Development changes can occur at any time in the life cycle of the design. Following design certification i.e. when all design verification has been completed and the product launched into production, changes to the product to incorporate design changes are generally classed as 'modifications'.

Changes to design documents are not design changes unless the characteristics of the product are altered. Changes in the presentation of design information or to the system of measurement (Imperial units to metric units) are not design or development changes.

Why is this necessary?

This requirement responds to the Process Approach Principle.

You need to control design changes to permit desirable changes to be made and to prohibit undesirable changes from being made. Change control during the design process is a good method of controlling costs and timescales because once the design process has commenced every change will cost time and effort to address. This will cause delays whilst the necessary changes are implemented and provides an opportunity for additional errors to creep into the design. 'If it's not broke don't fix it!' is a good maxim to adopt during design. In other words don't change the design unless it already fails to meet the requirements or you have discovered the requirements to be wrong. Designers are creative people who love to add the latest devices, the latest technologies, to stretch performance and to go on enhancing the design regardless of the timescales or costs. One reason for controlling design changes is to restrain the otherwise limitless creativity of designers in order to keep the design within the budget and timescale.

How is this implemented?

The imposition of change control is often a difficult concept for designers to accept. They would prefer change control to commence after they have completed their design rather than before they have started. They may argue that until they have finished there is no design to control. They would be mistaken. Designs proceed through a number of stages (as described previously under design reviews). Once the design requirements have been agreed, any changes in the requirements should be subject to formal procedures. When a particular design solution is complete and has been found to meet the requirements at a design review, it should be brought under *change control*. Between design reviews the designers should be given complete freedom to derive solutions to the requirements. Between the design reviews there should be no change control on incomplete solutions.

Design changes will result in changes to documentation but not all design documentation changes are design changes. This is why design change control should be treated separately from document control. You may need to correct errors in the design documentation and none of these may materially affect the product. The mechanisms you employ for such changes should be different from those you employ to make changes that do affect the design. By keeping the two types of change separate you avoid bottlenecks in the design change loop and only present the design authorities with changes that require *their* expert judgment.

Identifying and recording design changes

The documentation for design changes should comprise the change proposal, the results of the evaluation, the instructions for change and traceability in the changed documents to the source and nature of the change. You will therefore need:

- A Change Request form which contains the reason for change and the results of the evaluation – this is used to initiate the change and obtain approval before being implemented.
- A Change Notice that provides instructions defining what has to be changed – this is issued following approval of the change as instructions to the owners of the various documents that are affected by the change.
- A Change Record that describes what has been changed – this usually forms part of the document that has been changed and can be either in the form of a box at the side of the sheet (as with drawings) or in the form of a table on a separate sheet (as with specifications).

Where the evaluation of the change requires further design work and possibly experimentation and testing, the results for such activities should be documented to form part of the change documentation.

At each design review a design baseline should be established which identifies the design documentation that has been approved. The baseline should be recorded and change control procedures employed to deal with any changes. These change procedures should provide a means for formally requesting or proposing changes to the design. For complex designs you may prefer to separate proposals from instructions and have one form for proposing design changes and another form for promulgating design changes after approval. You will need a central registry to collect all proposed changes and provide a means for screening those that are not suitable to go before the review board, (either because they duplicate proposals already made or because they may not satisfy certain acceptance criteria which you have prescribed). On receipt, the *change proposals* should be identified with a unique number that can be used on all related documentation that is subsequently produced. The change proposal needs to:

- Identify the product of which the design is to be changed
- State the nature of the proposed change

- Identify the principal requirements, specifications, drawings or other design documents which are affected by the change
- State the reasons for the change either directly or by reference to failure reports, nonconformity reports, customer requests or other sources
- Provide for the results of the evaluation, review and decision to be recorded

Identifying and recording modifications

As *modifications* are changes to products resulting from design changes, the identity of modifications needs to be visible on the product that has been modified. If the issue status of the product specification changes, you will need a means of determining whether the product should also be changed. Not all changes to design documentation are design changes that result in product changes and not all product changes are modifications. (Nonconformities may be accepted which change the product but not the design.) Changes to the drawings or specifications that do not affect the form, fit or function of the product are usually called 'alterations' and those which affect form, fit or function are 'modifications'. Alterations should come under 'document control' whereas design changes should come under 'configuration control'. You will therefore need a mechanism for relating the modification status of products to the corresponding drawings and specifications. Following commencement of production the first design change to be incorporated into the product will usually be denoted by a number such as Mod 1 for hardware and by Version or Release number for software. The practices for software differ in that versions can be incremented by points such as 1.1, 1.2 etc., where the second digit denotes a minor change and the first digit a major change. This modification notation relates to the product whereas, issue notation relates to the documentation that describes the product. You will need a modification procedure that describes the notation to be used for hardware and software.

Within the design documentation you will need to provide for the attachment of modification plates on which to denote the modification status of the product.

Prior to commencement of production, design changes do not require any modification documentation, the design changes being incorporated in prototypes by rework or rebuild. However, when product is in production, instructions will need to be provided so that the modification can be embodied in the product. These modification instructions should detail:

- The products that are affected by part number and serial number
- The new parts that are required
- The work to be carried out to remove obsolete items and fit new items or the work to be carried out to salvage existing items and render them suitable for modification

- The markings to be applied to the product and its modification label
- The tests and inspections to be performed to verify that the product is serviceable
- The records to be produced as evidence that the modification has been embodied

Modification instructions should be produced after approval for the change that has been granted and should be submitted to the change control board or design authority for approval before release.

Review and evaluation of changes (7.3.7)

1994–2000 Differences

Previously the standard required all design changes and modifications to be approved by authorized personnel before their implementation.

The additional requirement for what amounts to an impact assessment, looks beyond design to affect of change on products in service.

The standard requires *the changes* to *be reviewed and approved before implementation, including the evaluation of the effect of changes on constituent parts and delivered product.*

What does this mean?

A change to a design that has not proceeded beyond a design review or verification stage is still in progress and therefore requires no approval. When a design is reviewed or verified it means that any change to the information upon which that decision was taken needs to be evaluated for its effect on the design and any product produced from that design that may be in production or in service.

Why is this necessary?

This requirement responds to the Factual Approach Principle.

By controlling change you control cost so it is a vital organ of the business and should be run efficiently. The requirement for changes to be approved before their implementation emphasizes the importance of this control mechanism. The requirement for evaluation of changes for impact on product in service is necessary to transfer any benefits from the change to customers. This is especially important if the reason for change was to improve safety, reliability or regulatory compliance.

How is this implemented?

Following the commencement of design you will need to set up a change control board or panel comprising those personnel responsible for funding the design, administering the contract and for accepting the product. All change proposals should be submitted to such a body for evaluation and subsequent approval or disapproval before the changes are implemented. Such a mechanism will give you control of all design changes. By providing a two-tier system you can also submit all design documentation changes through such a body. They can filter the alterations from the modifications and the minor changes from the major changes.

The change proposals need to be evaluated:

- To validate the reason for change
- To determine whether the proposed change is feasible
- To judge whether the change is desirable
- To determine the effects on performance, costs and timescales
- To determine the impact of the change on other designs with which it interfaces and in which it is used
- To examine the documentation affected by the change and consequently programme their revision
- To determine the stage at which the change should be embodied

The evaluation may need to be carried out by a review team, by suppliers or by the original proposer, however, regardless of who carries out the evaluation, the results should be presented to the change control board for a decision.

During development there are two decisions the board will need to make:

- Whether to accept or reject the change and
- When to implement the change in the design documentation

If the board accepts the change, the changes to the design documentation can either be submitted to the change control board or processed through your document control procedures. During development it is a common practice to accumulate design changes for incorporation into the design when design proving has been completed. If there are many of these changes a two or three stage process of incorporation may be desirable. In the event that the development model is deliverable to the customer, or as in the case of one-off systems, the changes need to be incorporated into the design before delivery, acceptance may take place against drawings and specifications extended by change notes. However, unless the change notes accurately reflect the final design configuration, the integrity of any certification of the product against a proven design cannot be assured. There is also a temptation to cut costs by not incorporating latent design changes into the design documentation. This may well avert delayed delivery but will have severe consequences should modifications be necessary later or should the changes affect the integrity of the supporting handbooks and manuals. So, deciding when to incorporate the changes is a very important consideration.

During production the change control board will need to make four decisions:

- Whether to accept or reject the change
- When to implement the change in the design documentation
- When to implement the modification in new product
- What to do with existing product in production, in store and in service

The decision to implement the modification will depend on when the design documentation will be changed and when new parts and modification instructions are available. The modification instructions can either be submitted to the change control board or through your document control procedures. The primary concern of the change control board is not so much the detail of the change but its effects, its costs and the logistics in its embodiment. If the design change has been made for safety or environmental reasons you may need to recall product in order to embody the modification. Your modification procedures need to provide for all such cases. With safety issues, there may be regulatory procedures that need to be implemented to notify customers, recall product, implement modifications and to release modified product back into service.

Verification and validation of design changes (7.3.7)

The standard requires design changes to *be verified and validated as appropriate before implementation.*

1994–2000 Differences

This is a new requirement that has no equivalent in the 1994 version.

What does this mean?

Design changes are no different than original designs in that they need to be verified and validated.

Why is this important?

This requirement responds to the Factual Approach Principle.

When a change is made to an approved design, any previous review, verification and validation may be invalidated by the change. Re-verification and validation may therefore be necessary.

How is this implemented?

Depending on the nature of the change, the verification may range from a review of calculations to a repeat of the full design verification programme. The changes may occur before the design has reached the validation phase and therefore not warrant any change to the validation programme. It is therefore necessary when evaluating a design change to determine the extent of any verification and validation that may need to be repeated. Some design changes warrant being treated as projects in their own right, recycling the full design process. Other changes may warrant verification on samples only or verification may be possible by an analysis of the differences with a proven design.

In some cases the need for a design change may be recognized during production tests or installation and in order to define the changes required you may wish to carry out trial modifications or experiments. Any changes to the product during production should be carried out under controlled conditions, hence the requirement that approval of design changes be given before their implementation. To allow such activities as trial modifications and experiments to proceed you will need a means of controlling these events. If the modification can be removed in a way that will render the production item in no way degraded, you can impose simple controls for the removal of the modification. If the item will be rendered unserviceable by removing the modification, alternative means may need to be determined otherwise you will sacrifice the product. It is for this reason that organizations provide development models on which to try out modifications.

Purchasing (7.4)

Purchasing process (7.4.1)

Ensuring purchased product conforms to specified requirements (7.4.1)

The standard requires the organization to *ensure that purchased product conforms to specified purchase requirements.*

What does this mean?

ISO 9000 defines a supplier as an organization or person that provides a product and in ISO 9000 a product can be services, hardware, software or processed materials. A supplier may therefore be a producer, distributor, retailer, vendor, contractor, subcontractor or service provider. Purchased product is any product or service that is purchased rather than freely given or otherwise acquired. Specified purchase requirements are those requirements that are specified by the customer, the organization or by statutes and regulations that apply to purchased product. This would include any requirements limiting the conditions or the source of supply.

> **1994–2000 Differences**
>
> Previously the standard required the supplier to establish and maintain documented procedures to ensure that purchased product conforms to specified requirements.
>
> The intent of the requirement remains unchanged.

Why is this necessary?

This requirement responds to the Factual Approach Principle.

All organizations have suppliers of one form or another in order to provide products and service to their customers. Some of them directly or indirectly impact the product being supplied to the organization's customers and others may have no impact at all such as office supplies. From the scope of the standard we draw the conclusion that the requirement is not intended to apply to products and service that have no impact on the customer but why would you not want to manage such purchasing activities as effectively as other purchasing activities?

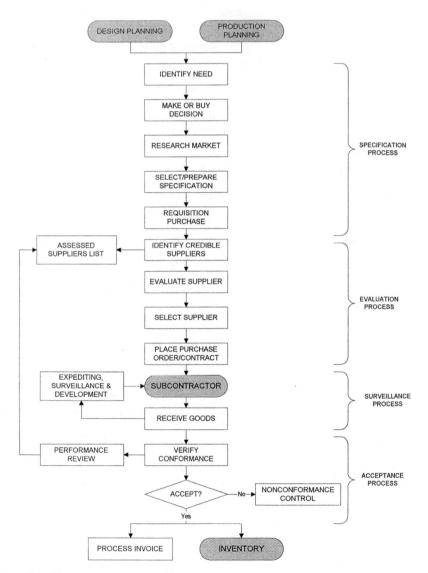

Figure 7.8 Procurement process flow

How is this implemented?

Once the make or buy decision has been made, control of any purchasing activity follows a common series of activities.

There are four key processes in the procurement cycle for which you should prepare procedures.

- The specification process which starts once the need has been identified and ends with a request to purchase.
- The evaluation process which starts with the request to purchase and ends with the placement of the order or contract.
- The surveillance process which starts with placement of order or contract and ends upon delivery of supplies.
- The acceptance process which starts with delivery of supplies and ends with entry of supplies on to the inventory and/or payment of invoice.

Whatever you purchase the processes will be very similar although there will be variations for purchased services such as subcontract labour, computer maintenance, consultancy services etc. Where the purchasing process is relatively simple, one route may suffice but where the process varies you may need separate routes so as to avoid *all* purchases, regardless of value and risk, going through the same process and incurring unnecessary costs and delay. A typical procurement process flow is illustrated in Figure 7.8.

Control of suppliers (7.4.1)

The standard requires *the type and extent of control applied to the supplier and the purchased product to be dependent upon the effect of the purchased product on subsequent product realization or the final product.*

What does this mean?

The requirement contains two quite separate requirements – one applying to the product and the other applying to the supplier.

Regarding the product, the type of control refers to whether the controls should act before, during or after receipt of product. The extent of control refers to whether it is remote or on the suppliers' premises and whether product is accepted on the basis of supplier data or is to be evaluated before authorizing delivery.

> **1994–2000 Differences**
>
> Previously the standard required suppliers to define the type and extent of control exercised by the supplier over subcontractors and goes on to require that these controls be dependent upon the type of product, the impact of the product on the quality of the final product and, where applicable, on the quality audit reports and/or quality records of the previously demonstrated capability and performance of subcontractors.
>
> The changed wording does not alter the intent of the requirement.

Regarding the supplier the type of control refers to whether or not to qualify the supplier and the extent of control refers to the degree to which the organization is involved with the supplier in managing the purchase.

Purchased product can have varying degrees of impact on the processes and products of the organization ranging from no impact to critical impact. A product with a critical impact would warrant stringent control over its purchase, whereas a product with negligible or no impact may warrant no more than a simple visual check on delivery to verify receipt of the right product.

Why is this necessary?

This requirement responds to the Mutually Beneficial Supplier Relationships Principle.

As it would not be prudent to exercise no control over suppliers, it would also be counterproductive to impose rigorous controls over every supplier and purchased product. A balance has to be made on the basis of risk to the processes in which the purchased product is to be used and the final product into which the purchased product may be installed.

How is this implemented?

Selecting the degree of control

You need some means of verifying that the supplier has met the requirements of your order and the more unusual and complex the requirements, the more control will be required. The degree of control you need to exercise over your suppliers depends on the confidence you have in their ability to meet your requirements. If you have high confidence in a particular supplier you can concentrate on the areas where failure is more likely. If you have no confidence you will need to exercise rigorous control until you gain sufficient confidence to relax the controls. The fact that a supplier has gained ISO 9000 registration for the products and service you require should increase your confidence, but if you have no previous history of their performance it does not mean they will be any better than the supplier you have used for years which is not registered to ISO 9000. Your supplier control procedures need to provide the criteria for selecting the appropriate degree of control and for selecting the activities you need to perform.

With suppliers of proprietary products, your choices are often limited because you have no privileges. Control over your suppliers is therefore exercised by the results of receipt inspection or subsequent verification. If your confidence in a supplier is low you can increase the level of verification and if high you can dispense with receipt verification and rely on in-process controls to alert you to any deterioration in supplier performance.

In determining the degree of control to be exercised you need to establish whether:

- The quality of the product or service can be verified on receipt using your normal inspection and test techniques. Sampling inspection on receipt should be used when statistical data is unavailable to you or you don't have the confidence for permitting ship-to-line. (This is the least costly of methods and usually applies where achievement of the requirements is measurable by examination of the end product.)
- The quality of the product can be verified on receipt providing you acquire additional equipment or facilities. (This is more costly than the previous method but may be economic if there is high utilization of the equipment.)
- The quality of the product can be verified by witnessing the final acceptance on the suppliers' premises. (If you don't possess the necessary equipment or skill to carry out product verification, this method is an economic compromise and should yield as much confidence in the product as the previous methods. You do, however, need to recognize that your presence on the supplier's premises may affect the results. They may omit tests that are problematical or your presence may cause them to be particularly diligent, a stance that may not be maintained when you are not present.)
- The verification of the product could be contracted to a third party. (This can be very costly and is usually only applied with highly complex products and where safety is of paramount importance.)
- The quality of the product can only be verified by the supplier during its design and manufacture. (In such cases you need to rely on what the contractor tells you and to gain sufficient confidence you can impose quality system requirements, require certain design, manufacturing, verification documents to be submitted to you for approval and carry out periodic audit and surveillance activities. This method is usually applied to one off systems or small quantities when the stability of a long production run cannot be achieved to resolve problems.)

In order to relate the degree of inspection to the importance of the item, you should categorize purchases as follows:

- If the subsequent discovery of nonconformity will *not* cause design, production, installation or operational problems of any nature, a simple identity, carton quantity and damage check may suffice. An example of this would be stationery.
- If the subsequent discovery of nonconformity will cause *minor* design, production, installation or operational problems, you should examine the features and characteristics of the item on a sampling basis. An example of this would be electrical, electronic or mechanical components.

- If the subsequent discovery of nonconformity will cause *major* design, production, installation or operational problems then you should subject the item to a complete test to verify compliance with all prescribed requirements. An example of this would be an electronic unit.

These criteria would need to be varied depending on whether the items being supplied were in batches or separate. However, these are the kind of decisions you need to take in order to apply practical receipt verification procedures.

Defining supplier controls

When carrying out supplier surveillance you will need a plan which indicates what you intend to do and when you intend to do it. You will also need to agree the plan with your supplier. If you intend witnessing certain tests the supplier will need to give you advanced warning of commencing such tests so that you may attend.

The quality plan would be a logical place for such controls to be defined. Some companies produce a Quality Assurance Requirement Specification to supplement ISO 9001 and also produce a Supplier Surveillance Plan. In most other cases the controls may be defined on the reverse side of the purchase order as standard conditions coded and selected for individual purchases. However don't impose onerous requirements on simple purchases. Requiring Year 2000 compliance or test samples for literature you purchase is rather ludicrous. Make provision for the relevant conditions to be selected by the buyer otherwise you run the risk of suppliers ignoring requirements that might be relevant.

Evaluation and selection of suppliers (7.4.1)

1994–2000 Differences

Previously the standard required the supplier to evaluate and select suppliers on the basis of their ability to meet subcontract requirements, including the quality system and any specific quality assurance requirements.

The intent of the requirement remains unchanged.

The standard requires the organization to *evaluate and select suppliers based on their ability to supply product in accordance with the organization's requirements and to establish criteria for selection, evaluation and re-evaluation.*

What does this mean?

In searching for a supplier you need to be confident that the supplier can provide the product or service you require. This means that the decision to select a supplier should be based on knowledge about that supplier's capability to meet your requirements. The decision should be based on facts gathered as a result of an evaluation against criteria that you have established.

Why is this necessary?

This requirement responds to the Mutually Beneficial Supplier Relationships Principle.

It would be foolish to select a supplier without first verifying that it was able to meet your requirements in some way or other. Failure to check out the supplier and its products may result in late delivery of the wrong product. It may also mean that you might not know immediately that the product does not meet your requirement and discover much later that it seriously impacts your commitments to your customer.

How is this implemented?

Selection process

The process for selection of suppliers varies depending upon the nature of the products and services to be procured. The more complex the product or service, the more complex the process. You either purchase products and services to your specification (custom) or to the supplier's (proprietary). For example you would normally procure stationery, fasteners or materials to the *supplier's specification* but procure an oil platform, radar system or road bridge to *your specification*. There are grey areas where proprietary products can be tailored to suit your needs and custom made products or services that primarily consist of proprietary products configured to suit your needs. There is no generic model, each industry seems to have developed a process to match its own needs. However we can treat the process as a number of stages some of which do not apply to simple purchases as shown in Table 7.1. At each stage the number of potential suppliers is whittled down to end with the selection of what is hoped to be the most suitable that meets the requirements. With 'custom' procurement this procurement cycle may be exercised several times. For instance there may be a competition for each phase of project feasibility, project definition, development and production. Each phase may be funded by the customer. On the other hand, a supplier may be invited to tender on the basis of previously demonstrated capability but has to execute project feasibility, project definition and development of a new version of a product at its own cost. Supplier capability will differ in each phase. Some suppliers have good design capability but lack the capacity for quantity production, others have good research capability but lack development capability.

You need to develop a supplier evaluation and selection process and in certain cases this may result in several closely related procedures for use when certain conditions apply. Do not try to force every purchase through the same selection process. Having purchasing policies that require three quotations for every purchase regardless of past performance of the current supplier is placing price before quality. Provide flexibility so that process

Table 7.1 Supplier evaluation and selection stages

Stage	Purpose	Proprietary	Tailored	Custom
Preliminary supplier assessment	To select credible suppliers	✓	✓	✓
Pre-qualification of suppliers	To select capable bidders		✓	✓
Qualification of suppliers	To qualify capable bidders			✓
Request for Quotation (RFQ)	To obtain prices for products/services	✓	✓	
Invitation to Tender (ITT)	To establish what bidders can offer			✓
Tender/Quote Evaluation	To select a supplier	✓	✓	✓
Contract Negotiation	To agree terms and conditions	✓	✓	✓

complexity matches the risks anticipated. Going out to tender for a few standard nuts and bolts would seem uneconomical. Likewise, placing an order for £1m of equipment based solely on the results of a third party ISO 9000 certification would seem unwise.

Preliminary supplier assessment

The purpose of the preliminary supplier assessment is to select a *credible* supplier and not necessarily to select a supplier for a specific purchase. There are millions of suppliers in the world, some of which would be happy to relieve you of your wealth given half a chance, and others that take pride in their service to customers and are a pleasure to have as partners. You need a process for gathering intelligence on potential suppliers and for eliminating unsuitable suppliers so that the buyers do not need to go through the whole process from scratch with each purchase. The first step is to establish the type of products and services you require to support your business, then search for suppliers that claim to provide such products and services. In making your choice, look at what the supplier says it will do and what it has done in the past. Is it the sort of firm that does what it says it does or is it the sort of firm that says what you want to hear and then conducts its business differently? Some of the checks needed to establish the credibility of suppliers are time consuming and would delay the selection process if undertaken only when you have a specific purchase in mind. You will need to develop your own criteria but typically unsuitable suppliers may be those that:

- are unlikely to deliver what you want in the quantities you may require
- are unable to meet your potential delivery requirements
- cannot provide the after-sales support needed
- are unethical
- do not comply with the health and safety standards of your industry
- do not comply with the relevant environmental regulations
- do not have a system to assure the quality of supplies
- are not committed to continuous improvement
- are financially unstable

You may also discriminate suppliers on political grounds such as a preference for supplies from certain countries or a requirement to exclude supplies from certain countries.

The supplier assessment will therefore need to be in several parts:

Technical assessment – This would check the products, processes or services to establish they are what the supplier claims them to be. Assessment of design and production capability may be carried out at this stage or be held until the pre-qualification stage when specific contracts are being considered.

Quality system assessment – This would check the certification status of the quality system, verifying that any certification was properly accredited. For non-ISO 9000 registered suppliers, a quality system assessment may be carried out at this stage either to ISO 9000 or the customer's standards.

Financial assessment – This would check the credit rating, insurance risk, stability etc.

Ethical assessment – This would check probity, conformance with professional standards and codes.

These assessments do not need to be carried out on the supplier's premises. Much of the data needed can be accumulated from a supplier questionnaire and searches through directories and registers of companies and you can choose to rely on assessments carried out by accredited third parties to provide the necessary level of confidence. (The Directories of Companies of Assessed Capability that are maintained by the Accreditation Agencies can be a good place to start.) The assessments may yield suppliers over a wide range and you may find it beneficial to classify suppliers as follows:

Class A ISO 9000 certified and demonstrated capability – This is the class of those certified suppliers with which you have done business for a long time and gathered historical evidence that proves their capability.

Class B Demonstrated capability – This is the class of those suppliers you have done business with for a long time and warrant continued patronage on the basis that its better to deal with those suppliers you know than those you don't. They may not even be contemplating ISO 9000 certification, but *you* get a good product, a good service and no hassle.

Class C ISO 9000 certified and no demonstrated capability – This is the class of those certified suppliers with whom you have done no business. This may appear a contradiction because ISO 9000 certification is obtained on the basis of demonstrated capability, but you have not established their capability to meet *your* requirements.

Class D Capable with additional assurance – This is the class of first time suppliers with which you have not done sufficient business to put in class B and where you may need to impose ISO 9000 requirements or similar to gain the confidence you need.

Class E Unacceptable performance that can be neutralized – This class is for those cases where you may be able to compensate for poor performance if they are sole suppliers of the product or service.

Class F No demonstrated capability – This is the class of those suppliers you have not used before and therefore have no historical data.

Class G Demonstrated unacceptable performance – This is the class of those suppliers that have clearly demonstrated that their products and services are unacceptable and it is uneconomic to compensate for their deficiencies.

Caution is advised on the name you give to this list of suppliers. All have been assessed but all may not have been visited or used. Some organizations refer to it as an Approved Suppliers List (ASL) or Approved Vendor List (AVL), but if you include unacceptable suppliers you cannot call it an Approved Vendor List. If it is in paper form, two lists may be preferable. Some organizations use coloured paper to distinguish between approved and unapproved suppliers. If the data is stored electronically, the fields can be protected to prevent selection of unacceptable suppliers.

If your requirements vary from project to project, suppliers approved for one project may not be approved for others. If your procurement requirements do not vary from product to product, you may well be able to maintain an AVL. Most will meet your minimum criteria for doing business with your company but may not be capable of meeting specific product/service requirements. Others you will include simply because they do supply the type of product/ service you require but their credibility is too low at present to warrant preferred status. In the process you have eliminated the 'cowboys' or 'rogues' – there is no point in adding these to the list because you have established that they won't change in the foreseeable future.

Pre-qualification of suppliers

Pre-qualification is a process for selecting suppliers for known future work. The design will have proceeded to a stage where an outline specification of the essential parameters has been developed. You know roughly what you want but not in detail. Pre-qualification is undertaken to select those suppliers that can demonstrate they have the capability to meet your specific requirements on quality, quantity, price and delivery. A supplier may have the capability to meet quality, quantity and price requirements but not have the capacity available when you need the product or service. One that has the capacity may not offer the best price and one that meets the other criteria may not be able to supply product in the quantity you require.

A list of potential bidders can be generated from the Assessed Suppliers List by searching for suppliers that match given input criteria specific to the particular procurement. However, the evidence you gathered to place suppliers on your Assessed Suppliers List may now be obsolete. Their capability may have changed and therefore you need a sorting process for specific purchases. If candidates are selected that have not been assessed, an assessment should be carried out before proceeding any further.

Once the list is generated a Request for Quotation (RFQ) or Invitation to Tender (ITT) can be issued depending on what is required. RFQs are normally used where price only is required. This enables you to disqualify bidders offering a price well outside your budget. ITTs are normally used to seek a line-by-line response to technical, commercial and managerial requirements. At this stage you may select a number of potential suppliers and require each to demonstrate its capability. You know what they do but you need to know if they have the capability of producing a product with specific characteristics and can control its quality.

When choosing a bidder you also need to be confident that continuity of supply can be assured. One of the benefits of ISO 9000 certification is that it should demonstrate that the supplier has the capability to supply certain types of products and services. However, it is not a guarantee that the supplier has the capability to meet *your* specific requirements. Suppliers that have not gained ISO 9000 registration may be just as good. (There is no evidence to demonstrate that ISO 9000 certified suppliers perform better than non-certificated suppliers.) You may not have a choice if the product or service you require can only be obtained from a non-registered contractor. Using an ISO 9000 registered supplier should enable you to reduce your supplier controls, so by using a non ISO 9000 registered supplier you will need to compensate by performing more quality assurance activities yourself, or employ a third party.

Depending on the nature of the work you may require space models, prototypes, process capability studies, samples of work as evidence of capability. You may also make a preliminary visit to each potential bidder but would not send out an evaluation team until the qualification stage.

Qualification of suppliers

Of those potential bidders that are capable, some may be more capable than others. Qualification is a stage executed to compile a short list of bidders following pre-qualification. A detail specification is available at this stage and production standard models may be required to qualify the design. Some customers may require a demonstration of process capability to grant production part approval.

During this stage of procurement a series of meetings may be held depending on the nature of the purchase. A pre-bid meeting may be held on the customer's premises to enable the customer to clarify the requirements with the bidders. A mid-bid meeting or pre-award assessment may be held on the supplier's premises at which the customer's Supplier Evaluation Team carries out a capability assessment on site. This assessment may cover:

- an evaluation of the product
- an audit of design and production plans to establish that, if followed, they will result in compliant product
- an audit of operations to verify that the approved plans are being followed
- an audit of processes to verify their capability
- an inspection and test of product (on or off site) to verify that it meets the specification

The result of supplier qualification is a list of capable suppliers that will be invited to bid for specific work.

ISO 9000 certification was supposed to reduce the amount of supplier assessments by customers and it has in certain sectors. However, the ISO 9000 certification whilst focused on a specific scope of registration is often not precise enough to give confidence to customers for specific purchases.

The evaluation may qualify two or three suppliers for a specific purchase. The tendering process will yield only one winner but the other suppliers are equally suitable and should not be disqualified because they may be needed if the chosen supplier fails to deliver.

Invitation to tender

Once the bidders have been selected, an Invitation to Tender (ITT) needs to be prepared to provide a fixed baseline against which unbiased competitive bids may be made. The technical, commercial and managerial requirements should be finalized and subject to review and approval prior to release. It is important that all functions with responsibilities in the procurement process review the tender documentation. The ITT will form the basis of any subsequent contract.

The requirements you pass to your bidders need to include as appropriate:

- The tender conditions, date, format, content etc.
- The terms and conditions of the subsequent contract
- A specification of the product or service that you require that transmits all of the relevant requirements of the main contract (see *purchasing specifications*)
- A specification of the means by which the requirements are to be demonstrated (see *purchasing specifications*)
- A statement of work which you require the supplier to perform – It might be design, development, management or verification work and will include a list of required deliverables such as project plans, quality plans, production plans, drawings, test data etc. (You need to be clear as to the interfaces both organizationally and technically.)
- A specification of the requirements which will give you an assurance of quality – This might be a simple reference to the appropriate ISO 9000 standard, but as this standard does not give you any rights you will probably need to amplify the requirements (see Q*uality management system requirements*)

In the tendering phase each of the potential suppliers is in competition, so observe the basic rule that what you give *one* must be given to *all!* It is at this stage that your supplier conducts the tender review defined in clause 7.2.2 of ISO 9001.

Tender/quote evaluation

On the due date when the tenders should have been received, record those that have been submitted and discard any submitted after the deadline. Conduct an evaluation to determine the winner – the supplier that can meet all your requirements (including confidence) for the lowest price. The evaluation phase should involve all your staff that were involved with the specification of requirements. You need to develop scoring criteria so that the result is based on objective evidence of compliance.

The standard does not require that you purchase from 'approved suppliers'. It does require that you maintain records of the results of supplier evaluations but does not prohibit you from selecting suppliers that do not fully meet your purchasing requirements. There will be some suppliers that fully meet your requirements and others that provide a product with the right functions but quality, price and delivery may be less than you require. If the demonstrated capability is lacking in some respects you can adjust your controls to compensate for the deficiencies.

In some cases your choice may be limited to a single source because no other supplier may market what you need. On other occasions you may be spoilt for choice. With some proprietary products you are able to select particular options so as to tailor the product or service to your requirements. It remains a proprietary product because the supplier has not changed anything just for you. The majority of products and services you will purchase from suppliers, however, is likely to be from catalogues. The designer may have already selected the item and quoted the part number in the specification. Quite often you are buying from a distributor rather than the manufacturer and so need to ensure that *both* the manufacturer and the distributor will meet your requirements.

Contract negotiation

After selecting a 'winner' you may need to enter contract negotiations in order to draw up a formal subcontract. It is most important that none of the requirements are changed without the supplier being informed and given the opportunity to adjust the quotation. It is at this stage that your supplier conducts the requirement review defined in clause 7.2.2 of ISO 9001. It is pointless negotiating the price of products and services that do not meet your needs. You will just be buying a heap of trouble! Driving down the price may also result in the supplier selling their services to the highest bidder later and leaving you high and dry!

Satisfying regulatory requirements

The first step in meeting this requirement is to establish a process that will identify all current regulatory requirements pertaining to the part or material.

You need to identify the regulations that apply in the country of manufacture and the country of sale. This may result in two different sets of requirements. For example a part may be manufactured in Mexico and sold in California or made in UK and sold in Syria. In one case the regulations on recycling materials may be tougher in the country of sale and in the other case, there may be restrictions prohibiting sale of vehicles containing materials from a particular country. It is difficult to keep track of changes in import and export regulations but using the services of a legal department or agency will ease the burden.

In order to ensure compliance with this requirement you need to impose on your suppliers through the purchase order, the relevant regulations and through examination of specifications, products and by on-site assessment, verify that these regulations are being met. It is not sufficient to merely impose the requirement upon your supplier through the purchase order. You can use the certified statements of authorized independent inspectors as proof of compliance instead of conducting the assessment yourself. However, such inspections may not extend to the product being supplied and therefore a thorough examination by your technical staff will be needed. Once deemed compliant, you need to impose change controls in the contract that prohibit the supplier changing the process or the product without your approval. This may not be possible when dealing with suppliers supplying product to their specification or when using offshore suppliers where the system of law enforcement cannot be relied upon. In such cases you will need to accurately define the product required and carry out periodic verification for continued compliance.

Criteria for periodic evaluation

For one-off purchases periodic re-evaluation would not be necessary. Where a commitment from both parties is made to supply products and services continually until terminated, some means of re-evaluation is necessary as a safeguard against deteriorating standards.

The re-evaluation may be based upon supplier performance, duration of supply, quantity, risk or changes in requirements and conducted in addition to any product verification that may be carried out. Suppliers are no different than customers in that their performance varies over time. People, organizations and technologies change and may impact the quality of the service obtained from suppliers. The increasing trend for customers to develop partnerships with suppliers has led to supplier development programmes where customers work with suppliers to develop their capability to improve process capability, delivery schedules or reduce avoidable costs. These programmes replace re-evaluations because they are ongoing and any deterioration in standards is quickly detected.

1994–2000 Differences

Previously the standard required that the supplier establish and maintain records of acceptable sub-contractors.

This modified requirement implies that such records should be more than a list of approved suppliers (the common interpretation) to a file of evaluation results.

Results of supplier evaluation (7.4.1)

The standard requires *the records of evaluations and any necessary follow-up actions to be maintained.*

What does this mean?

Records of evaluations are documents containing the results of the evaluation. This is not the Approved Supplier List or AVL used to select suppliers but the objective evidence that was used to make the decision as to whether a supplier should be listed in such a document.

Why is this necessary?

This requirement responds to the Factual Approach Principle.

Records of supplier evaluation are necessary in order to select suppliers on the basis of facts rather than opinion. They are also necessary for comparisons between competing suppliers as a mere listing provides little information on which to judge acceptability.

How is this implemented?

Although records of evaluations are not the same as a list of approved suppliers, there is a need for both. The list identifies which suppliers have been or not been evaluated and the records support the decision to include suppliers in the list or qualify suppliers in different categories.

Evaluation records

Evaluation records can be classified in three groups:

- Initial evaluation for supplier selection
- Supplier performance monitoring
- Re-evaluation to confirm approval status

The initial evaluation records would include the evaluation criteria, the method used, the results obtained and the conclusions. They may also include information relevant to the supplier such as supplier history, advertising literature, catalogues and approvals. These records may not contain actions and recommendations because the evaluation may have been carried out under a competitive tender. The actions come later, when re-evaluations are performed and continued supply is decided.

You should monitor the performance of all your suppliers and classify each according to prescribed guidelines. Supplier performance will be evident from audit reports, surveillance visit reports and receipt inspections carried out by you or the third party if one has been employed. You need to examine these documents for evidence that the supplier's quality system is controlling the quality of the products and services supplied. You can determine the effectiveness of these controls by periodic review of the supplier's performance. What some firms call 'vendor rating'. By collecting data on the performance of suppliers over a long period you can measure their effectiveness and rate them on a scale from excellent to poor. In such cases you should measure at least three characteristics, quality, delivery and service. Quality would be measured by the ratio of defective products to conforming products. Delivery would be measured by the number of days early or late and service would be measured by the responsiveness to actions requested by you on scale of excellent to poor. The output of these reviews should be in the form of updates to the list of assessed suppliers.

Re-evaluation records would include all the same information as the initial evaluation but in addition contain follow-up actions and recommendations, the supplier's response and evidence that any problems have been resolved.

Listing suppliers

It is important that you record those suppliers that should not be used due to previously demonstrated poor performance so that you don't repeat the mistakes of the past. Assessing suppliers is a costly operation. Having established that a supplier has or hasn't the capability of meeting your requirements you should enter their details in a database. The database should be made available to the purchasing authority thereby avoiding the necessity of re-assessments each time you wish to place an order. The database of assessed suppliers should not only identify the name and address of the company but also provide details of the products and service that have been evaluated. This is important because the evaluation performed to place suppliers on the list will have only covered particular products and services. Other products and services offered by the supplier may not have been acceptable. Some firms operate several production lines each to different standards. A split between military products and civil products is most common. Just because the military line met your requirement doesn't mean that the civil line will also meet your requirements. Calling it a List of Assessed Suppliers does not imply that it only lists approved firms – it allows you to include records of all firms with which you have done business and classify them accordingly. By linking purchases with the List of Assessed Suppliers you can indicate usage status e.g. current, dormant or unused.

You will need a process for generating and managing the database of Assessed Suppliers adding new suppliers, changing data and reclassifying suppliers that no longer meet your criteria.

Purchasing information (7.4.2)

Describing products to be purchased (7.4.2)

The standard requires purchasing information to *describe the product to be purchased.*

What does this mean?

Purchasing information is the information that identifies the product or service to be purchased and which is used to make purchasing decisions. Not all of this information may be conveyed to the supplier. Some information may be needed by buyers to select the correct product or service required.

Why is this necessary?

This requirement responds to the Process Approach Principle.

The supplier needs to know what the organization requires before it can satisfy the need and although the standard does not specifically require the information to be recorded, you need to document purchasing requirements so that you have a record of what you ordered. This can then be used when the goods and the invoice arrive to confirm that you have received what you ordered. The absence of such a record may prevent you from returning unwanted or unsatisfactory goods.

How is this implemented?

The essential purchasing information must be communicated to suppliers so that they know what you require, but it is not essential to submit your purchasing documents to your suppliers. In fact many purchases will be made from catalogues by telephone, quoting reference number and quantity required. Providing you have a record and can compare this with the goods received and the invoice, you are protected against paying for goods you didn't order.

Product identification

The product or service identification should be sufficiently precise as to avoid confusion with other similar products or services. The supplier may produce several versions of the same product and denote the difference by suffixes to the main part number. To ensure you receive the product you require you need to carefully consult the literature provided and specify the product in the same manner as specified in the literature or as otherwise advised by the supplier.

Purchasing specifications

If you are procuring the services of a supplier to design and/or manufacture a product or design and/or deliver a service, you will need specifications which detail all the features and characteristics which the product or service is to exhibit. The reference number and issue status of the specifications need to be specified in the event that they change after placement of the purchase order. This is also a safeguard against the repetition of problems with previous supplies. These specifications should also specify the means by which the requirements are to be verified so that you have confidence in any certificates of compliance that are supplied. For characteristics that are achieved using special processes you need to ensure that the supplier employs qualified personnel and equipment. Products required for particular applications need to be qualified for such applications and so your purchasing documents will need to specify what qualification tests are required.

Quality management system requirements

Management system requirements are only necessary inclusions in purchasing information when the quality of the product cannot be verified on receipt or when confidence in the product and the supplier is needed to permit the supplier to ship direct into stock or onto the production line.

Management system requirements can be invoked in your purchasing documents whether or not your supplier is registered to a management system standard, but doing so may cause difficulties. If the firm is not registered they may not accept the requirement or may well ignore it, in which case you will need to compensate by invoking surveillance and audit requirements in the order. If your purchasing documents do not reference the appropriate ISO 9000 standard or its equivalent and you have taken alternative measures to assure the quality of the supplies, you need not invoke quality management requirements in the order. There is little point in imposing ISO 9000 on non-registered suppliers when ordering from a catalogue. It only makes sense when the supplier is prepared to make special arrangements for your particular order – arrangements which may well cost you more for no added value. Remember that the requirements in clause 7.4.2 apply only where applicable.

Adequacy of purchasing requirements (7.4.2)

The standard *requires* the organization to *ensure the adequacy of specified purchase requirements prior to their communication to the supplier.*

What does this mean?

The adequacy of purchasing information is judged by the extent to which it accurately reflects the requirements of the organization for the products concerned. Communication of such requirements to

1994–2000 Differences
Previously the standard required the supplier to review and approve purchasing documents for adequacy of specified requirements prior to release.
This modified requirement does not change the intent.

the supplier can be verbal or through documentation and processed by post or electronically.

Why is this necessary?

This requirement responds to the Factual Approach Principle.

The acceptance of an order by a supplier places it under an obligation to accept product or service that meets the stated requirements. It is therefore important that such information is deemed adequate before being released to the supplier.

How is this implemented?

Prior to orders being placed the purchasing information should be checked to verify that it is fit for its purpose. The extent to which you carry out this activity should be on the basis of risk and if you choose not to review and approve all purchasing information, your procedures should provide the rationale for your decision. In some cases orders are produced using a computer and transmitted to the supplier directly without any evidence that the order has been reviewed or approved. The purchase order does not have to be the only purchasing document. If you enter purchasing data onto a database, a simple code used on a purchase order can provide traceability to the approved purchasing documents.

You can control the adequacy of the purchasing data in three ways:

- Provide the criteria for staff to operate under self-control.
- Check everything they do.
- Select those orders that need to be checked on a sample basis.
- Classify orders depending on risk and only review and approve those that present a certain risk.

A situation where staff operate under self control would be in the case of telephone orders where there is little documentary evidence that a transaction has taken place. There may be an entry on a computer database showing that an order has been placed with a particular supplier. So how would you ensure the adequacy of purchasing requirements in such circumstances? There follows a number of steps you can take:

- Provide buyers with read only access to approved purchasing data in the database.
- Provide buyers with read only access to a list of approved suppliers in the database.
- Provide a computer file containing details of purchasing transactions with read and write access.

- Provide a procedure that defines the activities, responsibilities and authority of all staff involved in the process.
- Train the buyers in the use of the database.
- Route purchase requisitions only to trained buyers for processing.

The above approach is suitable for processing routine orders, however, where there are non-standard conditions a more variable process needs to be developed.

Verification of purchased product (7.4.3)

Ensuring purchased product meets requirements (7.4.3)

The standard requires the organization to *establish and implement the inspection or other activities necessary for ensuring that purchased product meets specified purchase requirements.*

What does this mean?

Verification is one the fundamental elements of the control loop and in this case the verification serves to ensure the output from the purchasing process meets the purchasing requirement. Verification may be achieved by several means, inspection, test, analysis before or after product is delivered or by building confidence in the source of supply so that product may enter the organization without any physical inspection. The requirement does not state when such verification should be performed and clearly it can be before, during and after receipt of the product. The standard leaves it to the organization's discretion to choose the timing that is appropriate to its operations.

> **1994–2000 Differences**
>
> Previously this requirement was split into three separate requirements those for:
>
> (a) Receiving inspection and testing (clause 4.10.2)
> (b) Supplier verification at supplier's premises (clause 4.6.4.1)
> (c) Customer verification of subcontracted product (clause 4.6.4.2).
>
> Though less prescriptive the new requirement does not change the intent and is more concise.

Why is this necessary?

This requirement responds to the Factual Approach Principle.

When we purchase items as individuals it is a natural act to inspect what you have purchased before you use it. To neglect to do this may result in you forfeiting your rights to return it later if found defective or nonconforming. When we purchase items on behalf of our employers we may not be as tenacious, so the company has to enforce its own receipt inspection policy as a way of protecting itself from the mistakes of its suppliers. Another reason for inspecting product on receipt is that it is often the case that characteristics are not accessible for inspection or test after subsequent processing. Characteristics that have not been verified prior to or on receipt may never be verified.

How is this implemented?

There are several ways of verifying that purchased product meets requirements and these were outlined previously under *Selecting the degree of control*. Assessments by third parties alone would not give sufficient confidence to remove all receiving inspection for deliveries from a particular supplier. You need to examine product as well as the system until you have gained the confidence to reduce inspection and eventually remove it.

Timing of verification activities

If you have verified that product conforms to the specified requirements before it arrives you can receive product into your company and straight onto the production line. An example of this is where you have performed acceptance tests or witnessed tests on the supplier's premises. You may also have obtained sufficient confidence in your supplier that you can operate a 'just-in-time' arrangement but you must be able to show that you have a continuous monitoring programme that informs you of the supplier's performance.

If you have not verified that product meets requirements before it arrives you need to install a 'gate' through which only conforming items may pass. You need to register the receipt of items and then pass them to an inspection station equipped to determine conformance with your purchasing requirements. If items would normally pass into stores following inspection, as a safeguard you should also make provision for the store-person to check that all items received have been through inspection, rejecting any that have not. By use of labels attached to items you can make this a painless routine. If some items are routed directly to the user, you need a means of obtaining written confirmation that the items conform to the prescribed requirements so that at receipt inspection you can provide evidence that:

- Nothing comes into the company without being passed through inspection and
- Nothing can come out of inspection without it being verified as conforming

If the user is unable to verify that requirements have been met, you will need to provide either evidence that it has passed your receipt inspection or has been certified by the vendor.

Receiving inspection

The verification plans should prescribe the acceptance criteria for carrying out receipt inspection. The main aspects to cover are as follows:

- Define how the receipt inspection personnel obtain current purchasing requirements.
- Categorize all items that you purchase so that you can assign levels of receipt inspection based on given criteria.
- For each level of inspection, define the checks that are to be carried out and the acceptance criteria to be applied.
- Where dimensional and functional checks are necessary, define how the receipt inspection personnel obtain the acceptance criteria and how they are to conduct the inspections and tests.
- Define the action to be taken when product, the packaging or the documentation is found to be acceptable.
- Define the action to be taken when the product, the packaging or the documentation is found to be unacceptable.
- Define the records to be maintained.

Evaluation of supplier's statistical data

If the supplier supplies statistical data from the manufacturing process that indicates that quality is being controlled, then an analysis of this data based on assurances you have obtained through site evaluation can provide sufficient confidence in part quality to permit release into the organization.

Where you have required your suppliers to send a certificate of conformity (C of C) testifying the consignment's conformity with the order, you cannot omit all receiving checks. Once supplier capability has been verified, the C of C allows you to reduce the frequency of incoming checks but not to eliminate them. The C of C may need to be supported with test results therefore you would need to impose this requirement in your purchasing documents. However, take care to specify exactly what test results you require and in what format you require them presented because you could be provided with attribute data when you really want variables data.

Purchased labour

This requirement poses something of a dilemma when purchasing subcontract labour because clearly it cannot be treated the same as product. You still need to ensure, however, that the labour conforms with your requirements before deployment to the job. Such checks will include verification that the personnel provided have the requisite qualifications, skills and knowledge and they are who they say they are. These checks can be made on the documentary evidence provided such as certificates, but you will probably wish to monitor their performance because it is the effort you have purchased not the people. You will not be able to verify whether they are entirely suitable until you have evaluated their performance so you need to keep records of the personnel and their performance during the tenure of the contract.

Dealing with product audits on supplier's premises

Within your procedures you need to provide a means of identifying which items have been subject to inspection at the supplier's premises and the receipt inspection action to be taken depending on the level of that inspection. In one case, your representative on the supplier's premises may have accepted the product. In another case, your representative may have accepted a product from the same batch but not the batch that has been delivered. Alternatively your representative may have only performed a quality audit to gain a level of confidence. You need to specify the inspection to be carried out in all such cases. Even if someone has performed inspection at the supplier's premises, if there is no evidence of conformance the inspections are of little value. The fact that an inspection was carried out is insufficient. There has to be a statement of what was checked, what results were obtained and a decision as to whether conformance had been achieved. Without such evidence you may need to repeat some of the inspections carried out on the supplier's premises.

Verification on supplier premises (7.4.3)

1994–2000 Differences

Previously the standard required:

(a) the supplier to specify verification arrangements and the method of product release in the purchasing documents;

(b) the customer to be afforded the right to verify that subcontracted product conforms to specified requirement.

The intent of the requirement remains unchanged.

The standard requires that *where the organization or its customer intends to perform verification activities at the supplier's premises, the organization is to state the intended verification arrangements and method of product release in the purchasing information.*

What does this mean?

If you choose a verification method other than receipt inspection that involves a visit to the supplier's premises, the supplier has a right to know and the proper vehicle for doing this is through the purchasing information such as a contract or order.

Why is this necessary?

This requirement responds to the Factual Approach Principle.

The supplier needs to know if you or your customers intend to enter its premises to verify product before shipment so that they may make the necessary arrangements and establish that the proposed methods are acceptable to them.

How is this implemented?

Verification by the organization

The acceptance methods need to be specified at the tendering stage so that the supplier can make provision in the quotation to support any of your activities on site. When you visit a supplier you enter its premises only with their permission. The product remains their property until you have paid for it and therefore you need to be very careful how you behave. The contract or order is likely to only give access rights to products and areas related to your order and not to other products or areas. You cannot dictate the methods the supplier should use unless they are specified in the contract. It is the results in which you should be interested not the particular practices unless you have evidence to demonstrate that the steps they are taking will affect the results.

Verification by the customer

In cases where your customer requires access to your suppliers to verify the quality of supplies, you will need to transmit this requirement to your supplier in the purchasing information and obtain agreement. Where a firm's business is wholly that of contracting to customer requirements, a clause giving their customers certain rights will be written into their standard purchasing conditions. If this is an unusual occurrence, you need to identify the need early in the contract and ensure it is passed on to those responsible for preparing subcontracts. You may also wish to impose on your customer a requirement that you are given advanced notice of any such visits so that you may arrange an escort. Unless you know your customer's representative very well it is unwise to allow unaccompanied visits to your suppliers. You may for instance have changed, for good reasons, the requirements that were imposed on you as the main contractor when you prepared the subcontract and in ignorance your customer could inadvertently state that these altered requirements are unnecessary.

When customers visit your suppliers or inspect product on receipt, they have the right to reserve judgment on the final acceptance of the product because it is not under their direct control and they may not be able to carry out all the test and inspections that are required to gain sufficient confidence. Customer visits are to gain confidence and not to accept product. The same rules apply to you when you visit your suppliers. The final decision is the one made on receipt or some time later when the product is integrated with your equipment and you can test it thoroughly in its operating environment or equivalent.

Production and service provision (7.5)

Control of production and service provision (7.5.1)

Planning production and service provision (7.5.1)

The standard requires the organization to *plan and carry out production and service provision under controlled conditions.*

What does this mean?

The process referred to in this section of the standard is the result producing process, the process of implementing or replicating the design. It is the process that is cycled repeatedly to generate product or to deliver service. It differs from the design process in that it is arranged to reproduce product or service to the same standard each and every time. The design process is a journey into the unknown whereas the production process is a journey along a proven path with a predictable outcome. The design process requires control to keep it on course towards an objective, the production process requires control to maintain a prescribed standard.

There are two ways in which product quality can be controlled: by controlling the product that emerges from the producing processes or by controlling the processes through which the product passes. Process control relies upon control of the elements that drive the process, whereas product control relies upon verification of the product as it emerges from the process. In practice it is a combination of these that yields products of consistent quality. If you concentrate on the process output to the exclusion of all else, you will find there is a high level of rework of the end product. If you concentrate on the process using the results of the product verification, you will gradually reduce rework until all output products are of consistent quality. It will therefore be possible to reduce dependence on output verification.

Controlled conditions are conditions under which the outputs are predictable and are capable of being changed by a measurable degree. If the factors that affect process outputs could not be identified and changed, the process is not under control. There are usually eight factors that affect the control of any process.

- The quality of the people – competence to do the job with the required proficiency when required. If you can't identify the competency of personnel required and choose those with the required competence, you are not in control of the process unless you can compensate by changing other parameters. (Clause 6.2.1)
- The quality of the physical resources – capability of plant, machinery, equipment, tools. If you can't identify the physical resources required and choose or change them so that capability is improved, you are not in control of the process. (Clause 7.5.1c)
- The quality of the physical environment – level of temperature, cleanliness, vibration. If you can't identify the physical environment required or change it, you are not in control of the process. (Clause 6.4)

- The quality of the human environment – degree of physical stress, physiological stress, motivation. If you can't identify the human factors required in the work environment required and alter their effect, you are not in control of the process. (Clause 6.4)
- The quality of the information – degree of accuracy, currency, completeness, usability, validity. If you can't identify the information required and improve it, you are not in control of the process. (Clause 7.5.1a and b)
- The quality of materials – adequacy of physical properties, their consistency and purity. If you can't identify the materials required and change their properties, you are not in control of the process. (Clause 7.4)
- The quantity of resources – time, money, information, people, materials, components, equipment etc. If you can't identify the quantities required and adjust them to suit the demand, you are not in control of the process. (Clause 6.1)
- The quality of measurement – units, values, timing and integrity. If you can't identify the measurements to be taken, the units of measure, the target values and when to take them and control the integrity of measurement you are not in control of the process. (Clause 7.5.1d, e and 7.6)

Only three of these factors are addressed by clause 7.5.2 of the standard. The others are addressed by other clauses of the standard meaning that the list of items in clause 7.5.1 is not all that you would need to do to provide controlled conditions.

The use of the term *provision* in the requirement is not significant to its meaning. The term *process* would have been more consistent with the principles upon which the standard is based.

Why is this necessary?

This requirement responds to the Leadership Principle.

Controlled conditions enable the organization to achieve its objectives. If operations were carried out in conditions in which there were no controls, the outputs would be the result of chance and totally unpredictable.

How is this implemented?

The planning of production and servicing processes requires three levels:

- Identifying which processes are required to produce products and deliver services
- Designing, commissioning and qualifying these processes for operational use
- Routing the product through the appropriate qualified processes or running the service delivery process

Production planning

In order to identify the production processes required to produce a particular product you need a production requirement in the form of product specifications which define the features and characteristics of the product which are to be achieved. By studying these specifications you will be able to identify the processes required to turn raw materials and bought out components into a finished product. With manufactured products the processes may include, machining, welding, fabrication, assembly, forming, plating, painting, heat treatment etc.

The next stage is to design the processes that have been identified. In many cases, existing processes may well satisfy the need but process approval may be required if the tolerance on product characteristics is much less than the currently demonstrated process capability.

The plans that route an item through the various processes from raw material to finished product are often called route cards or shop travellers. You may need separate plans for each process and each part with an overall plan which ensures the product goes through the right processes in the right sequence. The number of plans is usually determined by the manner in which the specifications are drawn up. You may have drawings for each part to be made or one drawing covering several parts.

Unless products, processes and facilities are developed in parallel, the product will be unlikely to reach the market when required. This requires product and process development to proceed simultaneously with facility development and as a consequence the term 'simultaneous engineering' or 'concurrent engineering' has emerged to optimize the relationship between design and manufacturing functions. It is not a case of designing only those products for which facilities exist, but designing those products that will give you a competitive edge and laying down facilities that will enable you to fulfil that promise.

To ensure that the processes are carried out under controlled conditions the production plans need to:

● Identify the product in terms of the specification reference and its issue status
● Define the quantity required
● Define which section is to perform the work
● Define each stage of manufacture and assembly
● Provide for progress through the various processes to be recorded so that you know what stage the product has reached at any one time
● Define the special tools, processing equipment, jigs, fixtures and other equipment required to produce the product (General purpose tools and equipment need not be specified because your staff should be trained to select the right tool for the job.)

- Define the methods to be used to produce the product either directly or by reference to separate instructions
- Define the environment to be maintained during production of the product if anything other than ambient conditions
- Define the process specifications and workmanship standards to be achieved

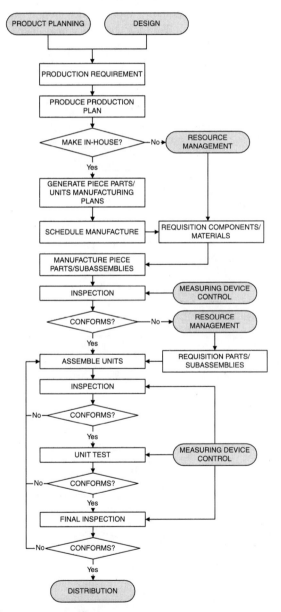

Figure 7.9 Production process flow

- Define the stages at which inspections and test are to be performed and the methods to be used
- Define any special handling, packaging, marking requirements to be met
- Define any precautions to be observed to protect health, safety and environment

These plans create a basis for ensuring that work is carried out under controlled conditions, but the staff, equipment, materials, processes and documentation must be up to the task before work commences. A simple

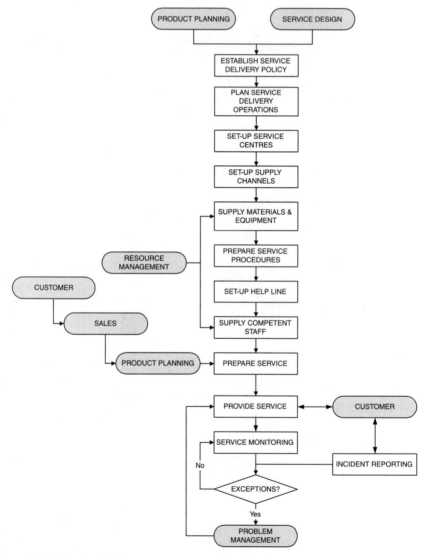

Figure 7.10 Service delivery process

production process is illustrated in Figure 7.9. The shaded boxes indicate interfaces external to the production process. The variables are too numerous to illustrate the intermediate steps.

Service planning

The variety of different types of services makes it impractical to lay down any prescription for how they should be planned apart from some fundamental provisions. A typical service delivery process flow is illustrated in Figure 7.10.

To ensure that the processes are carried out under controlled conditions the service delivery plans need to:

- Define the service objectives and targets
- Define the stages in the process to achieve these objectives
- Define the inputs and outputs for each stage in the process
- Define the resources required to generate these inputs and outputs
- Define the methods to be used to operate any equipment and generate the inputs and outputs
- Define the methods of measuring stage outputs
- Define the methods of ensuring the integrity of these measurements
- Define the information and resources required for each stage to be performed as planned
- Define the actions to be taken when problems are encountered
- Define the information provided to service users that indicates the operation and availability of the service
- Define the precautions to be observed to protect health, safety and environment

Availability of information that describes the product (7.5.1a)

The standard requires the organization to *control production and service provision through the availability of information that describes the characteristics of the product.*

1994–2000 Differences
This is a new requirement that has no equivalent in the 1994 version.

What does this mean?

This information tells you what to make or provide and the criteria the output must meet for it to be fit for its purpose. The information is the input to the production or service delivery process usually coming out of the design process but may be direct from customers. It may take the form of definitive specifications, drawings, layouts or any information that specifies the physical and functional characteristics that the product or service is required to meet.

Why is this necessary?

This requirement responds to the Process Approach Principle.

Information is one of the key factors needed to control processes. Without information specifying the product to be produced or the service to be delivered, there is no basis upon which to commence production.

How is this implemented?

In order to ensure the right information is available, there needs to be a communication channel opened between the product design and production process or the service design and the service delivery process as appropriate. Along this channel needs to pass all the information required to produce and accept the product or deliver the service. Provision also needs to be made for transmitting changes to this information in such a manner that the recipients can readily determine what the changes are and why they have been made. Often the design information is reissued, identified with a revision code leaving the recipient to work out what has changed and whether it affects what has gone before. The change management process therefore needs to take into account the factors that affect the effectiveness of the interfacing processes.

Availability of work instructions (7.5.1b)

1994–2000 Differences

Previously the standard required controlled conditions to include documented procedures defining the manner of production, installation and servicing where the absence of such instructions would adversely affect quality.

The change in wording does not change the intent of this requirement.

The standard requires the organization to *control production and service provision through the availability of work instructions where necessary.*

What does this mean?

Information is one of the key factors needed to control processes. In addition to information specifying the product characteristics to be achieved, information relating to how, when and where the activities required to convert the inputs into useable outputs are to be performed will be needed. This type of information is often termed as work instructions. There are two forms of work instructions – instructions that inform people what work to do and when to do it and instructions that inform people how to do work – the latter are often called procedures. This topic is addressed in more detail in Chapter 4.

The requirement implies that work instructions may not always be required. While it is true that documented work instructions may not always be necessary, it is hard to imagine any production or service work proceeding without there being either an instruction or an identified need. Some people take instructions from their managers, others take instruction from the situation, the equipment or other signals they receive.

Why is this necessary?

This requirement responds to the Process Approach Principle.

As people are not normally mind readers, they are unlikely to know what is required unless the work instructions come direct from the customer or the supplier. Once they know what is required they may need further instructions on how to carry out the work because it is not intuitive or learnt through education and training. Work instructions may also be necessary to ensure consistent results. In fact any operation that requires tasks to be carried out in a certain sequence to obtain consistent results should either be specified through work instructions or procedures or developed into a habit.

How is this implemented?

Work instructions can take many forms:

- Schedules indicating when work should be complete
- Plans indicating what work is to be performed and what resources are available
- Specifications indicating the results the work should achieve
- Process descriptions indicating the stages through which work must pass
- Procedures indicating how work should be performed and verified

There are instructions for specific activities and instructions for specific individuals – whether they are contractors or employees is not important – the same requirements apply. As each employee may perform different jobs, they may each have a different set of instructions that direct them to specific sources of information. Therefore it is unnecessary to combine all instructions into one document although they could all be placed in the same binder for easy access.

By imposing formal controls you safeguard against informality that may prevent you from operating consistent, reliable and predictable processes. The operators and their supervisors may know the tricks and tips for getting the equipment or the process to operate smoothly. You should discourage informal instructions because you cannot rely on them being used by others when those who know them are absent. If the tips or tricks are important, encourage those who know them to bring them to the process owner's attention so that changes can be made to make the process run smoothly all the time.

If you have a manufacturing process that relies on skill and training then instructions at the workstation are unnecessary. For example, if fixing a tool in a tool holder on a lathe is a skill, learnt during basic training, you don't need to provide instructions at each workstation where normal tool changes take place. However, if the alignment of the tool is critical and requires knowledge of a setting up procedure, then either documented instruction or training is necessary. Even for basic skills you can still provide standard machinery data books that are accessible near the workstation. There is merit in not providing basic textbooks to operators because the information is soon outdated and operators relying on such data instead of consulting the authorized data may inadvertently induce variation into the process.

Use of suitable equipment (7.5.1c)

1994–2000 Differences

Previously the standard required:

(a) suitable maintenance of equipment to ensure continued process capability;

(b) controlled conditions to include the use of suitable production, installation and servicing equipment.

There is no change in intent although, the removal of the phrase 'continued process capability', does imply a less stringent requirement.

The standard requires the organization to *control production and service provision through the use of suitable equipment.*

What does this mean?

Equipment is one of the key factors needed to control processes. Suitable equipment is equipment of the right type and capability to fulfil the requirements for which it is needed. Although the term equipment is used, the intent is to imply any physical resource that is needed to achieve the process objectives. It means that the resources have to be serviceable and capable of the performance, accuracy and precision required i.e. maintained, calibrated, qualified, verified or otherwise approved as appropriate.

Why is this necessary?

This requirement responds to the Process Approach Principle.

Process outputs cannot be achieved unless the physical resources that are essential to perform the work are fit for their purpose. In any other state, the human resources would be used to compensate for the inadequacies of the equipment – a state that can be sustained in some circumstances but not for long without degrading the quality of the work.

How is this implemented?

The equipment should be selected during the planning process. In selecting such equipment you should determine whether it is capable of producing, maintaining or handling conforming product in a consistent manner. You also need to ensure that the equipment is capable of achieving the specified dimensions within the stated tolerances. Process capability studies can reveal deficiencies with equipment that are not immediately apparent from inspection of the first off.

There may be documentation available from the supplier of the equipment that adequately demonstrates its capability, otherwise you may need to carry out qualification and capability tests to your own satisfaction. In the process industries the plant is specially designed and so needs to be commissioned and qualified by the user. Your procedures need to provide for such activities and for records of the tests to be maintained.

When equipment or plant is taken out of service either for maintenance or for repair, it should not be re-introduced into service without being subject to formal acceptance tests which are designed to verify that it meets your declared standard operating conditions. Your procedures need to provide for such activities and for records of the tests to be maintained.

Use of monitoring and measuring devices (7.5.1d)

The standard requires the organization to *control production and service provision through the availability and use of measuring and monitoring devices.*

What does this mean?

Measurement is one of the key factors needed to control processes. This means providing the devices needed to measure product features and monitor process performance and also providing adequate training and instruction for these devices to be used as intended.

Why is this necessary?

This requirement responds to the Process Approach Principle.

Product quality can only be determined if the devices needed to measure and monitor product and process characteristics are available and used.

> **1994–2000 Differences**
> Previously the standard required:
> (a) the use of suitable production, installation and servicing equipment;
> (b) the monitoring of suitable process parameters.
> Although not explicit the requirement for use of measuring and monitoring devices is implied in the previous requirements through the term *process control.*

How is this implemented?

When designing the process for producing product or delivering service you should have provided stages at which product/service features are verified and/or installed monitoring devices that indicate when the standard operating conditions have been achieved and whether they are being maintained. The devices used to perform measurements need to be available where the measurements are to be performed. The monitoring devices need to be accessible to process operators for information on the performance of the process to be obtained. The monitoring devices may be located in inaccessible places providing the signals are transmitted to the operators controlling the process.

Implementation of monitoring and measurement activities (7.5.1e)

The standard requires the organization to *control production and service provision through the implementation of monitoring and measurement.*

What does this mean?

Measurement is one of the key factors needed to control processes. Measurement and monitoring is the means by which product and process characteristics are determined. The specifications define the target values and the process description or plan defines when measurements should be taken to ascertain whether the targets have been met.

Why is this necessary?

This requirement responds to the Factual Approach Principle.

In order to control product quality the achieved characteristics need to be measured and the process operating conditions need to be monitored. All controls need a verification stage and a feedback loop. You cannot control production processes without performing some kind of verification.

How is this implemented?

Controlled conditions in production include in-process monitoring and in-process inspection and test. In a service delivery process they may include inspections of information, personnel and facilities as well as a review of process outputs.

The production of some products can be controlled simply by inspection after the product has been produced. In other cases, such as with the continuous production of food and drugs, you may need to monitor certain process parameters to be sure of producing conforming product. By observing the variability of certain parameters using control charts, you can determine whether the process is under control within the specified limits.

The purpose of monitoring the process is firstly to establish its capability of producing product correctly and consistently and secondly to alert the process operators to conditions that indicate that the process is becoming incapable of producing the product correctly and consistently.

Process monitoring can be achieved by observing sensors installed in the production process that measure key process parameters or, samples can be taken at discrete intervals and prescribed measurements taken. In both cases the measurements should be recorded for subsequent analysis and any decision made to allow the process to continue or to stop should also be recorded together with the reasons for the decision. The data to be recorded should be specified in advance on the forms or computer screens provided at the workstation. This will give personnel a clear indication of what to record, when and where to record it. It also simplifies auditing if data is required in all boxes on a form or computer screen. A blank box would then indicate an unusual occurrence that should be checked. The forms should also indicate the accept/reject limits so that the operator can easily judge when the process is out of control.

Operators should be trained to both operate the plant and control the process. As added assurance you should take samples periodically and subject them to a thorough examination. The sampling plan should be defined and documented and operators trained to determine what causes the results they observe. *Operators should therefore understand what causes the dots on the chart to vary.* Process control comes about by operators knowing what results to achieve, by knowing what results are being achieved and by being able to correct performance should the results not be as required. They need to understand what is happening during processing to cause any change in the results as they are being monitored. In the process specification you will need to define the parameters to be observed and recorded and the limits within which the process is to be controlled.

Release processes (7.5.1f)

The standard requires *the implementation of release activities.*

This greatly simplified requirement puts the emphasis on release processes, whereas the previous requirement highlighted only some stages where release controls were necessary. The implication is that the management system may well require an overhaul to identify such transition processes.

What does this mean?

Release activities are decision points where process output is confirmed as complete and moved onto the next stage in a process or to another process. These are sometimes called 'gates' through which product has to pass before being deemed acceptable for further processing or delivery.

1994–2000 Differences

Previously the standard required the supplier to:

(a) hold product until requirement inspection and tests had been completed;

(b) positively identify product where incoming product is released for urgent production purposes prior to verification;

(c) ensure incoming product is not used or processed until it has been inspected or otherwise verified as conforming;

(d) ensure only product that has passed the required inspections and tests is used or installed;

(e) stipulate appropriate methods for authorizing receipt to and dispatch from storage areas.

In this far less prescriptive requirement there is no change in intent.

Why is this necessary?

This requirement responds to the Process Approach Principle.

Within the chain of processes from customer requirement to delivery of product there are many interfaces between processes. Were there to be no decision points between processes, errors may pass from one process to another resulting in customer dissatisfaction.

How is this implemented?

In the production process there are several release points:

- Release from component storage; where components and materials are held pending completion of the input requirement
- Release from job set-up; where work is held pending verification of job set-up
- Release from in-process inspection; where product is held pending completion or rework, sample tests, repair etc.
- Release from final inspection; where product is held pending completion of all inspection stages, sampling etc.
- Release from finished product storage; where product is held pending receipt of customer order or customer instruction

Release from storage areas

The content of storage areas should be known at all time in order that you can be confident that only that which is in storage areas is of a known condition. Storage areas containing conforming items should be separate from those containing nonconforming items. It follows therefore that when an item is taken from a storage area the person taking it should be able to rely on it conforming unless otherwise stated on the label. If free access is given to add and remove items in such areas, this confidence is lost. If at any time the controls are relaxed, the whole stock becomes suspect.

There is often a need to supply items as free issue because the inadvertent loss of small value items is less than the cost of the controls to prevent such loss. This practice can be adopted only if the quality of the items can be determined wholly by visual inspection by the person using them.

There are however, issues other than quality that will govern the control of items in stock. Inventory control is a vital part of any business. Stock ties up capital, so the less stock that is held the more capital the firm has available to apply to producing output.

A common solution that satisfies both inventory control and quality control is to institute a stock requisition system. Authorization of requisitions may be given by a person's supervisor or can be provided via a work order. If someone has been authorized to carry out a particular job, this should authorize the person to requisition the items needed. Again for inventory control reasons you may wish to impose a limit on such authority, requiring the person to seek higher authority for items above a certain value.

Held product

In continuous production, product is inspected by taking samples from the line that are then examined whilst the line continues producing product. In such cases you will need a means of holding product produced between sampling points until the results of the tests and inspections are available. You will also need a means of releasing product when the results indicate that the product is acceptable. So a Product Release Procedure, or Held Product Procedure may be necessary.

Release from job set-ups

In setting up a job prior to commencing a production run, you need to verify that all the requirements for the part are being met. You will therefore need job-set-up instructions so as to ensure each time the production of a particular part commences, the process is set up against the same criteria. In addition, process parameters may change whenever there is material changeover, a job change or if significant time periods lapse between production runs.

Documentation verifying job set-ups should include instructions to perform the set-up and records that demonstrate that the set-up has been performed as required. This requires that you record the parameters set, the sample size and retain the control charts used that indicate performance.

Release from inspection

Every verification is a stage where product is verified as either conforming or nonconforming. Provisions are needed for signifying when product is ready for release either to the next stage in the process, into quarantine store awaiting decision or back into the process for rework or completion. Often this takes the form of an inspection label appropriately annotated. With services, release is often signified by an 'In-service' notice a 'Ready' indicator, illuminated sign or other indicator. In many cases however, it is only 'Out of Service' notices that are posted.

Delivery processes (7.5.1f)

The standard requires *the implementation of delivery activities*.

What does this mean?

Delivery is an activity that serves the shipment or transmission of product to the customer and is one part of the distribution process. Delivery may

> **1994–2000 Differences**
>
> Previously the standard required the supplier to ensure only product that has passed the required inspections and tests is dispatched.
>
> The previous delivery requirements were limited to protection measures.

include preparation for delivery such as packing, notification, transportation, customs, arrival at destination and unpacking on customer premises. In the consumer sector, this may involve agents, wholesalers, and retailers before the end user received the goods. In the service delivery process this means the fulfilment of the service and may include transmission of information and payment mechanisms. In the consumer goods market there may be intermediaries such as agents, wholesalers, retailers, resellers etc. which exist to distribute product to the customer.

Why is this necessary?

This requirement responds to the Process Approach Principle.

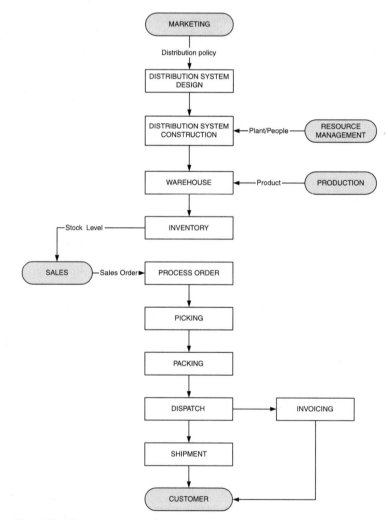

Figure 7.11 Distribution process flow

The process of moving goods from producers to customers is an important process in the management system. Although good product design, economic production and effective promotion are vital for success, these are useless if the customer cannot buy the product and take ownership. It is necessary to control delivery activities because conforming product may be degraded by the manner in which it is protected during transit and it may be delayed by the manner in which it is transported. You may be under an obligation to supply product by certain dates or within so many days of order and as a consequence control of the delivery process is vital to honour these obligations.

How is this implemented?

A typical distribution process is illustrated in Figure 7.11 indicating that like any process it needs to be designed and that the origin of the process inputs is the Marketing Process.

The distribution or marketing channel promotes the physical flow of goods and services along with ownership title, from producer to consumer or business user (Boone Louis E. and Kurtz David L, 2001)[3]. Often the logistics for moving goods to outlets where consumers are able to purchase them is a business in its own right but nevertheless starts out in the marketing process when determining the distribution strategy. There are several different distribution channels depending on the type of goods and the market into which they are to be sold as illustrated in Figure 7.12.

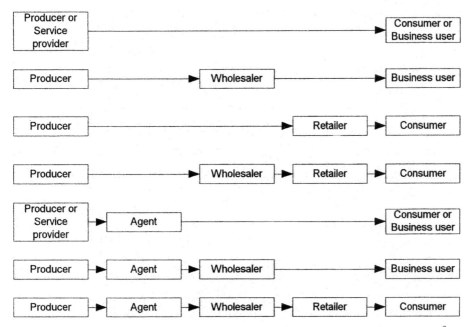

Figure 7.12 Distribution channels (Source: Adapted from Boonze and Kurtz 2001[3] Figure 13.2)

Delivery takes place between each of the parties in the distribution chain and for each party there are several aspects to the delivery process:

- Preparation of product such as cleaning and preservation
- Packing of product
- User information
- Product certification
- Labelling and transit information
- Handling
- Customer notification
- Transportation
- Tracking

Preparation and packing of product is addressed under preservation later in this chapter as the methods also apply to internal processing. However, within the delivery process there will be specific packing stages that are different in nature to internal packing stages.

Sometimes delivery is made electronically using a modem and telephone line. The product may be a software package, a document stored in electronic form or a facsimile. Protection of the product is still required but takes a different form. You need to protect the product against loss and corruption during transmission.

When shipping consumer goods it is necessary to include user information such as operating instructions, handbooks, warranty and return instructions.

Customers may require product certificates testifying the fulfilment of contracts or order requirement. Customs may require certain legal information on the outside of the package otherwise the consignment will be held at the port of entry and customers will be none too pleased.

The type of transport employed is a key factor in getting shipments to customers on time.

On-time delivery

To guarantee shipment on time, you either need to maintain an adequate inventory of finished goods, for shipment on demand or utilize only predictable processes and obtain sufficient advanced order information from your customer. Without sufficient lead-time on orders you will be unlikely to meet the target. There will be matters outside your control and matters over which you need complete control. It is the latter that you can do something about and take corrective action should the target not be achieved.

Firstly you need to estimate the production cycle time during the production trial runs in the product and process validation phase, assess risk areas and build in appropriate contingencies. An assessment of your supplier's previous delivery performance will also enable you to predict their future performance.

When new processes become stabilized over long periods and the frequency of improvement reduces as more and more problems are resolved, you will be able to reduce lead-time.

Your planning and delivery procedures need to record estimated and actual delivery dates and the data collected and analysed through delivery performance monitoring. When targets are not met you should investigate the cause under the corrective action procedures and formulate corrective action plans. Where the cause is found to be a failure of the customer to supply some vital information or equipment, it would be prudent not to wait for the periodic analysis but react promptly.

Customer notification

A means for notifying customer of pending delivery is often necessary. In some industries the supplier is linked with the customer electronically so that demands are transmitted from the customer to the supplier to trigger the delivery process. This does have its problems because the customer may need to change quantities and delivery dates due to variations in production. This does not mean the changes will always be to shorten delivery times but on occasions the delivery times may need to be extended owing to problems on the assembly line or as a result of problems with other suppliers. The customer may not have made provision to store your product so needs to be able to urgently inform you to hold or advance deliveries. If the customer reduced the quantity required from that previously demanded, you could be left with surplus product and consequently need protection through the contract for such eventualities.

Post delivery processes (7.5.1f)

The standard requires *the implementation of post-delivery activities.*

What does this mean?

Post delivery activities are those performed after delivery of the consignment to the customer and may include:

- Servicing
- Warranty claims
- Technical support
- Maintenance
- Logistics
- Installation

1994–2000 Differences

Previously the standard required the supplier to establish and maintain documented procedures for performing, verifying and reporting that servicing meets specified requirements.

The new requirement is far less specific but enlarges the scope of servicing.

Why is this necessary?

This requirement responds to the Customer Focus Principle.

Control of post delivery activities is just as important as pre-delivery if not more so as the customer may be losing use of the product and want prompt resolution to the problems encountered. Post delivery performance is often the principle reason why customers remain loyal or choose a competitor. Even if a product does give trouble, a sympathetic, prompt and courteous post delivery service can restore confidence.

How is this implemented?

The wide range of post delivery services makes a detailed analysis impractical in this book. However there are some simple measures that can be taken that would apply to all types of post delivery activities.

- Define the nature and purpose of the post delivery service.
- Define post delivery policies that cover such matters as handling complaints, offering replacement product, service/installation staff conduct.
- Establish conditions of post delivery contracts with customers.
- Specify objectives and measures for each feature of the service such as response time, resolution time.
- Communicate the policies and objectives and ensure their understanding by those involved.
- Define the stages in the process needed to achieve these objectives.
- Identify the information needs and ensure control of this information.
- Identify and provide the resources to deliver the service.
- Install verification stages to verify achievement of stage outputs.
- Provide communication channels for feeding intelligence into production and service design processes.
- Determine methods for measuring process performance.
- Measure process performance against objectives.
- Determine the capability of the process and make changes to improve performance.
- Determine process effectiveness and pursue continual improvement.

Validation of processes (7.5.2)

The standard requires the organization to *validate any production and service provision where the resulting output cannot be verified by subsequent measurement or monitoring.*

What does this mean?

Many processes do not present any difficulty in the verification of the output against the input requirements regardless of the tools, personnel, facilities or other means used to carry out the process. The resultant features and characteristics are relatively easily determined. However, there are some processes where the output is totally dependent upon the personnel, the equipment and the facilities and what is more, cannot be fully verified by examination of the end product at any stage of assembly. Among such processes are welding, soldering, adhesive bonding, casting, forging, forming, heat treatment, protective treatments and inspection and test techniques such as X-ray examination, ultrasonics, environmental tests, mechanical stress tests.

In service industries, special processes include correctness of financial or legal documents, software,

> **1994–2000 Differences**
>
> Previously the standard required special processes to be carried out by qualified operators and/or continuous monitoring and control of process parameters to ensure that the specified requirements are met.
>
> The previous requirement was phrased in such a way that the intent was unclear.

professional advice etc. In such cases, these processes are not separated for special treatment because all processes in the business may fall into this category.

Why is this necessary?

This requirement responds to the Factual Approach Principle.

If any of these factors upon which the performance of a process depends is less than adequate, deficiencies may not become apparent until long after the product is installed, used or enters service. Normally, product characteristics are verified before release but when this is not possible without destroying the product, the process needs to be qualified as capable of only producing conforming product.

How is this implemented?

To limit the potential for deficiencies to escape detection before the product is released, measures should be taken that ensure the suitability of all equipment, personnel, facilities and prevent varying conditions, activities or operations. A thorough assessment of the processes should be conducted to determine their capability to maintain or detect the conditions needed to consistently produce conforming product. The limits of capability need to be determined and the processes applied only within these limits.

You should produce and maintain a list of special processes that have been qualified as well as a list of the personnel who are qualified to operate them. In this way you can easily identify an unqualified process, an unauthorized person or an obsolete list if you have neglected to maintain it.

Where process capability relies upon the competence of personnel, personnel operating such processes need to be appropriately educated and trained and undergo examination of their competency. If subcontracting special processes you need to ensure that the supplier only employs qualified personnel and has qualified process equipment and facilities.

Where there is less reliance on personnel but more on the consistency of materials, environment and processing equipment, the particular conditions need to be specified and where necessary restrictions placed on the use of alternative materials, equipment and variations in the environment. Operating instructions should be used that define the set-up, operation and shut-down conditions and the sequence of activities required to produce consistent results. The resultant product needs to be thoroughly tested using such techniques that will enable the performance characteristics to be measured. This may involve destructive tests to measure tensile and compressive strength, purity, porosity, adhesion, electrical properties etc. In production, samples should be taken at set frequencies and the tests repeated.

In production you need to ensure that only those personnel, equipments, materials and facilities that were qualified are employed in the process otherwise you will invalidate the qualification and inject uncertainty into the results.

The records of qualified personnel using special processes should be governed by the training requirements. Regarding the equipment, you will need to identify the equipment and facilities required within the process specifications and maintain records of the equipment. This data may be needed to trace the source of any problems with product that was produced using this equipment. To take corrective action you will also need to know the configuration of the process plant at the time of processing the product. If only one piece of equipment is involved, the above records will give you this information but if the process plant consists of many items of equipment which are periodically changed during maintenance, you will need to know which equipment was in use when the fault was likely to have been generated.

Identification and traceability (7.5.3)

Identifying product (7.5.3)

The standard requires the organization to *identify the product by suitable means throughout product realization where appropriate.*

What does this mean?

The requirements for product identification are intended to enable products and services with one set of characteristics to be distinguishable from products or services with another set of characteristics.

The option of applying this requirement 'where appropriate' implies that there are situations where product identity is unnecessary. There are of course situations where attaching an identity to a product would be impractical such as in the chemical industries but the product nevertheless has an identity that is conveyed through the associated information. In the food industry, the biscuits on the conveyor might not carry an identity but the box into which they are packed does as does the instruction that ordered the biscuits to be produced. Thus identifying a product by suitable means might require the product to be labelled, or might require the container to be labelled. Services are somewhat different. Many are not identified other than by the nature of what the organization does by generic categories such as investment, mortgage, financial planning services of banks. Where there are differences for instance in interest

| 1994–2000 Differences |
| Previously the standard required the supplier to establish and maintain documented procedures where appropriate for identifying the product by suitable means from receipt and during all stages of production, delivery and installation. |
| The intent of the requirement remains unchanged. |

rates, the 'products' are given different names such as Instant Access Account, 90 Day account and so on.

Why is this necessary?

This requirement responds to the Process Approach Principle.

Product identity is vital in many situations to prevent inadvertent mixing, to enable reordering, to match products with documents that describe them and to do that basic of all human activities – to communicate. Without codes, numbers, labels, names and other forms of identification we cannot adequately describe the product or service to anyone else. The product must be identified in one way or another otherwise it cannot be matched to its specification.

How is this implemented?

Separate product identity is necessary where it is not inherently obvious. If products are so dissimilar that inadvertent mixing would be unlikely to occur, a means of physically identifying the products is probably unnecessary. 'Inherently obvious' in this context means that the physical differences are large enough to be visible to the untrained eye. Functional differences therefore, no matter how significant as well as slight differences in physical characteristics such as colour, size, weight, and appearance would constitute an appropriate situation for documented identification procedures.

Identifying product should start at the design stage when the product is conceived. The design should be given a unique identity, a name or a number and that should be used on all related information. When the product emerges into production, the product should carry the same number or name but in addition it should carry a serial number or other identification to enable product features to be recorded against specific products. If verification is on a go/no go basis, product does not need to be serialized. If measurements are recorded some means has to be found of identifying the measurements with the product measured. Serial numbers, batch numbers and date codes are suitable means for achieving this. This identity should be carried on all records related to the product.

Apart from the name or number given to a product you need to identify the version and the modification state so that you can relate the issues of the drawing and specifications to the product they represent. Products should either carry a label or markings with this type of information in an accessible position or bear a unique code number that is traceable to such information.

You may not possess any documents that describe purchased product. The only identity may be marked on the product itself or its container. Where there are no markings, information from the supplier's invoice or other such documents should be transferred to a label and attached to the product or the container. Information needs to be traceable to the products it represents.

The method of identification depends upon the type, size, quantity or fragility of the product. You can mark the product directly (provided the surface is not visible to the end user unless of course identity is part of the brand name) tie a label to it or the container in which it is placed. You can also use records remote from the product providing they bear a unique identity that is traceable to the product.

Marking products has its limitations because it may damage the product, be removed or deteriorate during subsequent processing. If applied directly to the product, the location and nature of identification should be specified in the product drawings or referenced process specifications. If applied to labels which are permanently secured to the product, the identification needs to be visible when the product is installed so as to facilitate checks without its removal. One situation which can be particularly irritating to customers is placing identification data on the back of equipment and then expecting the customer to state this identity when dealing with a service call thus causing delay while the customer dives under the desk to locate the serial number and drops the telephone in the panic!

Verification status (7.5.3)

The standard requires the organization to *identify the status of the product with respect to measurement and monitoring requirements.*

What does this mean?

Product status with respect to monitoring and measurement means an indication as to whether the product conforms or does not conform to specified requirements. Thus identifying product status enables conforming product to be distinguishable from nonconforming product.

Why is this necessary?

This requirement responds to the Factual Approach Principle.

Measurement does not change a product but does change our knowledge of it. Therefore it is necessary to identify which products conform and which do not so that inadvertent mixing, processing or delivery is prevented.

How is this implemented?

The most common method of denoting product status is to attach labels either to the product or to containers holding the product. *Green labels* for acceptable good and *Red labels* for reject goods. Labels should remain affixed until the product is either packed or installed. Labels should be attached in a way that prevents their detachment during handling. If labels need to be removed during further processing, the details should be transferred to inspection records so that at a later date the status of the components in an assembly can be checked through the records. At dispatch, product status should be visible. Any product without status identi-

> **1994–2000 Differences**
>
> Previously the standard requires the supplier to:
>
> (a) identify the inspection and test status of product by suitable means, which indicate the conformance or nonconformity of product with regard to inspection and tests performed;
>
> (b) maintain the identification of inspection and test status of the product, as defined in the quality plan and/or documented procedures throughout production, installation and servicing.
>
> The intent of the requirement remains unchanged.

fication should be quarantined until re-verified and found conforming. Once a product has passed through the product realization process and is in use, it requires no product status identity unless it is returned to the product realization process for repair or other action.

It should be possible when walking through a machine shop for example, to identify which products are awaiting verification, which have been verified and found conforming and which have been rejected. If by chance, some product was to become separated from its parent batch, it should still be possible to return the product to the location from whence it came. A machine shop is where this type of identification is essential – it is where mix-ups can occur. In other places, where mix-ups are unlikely, verification status identification does not need to be so explicit.

Identifying product status is not just a matter of tying a label on a product. The status should be denoted by an authorized signature, stamp, mark or other identity which is applied by the person making the accept/reject decision and which is secure from misuse. Signatures are acceptable as a means of denoting verification status on paper records but are not suitable for computerized records. Secure passwords and 'write only' protection has to be provided to specific individuals. Signatures in a workshop environment are susceptible to deterioration and illegibility that is why numbered inspection stamps with unique markings have evolved. The ink used has to survive the environment and if the labels are to be attached to the product for life, it is more usual to apply an imprint stamp on soft metal or bar code.

Small and fragile products should be held in containers and the container sealed and marked with the product status. Large products should either carry a label or have a related inspection record.

In some situations the location of a product can constitute adequate identification of product status. However these locations need to be designated as 'Awaiting Inspection, Accepted Product or Reject Product' or other such labels as appropriate to avoid the inadvertent placement of items in the wrong location. The location of product in the normal production flow is not a suitable designation unless an automated transfer route is provided.

When a service is out of service, tell your customers. Services that rely on products should carry a label or a notice when accessed. A bank cash machine is one example where a notice is displayed when the machine is out of service. In some cases customers may need to be informed by letter or telephone.

With software the verification status can be denoted in the software as a comment or on records testifying its conformance with requirements.

With documentation you can either denote verification status by an approval signature on the document or by a reference number, date and issue status that is traceable to records containing the approval signatures.

If you use stamps, you will need a register to allocate stamps to particular individuals and to indicate which stamps have been withdrawn. When a person hands in his stamp it is good practice to avoid using the same number for 12 months or so to prevent mistaken identity in any subsequent investigations.

Traceability (7.5.3)

The standard requires the organization to *control and record the unique identification of the product, where traceability is a requirement (see 5.5.7).*

What does this mean?

Traceability is a process characteristic. It provides the ability to trace something through a process to a point along its course either forwards through the process or backwards through the process and determine as necessary, its origin, its history and the conditions to which it was subjected.

Why is this necessary?

This requirement responds to the Factual Approach Principle.

One needs traceability to find the root cause of problems. If records cannot be found which detail what happened to a product then nothing can be done to prevent its recurrence. Although the standard only requires traceability when required by contract or law, it is key to enabling corrective action.

In situations of safety or national security it is necessary to be able to locate all products of a batch in which a defective product has been found so as to eliminate them before there is a disaster. It is also very important in the aerospace, automobile, medical devices and food and drugs industries – in fact, any industry where human life may be at risk due to a defective product being in circulation.

Traceability is also important to control processes. You may need to know which products have been through which processes and on what date if a problem is found some time later. The same is true of test and measuring equipment. If on being calibrated a piece of test equipment is found to be out of calibration then it is important to track down all the equipment which has been validated using that piece of measuring equipment. This in fact is a requirement of ISO 9001 Clause 7.6 but no requirement for traceability is specified.

> **1994–2000 Differences**
>
> Previously the standard requires that where, and to the extent that traceability is a specified requirement, the supplier is to establish and maintain documented procedures for unique identification of individual product or batches and goes on to require this identification to be recorded.
>
> The intent of the requirement remains unchanged.

How is this implemented?

Providing traceability can be an onerous task. Some applications require products to be traced back to the original ingot from which they were produced. Traceability is achieved by coding items and their records such that you can trace an item back to the records at any time in its life. The chain can be easily lost if an item goes outside your control. If for example, you provide an item on loan to a development organization and it is returned sometime later, without a certified record of what was done to it, you have no confidence that the item is in fact the same one, unless it has some distinguishing features. The inspection history may also be invalidated because the operations conducted on the item were not certified. Traceability is only helpful when the chain remains unbroken. It can also be costly to maintain. The system of traceability that you maintain should be carefully thought out so that it is economic. There is little point in maintaining an elaborate traceability system for the once in a lifetime event when you need it, unless your very survival or society's survival depends upon it.

The conventions you use to identify product and batches need to be specified in the product specifications and the stage at which product is marked specified in the relevant procedures or plans. Often such markings are automatically applied during processing, as is the case with printed circuits, mouldings, ceramics, castings, products etc. Process setting up procedures should specify how the marking equipment or tools are to be set up.

If you do release a batch of product prior to verification being performed and one out of the batch is subsequently found to be nonconforming, you will need to retrieve all other from the same batch. This may not be as simple as it seems. In order to retrieve a component which has subsequently been assembled into a printed circuit board, which has itself been fitted into a unit along with several other assemblies, not only would you need a good traceability system but also one that is constantly in operation.

It would be considered prudent to prohibit the premature release of product if you did not have an adequate traceability system in place. If nonconformity will be detected by the end product tests, allowing production to commence without the receipt tests being available may be a risk worth taking.. However, if you lose the means of determining conformance by premature release, don't release the product until you have verified it as acceptable.

Customer property (7.5.4)

Care of customer property (7.5.4)

1994–2000 Differences

This is a new requirement that has no equivalent in the 1994 version.

The standard requires the organization to *exercise care with customer property while it is under the organization's control or being used by the organization.*

What does this mean?

Customer property is any property owned or provided by the customer. The product being supplied may have been produced by a competitor, by the customer or even by your own firm under a different contract. Customer property is any property supplied to you by your customer and not only what is to be incorporated into product to be supplied to customers. Customer owned tooling and returnable packaging also constitutes customer-supplied product. The property being used may be supplied by the customer such as tools, software, and equipment or made available for the organization's use such as test and development facilities on customer premises.

Documentation is not considered customer property because it is normally freely issued and ownership passes from customer to supplier on receipt. However, if the customer requires the documentation to be returned at the end of the contract, it should be treated as customer property.

Why is this necessary?

This requirement responds to the Customer Focus Principle.

Anything you use that does not belong to you should be treated with due care particularly if it has been supplied for your use and is expected to be returned in good condition.

How is this implemented?

For customer property that is used on your own premises you should maintain a register containing the following details:

- name of product, part numbers, serial numbers and other identifying features
- name of customer and source of product if different
- delivery note reference, date of delivery
- receipt inspection requirements
- condition on receipt including reference to any rejection note
- storage conditions and place of storage
- maintenance specification if maintenance is required
- current location and name of custodian
- date of return to customer or embodiment into supplies
- part number and serial number of product embodying the customer supplied product
- dispatch note reference of assembly containing the product

These details will help you keep track of the customer supplied product whether on embodiment loan or contract loan (see Appendix A for definitions) and will be useful during customer audits or in the event of a problem with the item either before or after dispatch of the associated assembly.

Identification of customer supplied property (7.5.4)

The standard requires the organization to *identify customer property provided for use or incorporation into the product.*

What does this mean?

Identifying customer property means attaching labels or other means of identification that denote its owner.

> **1994–2000 Differences**
>
> Previously the general requirements for identification of product applied to customer supplied product.
>
> The intent of the requirement remains unchanged.

Why is this necessary?

This requirement responds to the Process Approach Principle.

If customer property carries an identity that distinguishes it from other product, it will prevent inadvertent disposal or unauthorized use.

How is this implemented?

Customer property may carry suitable identification but if not, labels, containers or other markings may be necessary to distinguish it from organization owned property. As customer property may have been supplied by the organization originally as in the case of a repair service, labels indicating the owner should suffice. In a vehicle service area for instance, a label is attached to the car keys rather than labelling the car itself.

When deciding the type of marking, consideration needs to be given to the conditions of use. Markings may need to be permanent in order to be durable under the anticipated conditions of use. It would be wise to seek guidance from the customer if you are in any doubt as to where to place the marking or how to apply it. Metal identification plates stamped with the customer's identity, date of supply, contract and limitations of use are durable and permanent.

Verification of customer supplied property (7.5.4)

1994–2000 Differences
Previously the standard required the supplier to establish and maintain procedures for verification of customer-supplied product provided for incorporation into the supplies or for related activities.
The intent of the requirement remains unchanged.

The standard requires the organization to *verify customer property provided for use or incorporation into the product*.

What does this mean?

Customers may supply product purchased from other suppliers for installation in an assembly purchased from your organization.

Why is this necessary?

This requirement responds to the Factual Approach Principle.

Product needs to be verified before incorporation into the organization's product regardless of its source firstly, to establish the condition of the item on receipt in the event that it is damaged, defective or is incomplete and secondly, to verify that it is fit for the intended purpose before use. If you fail to inspect the product on receipt you may find difficulty in convincing your customer later that the damage was not your fault.

How is this implemented?

When property is received from a customer it should be processed in the same way as purchased product so that it is registered and subject to receipt inspection. The inspection you carry out may be limited if you do not possess the necessary equipment or specification, but you should reach an agreement with the customer as to the extent of any receipt inspection before the product arrives. You also need to match any delivery note with the product because the customer may have inadvertently sent you the wrong product. Unless you know what you are doing it is unwise to energize the product without proper instructions from the customer.

Protection of customer supplied property (7.5.4)

The standard requires the organization to *protect customer property provided for use or incorporation into the product.*

What does this mean?

Protection means safeguarding against loss, damage, deterioration and misuse.

Why is this necessary?

This requirement responds to the Customer Focus Principle.

As the property will either be returned to the customer on completion of contract or will be incorporated into your products, it is necessary to protect the product from conditions that may adversely affect its quality.

> **1994–2000 Differences**
>
> Previously the standard required the supplier to establish and maintain procedures for storage of customer-supplied product provided for incorporation into the supplies or for related activities.
>
> Protection is a better term in this context than storage.

How is this implemented?

Where the customer supplied property is in the form of products that could be inadvertently degraded, they should be segregated from other products to avoid mixing, inadvertent use, damage or loss. Depending on the size and quantity of the items and the frequency with which your customer supplies such products you may require special storage areas. Wherever the items are stored you should maintain a register of such items, preferably separate from the store in inventory control or the project office for example. The authorization for releasing customer supplied property from stores may need to be different for inventory control reasons. You also need to ensure that such products are insured. You will not need a corresponding purchase order and they may not therefore be registered as stock or capital assets. If you receive customer-supplied property very infrequently, you will need a simple system that is only activated when necessary rather than being built into your normal system. Under such circumstances it is easy to lose these products and forget they are someone else's property. You need to alert staff to take extra care especially if they are high value items which cannot readily be replaced.

Maintenance of customer supplied property (7.5.4)

The standard requires the organization to *maintain customer property provided for use or incorporation into the product.*

Previously the standard required the supplier to establish and maintain procedures for maintenance of customer-supplied property provided for incorporation into the supplies or for related activities.

There is no change in requirement.

What does this mean?

Maintenance of customer supplied property means retaining the property in the condition in which it was originally provided.

Why is this necessary?

This requirement responds to the Process Approach Principle.

Customer supplied property that is issued for incorporation into supplies don't often require maintenance – however, items for use in conjunction with the contract may be retained for such a duration that maintenance is necessary.

How is this implemented?

If the property requires any maintenance you should be provided with a maintenance specification and the appropriate equipment to do the job. Maintenance may include both preventive and corrective maintenance but you should clarify with your customer which it is. You may have the means for preventive maintenance such as lubrication and calibration but not for repairs. Always establish your obligations in the contract regarding customer supplied property, because you could take on commitments for which you are not contractually covered if something should go wrong. You need to establish who will supply the spares and re-certify the equipment following repair.

Reporting problems to the customer (7.5.4)

1994–2000 Differences

Previously the standard required that any such product that is lost, damaged or is otherwise unsuitable for use be recorded and reported to the customer and again advises the supplier that verification by the supplier does not absolve the customer of the responsibility to provide acceptable product.

The intent of the requirement remains unchanged.

The standard requires *occurrence of any customer property that is lost, damaged or otherwise found to be unsuitable for use to be recorded and reported to the customer.*

What does this mean?

While customer property is on your premises, it may be damaged, develop a fault or become lost. Also when using customer property on customer premises, events may occur that result in damage or failure to the property.

Why is this necessary?

This requirement responds to the Customer Focus Principle.

It is necessary to record and report any damage, loss or failure to the customer so that as owners they may decide the action that is required. Normally, the organization does not have responsibility to alter, replace or repair customer property unless authorized to do so under the terms of the contract.

How is this implemented?

The customer is responsible for the product they supply wherever it came from in the first place. It is therefore very important that you establish the condition of the product before you store it or use it. In the event that you detect that the product is damaged, defective or is incomplete, you should place it in a quarantine area and report the condition to the customer. Even if the product is needed urgently and can still be used, you should obtain the agreement of your customer before using inferior product, otherwise you may be held liable for the consequences.

You could use your own reject note or nonconformity report format to notify the customer of a defective product but these are not appropriate if the product is lost. You also need a customer response to the problem and so a form that combined both a statement of the problem and of the solution would be more appropriate.

Preservation of product (7.5.5)

The standard requires the organization to *preserve conformity of product during internal processing and delivery to the intended destination* and goes on to require these measures *to include identification, handling, packaging, storage and protection.*

What does this mean?

These requirements are concerned with conformity control, i.e. ensuring that products remain conforming once they have been certified as conforming. They apply to service operations that involve the supply of product such as maintenance.

Identification in this context means identifying the product through the packaging and can apply at any stage in the product realization process. Handling refers to the manner by which product is moved by hand or by machine. Packaging refers to the materials employed to protect the product during movement and storage refers to the place where product is held pending use, shipment or further processing. Protection applies at all stages in product realization.

Why is this necessary?

This requirement responds to the Process Approach Principle.

As considerable effort will have gone into producing a conforming product, it is necessary to protect it from adverse conditions that could change the physical and functional characteristics. In some cases preservation is needed immediately the characteristics have been generated e.g. surface finish. In other cases, preservation is only needed when the product leaves the controlled environment e.g. food, chemicals and electrical goods. Preservation processes need to be controlled in order that product remains in its original condition until required for use.

How is this implemented?

Determination of preservation requirements commences during the design phase or the manufacturing or service planning phase by assessing the risks to product quality during its manufacture, storage, movement, transportation and installation. Packaging design should be governed by the requirements of clause 7.3 although if you only select existing designs of packaging these requirements would not be applicable.

The preservation processes should be designed to prolong the life of the product by inhibiting the effect of natural elements. While the conditions in the factory can be measured, those outside the factory can only be predicted.

Having identified there is a risk to product quality you may need to prepare instructions for the handling, storage, packing, preservation and delivery of particular items. In addition to issuing the instructions you will need to reference them in the appropriate work instructions in order that they are implemented when necessary. Whatever the method, you will need traceability from the identification of need to implementation of the provisions and from there to the records of achievement.

Identification

Packages for export may require different markings than those for the home market. Those for certain countries may need to comply with particular laws. Unless your customer has specified labelling requirements, markings should be applied both to primary and secondary packaging as well as to the product itself. Markings should also be made with materials that will survive the conditions of storage and transportation. Protection can be given to the markings while in storage and in transit but this cannot be guaranteed while products are in use. Markings applied to the product therefore need to be resistant to cleaning processes both in the factory and in use. Markings on packaging are therefore essential to warn handlers of any dangers or precautions they must observe. Limited Life Items should be identified so as to indicate their shelf life. The expiry date should be visible on the container and provisions should be made for such items to be removed from stock when their indicated life has expired.

While a well-equipped laboratory can determine the difference between products and materials the consumer needs a simple practical method of identification and labelled packets is often a reliable and economic alternative.

For products that start to deteriorate when the packaging seal is broken, the supplier's responsibility extends beyond delivery to the point of use. In such cases markings need to be applied to the containers to warn the consumers of the risks.

Handling

Handling provisions serve two purposes both related to safety. Protection of the product from the individual and protection of the individual handling the product. This latter condition is concerned with safety and addressed through other provisions, however, the two cannot and should not be separated and handling procedures should address both aspects.

Handling product can take various forms depending on the hazard you are trying to prevent from happening. In some cases notices on the product will suffice, such as 'LIFT HERE' or 'THIS WAY UP' or the notices on batteries warning of acid. In other cases you will need to provide special containers, or equipment. There follows a short list of handling provisions that your procedures may need to address:

- Lifting equipment
- Pallets and containers
- Conveyors and stackers
- Design features for enabling handling of product
- Handling of electrostatic sensitive devices
- Handling hazardous materials
- Handling fragile materials

Packaging

Packing processes should be designed to protect the product from damage and deterioration under the conditions that can be expected during storage and transportation. You will need a means of identifying the packaging and marking requirements for particular products and of identifying processes for the design of suitable packaging including the preservation and marking requirements. Depending on your business you may need to devise packages for various storage and transportation conditions, preservation methods for various types of product and marking requirements for types of product associated with their destination.

Unless your customer has specified packaging requirements, there are several national standards that can be used to select the appropriate packaging, marking and preservation requirements for your products. Your procedures should make provision for the selection to be made by competent personnel at the planning stage and for the requirements thus selected to be specified in the packing instructions to ensure their implementation.

Packing instructions should not only provide for protecting the product but also for including any accompanying documentation such as:

- Assembly and installation instructions
- Licence and copyright notices
- Certificates of conformity

- Packing list identifying the contents of the container
- Export documents
- Warranty cards

The packing instructions are likely to be one of the last instructions you provide and probably the last operation you will perform for a particular consignment. This also presents the last opportunity for you to make mistakes! They may be your *last* mistakes but they will be the *first* your customer sees. The error you made on component assembly probably won't be found, but the slightest error in the packaging, the marking, the enclosures will almost certainly be found therefore this process needs careful control. It may not be considered so skilled a process but all the same it is vital to your image.

Storage

In order to preserve the quality of items that have passed receipt verification they should be transferred to stockrooms in which they are secure from damage and deterioration. You need secure storage areas for several reasons:

- For preventing personnel from entering the stock rooms and removing items without authorization
- For preventing items from losing their identity (Once the identity is lost it is often difficult, if not impossible to restore complete identification without testing material or other properties.)
- For preventing vermin damaging the stock
- For preventing climatic elements causing stock to deteriorate

While loss of product may not be considered a quality matter, it is if the product is customer property or if it prevents you from meeting your customer requirements. Delivery on time is a quality characteristic of the service you provide to your customer and therefore secure storage is essential.

To address these requirements you will need to identify and specify the storage areas that have been established to protect product pending use or delivery. Although it need be only a brief specification, the requirements to be maintained by each storage area should be specified based on the type of product, the conditions required preserving its quality, its location and environment. Products that require storage at certain temperatures should be stored in areas that maintain such temperatures. If the environment in the area in which the room is located is either uncontrolled or at a significantly higher or lower temperature, an environmentally controlled storage area will be required.

All items have a limit beyond which deterioration may occur and therefore temperature, humidity, pressure, air quality, radiation, vibration etc. may need to be controlled. At some stage, usually during design or manufacturing or service planning, the storage conditions need to be defined and displayed. In many cases dry conditions at room temperature are all that is necessary but problems may occur when items requiring non-standard conditions are acquired. You will need a means of ensuring that such items are afforded the necessary protection and your storage procedures need to address this aspect. It is for this reason that it is wiser to store items in their original packaging until required for use. If packets need to be opened, they should be sealed again before return into storage.

Any area where product is stored should have been designated for that purpose in order that the necessary controls can be employed. If you store product in undesignated areas then there is a chance that the necessary controls will not be applied. Designation can be accomplished by placing notices and markers around the area to indicate the boundaries where the controls apply.

Each time the storage controller retrieves an item for issue, there is an opportunity to check the condition of stock. However, some items may have a slow turnover in certain storage areas e.g., where spares are held pending use. There is also a need to periodically check the overall condition of the stockroom for damage to the fabric of the building. Rainwater may be leaking on to packaging and go undetected until that item is removed for use.

Some items such as electrolytic capacitors and two part adhesives may deteriorate when dormant. Others such as rubber materials, adhesive tape and chemicals deteriorate with the passage of time regardless of use. These are often referred to as 'Shelf Life Items' or 'Limited Life Items'. Dormant electronic assemblies can deteriorate in storage and provision should be made to retest equipment periodically or prior to release if in storage for more than one year.

The assessment interval should depend on the type of building, the stock turnover, the environment in which the stock is located and the number of people allowed access. The interval may vary from storage area to storage area and should be reviewed and adjusted as appropriate following the results of the assessment.

Segregation

Segregation is vital in many industries where products can only be positively identified by their containers. It is also important to prevent possible mixing or exposure to adverse conditions or cross contamination. Examples where segregation makes sense are:

- Toxic materials
- Flammable materials
- Limited life items
- Explosives

Segregation is not only limited to the product but also to the containers and tools used with the product. Particles left in containers and on tools – no matter how small, can cause blemishes in paint and other finishes as well as violate health and safety regulations. If there are such risks in your manufacturing process then procedures need to be put in place that will prevent product mixing.

Segregation may also be necessary in the packaging of products not only to prevent visible damage but also to prevent electrical damage as with electrostatic sensitive devices. Segregation may be the only way of providing adequate product identity as is the case with fasteners.

Cleaning

Where applicable, preservation processes should require that the product be cleaned before being packed and preservative applied. In other cases the product may need to be stored in sealed containers in order to retard decay, corrosion and/or contamination.

Control of measuring and monitoring devices (7.6)

Determining monitoring and measurements to be undertaken (7.6)

1994–2000 Differences

Previously the standard required the supplier to determine the measurements to be made and the accuracy required.

The implication is that all physical and non-physical monitoring and measurements needed to demonstrate compliance with product requirements are to be determined.

The standard requires the organization to *identify the monitoring and measurement to be undertaken to provide evidence of conformity of product to determined requirements.*

What does this mean?

This requirement should strictly be located in section 8 but has been included in section 7 because it is believed that there are some applications where it does not apply. Clearly there are no applications where monitoring and measurement do not apply but there may be applications where physical calibration of measuring devices may not be applicable in the traditional sense of the word *devices*. The monitoring and measurements referred to are those required to carry out product verification rather than the measurements to calibrate a measuring device. The requirement is under product realization not a sub section, and therefore applies equally to product/service design, purchasing and production or service delivery. It should not be interpreted as only applying to the characteristics of a product that can be measured through examination. It applies equally to performance characteristics that are inherent in the product design such as durability, safety and security and to intangible characteristics such as courtesy, respect and integrity.

Measurement is the process of associating numbers with physical quantities and phenomena. Measurements may be made by unaided human senses in which case they are often called estimates or, more usually, by the use of instruments, which may range in complexity from simple rules for measuring lengths to highly sophisticated systems designed to detect and measure quantities entirely beyond the capabilities of human senses. A unit is the name of a quantity, such as kilogram or metre; a standard is the physical embodiment of a unit.

Determined requirements are those of the customer, the regulators and the organization as addressed previously in clause 7.2.1 of the standard. It is therefore not only a question of measuring the characteristics of the product but relating these characteristics to the defined requirements. For tangible product, the requirements may be expressed in performance terms (performance requirements) or in terms of form, fit and function (conformity requirements). Performance requirements may not be directly measurable. For instance safety requirements have to be translated into physical characteristics that are deemed to satisfy the requirement. You do not measure safety but the absence of hazard and therefore on a metal enclosure you would measure the absence of sharp edges and with food you would measure the absence of bugs. You can only search for what is known. Only when we know that a certain quantity of a substance is toxic can we search for it.

Where the product of a process is intangible the range of measurements varies widely. Knowledge is measured as the output of a course of study, skill or competence is measured as an output of training. Perceptions and behaviours are measured where they are vital to service quality. Comfort and convenience may be measured in a transport system.

Why is this necessary?

This requirement responds to the Factual Approach Principle.

The reason for requiring monitoring and measurements to be identified is so that you have a means of relating the requirements to the characteristics to be measured so as verify their achievement. If you did not identify the monitoring and measurements to be undertaken you would have no knowledge of whether or not requirements had been met before you delivered the product or service.

How is this implemented?

The measurements to be made should be derived from the characteristics defined in the product requirement. In some cases these may be directly measurable, such as size and weight, but often the characteristics need to be translated into measurable parameters. One way to identify the measurements is to produce a verification matrix showing the product characteristic, the measures, the units of measure, the target values and the level at which the measurements will be taken.

The product characteristic may be a specific dimension or an attribute. Length, mass and time are specific dimensions, response, safety, reliability, on-time delivery are attributes.

There are many different ways of expressing the units of measure.

Measure	Units
Length	Metres
Mass	Kilograms
Time	Seconds
Response	Time between receipt of call and engineer on site
Safety	Incidents per passenger mile
Reliability	Mean time between failures
Maintainability	Mean time to repair
On-time delivery	Percent delivered by agreed date
Conformity	Percent defective
Courtesy	Ratio of complaints to transactions

With tangible products the level of measurement may be at system, subsystem, equipment, component or material level. With intangible products the measurement may be at the relationship, encounter or transaction level. The relationship is the long term interaction between customer and supplier, the encounter tends to be the short term interaction involving a single purchase and the transaction is a specific activity between representatives of the customer and supplier. A single encounter may involve several transactions and a relationship may involve years of encounters.

The measurements to be made should be identified in test specifications, process specifications and drawings etc., but often these documents will not define how to take the measurements. The method of measurement should be defined in verification procedures that take into account the measurement uncertainty, the devices used to perform the measurements, the competency of the personnel and the physical environment in which measurements are taken. There may be a tolerance on variable parameters so as to determine the accuracy required. You may use general tolerances to cover most dimensions and only apply specific tolerances where it is warranted by the application.

Determining measuring and monitoring devices needed (7.6)

The standard requires the organization to *identify the measuring and monitoring devices needed to provide evidence of conformity of product to determined requirements.*

What does this mean?

The integrity of products depends upon the quality of the devices used to create and measure their characteristics. This part of the standard specifies requirements for ensuring the quality of such devices.

A device is something constructed for a particular purpose and need not be a piece of hardware. It could be software or a method or sensor that captures information. It includes devices used during design and development for determining product characteristics and for design verification. Some characteristics cannot be determined by calculation and need to be derived by experiment. In such cases the accuracy of devices you use must be controlled, otherwise the parameters stated in the resultant product specification may not be achievable when the product reaches production.

Wherever there is a measurement to be made, a parameter or phenomena to be monitored, there is always a device or sensor employed to sense the measurements. The device may be human senses (hearing, sight, touch, taste, smell) a physical instrument measuring mass, length, time, electric current, temperature etc., a perception obtained from surveys, interviews, questionnaires or behaviour obtained from psychometric tests or knowledge obtained from written examination. There may be others, but clearly measurement is a wide subject and beyond the scope of this book to explore in any detail.

The sensor senses what is taking place and registers it in a form suitable for transmission to a receiver. The measuring and monitoring device should encompass the sensor, the transmitter and the receiver because the purpose of measurement is to take decisions and without receipt of the information no decisions can be taken. Also, you need to be aware that the transmitter and receiver may degrade the accuracy and precision of the measurement.

Why is this necessary?

This requirement responds to the Process Approach Principle.

It is necessary to identify the measuring and monitoring device so that a device capable of the appropriate accuracy and precision is used to take the

---

1994–2000 Differences

Previously the standard required the supplier to:

(a) select the appropriate inspection, measuring and test equipment that is capable of the accuracy and precision necessary;

(b) identify any measuring requirement that exceeds the known state of the art in sufficient time for the needed capability to be developed.

Although less prescriptive the modified wording does not alter the intent of the requirement.

measurements or monitor the parameters. If the devices you use to create and measure characteristics are inaccurate, unstable, damaged or in any way defective the product will not possess the required characteristics and furthermore you will not know it. You know nothing about an object until you can measure it, but you must measure it accurately and precisely. The devices you use therefore need to be controlled.

How is this implemented?

When identifying measuring and monitoring devices you need identify the characteristic, the unit of measure, the target value and then choose an appropriate measuring or monitoring device. As the type of product may vary considerably, the range of measuring devices also varies widely. Considering that the term product in the ISO 9000 includes service, hardware, software and processed material, and that documents are considered to be software rather than information products, the range of characteristics for which measuring devices are required is enormous. It is relatively easy to identify measuring and monitoring devices for hardware product and processes material but less easy for services, software and information.

In many cases there will be a device available to do the measuring, but if you propose a new unit of measure a new sensor may be required.

Physical measurement

There are two categories of equipment that determine the selection of physical devices – *general purpose* and *special to type equipment*. It should not be necessary to specify all the general-purpose equipment needed to perform basic measurements that should be known by competent personnel. You should not need to tell an inspector or tester which micrometer, vernier calliper, voltmeter or oscilloscope to use. These are the tools of the trade and they should select the tool that is capable of measuring the particular parameters with the accuracy and precision required. However, you will need to tell them which device to use if the measurement requires unusual equipment or the prevailing environmental conditions require that only equipment be selected that will operate in such an environment. In such cases the particular devices to be used should be specified in the verification procedures. In order to demonstrate that you selected the appropriate device at some later date, you should consider recording the actual device used in the record of results. With mechanical devices this may not necessary because wear will be normally detected by periodic calibration well in advance of a problem with the operation of the device.

With electronic devices subject to drift with time or handling, a record of the device used will enable you to identify suspect results in the event of the device being found to be outside the limits at the next calibration. A way of reducing

Table 7.2   Service quality measures

Service provided	*Measures*
Telephone	Line availability
	Call out response time
	Time to reply to complaints
Water	Time to reply to complaints
	Supply connection time
	Water quality
Education	Class size
	Percentage of pupils achieving pass grades

the effect is to select devices that are several orders of magnitude more accurate that needed.

Service measurements

In the service sector there are many measurements that cannot be made using physical devices. The most common device is the customer survey either used directly by an interview with customers or by mail. Many service organizations develop metrics for monitoring service quality relative to the type of service they provide. Some examples are provide in Table 7.2.

Defining the measuring and monitoring processes (7.6)

The standard requires *processes to be established to ensure that monitoring and measuring can be carried out and are carried out in a manner consistent with the measuring and monitoring requirements.*

What does this mean?

A measurement process consists of the *operations* (i.e. the measurement tasks and the environment in which they are carried out) *procedures* (i.e. how the tasks are performed) *devices* (i.e. gauges, instruments, software etc. used to make the measurements) the *personnel* used to assign a quantity to the character-

> **1994–2000 Differences**
>
> Previously the standard required measuring equipment to be used in a manner that ensures that the measurement uncertainty is known and is consistent with the required measurement capability.
>
> The intent of the requirement remains unchanged.

istics being measured and the measurement system (i.e. the units of measure and the process by which standards are developed and maintained).

Why is this necessary?

This requirement responds to the Systems Approach Principle.

If the measurements of product and service are to have any meaning, they have to be performed in a manner that provides results of integrity – results that others inside and outside the organization can respect and rely upon as being accurate and precise. If the integrity of measurement is challenged and the organization cannot demonstrate the validity of the measurements, the quality of the product remains suspect.

How is this implemented?

Measurement process

Measurement begins with a definition of the measure, the quantity that is to be measured, and it always involves a comparison of the measure with some known quantity of the same kind. If the measure is not accessible for direct comparison, it is converted or 'transduced' into an analogous measurement signal. As measurement always involve some interaction between the measure and the observer or observing instrument, there is always an exchange of energy, which, although in everyday applications is negligible, can become considerable in some types of measurement and thereby limit accuracy (Measurement, ©1994–1999)[4].

Any measuring requirement for a quantity requires the measurement process to be capable of accurately measuring the quantity with consistency. For this to happen, the factors that affect the result need to be identified and a process designed that takes into account the variations in these factors and delivers a result that can be relied upon as being accurate within defined limits.

Controlling measurements

One necessary measuring and monitoring requirement is that the measurements carried out are controlled i.e. regulated in a manner that will ensure consistent results. Control in this instance means several things:

- Knowing what devices are used for product verification purposes so that you can distinguish between controlled and uncontrolled devices – you will need to maintain a list of devices for this purpose.
- Knowing where the equipment is located so that you can recall it for calibration and maintenance – you will need a recall notice for this purpose.
- Knowing who the current custodian is so that you have a name to contact.

- Knowing what condition it is in so that you can prohibit its use if the condition is unsatisfactory – you will need a defect report for this purpose.
- Knowing when its accuracy was last checked so that you can have confidence it its results – calibration records and labels fulfil this need.
- Knowing what checks have been made using the instrument since it was last checked so that you can repeat them should the instrument be subsequently found out of calibration – this is only necessary for instruments whose accuracy drifts over time i.e. electronic equipment. (It is not normally necessary for mechanical devices. You will need a traceability system for this purpose.)
- Knowing that the measurements made using it are accurate so that you rely on the results – a valid calibration status label will fulfil this purpose.
- Knowing that it is only being used for measuring the parameters for which it was designed so that results are reliable and equipment is not abused. The abuse of measuring devices needs to be regulated primarily to protect the device but also if high pressures and voltages are involved, to protect the user. Specifying the devices to be used for making measurements in your work instructions will serve to prevent the abuse of devices.

You may not need to know all these things about every device used for product verification but you should know most of them. This knowledge can be gained by controlling:

- the selection of measuring devices
- the use of measuring devices
- the calibration of measuring devices

You may know where each device is supposed to be, but what do you do if a device is not returned for calibration when due? Your procedures should track returns and make provision for tracking down any maverick devices, because they could be being used on product acceptance. A model process flow for control of measuring and monitoring devices is illustrated in Figure 7.13.

Measurement uncertainty

There is uncertainty in all measurement processes. There are uncertainties attributable to the measuring device being used, the person carrying out the measurements and the environment in which the measurements are carried out. When repeated measurements are taken with the same device on the same dimension of the same product and the results vary, this is measurement uncertainty. When you make a measurement with a calibrated instrument you need to know the specified limits of permissible error (how close to the true value the measurement is). If you are operating under stable environmental

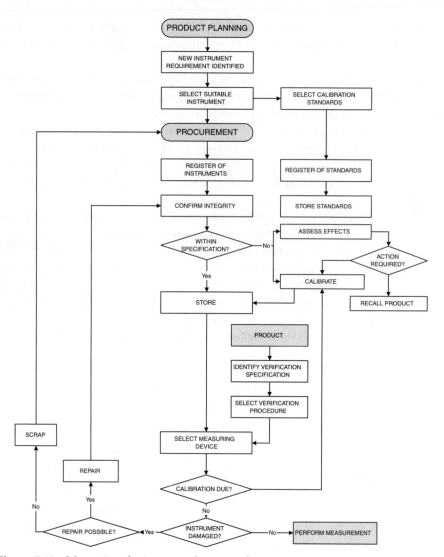

Figure 7.13 Measuring device control process flow

conditions, you can assume that any calibrated device will not exceed the limit of permissible error. Stable conditions exist when all variation is under statistical control. This means that all variation is due to common causes only and none due to special causes. In other cases you will need to estimate the amount of error and take this into account when making your measurements. Test specifications and drawings etc. should specify characteristics in true values, i.e. values that do not take into account any inherent errors. Your test and inspection procedures, however, should specify the characteristics to be measured taking into account all the errors and uncertainties that are attributable to the equipment, the personnel and the environment when the measurement system is in statistical control. This can be achieved by tightening the tolerances in order to be confident that the actual dimensions are within the specified limits.

Controlling variation in measurement processes

Measurement processes must be in statistical control so that all variation is due to common cause and not special cause. It is often assumed that the measurements taken with a calibrated device are accurate and indeed they are if we take account of the variation that is present in every measuring system and bring the system under statistical control. Variation in measurement processes arises due to bias, repeatability, reproducibility, stability and linearity.

Bias is the difference between the observed average of the measurements and the reference value.

Repeatability is the variation in measurements obtained by one appraiser using one measuring device to measure an identical characteristic on the same part.

Reproducibility is the variation in the average of the measurements made by different appraisers using the same measuring instrument when measuring an identical characteristic on the same part.

Stability is the total variation in the measurements obtained with a measurement system on the same part when measuring a single characteristic over a period of time.

Linearity is the difference in the bias values through the expected operating range of the measuring device.

It is only possible to supply parts with identical characteristics if the measurement processes as well as the production processes are under statistical control. In an environment in which daily production quantities are in the range of 1,000 to 10,000 units, inaccuracies in the measurement processes that go undetected can have a disastrous impact upon customer satisfaction and consequently profits.

Measurement laboratories

In order to maintain the integrity of measurement, physical measurements need to be undertaken in a controlled environment often referred to as a 'laboratory'. The controlled environment consists of a workspace in which the temperature, humidity, pressure, cleanliness, access and the integrity of the measuring devices and supporting equipment is controlled and the personnel qualified. Such areas can be assessed separately to other areas of the organization against international metrological standards. Other organizations are established solely for the purpose of providing measurement services to industry and therefore undertake certification of measurement devices – testifying the devices have been calibrated against standards traceable to national or international standards. Here we enter the world of accreditation as opposed to certification.

Accreditation and certification

Laboratory accreditation is defined by ISO as formal recognition that a laboratory is competent to carry out specific tests or specific types of tests. The key words in this definition are 'competent' and 'specific tests'. Each accreditation recognizes a laboratory's technical capability (or competence) to do specific tests, measurements, or calibrations. In that sense, it should be recognized as a stand-alone form of very specialized technical certification, as distinct from a purely quality system certification as provided by ISO 9000. An accredited organization is authorized to issue certificates of conformity to national or international standards. ISO 9000 certification does not authorize organizations to issue such certificates. Accreditation is awarded for a specific scope of service or range of products as is certification, except that for laboratory accreditation they are accredited for very specific tests or measurements – usually within specified ranges of measurement – with associated information on uncertainty of measurement and for particular product and test specifications. An ISO 9000 certificate for a laboratory does not accurately specify the performance characteristics of the product that the certificated organization is capable of supplying.

Use of laboratories

Wherever physical measurement is performed you need to be confident in the results and therefore whether the measurements are performed in-house or by external laboratories, both areas should meet the same standards in order that results are consistently accurate and precise. Wherever the calibration is performed, the same standards should therefore apply. Calibrating equipment in-house should not absolve you from complying with the same requirements that you would need to impose on an external test house.

The standard that applies to measurement laboratories is now ISO/IEC 17025. Previously ISO Guide 25 applied but this is now being replaced by ISO/IEC 17025. Laboratories meeting the requirements of ISO/IEC 17025, for calibration and testing activities, will comply with the relevant requirements of ISO 9001 when they are acting as suppliers producing calibration and test results. However, laboratories meeting the requirements of ISO 9001 would not meet the requirements of ISO/IEC 17025. Therefore in-house laboratories should be assessed against ISO/IEC 17025 to obtain the same level of confidence as obtained from external laboratories.

Calibrating and verifying measurements (7.6a)

The standard requires measuring and monitoring devices to *be calibrated or verified at specified intervals or prior to use, against measurement standards traceable to international or national standards.*

What does this mean?

In a measurement system the physical signal is compared with a reference signal of known quantity. The reference signal is derived from measures of known quantity by a process called calibration. The known quantities are based on standards that in the majority of cases are agreed internationally.

The International System of Units was adopted by the 11th General Conference on Weights and Measures in 1960, it is abbreviated SI in all languages. Several base measuring units are defined, the three primary ones being mass, length and time. Since 1983 the standard for the unit of **length**, the metre, has been defined as the distance travelled by light in a vacuum in 1/299,792,458 second. The standard for the unit of **mass**, the kilogram, is a cylinder of platinum-iridium alloy kept by the International Bureau of Weights and Measures, located in Sèvres, near Paris. The standard for the unit of **time**, the second, is defined as the duration of 9,192,631,770 cycles of the radiation associated with a specified transition, or change in energy level, of the cesium-133 atom (Metric systems, ©1994–1999)[5]. All physical measurements should be traceable to these standards and their derivatives. This means that an instrument will give the same reading when measuring a quantity under the same environmental conditions, wherever the measurement is taken.

With non-physical measurement systems there is still a need for calibration but we tend to use the term integrity. The reference signal of known quantity is the standard and you can derive standards for anything – the only proviso is that they are agreed by

1994–2000 Differences

Previously the standard required the supplier to:

(a) calibrate and adjust all inspection, measuring and test equipment at prescribed intervals, or prior to use, against certified equipment having a known valid relationship to nationally recognized standards;

(b) calibrate inspection, measuring and test equipment used to demonstrate the conformance of product to the specified requirements;

(c) define the frequency of checks, check method, acceptance criteria and action to be taken when results are unsatisfactory;

(d) check and recheck at prescribed intervals, comparative references used as suitable forms of inspection to prove that they are capable of verifying the acceptability of product prior to release for use during production, installation and servicing;

(e) establish the extent and frequency of checks on comparative references and to maintain records as evidence of control.

The intent of the requirement remains unchanged.

those who benefit from the measurements. Therefore if you set out to measure customer satisfaction the standard used needs to be agreed with the customer. Standards that are not agreed by those they affect lack integrity.

Why is this necessary?

This requirement responds to the Factual Approach Principle.

Variations can arise in measurements taken in different locations due to the measuring device not being calibrated to the same standards as other devices. With the introduction of the SI system of units, this variation could be eliminated providing the quantity used to calibrate the measuring device was traceable to national or international standards.

How is this implemented?

Calibration of measuring and monitoring devices

Calibration is concerned with determining the values of the errors of a measuring instrument and often involves its adjustment or scale graduation to the required accuracy. You should not assume that just because a device was once accurate it would remain so forever. Some devices if well treated and retained in a controlled environment will retain their accuracy for very long periods. Others if poorly treated and subjected to environmental extremes will lose their accuracy very quickly. Ideally you should calibrate measuring devices before use in order to prevent an inaccurate device being used in the first place and afterwards to confirm that no changes have occurred during use. However, this is often not practical and so intervals of calibration are established which are set at such periods as will detect any adverse deterioration. These intervals should be varied with the nature of the device, the conditions of use and the seriousness of the consequences should it produce incorrect results.

It is not necessary to calibrate all measuring and monitoring devices. Some devices may be used solely as an indicator such as a thermometer, a clock or a tachometer – other equipment may be used for diagnostic purposes, to indicate if a fault exists. If such devices are not used for determining the acceptability of products and services or process parameters, their calibration is not essential. However, you should identify such devices as for 'Indication Purposes Only' if their use for measurement is possible. You don't need to identify all clocks and thermometers fixed to walls unless they are used for measurement.

There are two systems used for maintaining the accuracy and integrity of measuring devices – a calibration system and a verification system. The calibration system determines the accuracy of measurement and the verification system determines the integrity of the device. If accuracy is important then the device should be included in the calibration system. If accuracy is not an issue but the device's form, properties or function is important then it should be included in the verification system. You need to decide the system in which your devices are to be placed under control and identify them accordingly.

There are two types of devices subject to calibration – those that are adjustable and those that are not. An adjustable device is one where the scale or the mechanism is capable of adjustment (e.g. micrometer, voltmeter, load cell). For non-adjustable devices, a record of the errors observed against a known standard can be produced which can be taken into account when using the device (e.g. slip gauge, plug gauge, surface table, thermometer).

Comparative references are not subject to calibration. They are, however, subject to verification. Such devices are those which have form or function where the criteria is either pass or fail i.e. there is no room for error or where the magnitude of the errors does not need to be taken into account during usage. Such devices include software, steel rules/tapes, templates, forming and moulding tools. Devices in this category need carry no indication of calibration due date. The devices should carry a reference number and verification records should be maintained showing when the device was last checked. Verification of such devices include checks for damage, loss of components, function etc.

Some electronic equipment has self-calibration routines built in to the start-up sequence. This should be taken as an indication of serviceability and not of absolute calibration. The device should still be subject to independent calibration at a defined frequency. Note that **Use – not function – determines need for calibration.**

Traceability

If you calibrate your own devices you will need (in addition to the 'working standards' which you use for measurement) calibration standards for checking the calibration of the working standards. The calibration standards should also be calibrated periodically against national standards held by your national measurement laboratory. This unbroken chain ensures that there is compatibility between measurements made in different locations using different measuring devices. By maintaining traceability you can rely on obtaining the same result (within the stated limits of accuracy) wherever and whenever you perform the measurement providing the dimensions you are measuring remain stable. The relationship between the various standards is illustrated in Figure 7.14.

Determining calibration frequency

ISO 10012 requires that measuring equipment be confirmed at appropriate intervals established on the basis of stability, purpose and usage. With new equipment it is customary to set the frequency at 12-month intervals unless

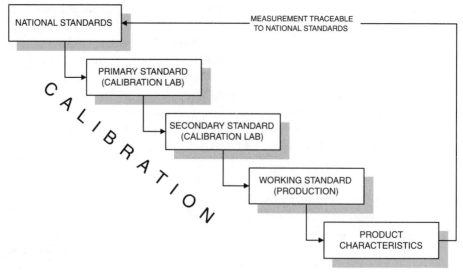

Figure 7.14 Traceability of standards

recommended otherwise by the manufacturer. Often this frequency remains despite evidence during calibration that accuracy and precision is no longer stable. Such action indicates that the calibration staff have not been properly trained or that cost rather than quality is driving calibration services. Calibrations should be performed prior to any significant change in accuracy that can be anticipated. The results of previous calibrations will indicate the amount of drift – if drift is detected, the intervals of confirmation should be shortened. Conversely, if drift is not detected, the intervals may be lengthened if two previous confirmations indicate such action would adversely affect confidence in the accuracy of the device. Environment, handling, frequency of use and wear are factors that can affect the stability of devices, therefore regardless of the calibration results, both previous and future conditions need to be taken into account. In order to demonstrate you have reviewed the results and determined the appropriate calibration frequency, provision should be made on the calibration records for the frequency to be decided at each calibration. Specifying a date is insufficient if the calibration instructions specify a frequency because it is unreasonable to expect the person subsequently performing calibration to detect whether any change has been made.

Reference materials

Comparative references are devices that are used to verify that an item has the same properties as the reference. They may take the form of colour charts or materials such as chemicals which are used in spectrographic analysers or those used in tests for the presence of certain compounds in a mixture or they could be materials with certain finishes, textures etc. Certificates should be produced and retained for such reference material so that their validity is known to those who will use them. Materials that degrade over time should be dated and given a use by date. Care should be taken to avoid cross contamination and any degradation due to sunlight (as can happen with colour charts). A specification for each reference material should be prepared so that its properties can be verified.

Recording the basis for calibration (7.6a)

The standard requires that *where no international or national standards exist, the basis used for calibration or verification be recorded*.

> **1994–2000 Differences**
>
> Previously the standard required the supplier to document the basis used for calibration where no nationally recognised standards exist.
>
> The intent of the requirement remains unchanged.

What does this mean?

For physical and chemical measurements that are based on the fundamental units of measure (metre, kilogram, second, ampere etc.) there are national or international standards but for other measures no national or international standard may exist. Each industry has developed a series of measures by which the quality of its goods and services are measured and has accordingly developed standards that represent agreed definitions of the measures. In the service sector involving interrelationships between people, standards become more difficult to define in quantitative terms and therefore may be defined qualitatively. For instance, the performance of a person handling customer calls may be defined by a series of results to be achieved. In setting the standard, the effort is focused on defining what a good job looks like.

Why is this necessary?

This requirement responds to the Factual Approach Principle.

Without a sound basis for comparison, the effort of measurement is wasted.

How is this implemented?

In some situations there may be no national standard against which to calibrate your devices. If you face this situation, you should gather together a group of experts within your company or trade association and establish by investigation, experimentation and debate what constitutes the standard. Having done this you should document the basis of your decisions and produce a device or number of devices that can be used to compare the product or result with the standard using visual, quantitative or other means. The device may be a physical instrument but could be information such as a set of agreed criteria.

Where you devise original solutions to the measurement of characteristics, the theory and development of the method should be documented and retained as evidence of the validity of the measurement method. Any new measurement methods should be proven by rigorous experiment to detect the measurement uncertainty and cumulative effect of the errors in each measurement process. The samples used for proving the method should also be retained so as to provide a means of repeating the measurements should it prove necessary.

<table>
<tr><td>

1994–2000 Differences

Previously the standard required that all inspection, measuring and test equipment be calibrated and adjusted.

The intent of the requirement remains unchanged.

</td><td>

Adjustment of devices (7.6b)

The standard requires measuring equipment to *be adjusted or re-adjusted as necessary.*

What does this mean?

Adjustment is only possible with devices that have been designed to be adjustable.

</td></tr>
</table>

Why is this necessary?

This requirement responds to the Process Approach Principle.

When a measuring device is verified, it may be found within specification and adjusted if the parameters have drifted towards the upper or lower limits. If the device is found outside specification it can be adjusted or re-adjusted (on subsequent occasions) within the specified limits.

How is this implemented?

Mechanical devices are normally adjusted to the null position on calibration. Electronic devices should only be adjusted if found to be outside the limits. If you adjust the device at each calibration you will not be able to observe drift. Adjustments, if made very frequently, may also degrade the instrument. If the observed drift is such that the device may well be outside the specified limits by the next calibration, adjustment will be necessary.

In addition to calibrating the devices, you will need to carry out preventive and corrective maintenance in order to keep them in good condition. Preventive maintenance is maintenance to reduce the probability of failure –

such as cleaning, testing, inspecting, replenishment of consumables etc. Corrective maintenance is concerned with restoring a device (after a failure has occurred) to a condition in which it can perform its required function. These activities may cover a wide range of skills and disciplines depending on the nature of the measuring devices you use. It will include software development skills if you use test software for instance, or electronic engineering if you use electronic equipment. You can of course subcontract the complete task to a specialist who will not only maintain the equipment but, on request, carry out calibration. Take care to confirm that the supplier is qualified to perform the calibrations to national standards and to provide a valid certificate of calibration.

Indicating calibration status (7.6c)

The standard requires measuring devices to *be identified to enable the calibration status to be determined.*

What does this mean?

Calibration status is the position of a measuring device relative to the time period between calibrations. If the date when calibration is due is in the future, the device can be considered calibrated – if the current date is beyond the date when calibration is due, the device is not necessarily inaccurate but

> **1994–2000 Differences**
> Previously the standard required the supplier to identify inspection, measuring and test equipment with a suitable indicator or approved identification record to show the calibration status.
>
> The intent of the requirement remains unchanged.

remains suspect until verified. However, devices can also be suspect if dropped or damaged even when the date of calibration is due is in the future. The requirement only applies to physical devices subject to wear, drift or variation with use or time.

Why is this necessary?

This requirement responds to the Factual Approach Principle.

While a robust calibration system should ensure no invalid devices are in use, system failures are a possibility. As the consequences of failure are greater than the effort involved in checking the validity of devices before use, it is prudent to provide a means for checking calibration status.

How is this implemented?

All devices subject to calibration should display an identification label that either directly or through traceable records, indicates the authority responsible for calibrating the device and the date when the next calibration is due. Don't state the actual calibration date because this would be no use without the user knowing the calibration frequency. Measuring equipment should indicate its calibration status to any potential user. Measuring instruments too small for calibration status labels showing the due date may be given other types of approved identification. It is not mandatory that users identify the due date solely from the instrument itself but they must be able to determine that the instrument has been calibrated. Serial numbers alone do not do this unless placed within a specially designed label that indicates that the item has been calibrated or you can fix special labels that show a circular calendar marked to show the due date. If you do use serial numbers or special labels then they need to be traceable to calibration records that indicate the calibration due date.

Devices used only for indication purposes or for diagnostic purposes should also display an identity that clearly distinguished them as not being subject to calibration. If devices are taken out of use for prolonged periods, it may be more practical to cease calibration and provide a means of preventing inadvertent use with labels indicating that the calibration is not being maintained. You may wish to use devices that do not fulfil their specification either because part of the device is unserviceable or because you were unable to perform a full calibration. In such cases, you should provide clear indication to the user of the limitation of such devices.

Safeguarding measuring and monitoring devices (7.6d)

1994–2000 Differences

Previously the standard required the supplier to safeguard inspection, measuring and test facilities including both test hardware and test software from adjustments that would invalidate the calibration setting.

The intent of the requirement remains unchanged.

The standard requires measuring and monitoring devices to *be safeguarded from adjustments that would invalidate the measurement result.*

What does this mean?

Once a device has been calibrated or verified there need to be safeguards in place to prevent unauthorized or inadvertent adjustment.

Why is this necessary?

This requirement responds to the Factual Approach Principle.

The purpose of this requirement is to ensure that the integrity of the measurements is maintained by precluding errors that can occur if measuring equipment is tampered with.

How is this implemented?

To safeguard against any deliberate or inadvertent adjustment to measuring devices, seals should be applied to the adjustable parts or where appropriate to the fixings securing the container. The seals should be designed so that tampering will destroy them. Such safeguards may not be necessary for all devices. Certain devices are designed to be adjusted by the user without needing external reference standards, for example zero adjustments on micrometers. If the container can be sealed then you don't need to protect all the adjustable parts inside.

Your procedures need to specify:

- Those verification areas that have restricted access and how you control access
- The methods used for applying integrity seals to equipment
- The authority permitted to apply and break the seals
- The action to be taken if the seals are found to be broken either during use or during calibration

Protection of measuring and monitoring devices (7.6e)

The standard requires measuring and monitoring devices to *be protected from damage and deterioration during handling, maintenance and storage.*

What does this mean?

Each measuring and monitoring device has a range within which accuracy and precision remains stable – use the device outside this range and the readings are suspect.

Why is this necessary?

> **1994–2000 Differences**
> Previously the standard required the supplier to ensure that the handling, preservation and storage of inspection, measuring and test equipment is such that the accuracy and fitness for use is maintained.
> The intent of the requirement remains unchanged.

This requirement responds to the Process Approach Principle.

Physical measuring and monitoring devices can be affected by inappropriate handling, maintenance and storage and thus jeopardize their integrity. Often measuring devices are very sensitive to vibration, dirt, shock and tampering and thus it is necessary to protect them so as to preserve their integrity.

How is this implemented?

When not in use, measuring devices should always be stored in the special containers provided by the manufacturer. Handling instructions should be provided with the storage case where instruments may be fragile or prone to inadvertent damage by careless handling. Instruments prone to surface deterioration during use and exposure to the atmosphere should be protected and moisture absorbent or resistant materials used. When transporting measuring devices you should provide adequate protection. Should you employ itinerant service engineers, ensure that the instruments they carry are adequately protected as well as calibrated.

Action on equipment found out of calibration (7.6)

1994–2000 Differences

Previously the standard required the supplier to assess and document the validity of previous inspection and test results when inspection, measuring and test equipment is found to be out of calibration.

The intent of the requirement remains unchanged.

The standard requires the validity of previous measuring results to *be assessed and recorded when equipment is found not to conform to requirements and for appropriate action to be taken on the equipment and any product affected.*

What does this mean?

This is perhaps the most difficult of requirements to meet for some organizations. It is not always possible or practical to be able to trace product to the particular devices used to determine its acceptability. The requirements apply not only to your working standards but also to your calibration standards. When you send calibration standards away for calibration and they are subsequently found to be inaccurate, you will need a method of tracing the devices they were used to calibrate. If you have a small number of measuring devices and only one or two of each type, it may not be too difficult to determine which products were accepted using a particular device. In large organizations that own many pieces of equipment that are constantly being used in a variety of situations, meeting the requirements can be very difficult.

Why is this necessary?

This requirement responds to the Process Approach Principle.

If a measurement has been taken with a device that is subsequently found inaccurate, the validity of the measurement is suspect and therefore an assessment is needed to establish the consequences. In most cases the devise used is accurate to an order of magnitude greater than that required, therefore, if found outside tolerance, it may not mean that the product measured is nonconforming. However, if measurements are taken at the extreme of device accuracy, the product may well be nonconforming if the device is found to be inaccurate.

How is this implemented?

One way of meeting this requirement is to record the type and serial number of the devices used to conduct measurements but you will also need to record the actual measurements made. Some results may be made in the form of ticks or pass/fail and not by recording actual readings. In these cases you will have a problem in determining whether the amount by which the equipment is out of specification would be sufficient to reject the product. In extreme circumstances, if the product is no longer in the factory, this situation could result in your having to recall the product from your customer or distributor.

In order to reduce the effect, you can select measuring devices that are several orders of magnitude more accurate than your needs so that when the devices drift outside the tolerances, they are still well within the accuracy you require. There still remains a risk that the device may be wildly inaccurate due to damage or malfunction. In such cases you need to adopt the discipline of re-calibrating devices that have been dropped or are otherwise suspect before further use.

You need to carefully determine your policy in this area paying particular attention to what you are claiming to achieve. You will need a procedure for informing the custodians of unserviceable measuring devices and one for enabling the custodians to track down the products verified using the unserviceable device and assess the magnitude of the problem. You will need a means of ranking problems in order of severity so that you can resolve the minor problems at the working level and ensure that significant problems are brought to the attention of the management for resolution. It would be irresponsible for a junior technician to recall six months production from customers and distributors based on a report from the calibration laboratory. You need to assess what would have happened if you had used serviceable equipment to carry out the measurements. Would the product have been reworked, repaired, scrapped or the requirement merely waived. If you suspect previously shipped product to be nonconforming and now you have discovered that the measurements upon which their acceptance was based were inaccurate, you certainly need to notify your customer. In your report to your customer, state the precise amount by which the product is outside specification so that the customer can decide whether to return the product – remember the product specification is but an interpretation of what constitutes fitness for use. Out of 'spec' doesn't mean unsafe, unusable, un-saleable etc.

Calibration and verification records (7.6)

The standard requires *records of the results of calibration and verification to be maintained.*

What does this mean?

Records of the results of calibration and verification are those records indicating the accuracy of the device prior to any adjustment and records after adjustment.

Why is this necessary?

This requirement responds to the Factual Approach Principle.

It is important to record calibration and verification in order to determine whether the device was outside the prescribed limits when last used. It also permits trends to be monitored and the degree of drift to be predicted.

Calibration records are also required in order to notify the customer if suspect product or material has been shipped.

How is this implemented?

Calibration and verification records are records of activities that have taken place. Records should be maintained not only for proprietary devices but also for devices you have produced and devices owned by customers and employees.

These records should include where appropriate:

- The precise identity of the device being calibrated/verified (type, name, serial number, configuration if it provides for various optional features)
- The name and location of the owner or custodian
- The date calibration was performed
- Reference to the calibration/verification procedure, its number and issue status
- The condition of the device on receipt
- The results of the calibration/verification in terms of readings before adjustment and readings after adjustment for each designated parameter
- The date fixed for the next calibration/verification
- The permissible limits of error
- The serial numbers of the standards used to calibrate the device
- The environmental conditions prevailing at the time of calibration
- A statement of measurement uncertainty (accuracy and precision)
- Details of any adjustments, servicing, repairs and modifications carried out
- The name of the person performing the calibration/verification
- Details of any limitation on its use

The records required are only for formal calibrations and verification and not for instances of self-calibration or zeroing using null adjustment mechanisms. Whilst calibration usually involves some adjustment to the device, non-adjustable devices are often verified rather than calibrated. However, it is not strictly correct to regard all calibration as involving some adjustment. Slip gauges and surface tables are calibrated but not adjusted. An error record is produced to enable users to determine the uncertainty of measurement in a particular range or location and compensate for the inaccuracies when recording the results.

Software validation (7.6)

The standard requires *confirmation of the ability of software used for measuring and monitoring of specified requirements to satisfy intended application to be undertaken prior to initial use and reconfirmed as necessary.*

What does this mean?

These requirements apply not only to production, installation and servicing but also to design, development and operations.

Why is this necessary?

This requirement responds to the Factual Approach Principle.

Software is used increasingly to drive equipment used for measurement or to interpret results. The integrity of the software therefore has a bearing on the integrity of the measurement and therefore needs to be verified prior to use. Although software does not degrade or wear out, it can be corrupted such that it no longer does the job it was intended to. In many cases software malfunction will be apparent by the absence of any result at all, but in some cases, a spurious result may be generated that appears to the observer as correct. Re-confirmation is necessary therefore after a period where the equipment may have been used in situations where intended or unintended changes to the configuration could have been made.

1994–2000 Differences

Previously the standard required:

(a) the supplier to control, calibrate and maintain test software used to demonstrate the conformance of product to the specified requirements;

(b) test software used as suitable forms of inspection, to be checked and rechecked at prescribed intervals to prove that they are capable of verifying the acceptability of product prior to release for use during production, installation and servicing;

(c) the supplier to establish the extent and frequency of such checks and to maintain records as evidence of control.

The intent of the requirement remains unchanged.

How is this implemented?

The integrity of software is critical to the resultant product whether it be a deliverable product to a customer or a product being developed or in use. The design of software should be governed by the requirements of Clause 7.3 although this is not mandated by the standard, indeed, if these requirements are applied, the design verification requirements should adequately prove that the software is capable of verifying the acceptability of product. However, the design control requirements may be impractical for many minor verification devices. The hardware that provides the platform for the software should also be controlled, and whilst it may not measure any parameters, its malfunction could result in nonconforming product being accepted. Complex hardware of this nature should be governed by the design controls of Clause 7.3 if designed in-house because it ensures product quality. If bought out, you should obtain all the necessary manuals for its operation and maintenance and it should be periodically checked to verify it is fully operational.

To control software you need to consider what it is that you need to control. As a minimum you should control its use, modification, location (in terms of where it is installed), replication and disposal.

Use is controlled by specifying the software by type designation and version in the development and production test procedures or a register that relates products to the software that has to be used to verify its acceptability. You should also provide procedures for running the software on the host computer or automatic test equipment. They may of course be menu driven from a display screen and keyboard rather than paper procedures.

Modifications should be controlled in a manner that complies with the requirements of clauses 7.3.7 of the standard.

The location could be controlled by index, register, inventory or other such means which enables you to identify on what machines particular versions of the software are installed, where copies and the master tapes or disks are stored.

Replication and disposal could be controlled by secure storage and prior authorization routines where only authorized personnel or organizations carry out replication and disposal.

Summary

In this chapter we have examined the requirements contained in section 7 of ISO 9001. This is the largest section of the standard and covers the result-producing process of an organization. Most of the requirements contained in the 1994 version of ISO 9001 are included in this section. We have examined the product realization processes both in general and specific terms through a series of processes that took us from receipt of a customer enquiry to post delivery activities. However, we have learnt that these processes are not necessarily triggered by customer orders and can also be triggered by a marketing process feeding requirements that have been derived from an understanding of market needs into a design process. This changes contract review into product requirement review and brings in all those functions that might have been excluded from the management system such as marketing, sales and design. We have learnt that we cannot ignore the first two requirements of clause 7.6 as they apply to all organizations and that the integrity of every device used to determine whether or not a requirement has been met does need to be managed. A recurring theme through this section of the standard is the absence of requirements for documented procedures. Taking one example to illustrate this trend; instead of requiring organizations to establish and maintain documented procedures for customer communication, the standard requires the organization to determine and implement effective arrangements for communicating with customers, thereby focusing on results rather than on the documentation. Much of the prescriptive style has disappeared and the requirements have become more generic. We have learnt that every one of the requirements is important and examined several solutions to meeting them. We have also seen how each of the product realization clauses can be linked together to form a cycle that covers the core business processes – processes that need to be managed effectively to achieve and sustain customer satisfaction.

Product Realization Questionnaire

Planning product realization

1 How do you plan and develop the processes required for product realization?
2 How do you ensure that planning of the realization processes is consistent with the other requirements of the organization's management system?
3 How do you determine the quality objectives and requirements for the product?
4 How do you determine the product specific processes that are needed?
5 How do you determine the product specific documents that are needed?
6 How do you determine the product specific resources that are needed?
7 How do you determine the product specific verification, validation, monitoring, inspection and test activities that are needed?
8 How do you determine the criteria for product acceptance?
9 How do you determine the records needed to provide evidence that the realization processes and resulting product meet requirements?
10 How do you ensure the product realization planning is in a form suitable for the organization's method of operations?

Customer related processes

11 How do you determine customer specified requirements including those requirements for delivery and post delivery activities?

12 How do you determine product requirements not specified by the customer but necessary for known intended use?

13 How do you determine statutory and regulatory requirements related to the product?

14 How do you determine the organization's requirements that apply to the product?

15 How do you review the requirements related to the product?

16 How do you ensure that product requirement reviews are conducted prior to the decision or commitment to supply a product to the customer?

17 How do you ensure that product requirements are defined?

18 How do you ensure that contract or order requirements differing from those previously expressed are resolved?

19 How do you ensure that the organization has the ability to meet defined requirements?

20 What records are maintained of the results of product requirements review?

21 How do you ensure that where the customer provides no documented statement of requirement, the customer requirements are confirmed before acceptance?

22 How do you ensure that where product requirements are changed, the relevant documents are amended and the relevant personnel are made aware of the changed requirements?

23 How do you communicate product information to customers?

24 How do you handle customer enquiries?

25 How do you process contracts or orders?

26 How do you handle amendments to customer requirements?

27 How do you handle customer feedback including customer complaints?

Design and development

28 How do you control design and development of the product?

29 How do you plan design and development of the product?

30 How do you determine the necessary stages of design and development for a particular product?

31 How do you determine the review, verification and validation activities appropriate to each design and development stage?

32 How do you determine the responsibilities and authorities for design and development activities?

33 How do you manage the interfaces between different groups involved in the design and development process?

34 How do you ensure that planning output is updated, as appropriate, as the design and development progresses?

35 How do you ensure that design inputs relating to product requirements are determined?

36 What records are maintained of design inputs?

37 How do you ensure that design inputs include functional and performance requirements?

38 How do you ensure that design inputs include applicable statutory and regulatory requirements?

39 How do you ensure that design inputs include applicable information derived from previous similar designs?

40 How do you ensure that design inputs include any other requirements essential for design and development?

41 How do you ensure that design inputs are reviewed for adequacy?

42 How do you ensure that the outputs of design and development are provided in a form that enables verification against the design and development inputs?

43 How do you ensure that design and development outputs meet the design and development input requirements?

44 How do you ensure that design and development outputs provide appropriate information for purchasing, production and service provision?

45 How do you ensure that design and development outputs contain or reference product acceptance criteria?

46 How do you ensure that design and development outputs define the characteristics of the product that are essential to its safe and proper use?

47 How do you ensure that design and development outputs are approved prior to release?

48 How do you ensure that systematic reviews of design and development are performed at suitable stages?

49 How do you ensure that design reviews are conducted to evaluate the ability of the results of the design and development to fulfil requirements?

50 How do you ensure that participants in design reviews include representatives of functions concerned with the design and development stage(s) being reviewed?

51 What records are maintained of the results of the design reviews and the actions arising from the review?

52 How do you ensure that design and development verification is performed to ensure the output meets the design and development inputs?

53 How do you ensure that the results of design verification and any required actions are recorded?

54 How do you ensure that design and development validation is performed to confirm that resulting product is capable of fulfilling the requirements for the specified application or intended use?

55 How do you ensure that wherever applicable, design validation is completed prior to the delivery or implementation of the product?

56 What records are maintained of design validation and subsequent follow-up actions?

57 How do you identify design and development changes?

58 What records are maintained of design and development changes?

59 How do you ensure that design changes are reviewed and approved before implementation?

60 How do you ensure that before implementation of design changes the effect of these changes on constituent parts and delivered product is evaluated?

61 How do you ensure that design changes are verified and validated as appropriate before implementation?

Purchasing

62 How do you ensure that purchased product conforms to specified purchase requirements?

63 How do you control suppliers and purchased product?

64 How do you evaluate and select suppliers?

65 What criteria have been established for selection, evaluation and re-evaluation of suppliers?

66 How do you ensure purchasing information describes the product to be purchased?

67 What activities are carried out to verify that purchased product meets specified purchase requirements?

Production and service provision

68 How do you ensure production and service provision is planned and carried out under controlled conditions?

69 How do you ensure work instructions are available where necessary to control production and service provision?

70 How do you ensure that information describing the characteristics of the product is available to control production and service provision?

71 How do you ensure suitable equipment is used to control production and service provision?

72 How do you ensure measuring and monitoring devices are available and used to control production and service provision?

73 How do you ensure that planned monitoring and measurement provisions are implemented?

74 What release activities are implemented to control production and service provision?

75 What delivery activities are implemented to control production and service provision?

76 What post-delivery activities are implemented to control production and service provision?

77 How do you validate production and service provision where the resulting output cannot be verified by subsequent measurement or monitoring?

78 How do you ensure the product is identified by suitable means throughout product realization?

79 How do you preserve conformity of product during internal processing and delivery to the intended destination?

Control of monitoring and measuring devices

80 How do you identify the monitoring and measurements necessary to provide evidence of conformity of product to determined requirements?

81 How do you identify the measuring and monitoring devices needed to provide evidence of conformity of product to determined requirements?

82 What processes have been established to ensure that monitoring and measuring can be carried out and are carried out in a manner consistent with the measuring and monitoring requirements?

83 How do you ensure measuring and monitoring devices are calibrated or verified at specified intervals or prior to use, against measurement standards traceable to international or national standards?

84 What records are maintained of the basis used for calibration or verification where no international or national standards exist?

85 How do you ensure valid results are maintained when measuring equipment is adjusted or re-adjusted?

86 What provisions have been made to enable the calibration status of measuring devices to be determined?

87 How do you ensure measuring and monitoring devices are safeguarded from adjustments that would invalidate the measurement result?

88 How do you ensure measuring and monitoring devices are protected from damage and deterioration during handling, maintenance and storage?

89 What action is taken with previous measuring results when measuring and monitoring equipment is found not to conform to requirements?

90 What records are maintained of the results of measuring and monitoring equipment calibration and verification?

91 How do you ensure that software used for measuring and monitoring of specified requirements satisfies the intended application?

Product Realization – Food for Thought

1 Do your marketing, sales and design processes include provisions for measuring the extent to which the process objectives are being achieved?

2 Are you confident that your sales personnel will not commit the organization beyond the capability of its processes?

3 When preparing plans for product realization how do you know you have taken account of all the factors that will affect successful implementation?

4 How do you know that the plans made for fulfilling product requirements will reach those who will create the product and process features necessary for successful implementation?

5 Do you assume customers will define the characteristics necessary to give satisfaction or do you recognize they are not experts and endeavour to find out what their expectations really are?

6 How do you know you have identified all the relevant regulations that apply to the customer transaction?

7 Would your customer expect you to proceed knowing there are issues to be resolved or to wait while you sought resolution?

8 However simple the order, do you always confirm understanding before proceeding?

9 How confident are you that the sales literature does not lead potential customers to expect more than you are prepared to provide?

10 Is customer feedback collected from all the points of contact with customers or only through the mailbox?

11 At what point do you bring design under control, before the design is released or before you spend money?

12 Are you confident that you won't make the same mistakes on the next new design as you did on the last design?

13 How do you stop your designers reinventing solutions to problems solved previously?

14 How do you ensure that design weaknesses revealed through risk analysis techniques are eliminated, reduced or at least controlled before the design is released?

15 What research is performed to discover the probability of success with new designs?

16 Is your purchasing process sufficiently flexible to prevent inappropriate conditions being placed on your suppliers?

17 Does your supplier selection procedure permit value-based decisions to be made or is it one size that fits all?

18 How do you know that the products you purchase for incorporation into supplies will satisfy the regulatory conditions that apply to the item you deliver to your customer?

19 How do your receipt inspectors know of the decisions your supplier verification personnel have made on the shipments received?
20 How do you know the processes are capable of achieving the required product or service features before commencing production or service delivery?
21 Does your system include all the distribution channels that have been established for delivering product to customers?
22 If a product was returned because of a failure, are you confident that you could find out what work has been done on it as it passed through the production process?
23 If an item of customer property was recalled, could you find it and return it in its original condition if requested to do so?
24 Have you put in place methods that will ensure the integrity of all of the devices used for monitoring and measurement?

Bibliography

1. Hoyle, David, (1996). *ISO 9000 Quality System Development Handbook,* Butterworth Heinemann.
2. Lyon, D.D., (2000). *Practical CM – Best Configuration Management Practices,* Butterworth Heinemann.
3. Boone Louis E. and Kurtz David L., (2001). *Contemporary marketing 10th Edition,* Harcourt College Publishers.
4. Subject – Measurement (©1994–1999). *Britannica® CD 99 Multimedia Edition* ©, Encyclopædia Britannica, Inc.
5. Subject – Metric system (©1994–1999). *Britannica® CD 99 Multimedia Edition* ©, Encylopædia Britannica, Inc.

Chapter 8
Measurement, analysis and improvement

> There can be no improvement where there are no standards . . .
> standards exist only to be superseded by better standards. Every
> standard, every specification and every measurement cries out for
> constant revision and upgrading
>
> *Masaaki Imai*

Summary of requirements

Measurement, analysis and improvement processes are vital to the achievement of quality. Until we measure using devices of known integrity, we know little about a process or its outcomes. But if we measure using instruments that are unfit for purpose, we will be misled by the results. With the results of valid measurement we can make a judgement on the basis of facts. The facts will tell us whether we have met the target. Analysis of the facts will tell us whether the target can be met using the same methods or better methods or whether the target is the right target to aim for. Measurements without a target value to compare results of measurement are measurements without a purpose. The target value is therefore vital but arbitrary values demotivate personnel. Targets should always be focused on purpose so that through the chain of measures from corporate objectives to component dimensions there is a soundly based relationship between targets, measures, objectives and the purpose of the organization, process or product.

Measurement tells us whether there has been a change in performance. Change is a constant. It exists in everything and is caused by physical, social or economic forces. When we measure the same parameter on different items we expect slight variation. However, if we measure the same parameter using the same device we might not expect there to be a change, but the inaccuracies inherent in the measuring system will lead to a variation in readings. To understand change we need to understand its cause. Some change is represented by variation about a norm and is predictable – it is a natural phenomenon of a process and when it is within acceptable limits it is tolerable. Other change is represented by erratic behaviour and is not predictable but its cause can be determined and eliminated through measurement, analysis and improvement.

Measurement, analysis and improvement are strictly sub-processes within each business process. However parent processes will often capture data from monitoring and measurements within sub-processes. This may happen when assessing a variety of data from individual processes to determine customer satisfaction or for discovering common cause problems and subsequently devising company wide improvement programmes.

There is a sort of logic in the structure of the requirements in this section but there are some gaps. It would have assisted understanding if the same terms as used in clause 8.1 had been used in the headings of clauses 8.2 to 8.5. In that way the relationships would have been more obvious. The general requirements of clause 8.1 are amplified by clauses 8.2 to 8.5 so the requirements in clause 8.1 are not separate to those in clauses 8.2 to 8.5 with the exception of clause 8.3 on the control of nonconforming product and those on statistical techniques. This later requirement is stated once because it applies to all monitoring, measurement and analysis processes. Clause 8.3 on nonconforming product appears in section 8 not because it has anything to do with measurement, analysis and improvement but because its inclusion in section 7 would imply that it could be excluded from the management system (see ISO 9001 clause 1.2).

It should not be assumed that section 8 includes all requirements on measurement, analysis and improvement.

Measurement and monitoring is also addressed by:

- Management representative (5.5.2) – in the context of reporting on system performance
- Management review (5.6) – in the context of reviewing system adequacy
- Control of monitoring and measurement devices (7.6)
- Design and development verification (7.3.5)
- Design and development validation (7.3.6)
- Verification of purchased product (7.4.3)

Analysis is also addressed by:

- Management review (5.6) – in the context of changes that could affect the management system
- Control of design and development changes (7.3.7) – in the context of evaluation of the effects of change

1994–2000 Differences
Previously the standard required:

(a) suppliers to establish and maintain documented procedures for inspection and testing activities in order to verify that the specified requirements for product are met;
(b) the required inspecting and testing and the records to be established and detailed in the quality plan or documented procedures;
(c) the supplier to ensure that production, installation and servicing processes were carried out under controlled conditions that included the monitoring of suitable process parameters and product characteristics;
(d) identify the need for statistical techniques required for establishing, controlling and verifying process capability and product characteristics;
(e) establish and maintain documented procedures to implement and control the application of statistical techniques.

The modified requirement goes beyond inspection and test to embrace all measurement and monitoring not only of product but also of equipment, environment and materials and will impact those systems in which measurement is limited to product inspection and test.

- Control of monitoring and measuring devices (7.6) – in the context of measurement systems

Improvement is also addressed by:

- Management review (5.6) – in the context of changes to quality policy
- Control of design and development changes (7.3.7)
- Internal communication (5.5.3) – in the context of communicating the effectiveness of the management system
- Provision of resources (6.1) in the context of resources needed for continual improvement

Monitoring, measurement, analysis and improvement processes (8.1)

Processes to demonstrate conformity (8.1)

The standard requires the organization *to plan and implement the monitoring, measurement, analysis and improvement processes needed to demonstrate conformity of the product including determination of applicable methods such as statistical techniques and the extent of their use.*

What does this mean?

The requirement for monitoring, measurement, analysis and improvement processes to be planned means that these activities should not be left to chance. It is odd that the requirements are limited to the processes needed to demonstrate conformity of the product and not all processes. However, this should not be taken too literally, because almost every process in an organization will impact the product either directly or indirectly. For example, if training processes are not monitored, untrained staff could produce nonconforming product. If management processes are not monitored result-producing processes may be starved of resources and consequently impact the product.

The monitoring processes identified in the standard that are needed to demonstrate conformity of product are:

- The monitoring of customer satisfaction (8.2.1)
- Monitoring of product (8.2.4) including design and development review (7.3.4)

These are the processes that keep operations and operating conditions under periodic or continual observation in order to be alerted to events before they occur. This is so that action can be taken to prevent nonconformity. Typical monitoring processes are those employed to check that machines are functioning correctly, that processes are under statistical control, that there are no serious bottlenecks or other conditions that may cause abnormal performance.

The measurement processes identified in the standard that are needed to demonstrate conformity of product are:

- Measurement of product (8.2.4) including:
  - Design and development verification (7.3.5)
  - Design and development validation (7.3.6)
  - Verification of purchased product (7.4.3)
  - Control of monitoring and measuring devices (7.6)

These are the processes that determine the characteristics of product in order to establish whether the product meets defined requirements. Typical measurement processes involve physical measurement of a product using inspection, test or demonstration techniques, or non-physical measurement of services using observation or examination techniques. These processes are found in design, production and service delivery operations.

The analysis processes identified in the standard to demonstrate conformity of product are:

- Design and development review (7.3.4) (This is both a monitoring and an analysis process.)
- Corrective action (8.5.2)
- Preventive action 8.5.3)

These are those processes that convert product data into knowledge from which decisions of conformity against prescribed standards can be made. Typical analysis processes are chemical and microbiological analysis to ascertain the properties or composition of a substance, stress analysis to ascertain the load bearing capacity of a structure. Other types of analysis may be used to compare current designs with previously validated designs, determine time dependent characteristics, assess vulnerability, susceptibility and durability.

The improvement processes needed to demonstrate conformity of the product are those processes that eliminate the cause of nonconformities and prevent their occurrence. These include the corrective action processes and preventive action processes. (These are dealt with under the relevant headings.)

There are various ways of monitoring, measuring and analysing things and some methods are better than others. The standard requires that applicable methods be determined and one field of data collection and analysis that can be used to demonstrate conformity of the product is to use statistical techniques. Any technique that uses statistical theory to reveal information is a statistical technique. However, there is a difference between statistical theory and statistics. Any set of figures that are intended to describe an entity or phenomena can be regarded as statistics. When one makes a prediction from these figures that attributes a particular quality to an entity or phenomena one needs to apply statistical theory for the prediction to be valid. Techniques such as Pareto analysis, histograms, correlation diagrams, matrix analysis are regarded as statistical techniques but although numerical data is used, there is no probability theory involved. These techniques are used for problem solving not for making product acceptance decisions. Other techniques such as SPC, reliability prediction and maintainability prediction use probability theory to provide a result which may not be absolute fact but which is the most probable result that can be deduced from the facts about a product or a number of products.

Why is this necessary?

This requirement responds to the Factual Approach Principle.

Monitoring, measurement, analysis and improvement processes are necessary to control the quality, cost and delivery of output. Where monitoring and measurement processes needed to demonstrate conformity of the product are performed, they should form part of a plan the intention of which is to discover whether the product conforms to requirements. Having discovered that information, it should also be planned that the information is passed through analysis processes on to the decision-makers so that decisions on product acceptability are made on the basis of fact and not opinion. Also as part of the plan, it is necessary to make provision for dealing with unacceptable product, either making it conform or preventing its unintended use or further processing.

How is this implemented?

Planning the monitoring, measurement and analysis processes

Whether monitoring or measuring, the processes are very similar and consist of a uniform series of elements (Juran, J. M., 1995)[1].

- The characteristic to be measured or monitored
- The units of measure
- The standard or specification to be achieved
- The sensor for detecting variance
- The human and physical resources for collecting, analysing, transmitting and presenting the data
- Interpretation and verification of results
- Decision on the action needed
- Taking action

Some of these elements where addressed in Chapter 7 under *Control of measuring and monitoring devices.*

In planning the monitoring and measurement processes needed to demonstrate conformity of the product the first thing to do is to identify the characteristics that need to be achieved and then determine how and where they are going to be verified. It is also necessary to determine the conditions that affect the achievement of these characteristics such as key process parameters and establish how these will be monitored.

A useful approach is to develop for each product a Verification Matrix that identifies the requirement to be achieved, the level at which the requirement is achieved and the method to be employed. Some requirements may be verified during design verification and not require confirmation during production because they are inherent features of the design. Other requirements may need to be reconfirmed on each product due to variations in materials or processes. Some characteristics may be only accessible for verification at the component or subassembly levels whereas others can be verified at end product level.

Another useful approach that is used in the automotive industry is a control plan. The aim of the control plan is to ensure that all process outputs will be in a state of control by providing process monitoring and control methods that control product and process characteristics. Apart from product identification data, the type of information contained in a control plan for each manufacturing operation is as follows:

- Operation description
- Characteristic
- Specification
- Measurement technique

- Sample size and frequency
- Control method (control chart, 100% inspection, functional test, check sheet etc.)
- Reaction plan (what to do in the event of a nonconformity)

For each production process, there should be a process specification that defines the standard operating conditions that need to be maintained and the means by which variation in these conditions is to be detected. Various instruments may be needed to provide a visual indication of operating conditions and the specification should also indicate the frequency of checks if they are located remote from the operator.

Determining measurement methods

The standard does not require you to use statistical techniques but identify the need for them. Within your procedures you will therefore need a means of determining when statistical techniques will be needed to determine product characteristics and process capability. One way of doing this is to use check lists when preparing customer specifications, design specifications and verification specifications and procedures. These check lists need to prompt the user to state whether the product characteristics or process capability will be determined using statistical techniques and if so which techniques are to be used.

Techniques for establishing and controlling process capability are essentially the same – the difference lies in what you do with the results. Firstly you need to know if you can make the product or deliver the service in compliance with the agreed specification. For this you need to know if the process is capable of yielding conforming product. Statistical Process Control techniques (SPC) will give you this information. Secondly you need to know if the product or service produced by the process actually meets the requirements. SPC will also provide this information. However, having obtained the results you need the ability to change the process in order that all product or service remains within specified limits and this requires either real-time or off-line process monitoring to detect and correct variance. To verify process capability you periodically rerun the analysis by measuring output product characteristics and establishing that the results demonstrate that the process remains capable.

When carrying out quality planning you will be examining intended product characteristics and it is at this stage that you will need to consider how achievement is to be measured and what tool or technique is to be used to perform the measurement. When you have chosen the tool you need to describe its use in the control plan.

Where statistical techniques are used for establishing, controlling and verifying process capability and product characteristics, procedures need to be produced for each application. You might for instance need a Process Control

Procedure, Process Capability Analysis Procedure, Receipt Inspection Procedure, and a Reliability Prediction Procedure etc. The procedures need to specify when and under what circumstances the techniques should be used and provide detail instruction on the sample size, collection, sorting and validation of input data, the plotting of results and application of limits. Guidance will also need to be provided to enable staff to analyse and interpret data, convert data and plot the relevant charts as well as make the correct decisions from the evidence they have acquired. Where computer programs are employed, they will need to be validated to demonstrate that the results being plotted are accurate. You may be relying on what the computer tells you rather than on any direct measurement of the product.

Processes to ensure conformity of management system (8.1)

The standard requires the organization *to plan and implement the monitoring, measurement, analysis and improvement processes needed to ensure conformity of the quality management system including determination of applicable methods such as statistical techniques and the extent of their use.*

What does this mean?

Conformity of the management system means that the system has been designed with the capability of implementing the defined policies and fulfilling the established objectives and targets and is being operated in a manner consistent with these policies, objectives and targets.

The monitoring processes identified in the standard to ensure conformity of the management system are:

- Reporting on management system performance (5.5.2)
- Review of system adequacy (5.6)
- Internal audit (8.2.2)
- Monitoring of processes (8.2.3)

(Note: System adequacy is interpreted as a state where the system delivers the required outputs. They

---

1994–2000 Differences

Previously the standard required:

(a) procedures for corrective action;
(b) procedures for preventive action;
(c) procedures for planning and implementing internal quality audits.

Previously the requirements focused on nonconforming product and conformity of activities to planned arrangements. This new requirement extends improvement activities to those related to all aspects of improved efficiency and effectiveness. It clearly extends the application of statistical techniques to any measurement and monitoring activities and therefore will impact those systems where their use was limited to product conformity and process capability.

may not be produced efficiently or be the right outputs but they are the ones required.)

More generally in this context the monitoring processes are those that keep operations and operating conditions under periodic or continual observation. The reason for doing this is to be alerted to events before, during or immediately after they occur so that action can be taken to prevent or minimize their effects. Typical monitoring processes are those employed in the utility industries where advanced warning of potential or actual problems is needed to maintain the supply of electricity, water and gas to consumers. Management monitor expenditure or rate of expenditure to forecast whether it will be able to meet their current and future commitments. Operators monitor machines to check that they are functioning correctly, that processes are under statistical control. Distribution staff may monitor on-time delivery and ring the alarm bells when this drops below the norm.

The measurement processes identified in the standard to ensure conformity of the management system are:

- Validation of processes (7.5.2)
- Measurement of processes (8.2.3)

The measurement processes needed to ensure conformity of the management system are those processes that measure the performance of the business processes. Every process should not only contain provision for measuring output but for measuring whether the process objectives are being achieved. Audits are one means of verifying that the management system conforms in both its design and implementation. Such audits would not only determine if procedures were being followed but whether the desired results were being achieved and any regulations complied with. (Audits are dealt with separately under the relevant heading.)

The analysis processes to ensure conformity of the management system are:

- Internal audit (8.2.2) This is in the context of audits of implementation.
- Analysis of data (8.4).

More generally the analysis processes needed to ensure conformity of the management system are those processes that convert process data into knowledge from which decisions of conformity against prescribed standards can be made. Examples include the analysis of variation in processes, process capability studies, behavioural analysis, organizational analysis, workflow analysis, analysis of constraints, risk analysis, hazard analysis and defect analysis.

The improvement processes needed to ensure conformity of the management system are the corrective action processes that reduce variation in process performance and restore the status quo. (Corrective action is dealt with separately under the relevant heading.)

The statistical techniques in this context are those used for measuring process capability.

Why is this necessary?

This requirement responds to the Factual Approach Principle.

As the management system is the means by which the organization achieves its objectives, it is necessary to ensure that the processes are well designed and are operating properly. Much of the focus in the 1994 version of ISO 9001 was on measuring product and auditing procedures. It has been widely accepted that both these techniques are not only ineffective in ensuring customer satisfaction but are also uneconomic A more effective technique is to monitor and measure processes and strive to reduce variation in these processes. By setting up processes that are capable of delivering conforming output and then monitoring, measuring and improving these processes so that process capability is assured, less dependence needs to be put on measuring product and auditing procedures and as a result less resources are utilized.

How is this implemented?

These requirements are expanded in the other sections of clause 8 of the standard and therefore the methods for implementing them are addressed under the appropriate heading.

Processes to continually improve the effectiveness of the management system (8.1)

The standard requires the organization *to plan and implement the monitoring, measurement, analysis and improvement processes needed to continually improve the effectiveness of the quality management system including determination of applicable methods such as statistical techniques and the extent of their use.*

> **1994–2000 Differences**
> This is a new requirement that has no equivalent in the 1994 version.

What does this mean?

The Monitoring and measurement processes identified in the standard to continually improve the effectiveness of the management system are:

- Management review (5.6)
- Review of requirements related to product (7.2.2)
- Monitoring and measurement of processes (8.2.3)

Continual improvement of the effectiveness of the management system is addressed in more detail against clause 8.5.1 of the standard. However it is important to distinguish between improving the management system and improving the effectiveness of the management system. The management system can be improved by correcting deficiencies in process design and implementation but this is improving conformity – making the process perform as it should do. Effectiveness is about doing the right things therefore improving the effectiveness of the management system means making the objectives, standards or targets established for activities, tasks or processes meet the needs of the organization to accomplish its purpose or mission. The objectives, targets and standards focus action therefore if they are not the right objectives, targets and standards the action, no matter how well it is performed, will be the wrong action for the organization. It may be the right action in another organization or in different circumstances.

The only analysis process that serves continual improvement in system effectiveness is the process for scanning the environment for changes that impact the objectives and targets that have been established. This is addressed by clause 5.6.2f.

The improvement process for improving the effectiveness of the management system is the *change management process*. This process would be triggered by the results of scanning the environment for changes as stated above and would manage the change through the organization.

Why is this necessary?

This requirement responds to the Continual Improvement Principle.

Many organizations are managed as a series of functions. A functional hierarchy is a common approach to organizational design. However, the structure tends to dictate the way objectives are set and therefore each function sets its objectives based upon what it believes is necessary to meet the organization's purpose and mission. This often leads to conflicting objectives where one function pursues objectives that compromise other functions. When functional objectives are based upon quotas such as numbers of orders processed, number of designs produced, number of products produced, the challenge is to do more rather than do better. Effectiveness is not a measure of meeting quotas but fulfilling purpose. It is therefore necessary to monitor and measure the effectiveness of the system as a whole – not the functions. A typical example is where the purchasing function is measured on the costs of purchased product and naturally strives to drive down suppliers on price. The net result is that either the supplier goes out of business or uses sub standard materials and takes risks. The results submitted by the purchasing function to the Executive look good – it has halved the purchasing costs but production can't make the product and warranty costs go up. This is why it is necessary to manage the system as a series of processes not as a series of functions.

How is this implemented?

The methods for improving the effectiveness of the management system are dealt with under the section on improvement.

Customer satisfaction (8.2.1)

The standard requires the organization *to monitor information relating to customer perception as to whether the organization has met customer requirements and requires the methods of obtaining and using this information to be determined.*

> **1994–2000 Differences**
> This is a new requirement that has no equivalent in the 1994 version.

What does this mean?

By combining definitions of the terms 'customer satisfaction' and 'requirement' ISO 9000 defines customer satisfaction as the customer's perception of the degree to which the customer's stated or implied needs or expectations have been fulfilled.

In order to satisfy customers you therefore have to go beyond the stated requirements. Customers are people and people differ in their perceptions as to whether the transaction has been satisfactory. The term perception is used because satisfaction is a subjective and human condition unlike acceptance that is based on objective evidence. Customers may accept a product but not be wholly satisfied with it or the service they have received. Whether or not you have done your utmost to please the customer, if the customer's perception is that you have not met their expectations, they will not be satisfied. You could do exactly the same for two customers and find that one is ecstatic about the products and the services you provide and the other is dissatisfied.

Information relating to customer perception is any meaningful data from which a judgement can be made about customer satisfaction and would include compliments, complaints, sales statistics, survey results etc. The requirement refers to the monitoring of customer perception rather than the measurement of customer satisfaction. One difference is that monitoring involves systematic checks on a periodic or continuous basis, whereas measurement may be a one-off event.

Why is this necessary?

This requirement responds to the Factual Approach Principle.

The primary purpose of the management system is to enable the organization to achieve its objectives one of which will be the creation and retention of satisfied customers. It therefore becomes axiomatic that customer satisfaction needs to be monitored.

How is this implemented?

There are several ways of monitoring information relating to customer perceptions ranging from unsolicited information to customer focus meetings.

Repeat orders

The number of repeat orders (e.g. 75% of orders are from existing customers) is one measure of whether customers are loyal but this is not possible for all organizations particular those that deal with consumers and do not capture their names. Another measure is the period over which customers remain loyal (e.g. 20% of our customers have been with us for more than 10 years). A marked change in this ratio could indicate success or pending disaster.

Competition

Monitoring what the competition is up to is an indicator of your success or failure. Do they follow your lead or are you always trying to catch up? Monitoring the movement of customers to and from your competitors is an indicator of whether your customers are being satisfied.

Referrals

When you win new customers find out why they chose your organization in preference to others. Find out how they discovered your products and services. It may be from advertising or maybe, your existing customers referred them to you.

Demand

Monitoring the demand for your products and services relative to the predicted demand is also an indicator of success or failure to satisfy customers. It could also be an indicator of the effectiveness of your sales promotion programme, therefore analysis is needed to establish which it is.

Effects of product transition

When you launch a new product or service, do you retain your existing customers or do they take the opportunity to go elsewhere?

Surveys

There are several types of survey than can be used. There is the impersonal form and the personal form. The impersonal form relies on responses to questionnaires and seeks to establish customer opinion on a number of topics ranging from specific products and services to general perceptions about the organization. The questionnaires can be sent to customers in a mail shot, included with a shipment or filled in before a customer departs (as with hotels and training courses). These questionnaires are somewhat biased because they only gather information on the topics perceived as important to the organization.

It should be noted that questionnaires by themselves are not an effective means of gathering customer opinion. Customers don't like them and are not likely to take them seriously unless they have a particular issue they want to bring to your attention. It is much better to talk face to face with your customer using an interview checklist. Think for a moment how a big customer like Ford and General Motors would react to thousands of questionnaires from their suppliers. They would either set up a special department just to deal with the questionnaires or set a policy that directs staff not to respond to supplier questionnaires. Economics alone will dictate the course of action that customers will take.

The personal form of survey is conducted through interview such as a customer service person approaching a customer with a questionnaire while the customer is on the organization's premises. This may apply to hotels, airports, entertainment venues and large restaurants. With this method there is the opportunity for dialogue and capturing impromptu remarks that hide deep-rooted feelings about the organization.

Focus meetings

A personal form of obtaining information on customer satisfaction is to arrange to meet with your customer. Seek opinions from the people within the customer's organization such as from Marketing, Design, Purchasing, Quality Assurance and Manufacturing departments etc. Target key product features as well as delivery or availability, price and relationships. This form is probably only suitable where you deal with other organizations.

Complaints

The process for handling customer complaints is addressed in Chapter 7 under *Customer Feedback*. Here the topic is *monitoring* and therefore you should be looking at the overall number of complaints, the upward or downward trends and the distribution of complaints by type of customer, location and nature of complaint. Coding conventions could be used to assign complaints to various categories covering the product (or parts thereof) packaging, labelling, advertising, warranty, support etc.

Any complaint, no matter how trivial, is indicative of a dissatisfied customer. The monitoring methods need to take account of formal complaints submitted in writing by the customer and verbal complaints given in conversation via telephone or meeting. Everyone who comes into contact with customers should have a method of capturing customer feedback and communicating it reliably to a place for analysis.

Compliments

Compliments are harder to monitor because they can vary from a passing remark during a sales transaction to a formal letter. Again, all personnel who come into contact with customers should have a non-intrusive method for conveying to the customer that the compliment is appreciated and will be passed on to the staff involved.

Internal audit (8.2.2)

Auditing for conformance with planned arrangements (8.2.2a)

1994–2000 Differences
Previously the standard required the supplier to carry out audits to verify whether quality activities and related results comply with planned arrangements.
This new requirement focuses on the design of the management system rather than its implementation and implies that the management system needs to be designed to meet both clause 7.1 and 4.1 as well as achieve the objectives required by clause 5.4.1.

The standard requires the organization *to conduct internal audits at planned intervals to determine whether the quality management system conforms to the planned arrangements (see 7.1).*

What does this mean?

ISO 9000 defines an audit as a systematic, independent and documented process for obtaining audit evidence and evaluating it objectively to determine the extent to which agreed criteria are fulfilled. In other words an audit is an examination of performance to determine whether defined performance standards have been met. Audits are a means of verification and as such involve monitoring and measurement. Both these words are used in the standard and it seems as though they are intended to convey different concepts but are actually part of the same concept (see Chapter 2).

The Planned arrangements in this context are the agreed criteria and these are the intentions of management as expressed by the quality policy, quality objectives and particular requirements for products. The purpose of this audit is therefore to establish that the management system has been designed to implement the agreed quality policy, quality objectives and product requirements i.e. does it possess all the characteristics necessary for it to fulfil its purpose? Principal among these characteristics are the organization's processes.

Clause 7.1 refers to clause 4.1 and therefore, the audit should verify that in designing the management system, the organization has identified all the necessary processes, determined their sequence and interaction, the criteria and methods for effective operation and control, provided the necessary information and resources and installed the necessary monitoring, measurement analysis and improvement processes.

Planned intervals can be any time interval and as the quality policy is unlikely to change very much in a five-year period, annual audits may not detect any significant variations. Quality objectives also may change once a year and so quarterly audits may not detect any significant change. However, product requirements vary with every new product and therefore the intervals of audit need to be set relative to changes in policies, objectives and products rather than a set frequency.

Why is this necessary?

This requirement responds to the Factual Approach Principle.

The purpose of quality audits is to establish, by an unbiased means, factual information on quality performance. Quality audits are the measurement component of the quality system. Having established a quality system it is necessary to install measures that will inform management whether the system is being effective. Installing any system without some means of being able to verify whether it is doing its intended job is a waste of time and effort. Audits gather facts, they should not change the performance of what is being measured and should always be performed by someone who has no influence over what is being measured. Audits should not be performed to find faults, to apportion blame or to investigate problems; other techniques should be used for these purposes. One of the most common deficiencies as Deming points out (Deming, W. Edwards, 1982)[2] is that a goal without a method for reaching it is useless, but it is a common practice for management to set goals without describing how they are going to be accomplished. A management system audit is needed to reveal such deficiencies.

How is this implemented?

As indicated above, this audit should be triggered by a change in policy, objectives or product requirements. A practical approach would therefore be to design three types of management system audits or System Audits. The audits should be designed to verify that the system is capable of:

- implementing the agreed policies (a policy audit)
- enabling the organization to achieve the agreed objectives (a strategic audit)
- enabling the organization to meet specific product requirements (a project or product audit)

Policy audit

The policy audit should establish that:

- the corporate policies are derived from an analysis of the factors critical to accomplishment of the organization's purpose (Are they soundly based?)
- the corporate policies are communicated throughout the organization (Does everyone understand them?)
- measures have been established for determining whether the corporate policies are being implemented (How will we know if they are not being implemented?)
- the operational policies do not conflict with the corporate policies (How do departmental policies relate to corporate policies?)

Strategic audit

The strategic audit should establish that:

- there is a defined process for establishing the organizations goals and objectives
- an analysis of current and future needs of customers and other interested parties has been carried out
- the requirements which the organization needs to meet to fulfil its mission have been determined
- objectives have been established for achieving these requirements
- priorities for action have been set
- the products, services and projects that need to be developed or abandoned to achieve these objectives have been identified
- the risks to success have been quantified
- the processes for achieving the objectives have been designed and constructed
- the information, resources, criteria and methods for effective operation of these processes have been identified, developed and provided
- the necessary monitoring, measurement, analysis and improvement processes have been designed and installed

Project or product audit

The project audit should be conducted for each new project (i.e. an undertaking that requires the development of new or modified products, processes, services). The project audit should establish that:

- any changes to the management system processes that are needed to achieve specific product requirements have been identified
- the processes have been modified or new processes designed
- the information, resources, criteria and methods for effective operation and control of these processes have been identified, developed and provided
- the necessary monitoring, measurement, analysis and improvement processes have been designed and installed

By judicious implementation of these system audits, the integrity of the management system will be confirmed.

Auditing for compliance (8.2.2a)

The standard requires the organization *to conduct internal audits at planned intervals to determine whether the quality management system conforms to the requirements of this International Standard.*

What does this mean?

ISO 9001 contains a series of requirements for which there are numerous solutions depending on the nature of the organization and its markets, products and services. As the organization, its processes and products change, periodic confirmation that the system conforms to the standard is necessary to verify it remains in conformity.

> **1994–2000 Differences**
> Previously the standard required the supplier to carry out audits to verify whether quality activities and related results comply with planned arrangements.
>
> The planned arrangements could have been the intent to meet the requirements of ISO 9001, therefore there is no change in intent.

Why is this necessary?

This requirement responds to the Factual Approach Principle.

It is debatable whether this requirement is really necessary. If the organization has conducted system audits of the type described above, has conducted implementation audits of the type described below and is conducting management reviews, it will know whether the management system is effective. There is therefore no justification for verifying that the system conforms to the requirements of ISO 9001 because it puts the emphasis on conformity rather than performance. It suggests that if the management system was deemed effective by the management review but an ISO 9001 conformity audit revealed that certain requirements were not being met, the system should be changed simply to bring it into conformity with the standard. Why would anyone want to do this? The system could be focused on the wrong objectives, but it does not require a complete ISO 9000 audit for this to be discovered.

The argument for this requirement is that all organizations should have control over their own operations and not rely upon external Certification Bodies to detect system nonconformities. It would therefore be logical for organizations to perform internal audits against the same standards as the external bodies and only use the external bodies as confirmation that they meet the requirements of the standard. Having performed an initial assessment against the requirements of ISO 9001, one should only need to repeat the assessment when the system changes.

How is this implemented?

As the requirement is placed under the heading of internal audit, the Certification Body audit cannot be a substitute even though it is performed with the same purpose in mind. There is a school of thought that believes a Certification Body audit will ultimately reduce to a confirmation that the internal conformity audit has been carried out by competent personnel and has demonstrated that the system is in conformity with the requirement of ISO 9001. This is not beyond the bounds of possibility. All it needs is for the Certification Body to recognize the competence and impartiality of the internal auditors, reduce their certification costs and a new auditing regime will emerge.

Conformity with the requirements of ISO 9001 can be confirmed in one of two ways:

(a) by performing a full internal system audit against ISO 9001
(b) by analysing the results of policy, strategic, project and process audits and determining conformity by correlation

In order to meet this requirement by analysis of data, rather than audit you would first need a matrix showing all the requirements of ISO 9001 against the processes in which the requirements were implemented. As there are over 250 requirements, this would be a large and complicated matrix so one solution is to compile the matrix as a series of layers. The first layer would list the ISO 9001 requirements as a series of clauses against the core business processes. For each process a list of applicable requirements can then be identified and cross-referenced to the process stage where it is implemented. The audit results from the policy, strategic, project and process audits can then be cross-referenced and through data synthesis, conformity with the requirements of ISO 9001 can be confirmed. A report can be printed and the assumptions, conclusions and recommendations added.

Auditing for effective implementation and maintenance (8.2.2b)

The standard requires the organization *to conduct internal audits at planned intervals to determine whether the quality management system is effectively implemented and maintained.*

What does this mean?

Effective implementation should not be confused with system effectiveness. The evaluation of system effectiveness serves to explore better ways of doing things, whereas, an evaluation of effective implementation serves to explore whether the processes are being run as intended and are achieving their purpose i.e. people are doing what they are required to do and the results are having the desired effect. A process may be run as intended but not achieve the desired results indicating a design weakness in the process.

Effectively maintained means that the processes continue to remain capable despite changes in the quantity, condition or nature of the human, physical and financial resources.

In the past it has been assumed that if people were found to be following the procedures as documented, the system was effective. Conversely, if the people were not found to be following the procedures, the system was somehow ineffective. But this was not the reason for the system i.e. it was not the purpose of the system to force people to follow procedures. The purpose was to ensure results, therefore a system is effective only if it can be demonstrated that the desired results are being achieved.

Why is this necessary?

This requirement responds to the Factual Approach Principle.

In order to manage the organization effectively, it is necessary to know whether the system for achieving the organization's objectives does the job for which it has been designed. Management also needs a system that does not collapse every time something changes – the system has to be robust. It has to cope with changes in personnel, changes in customer requirements, changes in the environment and in resources. Consequently to remain robust the system has to be effectively maintained.

How is this implemented?

The management system comprises a series of interconnected processes and each contributes to its overall effectiveness. This requirement can be met in one of three ways:

(a) by system implementation audits
(b) by process audits conducted by personnel external to the process
(c) by process audits conducted by personnel operating the process

System implementation audit

There are two ways for conducting the system implementation audit:

(a) by planning a series of audits that will cover the entire system in one cycle
(b) by analysing the results of process audits and determining effectiveness by correlation

If the system implementation option is chosen, you should not need to build into each process an audit mechanism. The analysis option is only an option when each process has a build-in audit mechanism.

Process audit

The traditional practice has been for processes to embody provisions for product measurement and process monitoring that is results-oriented. The measures are related to what is being processed – not the extent to which the rules are being followed. The internal audit has taken on this role but it misses the crucial question of establishing the efficiency of the process. Results were not matched with the effort used to produce them. A process is not efficient if it achieves the required results by wasting resources. It is therefore necessary to periodically examine whether:

● the activities are being performed as planned
● the resources are being effectively utilized

Such audits would examine activities not only to verify that the prescribed actions and decisions have been taken but also to verify the time and effort taken to perform them. The plans and specifications should define targets for time and effort so that the audit is against agreed targets and does not become a witch hunt. The audits could be performed by personnel external to the process, such as internal auditors or managers or in fact be performed by the supervisors of the process.

Planning audits (8.2.2)

The standard requires the audit programme *to be planned taking into consideration the status and importance of the processes and areas to be audited as well as the results of previous audits.*

1994–2000 Differences

Previously the standard required the supplier to schedule audits on the basis of the status and importance of the activity.

The additional requirement for audit planning to take into account previous audit results is merely a clarification as the status of an activity would include previous performance. There will be impact only where audits were planned without evaluating past performance.

What does this mean?

The audit programme is defined in ISO 9000 as a set of one or more audits planned for a specific time frame and directed towards a specific purpose. The *programme* will therefore have dates on which the audits are to be conducted. As the programme should be directed at the purpose of the audits, there may be a need for different types of audit programmes depending on whether the audits are of the quality system, contracts, projects, processes, products or services. It would therefore be expected that all audits in a particular audit programme would serve the same purpose. The audit programme would also be presented as a calendar chart showing where and when the audits will take place.

Status has three meanings in this context – the first to do with the relative position of the process or area in the scheme of things; the second to do with the maturity of the process; the third to do with the performance of process.

On the importance of the process, you need to establish to whom is it important – to the customer, the managing director, the public or your immediate superior? You also need to establish the importance of the activity upon the effect of non-compliance with the planned arrangements. Importance also applies to what may appear minor decisions in the planning or design phase but if the decisions are incorrect it could result in major problems down stream. If not detected, getting the decimal place wrong, or the units of measure wrong can have severe consequences. Rather than check the figures or the units of measure, audits should verify that the appropriate controls are in place to detect such errors before it is too late.

The status and importance of the activities will determine whether the audit is scheduled once a month, once a year or left for three years – any longer and the activity might be considered to have no value in the organization.

Why is this necessary?

This requirement responds to the Process Approach Principle.

There is little point in conducting in-depth audits on processes that add least value. There is also little point auditing processes that have only just commenced operation. You need objective evidence of compliance and that may take some time to be collected. Where the results of previous audits have revealed a higher than average performance in an area, (such as zero nonconformities on more than two occasions) the frequency of audits may be reduced. However, where the results indicate a lower than average performance, (such as a much higher than average number of nonconformities) the frequency of audits should be increased.

How is this implemented?

An audit programme should be developed for each type of audit as indicated above. Therefore one might prepare audit programmes for:

- Management audits (a combination of policy audits and strategic audits)
- Project audits (for new developments)
- Product audits (for existing products and services)
- Process audits (for all the organization's processes)
- Conformity audits (for all regulations and standards that apply)

The conformity audits could focus on *all* regulatory requirements, not simply those of ISO 9001, because they serve the same purpose – to verify conformity with standards.

This requirement focuses on the criteria for choosing the areas, activities, processes etc. to audit and therefore following initial audits to verify that the system is in place and functioning as planned, subsequent audits should be scheduled depending on status and importance.

An audit of one requirement of a policy, standard, process, procedure, contract etc. in one area only will not be conclusive evidence of compliance if the same requirements are also applicable to other areas. Where operations are under different managers but performing similar functions you cannot rely on the evidence from only one area – management style, commitment and priorities will differ. In order to ensure that a particular audit programme is comprehensive you will need to draw up a matrix showing the areas/ processes/products etc. to be audited and the dates when the audits are to be carried out. Supporting each audit programme an analysis of the status and importance should be performed and the key aspects to be audited identified. The programme also has to include shift working so that auditors need to be very flexible. One audit per year covering 10% of the quality system in 10% of the organization is hardly comprehensive. However, there are cases where such an approach is valid. If sufficient confidence has been acquired after conducting a comprehensive series of audits over some time, the audit programme can be adjusted so that it targets only those areas where change is most likely, thus auditing more stable areas less frequently.

The management system will contain many provisions, not all of which may be verified on each audit. This may either be due to time constraints or work for which the provisions apply not being scheduled. It is therefore necessary to record those aspects that have or have not been audited and devise the programme so that over a one to three year cycle all provisions are audited in all areas at least once.

Defining audit criteria, scope, frequency and methods (8.2.2)

The standard requires *the audit criteria, scope, frequency and methods to be defined*.

What does this mean?

The audit criteria are the standards for the performance being audited. They may include policies, procedures, regulations or requirements. Examinations without such a standard are surveys – not audits.

The scope of the audit is a definition of what the audit is to cover – the boundary conditions including the areas, locations, shifts, processes, departments etc.

> **1994–2000 Differences**
>
> Previously the standard required the supplier to establish and maintain documented procedures for planning internal quality audits.
>
> This change defines the planning requirement in more detail but does introduce the concept that audit scope and methodology can differ and should therefore be defined for each audit.

The frequency is the interval over which the audit is to be repeated and can be daily, weekly, monthly, quarterly, annually or longer.

The methods are the manner by which the audit is to be planned, conducted, reported and completed.

In defining these aspects, they may be described through procedures, standards, forms and guides.

Why is this necessary?

This requirement responds to the Process Approach Principle.

Without defined methods of auditing it is likely that each auditor will choose a different way of performing the audit – some will be good and some not so good. In order to run an effective management system, auditing should aim for best practice and therefore defining auditing methods enables best practice to be defined for the benefit of the organization.

How is this implemented?

For each audit the auditor should as a matter of routine always define the standard against which the audit is to be carried out and the scope of the audit. The frequency of the audit should be defined in the audit programme and the method within the auditing procedures.

Selection of auditors (8.2.2)

1994–2000 Differences

Previously the standard required that internal quality audits be carried out by personnel independent of those having direct responsibility for the activity being audited.

This change implies that managers and supervisors can legitimately perform audits that satisfy ISO 9001 whereas previously any audits they performed would not be accepted owing to bias.

The standard requires the selection of auditors and the conduct of audits *to ensure objectivity and impartiality of the audit process and for auditors not to audit their own work.*

What does this mean?

This requirement means that auditors should be selected on the basis of their objectivity and impartiality – such that their association with the work being audited should not influence their judgement. The requirement suggests that anyone auditing their own work may be influenced to overlook, hide or ignore facts pertinent to the audit.

Why is this necessary?

This requirement responds to the Leadership Principle.

If personnel have personally produced a product, they are more likely to be biased and oblivious to any deficiencies than someone totally unconnected with the product. They may be so familiar with the product that they are blind to its full strengths and weaknesses. A second pair of eyes often catches the errors overlooked by the first pair of eyes. However, auditors are human and if there is a personal relationship between the auditor and the auditee, the judgement of the auditor may be prejudiced. Depending on the nature of any problems found, the auditor being a friend, relation or confidant of the auditee, may be reluctant to or may be persuaded not to disclose the full facts. Even a customer may fail to exercise objectivity when it is found that the cause of problems is the inadequacy of the customer requirement!

How is this implemented?

Apart from the requirement for auditors not to audit their own work, any other competent person could be selected as an auditor. The requirement for objectivity and impartiality does not mean that one must rule out supervisors, managers, friends, relations or internal customers as auditors. These conditions do not necessarily mean such a person cannot be objective and impartial – there is simply an inherent risk. This risk is overcome by the selection being made on a person's character and track record. It would be foolish to limit the selection of auditors to those who are totally independent because in some small organizations there may be no one who fits this criterion. The difficulty arises in demonstrating subsequent to the audit, that the selected auditor exercised objectivity and impartiality. In organizations that observe a set of shared values, where honesty and trust are prevalent and frequently reinforced, it should not be necessary to demonstrate that the selected auditors meet this criterion. For other organizations a solution is for the auditors to be selected on the basis of having no responsibility for the work audited and no personal relationship with any of the auditees concerned.

By being divorced from the audited activities, the auditor is unaware of the pressures, the excuses, the informal instructions handed down and can examine operations objectively without bias and without fear of reprisals. To ensure their objectivity and impartiality, auditors need not be placed in separate organizations. Although it is quite common for quality auditors to reside in a quality department, it is by no means essential. There are several solutions to retaining impartiality:

- Auditors can be from the same department as the activities being audited, provided they do not perform the activities being audited
- Separate independent quality audit departments could be set up staffed with trained auditors
- Audits could be carried out by competent personnel at any level

Audit procedures (8.2.2)

The standard requires *the responsibilities and requirements for planning and conducting audits and for reporting results and maintaining records to be defined in a documented procedure.*

What does this mean?

This means that the 'who, when, where, what, why and the how' of planning, conducting and reporting audits should be defined and documented. It also means that the methods of maintaining audit records following the audit should also be defined and documented.

Although the requirement calls for *a* documented procedure, it is not essential that your documentation be limited to a single document, because you may need policies, forms, guides and standards to describe the audit process.

Why is this necessary?

This requirement responds to the Process Approach Principle.

Auditing is a process and as such should be documented in order to achieve consistency, to record best practice and to provide the basis for improvement.

How is this implemented?

The audit procedures should cover the following:

- Preparing the annual audit programme
- The selection of auditors and team leader if necessary
- Planning particular type of audits
- Conducting the audit
- Recording observations
- Determining corrective actions
- Reporting audit findings
- Implementing corrective actions
- Confirming the effectiveness of corrective actions
- The forms on which you plan the audit
- The forms on which you record the observations and corrective actions
- Any warning notices you send out of impending audits, overdue corrective actions and escalation actions

The detail plan for each audit may include dates if it is to cover several days but the main substance of the plan will be what is to be audited, against what requirements and by whom. At the detail level, the specific requirements to be checked should be identified based upon risks, past performance and when it was last checked. *Overall plans* are best presented as programme charts and *detail plans* as check lists. Audit planning should not be taken lightly. Audits require effort from auditees as well as the auditor so a well-planned audit designed to quickly discover pertinent facts is far better than a rambling audit that jumps from area to area looking at this or that without any obvious direction.

Although check lists may be considered a plan, in the context of an audit they should be considered only as an aid to allow the auditor to follow trails that may lead to the discovery of pertinent facts. However, there is little point in drawing up a checklist then putting it aside. The checklist should represent the minimum aspects to be checked so that following the audit you have evidence indicating:

- those activities that were compliant
- those activities that did not comply
- those activities that were not checked
- those activities where there were opportunities for improvement

Audits of practice against procedure or policy should be recorded as they are observed and you can either do this in note form to be written up later or directly on to observation forms especially designed for the purpose. Some auditors prefer to fill in the forms after the audit and others during the audit. The weakness with the former approach is that there may be some dispute as to the facts if presented some time later. It is therefore safer to get the auditee's endorsement to the facts at the time they are observed. In other types of audits there may not be an auditee present. Audits of process documentation against policy can be carried out at a desk. One can check whether the documents of the quality system satisfy all the clauses of the standard at a desk without walking around the site, but you can't check whether the system is documented unless you examine the operations in practice. There may be many activities that make the system work that are not documented.

Taking action (8.2.2)

The standard requires management responsible for the area audited *to ensure that actions are taken without undue delay to eliminate the detected nonconformities and their causes.*

What does this mean?

Management responsible for the area audited are those who have the authority to cause change. An auditor may have interviewed a supervisor and found opportunities for improvement but the supervisor may not have the authority to agree to any changes – the auditor would therefore need to report the findings to the person who is authorized to take action.

Action without undue delay means that management are expected to act before the detected problem impacts subsequent results.

> **1994–2000 Differences**
>
> Previously the standard required management personnel responsible for the area to take timely corrective action on the deficiencies found during the audit.
>
> The intent of the requirement remains unchanged. However it may impact those organizations that limited corrective actions to removal of the problem rather than in addition to eliminating its cause.

Eliminating nonconformities and their causes means that managers should:

- Take remedial action to correct the particular nonconformity
- Search for other examples of nonconformity and establish how widespread the problem is
- Establish the route cause of the nonconformity and prevent its recurrence

Why is this necessary?

This requirement responds to the Leadership Principle.

There is simply no point in conducting audits and finding problems if management does not intend to take action to prevent such problems impacting results. It often arises that problems detected by internal audits are perceived by management to have no impact on results, so it delays taking any action.

How is this implemented?

To ensure actions are implemented without undue delay, the auditor needs to be sure that a failure to act will in fact impact performance of the process or the system. Management will not implement actions that have no effect on performance. It is therefore sensible for the auditor to explain the impact of the detected nonconformity within the audit report – possibly by using a classification convention from critical to minor.

Unless the auditee is someone with responsibility for taking the corrective action, the auditee's manager should determine the actions required. If the action required is outside that manager's responsibility, the manager and not the auditor should seek out the appropriate authority and secure a proposal. Your system manual should stipulate management's responsibility for taking action without undue delay.

A proposed action may not remove the non-compliance, it may be palliative leaving the problem to recur again at some future time. Target dates should be agreed for all actions and the dates should be met as evidence of commitment. Third party auditors will search your records for this evidence so you will need to impress on your managers the importance of honouring their commitments. The target dates also have to match the magnitude of the deficiencies. Small deficiencies which can be corrected in minutes should be dealt with at the time of the audit otherwise they will linger on as sores and show a lack of discipline. Others which may take 10–15 minutes should be dealt with within a day or so. Big problems may need months to resolve and require an orchestrated programme to be implemented. The actions in all cases when implemented should remove the problem i.e. restore compliance. An action should not be limited to generating another form or procedure because it can be rejected by another manager thereby leaving the deficiency unresolved.

Follow-up audits (8.2.2)

The standard requires follow-up activities *to include the verification of the actions taken and the reporting of verification results.*

What does this mean?

A follow-up audit is an action taken after the audit to verify that agreed actions from the audit have been completed as planned.

> **1994–2000 Differences**
>
> Previously the standard required that follow-up audit activities record the implementation and effectiveness of the corrective action taken.
>
> The intent of the requirement remains unchanged.

Why is this necessary?

This requirement responds to the Factual Approach Principle.

Verification of actions completed is a normal activity of any managed process. The audit remains open until completion of actions has been confirmed.

How is this implemented?

Follow-up action is necessary to verify that the agreed action has been taken and verify that the original nonconformity has been eliminated. Follow-up audits may be carried out immediately after the planned completion date for the actions or at some other agreed time. However, unless the audit is carried out relatively close to the agreed completion date, it will not be possible to ascertain if the action was carried out without undue delay.

The auditor who carries out the follow-up audit need not be the same that carried out the initial audit. In fact there is some merit in using different auditors in order to calibrate the auditors.

When all the agreed nonconformities have been eliminated the audit report can be closed. The audit remains incomplete until all actions have been verified as being completed. Should any action not be carried out by the agreed date, the auditor needs to make a judgment as to whether it is reasonable to set a new date or to escalate the slippage to higher management. For minor problems, when there are more urgent priorities facing the managers, setting a new date may be prudent. However, you should not do this more than once. Not meeting the agreed completion date is indicative either of a lack of commitment or poor estimation of time and both indicate that there may well be a more deep routed problem to be resolved.

Monitoring and measurement of processes (8.2.3)

Monitoring and measuring methods (8.2.3)

<table>
<tr><td>

1994–2000 Differences

Previously the standard required controlled conditions to include the monitoring and control of suitable process parameters during production, installation and servicing.

This new requirement extends process monitoring to all product realization processes but falls short of including all processes in the management system.

</td></tr>
</table>

The standard requires the organization *to apply suitable methods for monitoring and where applicable, measurement of the quality management system processes.*

What does this mean?

In all managed processes there will be stages where outputs are verified against inputs – these are product controls. There also need to be stages where the performance of the process itself is measured – these are process controls.

Monitoring is an on-going activity and, as stated at the beginning of this chapter, is the periodic or continual observation of operations to detect events before they occur so that action can be taken to prevent nonconformity. Measurement on the other hand implies that standards have been set and performance against those standards is being verified. For processes this may involve a range of parameters that are defined as being critical for the process to consistently deliver the correct results.

Why is this necessary?

This requirement responds to the Factual Approach Principle.

It is processes that produce products and therefore measuring products tells us whether the products are correct but does not tell us whether the process is achieving its objectives. Parameters such as the rate at which products are produced, the variability between product characteristics, the resources used by the process and the effect of the process on its environment are parameters that require process measurement.

How is this implemented?

There are several methods available for monitoring and measuring processes. The simplest monitoring method is visual observation by a person trained to detect variations that signal something is not quite right with a process. With industrial processes instruments may be installed to give the observer a visual indicator of performance. Data may be recorded on control charts so that the observer can tell when the performance is deteriorating. With management and administration processes, the observer (often the manager or supervisor) has formal or informal standards against which processes are monitored. Staff sometimes work in an environment in which they can't predict how their manager will react – an environment where the manager has not communicated the standards of performance expected. In other cases the staff work in a predictable environment – where the manager monitors performance against a standard known to the staff. In the former case the processes are not managed – they are reactive. In a managed process, monitoring would only look for the unpredictable where the immediate reaction is 'Why did that happen? or 'That shouldn't have happened' Management and administrative processes also lend themselves to management by data rather than observation. Provided that targets have been set, data can be collected, analysed and results produced to show whether performance is on track.

Whatever is being monitored or measured a soundly based method needs to be used to sense the variance from target, transmit the data, analyse it and compute factual results. The integrity of the measurements need to be sound i.e., there should be no filtering, screening or reduction of the raw data that is not planned and the personnel performing the measurement should be competent to do so.

Process capability (8.2.3)

The standard requires the monitoring and measurement methods *to demonstrate the ability of the processes to achieve planned results.*

> **1994–2000 Differences**
>
> This is a new requirement that has no equivalent in the 1994 version.

What does this mean?

The planned results are the performance requirements at corporate and system level that relate to a particular process. There are whatever the process has been designed to achieve but should include needs, expectations and obligations from outside the process that impinge upon the process.

To demonstrate ability means that either by observation or through validated records, evidence should be available which shows that the process is capable of achieving the planned results. A process is in control when the average spread of variation coincides with the nominal specification for a parameter. The range of variation may extend outside the upper and lower limits but the proportion of output within the limits can be predicted. This situation will remain as long as the process remains in statistical control. A process is in statistical control when the source of inherent variation is from common causes only i.e. a source of variation that affects all the individual values of the process output and appears random. Common cause variation results in a stable and repeatable distribution of results over time. When the source of variation causes the location, spread and shape of the distribution to change, the process is not in statistical control. These sources of variation are due to special or assignable causes and must be eliminated before commencing with process capability studies. It is only when the performance of a process is predictable that its capability to meet customer expectations can be assessed.

Why is this necessary?

This requirement responds to the Factual Approach Principle.

Monitoring and measurement should not be performed merely to acquire information; it should either be performed to establish that processes are achieving the results for which they have been designed or for establishing that the results for which the processes have been designed are not adequate to meet the organization's objectives. Without objectives and targets information from monitoring and measurement is merely interesting but not justification for action. Action should only be taken to bring performance in line with requirements or to change the requirements.

How is this implemented?

In monitoring and measuring processes there are three questions that the process manager needs to be able to answer:

- How do you know the process is performing as planned?
- How you do know the process is achieving the results in the best way?
- How do you know that the results being achieved are those necessary to fulfil organizational goals?

Achieving objectives

Provisions need to be put in place for each process that enable operations to be monitored and its performance to be measured against process objectives and targets. Objectives and targets need to be established for each process and these should be derived from an analysis of the factors that affect the ability of the process to deliver the desired results.

For example, the purpose of a purchasing process might be to acquire physical resources needed to fulfil the organization's objectives. An analysis of these objectives may reveal a need for a reliable supply of raw materials of consistent quality to be delivered in accordance with schedules that change monthly. A purchasing objective might be to secure a supply of the specific raw materials from a supplier who is capable of meeting the delivery schedules together with raw material quality, service quality and cost targets. These may include targets for response to changes in delivery schedules and raw material specification. Clearly a critical factor is the ability of the purchasing process to respond to change. Not only would the supplier have to respond to change but the internal stages of the purchasing process would also have to respond to change. Monitoring this process would involve observing how changes were received and transmitted through all the stages in the process and alerting staff to bottlenecks or other factors that could jeopardize meeting the targets. Measuring this process would involve checking that deliveries were being made on time and that the variation in cost and quality was also on target. Product measures would look at specific deliveries, whereas process measures would look at all deliveries for evidence that the purchasing objective was being met.

A process may be designed to deliver output that meets specification therefore a measure of performance is the ratio of conforming output to total output. If the ratio is less than 1 the process is not capable. Most processes fall into this category because some defective output is often produced, but it is possible to design processes so that they only produce conforming output. This does not mean perfect output but output that is within the limits defined for the process. The target yield for a process may be 97% implying that 100% is not feasible, therefore a yield of 98% is good and a yield of 96% bad – it depends what standards have been set.

This type of measurement requires effective data collection, transmission and analysis points so that information is routed to analysts to determine performance and for results to be routed to decision makers for action. With a process such as order processing, in addition to each order being checked (product verification) the process should be monitored and measured to establish it is meeting the defined objectives for processing time, customer communication etc. and that there is no situation developing that may jeopardize achievement of the order processing objectives. Therefore every process will have at least two verification stages – one in-line for verifying output quality and another for verifying process performance against objectives.

Achieving best practice

Each result requires resources and even when the required results are being achieved there may be better ways or more efficient ways of achieving them. Therefore targets may be set for efficiency and these too need to be monitored and measured. One method is to monitor resource utilization. Another is to conduct benchmarking against other processes to find the best practice.

Fulfilling purpose

The planned results include organizational objectives and therefore the process objectives should be reviewed periodically to verify they are the right objectives. A 99.73% (3 sigma) yield may have been a real challenge five years ago but today your competitors achieve 99.999998% (6 sigma) and therefore the objective needs to change for the organization to maintain its position in the market.

Monitoring and measurement of product (8.2.4)

Verifying conformity with product requirements (8.2.4)

1994–2000 Differences
Previously the standard required:

(a) the supplier to inspect, test and identify product as required by the quality plan or documented procedures;
(b) the supplier to carry out final inspection and testing in accordance with the quality plan and/or documented procedures;
(c) the quality plan or documented procedures for final inspection and testing to require that all the specified inspections and tests, including those specified either on receipt of product or in-process, have been carried out and that the data meets specified requirements.

Though less prescriptive the intent of the requirement remains unchanged.

The standard requires the organization *to monitor and measure the characteristics of the product to verify that product requirements have been met* and that these activities *be conducted at appropriate stages of the product realization process in accordance with the planned arrangements*.

What does this mean?

Activities that monitor and measure product are often referred to as inspection, test or verification activities. Appropriate stages of the product realization process means the stages at which:

● the achieved characteristics are accessible for measurement and
● an economic means of measurement can be performed and
● the correction of error is less costly than if the error is detected at later stages

It may be possible to verify some characteristics on the final product just prior to shipment but it is costly to correct errors at this late stage resulting in delayed shipment. It is always more economic to verify product at the earliest opportunity.

The planned arrangements in this case are the plans made for verifying product in terms of what is to be verified, who is to verify it, when is it to be verified, how it is to be verified, where is it to be verified and what criteria is to be used to judge conformity.

Product requirements are all the requirements for the product including customer, regulatory and the organization's requirements. Some of these may be met by inherent design features, others will be met in production, installation or service.

The forms of verification that are used in product and service development, should also be governed by these requirements as a means of ensuring that the product upon which design verification is carried out conforms with the prescribed requirements. If the product is non-compliant it may invalidate the results of design verification. Product verification also applies to any measuring and monitoring devices that you design and manufacture to ensure that they are capable of verifying the acceptability of product as required. Product verification is part of product realization and not something separate from it although the way the requirements are structured may imply otherwise. Whenever a product is supplied, produced or repaired, rebuilt, modified or otherwise changed, it should be subject to verification that it conforms to the prescribed requirements and any deficiencies corrected before being released for use.

Why is this necessary?

This requirement responds to the Factual Approach Principle.

One verifies product to establish that it meets requirements. If one could be certain that a product would be correct without it being verified, product verification would be unnecessary. However, most processes possess inherent variation due to common causes – variations that affect all values of process output and appear random. Although a process may be under statistical control, a special event could disturb performance and without checks on the output, its detection may go unnoticed. One can only check for those events we think might happen which is why our confidence in the 'system' is shaken when we discover a condition with a cause we had not predicted.

How is this implemented?

As product requirements may include characteristics that are achieved by design, production, installation or service delivery, a high-level verification matrix is needed to provide traceability from requirement to the means of verification. This will undoubtedly lead to there being a few characteristics that need to be verified only once by design verification with many of the others being verified in production or service delivery. Characteristics that do not vary only need to be checked once. For example a chair designed with four legs could not possibly be made with two, three or five legs when put into production, but a cup with a handle could emerge from the process without a handle!

Having established that characteristics vary, the stage at which they need to be verified should be determined. This leaves three possibilities; on receipt, in-process or on completion. Receipt verification was addressed under purchasing in Chapter 7. Here we address in-process and finished product verification.

In-process verification

In-process verification is carried out in order to verify those features and characteristics that would not be accessible to verification by further processing or assembly. When producing a product that consists of several parts, sub-assemblies, assemblies, units, equipments and subsystems, each part, sub-assembly etc. needs to be subject to final verification but may also require in-process verification for the reasons given above. Your plans should define all the in-process verification stages that are required for each part, sub-assembly, assembly etc. In establishing where to carry out the verification, a flow diagram may help. The verification needs to occur after a specified feature has been produced and before it becomes inaccessible for measurement. This doesn't mean that you should check features as soon as they are achieved. There may be natural breaks in the process where the product passes from one stage to another or stages at which several features can be verified at once. If product passes from the responsibility of one person to another, there should be a stage verification at the interface to protect the producer even if the features achieved are accessible later. Your verification plans should:

- Identify the product to be verified
- Define the specification and acceptance criteria to be used and the issue status which applies
- Define what is to be verified at each stage. (Is it all work between stages or only certain operations? The parameters to be verified should include those that are known to be varied by the manufacturing processes. Those that remain constant from product to product, need verifying once only usually during design proving.)
- Define the verification aids and test equipment to be used. (There may be jigs, fixtures, gauges and other aids needed for verification. Standard measuring equipment would not need to be specified because your verification staff should be trained to select the right tools for the job. Any special measuring devices should be identified.)
- Define the environment for the measurements to be made if critical to the measurements to be made
- Identify the organization that is to perform the verification
- Make provision for the results of the verification to be recorded

Finished product verification

Finished product verification is in fact the last verification of the product that you will perform before dispatch but it may not be the last verification before delivery if your contract includes installation. There are three definitions of finished product verification:

- The verification carried out on completion of the product – afterwards the product may be routed to stores rather than to a customer.
- The last verification carried out before dispatch – afterwards you may install the product and carry out further work.

- The last verification that you as a supplier carry out on the product before ownership passes to your customer – this is the stage when the product is accepted and consequently the term *product acceptance* is more appropriate and tends to convey the purpose of the verification rather than the stage at which it is performed.

There are two aspects to finished product verification. One is checking what has gone before and the other is accepting the product.

Final verification and test checks should detect whether:

- All previous verification activities have been performed
- The product bears the correct identification, part numbers, serial numbers, modification status etc.
- The as-built configuration is the same as the issue status of all the parts, sub-assemblies, assemblies etc. specified by the design standard
- All recorded nonconformities have been resolved and remedial action taken and verified
- All concession applications have been approved
- All verification results have been collected
- Any result outside the stated limits is either subject to an approved concession, an approved specification change or a retest that shows conformance with the requirements
- All documentation to be delivered with the product has been produced and conforms to the prescribed standards

Evidence of conformity (8.2.4)

The standard requires *evidence of conformity with the acceptance criteria to be maintained.*

What does this mean?

Evidence of conformity is the information recorded during product verification that shows the product to have exhibited the characteristics required.

Why is this necessary?

This requirement responds to the Factual Approach Principle.

At a point in the process, product will be presented for delivery to the next stage in the process or to a customer. At such stages a decision is made whether or not to release product and this decision needs to be made on the basis of facts substantiated by objective evidence.

How is this implemented?

This requires that you produce something like an Acceptance Test Plan which contains, as appropriate, some or all of the following:

- Identity of the product to be verified
- Definition of the specification and acceptance criteria to be used and the issue status that applies
- Definition of the verification aids and measuring devices to be used
- Definition of the environment for the measurements to be made
- Provision for the results of verification to be recorded – these need to be presented in a form that correlates with the specified requirements

Having carried out these verification activities, it should be possible for you to declare that the product has been verified and objective evidence produced that will demonstrate that it meets the specified requirements. Any concessions given against requirements should also be identified. If you can't make such a declaration, you haven't done enough verification. Whether or not your customer requires a certificate from you testifying that you have met the requirements, you should be in a position to produce one. The requirement for a certificate of conformance should not alter your processes, your quality controls or your procedures. Your management system should give you the kind of evidence you need to assure your customers that your product meets their requirements without having to do anything special.

Your verification records should be of two forms – one which indicates what verification activities have been carried out and the other which indicates the results of such verification. They may be merged into one record but when parameters need to be recorded it is often cleaner to separate the progress record from the technical record. Your procedures, quality plan or product specifications should also indicate what measurements have to be recorded.

Don't assume that because a parameter is shown in a specification that an inspector or tester will record the result. A result can be a figure, a pass/fail or just a tick. Be specific in what you want recorded because you may get a surprise when gathering the data for analysis. If you use computers, you shouldn't have the same problems but beware, too much data is probably worse than too little! In choosing the method of recording measurements, you also need to consider whether you will have sufficient data to minimize recovery action in the event of the measuring device subsequently being found to be out of calibration. As a general rule, only gather that data you need to determine whether the product meets the requirements or whether the process is capable of producing a product that meets the requirements. You need to be selective so that you can spot the out of tolerance condition. All verification records should define the acceptance criteria, the limits between which the product is acceptable and beyond which the product is unacceptable and therefore nonconforming.

Identifying the person(s) authorizing release (8.2.4)

The standard requires *records to indicate the person(s) authorizing release of product.*

What does this mean?

The person authorizing release of the product is the one whose permission is needed before product can pass beyond a defined stage. Release conditions may include conformity to specification and quantity. Product may be held until the required quantity has been produced. When a product is 'in-process' the

> **1994–2000 Differences**
> Previously the standard requires that records identify the inspection authority responsible for the release of conforming product.
> The intent of the requirement remains unchanged.

operator is working on it. Product may be piling up in the output basket, but until the operator indicates it can be released, it remains under his or her control. This requirement means that such decisions are to be recorded in a manner that is traceable to the person who made them. With hardware, software and processed material this often means a signature or stamp on verification records or labels attached to the product. With documentation, it is an approval signature on a document or accompanying forms.

This requirement implies that there will always be a person in the process who decides when product should or should not be released. This may not always be so. With automated processes equipped with product verification instrumentation, the product may well pass straight into dispatch and onto the customer without any human intervention. The person releasing product in this case is the person controlling the process.

Why is this necessary?

This requirement responds to the Factual Approach Principle.

Within an organization you may wish to identify the individual responsible so that you can go back to ask questions. This is more likely in the case of a reject decision as opposed to an acceptance decision. It is also necessary to be able to demonstrate (particularly with food and drugs) that product was released by someone who was aware of the consequences of their actions and were acting responsibly. An organization's reputation could be easily damaged if it emerged that the person releasing product into the food chain was unqualified.

How is this implemented?

There are two parts to this requirement. The first is that the person who releases product is identified and the second that this person is authorized to release product. It is not enough for there to be a signature on a document, on a record or on a label. The signature has to be of a person who has the right to release the product. The signature therefore needs to be legible or at least traceable to the individual.

Some organizations maintain a list of authorized signatures as a means of being able to trace signatures to names of people who carry certain authority. If you have a large number of people signing documents and records and there is a possibility that the wrong person may sign a document, the list is a good tool for checking that there has been no abuse of authority. Otherwise, the name of the individual and his or her position below or alongside the signature should be adequate. The management system should have in-built provision for preventing the wrong people releasing product. When such provisions have been made, the authorized person could under certain circumstances be influenced to release bad product – it is only the strength of the shared values that would prevent such transgression.

Product release approval (8.2.4)

The standard *requires that unless otherwise approved by a relevant authority and where applicable, by the customer, product release and service delivery is not to proceed until the planned arrangements have been satisfactorily completed.*

What does this mean?

This requirement can impose unnecessary constraints if taken literally. Many activities in planned arrangements are performed to give early warning of nonconformities. This is in order to avoid the losses that can be incurred if failure occurs in later tests and inspections. The earlier you confirm conformance the less costly any rework will be. One should therefore not hold shipment if later activities have verified the parameters, whether or not earlier activities have been performed. It is uneconomic for you to omit the earlier activities, but if you do, and the later activities can demonstrate that the end product meets the requirements, it is also uneconomic to go back and perform those activities that have not been completed. Your planned arrangements could cover installation and maintenance activities which are carried out after dispatch and so it would be unreasonable to insist that these activities were completed before dispatch or to insist on separate plans just to sanitize a point. A less ambiguous way of saying the same thing is to require no product to be dispatched until objective evidence has been produced to demonstrate that it meets the product requirements and that authorization for its release has been given.

If planned arrangements cannot be achieved, a concession might be obtained from the recipient to permit release of product that did not fully meet the requirements. The recipient could be the owner of the process receiving product for processing or the external customer receiving product in response to an order.

> **1994–2000 Differences**
> Previously the standard required the supplier to ensure:
>
> (a) that no product be dispatched until all the activities specified in the quality plan or documented procedures have been satisfactorily completed and the associated data and documentation are available and authorized;
> (b) that only product that has passed the required inspections and tests (or released under an authorized concession) is dispatched, used or installed.
>
> The intent of the requirement remains unchanged.

Why is this necessary?

This requirement responds to the Factual Approach Principle.

Having decided on the provisions needed to produce product that meets the needs and expectations of customers, regulators and the organization itself, it would be pretty foolish to permit release of product before confirming that all that was agreed to be done has been done. However, circumstances may arise where nonconforming product has been produced and instead of shipping such product without informing the intended recipient, an organization committed to quality would seek permission to do so.

How is this implemented?

You need four things before you can release product whether it be to the stores, to the customer, to the site for installation or anywhere else:

- Sight of the product
- Sight of the requirement with which the product is to conform including its packaging, labelling and other product related requirements
- Sight of the objective evidence that purports to demonstrate that the particular product meets the requirement

- Sight of an authorized signatory or the stamp of an approved stamp-holder who has checked that the particular product, the evidence and the requirement are in complete accord

Once the evidence has been verified, the authorized person can make the release decision and endorse the appropriate record indicating readiness for release. Should there be any discrepancies, they should be validated and if proven valid, the nonconforming product process should be initiated.

Control of nonconforming product (8.3)

Preventing unintended use (8.3)

1994–2000 Differences

Previously the standard required the supplier to:

(a) establish and maintain documented procedures to ensure that product that does not conform to specified requirements is prevented from inadvertent use or installation;

(b) provide for identification, documentation, evaluation, segregation, disposition of nonconforming product and for notification to the functions concerned.

The requirement remains unchanged.

The standard requires the organization to ensure that *product which does not conform to product requirements is identified and controlled to prevent unintended use or delivery and goes on to require the controls and related responsibilities for dealing with nonconforming product to be defined in a documented procedure.*

What does this mean?

Nonconforming product is product that does not conform to agreed product requirements when subject to either planned or unplanned verification. Product requirements are not limited to customer requirements (see also Chapter 7) therefore a nonconforming product is one that fails to meet the:

- Specified customers requirements
- Intended usage requirements
- Stated or implied needs
- Organization's own requirements
- Customer expectations

A product is judged either conforming or nonconforming at a verification stage. A product could also be judged nonconforming if it becomes damaged or fails at any other stage but is normally considered unserviceable. Unserviceable products however are not necessarily nonconforming – they may simply lack lubrication or calibration. A piece of test equipment, the calibration date of which has expired, is not nonconforming – it is merely unserviceable. When checked against a standard it may be found to be out of calibration and then it is nonconforming, but it could be found to be within the specified calibration *limits*.

A product may be suspected of being nonconforming as might be the case with a batch of product that has failed the sampling inspection. Only the samples checked are definitely nonconforming – the others in the batch are only suspected as being nonconforming. We should therefore look further than the product that has been found to be nonconforming and seek out other products that may possess the same characteristics as those found to be nonconforming. These other products may have already been released to customers. This latter situation can arise if you discover the measuring or processing equipment to be inaccurate or malfunctioning. Any product that has passed through that process since it was last confirmed as serviceable is now suspect. Another example of suspect product is when product is mishandled but shows no obvious signs of damage. This may arise when product is dropped or not handled in stipulated clean conditions or in accordance with electrostatic safe handling procedures. Suspect product should be treated in the same manner as nonconforming product and quarantined until dispositioned. However, until nonconformity can be proven, the documentation of the nonconformity merely reveals the reason for the product being suspect.

This requirement relates to the controls exercised over the product itself whereas clause 8.5.2. on corrective action addresses the measures needed to prevent recurrence of the nonconformity. The scope of procedures for control of nonconforming product should therefore focus on the product not the cause.

Why is this necessary?

This requirement responds to the Process Approach Principle.

Nonconforming product needs to be prevented from use or delivery, simply because the organization should not knowingly supply nonconforming product.

How is this implemented?

The only sure way of preventing inadvertent use of nonconforming product is to destroy it, but that may be a little drastic in some cases. It may be possible to eliminate the nonconformity by repair, completion of processing or rework. A more practical way of preventing the inadvertent use or installation of nonconforming or unserviceable products is to identify the product as *nonconforming* or *unserviceable* and then place it in an area where access to it is controlled. These two aspects are covered further below.

Identifying nonconforming product

The most common method is to apply labels to the product that are distinguishable from other labels. It is preferable to use red labels for nonconforming and unserviceable items and green labels for conforming and serviceable items. In this way you can determine product status at a distance and reduce the chance of confusion. You can use segregation as a means of identifying nonconforming product but if there is the possibility of mixing or confusion then this means alone should not be used.

On the labels themselves you should identify the product by name and reference number, specification and issue status if necessary and either a statement of the nonconformity or a reference to the service or nonconformity report containing full details of its condition. Finally the person or organization testifying the nonconformity should be identified either by name or inspection stamp.

Unlike products, nonconforming services are usually rendered unavailable for use by notices such as 'Out of Order' or by announcements such as 'Normal service will be resumed as soon as possible' Products are often capable of operation with nonconformities whereas services tend to be withdrawn once the nonconformity has been detected however trivial the fault.

Controlling nonconforming product

To control nonconforming product you need to:

(a) know when it became nonconforming
(b) know who decided it was nonconforming
(c) know of its condition
(d) know where it is located
(e) know that it is not being used

On detection of a nonconformity, details of the product and the nonconformity should be recorded so as to address a), b) and c) above.

Segregating a nonconforming product (or separating good from bad) places it in an area with restricted access and addresses d) and c) above. Such areas are called quarantine areas or quarantine stores. Products should remain in quarantine until disposal instructions have been issued. The store should be clearly marked and a register maintained of all items that enter and exit the store. Without a register you won't be able to account for the items in store, check whether any are missing, or track their movements. The quarantine store may be contained within another store providing there is adequate separation that prevents mixing of conforming and nonconforming articles. Where items are too large to be moved into a quarantine store or area, measures should be taken to signal to others that the item is not available for use and cordons or floor markings can achieve this. With services the simplest method is to render the service unavailable or inaccessible.

Documented procedures

Documented procedures should specify the authorities who make the disposition, where it is to be recorded and what information should be provided in order that it can be implemented and verified as having been implemented.

In order to implement these requirements your nonconformity control procedures should include the following actions:

- Specify how product should be scrapped, or recycled, the forms to be used, the authorizations to be obtained
- Specify the various repair procedures, how they should be produced, selected and implemented
- Specify how modifications should be defined, identified and implemented
- Specify how production permits (deviations) and concessions (waivers) should be requested, evaluated and approved or rejected
- Specify how product should be returned to its supplier, the forms to be completed and any identification requirements in order that you can detect product on its return
- Specify how regrading product is to be carried out, the product markings, prior authorization and acceptance criteria

When making the disposition your remedial action needs to address:

- action on the nonconforming item to remove the nonconformity and
- a search for other similar items which may be nonconforming (i.e. suspect product) and
- action to recall product containing suspect nonconforming product

If you need to recall product that is suspected as being defective you will need to devise a *Recall Plan*, specify responsibilities and time-scales and put the plan into effect. Product recall is a *Remedial Action* not a *Corrective Action* because it does not prevent a recurrence of the initial problem.

Defining responsibility

The decision on product acceptance is a relatively simple one because there is a specification against which to judge conformance. When product is found to be nonconforming there are three decisions you need to make based on the following questions:

- Can the product be made to conform?
- If the product cannot be made to conform, is it fit for use?
- If the product is not fit for use, can it be made fit for use?

The authority for making these decisions will vary depending on the answer to the first question. If, regardless of the severity of the nonconformity, the product can be made to conform simply by rework or completing operations, these decisions can be taken by operators or inspectors, providing rework is economical. Decisions on scrap, rework and completion would be made by the fund-providing authority rather than the design authority. If the product cannot be made to conform by using existing specifications, decisions requiring a change or a waiver of a specification should be made by the authority responsible for drawing up or selecting the specification.

It may be sensible to engage investigators to review the options to be considered and propose remedial actions for the authorities to consider. In your procedures you should identify the various bodies that need to be consulted for each type of specification. Departures from customer requirements will require customer approval; departures from design requirements will require design approval; departures from process requirements will require process engineering approval etc. The key lies in identifying who devised or selected the requirement in the first place. All specifications are merely a substitute for knowledge of fitness for use – any departure from such specification must be referred back to the specification authors for a judgement.

Correction of nonconforming product (8.3a)

1994–2000 Differences

Previously the standard required the supplier to:

(a) review nonconforming product in accordance with documented procedures and advises that it may be reworked, accepted, re-graded, rejected or scrapped;

(b) define the responsibility for review and authority for the disposition of nonconforming product.

The intent of the requirement remains unchanged.

The standard requires the organization when appropriate to *deal with nonconforming product by taking action to eliminate the detected nonconformity.*

What does this mean?

Action to remove the detected nonconformity is a remedial action and can include the completion of operations, rework, repair or modification. Sometimes a product may be inadvertently submitted for verification before all operations have been completed. Rework means the continuation of processing that will make an item conform to specification. Rework requires only normal operations to complete the item and does not require any additional instructions. Rework when applied to documents means correcting errors without changing the original requirement. Repair is an action that restores an item to an acceptable condition but unlike rework, it may involve changing the product so that it differs from the specification but fulfils the intended use requirement. Modification may involve changing the requirement as would be the case if the product requirement was found to be incorrect when assembling or operating product.

In some cases it may not be cost effective to attempt to eliminate the nonconformity and therefore such action would be inappropriate and the product should be disposed of.

Why is this necessary?

This requirement responds to the Process Approach Principle.

Remedial action is warranted when there are cost benefits from attempting to eliminate the nonconformity.

How is this implemented?

To implement this requirement you will need a form or other such document in which to record the decision and to assign the responsibility for the remedial action. When deciding on repair or rework action, you may need to consider whether the result will be visible to the customer on the exterior of the product. Rework or repairs that may not be visible when a part is fitted into the final assembly might be visible when these same parts are sold as service spares. To prevent on-the-spot decisions being at variance each time, you could:

(a) Identify in the drawings, plans etc. those products that are supplied for service applications: i.e. for servicing, maintenance and repair
(b) Provide the means for making rework invisible where there are cost savings over scrapping the item
(c) Stipulate on the drawings etc. the approved rework techniques

Authorizing use of nonconforming product (8.3b)

The standard requires the organization when appropriate to *deal with nonconforming product by authorizing its use, release or acceptance under concession by a relevant authority and where applicable by the customer.*

What does this mean?

If you choose to accept a nonconforming item as it is without rework, repair etc., then you are in effect granting a *concession* or waiving the requirement *only* for that particular item. If the requirements cannot be achieved at all then this

1994–2000 Differences

Previously the standard
required that where
required by the contract:

(a) the proposed use or
repair of product
which does not
conform to specified
requirements be
reported for
concession to the
customer or
customer's
representative;
(b) the supplier records
the description of
nonconformity that has
been accepted, and of
repairs, to denote the
actual condition.

Though less prescriptive,
the intent of the
requirement remains
unchanged.

is not a situation for a concession but a case for a change in requirement. If you know in advance of producing the product or service that it will not conform with the requirements, you can then request a deviation from the requirements. This is often referred to as a *production permit*. Concessions apply *after* the product has been produced. Production permits apply *before* it has been produced. Both are requests that should be made to the acceptance authority for the product.

The relevant authority is the authority that specified the requirement that has not been met. This authority could therefore be the customer, the regulator or the designer.

Why is this necessary?

This requirement responds to the Process Approach Principle.

Product that does not conform to requirement may be fit for use. All specifications are but a substitute for knowledge of fitness for use. Any departure from such specification should be referred back to the specification authors for a judgment.

How is this implemented?

In order to determine whether a nonconforming product could be used, an analysis of the conditions needs to be made by qualified personnel. There are two ways of doing this. Either you refer all such nonconformities to the relevant authority or the authority appoints representatives who are capable of making these decisions within prescribed limits. A traditional method is to classify nonconformities, assign authority for accepting concessions for each level and define the limits of their authority. These levels could be as follows:

• Critical Nonconformity (a departure from the requirements which renders the product or service unfit for use)
• Major Nonconformity (a departure from the requirements included in the contract or market specification)
• Minor Nonconformity (a departure from the requirements not included in the contract or market specification)

The only cases where you need to request concessions from your customer are when you have deviated from one of the customer requirements and cannot make the product conform. Even when you repair a product, providing it meets all of the customer requirements, there is generally no need to seek a concession from your customer. While it is generally believed that non-conformities indicate an out of control situation, provided that you detect and rectify them before release of the product, you have quality under control and have no need to report nonconformities to your customer.

In informing your customer when nonconforming product has been shipped you obviously need to do this immediately you are certain that there is a nonconformity. If you are investigating a suspect nonconformity it only becomes a matter for reporting to your customer when the nonconformity remains suspect after you have concluded your investigations. Alerting your customer every time you think there is a problem will destroy confidence in your organization. Customers appreciate zeal but not paranoia!

Action to preclude use or application (8.3c)

The standard requires the organization when appropriate to *deal with nonconforming product by taking action to preclude its original intended use or application*.

> **1994–2000 Differences**
>
> Previously the standard required the nonconformity to be regraded, rejected or scrapped.
>
> The intent of the requirement remains unchanged.

What does this mean?

Precluding intended use or application means either scrapping the product so no one can use it or regrading it so that it may be used in other applications. In some cases products and services are offered in several models, types or other designations but are basically of the same design. Those which meet the higher specification are graded as such and those which fail may meet a lower specification and can be *regraded*. The grading should be reflected in the product identity so that there is no confusion.

Why is this necessary?

This requirement responds to the Process Approach Principle.

If a nonconforming product cannot be made conforming or accepted as is, some other action is needed to prevent inadvertent use and this leaves the two options stated.

How is this implemented?

Regrading can be accomplished by assigning a new identity to the product. Scrapping an item should not be taken lightly – it could be an item of high value. Scrapping may be an economical decision with low cost items, whereas the scrapping of high value items may require prior authorization as salvage action may provide a possibility of yielding spares for alternative applications.

Records of nonconformity (8.3)

1994–2000 Differences
Previously the standard required the description of the accepted nonconformity and the repairs undertaken to be recorded to denote the actual condition.
The intent of the requirement remains unchanged.

The standard requires *records of the nature of non-conformities and any subsequent actions taken, including concessions to be maintained.*

What does this mean?

The records of nonconformities are the documented details of the product (its identity), the specific deviations from requirements (what it is and what it should have been), the condition under which the nonconformity was detected (the environmental or operating conditions – what was happening at the time the nonconformity was detected), the time and date of detection, the name of the person detecting it and the actions taken with reference to any instructions, revised requirements and decisions.

Why is this necessary?

This requirement responds to the Factual Approach Principle.

Records of nonconformities are needed for presentation to the authorities responsible for deciding on the action to be taken and for subsequent analysis. Without such records, decisions may be made on opinion resulting in the means for identifying opportunities for improvement being absent.

How is this implemented?

There are several ways in which you can document the presence of a nonconformity. You can record the condition:

- on a label attached to the item
- on a form unique to the item such as a nonconformity report
- of functional failures on a failure report and physical errors on a defect report

- in a logbook for the item such as an inspection history record or snag sheet
- in a logbook for the workshop or area

The detail you record depends upon the severity of the nonconformity and to whom it needs to be communicated. In some cases a patrol inspector or quality engineer can deal with minor snags on a daily basis as can an itinerant designer. Where the problem is severe and remedial action complicated, a panel of experts may need to meet. Rather than gather around the nonconforming item, it may be more practical to document the remedial action on a form. In some cases the details may need to be conveyed to the customer off site and in such cases a logbook or label would be inappropriate. It is important when documenting the nonconformity that you record as many details as you can because they may be valuable to any subsequent investigation in order to help diagnose the cause and prevent its recurrence.

Re-verification of corrected product (8.3)

The standard requires *nonconforming product to be subject to re-verification after correction to demonstrate conformity to the requirements.*

What does this mean?

Any rework, repair, modification or other action taken to correct the nonconformity will change the product and therefore it needs to be subject to re-verification. This may involve verification against different requirements to the original requirements.

> **1994–2000 Differences**
>
> Previously the standard required the supplier to re-inspect repaired or reworked product in accordance with the quality plan and/or documented procedures.
>
> The intent of the requirement remains unchanged.

Why is this necessary?

This requirement responds to the Factual Approach Principle.

If a nonconforming product is accepted as is without correction, no re-verification is necessary, but if the product is changed the previous verification is no longer valid.

How is this implemented?

Any product that has had work done to it should be re-verified prior to it being released to ensure the work has been carried out as planned and has not affected features that were previously found conforming. There may be cases where the amount of re-verification is limited and this should be stated as part of the remedial action plan. However, after rework or repair the re-verification should verify that the product meets the original requirement, otherwise it is not the same product and must be identified differently.

The verification records should indicate the original rejection, the disposition and the results of the re-verification in order that there is traceability of the decisions that were made.

Consequences of nonconformity (8.3)

1994–2000 Differences

Previously the standard required the procedures for corrective action to include the effective handling of reports of product nonconformities.

This new requirement implies that a process is needed to manage the consequences of detecting nonconforming product such as informing customers, product recall etc.

The standard requires the organization *to take action appropriate to the effects or potential effects of the nonconformity when nonconforming product is detected after delivery or use has started.*

What does this mean?

A nonconformity may be detected by a subsequent user of the product either within the organization or by the customer. Also a nonconformity might be detected prior to release and implicate products already in use such as when subsequent analysis reveals inaccurate measurements or when verification methods or acceptance criteria change. Such product may not have failed in service because it has not been used in a manner needed to cause failure but if part of the same batch or lot contains a common cause nonconformity all product is suspected. Action taken as a result of latent nonconformity may involve product recall, product alerts or the issue of instructions for correction.

Why is this necessary?

This requirement responds to the Customer Focus Principle.

The requirement acknowledges that problems may be detected after shipment or use that need action to prevent undesirable effects.

How is this implemented?

Nonconformities detected by internal or external users indicate that the controls in place are not effective and should give cause for concern. Details should be recorded and an investigation conducted to establish why the planned verification did not detect the problem. Action should then be taken to improve the verification methods by changing procedures, acceptance criteria, equipment or retraining personnel.

When a nonconformity is detected by verification personnel in a product where products of the same type are in use, an analysis is needed to establish whether the nonconformity would previously have escaped detection. If not, there is no cause for alarm but if something has now changed to bring the nonconformity to light, an evaluation of the consequences needs to be conducted. It may only be a matter of time before the user detects the same nonconformity.

The procedures should cover:

- The method of receiving and identifying returned product
- The method of logging reports of nonconformities from customers and other users
- The process of responding to customer requests for assistance
- The process of dispatching service personnel to the customer's premises
- A form on which to record details of the nonconformity, the date, customer name etc.
- A process for acknowledging the report in order that the customer knows you care
- A process for investigating the nature of the nonconformity
- A process for replacing, or repairing nonconforming product and restoring customer equipment into service
- A process for assessing all products in service that are nonconforming, determining and implementing recall action if necessary

Analysis of data (8.4)

Collecting and analysing appropriate data (8.4)

The standard requires the organization to *determine, collect and analyse appropriate data to demonstrate the suitability and effectiveness of the quality management system including data generated as a result of monitoring and measurement and from other relevant sources.*

What does this mean?

The suitability of the management system as stated previously is whether it represents the best way of doing things rather than whether it is fit for purpose – this is expressed by the requirement for the management system to be adequate in clause 5.6. (The omission of the word 'adequacy' in this clause is perhaps an oversight.) The effectiveness of the management system is whether the purpose for which it was designed matches the needs of the organization.

1994–2000 Differences

Previously the standard required:

(a) documented procedures for the collection of records;

(b) the supplier to use appropriate sources of information to detect and eliminate potential causes of nonconforming product;

(c) the management representative to report on the performance of the quality system as a basis for improvement of the quality system.

The previous requirements only addressed two aspects of the data collection and analysis processes, but the responsibility placed on the management representative covered the gap without specifying a particular action. The standard is now more explicit.

Appropriate data would be any data generated from the processes of the management system that assist in the determination of their suitability and effectiveness.

The standard does not indicate what data may be needed – the organization is required to determine the data needed, to collect and then analyse it in order to provide a basis for determining the performance of the management system.

Why is this necessary?

This requirement responds to the Factual Approach Principle.

The requirements in clause 5.6 indicate a need for data on which to judge whether the system is suitable, adequate and effective – this requirement addresses this need.

How is this implemented?

Determining what data to collect

Suitability is concerned with doing things in the most appropriate way – perhaps the best way. If the system enabled staff to waste resources or under-utilize physical and human resources and under-utilize knowledge and capability, the output may conform to requirements but productivity would be down, bottlenecks would occur in processes and there would be a struggle to meet delivery targets without certain staff working flat out. System suitability cannot be examined if one perceives the system to be a set of documents – it is only possible if one perceives the system as encompassing everything the organization needs to fulfil its mission.

Effectiveness is concerned with doing the right things rather than with doing things right. So if the system enables management to stop the development of products for which there was no requirement, discover a potential safety problem, anticipate customer needs ahead of the competition, cut waste by 50%, successfully defend a product liability claim, meet all the delivery targets agreed with the customer, you would probably say that the system was pretty effective. If on the other hand the system allows the shipment of defective products every day, loses one in three customers, allows the development of unsafe products to reach the market, or the failure of a revolutionary power plant, you would probably say that the system was pretty ineffective. So the first thing you need to do is establish what you want the quality system to do, because without a yardstick as a measure, you can't determine whether the system is effective or not. Many systems are only designed to meet the standard with the result that you can deliver defective product providing you also deliver some which are not defective.

As with many of these requirements, the place to start is to assess each process and determine:

- the data needed to establish that the process is achieving its objectives
- the data needed to establish that the process is being run in the best way
- the data needed to establish that the process objectives remain relevant to the organizational goals

Data on achievement of objectives might include statistics on percent conforming, throughput, response time etc. Data on best practice may include measures of productivity, quality costs – the cost of prevention, appraisal and failure costs or benchmarking data from competitors or similar industries. Data on relevance of objectives may include contrasting the objectives and targets with the organization's objectives.

Data collection

Plan the data requirements carefully so that you:

- only collect data on events that you intend to analyse
- only analyse data with the purpose of discovering problems
- only provide solutions to real problems
- only implement solutions that will improve performance

To analyse anything, you need data. Without data you cannot know if your processes are under control and if your customers are satisfied. It is not sufficient to claim that you have had no problems unless you are confident that the processes in place will alert you to problems should they arise. You also need to take care to avoid the 'garbage in /garbage out' syndrome. Your analysis will only be as good as the data with which you are provided. If you want to determine certain facts, you need to ensure that the means exist for the necessary information to be obtained. To do this you may need to change the input forms or provide new forms on which to collect the data. The data needed for corrective action is rarely of use to those providing it therefore design your forms with care. Reject any incomplete forms as a sign that you are serious about needing the data. A sure sign that forms have become obsolete is the number of blank boxes. It is also better to devise unique forms for specific uses rather than rely on general multipurpose forms because the latter have a tendency to degrade the reliability of the data.

Methods are needed to collect the data from the sensors and transmit it to the analysis stations. This may involve not only collecting data locally for immediate analysis for control purposes, but also transmission to central analysis stations. At such stations the data on all factors affecting performance may be aggregated and information produced for use in measuring overall performance relative to objectives. For example, a common target may be set for all processes relative to utilization, nonconformities, response time etc. Some processes may be better than others but when aggregated show that the corporate objectives are not being achieved. A computer network can aid data collection by enabling remote access and collection into interlinked databases. However, many organizations still rely on paper records and therefore you will need a means of enabling such records to be either submitted to the analysis points or collected from source. To achieve this you will need to insert submission or collection instructions in the relevant procedures that specify the records.

Many organizations use a Nonconformity Report to collect information on nonconformities. One report may deal with remedial action and another separate report may address corrective action in order to prevent the recurrence of one or more nonconformities. In this way you are not committed to taking action on every incident but on a group of incidents where the action and its cost can be more easily justified.

This requirement is similar to that in clause 4.14.3 under preventive action as the data collected for preventive action serves a similar purpose. In one case an analysis of company level data serves to identify overall trends and predict potential failures that will affect achievement of the goals. In the preventive action case, the data serves to identify local and overall trends and predict potential failures that will affect achievement of specified requirements for the product, process and the quality system. It would be sensible to develop a data collection and analysis system that serves all levels in the organization with criteria at each level for reporting data upwards as necessary. You should not treat this requirement separately from that for preventive action because the same data should be used.

A general plan of action would include the following actions:

- Identify the key parameters to be measured.
- Locate where in the process they are achieved.
- Install data collection methods in relevant procedures.
- Collect and analyse the data.
- Use suitable presentation techniques to draw attention to the results.

In collecting the data, care should be taken to avoid data paralysis. The various quality tools can be used to prioritize the identified problems and corresponding decisions. As with all data collection tasks, you should show a direct correlation between what you are collecting and the goals to be achieved. All conclusions should lead to positive action otherwise the effort has been futile.

Evaluating where improvements in effectiveness can be made (8.4)

The standard requires the organization to *evaluate where continual improvement of the effectiveness of the quality management system can be made.*

> **1994–2000 Differences**
>
> This is a new requirement that has no equivalent in the 1994 version.

What does this mean?

Juran writes on improvement thus 'Putting out fires is not improvement of the process – Neither is discovery and removal of a special cause detected by a point out of control. This only puts the process back to where it should have been in the first place (Deming, W. Edwards, 1982)[3]. 'Continual improvement in the effectiveness of the management system is concerned with identifying where the objectives, standards or targets established for activities, tasks or processes are below those needed for the organization to accomplish its purpose or mission. At one level this means changing the targets so that they are harder to meet and at another level it means changing the objectives so that work is driven in a new direction.

Why is this necessary?

This requirement responds to the Continual Improvement Principle.

The analysis of the external environment (customers, markets, regulations, economy, society) will indicate whether the organization's objectives are relevant or whether they need to change. If the management system continues driving the organization against existing objectives, it will fail to satisfy customers and other interested parties, therefore improvement in the effectiveness of the management system is needed. There may be cases where no specific objectives are set for some aspects that affect organizational performance. For example managers may be desensitized to the level of rejects, the level of waste, scrap, delays, absenteeism, illness believing there is nothing that can be done to change it but by default, objectives have been set to maintain the status quo – if no objectives are set, any level of performance is acceptable!

In evaluating the effectiveness of the management system, those areas where objectives have not been specified become opportunities for improvement.

How is this implemented?

Implementation of this requirement needs a two-pronged approach. A review of established objectives and a review of performance attributes that have no objectives.

Reviewing established objectives

An approach to take is to:

- Identify the objectives and targets that have been established for each process and sub-process
- Establish whether these targets are being achieved
- Analyse the processes to determine the potential for raising the targets or eliminating targets on the basis that they no longer serve the organization's goals
- Assess the feasibility of meeting the raised targets or the impact of eliminating inappropriate targets
- Present the case to management for change

Reviewing uncontrolled performance attributes

One approach is to undertake the following actions:

- Analyse each process and identify all process outcomes – i.e. Tangible and intangible outputs and effects on all interested parties.
- Identify the outcomes for which no objectives and targets have been set. (Some outcomes may have objectives but no targets and are therefore not being measured.)
- Assess the significance of the outcome in terms of impact (both short and long term) on the organization's goals.
- Make proposals for setting objectives and plans for those outcomes that impact the organization's goals.

Analysis of customer satisfaction data (8.4a)

The standard requires *analysis of data to provide information relating to customer satisfaction.*

What does this mean?

This requirement seeks to take the data generated by the monitoring process addressed in clause 8.2.1 and through analysis produce meaningful information on whether customers are in fact satisfied with the products and services offered by the organization.

Why is this necessary?

This requirement responds to the Factual Approach Principle.

Customer satisfaction is not something one can monitor directly by installing a sensor. One has to collect and analyse data to draw conclusions.

> **1994–2000 Differences**
>
> This is a new requirement that has no equivalent in the 1994 version.

How is this implemented?

We can now look at the ways by which data can be collected relative to the different techniques of monitoring customer satisfaction:

- Repeat orders – this data can be collected from the order processing process
- Competition – this data is more subjective and results from market research
- Referrals – this data can be captured from sales personnel during the transaction or later on follow-up calls
- Demand – this data can be collected from sales trends
- Effects of product transition – this data can be collected from sales trends following new product launch
- Surveys – this data can be collected from survey reports
- Focus meetings – this data can be collected from the meeting reports
- Complaints – this data can be collected from complaints recorded by customers or by staff on speaking with customers
- Compliments – this data can be collected from written compliments sent in by customers or by staff on speaking with customers

As indicated above there are several sources of data, several ways in which it can be collected and several functions involved. Provisions need to be made for transmitting the data from the processes where it can be captured to the place where it is to be analysed. It is evident that sales and marketing personnel are involved and as information on customer perceptions is vital for these functions to manage their own operations effectively, it may be appropriate to locate the analysis process within one of these departments. In some organizations, customer support groups are formed to provide the post-sales interface with customer and in such cases they would probably perform the analysis.

The process

The integrity of your process for determining customer satisfaction is paramount otherwise you could be fooling yourselves into believing all is well when it is far from reality. The process therefore needs to be free from bias, prejudice and political influence.

In defining the process you will need to:

- determine the sources from which information is to be gathered
- determine the method of data collection – the forms, questionnaires and interview check lists to be used
- determine the frequency of data collection
- devise a method for synthesizing the data for analysis
- analyse trends
- determine the methods to be used for computing the customer satisfaction index
- establish the records to be created and maintained
- identify the reports to be issued and to whom they should be issued
- determine the actions and decisions to be taken and those responsible for the actions and decisions

Pareto analysis can be used to identify the key areas on which action is necessary. For example it may turn out that 80% of the sales come from repeat orders indicating a slow down in the number of new customers. Also 80% of the complaints may be from one market sector with only 20% of the sales – an indication that 80% of customers may be satisfied. Alternatively, 80% of the compliments may come from 20% of the customers but as they represent 80% of the sales it may prove very significant. The important factor is to look for relationships that indicate major opportunities and not insignificant opportunities for improvement. Use the results to derive the business plans, product development and process development plans for current and future products and services.

Frequency of measurement

Frequency needs to be adjusted following changes in products and services and major changes in organization structure such as mergers, downsizing, plant closures etc. Changes in fashion and public opinion should also not be discounted. Repeating the survey after the launch of new technology, new legislation or changes in world economics affecting the industry may also affect customer perception and consequently satisfaction.

Trends

To determine trends in customer perception you will need to make regular measurements and plot the results preferably by particular attributes or variables. The factors will need to include quality characteristics of the product or service as well as delivery performance and price. The surveys could be linked to your improvement programmes so that following a change, and allowing sufficient time for the effect to be observed by the customer, customer feedback data could be secured to indicate the effect of the improvement.

Customer dissatisfaction will be noticeable from the number and nature of customer complaints collected and analysed as part of your corrective action procedures. This data provides objective documentation or evidence and again can be reduced to indices to indicate trends.

By targeting the final customer using data provided by intermediate customers, you will be able to secure data from the users but it may not be very reliable. A nil return will not indicate complete satisfaction so you will need to decide whether the feedback is significant enough to warrant attention. Using statistics to make decisions in this case may not be a viable approach because you will not possess all the facts!

Customer satisfaction index

A customer satisfaction index that is derived from data from an independent source would indeed be more objective. Such schemes are in use in North America, Sweden and Germany. A method developed by Professor Claes Fornell has been in operation for 10 years in Sweden and is now being used at the National Quality Research Center of the University of Michigan Business School. Called the American Customer Satisfaction Index (ACSI) it covers seven sectors, 40 industries and some 189 companies and government agencies. It is sponsored by the ASQC and the University of Michigan Business School with corporate sponsorship from Federal Express, Sears Roebuck, Florida Power and Light and others. The index was started in 1994 (American Society for Quality, 2001)[4] and using data obtained from customer interviews, sector reports are published indicating a CSI for each listed organization thereby providing a quantitative and independent measure of performance useful to economists, investors and potential customers (US Government, 2001)[5].

Analysis of conformance to customer requirements (8.4b)

The standard requires *analysis of data to provide information relating to conformity to product requirements.*

What does this mean?

Data relating to conformity to product requirements is data generated from monitoring and measuring product characteristics. It comprises the results of all verification activities including those generated during design, purchasing, production, installation and operation. The data collected from customer feedback is also included where the cause of the complaint is product nonconformity. The requirement focuses on conformity and therefore the degree of variation is not relevant. A product either conforms or does not conform and it is this that is required to be analysed. The next requirement deals with variation.

Why is this necessary?

This requirement responds to the Factual Approach Principle.

When setting your quality objectives, targets should be established for product conformity as a measure of achievement. Data needs to be collected and analysed for all products in order to determine whether these objectives are being achieved.

How is this implemented?

Data on conformity and nonconformity can be collected from the product verification points in each process but it is also important to collect data on the size of the population involved. In general terms it is important to know the overall ratio of conforming product to nonconforming product i.e. of a quantity of products, how many were conforming and how many nonconforming. The data could also relate to specific product characteristics such as reliability, safety, power output, strength etc.

A concept that has become very popular is the sigma value – a measure of the capability of a process to produce conforming product (see Chapter 2 under *Six sigma*).

Analysis of product and process characteristics (8.4c)

The standard requires *analysis of data to provide information relating to characteristics and trends of processes and product including opportunities for preventive action.*

What does this mean?

The data that can provide information relating to characteristics and trends of processes and product comprises all the product and process measurements taken. The measurements provide useful data for indicating variation in product conformity and process capability. Variation is measured when the characteristics are variable such as dimensions, voltage, power output and strength.

Opportunities for preventive action may arise when the trend in a series of measured values indicates deterioration in performance and if the deterioration were allowed to continue, nonconformity would result.

Why is this necessary?

This requirement responds to the Factual Approach Principle.

The purpose behind the requirement is to generate information that can be used to bring about an improvement in product and process quality. It is only by analysing trends that the opportunity for improvement is revealed. A series of figures may appear random at first glance but on closer analysis proves the process to be out of control. The points on a graph may indicate measurements are within limits but further analysis may reveal that a change has occurred that if ignored, may result in the process generating nonconforming product in the future. Data analysis is therefore useful for assessing current performance and predicting future performance.

> **1994–2000 Differences**
>
> Previously the standard required the supplier to monitor suitable process parameters and product characteristics.
>
> The intent of the requirement has changed from monitoring data for control purposes to analysing data for control and improvement purposes. It also extends the applicability of the requirement beyond production to all processes including in-service performance.

How is this implemented?

Measurements of product and process characteristics should be collected but remember to collect only data that is useful in improving conformity or capability. Just because it can be measured does not mean that it should be! In automated processes, the machine performs the analysis and adjusts the process. In operator controlled processes, the operator takes the measurements, conducts the analysis and makes the adjustments often using control charts such as Average and Range Charts, Median Charts, p-Charts, np-Charts etc. The characteristics measured are taken from the product specification. In management controlled processes, the data needs to be collected, reduced, analysed, interpreted and presented in a suitable form before any meaningful information can be transmitted to decision makers. The data may come from many processes and locations. Analysing the Staff Development process for instance may require data from all managers on staff numbers, development needs, training programmes etc. to be consolidated and interpreted before meaningful results will emerge. The output may be in the form of histograms showing the levels of competence in each department, the cost of training per employee, the proportion of turnover spent on training etc. All information should relate to specific product or process characteristics to prevent the management being inundated with reports that add no value.

A methodical approach would be to generate a list for each product and process that includes:

- the product or process characteristics
- the location(s) of the data capture point(s)
- the method of capturing measurement data (automated, operator, manager)
- the form in which the data is transmitted to the analysis point (raw data, reports, surveys etc.)
- the unit responsible for data analysis
- the methods used to extract meaningful information from the data
- the form in which the resultant analysis is transmitted to decision makers
- the frequency of reporting
- the levels through which the information must pass before reaching the decision makers
- the unit responsible for making decisions

Data on product characteristics may be analysed and acted upon by the operator and therefore do not warrant separate indication of each characteristic. However, some characteristics such as reliability and availability are not measured by operators but from field data or service centres. For processes the characteristics will be key performance measures against the process objectives. Where a process involves many departments, extracting and analysing the data can be a complex process in itself. Juran uses the analogy of telephone transmission to illustrate the problems with communication (Juran, J. M., 1995)[6].

- The amplifier – restoring intensity of a signal that has become weak over long distances
- The filter – a device for admitting a selected part of the spectrum and to reject all else
- Redundancy – multiple transmission channels to increase reliability
- Shielding – a device to keep noise from invading the message, keeps the message secure and keeps out cross talk

Depending on the significance of the information, all of these devices may be active in the channels transmitting information of product and process performance. Some of the devices may be installed deliberately to safeguard information from outsiders. Other devices may be used covertly to prevent information from reaching the top management. In the list described above, the penultimate bullet is inserted to bring such ploys out into the open. If the information is based upon fact and is relevant to the product and process objectives, it should be allowed free passage. Redundancy may be warranted when the information is of vital importance to the business and some means of validating the facts is needed.

Analysis of supplier data (8.4d)

The standard requires *analysis of data to provide information relating to suppliers.*

What does this mean?

Information relating to suppliers includes that related to their performance regarding product and service quality, delivery and cost.

Why is this necessary?

This requirement responds to the Factual Approach Principle.

Suppliers are a key contributor to the performance of an organization and therefore information on the performance of suppliers is necessary to determine the adequacy, suitability and effectiveness of the management system.

> **1994–2000 Differences**
>
> Previously the standard required the type and extent of control exercised by the supplier over subcontractors to be dependent upon records of the previously demonstrated capability and performance of subcontractors.
>
> The previous requirement implied that supplier performance data should be collected for control purposes but the intent has now changed to analysing data for control and improvement purposes.

How is this implemented?

There are several aspects of the purchasing process that can be analysed and used to reveal information about suppliers in order to determine their performance and opportunities for improvement. However, the resources allocated to the analysis need to be appropriate to the potential risks to the organization and its customers. It is therefore necessary to focus on those suppliers that indicate the greatest risk to the organization's performance.

Order value

One group of suppliers at risk are those that provide the highest value of products and services. High order value implies significant investment by the organization because such decisions are not taken lightly. Should the supplier fail, the organization may not be able to recover sufficiently to avoid dissatisfying its customers.

The supplier database should identify the value of orders with suppliers and from an examination of this data, a Pareto analysis may reveal the proportion of suppliers that receive the highest value of orders. The performance of those in the top 20% in the order value list will obviously have more effect on the organization than the performance of the other 80% and may warrant closer attention. If you establish the effort spent on developing these suppliers as opposed to the others, it may reveal that the priorities are wrong and need adjustment.

Order quantity

Another group at risk are those suppliers that process the greatest number of orders. If there is a systemic fault in their processes, many deliveries may contain the same fault. It is possible that some of the high order value suppliers are the same as the high order quantity suppliers such as those supplying consumables. The performance of the top 20% in the order quantity list may affect all your products especially if the product is a raw material, fasteners, adhesives or any item that forms the basis of the products physical nature.

Quality risk

The third group at risk are those suppliers that supply products or services that a product failure modes analysis has shown are mission critical regardless of value or quantity. You may only need a few of these and their cost may be trivial, but their failure may result in immediate customer dissatisfaction. The FMEA should show the probability of failure and therefore the Pareto analysis could reveal the top 20% of products that are critical to the organization in terms of quality.

Delivery risk

The fourth group at risk are those suppliers that must meet delivery targets. Some items are on a long lead time with plenty of slack, others are ordered when stocks are low and others are ordered against a schedule that is designed to place product on the production line just-in-time to be used. It is the latter that are most critical although a JIT scheme does not have to be in place for delivery to be critical. The top 20% of these suppliers deserve special attention, regardless of value, quantity or product quality risk. A late delivery may have ramifications throughout the supply chain.

Suppliers per item

The fifth group of suppliers is not necessarily a group at risk. Many organizations insist on having more than one qualified supplier for a given item or service just in case a supplier under performs. As Deming points out *'A second source for protection in case of ill luck puts one vendor out of business temporarily or forever, is a costly policy. There is lower inventory and a lower total investment with a single supplier than with two'* (Deming, W. Edwards, 1982)[7] An analysis of purchased items by supplier will reveal how many items are sourced from more than one supplier. Those items sourced from the most number of suppliers are therefore candidates for a supplier reduction programme.

Costs

Cost is also a factor but often only measured when there is a target for suppliers to reduce costs year-on-year. An analysis of these suppliers may reveal the top 20% that miss the target by the greatest amount.

Once the top 20% have been identified in each group, further analysis should be carried out to establish how each of these suppliers performs on quality, cost and delivery, the amount of effort spent in developing these suppliers and the degree to which these suppliers respond to requests for action.

A common method of assessing suppliers was to send out questionnaires that gathered data about the supplier. These add little value apart from gathering data. A measure of how many of your suppliers have ISO 9000 certification does not reveal anything of value because it does not indicate their performance. Analysis of supplier data should only be performed to obtain facts from which decisions are to be made to develop the supplier or terminate supply.

Improvement (8.5)

Continual improvement (8.5.1)

The standard requires the organization to *continually improve the effectiveness of the quality management system through use of the quality policy, quality objectives, audit results, analysis of data, corrective and preventive actions and management review.*

> **1994–2000 Differences**
>
> This is a new requirement that has no equivalent in the 1994 version.

What does this mean?

There are eight requirements for continual improvement in the standard including the one above:

1 The organization shall establish, document, implement and maintain a management system and continually improve its effectiveness.
2 The organization shall implement actions necessary to achieve continual improvement of the processes needed for the management system.
3 Top management shall provide evidence of its commitment to continually improving the effectiveness of the management system.
4 Top management shall ensure that the quality policy includes a commitment to continually improve the effectiveness of the management system.
5 The organization shall determine and provide the resources needed to continually improve the effectiveness of the management system.
6 The organization shall plan and implement the monitoring, measurement, analysis and improvement processes needed to continually improve the effectiveness of the management system.

7 The organization shall determine, collect and analyse appropriate data to evaluate where continual improvement of the management system can be made.

8 The organization shall continually improve the effectiveness of the management system through the use of the quality policy, quality objectives, audit results, analysis of data, corrective and preventive actions and management review.

Requirement 1 is duplicated by requirement 8. Requirement 2 omits reference to *effectiveness* therefore improvement can be interpreted as applying to improved efficiency as well as effectiveness. Requirements 3 and 4 are linked in that they relate to policy. Requirement 6 serves to identify opportunities for improvement of which requirement 7 forms a part and requirement 5 provides the means by which improvement are to be made. They are therefore not separate requirements but are all derivatives of the first requirement, each focusing on either the whole or a part of the improvement process.

Why is this necessary?

This requirement responds to the Continual Improvement Principle.

The policies, objectives and targets maybe those that are set on the basis of existing capability and performance – what was achieved last year. They may be those that were set last time customer needs and expectations were evaluated or the prevailing regulations determined. These may no longer be the policies, objectives and targets that are required to keep the organization focused on its purpose and mission. The *goal posts* may have moved! The competition may have pushed forward the frontiers of technology, innovation, and performance. The market may have changed, the economic and social climate changed and in order to stay ahead of the competition, the organization has to aim for different objectives and targets, to set new policies that will form different behaviours. On the premise that for a system to be effective it has to fulfil its purpose and in the environment in which the system operates, the route towards that fulfilment is always changing; the system will never be totally effective – there will always be a new goal to aim for. It is therefore necessary to continually improve the effectiveness of the management system even though by the time the system is effective the goal posts will have moved. There is nothing more certain in life than death, taxes and change!

How is this implemented?

This particular requirement duplicates that contained in the first para of clause 5.4.2 because clause 5.4.1 required objectives consistent with policy and clause 5.3 required policy to address continual improvement, therefore plans for continual improvement would be required. Planning for improvement is also addressed by clause 8.1 and 8.5.1 so there is no shortage of clauses related to improvement planning. They all amount to the same thing – there is not a lot of difference between them but the most informative reference is that in Annex B of ISO 9004 where an improvement methodology is described.

Continual improvement was addressed in chapter 4 but to understand the implications of this requirement it is necessary to understand:

- the composition of a management system
- the types of improvement
- the difference between random and continuous improvement

The meaning of a management system was addressed in Chapter 2 so we have learnt that a management system is much more than a set of documents. As a management system consists of the processes required to deliver the organization's products and services as well as the resources, behaviours and environment upon which they depend, it follows that in continually improving the management system, you need to continually improve the processes, resources, behaviours and the physical and human environment within the organization.

Improvement can be random and unstructured – arising from fire fighting measures, reactions to situations that have got out of control or to threats that appear on the horizon that must be dealt with in order to survive – but this is not strictly improvement, it merely restores performance to where it should have been in the first place. ISO 9000 requires a continual quest for improvement and this will only come about if you are continually measuring performance and acting upon the results so as to improve conformity and improve capability. The frequency by which performance is measured should be appropriate to the parameter concerned. Some parameters change by the second, others by the year. The frequency of measurement should provide factual data that if acted upon will move the organization forward incrementally or in great steps. What should not happen is that the measurements are taken too late to halt a significant decline in performance.

Improvement plans do not need to be consolidated into documents with the title Continual Improvement Plan. Separate plans may exist, focused on general or specific improvements. For example there may be:

- New product development plans
- New process development plans
- New system development plans
- Corrective action plans
- Preventive action plans
- Staff development plans
- Plant development plans

All these plans aim to provide the organization with an improved capability and for data management purposes, it may help to catalogue these plans under *Improvement* as well as product, process, department, division or corporate headings etc.

Corrective Action (8.5.2)

Eliminating the cause of actual nonconformities (8.5.2)

1994–2000 Differences

Previously the standard required:

(a) corrective action procedures to include determining the corrective action needed to eliminate the cause of nonconformities;

(b) any corrective action taken to eliminate the causes of actual nonconformities is to a degree appropriate to the magnitude of problems and commensurate with the risks encountered.

The intent remains unchanged because corrective action was defined in ISO 8402 as action taken to prevent recurrence of nonconformity.

The standard requires the organization to *take action to eliminate the cause of nonconformities in order to prevent recurrence and requires the actions to be appropriate to the effects of the nonconformities encountered.*

What does this mean?

Corrective action is the pattern of activities that traces the symptoms of a problem to its cause, produces solutions for preventing the recurrence of the problem, implements the change and monitors that the change has been successful. Corrective action provides a feedback loop in the control cycle. *Inspection* detects nonconformity – *nonconformity control* identifies, segregates and rectifies the nonconforming item and *corrective action* serves to prevent the nonconformity from recurring. Whilst the notion of *correction* implies that it could be as concerned with the nonconforming item as with the cause of nonconformity, correcting the nonconforming item is a remedial action. It doesn't stop it recurring. ISO 9000 does not use the term remedial action except in the context of a repair. The term in ISO 9000 used for correcting the nonconformity is *correction* – which is a little too similar to the term corrective action to avoid confusion. Preventing the recurrence of nonconformity is a corrective action. A problem has to exist for you to take corrective action. When actual problems don't exist but there is a possibility of failure, the action of preventing the occurrence of nonconformity (or any problem for that matter) is a *preventive action*. So we have Remedial Action, Corrective Action and Preventive Action, each with a different meaning. Remedial Action is covered by clause 8.3, Corrective Action by 8.5.2 and Preventive Action by clause 8.5.3 of the standard.

Let us take a medical analogy. You have a head cold so you go to the doctor for advice. The doctor prescribes a remedy – 'take two pills three time a day and the cold symptoms should subside'. You do as the doctor advises and indeed the cold symptoms subside. This is remedial action. You then return to the doctor year after year with the same problem and ask the doctor to prescribe a means of preventing the cold symptoms from recurring each year. The doctor prescribes a course of injections that will prevent the symptoms occurring. You take the course of injections and behold, you do not feel cold symptoms ever again! This is corrective action. You observe over the years that the course of injections work providing you continue with the regime. You have a daughter who has never had a head cold and, mindful of the treatment you are given, wish to preserve your daughter from the suffering you have had over the years. You seek the doctor's advice which is that you enter your daughter on to a course of injections to safeguard against the risk of attracting the cold virus. Your daughter undertakes the prescribed course of treatment and never experiences a head cold. This is preventive action.

Although the natural inclination is to think of nonconformities in the context of product and manufacturing process, any departure from a requirement is a nonconformity. It follows therefore that any failure to meet the organization's objectives is a nonconformity and its cause should be eliminated.

Action appropriate to the effects of the nonconformities encountered, means that if the nonconformity is a random occurrence and of insignificant consequence, no corrective action might be needed e.g. if a person makes a mistake and knows a mistake has been made – there is no pattern of behaviour that would suggest it would occur again. If there is frequent occurrence of nonconformity this indicates a systemic problem that can be prevented from recurrence by retraining, changing work practices or modifying product or process design. It is therefore not practical to attempt action to prevent recurrence for each nonconformity.

Why is this necessary?

This requirement responds to the Process Approach Principle.

Nonconformities are caused by factors that should not be present in a process. There will always be variation but variation is not nonconformity. Nonconformity is when the variation exceeds the limits permitted. The factors that cause nonconformity on one occasion will (unless removed) cause nonconformity again and again. As the objective of any process must be to produce conforming output, it follows therefore that it is necessary to eliminate the causes of nonconformity. This does not simply apply to products of the production process but to products of all processes – business management, marketing, sales, finance etc.

How is this implemented?

The other requirements in this clause identify most of the steps needed to eliminate the cause of nonconformity. There are one or two stages that have been omitted. A more complete list of steps is shown in Table 8.1, they will be addressed later in this chapter.

Table 8.1 Steps in the corrective action process

Step	Action	Clause 8.5.2 requirement
1	Collect the nonconformity data and classify	Reviewing nonconformities
2	Conduct Pareto analysis to identify the vital few and trivial many	
3	Organize a Diagnostic Team	
4	Postulate causes and test theories	Determining the cause
5	Determine the root cause of nonconformity	
6	Determine the effects of nonconformity and the need for action	
7	Determine the action needed to prevent nonconformity recurring	Evaluating the action needed
8	Organize an Implementation Team	
9	Create or choose the conditions which will ensure effective implementation	Implementing the action needed
10	Implement the agreed action	
11	Record the results of Pareto analysis	
12	Record the causes of nonconformity	
13	Record the criteria for determining severity or priority	Records of results
14	Record the proposed actions to be taken	
15	Record the actions actually taken	
16	Record the results of actions taken	
17	Assess the actions taken	
18	Determine whether the actions were those required to be taken	
19	Determine whether the actions were performed in the best possible way	Reviewing corrective actions
20	Determine whether the nonconformity has recurred	
21	If nonconformity has recurred repeat steps 1 to 14	

As the sources of nonconformity are so varied, it may not be practical to have a single corrective action procedure. It may be more practical to embody corrective action provisions in the following procedures:

- Failure investigation procedure
- Nonconforming material review procedure
- Customer complaints procedure
- Document change procedure
- Specification change procedure
- Maintenance procedures

Reviewing nonconformities (8.5.2a)

The standard requires *the documented procedure for corrective action to define requirements for reviewing nonconformities (including customer complaints).*

What does this mean?

As indicated above, the review of nonconformities means that nonconformity data should be collected, classified and analysed. The reference to customer complaints is that every customer complaint is a nonconformity with some requirement. They may not all be product requirements. Some may relate to delivery, to the attitude of staff or to false claims in advertising literature. Any complaint implies that a requirement (expectation, obligation or implied need) has not been met even if that requirement had not been determined previously. We have to accept that we could have overlooked something. Just because it was not written in the contract does not mean the customer is wrong.

> **1994–2000 Differences**
>
> Previously the standard required the procedures for corrective action to include effective handling of customer complaints and reports of nonconformity.
>
> The implication is that all nonconformities needs to be identified not only those related to product.

Why is this necessary?

This requirement responds to the Continual Improvement Principle.

A review is another look at something therefore the first view of the nonconformity was when it was detected and recorded. The second view of it should aim to:

1 establish if the nonconformity had been predicted in the planning phase
2 establish why the preventive action measures were not effective
3 prevent it from happening again where possible

How is this implemented?

Your corrective action procedures need to cover the collection and analysis of product nonconformity reports and the collection and analysis of process data to reveal process nonconformities. The standard does not require you to take corrective action on every nonconformity. Here it is suggested that the decision to act should be *appropriate to the effects of the nonconformities encountered*. It is therefore implying that you only need act on the vital few. To find the vital few nonconformities out of the total population that provide the bulk of improvement potential a Pareto analysis should be conducted. A Pareto analysis is a management tool that finds a few needles in a haystack of trivia, e.g. most of the wealth is concentrated in few hands or 10% of customers account for 60% of sales. (For an explanation of the Pareto principle and its origins see Juran (1995) on Quality by design). When dealing with nonconformity, the question we need an ask is 'What are the few sources of nonconformities that comprise the bulk of all nonconformities? If we can find these nonconformities and eliminate their cause, we will reduce variation significantly.

The first step is to assign a short description to the nonconformity such as dry solder joint, hole not plated, broken track, incorrect part number, dirty terminal etc. The next step is to sort the nonconformities by product and process. Then rank the nonconformities in order of occurrence so that the nonconformity having the most occurrences would appear at the top of the list. The result might be that for a particular product or process a few types of nonconformity would account for the greatest proportion of nonconformities. An example is given in Table 8.2. Here we see there are fifteen types of nonconformity with just four types accounting for 76% of the total. It follows therefore that if we eliminate the bottom four causes of nonconformity

Table 8.2 Pareto analysis

Nonconformity type	Frequency	%	Cumulative %
Too much solder	400	34.19	34.19
Lifted tracks	230	19.66	53.85
Solder bridge	180	15.38	69.23
Dirty terminals	90	7.69	76.92
Component not flat on board	70	5.98	82.91
Cracked insulation	40	3.42	86.32
Uncropped component legs	30	2.56	88.89
Under spec plating thickness	30	2.56	91.45
Too little solder	20	1.71	93.16
Dry joints	20	1.71	94.87
Unplated holes	20	1.71	96.58
Broken tracks	10	0.85	97.44
Incorrect component fitted	10	0.85	98.29
Incorrect part number	10	0.85	99.15
Damage edge connector	10	0.85	100.00
Total nonconformities	1170		

productivity would increase by a mere 3 %. However, if we eliminate the four most dominant types of nonconformity, productivity would increase by a staggering 76%.

Another way of ranking the nonconformities is by seriousness. Not all nonconformities will have the same effect on product quality. Some may be critical and others insignificant. By classification of nonconformities in terms of criticality a list of those most serious nonconformities can be revealed using the Pareto analysis. Even though the frequency of occurrence of a particular nonconformity may be high, it may not affect any characteristic that impacts customer requirements. This is not to say the cause should not be eliminated but there may be other more significant problems to eliminate first.

Before managers will take action, they need to know:

- What is the problem or potential problem?
- Has the problem been confirmed?
- What are the consequences of doing nothing i.e. what effect is it having?
- What is the preferred solution?
- How much will the solution cost?
- How much will the solution save?
- What are the alternatives and their relative costs?
- If I need to act, how long have I got before the effects damage the business?

Whatever you do, don't act on suspicion, always confirm that a problem exists or that there is a certain chance that a problem will exist if the current trend continues. Validate causes before proclaiming action!

Customer complaints and returned product

The customer can be mistaken and customer complaints therefore need to be validated as genuine nonconformities before entering the corrective action process. Parts returned from dealers, customer manufacturing plants etc. may not be nonconforming. They may be obsolete, surplus to requirements, have suffered damage in handling or have been used in trials etc. Products may have failed under warranty and not be logged as a complaint but nonetheless they are nonconforming. Whatever the reason for return, you need to record all returns and perform an analysis to reveal opportunities for corrective action when appropriate. You should process these items as indicated previously but prior to expending effort on investigations, you should establish your liability and then investigate the cause of any nonconformities for which you are liable.

Nonconformity reduction

Previously it was suggested that action be taken on the vital few non-conformities that dominated the population. If this plan is successful these nonconformities will no longer appear in the list the next time the analysis is repeated. As the vital few nonconformities are tackled, the frequency of occurrence will begin to decline until there are no nonconformities left to deal with. This is nonconformity reduction (or special cause removal) and can be applied to specific products or processes. If you were to aggregate the nonconformities for all products and processes you would observe that it is quite possible to take corrective action continuously and still not reduce the number of nonconformities – no matter how hard you try you cannot seem to reduce the number. This is because the objectives and targets keep changing. They rarely remain constant long enough to make valid comparisons from year to year. There is always some new process, practice or technology being introduced that triggers the learning cycle all over again.

Determining the cause of nonconformities (8.5.2b)

1994–2000 Differences
Previously the standard required the supplier to investigate the cause of nonconformities relating to product, process and quality system and to record the results of the investigation.
The intent of the requirement remains unchanged.

The standard requires *the documented procedure for corrective action to define requirements for determining the causes of nonconformity.*

What does this mean?

The cause of nonconformity is the reason it occurred. What you observe when detecting nonconformity is the effect of the cause. A product is damaged, the immediate cause might be poor packaging or poor handling but these too have their causes and although they may appear unconnected there maybe a common cause which, if eliminated, resolves two problems of concern.

There are three types of corrective action, product related, process related and system related. Product-related nonconformities can be either internal or external and you will have nonconformity reports to analyse. Process-related nonconformities may arise out of product nonconformity but if you expect something less than 100% yield from the process, the reject items may not be considered *nonconformities*. They may be regarded as *waste*. Unlike products, process nonconformities are often not recorded in the same way and therefore the data is not as readily accessible. By analysing the process you can find the cause of low yield and improve performance of the process. Product and process nonconformities may be detected at planned verification stages and may also be detected during product and process audits. System-related nonconformities could arise out of internal and external system audits but arise equally as a result of tracing the root cause of a problem to a system inadequacy.

Why is this necessary?

This requirement responds to the Continual Improvement Principle.

All nonconformities are caused – all causes within your control can be avoided – all that is needed is concerted action to prevent recurrence. Nonconformity costs money and wastes resources. The fewer the non-conformities the more resources available for producing productive output.

How is this implemented?

Discovering the cause

To eliminate the cause of nonconformity the cause needs to be known and therefore the first step is to conduct an analysis of the symptoms to determine their cause. Simply asking why an event occurred might reveal a cause but don't accept the first reason given because there is usually a reason why this previous event occurred. Toyota discovered that asking *why* successively five times will invariably discover the root cause. There may be more or less than five steps to the root cause but it is critical to stop only when you can't go any further. The following example illustrates the technique.

A trainer arrives to conduct a training course to discover that the materials have not been delivered from head office as she expected them to be.

1 *Why were the materials not delivered? – Answer – because the administrators thought the trainer would bring her own materials*
2 *Why did they think the trainer would bring her own materials? – Answer – because they had not been informed otherwise*
3 *Why weren't the administrators given the correct information? – Answer – because the office manager had not communicated the agreed division of responsibility when setting up training courses.*
4 *Why had the office manager not communicated the agreed division of responsibility? Answer – because the office manager had put other matters before internal communication in his order of priorities.*
5 *Why had the office manager not got his priorities right? Answer – because he was not yet competent*
6 *Why was the office manager not yet competent? Answer – because the top management had made the appointment in haste*
7 *Why had top management made the appointment in haste? Answer – because they were not applying leadership*

Therefore a lack of leadership (the 2nd quality management principle) is the root cause. It took seven questions to get there but if we had stopped at question 3, and made the assumption that giving the administrators the correct instructions would prevent recurrence of the problem, we would be wrong. If the office manager forgot to issue the instructions, it indicates that he did not complete the process that commenced when the division of responsibility was agreed. This is quite typical. A meeting is held and agreements reached and when everyone departs they get on with what they were doing before the meeting, not realizing that a process has been initiated that needs to continue and be completed outside the meeting. If the staff were competent, they would complete the process before moving on. The root cause of most problems can be traced to lack of application of one or more of the eight quality management principles.

Another technique is the cause and effect diagram (Aka Ishikawa Diagram or fishbone diagram). This is a graphical method of showing the relationship between cause and effect. Each type of nonconformity (an effect) would be analysed to postulate the causes so for example the question would be put to a diagnostic team – What could cause too much solder on a joint? The team would come up with a number of possibilities. Each one would be tested either by experiment or further examination of the soldering process and a root cause established.

Some nonconformities appear random but often have a common cause. In order to detect these causes, statistical analysis may need to be carried out. The causes of such nonconformities are generally due to non-compliance with (or inadequate) working methods and standards. Other nonconformities have a clearly defined special or unique cause that has to be corrected before the process can continue. Special cause problems generally require the changing of unsatisfactory designs or working methods. They may well be significant or even catastrophic. These rapidly result in unsatisfied customers and loss of profits. In order to investigate the cause of nonconformities you will need to:

1 Identify the requirements which have not been achieved
2 Collect data on nonconforming items, the quantity, frequency and distribution
3 Identify when, where and under what conditions the nonconformities occurred
4 Identify what operations were being carried out at the time and by whom

Common problem solving tools

There are many tools you can use to help you determine the root cause of problems. These are known as *disciplined problem solving methods*.

Disciplined methods are those proven methods that employ fundamental principles to reveal information. There are two different approaches to problem solving. The first is used when data are available as is the case when dealing with nonconformities. The second approach is when not all the data needed are available.

The seven quality tools in common use are as follows:

- Pareto diagrams – used to classify problems according to cause and phenomenon
- Cause and effect diagrams – used to analyse the characteristics of a process or situation
- Histograms – used to reveal the variation of characteristics or frequency distribution obtained from measurement
- Control charts – used to detect abnormal trends around control limits
- Scatter diagrams – used to illustrate the association between two pieces of corresponding data
- Graphs – used to display data for comparative purposes
- Check-sheets – used to tabulate results through routine checks of a situation

The further seven quality tools for use when not all data are available are:

- Relations diagram – used to clarify interrelations in a complex situation
- Affinity diagram – used to pull ideas from a group of people and group them into natural relationships
- Tree diagram – used to show the interrelations among goals and measures
- Matrix diagram – used to clarify the relations between two different factors (e.g. QFD)
- Matrix data-analysis diagram – used when the matrix chart does not provide information in sufficient detail
- Process decision program chart – used in operations research
- Arrow diagram – used to show steps necessary to implement a plan (e.g. PERT)

The source of causes is not unlimited. Nonconformities are caused by one or more of the following:

- Deficiency in communication
- Deficiencies in documentation
- Deficiencies in personnel training and motivation
- Deficiencies in materials
- Deficiencies in tools and equipment
- Deficiencies in the operating environment

Each of these is probably caused by not applying one or more of the eight quality management principles.

Once you have identified the root cause of the nonconformity you can propose corrective action to prevent its recurrence. Eliminating the cause of nonconformity and preventing the recurrence of nonconformity are essentially the same thing.

Evaluating the need for action (8.5.2c)

1994–2000 Differences

This is a new requirement that has no equivalent in the 1994 version.

The standard requires *the documented procedure for corrective action to define requirements for evaluating the need for action to ensure that nonconformities do not recur.*

What does this mean?

All nonconformities are the result of something not going to plan no matter how insignificant the problem. Whether action is taken depends upon the effects of the nonconformity. The plan may not be right, the deviation from plan may have no effect at all, it may be a one-off – unlikely to recur but on the other hand it may be disastrous and likely to recur unless something is done about it. An evaluation of the need for action is therefore necessary to determine if action should be taken and if so when that action should be taken.

Why is this necessary?

This requirement responds to the Continual Improvement Principle.

With a multitude of problems to resolve, some method of determining priorities is needed and rather than require the recurrence of all nonconformities to be prevented, the standard requires quite sensibly an evaluation to determine the need for action.

How is this implemented?

In reviewing the nonconformity data, you can rank nonconformities by class or cost so that you reveal the most important problems to tackle. A simple classification is to classify nonconformities on the basis of affecting form, fit or function and this is sufficient for most purposes. However there are various degrees of fit, form and function. In the automotive industry a severity ranking as shown in Table 8.3 is used when conducting a Failure Mode and Effects Analysis (FMEA).

Although used in the design phase, these criteria can be applied in the production and operational phases to rank nonconformities – those detected before and after shipment. Clearly a nonconformity that falls into any category above Low, (6–10) is a candidate for immediate corrective action. However, many nonconformities may not have these effects and would therefore receive a ranking of 1 but this does not mean that such nonconformities are not important to other processes.

Table 8.3 Failure severity ranking

Effect	Severity	Ranking
Hazardous without warning	Very high severity ranking when a potential failure mode affects safe vehicle operation and/or involves non-compliance with government regulation without warning	10
Hazardous with warning	Very high severity ranking when a potential failure mode affects safe vehicle operation and/or involves non-compliance with government regulation with warning	9
Very high	Vehicle/item inoperable, with loss of primary function	8
High	Vehicle/item operable, but at reduced level of performance. Customer dissatisfied	7
Moderate	Vehicle/item operable, but Comfort/Convenience item(s) inoperable. Customer experiences discomfort	6
Low	Vehicle/item operable, but Comfort/Convenience item(s) operate at reduced level of performance. Customer experiences some dissatisfaction	5
Very low	Fit and Finish/Squeak and Rattle item does not conform. Defect noticed by most customers.	4
Minor	Fit and Finish/Squeak and Rattle item does not conform. Defect noticed by *average* customers	3
Very minor	Fit and Finish/Squeak and Rattle item does not conform. Defect noticed by discriminating customers	2
None	No effect	1

Determining and implementing actions (8.5.2d)

The intent of the requirement remains unchanged.

The standard requires *the documented procedure for corrective action to define requirements for determining and implementing the corrective action needed.*

What does this mean?

The action needed is the action that will eliminate the cause of the nonconformity and therefore prevent its recurrence. You would think that after many years eliminating causes on nonconformity, there would be no nonconformities left, but you would be wrong, primarily because most of what purports to be corrective action is little more than remedial action. There are countless corrective action procedures being implemented that do not get close to eliminating the cause of nonconformity. They focus on the immediate cause and not the root cause.

Why is this necessary?

This requirement responds to the Continual Improvement Principle.

Getting at the root of the problem is crucial to corrective action. Action on the immediate cause is only a palliative – a temporary measure. Fixing the immediate cause will result in another nonconformity eventually appearing somewhere else.

How is this implemented?

It is important to distinguish between three separate actions when dealing with nonconformity:

- Action to remove the specific nonconformity in the nonconforming item (this is addressed by clause 8.3 covering the control of nonconforming product)
- Action to discover other occurrences of the nonconformity (this should also be covered by the provisions to meet clause 8.3)
- Action to prevent recurrence in the short term (this is the local action taken on the immediate cause)
- Action to prevent recurrence in the long term (this is the action taken on the root cause)

At the time you review a nonconforming product you should consider whether other similar products could be affected. Some of these products might already exist, others may be in the process of being produced and others in the process of being designed. For example, a nonconformity might be that a component was fitted the wrong way round.

1 The first action is to remove the component and fit a new one the right way round.
2 The second action is to search for other assemblies and replace the component. Some regard this as remedial action because it is searching for like items. Others regard it as corrective action because it is preventing a recurrence of a problem in the same and similar products. There are also

some people who regard it as preventive action because although the nonconformity has occurred in a specific product or process, it is only a potential nonconformity for other products or processes.

3 The third action is to display warning notices to alert operators and show them how to identify correct component orientation.
4 The fourth action is to install mistake-proofing measures.
5 The fifth action is to introduce into the design process a Process Failure Mode Effects Analysis that will detect when mistake-proofing is needed.

When corrective actions require interdepartmental action, it may be necessary to set up a corrective action team to introduce the changes. Each target area should be designated to a person with responsibility in that area and who reports to a team leader. In this way the task becomes a project with a project manager equipped with the authority to make the changes through the department representatives.

Take care not to degrade other processes by your actions. The corrective action plan should detail the action to be taken to eliminate the cause and the date by which a specified reduction in nonconformity is to be achieved. You should also monitor the reduction therefore the appropriate data collection measures need to be in place to gather the data at a rate commensurate with the production schedule. Monthly analysis may be too infrequent. Analysis by shift may be more appropriate.

Your management system needs to accommodate various corrective action strategies, from simple intradepartmental analysis with solutions that affect only one area, procedure, process or product, to projects that involve many departments, occasionally including suppliers and customers. Your corrective action procedures need to address these situations in order that when the time comes you are adequately equipped to respond promptly.

Recording results of actions taken (8.5.2e)

The standard requires *the documented procedure for corrective action to define requirements for recording results of action taken.*

What does this mean?

If taken literally this requirement means that one need only record whether the action had the desired effect. But we are interested in not only doing what the standard prescribes but also doing what is necessary for effective process management. Records of all the intentions and actions relative to the elimination of nonconformity should be generated.

1994–2000 Differences

Previously the standard required the supplier to apply controls to ensure that corrective actions are taken.

This additional requirement is more explicit and may impact those organizations that only record the action to be taken not the actual action that is taken.

Why is this necessary?

This requirement responds to the Factual Approach Principle.

Records are necessary in this case to chart the trail from nonconformity to root cause and back again to effective action. This is so that you can check through the logic of the analysis and subsequent actions and verify that the planned action was implemented.

How is this implemented?

Through the corrective action process there are several things that should be recorded:

- The results of Pareto analysis
- The likely causes
- The root cause
- The criteria for determining severity or priority
- The tests conducted to validate the root cause
- The actions proposed to eliminate the cause
- The actions taken
- The results of the actions taken

In order for it to be possible to verify the actions taken, records need exist to provide traceability. For example if your Corrective Action Report (e.g. CAR023) indicates that procedure XYZ requires a change, a reference to the Document Change Request (e.g. DCR134) initiating a change to procedure XYZ will provide the necessary link. The Change Request can reference the Corrective Action Report as the reason for change. If you don't use formal change requests, the Amendment Instructions can cross-reference the Corrective Action Report. Alternatively, if your procedures carry a change record, the reason for change can be added. There are several methods to choose from, but whatever the method you will need some means of tracking the implementation of corrective actions. This use of forms illustrates one of the many advantages of form serial numbers.

Reviewing corrective action taken (8.5.2f)

The standard requires the documented procedure for corrective action *to define requirements for reviewing corrective action taken.*

What does this mean?

The review of corrective actions means establishing that the actions have been effective in eliminating the cause of the nonconformity.

Why is this necessary?

This requirement responds to the Factual Approach Principle.

Every process should include verification and review stages not only to confirm that the required actions have been taken but also that the desired results have been achieved. It is only after a reasonable time has elapsed without a recurrence of a particular nonconformity that you can be sure that the corrective action has been effective.

> **1994–2000 Differences**
> Previously the standard required to apply controls to ensure that corrective action is effective.
>
> The modified wording weakens the intent of the requirement from implying periodic review for effectiveness to a one-off activity.

How is this implemented?

This requirement implies four separate actions:

- A review to establish what actions were taken
- An assessment to determine whether the actions were those required to be taken
- An evaluation of whether the actions were performed in the best possible way
- A investigation to determine whether the nonconformity has recurred

The effectiveness of some actions can be verified at the time they are taken but quite often the effectiveness can only be checked after a considerable lapse of time. Remember it took an analysis to detect the nonconformity therefore it may take further analysis to detect that the nonconformity has been eliminated. In such cases the Corrective Action Report should indicate when the checks for effectiveness are to be carried out and provision made for indicating that the corrective action has or has not been effective.

Some corrective actions may be multidimensional in that they may require training, changes to procedures, changes to specifications, changes in the organization, changes to equipment and processes – in fact so many changes that the corrective action becomes more like an improvement programme. Checking the effectiveness becomes a test of the system carried out over many months. Removing the old controls completely and committing yourselves to an untested solution may be disastrous therefore it is often prudent to leave the existing controls in place until your solution has been proven to be effective.

The nonconformity data should be collected and quantified using one of the seven quality tools, preferably the Pareto analysis. You can then devise a plan to reduce the 20% of causes that account for 80% of the nonconformities.

Preventive action (8.5.3)

Eliminating the cause of potential nonconformities (8.5.3)

1994–2000 Differences

Previously the standard required:

a) the supplier to use appropriate sources of information to eliminate potential causes of nonconforming product;

b) that any preventive action taken to eliminate the causes of potential nonconformities is to a degree appropriate to the magnitude of problems and commensurate with the risks encountered.

The intent of the requirement remains unchanged except the scope is widened beyond nonconforming product to include any situation that may cause a requirement to be unfulfilled.

The standard requires the organization to *determine action to eliminate the causes of potential nonconformities in order to prevent their occurrence and for such actions to be appropriate to the effects of the potential problems.*

What does this mean?

The difference between corrective and preventive action was previously addressed under corrective action. When actual problems don't exist but there is a possibility of failure, the action of preventing the occurrence of a nonconformity (or any problem for that matter) is a preventive action. Potential nonconformities might arise due to the inherent nature of the product or the process or its design, production, installation or operation. The way a product has been designed or the way it is intended to produce, install or maintain a product might lead to its failure either during production, installation or maintenance or its failure when in service.

Action to eliminate a potential nonconformity could be any action taken to anticipate failure in products and processes and remove the cause. If one cannot conceive of a mode of failure no action could possibly be taken. This is often regarded as operating within the 'state of the art'. There may be a time in the future when the risk of failure is known but one cannot plan for events about which one has no knowledge. This means of course that if there is evidence in the organization or in the public domain of a mode of failure that could occur with the organization's products or processes, preventive action needs to be taken. The grey areas arise where such evidence remains unproven. Many organizations are reluctant to take action on the basis of opinion especially when the action may be costly. It is an area where the organization's values can be tested and where moral or ethical judgements may need to be made.

Even if one does not have a crystal ball to look into the future, the present can provide a wealth of information. Knowledge of current performance can provide the basis for predicting future performance (except for the value of investments of course!). Monitoring performance and observing an undesirable trend, then taking action before a failure occurs is taking *preventive action* even though there is no evidence that the occurrence could be imminent.

Risk analysis, failure modes analysis, hazards analysis, stress analysis, reliability predictions or any similar type of analysis performed to identify design weaknesses is a preventive action *if* action is taken as a result of the analysis. Performing the analysis and doing nothing with the results is negligent. Preventive action can also be any action taken to ensure success. Research, planning, training, preparation, organizing and resourcing are all activities which if done well will prevent nonconformities arising.

Actions appropriate to the effects of the potential problems means that the probability of occurrence, the significance of the effects and the certainty of eliminating the cause should be taken into account when deciding on the action required.

Why is this necessary?

This requirement responds to the Continual Improvement Principle.

Regardless of the attitude of people towards quality, they all desire to be successful. No one really wants to fail but without foresight brought about by instinct, experience, diligence or luck, they will invariably fail. Organizations cannot put their results at risk and expect success to be achieved by chance. They have to take preventive action of the type described above if they are to succeed.

How is this implemented?

The other requirements in this clause identify most of the steps needed to eliminate the cause of a potential nonconformity. However, there are one or two stages that have been omitted. A more complete list of steps is given in Table 8.4, they will be addressed later in this chapter.

It makes no sense to have a procedure with the title Preventive Action Procedure because the above sequence of actions do not occur in isolation. They are part of and embedded within other actions and processes. The saying 'Look before you leap' is a preventive action but developed into a habit by the time we are teenagers. We sometimes forget or are distracted and don't look before we leap but it is not something where we stop and say to ourselves, 'Now what's the next step – oh yes; I must now look before I leap' We just do it without a conscious thought. The first 12 actions in Table 8.4 might form the basis of an FMEA Procedure with the other 12 actions being implemented by other processes. For example the records will be generated from planned verification activities, not special preventive action activities. The diagnostic and implementation teams will not be special teams but the normal design and production staff acting in their normal roles. There may be a need on occasions for a special task force to resolve a particularly difficult problem but most of the time, preventive action will be performed as a routine part of your job.

Table 8.4 Steps in the preventive action process

Step	Action	Clause 8.5.3 requirement
1	Determine the objectives of the product, process, task or activity	
2	Organize a Diagnostic Team	
3	Perform an analysis to determine the factors critical to the achievement of these objectives	
4	Determine how the factors might act to adversely affect the product, process, task or activity (the mode of failure)	Determining potential nonconformities and their causes
5	Determine the potential effect of such condition on the achievement of the objectives	
6	Determine the severity of the effect on meeting the objectives	
7	Assess the probability of this condition occurring	
8	Postulate causes and test theories	
9	Determine the root cause of potential nonconformity	
10	Identify the provisions currently in place that will prevent this adverse condition occurring or detect it before it has a detrimental effect on performance	
11	Assess the probability that these provisions will prevent the occurrence of this condition or of detecting it before it has a detrimental effect on performance	Evaluating the action needed
12	Determine any additional action needed to prevent the occurrence of the potential nonconformity	
13	Organize an Implementation Team	
14	Create or choose the conditions which will ensure effective implementation	Implementing the action needed
15	Implement the agreed action	
16	Record the results of all the analysis	
17	Record the causes of potential nonconformity	
18	Record the criteria for determining severity or priority	Records of results
19	Record the proposed actions to be taken	
20	Record the actions actually taken	
21	Determine whether the actions were those required to be taken	
22	Determine whether the actions were performed in the best possible way	Reviewing preventive actions
23	Determine whether the nonconformity has occurred	
24	If nonconformity has occurred, undertake corrective action and review the preventive action methods	

Preventive action provisions may therefore be embodied in the following types of procedures:

- Business planning procedures
- Design planning procedures
- Production planning procedures
- Resource planning procedures
- Risk assessment procedures
- Hazard analysis procedures
- Training procedures
- Performance analysis procedures
- Design review procedures
- Design analysis procedures (reliability, safety, maintainability etc.)
- Supplier/subcontractor performance review procedures
- Management review procedures

The actions in Table 8.4 could be included in a general planning guide. It would be foolish to make them policies because they describe a general methodology and there will be occasions when not all apply.

Determining potential nonconformities (8.5.3a)

The standard requires *a documented procedure that defines requirements for determining potential nonconformities and their causes.*

What does this mean?

Potential nonconformities are those that have not occurred, therefore the determination of potential nonconformities is a quest to discover inherent characteristics of products and processes that if not changed will eventually result in actual nonconform-

> **1994–2000 Differences**
>
> Previously the standard required the supplier to use appropriate sources of information to detect potential causes of nonconforming product. The intent of the requirement remains unchanged.

ities. As a nonconformity is non-fulfilment of a requirement, it follows that any requirement placed on or within the organization that may not be fulfilled is a potential nonconformity. As indicated above, the determination of potential nonconformities involves the analysis and evaluation of risk. Once risks are known and the effect on the product, process or organization established, action can be taken to eliminate, reduce or control these risks.

Why is this necessary?

This requirement responds to the Continual Improvement Principle.

The prevention of potential nonconformities cannot be relied upon to occur by chance – it has come about by systematic analysis of products and processes and their interrelationships both inside and outside the organization.

How is this implemented?

As indicated in Table 8.4, there are 8 steps to determining potential nonconformities and their causes. Each step will now be addressed briefly.

Determining objectives

As a nonconformity is non-fulfilment of a requirement, the first step is to determine what those requirements are. In some cases they will be product requirements, in others they will be process objectives or at a higher level the corporate objectives or quality objectives. It is necessary when considering the requirements for preventive action to avoid limiting your imagination to products because the potential for failure is just as present in the organization and its processes as in products – in fact it is these very weaknesses that are likely to be the cause of potential product nonconformities. Such objectives therefore will include the following:

- Corporate objectives (clause 5.4.1)
- Product requirements (clause 7.2.1)
- Process objectives (clause 4.1c)

As the product will comprise units, components, materials etc., each of these will be defined by requirements. As each process will comprise sub-processes, tasks and activities, each of these will be defined by objectives and input or entry requirements.

Organizing diagnostic teams

As indicated previously, specially organized diagnostic teams may not be needed because the prevention of nonconformity is the job of the product or process design team. It is usually a one-off activity. Once the provisions are put in place to prevent nonconformity, the team moves on to other things. At the corporate level, a team of senior managers or a research team may be needed to analyse the organization as a whole to discover risks to achievement of its objectives. At the sub-process and task level a team approach may also be necessary but at the activity level, it is the individual who should assess the risks, anticipate problems and either put in place provisions to prevent failure or take precautions.

Analysis of critical success factors

With every organization, process or product there are some critical factors upon which their success depends. The success of a book is not whether there is an unwanted printing mark on a page – it is whether the book lives up to the readers expectations and that is more to do with the substance than with materials. The success of electronic equipment is dependent upon appearance, function and reliability. The success of an automobile depends upon appearance, function, safety, reliability and maintainability. In most cases these factors will be defined in the product specification and will be the functions that the product is required to perform. With processes, success may depend upon throughput, resource consumption, traceability and/or response. With the organization, success may depend upon market intelligence, retaining competent people, short product development timescales, the quality of conformity or service standards – these will be the organizations objectives.

Answering the key question – 'What affects our ability to fulfil our mission or achieve our objectives?' reveals the critical success factors.

Failure modes

By taking each factor, one at a time and asking one or more of the following questions you develop a series of failure modes – the outward appearance of a specific failure effect (Smith, David, 1997)[8] :

- How might this part or process fail to meet the requirements?
- What could happen which would adversely affect performance?
- What would an interested party consider to be unacceptable?

Previous experience is a good starting point for determining what could go wrong but often these failures only arise under certain conditions. When a product is stressed by being subject to extreme environmental conditions, it may fail. When a process is overloaded or under-resourced or the operators are put under pressure, certain failures might occur. This can be presented as a Fault Tree diagram that describes the combination of events leading to a defined product/process/organization failure. For a description of this analysis see (Smith, David, 1997)[9].

Failure effects

For each failure mode, determine the effect of the failure through the hierarchy to the end product, the system and the external interfaces. The effect should be described in terms of what the customer might experience or the impact on overall organizational performance. A component may distort under load resulting in a failure of the assembly of which it is a part and consequently cause customer dissatisfaction. A process may deliver output late that in turn injects delays into other processes, which ultimately causes the organization to lose a customer. The omission of safety checks could endanger operators and subsequently put the line out of service or in breach of government regulations. The omission of records could leave a process down stream without necessary input data. This in turn could result in decisions being made without the full facts being available thus impacting work priorities that divert effort away from key projects.

Severity

Once the effects of failure have been identified, it does not follow that you have to act upon all of them. Some will have more impact than others and the next step is therefore to assess the severity of the effect. The same classification conventions used in evaluating the need for corrective action can be used.

Probability of occurrence

A potential nonconformity is one that could occur but the probability of occurrence might be as low as 1 in 1,000,000 or as high as 1 in 2. With electronic components, standard failure rate data can be used to predict the probability of failure. With other failure effects you will have to rely on past experience and this is where the records from previous projects are useful. Simply asking the question – 'When did we last experience this type of problem?' might bring forth useful information.

Determining cause

The diagnostic effort needed to determine the potential cause of the identified mode of failure can be considerable and therefore it is prudent to determine the probability of occurrence first so that the diagnostic effort can be focused on the failures with highest probability of occurrence.

Here once again the '5 Why's' technique is useful to get at the root cause. In some cases it may be necessary to experiment using Design of Experiments (DOE) technique in order to determine which causes are the major contributors.

Evaluating the need for action (8.5.3b)

1994–2000 Differences

This is a new requirement that has no equivalent in the 1994 version.

The standard requires *a documented procedure that defines requirements for evaluating the need for action to prevent occurrence of nonconformities.*

What does this mean?

The likelihood that an event might occur is not a command to take action for provisions may already be in place to prevent its occurrence, reduce or control its effects. The requirement therefore means that in evaluating the need for action, the existing provisions should be evaluated and on this basis, requirements for action to prevent the occurrence of nonconformity should be determined.

Why is this necessary?

This requirement responds to the Continual Improvement Principle.

The existing provisions may not adequately prevent the occurrence of nonconformity and therefore it is necessary to determine the additional actions that are needed. Events are not always mutually exclusive and therefore provisions designed to eliminate, reduce or control one failure mode may well eliminate, reduce or control others.

How is this implemented?

Adequacy of current provisions

All existing processes should include provisions for verifying output and monitoring progress even if they are informal. However, if the processes have evolved over a long period it is also likely that there will be many more controls in place. Every requirement of the 1994 version of ISO 9001 will, if implemented, impose control over the process. Such controls should have been installed to prevent failure but many were often installed just to meet the requirements of the standard and get the *badge on the wall*. If you now re-examine these controls from the perspective of establishing the failure modes they prevent, you will at least give justification to those that serve a useful purpose and provide an action list for those that don't.

Table 8.5   Contrasting preventive and detection measures

Preventive measures	Detection measures
Planning	Material testing
Training	Component inspection
Safety factors	Assembly testing
Component derating	Prototype testing
Component redundancy	Receipt inspection
Product identification	Design review
Mistake proofing	Peer review
Warning notices	Alarms
	Alerts

Existing controls can be classified as those that prevent occurrence and those that detect occurrence. Table 8.5 illustrates the difference. There are two types of detection measures – those that detect a failure and lead to a permanent change and those that detect a failure and lead to a restoration action such as to reset the product or process or to replenish consumables.

Probability of detection

You can go a step further and rank the probability that the existing provisions will detect the failure. The ranking could range from 'Certainty of detection' to Absolute uncertainty of detection' with variations in between. Examine the existing provisions to see whether there are any alarms, alerts or reporting arrangements that would bring potential problems to the attention of management.

What may appear trivial on a case-by-case basis may well be significant when taken over a longer period or a larger population. Determining this deterioration requires some detective work that focuses on processes and not on specific products. Managers have a habit of reacting to events particularly if they are serious nonconformities in the form of a customer complaint. What we are all poor at is perceiving the underlying trends that occur daily and gradually eat away at our profits. If there is no means of alerting management to these trends clearly something is missing.

Determining additional provisions

The next stage is to determine what additional provisions, if any, are necessary. If the event would not be detected by current provisions and its severity and the probability of occurrence is high – additional provisions are needed. If the event would not be detected by current provisions and its severity is negligible and its probability of occurrence unlikely – no action may be necessary unless all other potential causes of nonconformity have been eliminated.

Determining and implementing preventive action (8.5.3c)

1994–2000 Differences

Previously the standard required:

(a) preventive action procedures to include the determination of steps needed to deal with any problems requiring preventive action;
(b) initiation of preventive action.

The intent of the requirement remains unchanged.

The standard requires *a documented procedure that defines requirements for determining and implementing action needed to prevent occurrence of nonconformities.*

What does this mean?

Action to prevent a potential nonconformity may be in the form of a redesign of a product or process, the introduction of new routines, precautions, procedures, techniques or methods or involve changing the behaviour of personnel including management. The work environment may be the cause of some problems – changing it should not be ruled out.

Why is this necessary?

This requirement responds to the Continual Improvement Principle.

The most cost effective action one can take in any organization is an action designed to prevent problems from occurring. It is always cheaper to do a job right the first time rather than do it over (Crosby, Philip, 1979)[10]. Preventive action therefore saves money even though there is a price to pay for the discovery of potential nonconformities. Once the analysis has been performed a few times, a pattern will begin to emerge where provisions made to handle one situation will prove suitable for other situations and so it will get easier until the analysis almost becomes a habit.

How is this implemented?

The action necessary to eliminate, reduce or control the effects of a potential nonconformity may be as simple as applying existing techniques or methods to a new product or process. In other cases it might involve designing new techniques and methods – something that may require additional resources and a development team. If the solution requires the involvement of more than one function, the formation of a multidisciplinary team may be necessary. This is not the same as a multifunctional team where representatives from each function meet to discuss a problem then go back to their departments and get on with what they were doing. A multidisciplinary team comprises people of different disciplines, brought together to pool their skills and knowledge. They may all be from the same function but the focus is on getting the problem solved, not playing departmental politics.

The steps you need to take to deal with specific problems will vary depending on the nature of the problem. The part that can be proceduralized is the planning process for determining the preventive action needed. A typical process may be as follows:

- Devise a strategy for eliminating the cause together with alternative strategies, their limitations and consequences.
- Gain agreement on the strategy.
- Prepare an improvement plan which if implemented would eliminate the potential problem and not cause any others.
- Prepare a timetable and estimate resources for implementing the plan.
- Gain agreement of the improvement plan, timetable and resources before going ahead.

Some plans may be very simple and require no more than an instruction to implement an existing procedure. Others may be more involved and require additional resources. By incorporating the actions into a formal improvement plan you are seen to operate a coherent and co-ordinated improvement strategy rather than a random and unguided strategy. While those on the firing line are best equipped to notice the trends, any preventive action should be co-ordinated in order that the company's resources are targeted at the problems that are most significant.

Mistake-proofing

Mistake proofing is a means to prevent the manufacture or assembly of nonconforming product. Mistakes are inadvertent errors and arise through human fallibility. We all occasionally forget things and we can either make actions mistake-proof in order that they can only be performed one way or we can provide signals to remind us of what we should be doing. The terms foolproofing and Poka-Yoke (coined by Shigeo Shinto) are also used to describe the same concepts.

Mistake-proofing can be accomplished by product design features in order that the possibility of incorrect assembly, operation or handling is avoided. In such cases the requirements for mistake-proofing need to form part of the design input requirements for the part. The Design FMEA should be analysed to reveal features that present a certain risk that can be contained by redesign with mistake proofing features.

Mistake-proofing can also be accomplished by process design features such as sensors to check the set-up before processing, audible signals to remind operators to do various things. However, signals to operators are not exactly mistake-proof, only a mechanism that prevents operations commencing until the right conditions have been set, is proof against mistakes. In cases where computer data entry routines are used, mistake-proofing can be built-into the software such that the operator cannot bypass a stage.

Recording the results of preventive action (8.5.3d)

1994–2000 Differences

Previously the standard required that the preventive action procedures confirm that the relevant information on actions taken including changes to procedures is submitted for management review.

Though not explicit as to records, the previous requirement could not be implemented without records being available, therefore the intent of the requirement remains unchanged.

The standard requires *a documented procedure that defines requirements for recoding of results of action taken to prevent occurrence of nonconformities.*

What does this mean?

If taken literally this requirement means that one need only record whether the action had the desired effect and as we are addressing potential nonconformities, a record of the absence of nonconformities would seem to address this issue. However, in addition (and not in place of), other records are necessary for effective process management. Records of all the intentions and actions relative to the elimination of potential nonconformity should be generated.

Why is this necessary?

This requirement responds to the Factual Approach Principle.

Records of the actions taken en route to discover and eliminate potential nonconformities serve a number of important uses:

- They show due diligence and consideration to matters that affect customer satisfaction and compliance with regulations.

- They can be used as evidence in any prosecution against the organization.
- They provide a basis for comparison of actual nonconformity against predicted nonconformity and therefore a means to improve product and process design techniques.

How is this implemented?

Through the preventive action process there are several things that should be recorded:

- The objectives or requirements of the product, process or organization
- The critical success factors
- The modes of failure, their cause and effect, their severity and probability of occurrence (FMEA and FTA)
- The criteria for determining severity
- Current provisions to detect nonconformity
- The probability that current provisions will detect the nonconformity
- The actions proposed to eliminate the cause
- The actions taken
- The results of an analysis of nonconformity data showing the effectiveness of actions taken

Reviewing preventive action (8.5.3e)

The standard requires *a documented procedure that defines requirements for reviewing actions taken to prevent occurrence of nonconformities.*

What does this mean?

The review of preventive actions means establishing that the actions have been effective in preventing the occurrence of the nonconformity.

Why is this necessary?

This requirement responds to the Process Approach Principle.

A lot of effort goes into preventing problems and therefore it is necessary to periodically review results to establish whether this effort is being effectively applied. Is the effort focusing on the right things or does it repeatedly fail to prevent any significant problems occurring?

1994–2000 Differences

Previously the standard required:
a) the application of controls to ensure preventive action is effective;
b) the preventive action procedures to confirm that the relevant information on actions taken including changes to procedures is submitted for management review.

The modified wording weakens the intent of the requirement from implying periodic review for effectiveness to a one-off activity.

How is this implemented?

This requirement implies four separate actions:

- A review to establish what actions were taken
- An assessment to determine whether the actions were those required to be taken
- An evaluation of whether the actions were performed in the best possible way
- A investigation to determine whether the nonconformity has occurred

The first action is to trace forward from the failure analysis in order to locate evidence that the planned action was taken. The action taken may not be the same as planned simply because a better solution emerged and the FMEA was not updated (a common weakness but not drastic). The review should cause the FMEA to be updated but a more important issue is whether the *better solution* had the desired effect. An analysis of performance over a set time interval may reveal the evidence. It will show whether there are non-conformities occurring and if so, the preventive action has not been 100% effective. However a study of actual nonconformities will reveal whether:

- the root cause matches that in the FMEA
- the nonconformity is one that had been anticipated
- the solution merely created another problem

The fact that nonconformities occur should not necessarily be cause for despair. If a process is very mature and the organization stable, there perhaps should be no nonconformities. But life is never thus. There is always change and some of it we can predict and some we cannot. A lot of what is needed to prevent potential nonconformity is to do with imagination, knowledge and commitment. You need imagination to postulate the modes of failure, knowledge to confirm your suspicions and isolate the causes and commitment to do something about it, especially where cost is involved and it is uncertain as to whether nonconformity will occur. There are costs versus benefits and often the benefits are external to the organization rather than internal such as protection of the environment and safety of people. The management has to balance the costs and make value judgements which if they share good values, the decisions will always fall in favour of the external parties (employees are external parties in this situation).

Summary

In this chapter we have examined the requirements contained in section 8 of ISO 9001. We have discovered that measurement is key to performance, for without measurement we have no idea how we are performing and where we need to focus our effort to improve performance. We have learnt that the measurement, analysis and improvement processes are not unique to section 8 and have rationalized the duplication in the standard in this area. We have examined different ways of monitoring customer satisfaction and of performing internal audits and have discovered that many changes are likely to be needed in order to make both these processes effective. We have learnt that the requirements covering product measurement are less verbose but just as important as those in the 1994 version. We have also learnt that the requirements for process measurement are far more challenging and will require significant change for many – extending process management into all facets of the organization, perhaps for the first time. While the nonconformity control, corrective and preventive action requirements are not new, we have taken a fresh look at how these requirements can be implemented. We have examined the data analysis and continual improvement requirements and discovered that the search for improvement opportunities will need to extend beyond product-related issues and into the boardroom – questioning policies and objectives, strategies and goals. However once the improvement opportunities are identified, new levels of performance are within our reach because we have built change processes into the management system that ensure improvements are process-oriented rather than function-oriented and to ensure that the integrity of the system is maintained throughout the transition.

Measurement, analysis and improvement questionnaire

Monitoring, measurement, analysis and improvement processes

1 How do you plan and implement the monitoring, measurement, analysis and improvement processes needed to demonstrate conformity of the product?
2 How do you plan and implement the monitoring, measurement, analysis and improvement processes needed to ensure conformity of the management system?
3 How do you plan and implement the monitoring, measurement, analysis and improvement processes needed to continually improve the effectiveness of the management system?
4 How do you determine the methods necessary to monitor, measure, analyse and improve products and processes?
5 To what extent are statistical techniques used in the monitoring, measurement, analysis and improvement of products and processes?

Monitoring and measurement

6 How do you monitor customer perception as to whether the organization has met customer requirements?

7 How are data on customer perceptions obtained and used?

8 What methods are used to determine whether the management system conforms to the planned arrangements?

9 How do you ensure that the management system conforms to the requirements of ISO 9001?

10 How do you ensure that the management system is effectively implemented and maintained?

11 How do you ensure that the audit programme is planned, taking into consideration the status and importance of the processes and areas to be audited?

12 How do you ensure that the audit programme is planned taking into consideration the results of previous audits?

13 In what documents are the audit criteria, scope, frequency and methods defined?

14 How do you ensure audits are conducted with objectivity and impartiality?

15 In what documents are the responsibilities and requirements for planning and conducting audits defined?

16 In what documents are the requirements for reporting audit results and maintaining records defined?

17 How do you ensure that the management responsible for the area audited take actions to eliminate the detected nonconformities and their causes without undue delay?

18 How do you ensure that audit follow-up activities include the verification of the actions taken and the reporting of verification results?

19 How do you ensure that suitable methods for monitoring and where applicable, measurement of the management system processes are applied?

20 How do you ensure that the monitoring and measurement methods demonstrate the ability of the processes to achieve planned results?

21 How do you ensure that the organization monitors and measures the characteristics of the product to verify that product requirements have been met?

22 How do you ensure that product verification activities are conducted at appropriate stages of the product realization process in accordance with the planned arrangements?

23 How do you ensure that evidence of conformity with the acceptance criteria is maintained?

24 How do you ensure that records of product verification identify the person(s) authorizing release of product?

25 How do you ensure that (unless otherwise approved by a relevant authority and where applicable, by the customer) product release and service delivery does not proceed until the planned arrangements have been satisfactorily completed?

Control of nonconforming product

26 How do you ensure that product which does not conform to product requirements is identified and controlled to prevent unintended use or delivery?

27 In what documents are the controls and related responsibilities for dealing with nonconforming product defined?

28 How do you ensure that appropriate action is taken to eliminate the detected nonconformities?

29 What records are maintained of the nature of nonconformities and any subsequent actions taken, including concessions?

30 How do you ensure that nonconforming product is subject to re-verification after correction in order to demonstrate conformity to the requirements?

31 How do you ensure that action is taken appropriate to the effects or potential effects of the nonconformity when nonconforming product is detected after delivery or use has started?

Analysis of data

32 How do you determine, collect and analyse data to demonstrate the suitability and effectiveness of the management system?

33 How do you evaluate where continual improvement of the effectiveness of the management system can be made?

34 What analysis of data is performed to provide information relating to customer satisfaction?

35 What analysis of data is performed to provide information relating to conformity to product requirements?

36 What analysis of data is performed to provide information relating to characteristics and trends of processes and product?

37 What analysis of data is performed to provide opportunities for preventive action?

38 What analysis of data is performed to provide information relating to suppliers?

Improvement

39 What methods are employed to continually improve the effectiveness of the management system?

40 How do you ensure that action is taken to eliminate the cause of nonconformities in order to prevent recurrence?

41 How do you ensure that corrective actions are appropriate to the effects of the nonconformities encountered?

42 In what documents are the requirements defined for reviewing nonconformities (including customer complaints)?

43 In what documents are the requirements defined for determining the causes of nonconformity?

44 In what documents are the requirements defined for evaluating the need for action to ensure that nonconformities do not recur?

45 In what documents are the requirements defined for determining and implementing the corrective actions needed?

46 In what documents are the requirements defined for recording results of corrective actions taken?

47 In what documents are the requirements defined for reviewing corrective action taken?

48 How do you ensure that action is taken to eliminate the causes of potential nonconformities in order to prevent their occurrence?

49 How do you ensure that preventive actions are appropriate to the effects of the potential problems?

50 In what documents are the requirements defined for determining potential nonconformities and their causes?

51 In what documents are the requirements defined for evaluating the need for action to prevent occurrence of nonconformities?

52 In what documents are the requirements defined for determining and implementing action needed to prevent occurrence of nonconformities?

53 In what documents are the requirements defined for recording of results of action taken to prevent occurrence of nonconformities?

54 In what documents are the requirements defined for reviewing actions taken to prevent occurrence of nonconformities?

Measurement, analysis and improvement – food for thought

1 Do you manage the system as a series of processes or as a series of functions?

2 If no objectives are set for a process, will any level of performance be acceptable?

3 Only when you have put out all the fires can you improve the process.

4 Do you act on suspicion, or always confirm that a problem exists or might exist before taking action?

5 Have you discovered any root cause of a problem that cannot be traced to lack of application of one or more of the eight quality management principles?

6 Performing the analysis and doing nothing with the results is negligent.

7 Organizations cannot put their results at risk and expect success to be achieved by chance.

8 Have you re-examined existing controls from the perspective of establishing the failure modes they prevent?

9 Have you equipped every process with provisions for measuring its performance?

10 How often do you check that your objectives and targets are still relevant to the organization's goals?

11 If the questions in your customer satisfaction questionnaires were generated internally, how do you expect to obtain unbiased results?

12 When was the last time your internal audit programme found something that led to improved performance?

13 If you discontinued your internal audit programme, would anyone other than the internal or external auditors demand its reinstatement?

14 If your auditing approach has been to verify compliance with procedures, what approach are you intending to take now that the system has to enable the organization to achieve its objectives?

15 Do you consider that the system is effectively implemented if people are following the documented procedures or would you also verify that the planned results are being achieved?

16 Would you accept a box of 1000 components by simply checking one sample, if not why would you base your audit conclusions on a few unrepresentative samples?

17 Why shouldn't the manager perform the internal audits, and if you should think he or she is not competent to do so, why do you trust him/her to manage the function?

18 How do you know that each of the processes is achieving the planned results?

19 When was the last time you changed your operating methods in order to increase resource utilization?

20 Do you continue with the current level of product verification regardless of detecting no nonconformities?

21 Are you sure that those examining products or services for conformity apply the same criteria as those using them?

22 Is the data used by management to make decisions generated from the processes of the management system and if not why not?

23 Are there any data collection routines that are not triggered by a process in the management system?

24 How continuous is your continual improvement process?

25 When was the last time a problem recurred?

26 When did asking the question What if . . . become a habit?

Bibliography

1. Juran, J. M., (1995). *Managerial Breakthrough Second Edition*, McGraw-Hill.
2. Deming, W. Edwards, (1982). *Out of the crisis*, MITC.
3. Deming, W. Edwards, (1982). *Out of the crisis*, MITC.
4. American Society for Quality, (2001). http://acsi.asq.org/.
5. US Government, (2001). http://www.census.gov/mso/www/npr/acsi.htm.
6. Juran, J. M., (1995). *Managerial Breakthrough Second Edition*, McGraw-Hill.
7. Deming, W. Edwards, (1982). *Out of the crisis*, MITC.
8. Smith, David, (1997). *Reliability, Maintainability and Risk Fifth Edition*, Butterworth Heinemann.
9. Smith, David, (1997). *Reliability, Maintainability and Risk Fifth Edition*, Butterworth Heinemann.
10 Crosby, Philip, (1979). *Quality Is Free*, McGraw-Hill..

Appendix A
Glossary

The terms below are those used in this book for which alternative definitions may be provided in ISO 9000. For other terms the reader is directed to ISO 9000.

Acceptance criteria. The standard against which a comparison is made to judge conformance.

Accreditation. A process by which organizations are authorized to conduct certification of conformity to prescribed standards.

Adequate. Suitable for the purpose.

Approved. Something that has been confirmed as meeting the requirements.

Assessment. The act of determining the extent of compliance with requirements.

Assurance. Evidence (verbal or written) that gives confidence that something will or will not happen or has or has not happened.

Audit. An examination of results to verify their accuracy by someone other than the person responsible for producing them. (see also ISO 9000 clause 3.9.1)

Authority. The right to take actions and make decisions.

Authorized. A permit to do something or use something that may not necessarily be approved.

Benchmarking. A technique for measuring an organization's products, services and operations against those of its competitors resulting in a search for best practice that will lead to superior performance.

Calibrate. To standardize the quantities of a measuring instrument.

Certification body. *See Registrar.*

Certification. A process by which a product, process, person or organization is deemed to meet specified requirements.

Class. A group of entities having at least one attribute in common or a group of entities having the same generic purpose but different functional use.

Clause of the standard. A numbered paragraph or subsection of the standard containing one or more related requirements such as 7.2.2. N.B. each item in a list is also a clause.

Codes. A systematically arranged and comprehensive collection of rules, regulations or principles.

Commitment. An obligation a person or organization undertakes to fulfil i.e. doing what you say will do.

Common cause. Random variation caused by factors that are inherent in the system.

Competence. The ability to demonstrate *use* of education, skills and behaviours to achieve the results required for the job.

Competence-based assessment. A technique for collecting sufficient evidence that individuals can perform or behave to the specified standards in a specific role (Shirley Fletcher).

Competent. An assessment decision that confirms a person has achieved the prescribed standard of competence.

Concession. Permission granted by an acceptance authority to supply product or service that does not meet the prescribed requirements (see also ISO 9000 clause 3.6.11).

Concurrent engineering. *See Simultaneous engineering.*

Continual improvement. A recurring activity to increase the ability to fulfil requirements. (ISO 9000).

Contract. An agreement formally executed by both customer and supplier (enforceable by law) which requires performance of services or delivery of products at a cost to the customer in accordance with stated terms and conditions. Also agreed requirements between an organization and a customer transmitted by any means.

Contract loan. An item of customer-supplied property provided for use in connection with a contract that is subsequently returned to the customer.

Contractual requirements. Requirements specified in a contract.

Control. The act of preventing or regulating change in parameters, situations or conditions.

Control charts. A graphical comparison of process performance data to computed control limits drawn as limit lines on the chart.

Control methods. Particular ways of providing control which do not constrain the sequence of steps in which the methods are carried out.

Control procedure. A procedure that controls product or information as it passes through a process.

Controlled conditions. Arrangements that provide control over all factors that influence the result.

Core competence. A specific set of capabilities including knowledge, skills, behaviours and technology that generate performance differentials.

Corrective action. Action planned or taken to stop something from recurring (see also ISO 9000 clause 3.6.5).

Corrective maintenance. Maintenance carried out after a failure has occurred and is intended to restore an item to a state in which it can perform its required function.

Criteria for workmanship. Acceptance standards based on qualitative measures of performance.

Critical Success Factors. Those factors upon which the achievement of specified objectives depend.

Cross-functional team. *See Multidisciplinary team.*

Customer. Organization that receives a product or service – includes, Purchaser, consumer, client, end user, retailer or beneficiary. (ISO 9000)

Customer complaints. Any adverse report (verbal or written) received by an organization from a customer.

Customer feedback. Any comment on the organization's performance provided by a customer.

Customer supplied product. Hardware, software, documentation or information owned by the customer which is provided to an organization for use in connection with a contract and which is returned to the customer either incorporated in the supplies or at the end of the contract.

Data. Information that is organized in a form suitable for manual or computer analysis.

Define and document. To state in written form, the precise meaning, nature or characteristics of something.

Demonstrate. To prove by reasoning, objective evidence, experiment or practical application.

Department. A unit of an organization that may perform one or more functions. Units of organization regardless of their names are also referred to as functions *(see Functions)*.

Design. A process of originating a conceptual solution to a requirement and expressing it in a form from which a product may be produced or a service delivered.

Design and Development. Design creates the conceptual solution and development transforms the solution into a fully working model (see also ISO 9000 3.4.4).

Design of experiments. A technique for improving the quality of both processes and products by effectively investigating several sources of variation at the same time using statistically planned experiments.

Design review. A formal documented and systematic critical study of a design by people other than the designer.

Disposition. The act or manner of disposing of something.

Documented procedures. Procedures that are formally laid down in a reproducible medium such as paper or magnetic disk.

Effectiveness of the system. The extent to which the system fulfils its purpose.

Embodiment loan. An item of customer-supplied property provided for incorporation into product that is subsequently supplied back to the customer or a party designated by the customer.

Employee empowerment. An environment in which employees are free (within defined limits) to take action to operate, maintain and improve the processes for which they are responsible using their own expertise and judgment.

EMS. Environmental management system.

Ensure. To make certain that something will happen.

Establish and maintain. To set-up an entity on a permanent basis and retain or restore it in a state in which it can fulfil its purpose or required function.

Evaluation. To ascertain the relative goodness, quality or usefulness of an entity with respect to a specific purpose.

Evidence of conformance. Documents which testify that an entity conforms with certain prescribed requirements.

Executive responsibility. Responsibility vested in those personnel who are responsible for the whole organization's performance. Often referred to as top management.

Failure mode effects analysis (FMEA). A technique for identifying potential failure modes and assessing existing and planned provisions to detect, contain or eliminate the occurrence of failure.

FIFO. First in first out. A term used to describe a method of inventory control.

Final inspection and testing. The last inspection or test carried out by the organization before ownership passes to the customer.

Finite element analysis. A technique for modelling a complex structure.

First party audits. Audits of a company or parts thereof by personnel employed by the company. These audits are also called Internal Audits.

Follow-up audit. An audit carried out following and as a direct consequence of a previous audit to determine whether agreed actions have been taken and are effective.

Force majeure. An event, circumstance or effect that cannot be reasonably anticipated or controlled

Functions. In the organizational sense, a function is a special or major activity (often unique in the organization) which is needed in order for the organization to fulfil its purpose and mission. Examples of functions are design, procurement, personnel, manufacture, marketing, maintenance etc.

Geometric dimensioning and tolerancing. A method of dimensioning the shape of parts that provides appropriate limits and fits for their application and facilitates manufacturability and interchangeability.

Grade. Category or rank given to entities having the same functional use but different requirements for quality; e.g. hotels are graded by star rating, automobiles are graded by model (see also ISO 9000 clause 3.1.3).

IAF. International Accreditation Forum

Identification. The act of identifying an entity, i.e. giving it a set of characteristics by which it is recognizable as a member of a group.

Implement. To carry out a directive.

Implementation Audit. An audit carried out to establish whether actual practices conform to the documented quality system. N.B. also referred to as a Conformance Audit or Compliance Audit.

Importance of activities in auditing. The relative importance of the contribution an activity makes to the fulfilment of an organization's objectives.

Indexing. A means of enabling information to be located.

In-process. Between the beginning and the end of a process.

Inspection. The examination of an entity to determine whether it conforms to prescribed requirements (see also ISO 9000 clause 3.8.2).

Inspection authority. The person or organization that has been given the right to perform inspections.

Inspection, measuring and test equipment. Devices used to perform inspections, measurements and tests.

Installation. The process by which an entity is fitted into larger entity.

Intellectual property. Creations of the mind: inventions, literary and artistic works, and symbols, names, images, and designs used in commerce. Intellectual property is divided into two categories: Industrial property and Copyright.

Interested party. Person or group having an interest in the performance or success of an organization – includes: Customers, owners, employees, contractors, suppliers, investors, unions, partners or society.

ISO. International Organization for Standardization.

Issues of documents. The revision state of a document.

Manage Work. To manage work means to plan, organize and control the resources (personnel, financial and material) and the tasks required to achieve the objective for which the work is needed.

Management representative. The person management appoints to act on their behalf to manage the quality system.

Master list. An original list from which copies can be made.

Measurement capability. The ability of a measuring system (device, person and environment) to measure true values to the accuracy and precision required.

Measurement uncertainty. The variation observed when repeated measurements of the same parameter on the same specimen are taken with the same device.

Modifications. Entities altered or reworked to incorporate design changes.

Monitoring. To check periodically and systematically. It does not imply that any action will be taken.

Motivation. An inner mental state that prompts a direction, intensity and persistence in behaviour.

Multidisciplinary team. A team comprising representatives from various functions or departments in an organization, formed to execute a project on behalf of that organization.

Nationally recognized standards. Standards of measure that have been authenticated by a national body.

Nature of change. The intrinsic characteristics of the change (what has changed and why).

Objective. A result is to be achieved usually by a given time.

Objective evidence. Information that can be proven true, based on facts obtained through observation, measurement, test or other means (see also ISO 9000 clause 3.8.1).

Obsolete documents. Documents that are no longer required for operational use. They may be useful as historic documents.

OEM. Original Equipment Manufacturer.

Operating procedure. A procedure that describes how specific tasks are to be performed.

Organizational goals. Where the organization desires to be, in markets, in innovation, in social and environmental matters, in competition and in financial health.

Organizational interfaces. The boundary at which organizations meet and affect each other expressed by the passage of information, people, equipment, materials and the agreement to operational conditions.

Plan. Provisions made to achieve and objective.

Planned arrangements. All the arrangements made by the organization to achieve the customer's requirements. They include the documented policies and procedures and the documents derived from such policies and procedures.

Policy. A guide to thinking, action and decision.

Positive recall. A means of recovering an entity by giving it a unique identity.

Positively identified. An identification given to an entity for a specific purpose which is both unique and readily visible.

Potential nonconformity. A situation that if left alone will in time result in nonconformity.

Predictive maintenance. Work scheduled to monitor machine condition, predict pending failure and make repairs on an as-needed basis.

Pre-launch. A phase in the development of a product between design validation and full production (sometimes called pre-production) during which the production processes are validated.

Prevent. To stop something from occurring by a deliberate planned action.

Preventive action. Action proposed or taken to stop something from occurring (see also ISO 9000 clause 3.6.4).

Preventive maintenance. Maintenance carried out at predetermined intervals to reduce the probability of failure or performance degradation; e.g. replacing oil filters ate defined intervals.

Procedure. A sequence of steps to execute a routine activity (see also ISO 9000 clause 3.4.5).

Process. A set of interrelated tasks, behaviours and resources that achieves a result (see also ISO 9000 clause 3.4.1).

Process capability. The ability of a process to maintain product characteristics within preset limits.

Process Description. A set of information that describes the characteristics of a process in terms of its purpose, objectives, design features, inputs, activities, resources, behaviours, outputs, constraints and the measurements undertaken to obtain data with which to manage the process.

Process parameters. Those variables, boundaries or constants of a process that restrict or determine the results.

Product. Anything produced by human effort, natural or Man made processes. Result of activities or processes (ISO 9000–2).

Product realization. All those processes and resources necessary to transform a set of requirements into a product or service that fulfils the requirements.

Production. The creation of products.

Proprietary designs. Designs exclusively owned by the organization and not sponsored by an external customer.

Prototype. A model of a design that is both physically and functionally representative of the design standard for production and used to verify and validate the design.

Purchaser. One who buys from another.

Purchasing documents. Documents that contain the organization's purchasing requirements.

Qualification. Determination by a series of tests and examinations of a products, related documents and processes that the product meets all the specified performance capability requirements.

Quality. The degree to which a set of inherent characteristics fulfils a need or expectation that is stated, general implied or obligatory (ISO 9000).

Quality assurance. Part of quality management focused on providing confidence that quality requirements will be fulfilled (ISO 9000).

Quality characteristics. Any characteristic of a product or service that is needed to satisfy customer needs or achieve fitness for use.

Quality conformance. The extent to which the product or service conforms with the specified requirements.

Quality control. A process for maintaining standards of quality that prevents and corrects change in such standards so that the resultant output meets customer needs and expectations (see also ISO 9000 clause 3.2.10).

Quality costs. Costs incurred because failure is possible. The actual cost of producing an entity is the no failure cost plus the quality cost. The no failure cost is the cost of doing the right things right first time. The quality costs are the prevention, appraisal and failure costs.

Quality function deployment. A technique to deploy customer requirements (the true quality characteristics) into design characteristics (the substitute characteristics) and deploy them into subsystems, components, materials and production processes. The result is a grid or matrix that shows how and where customer requirements are met.

Quality improvement Part of quality management focused on increasing the ability to fulfil quality requirements (ISO 9000).

Quality management system. The set of interconnected processes used by the organization to achieve its objectives (see also ISO 9000 3.2.3).

Quality management system requirements. Requirements pertaining to the design, development, operation, maintenance and improvement of quality management systems.

Quality objectives. Those results which the organization needs to achieve in order to improve its ability to meet needs and expectations of all the interested parties.

Quality planning. Provisions made to achieve the needs and expectations of organization's interested parties and prevent failure.

Quality plans. Plans produced to define how specified quality requirements will be achieved, controlled, assured and managed for specific contracts or projects.

Quality problems. The difference between the achieved quality and the required quality.

Quality requirements. Those requirements which pertain to the features and characteristics of a product or service which are required to be fulfilled in order to satisfy a given need.

Quarantine area. A secure space provided for containing product pending a decision on its disposal.

Registrar. An organization that is authorized to certify organizations. The body may be accredited or non-accredited.

Registration. A process of recording details of organizations of assessed capability that have satisfied prescribed standards.

Regulator. A legal body authorized to enforce compliance with the laws and statutes of a national government

Regulatory requirements. Requirements established by law pertaining to products or services.

Remedial action. Action proposed or taken to remove a nonconformity (see also Corrective and preventive action).

Representative sample. A sample of product or service that possesses all the characteristics of the batch from which it was taken.

Requirement of the standard. A sentence containing the word *shall*. N.B. Some sentences contain multiple requirements such as to establish, document and maintain. This is in fact three requirements.

Responsibility. An area in which one is entitled to act on one's own accord.

Review. Another look at something.

Scheduled maintenance. Work performed at a time specifically planned to minimize interruptions in machine availability; e.g. changing a gearbox when machine is not required for use (includes predictive and preventive maintenance).

Shall. A provision that is binding.

Should. A provision that is optional.

Simultaneous engineering. A method of reducing the time taken to achieve objectives by developing the resources needed to support and sustain the production of a product in parallel with the development of the product itself. It involves customers, suppliers and each of the organization's functions working together to achieve common objectives.

Six sigma. Six standard deviations.

SMS. Safety management system.

Special cause. A cause of variation that can be assigned to a specific or special condition that does not apply to other events.

Specified requirements. Requirements prescribed by the customer and agreed by the organization or requirements prescribed by the organization that are perceived as satisfying a market need.

Stakeholder. A person or organization that has freedom to provide something to or withdraw something from an enterprise.

Statistical control. A condition of a process in which there is no indication of a special cause of variation.

Status.   The relative condition, maturity or quality of something.

Status of an activity (in auditing).   The maturity or relative level of performance of an activity to be audited.

Subcontract requirements.   Requirements placed on a subcontractor that are derived from requirements of the main contract.

Subcontractor.   A person or company that enters into a subcontract and assumes some of the obligations of the prime contractor.

System Audit.   An audit carried out to establish whether the quality system conforms to a prescribed standard in both its design and its implementation.

System effectiveness.   The ability of a system to achieve its stated purpose and objectives.

Technical interfaces.   The physical and functional boundary between products or services.

Tender.   A written offer to supply products or services at a stated cost.

Theory of constraints.   A thinking process optimizing system performance. It examines the system and focuses on the constraints that limits overall system performance. It looks for the weakest link in the chain of processes that produce organizational performance and seeks to eliminate it and optimize system performance.

TQM.   Total quality management.

Traceability.   The ability to trace the history, application, use and location of an individual article or its characteristics through recorded identification numbers (see also ISO 9000 3.5.4).

Unique identification.   An identification that has no equal.

Validation.   A process for establishing whether an entity will fulfil the purpose for which it has been selected or designed (see also ISO 9000 3.8.5).

Value engineering.   A technique for assessing the functions of a product and determining whether the same functions can be achieved with fewer types of components and materials and the product produced with less resources. Variety reduction is an element of value engineering.

Verification.   The act of establishing the truth or correctness of a fact, theory, statement or condition (see also ISO 9000 clause 3.8.4).

Verification activities.   A special investigation, test, inspection, demonstration, analysis or comparison of data to verify that a product or service or process complies with prescribed requirements.

Verification requirements.   Requirements for establishing conformance of a product or service with specified requirements by certain methods and techniques.

Waiver.   *See Concession.*

Work environment. is a set of conditions under which people operate and include physical, social and psychological environmental factors (ISO 9000:2000).

Work instructions. Instructions that prescribe work to be executed, who is to do it, when it is to start and be complete and if necessary how, it is to be carried out.

Workmanship criteria. Standards on which to base the acceptability of characteristics created by human manipulation of materials by hand or with the aid of hand tools.

Zero defects. The performance standard achieved when every task is performed right first time with no errors being detected downstream.

Appendix B
Related web sites

Articles and publications

An excellent range of articles and publications on ISO 9000:2000 at http://www.transition-support.com

Articles from Quality World at http://www.iqa.org

Purchase past articles from ASQ Journals at http://qic.asq.org/infosearch.html

An excellent range of books on ISO 90000, ISO 14000 and related topics at http://www.bh.com

Information on the fathers of scientific management at http://www.accel-team.com/scientific/index.html

Information about W. Edwards Deming at http://www-caes.mit.edu/products/deming/index.html

Article from Dr J. M. Juran at http://www.juran.com/research/back_articles.html

Auditing

Transition arrangements for registered auditors at http://www.lrqa.co.uk/

Information on auditing practices at www.iqnet-certification.com

The official line from the International Accreditation Forum on the transition at http:// www.iaf.nu

Benchmarking

Information on benchmarking from the American Productivity Centre http://www.apqc.org/

Competence

The Institute of Personnel Development at http://www.ipd.co.uk/
Information from the International Labour organization at http://www.ilo.org/public/spanish/region/ampro/cinterfor/temas/complab/xxxx/ing/xxiii/index.htm

Customer satisfaction

The American customer satisfaction index at http://acsi.asq.org/
http://www.census.gov/mso/www/npr/acsi.htm

Customer service standards

US Bureau of the Census customer service standards at http://www.euroqual.org/euroqual_main/mainindex.html

Process Management

Articles on process management and ISO 9000 at http://www.dti.gov.uk/

Product recall

Recalls notified by UK Trading Standards at http://www.tradingstandards.net/pages/recall.htm
Recall notices from the UK Department of Transport, Vehicle Inspectorate at http://www.automotive.co.uk/fleetnews/start.htm
Recall notices from USA at http://fullcoverage.yahoo.com/Full_Coverage/US/Consumer_News_and_Recall_Information/

Related initiatives

UK's manufacturing industry initiative at http://www.fitforthefuture.co.uk/
Tomorrows company at http://www.tomorrowscompany.co.uk/whatis_tia.html
Information form the European Organization for Quality at http://www.eoq.org/start.html

Sector schemes

Telecommunications sector scheme at http://questforum.asq.org/
mainhome.html

Automotive sector scheme at http://www.iaob.org/#IATFcomm

Six sigma

A good range of articles on six sigma at http://www.qualityamerica.com/six_
sigma.html

Standards

Mil Std 9858 can be obtained at http://assist.daps.mil/eAccess/index.cfm?i-
dent_number=7775

ISO standards can be obtained at http://www.iso.ch

British standards can be obtained at http://www.bsi-global.com/

Access news from the technical committee that created ISO 9000 at http:/
/www.tc176.org/

Standards on Investors in People at http://www.iipuk.co.uk/

Index